Timberwol

The History of
The 104th Infantry Division
1942 - 1945

By

LEO A. HOEGH
and

HOWARD J. DOYLE

WASHINGTON
INFANTRY JOURNAL PRESS

COPYRIGHT 1946 BY INFANTRY JOURNAL, INC.

FIRST EDITION

JULY 1946

PRINTED IN THE UNITED STATES OF AMERICA

DEDICATION

This history is the story of a fighting combat Division. It is fitting that this history be dedicated to those of our gallant comrades who went forth with us to battle, but when the battle had ended, did not return. It is to those brave officers and men who, from the canals of Holland to the banks of the Mulde have written a tale of courage that we offer this history as our tribute. We know that no word of ours can pay them adequate honor; rather is it from their names and their deeds that honor comes to us.

Now that peace has been won, the 104th has formed for its last parade. Though the flags have been furled and each of us has gone his separate way, we shall never forget that many of this Division keep their ranks formed forever as they lie sleeping in the fields of Henri Chapelle.

TO ALL TIMBERWOLVES:

To have served as your commander during two years of war is a distinct honor. Your wholehearted response to the vigorous demands made upon you for the highest type of Discipline, Teamwork and Combat Training, resulted in our welding together a fighting Division, second to none in battle efficiency.

During six and one-half months of continuous combat in Holland and Germany, you participated with outstanding success in spearheading five major Offensives. You always attained your objectives and you never gave ground.

You have proudly upheld the soldierly reputation of our Division. In future life, I know that you will continue to uphold the traditions of our Division and our Country.

I wish to pay tribute to our gallant dead, to whom we dedicate "TIMBERWOLF TRACKS". They made our success possible. It is our proud boast, that we have always lived up to our battle slogan, "NOTHING IN HELL CAN STOP THE TIMBERWOLVES".

My thanks to you all for your unfailing loyal support.

Sincerely,

Terry Allen

October 31, 1945

TO THE OFFICERS AND MEN OF THE 104TH INFANTRY DIVISION:

The deep appreciation of a grateful nation goes out to
you men of the Timberwolf Division who, by your heavy fighting
overseas, did so much to smash the powerful German army.

Since activation in September, 1942, in Oregon, the
104th has carried its banner high, earning a reputation as one
of our bravest fighting units. The division gave early indication
of this combat prowess during its training and maneuvers in Oregon,
California and Colorado. I had the good fortune to see the division
in training at Camp Carson, Colorado.

After your arrival in Europe you received your baptism of
fire in Holland when the 104th formed a vital link in the drive to
the Maas River. You turned from this bitter campaign to the fierce
fight for the Roer River line. In February, 1945, demonstrating
great tactical ability, the Timberwolves crossed the Roer and swept
irresistibly to Cologne. After crossing the Rhine, the 104th raced
to Paderborn, then to the Mulde, where you met the Russians as the
war ended. I saw the division near Leipzig, just before the German
surrender.

As your division goes through the process of inactivation,
your soldiers who take up new tasks will, I am confident, perform
them with the same self-reliance, initiative and loyalty which have
become a part of the division's tradition.

A grateful America joins me in commending you for your
heroic contribution to the cause of our country.

ROBERT P. PATTERSON
Secretary of War.

CONTENTS

BELGIUM · HOLLAND

23 October — 8 November 1944

Battle Of The Dykes
Freeing Of The Port Of Antwerp
Zundert · Oudenbosch · Mark River
Standaarbuiten · Zevenbergen
Klundert · Moerdijk · Maas River

LANDED CHERBOURG

7 September 1944 — October 1944

Valognes Staging Area
Red Ball Express

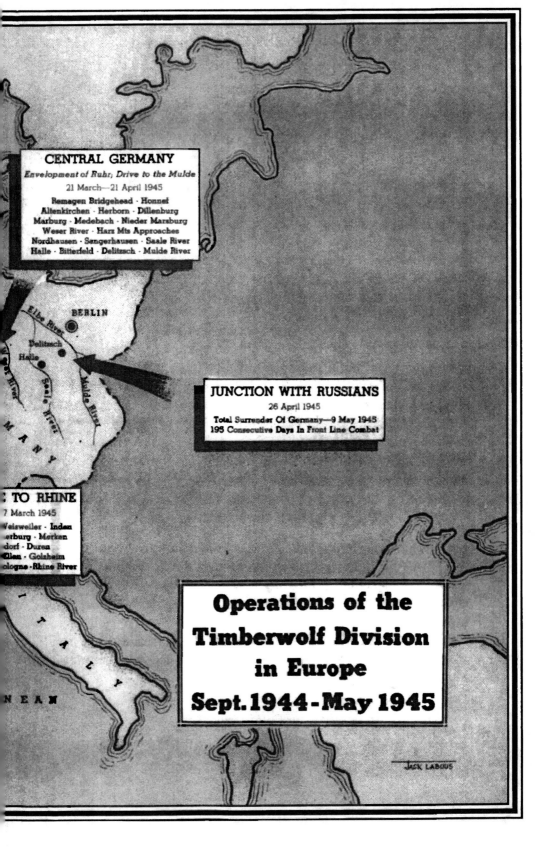

CENTRAL GERMANY

Envelopment of Ruhr; Drive to the Mulde

21 March—21 April 1945

Remagen Bridgehead · Honnef
Altenkirchen · Herborn · Dillenburg
Marburg · Medebach · Nieder Marsburg
Weser River · Harz Mts Approaches
Nordhausen · Sangerhausen · Saale River
Halle · Bitterfeld · Delitzsch · Mulde River

BERLIN

Elbe River

Delitzsch

Halle

Saale River

Mulde River

GERMANY

JUNCTION WITH RUSSIANS

26 April 1945

Total Surrender Of Germany—9 May 1945
195 Consecutive Days In Front Line Combat

: TO RHINE

7 March 1945

Weisweiler · Inden
erburg · Merken
dorf · Duren
llen · Golzheim
cologne · Rhine River

ITALY

NEAN

**Operations of the
Timberwolf Division
in Europe
Sept. 1944 - May 1945**

JACK LABOUS

FOREWORD

"The most rigorous service which a soldier is called upon to perform is the duty of a ground combat soldier. He is the man who must wade in the mud, endure heat and cold, and sleep on the ground. That is the toughest kind of service." These words, spoken from the floor of the United States Senate on April 19th, 1945 reflect the sincere feeling of the American people toward the Queen of Battles.

Through the medium of TIMBERWOLF TRACKS, it is our intention to present an honest commentary on the fighting in Europe incurred by the U. S. Infantryman . . . specifically the ground combat soldier who wore the green and silver patch of the Timberwolf. His lot was not a glamorous one; he fought, ate, slept in mud, snow and hail; his battle-weary body answered the call to move up time and time again while his tortured mind heroically withstood the numbing shock of having time-honored buddies fall by the wayside. His moments of praise were fleeting and none too consoling—still he wore the blue and silver Combat Infantryman Badge with an intense burning pride and he gloried in the record and achievements of his "outfit." His was the supreme satisfaction of a job well done.

The 104th Infantry Division did not win the war. We make no such far-reaching claim . . . but the Timberwolves did play a most effective role in crushing the iron fist of Nazidom. The record, compiled by the men of this fighting division, is in the words of the Commanding General "second to none". It is appropriate that such a record be preserved. In the following pages, Americans may find a justifiable gratefulness that such men as these stood so valorously between them and slavery.

PHASE I

"GET SMART . . . GET TOUGH!"

The following was written on July 16, 1944, when mornings were spent in walking out to some distant area and having—

BATTLE DRILL

"Now there's one thing in this Army that I'm sure we all dislike,
And it starts out every morning, with a speedy five-mile hike.
They teach us how to hit the dirt, and they teach us how to kill;
And we never do stop runnin' when we're having Battle Drill.

The enemy sits upon a hill, and waits for us to fight.
While the Sergeants are decidin'—"Flankers left" or "flankers right."
And a couple of "looies" watchin', just to pick out all the flaws,
As we crawl upon our faces, thru a half-a-dozen draws.

And when the draws no longer our position can conceal,
We have no other choice then but to cross the open field.
It's then that we all realize, that its death with whom we flirt,
And we're in for plenty practice for the hittin' of the dirt.

We hit the ground and scrape our noses in the sand and then,
We're up upon our feet—ten yards—and hit the dirt again.
This keeps up forty times or more, till we are black and blue,
They expect us to do all of this—and then some fighting too?

Next we assault the damned old hill, just wishin' it would stop.
We run up on the steepest side—and pass out on the top.
But before we can hike back to camp, and continue with our classes;
We have to sit and listen, while they all critique our ———."

Pfc. Edward J. Apple, Jr.
Company L, 414th Infantry

ACTIVATION

ON 15 September 1942 a new fighting unit took its place in the expanding Army of the United States when the 104th Infantry Division was formally activated with ceremonies held at Camp Adair, Oregon. At 1000 on that brisk, clear Oregon day, 684 officers and 1,435 enlisted men, then in the Division, marched to the central parade grounds, and stood at attention before the speakers' platform while the officers who were to command the Division mounted the stand. On the platform which was backed with replicas of regimental and battalion shields and the silver insignia of the 104th Division stood Major General Charles H. White, IX Corps Commander, Major General Gilbert R. Cook, Division Commander, Major General James L. Bradley, 96th Infantry Division Commander, Brigadier General Herman F. Kramer, Assistant Division Commander, Brigadier General William C. Dunckel, Commander of the 104th Division Artillery, Colonel H. C. Mandell, Chief of Staff, and other dignitaries. As the first notes of a bugle sounded the Division Commander's party reached the platform and the troops in the field came to attention. Lieutenant Colonel Frank Worthington, Division Chaplain, pronounced the invocation and Lieutenant Colonel A. M. Button read the orders of activation. Then, General Kramer, after listing the Division's component units and describing the various insignias, presented the Division to General Cook, who spoke:

We are not a lone wolf, we are a fighting team. We fight in packs, in teams. . . .

Activation! I wonder what that means to each of you. To me it means that we have definitely taken on certain responsibilities and duties, and also it might be called a birthday. A peculiar birthday though, because I am looking at the fathers and trainers of the filler replacements due us. Nevertheless it is our birthday. We stand on our own feet now. And those responsibilities settle definitely on the officer cadre which is approximately full strength, and on the enlisted cadre. They are responsible for developing and training filler replacements— men who know and recognize no obstacle when it comes to getting results, and— results in battle are what count.

We, the cadre, also are responsible for training the filler replacements which will come from all parts of the United States. We are responsible for teaching them comfort and welfare on the field of battle—"How to kill and how not to be killed!"

Now lastly, to the ladies of the Division. To them we pledge that our training will be such that we will not uselessly sacrifice the life of a single man charged to our care. . . .

Gentlemen, I assure you all that this is the proudest moment of my life. I am proud to command the 104th Division, the Timberwolf Division.

Activation Ceremonies

Camp Adair, September 15, 1942

General White spoke next:

The birthday of a large strong fighting unit is an historic event. That is what we are witnessing today. This fact will be born into your consciousness with each successive year. Years hence, as followed similarly after the last war, there will be formed a 104th Division Association to which you men now and others to join the Division, will proudly bear allegiance. . . .

In the service of our country is found the greatest brotherhood known to mankind. Sharing the same dangers, hardships and pleasures together, there is born the strongest of all human bonds. . . .

It is also the finest and noblest fellowship that you belong to. . . . You share a task with men of every type and every social station and are admitted to a fellowship so rare as almost to justify war. . . .

We have a job to do. We will do it. Let us sink all small petty considerations and fix our minds and efforts on the noble ideal set before us, the preservation of this great Republic. Again it is to be said, we are taking part in an historic event. There will be other glorious ones to follow, to create the history of the 104th Infantry Division.

Major L. T. Jenks, assistant Division Chaplain, pronounced the benediction and immediately thereafter General Kramer called to the cadre: "Wolverines—hunt your lair." With that charge, the men double-timed from the activation field. The 104th Infantry Division was born.

General Orders No. 1 of the Division was published on 15 September:

HEADQUARTERS 104TH INFANTRY DIVISION
Camp Adair, Oregon

15 September, 1942

GENERAL ORDERS
No. 1

1. The 104th Inf Div is activated this date at Cp Adair, Oreg., in compliance with Ltr AG 320.2 (5-26-42) MR-M-GN, TAGO, June 9/42, Sub: "Ordering Into Active Serv Certain OR Divs During Aug and Sept, 1942", and is organized in accordance with T/O indicated and the following elements:

Hq 104th Inf Div	T/O 7-1
Hq Co, 104th Inf Div	T/O 7-2
MP Plat, 104th Inf Div	T/O 19-7
104th Cav Rcn Tr	T/O 2-67
104th Sig Co	T/O 11-7
413th Inf	T/O 7-11
414th Inf	T/O 7-11
415th Inf	T/O 7-11
Hq & Hq Btry, 104th Inf Div Arty	T/O 6-10
385th FA Bn (L)	T/O 6-25
386th FA Bn (L)	T/O 6-25
929th FA Bn (L)	T/O 6-25
387th FA Bn (M)	T/O 6-35
329th Engr Bn	T/O 5-15
329th Med Bn	T/O 8-15
429th QM Bn	T/O 10-15

Ord Co 104th Inf Div (Provisional pending the issue of appropriate T/O)

2. Under Auth contained in par 1 SO 223 WD/42, I hereby assume comd of the 104th Inf Div.

3. BRIG GEN HERMAN F. KRAMER, 04904, USA, is announced as Asst Div Comdr.

4. BRIG GEN WILLIAM C. DUNCKEL, 06676, USA, is announced as Div Arty Comdr.

5. The following O are det in the GSC with trs and asgd to duty as follows:

COL HAROLD C. MANDELL, 04618, Cav. C of S
LT COL BURWELL B. WILKES, Jr, 0245960, CWS, Cml O
LT COL CHESTER W. OTT, 018338, CE, Engr O
LT COL LOGAN W. BOYD, 010387, IGD, IG
LT COL FRED L. THORPE, 016935, QMC, QM
LT COL RALPH E. WILLEY, 0213781, Sig C, Sig O
LT COL CLARENCE A. McINTYRE, 016557, MC, Surg
MAJ LEO' W. BELCHER, 0221055, FD, FO
MAJ FRANK J.T. WORTHINGTON, 0348362, Ch Corps, Ch
MAJ JOHN W. BONNER, 0318553, JAGD, JA
MAJ JAMES D. WILLIAMSON, 0279313, Ord Dept, Ord O
CAPT RAYMOND M. CRISSWELL, 0339639, CMP, PM
CAPT RALPH D. HAPHEY, Inf, Hq Comdt

GILBERT R. COOK (signed)
Major General, U.S. Army
Commanding

DISTRIBUTION "A"

Unit commanders assigned by General Cook on the day the Division was activated were as follows:

Captain Robert D. Haphey, Headquarters Company.
Captain Raymond M. Crisswell, MP Platoon.
Lieutenant Colonel Ralph E. Willey, 104th Signal Company.
Captain Edwin C. Haggard, 104th Reconnaissance Troop.
Captain Charles W. Doubleday, Jr., Ordnance Company.
Colonel Welcome P. Waltz, 413th Infantry.
Colonel Anthony J. Touart, 414th Infantry.
Colonel John H. Cochran, 415th Infantry.
Captain Robert C. Ingalls, Headquarters Battery, 104th Infantry Division Artillery.
Lieutenant Colonel Robert S. McClenaghan, 385th FA Battalian.
Lieutenant Colonel Wendell P. Sammet, 386th FA Battalion.
Lieutenant Colonel Fay W. Lee, 387th FA Battalion.
Lieutenant Colonel Thomas C. Bourke, 929th FA Battalion.
Lieutenant Colonel Chester W. Ott, 329th Engineer Battalion.

Early History

Three years after the end of World War I, in July 1921, the 104th was organized under the provisions of the National Defense Act as a reserve Infantry Division with personnel to be drawn from the Western states of Idaho, Montana, Wyoming, Utah and Nevada. Twenty-two years after the close of World War I, men from all parts of the United States came West to join the ranks of the 104th Division, now no longer a reserve Division but a combat outfit, ready for training to play a vital role in World War II.

To those men who were reserve officers during the twenty-one years following the organization the Division, among other things, owes its insignia, the head of a gray timberwolf against a background of green. But the name Timberwolf, by which the Division is now known, was assumed at the date of its activation. Before that time the 104th Division had been known as the Frontier Division.

It was on 20 August 1921, the month following authorization of the organization of the 104th Division, that Colonel F. L. Knudsen arrived at Fort Douglas, Utah, to assume his duties as the Division's first Chief of Staff. With him came one enlisted clerk. During the next nine months, Colonel Knudsen completed the organization, allocating the units to the five states in the area, and by 22 May the units of the Division were taking shape and the Division staff was fairly complete.

In July 1922, officers from the five states gathered at Fort Douglas, and it was there that the first training camp was held. The following year saw a reallocation of the units of the Division. By this time it had become apparent that the allocation of units by states was not satisfactory, and the units were allotted on the basis of population. Following the reorganization, Colonel Knudsen was succeeded by Colonel T. M. Anderson, who became Chief of Staff on 31 August 1923.

The Timberwolf insignia of the Division came into being in 1924 and was designed by Charles Livingston Ball, artist and authority on wildlife. The design was submitted to the War Department and a letter dated 16 August 1924, addressed to the Quartermaster General and sent from The Adjutant General, reads as follows:

1. The Secretary of War approves the following shoulder sleeve insignia for wear as a part of the uniform of the 104th Infantry Division.
     SHOULDER SLEEVE INSIGNIA—On a balsam green disc 2½ inches in diameter the head of a timberwolf in gray.

2. The above description and inclosure are furnished you with instructions to have drawing made indicating the tinctures and to send a copy of the same to the commanding general, Ninth Corps Area.

In 1924 the War Department approved the name of Frontier Division and the same was adopted by the Division. (Later, Timberwolf Division was substituted on 15 September 1942.)

Headquarters of the 104th Infantry Division, in the years before World War II, was located in Salt Lake City, Utah. When the Division was activated, however, the camp selected for its training was Camp Adair, Oregon, located in the Willamette Valley near Salem, just north of Corvallis and west of Albany.

General Cook, recently returned from duty in Hawaii, opened his headquarters as commanding general of the Division at Camp Adair, Oregon, on 7 August 1942. The strength report for August shows a total of thirty-one officers and eight enlisted men. The first officer assigned to the Division to report at Camp Adair was Captain Clyde L. Pennington (now Lieutenant Colonel), Division Automotive Officer, who arrived on 31 July; the first enlisted man to report was Staff Sergeant William E. Allen. New officers and enlisted men now began arriving in increasing numbers, rapidly filling the training nucleus of the Division. Most of the officer and enlisted cadre came from the 90th Infantry Division, then located at Camp Barkeley, Texas. On 15 August the Division strength report showed 185 officers and 1,430 enlisted men.

In the south part of Camp Adair the area was completed and occupied by the 96th Infantry Division; in the north, the area consisted of partially finished buildings, numerous lumber piles and impassable streets, hub-high in dust. The sightseeing trip would have been nice but there were no "sights" other than the so-called streets which were to connect the unit areas. The officers and men were seen in Corvallis, Albany, and Salem saying "Pardon me, Madam, but are you the lady who has an apartment to rent?" or "Do you know of an available house?" Soon Western Union was forwarding wires that read: "HONEY, COME AT ONCE. EVERYTHING SET." Thus it was that World War II had its beginning for the 104th Infantry Division.

After the cadre officers and enlisted men had arrived, and by the latter part of August the officer ranks were filled from all parts of the United States, many coming directly from OCS at Fort Benning, Georgia. They looked natty, with their shiny new bars, new blouses and pinks. They had spent several months learning how to be officers and sought now to make a good impression. They were greeted with a snappy salute and a pick and shovel as an initiation present from each unit. One young officer remarked, "And to think I spent ninety days in school learning to be an officer just to come to this."

The carpenters hired by contractors found their efforts supplemented by non-union labor in uniform. The skill of the non-union labor in building furniture, blackboards, etc., was so successful that soon the

Follow Me!

contractors had to guard their lumber piles to insure against "moonlight requisitioning." It was discovered that OCS grads made fine pick and shovel men. Someone facetiously suggested that a pick and shovel be adopted for the Division insignia.

The cadremen had completed construction of office desks, chairs and file cabinets, but now they were confronted with the problem of equipping the ninety-six dayrooms in the Division area. Soon there appeared in newspapers of all surrounding communities pleas for second hand furniture and recreational equipment. The people of Willamette Valley quickly responded and the dayrooms were equipped with tables, overstuffed chairs, davenports, reading lamps, bookcases, ping pong tables, magazines and many other articles.

Another phase of the early days of the Division can be described as a period of concentrated learning when all cadremen attended company, battalion, regimental, and division schools. Reams and reams of paper were used in outlining every military subject known to man. The 414th

10

Infantry officers circulated throughout the Division the following poem:

> Indeed, what manner of men are we,
> Who fight our wars with analyses;
> We seek our foes in foreign lands,
> And put them down with lesson plans.
> We found that after our induction,
> War was nothing but instruction;
> And if we do not plan our prattle,
> We surely will be lost in battle;
> Rifles, guns and hand grenades,
> Now give way to training aids;
> Forget about the ammunition,
> Is your pencil in condition?
> Do not call for transportation,
> Paper work will save the nation.
> So if the foe attempts to pass,
> We drop our guns and call a class;
> And then if any remain alive,
> They are choked to death with 21-5.

In October the rains came. Farmers of Benton and Polk Counties in Oregon's Willamette Valley had indulged in occasional wry smiles when the War Department talked of building a big training camp there. The Army would learn by experience, as had they and their forebears for generations, why the Willamette Valley farmers had come to be called Webfeet. The 104th Division did learn. Men slogged through rain, sometimes snow, plunged through swollen streams, and bivouacked in dripping forests. Gun crews and truck drivers pushed and pulled and cursed to coax their ponderous vehicles from the sticky mud. The old-timers said: "Do not worry, it rains, but you never get wet." Timberwolves soon found that the reason the old-timers never got wet was because they stayed indoors all winter. But such was not the lot of the 104th; they were to remain outside most of the time and they learned that one does get wet when exposed to Oregon's average rainfall of forty inches.

TRAINING AT CAMP ADAIR

After activation, rumors came thick and fast as to the date "fillers" would arrive. The month of October found the contractors moving out of the Division area and turning everything over to the military. Then followed the period of orientation in how to operate the several types of furnaces. Everyone learned the Army method of firing the Furnace, Hot Air, Model M-1.

November was heralded by the arrival of those long-overdue fillers. After several schools on how to receive a filler, perform medical inspections, quarter and feed him, orient him, and make him feel at home, the first trainload arrived. The hour was late, the weather wet, and the band blared "There'll Be a Hot Time in the Old Town Tonight." The train pulled to a halt and the procession of GI's started. This process continued during November and on into December. On 15 December the strength report showed a total of 819 officers, twenty-one warrant officers and 15,112 enlisted men and by 1 January the report showed 840 officers, twenty-two warrant officers and 16,261 enlisted men.

Basic training for the newly arrived recruits started on 14 December and the soldiers soon learned why the natives along the Willamette Valley hibernated each winter. Raincoats were part of the regular uniforms as the doughboys sloshed along over the sodden countryside and learned to throw themselves in the cold mud with disregard. Artillerymen swore as they shifted trails or pulled their pieces and trucks from the mire, and all hands worked constantly on equipment which rusted in a matter of minutes. Before the 329th Engineers had learned the use of the "weasel" it was called out to assist in flood relief when the Willamette River went slightly berserk following the heavy January rains. For the heroic work of saving the lives of several people, Governor Charles A. Sprague cited the Engineers by letter on 22 January.

The first medal for heroism awarded to any member of the Division was formally presented in November 1942 by Major General Cook to Sergeant Clarence D. Leach of the 104th Division Artillery. Sergeant Leach received the Soldier's Medal for heroism "above and beyond the call of duty" in risking his life in flames that enveloped an Army truck on 2 September. After rolling on the ground to smother a fire in his clothing, he drove the truck to safety.

During "basic," men could be seen marching in every direction and in every formation. They were learning to become fighting soldiers. As motorists rode on highway 99-W past the cantonment, they saw some of the grimmest training that American soldiers could get. Cold steel flashed in the sunlight or pierced the fog. Whatever the weather, the infantrymen were attacking dummies with the bayonet. All the men learned their weapons and in January they were firing record courses in the driving rain and blinding snow.

Basic training ended on 13 March and the physically hardened Timberwolves commenced their "unit" training on 14 March. The objective of the training was to produce well-trained, hard-hitting units, efficient in the practical application of tactical doctrine to combat situations. Units took to the field. It was a rough time as the men slept on the ground, ate out of messkits and washed and shaved from steel helmets. During this period Prune Ridge took on a new meaning. Calamine lotion (for poison oak) became the most popular face cream for the Timberwolves. Prune Ridge and the surrounding hills were taken from the north, south, east and west and finally by air attack. So many foxholes and slit trenches were dug there that it began to resemble the result of a volcanic eruption.

Under the heading "Weather Report," Technical Sergeant William Farrel, G Company, 414th Infantry, recalls what to him was the most predominant feature of the Timberwolves' training in and around Camp Adair:

The most outstanding feature of Camp Adair was the weather that I believe all will remember. Natives told us that it never rained in Oregon. But the old adage was broken for it continually rained from the time we arrived until almost the time we moved out to go on maneuvers. Camp Adair received the nickname Swamp Adair. Continually we worked, marched, and trained in knee-deep mud.

Some of the landmarks most all will remember are Coffin Butte, Prune Ridge, and the town of Airley which was Off Limits for all military personnel. Airley had a hamburger stand and about three houses with four or five civilians living there. Everyone disliked the place because in passing through, it reminded one of the fact that there was about eight or ten miles to camp and lots more walking to take place. Coffin Butte was a hill much admired by GIs at first from the barracks windows, but as we advanced along in our training our previous opinion changed because then we used the hill as a playground for squad and platoon tactics. Prune Ridge, an outstanding spot about five miles from camp proper, will long remain in our memories. Many a wet day and night was spent on this ridge sleeping on the drenched terrain and playing soldier.

Basic training was about the same in Camp Adair as in any other camp except for the climatic conditions. I for one will not forget the day on the range when the snow covered our rifles and one could hardly see the target. Personally I don't see how anyone qualified but most of us did. Everyone was eager to learn during basic training. We knew that what we learned then would be of help to us in months to come. Our days were filled with classes, close order drill, weapons familiarization, and all the basic subjects necessary to help one become a good infantryman. Our evenings were at times spent in the field studying the compass, learning night movements of smaller units, and studying night discipline in order to make us efficient night fighters.

Despite weather conditions, the Timberwolves, to a man, learned infantry tactics from A to Z. Oregon terrain bothered not a few, the outstanding being Sergeant Arthur C. Patterson of B Battery, 929th Field Artillery Battalion, who recalls the sinking sands of a sumphole:

. . . Another thing that always got us, at every position, we had to dig a latrine and a sump for the kitchen. And that was some job, for as soon as you would get down a way, the sides of the hole would cave in. Also characteristic were digging foxholes in each position, and sweating out long chow lines. One really had to be fast at eating or you would have a nice covering of dust on your food. Oh, yes, those were the good old days.

We used to run across a snake now and then. Especially in the rocky parts. One of the boys got the surprise of his life to find one in his bedroll, as he was ready to hit the sack. All you could see was a cloud of dust.

The best part of the maneuvers was when we got a break after a four or five day problem. That's when we could go to the shower unit and get cleaned up. We would also have our PX and we stacked up with candy for the next problem. Movies at night and an occasional swim helped immeasurably.

Award of the Silver Star for gallantry in action 23 November 1942 at Guadalcanal was conferred upon Brigadier General Bryant E. Moore, Assistant Division Commander, before the assembled Timberwolf Division on 15 March 1943 and for the first time since its activation the Division passed in review. In the driving rain at the colorful and impressive ceremony, General Cook placed the medal upon General Moore's chest. General Moore had joined the Division in February, having come direct from Guadalcanal to assume his new command. He also received the Distinguished Service Medal at Camp Adair, the award having been made on 29 March 1942.

The first week in May all personnel of the Division took the Army Ground Forces physical training tests. The thirty-three pushups, the 150-yard dash, the pig-a-back race, and the four mile march in fifty minutes made up part of the rugged test. The physical toughness which had been acquired by the men of the 104th was evidenced by the high score of the Division: 91.6 per cent.

Each infantry and engineer platoon successfully completed the Army Ground Forces platoon firing problem. Upon completion of the unit training period on 29 May, the program of combined training began. The Division training memorandum outlined the general mission: "To weld the units of the Division into a mentally and physically hardened team capable of taking the field for a prolonged period of time, prepared for action in a combat zone." This training period was divided into three phases. From 30 May to 17 July, the infantry, artillery, and engineers worked together in combat team exercises. From 18 July to 31 July, attack of a fortified area and river crossings were completed by each unit, and from 1 August to 7 August, preparations for movement to the Oregon maneuver area were completed.

On 26 July, Major General Alexander M. Patch Jr., commander of the IV Corps, and other dignitaries including the Governor and high state officials from Oregon witnessed an assault of a fortified area. Two battalions of infantry, supported by two artillery battalions, reduced a series of pillboxes fashioned after the types used by the Nazis along their Westwall. Dust from explosions and a thick chemical fog rose 500 feet into the air as the combat teams placed bangalore tor-

Major General Gilbert R. Cook, left, and Major General Alexander M. Patch talk to a member of the attack force during the Camp Adair maneuvers

pedoes in the enemy barbed wire and blew it apart. Then specialists armed with flame throwers and explosives neutralized the pillboxes. It was a one-sided problem with no opposition, but it acclimated the soldiers to the noise and flash of live ammunition. That night General Patch witnessed the 414th Infantry, supported by the 329th Engineer Battalion, crossing the Willamette River. Teamwork was constantly being stressed. The observers commented: "Brilliantly displaying the battle tactics learned in months of hard training, units of the Timberwolf Division gave visible evidence of the gathering might which is bringing nearer the day of victory."

In June, the toughest enlisted men in the Division were uncovered following the three-day physical fitness and mental alertness test. The need for superior scouts was constantly being reported from the combat zones. Judging the men on their physical condition, knowledge of weapons, map and compass reading, ability to read aerial photos, use of field expedients, and ability to swim, 103 of 317 top Timberwolves were selected—the Division's first Wolf Scouts. Among the standout stalwarts were: Sergeant Wright, Pfc. Scuza, Private Puskus, Private Bundell, Private Evers, Pfc. Blondell, Pfc. Eaton, Sergeant Hanan, Private Taylor, Private Church, Pfc. Ray, Private Lipscomb, Corporal Jackson, Private Jenkins, Private Lewis and Pfc. Dodson.

In August of 1943, with many months of back-breaking training toil past, the Division found its strength at 12,000 officers and enlisted men. Many of the men had been discharged because of age or physical ailment and some had been transferred to other units.

DIVISION ACTIVITIES

In addition to the forty-eight hours of vigorous training each week, the Division from its inception participated in many sports and other activities. Three basketball leagues were organized and games were played four nights a week to determine the Division championship. In the Infantry League were entered: Gulls (413th Infantry), Mountaineers (414th Infantry), Geysers (415th Infantry), Engineers (329th Engineer Battalion), Pillrollers (329th Medical Battalion). In the Artillery League were entered: Bees (385th Field Artillery Battalion), Boneheads (386th Field Artillery Battalion), Falcons (929th Field Artillery Battalion), Redlegs (387th Field Artillery Battalion), and the Generals (Division Artillery). In the Special Troops League were entered: Headquarters Company (104th Division Headquarters Company), Snoopers (104th Reconnaissance Troops), Storekeepers (104th Quartermaster Company), Sigs (104th Signal Company), Balls o' Fire (804th Ordnance Company). The Camp Adair *Sentry* carried the following headlines about the tourney:

MOUNTAINEERS KEEP RECORD CLEAR BY SCORING 4TH STRAIGHT WIN AT EXPENSE OF PILLROLLERS 46-9

ENGINEERS PUT UP A WHALE OF A BATTLE IN THE INFANTRY LEAGUE TILT WITH GEYSERS OF THE 415TH, BUT ARE FINALLY DOWNED 36-14

SNOOPERS TRIP STOREKEEPERS 38-33 AND DRAW TO WITHIN ONE HALF GAME OF THE LEADING HEADQUARTERS COMPANY REDLEGS OF THE ARTILLERY LOSE 31-14 TO THE LEADING BONEHEADS

GULLS STRENGTHEN CLAIM TO SECOND PLACE PUTTING THE PILLROLLERS INTO DEEPER LAST PLACE BY A SCORE 70-32

DRIVING BONEHEADS WIN OVER BEES 29-17 AND BREAK THEIR LEADERSHIP DEADLOCK WITH IDLE REDLEGS

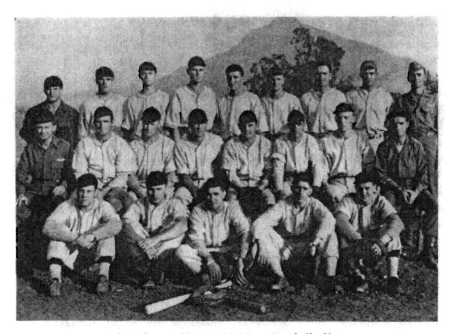

413th Infantry Team, Division Baseball Champs

REDLEGS STOP THE GENERALS 29-13

STOREKEEPERS PROVE MUCH HOTTER THAN BALLS O' FIRE WITH SCORE 35-7

THE POWERFUL MOUNTAINEERS FINALLY DROP THEIR FIRST GAME LOSING TO 2D PLACE GULLS 34-28 AFTER A RIP ROARING DRAMATIC MELEE IN WHICH THE SCORE WAS TIED 4 TIMES DURING THE LAST 2 MINUTES OF PLAY

HEADQUARTERS COMPANY MIX UP THE SIGS 32-10

REDLEGS ONCE AGAIN CRUSH BONEHEADS 36-17 AND CLINCH ARTILLERY LEAGUE

MOUNTAINEERS DE-SPOUT THE GEYSERS 36-14 TO CINCH INFANTRY LEAGUE

DIVISION HEADQUARTERS COMPANY CLINCHES SPECIAL TROOPS LEAGUE WINNING 11 LOSING 0

The 414th Mountaineers, the 387th Field Artillery Redlegs and the 104th Division Headquarters Company began their playoffs for the

17

Division basketball championship on 1 March. The Redleg team scored a stunning 18-15 victory over the favored undefeated Division Headquarters team in the initial playoff. More than 2,000 officers and enlisted men watched the 414th Mountaineers defeat the 387th Redlegs 29 to 25 and win the Division title. With fifty-five seconds to go the Redlegs led 25-23 but were overcome in the closing seconds.

On 4 March the Timberwolves organized a powerful baseball team with Sergeant Jack Knott as team manager and coach. Sixty men answered the first call. From this large list of horsehide hopefuls were selected the following members: Gregory, Frye, Bell, Sabrinsky, Connors, Armstrong, Calhoun, Butler, Jones, Langsam, Knott, Quin, Soupsus, O'Doul, Hohle, Bertucci, Perez, Rich, Karlin. Many of them were ex-big leaguers including Sergeant Knott, for several years with the St. Louis Browns and Connie Mack's Athletics; Beau Bell, formerly with St. Louis, Detroit, and Cleveland; Lieutenant Joe Quin, a former right-hander for the Washington Senators.

In the initial game on 29 April, the Timberwolves defeated the University of Oregon 4 to 3. Beau Bell slashed a double in the seventh inning to give the Timberwolves the decision. It was not long before the Timberwolves were recognized as the outstanding baseball team in the West. The following headlines show the team's success:

WOLF PACK TRAMPLES CASCADE STARS 7-2
GREGORY STARS WITH LANGSAM GETTING CREDIT FOR WIN

VICTORY MAD TIMBERWOLF DIVISION BASEBALL TEAM EASILY
SUBDUES OREGON STATE COLLEGE 8-4

TIMBERWOLF CLUB TURNS IN 4TH AND 5TH STRAIGHT WINS
DEFEATING COMMERCIAL IRON WORKS AND
PORTLAND UNIVERSITY

TIMBERWOLVES WIN STATE SEMIPRO BASEBALL TOURNAMENT
WITH 4-0 WIN OVER PORTLAND

TIMBERWOLVES TOPPLE PORTLAND AIRBASE 17-1

In July, the Timberwolves ended their season with two titles, the Oregon State Semipro and Northwest Service Teams championships, the latter being climaxed when the team defeated Fort Lewis two games out of three. Of the games scheduled, the Timberwolves won twenty-four, lost only two.

The Division also had a powerful basketball squad. Members of the team included: Pfc. Loren Garrett (Missouri), Sergeant Clark Brown

(Iowa), Lieutenant Herb Brown (Indiana), Lieutenant Gene Badgley (Iowa), Lieutenant Joe Quin (Seton Hall), Lieutenant Sam Coster (West Point), Lieutenant Bob Duffy, coach and player (California), Lieutenant Lloyd Evanson (North Dakota), Lieutenant McElmurry (Oklahoma), Private Waxman, Sergeant L. Burnick, and Corporal Kuklin. Playing the leading basketball teams in the West, the team climaxed its season with a 58 to 38 win over the 96th Division hoopsters for the Post championship.

Other athletic events saw the 413th Seagulls win the Division base-ball and softball championships. In the boxing tournament the 413th, 414th, and 415th tied for championship honors. Individual winners were: Al Sorenson, 414th Infantry, bantamweight; Frank La Bella, 413th Infantry, junior welterweight; Vincent Fazio, 415th Infantry, junior lightweight; Henry Gutterie, 415th Infantry, lightweight; Nat Weintraub, 413th Infantry, middleweight; Warren Morris, 414th Infan-try, featherweight; Bobby Moses, 413th Infantry, welterweight; Wayne Seibert, 414th Infantry, light-heavyweight; and Charles Watts, 415th Infantry, heavyweight.

The Division troops took part in many civic affairs in the neighboring communities. The Division band played at a number of ship launchings at the Kaiser shipyards in Portland. Timberwolves sponsored several radio programs and the Division was guest to many dignitaries includ-ing Governors Snell and Sprague of Oregon. On 20 April, the Timber-wolves "invaded" Portland as a part of the second War Loan Drive. Eight hundred men from the 104th Division moved by trucks to the metropolis and set up their guns on the busy streets. Attracting huge crowds, the Division assisted materially in boosting the bond sales.

Citizens of Corvallis, Salem, Albany, Eugene, Portland and other communities near the camp were gracious in their reception. USO clubs were established in all towns and various civic and fraternal organiza-tions entertained the soldiers on their visits to the communities. In March 1945 Mrs. C. D. Winston, in a letter to the editor of the Portland *Oregonian*, expressed her sentiments and those of the people in the Willamette Valley.

To the Editor: Just two years ago, families of the 104th Division were living right here with hundreds of us in Corvallis. We knew the boys and their wives and their children. Lt. Sam Peck and his wife lived with me. Sam had his 21st birthday at my house, and I'll always consider those two my special children. I'd never seen them before that Sunday they came up from the USO to my house to stay overnight just until they could find an apartment. They stayed ten months.

We had some good times together. Once I had dinner with them at the officers' mess. Another time Mae and I watched the entire division march in review on the field at Camp Adair on one of the coldest, windiest, wettest days Oregon can produce. In our line of vision, each passing column slipped in the mud in just the same spot and in just the same way each time. I remember how much harder it was for the short-legged men to keep up.

On another occasion, we saw the "graduation exercises" of the division. This time it was a beautiful, bright, spring day when the slopes of an Oregon hillside became a mock battlefield. There was the long ditch that would stop the tanks; over there were the pillboxes of the enemy they were to attack, and up on another hillside an abandoned group of farm buildings had become a little German village—Insdorf (or some such name) was on the marker.

The boys bobbed up out of their foxholes unexpectedly here and there as they ran forward toward the pseudo-enemy lines. A constant roar of gunfire, with injections of staccato reports of machine guns filled the air: flares went up telling the men of the stages of battle; flame throwers were seen off yonder. One of the men had a dog that was faithfully following him into the battle. The battle was won, of course, at the right time, and down in one corner of the field all the hay was raked off the big gun which until that time no one of us had seen.

Yes, Insdorf (or whatever it was) was taken without a casualty. Eschweiler was taken by the 104th Division at a heavier cost, and now they have marched into Cologne.

One day Mae had a party at my house for the young officers of Sam's company. They were there with their wives and sweethearts, and it was a gala evening. One young lieutenant was to be married to the girl who was with him that night. She is now living in the Willamette Valley with her son, but the young lieutenant will never see his baby, for he was recently killed in Europe.

Wherever go the boys of the 104th and whatever they do will always concern us in Corvallis who witnessed the birth of the outfit. They'll always be our bunch of boys.

MRS. C. D. WINSTON,
2720 Orchard Street,
Corvallis, Ore.

MANEUVERS

With its basic and unit training completed, the Timberwolf Division moved out of Camp Adair on 6 and 7 August to the Oregon desert in the vicinity of Sisters-Bend, Oregon. The officers and men had completed small unit training and were now to engage in Division, Corps, and Army maneuvers. On 7 August the Division closed in its assembly area. The strength report showed a total of 934 officers, thirty-eight warrant officers and 10,713 enlisted men. Actual maneuvers started on 10 August with the "D" series—the Division problems in which combat teams of the Division maneuvered against one another. There were six problems in the series, which came to a close on 26 August. On 1 September, the Division entrucked and moved to its new assembly area, near Hampton, east of Bend, Oregon. After camping two weeks on the sage-covered desert, the 104th Division began its maneuvers on 13 September. The 91st Infantry Division, the 96th Infantry Division, the

705th Tank Destroyer Battalion, the 644th Tank Destroyer Battalion, and many other tank, engineer and antiaircraft units participated in the maneuvers being conducted by IV Corps, then commanded by Major General Alexander M. Patch, Jr.

At dusk on 13 September, the Timberwolves covered their desert-tanned bodies with fatigues, their puptents with sage, and began scooping foxholes to satisfy the umpires who were descending upon them. At 1600 on 14 September, the restraining line was lifted and Problem M-1, the defense of Hampton, got under way. The Timberwolves were the Reds, the 91st and 96th the Blues. Wailing sirens from circling artillery cub planes ended the problem in the afternoon of 15 September.

M-1 was scarcely under way when rumor had it that the War Department was ordering the suspension of maneuvers because of wear and tear on tires, but the problems came and went, with new speculation at the end of each one. Towards the end of maneuvers, the rubber-tire rumor gave way to others: "The 104th Division is going to Camp White"; "the 104th is going to Camp San Luis Obispo"; "the Division is going to Fort Dix"; and so on.

On 18 September, defensive problem M-2 began with the 104th defending Glass Butte. A familiar sight was a column of dust, marching across country propelled by GI's with makeshift respirators tied around their heads. So dense at times was the powdered dust that it was difficult to breathe.

For the first time the Division changed its colors from Red to Blue and in conjunction with the 91st Infantry Division launched its attack on Wagontire. M-3 ended on 29 September.

Next was M-4, Christmas Tree Lake, in which the Division, again as part of the Blue force, advanced forty miles in three days and nights. What a relief it was when the sirens ended the problem at 1600 on 6 October.   -

Again on Problem M-5 the 104th Division was on the offensive with the mission of seizing Horse Ridge and Bear Creek Buttes. Successive objectives of Seven Mile Ridge, Cougar Mountain, North Table Mountain, Squaw Butte and Watkins Butte were seized in the thirty-eight-mile advance.

Probably the most delightful and comforting experience during the entire maneuvers was the sagebrush campfires, plentiful and easy to kindle. Not only did it dispel the bite of the desert night, but it furnished light for the poker groups huddled over a GI blanket. To those who sat silently staring into its burning embers, it was a magic crystal of times and events to come, or it was the reminiscent background to other times and places. "Fires out" came last on our list of tactical

On Camp Carson Lake, 329th Engineers blow up large underwater obstacle as part of invasion maneuvers

preparations for the next problem, and even after it had been covered we continued to linger, reluctant to bid farewell to an old friend.

M-6: The 104th organized and occupied positions to defend Horse Ridge and Bear Creek Butte. M-7: Timberwolves forced a crossing over the Deschutte River and attacked Kline Butte. The days had grown chilly and the nights cold on the great Oregon desert when the final problem ended 1700 on 30 October. Our memories of the Oregon maneuvers were many. Tasty venison supplementing GI chow. The painful positions and long hours on Camp Adair's marksmanship courses had paid off well for each chow line. The howling coyotes, the traveling PX's, the sawmill swimming hole, bathing in the Deschutte, off-limits Sisters, Alkali Lake, and many other items made up our memoirs.

Major General Terry Allen Assumes Command

On 15 October 1943 Major General Terry de la M. Allen, already a seasoned veteran of World War II, after service in the African and the European Theaters as commander of the Fighting 1st Division, assumed command of the Timberwolves. Major General Gilbert R. Cook was dropped from the roster of the 104th on 19 October when he took command of the XII Corps. The sound basic training received under the able leadership of Major General Cook was reflected later on the battlefield.

Upon taking command General Allen paid the following tribute to the men of the 104th Division: "This is as completely fine a potential combat unit as I have ever seen. I have not seen better spirit or a more thorough response to training."

For a successful combat division, General Allen pointed out that discipline, technique, physical toughness and a belief in your units are essential.

On 7 November the Division moved by train from Bend, Oregon, to Camp Hyder in the California-Arizona maneuver area. Camp was set up near Hyder, Arizona, located in the desert on the Southern Pacific Railroad between Yuma and Phoenix. On 29 November the Division moved to Camp Horn, six miles to the west of Hyder, and there the 104th began its thirteen-week desert training program. General Allen opened the period by outlining to all commissioned and noncommissioned officers the accomplishments and work he expected. Night operations, weapon proficiency, reconnaissance, rapid maneuver, combat exercises and battle drill were especially emphasized. "GET SMART AND GET TOUGH" was the motto of our training and the Timberwolves soon acquired a confident belief in themselves and their units. The principle of "Find 'em, fix 'em and fight 'em" was firmly inculcated in our combat units.

On 6 January the Legion of Merit was presented by General Patch, Commander of IV Corps, to General Allen for outstanding service in commanding the 1st Infantry Division in Sicily.

While on the desert the Division adopted for its motto, "NOTHING IN HELL CAN STOP THE TIMBERWOLVES," and likewise the Division song was written by Lieutenant Colonel Robert C. Ingalls, S-3 Division Artillery, and Captain Oates A. Pynes, 387th Field Artillery Battalion:

"RALLY THE PACK"
(To the melody of "Rambling Wreck from Georgia Tech")

From way up north in Oregon to Southlands far away
We've moved across the desert sands afightin' all the way
We'll climb the highest mountain in any state or land
We'll swing along by combat-team a-fightin' hand to hand.

CHORUS:

Oh, this is our night to howl boys, just follow us with will
The Timberwolves are on the prowl, we're closing in to kill
We're a hellava gang to fight with, just follow us and see
Hey, The 104th will lead the way from hell to victory.

We'll find the foe and fix him there with fire from shot and shell
Then move around on every flank and give him bloody hell
Oh rally the pack to counter-attack we fight with might and main
Hey, The Infantry, Artillery, and Cavalry all the same.

CHORUS: Repeat

Oh the Engineers and Signal Corps, the Quartermaster too
The Special Troops and Medics they will fight along with you
The Ordnance keeps 'em rollin', the MP's all in line
You'll find our gang is sluggin' on, and never markin' time.

CHORUS: Repeat

Tales of maneuvers don't bring many enthusiastic stories, but to Staff Sergeant John Ferraro, Company M, 413th Infantry, it was the most miserable time of his life. In his opinion the Army could do nothing right—and from his commentary on the Oregon maneuvers, we get the average doughboy's feeling for all those dry-runs which, at the time, seemed ridiculous.

Around the middle of July, a new phase of Army life came to us—maneuvers. Although at that time it was only rumor, a GI sense of intuition told us that something was up. The commonplace Army bitching followed. I heard a lot about maneuvers, how rough it was, so naturally I didn't look forward to it. We watched the latter part of July turn those ugly rumors into fact. Oh, how that hurt! Finally, they told us we would maneuver around Bend, Oregon and we first bivouacked in a beautiful forest. This was the life! Yes—for the first day or so. Then came orders to move out.

I was gunner with the 81mm mortars. We moved out for a few miles with the guns on carriers. It was interesting to see how well our vehicles were spaced out and how our boys maneuvered those jeeps and trucks on the twisting roads. Calling them roads was a masterpiece of overstatement, and the dust was four inches thick. When the order came to halt and go on from there off carriers, we all became part of that dust. My nostrils thrived on it; my eyes were constantly at half mast, and it was about an inch thick on my face. I thought—oh those lucky fellows on trucks, but when I saw them they were no different. But, all in all, so far it was fun . . . it says here. We were very green as yet and we didn't mind it. Our training in garrison surely taught us plenty. My first experience, and a well learned one, was one I will never forget because it almost cost me my back. We had just moved out of a forest into the open and we were pretty well bunched up. Just as our sergeant told us to scatter, an enemy plane dove on us. We had plenty of ground to disperse over, and as I ran, the bipod I was carrying dug into my shoulder with each step, and when I hit the ground flat on my stomach, I forgot to throw it away from me. It felt as though a 250-pounder had jumped on me with both feet. I was really mad at my own carelessness and stupidity. I got up bitching and spitting Oregon soil. We had our umpire with us and just as we crossed the opening to move into another forest, we were told an artillery concentration was falling on us. We all hit the dirt and were supposed to dig in. I forgot because I was gabbing with my buddy and laughing about it. The next thing I knew, both of us were dead—technically! Well, if you remember those maneuvers, we didn't have it easy for those next few days while we were supposed to be dead. Between KP and latrine digging, I started looking for the smallest hill to go over. Finally, we rejoined our outfit and took mental harassment for our stupidity.

We attacked our objective a few hours later and completed taking it. A slight downpour for an hour or so got things a little muddy. We dug in and were told to hold our objective for the night. By now C rations were a steady diet. We had them for breakfast and dinner, but the poop had us getting a hot supper. It never came. Then more rain. We were to stay on the alert all night because our planes spotted the enemy making preparations for an attack. It was miserable; no supper, wet to the skin, and up to our ankles in mud and water. To me, it seemed foolish, for I figured half our men would come down with pneumonia, but surprisingly none did. The next morning, with the dawn, came a counter-attack. We couldn't hold. We were to retreat to an alternate defensive position—way back. No sleep and still wet, I was ready to call it quits. Finally reaching our defensive position we dug in. I dug and dug and dug, and soon—blisters. Boy was I tired! I asked my officer if this was what we went through in combat and he said it was as far as he knew, if not worse. I was really learning to be rough and tough and the more we went on the more I became accustomed to digging, hitting the dirt, camouflaging and carrying my bipod. Never will I forget my first gun position; I thought I had a beauty. I lay back and relaxed, waiting for compliments. My officer walked up and started enumerating my mistakes. When he got through it seemed as though I just had a hole in the ground and that's all. But now I was beginning to learn what the maneuvers were for—to enable you to make your mistakes now and get you rough and tough for combat operations.

One night, I was picked for a patrol into the enemy lines. We removed our helmets and leggins, wore wool knit caps, tied our pants legs down, and blackened our faces. We moved out around midnight. The enemy wasn't very much on the alert, so we infiltrated through their lines without any trouble. We got our information and were on the way back when all hell broke loose. I was captured and from then until our first rest period I dug latrines, did KP and marched until I thought my feet would fall off. By this time I was thoroughly disgusted with maneuvers and the Army. I was mad at the Army while actually what was burning me up was my own stupidity.

What was the use of digging holes, marching and learning how to do things quietly when we didn't have to? I could do all that when the time came. I never really thought I would be going overseas—naive character that I was. What really got me down was the eating, especially when the enemy cut us off from our kitchen. I was so hungry I figured I couldn't go very much farther—but I did, and plenty. When our K and C rations finally came, they tasted like filet de mignon.

What seemed really crazy was learning to fight at night. Who ever heard of fighting at night? How the hell could we tell where we were going, where the enemy was, or what we were walking into? I figured the man that was sitting and waiting for you could see you but you wouldn't see him . . . need I say more? These crazy officers; any sensible man could see it wouldn't work. But all the bitching I did was futile. We were to learn how to fight at night— damning the maneuvers. How many nights I was wet and cold to the skin, I can't remember. And the mud—hell, that was part of me. I used to think and pray: "Isn't this ever going to end?" When I had to shave in cold water, I really blew my top, then someone would say, "Okay, wash them dirty clothes." What the hell! Can't they even get our clothes washed? But we were really getting tough . . . that I mustn't forget.

Another thing: I don't believe we ever went around any hills. Boy, I used to curse those hills when I got about half way up. That damned bipod seemed as though it was pulling me down. One incident I will never forget. We had moved out across a plain to attack a hill; rather a mountain, because it was really tall. There wasn't any firing going on—seemed funny to me. Maybe a trap. We got almost to the top and one of these affable umpires turned and said to our commanding officer, "No one is here, this must be the wrong hill." That did it! What a man—he could have told us at the bottom of the hill but waited until we were on the top. I could have gleefully knocked hell out of him for that. That's the Army for you, always doing it the wrong way. I'd sooner be overseas—I thought.

Something else that got me down was the size of the shovel they issued us. I remember one day when we were in a hurry to dig in because of imminent enemy attack. I was digging with my shovel, large size M-1—when my sergeant walked up and started chewing because I was so slow. It annoyed me so I asked him why he didn't get me a spoon, I could dig much faster. He did. We stayed there that night. About two in the morning, when I was doing okay in dreamland I was awakened by a lot of yelling and a not too gentle boot placed in a tender spot. It was our sergeant yelling, "Come on, let's go, we have to move out." Say, wasn't that nice; get out of a nice warm bed into the cold and run your fanny off. Leaving in a hurry, I forgot my blankets but not that heavy M-1. That came first, at the risk of freezing. I guess they figured I could take it. Then came the dry runs; aren't they ever going to give us any ammo? If I fired one round, I fired a million—all dry. I was even dry running in my sleep I guess.

My only consolation was a hot meal and my mail, that is, when I received it. Worse than that I was losing my money during rest periods. Oh, those dice. I recall the night we went to see a movie. We all sat on a little hill looking down at the makeshift screen. There I was, all excited and anxious to see my first movie in months. Time came for the movie and surely something had to go wrong. On came the picture but no sound. At this point, I realized that such things didn't seem to bother me like they used to . . . I must be getting indoctrinated. I was bitching when I crawled in the bed. Oh, a beautiful bed. You can't imagine the luxury; a blanket spread on the nice soft ground with the little boulders for your pillow. What a life! Does this go on forever? I wondered if they were accepting transfers to the Air Corps.

One joyful thing on maneuvers I won't forget is the time they attached our section of mortars to a company occupying a hill to the left of a road used by the enemy. We were told to strike at the convoy, capture what we could and move back to our hill. It was really fun. It started raining pretty hard that day and we had made shelters for ourselves to keep dry. The enemy had attacked the rest of our unit and pushed them back some eight or nine miles. The enemy didn't know our position. That evening the moon came out and we could see the road very plain. It made a dip in front of our lines and the rain turned it into a quagmire. The enemy convoy was to use that road to move forward. We watched their first few trucks try, but they bogged down and had to stay there. The other vehicles turned around and went out another way. In the morning, to the enemy's surprise, we attacked them and much to our surprise and joy, we had a kitchen truck. For two days, we had hot meals three times a day and snacks in between. That was *my* type of maneuvers. But I changed my mind a few hours later. The enemy found us, chased us back, and we lost two of the vehicles in the same mud. That meant carrying our guns, and once again our bedding equipment stayed with the enemy. The best part of eating at night was you didn't see what you were eating. Everything went into one; dessert, meat, potatoes and anything else you had; even dirt sometimes if you weren't careful. Finally, we heard maneuvers were over. Was I happy! Rumors flying all over, all kinds. I figured, good old garrison. Then officially we were told we were going to Arizona. What for? Yes, you guessed it, maneuvers again. Arizona maneuvers. Won't I ever get away from these damned maneuvers?

The arduous training in the Horn area was completed on 9 February and the Division moved northwest of Yuma for Corps maneuvers. We left behind us the wide open wastelands of Horn, the pyramidal tent homes, sand and dust storms, and memories of the pleasant weekend visits to Yuma and Phoenix. The Division had no sooner closed in sunny California northwest of Yuma than the rains came. All Califor-

Seagull Boxing Team, Division Champions

nians went into mourning. During the next two weeks the Division was engaged in maneuvers with the 80th Division. On 18 February, the Timberwolves commenced their attack against the fortied positions at Palen Pass, the formidable obstacle which had never been "captured." Taking advantage of its night operations and its physical toughness training, the Timberwolves scaled the high ridges and fighting by night accomplished its mission of seizing Palen Pass. The maneuvers ended with the next problem, during which the Division fought a delaying action for four days. On 4 March the Division moved to Camp Granite, California. Our new home did not differ greatly from Hyder or Horn except that the wind blew more severely. Timberwolves were seen in Idaho, Palm Springs and even Los Angeles. Movement rumors began to rumble—Fort Dix, Camp Devens, San Luis Obispo, and Fort Lewis. No mention was made of Camp Carson, Colorado, but on 15 March the Timberwolves were on their way to Colorado Springs.

Many changes had been made in the staff of the Division during the eighteen months following its activation. Major General Cook had been succeeded by General Allen on 15 October; Brigadier General Kramer, Assistant Division Commander, was succeeded by Brigadier General Moore on 6 February. Brigadier General William C. Dunckel, Division Artillery Commander, left the Division and Brigadier General William Woodward on 29 December assumed command. Colonel Harold Mandel, Chief of Staff, was succeeded by Lieutenant Colonel B. R. DeGraff on 2 October. Lieutenant Colonel Burwell B. Wilkes, AC of S, G-1, was succeeded by Major William J. Boydston on 24 April 1943. Major

Infantry Day—1944

Boydston was succeeded by Major Basil E. Williams on 14 October 1943. Major Williams gave way to Lieutenant Colonel Scott T. Rex on 13 December 1943.

Other changes transferred Lieutenant Colonel Charles T. Senay, AC of S, G-2, who was succeeded by Lieutenant Colonel Howard E. Pearson on 4 November 1942. Lieutenant Colonel James E. Bowen, Jr., AC of S, G-3, was succeeded by Major Leo A. Hoegh on 25 November 1943. Lieutenant Colonel Herbert B. Enderton left and Lieutenant Colonel DeGraff became AC of S, G-4, on 11 November 1942. Major Clyde L. Pennington on 2 October 1943 took over this position from Colonel DeGraff.

Camp Carson, lying in the evening shadows of Pike's Peak, was surrounded by renowned scenic and historic spots, Wacs, and mules. Here, to the ranks of the Division, came thousands of the ASTP and Air Corps who embarked on a five-weeks training program covering eleven basic infantry subjects. Under Lieutenant Colonel Floyd, the training regiment was established to carry on the program. On 7 May, the training regiment was dissolved and the new Timberwolves carried on with training in their parent organizations. Outstanding in the Carson training were numerous night attacks, amphibious training, malaria training, range firing, and the eighty-eight-hour specialized weapons courses. The three most significant phases and the longest ones to be remembered by the troops were: battle drill, POM, and TAT.

An active athletic program also went on in which new champions were made. The 413th Infantry won the Division boxing crown before a crowd of 7,000 officers and enlisted men. Individual crowns went to: Private John Matthews, 413th Infantry, bantamweight; Private Jimmy Sprouse, 415th Infantry, featherweight; Private Al Calderon, 413th Infantry, lightweight; Pfc. Frankie LaBella, 413th Infantry, lightweight; Staff Sergeant Joseph Mariano, 415th Infantry, junior lightweight; Private John Accettero, 415th Infantry, welterweight; Private John Cruikshank, 413th Infantry, middleweight; Private Ray Bracamote, 413th Infantry, light-heavyweight; Staff Sergeant Minor Bounds, 414th Infantry, heavyweight. The Seagulls copped the baseball and basketball titles, with the Antitank Company 415th Infantry taking the softball title.

On 15 June 1944, the 104th Division passed in review at Camp Carson in observance of Infantry Day. As the 15,000 fighting men passed the reviewing stand, thousands of civilians from the Rocky Mountain region understood why General Allen was proud of his Timberwolf Division and why the men of the Division called themselves the "fightin'est" outfit in the Army. During the review, presentation was made of Expert Infantryman Badges to over 4,714 infantrymen who had successfully completed the difficult test, and plaques to the outstanding infantry platoons and artillery battery. In observance of Infantry Day, General Allen spoke: "When this war started, too many people had the idea that the only man worth anything must fly a plane or drive a tank. The infantryman was overlooked as an effort was made to glamorize the striking power of the planes and machines. Now we know from experience, and it will become increasingly evident in European operations, that this war will be won by the infantry; the man who can strike on the ground, engage the enemy hand to hand and hold ground once won. That is why the infantry has to be there, the toughest soldiers in the Army."

The Camp Carson *Mountaineer* and newspapers throughout the Rocky Mountain area carried banner stories:

FULL DRESS REVIEW PROVES 104TH TOUGHENED OUTFIT

One of the most inspiring reviews ever held at Camp Carson was witnessed last Thursday when the 104th Infantry Division was reviewed by Major General Allen in observance of Infantry Day. Civilians left Camp Carson with a better knowledge of why the Infantry is called the "Queen of Battles."

General Allen with Under Secretary of War Patterson when the Congressional Committee visited Camp Carson to inspect the Timberwolves

On 17 May, Lord Halifax, British Ambassador, presented to General Allen in Denver, Colorado, the Order of the Commander of the Bath, Military Division, one of the top honors the King of England can grant. The award was presented for his leadership in Tunisia and Sicily. In June, Under Secretary of War (now Secretary of War) Robert P. Patterson and a congressional committee inspected the 104th Division. After reviewing the mock battle by the 3d Battalion, 413th Infantry, and other training events, Patterson stated: "I am certain that the 104th Division will do its share in upholding the traditions of the Army of the United States."

The Division's training at Camp Carson culminated with the Division test conducted by XVI Corps. Results of the test showed that the 104th Division was ready for combat—*the Timberwolves were set.*

PHASE II

APO 104

FRANÇAIS À 104

Our tents pitched by the hedgerow in the quaint French countryside;
Latrines and garbage pits galore, displayed our Army pride.
And we dug them in the open for the German planes to see,
As we hung our shiny mess-kits on a nearby apple tree.

We may not have entered Normandy while bayonets were drawn;
It was only D plus 90 and the Jerry foe had gone.
Our only present danger lay within the hedge and field,
'Twas Nazi booby traps and mines—ingeniously concealed.

Now the guards had ammunition—but no one around to shoot.
And we lived like Kings and Princes eating twenty dollar fruit.
For now we all had found the land of opportunity,
With a million dollar fortune hanging on each apple tree.

On hikes and marches we all saw, the country round about.
With both hands in our pockets, and our shirt-tails hanging out.
The ammunition that we found, would stop a flying rocket;
And every soldier had a four-inch blade in every pocket.

But the thing that bothers us the most, since we came overseas,
Is policin' up the area, beneath the apple trees.
Each morning after reveille, we take our helmets steel.
And pick up all the apples that have fallen in the field.

Our modesty is hindered, by the milk maid every day.
Now some would wait around the *Place* until she went away,
But some who had been seated 'fore the damsel came around,
Would sit there pink and flustered with their guard completely down.

Now we can stand not seeing combat—tho' it's where we'll prob'ly be,
We can stand the milk-maid watchin', while we lose our modesty,
But please God—and General Allen—we will never see a tree,
Next Summer, when it's Apple-pickin' time in Normandy.

Pfc. Edward J. Apple, Jr.
Company L, 414th Infantry

GANGPLANK FEVER

STOP your problem and move your troops to their barracks at once, the Division has been alerted for movement overseas." This was the directive received by Lieutenant Colonel William M. Summers, Commander, 3d Battalion, 413th Infantry, at 2200 16 July 1944, as his battalion was preparing to seize Hill A on the Camp Carson reservation. All units of the Division were immediately notified that "War Department letter 370.5 (11 July 1944) OB-S-E-M, subject: Movement Orders, Shipment 9599, dated 12 July 1944 and TWX, Headquarters Second Army, 160305Z," had been received directing the 104th Infantry Division to proceed by rail 15 August 1944 from Camp Carson, Colorado to Camp Kilmer, New Jersey for processing and subsequent movement to overseas destination. The intensive training of the Division was soon to be tested in combat.

The advance party under Brigadier General Bryant E. Moore, Assistant Division Commander, left Camp Carson by rail on 10 August, arrived at Fort Hamilton, New York, and sailed on 17 August 1944. The remainder of the Division, in twenty-four trains, moved out of Camp Carson between 15 and 17 August, closing in Camp Kilmer, New Jersey on 20 August. The trainloads of Timberwolves followed several different routes, some pulling into Camp Kilmer by way of Canada, some straight through Pennsylvania, and others swinging north from Washington, D. C. During the short stay at Camp Kilmer, each man was processed for overseas shipment—a final clothing, weapon, and equipment check. Some of the highlights of our stay at Camp Kilmer included trips to New York, Brooklyn and surrounding communities, ship drill, and the excellent USO shows, including the performance of Marlene Dietrich. The entire Division assembled at the open amphitheater on 24 August for final religious ceremonies in the United States. During this solemn hour the Division chaplains asked Almighty God for His blessing and guidance of our gallant men.

On 25 and 26 August the Division filed into coaches at Camp Kilmer and rode to New York harbor. Marching onto ferry boats, the men, heavily loaded, rode silently to the piers. By early morning 27 August all troops were loaded; the 413th Infantry Regiment, Headquarters and Headquarters Battery, 104th Division Artillery and 385th Field Artillery Battalion on the USS *Lejeune;* the 414th Infantry Regiment, 3d Battalion 415th Infantry Regiment, 386th and 929th Field Artillery Battalions, 104th Headquarters Company, 104th Quartermaster Company, 804th Ordnance Company and 329th Medical Battalion on the USS *George Washington*; 415th Infantry Regiment, less 3d Battalion,

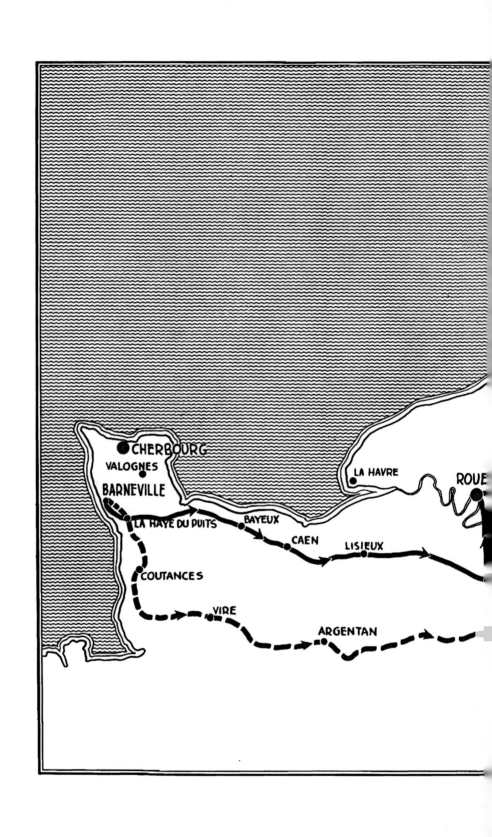

BELGIUM

VILVORDE

BRUXELLES

MONS

CHARLEROI

FRANCE

CAMBRAI

AMIENS

ST QUENTIN

BEAUVAIS

COMPIEGNE

CHANTILLY

RIVER

PARIS

VERSAILLES

ROUTE FROM BARNEVILLE, FRANCE
TO VILVORDE, BELGIUM
1 ⟶ MOTOR ROUTE ⟶
2 ➤- RAIL ROUTE ➤-

on USAT *Cristobal;* 387th Field Artillery Battalion on SS *Ocean Mail.*
Who can forget that long hard pull through the pier, up the plank and
down to the hold?

At noon on this bright Sunday the ships slipped away from the docks
and the Timberwolves were on their way. For many of our men it was
farewell to a beloved homeland. Fifty-six ships made up the convoy,
including troop transports, freighters, battered tankers, aircraft carriers
and destroyer escorts. During the voyage, ship drill, air raid, gas mask
drill, French classes, calisthenics and care of weapons composed the
training program. Pfc. Bernard F. Engel, Service Company, 413th
Infantry Regiment, describes the voyage:

Saturday night, 26 August, overstuffed duffel bags—there was a Timberwolf
under each one, but you couldn't see him—staggered down to the depot, boarded
red Pennsy coaches, and made a non-stop trip to a northern Jersey pier. Here
the duffel bags, in most cases still accompanied by men, clambered onto barges
and ferries and rode over to a covered shed on a South Brooklyn dock. A sleepy
Transportation Corps band played brassy marches as panting Wolves dragged
their basic allowance of clothing and equipment, with heavy additions, down the
long shed to a coffee and doughnut send-off conducted by American Red Cross
women . . . bless 'em!

The gangplank yawned behind us as we gulped the coffee. Then port noncoms arrived with rosters, and from Master Sergeant A to Private Z we moved
up the plank and onto our ship, the *Lejeune.*

Each man wormed his way onto a bunk, depositing his duffel bag at the foot
and curling himself into what was left of the space. "Takes up as much room
as my wife and is a damsight quieter," said one Wolf.

The next morning the *Lejeune* started moving about 1100 and by noon we
were waving goodbye to the thousands of bathers clustered on Coney Island.
By nightfall we were well out at sea.

The first day at sea was OK. We sat on the deck and played cards, read
books from the ship's library or watched the other ships in our convoy. Each
ship changed its position in the formation several times daily, presumably to
throw Nazi submarines off the track.

Old Man Atlantic got to feeling his oats Monday night and Tuesday was a
sad day for many a landlubber soldier—and also for the crew, most of whom
were fresh from boot camp. Almost everyone swore he could control his stomach
by lying in his bunk or by sitting up or by walking around the open deck—but
almost everyone was seasick.

The water calmed down and the remainder of the trip was a pretty fair vaca-
tion. Most companies had a few lectures on how to unfold a gas cape and there
were daily weapons inspections, but the remainder of our time was our own.
We spent the days acquiring sunburn and watching amateur talent shows and
boxing matches at night.

Timberwolves kept an eye on the sailors. Many a poop-deck discussion argued
the merits of Navy duty. Navy gun crews ran through daily antiaircraft drills,
usually dry-run style. The practice of assigning ten men to polish six feet of
brass railing reminded soldiers of many an Army detail. The crew declared that

the *Lejeune* was a well-built German ship which had been interned in Brazil when war broke out; it was registered 18,000 tons and could do 22 knots.

We learned to use "head" for "latrine" and were amused by colorful sea commands—"Now hear this . . . !"

Blackout regulations were strict and all portholes were sealed. "The smoking lamp is out on all weather decks" became a familiar evening order, and it was forbidden to throw trash in the water as submarines could track a wake of "Milky Way" wrappers and orange peelings.

Rumors had us going anywhere and everywhere with "we're just off Iceland" and "we're going through Gibraltar tomorrow" being the most prominent until we passed Portland Cape, England, on Monday night and woke up in the harbor of Cherbourg on Tuesday morning 7 September.

Shouldering our duffel bags once more, we loaded onto barges and rode to shore. We filed through the ruins of the railroad depot and loaded onto trucks for the trip to the Normandy staging area near Valognes, some twenty miles from Cherbourg.

Before "Ou est l'Hotel?" and "Comment ça va?" were mastered, land was sighted the afternoon of 6 September, and the following day the Division, less 415th Infantry Regiment and 387th Field Artillery Battalion, anchored at the great French harbor of Cherbourg, the USAT *Cristobal* and SS *Ocean Mail* anchoring at Utah Beach. The largest convoy and the first to proceed directly from the United States to France had arrived safely. Our mail was addressed: APO 104, c/o Postmaster, New York, New York.

NORMANDY

Dark, cold, and drizzling days did not dampen our spirits of adventure, but did add materially to our discomfort. When steel helmets were put on, we knew that it was now not for practice. Again overloading ourselves with our cumbersome duffel bags, everyone moved onto flat barges and landing craft which took us to land. All about us we could see the destruction of war. The once great French port of Cherbourg was in ruins. By foot and by motor the Division moved to its bivouac area near the village of Valognes. Along the narrow roads appeared signs, "Mines cleared to verges," and in the fields, "ACHTUNG! MINEN!", impressing us as did the battered 88's and Mark IV's, foxholes, barbed wire and gutted buildings. Pfc. Daniel L. McLoone, Headquarters Company, 1st Battalion, 415th Infantry, stated:

My first step on foreign land resulted in a loud splash as my foot hit the water-covered steel pier. After a long trek over the wet pier—we reached land— Utah Beach. Land that only a few months before saw one of the mightiest and bloodiest battles of the war. Land you had read about in history and in newspapers. Land blistered and seared by a Martian torch.

As we marched down the mud roads and through the first shell-torn, deserted coast town, there was only silence. The silence breaks when you see a Frenchman up the road—now is the time for you to try those phrases you learned. "Bon jour" you say, with a strictly American pronunciation, and feel elated when he tips his hat and replies with what you later learn to be "Bon jour." Later, too, you learn different and much more "practical" phrases.

Mud! Yes, Pop knew what he was talking about when he told me about French mud. All of a sudden everyone seems to be talking about America—how beautiful it is—expressing in words, probably for the first time, love for our great country. As we skidded through the mud and felt the pelting rain soaking clothes and chilling bodies, our misery is increased with nightfall.

On and on we walked, but at last we see trucks—big GI trucks. No more walking—we hoped. Finally the tailgate is lowered and we have arrived at our destination . . . or have we? Walking, sliding, and tumbling for several more miles, we finally reach our home—Area H.

Darkness hindered our tent pitching but finally it's done and we lay under slightly damp blankets—sleeping our first night in France—dreaming of our last night in America.

That night puptents were pitched and all crawled into bed early, tired and wet. For many of us the day recalled the Webfoot training days in Oregon. We were all impressed that mines, tanks, and the destructive powers of war were not just propaganda, but were real.

During the next few days, the outfit became familiar with the countryside of Normandy, with its small grain fields, pasture and hay lands divided by hedgerows, its old stone houses, historic and quaint churches and its simple peasant customs. "OFF LIMITS" signs barred our observation in Cherbourg, Valognes and other larger communities, but this was offset by movies, USO shows and "calvados." Everyone tried out his newly acquired language on the natives with little or no results. French children had acquired three profitable phrases—"Cigarette pour Papa," "Bonbon" and "Gum." It wasn't long until our puptent dwellings had straw and board floors, but despite this improvement, the damp soil of Normandy kept us reminded of our early days in Oregon.

Sergeant George Greenberg, Company C, 415th Infantry, recalls a few highlights on our stay near Valognes:

This was our first stop on our tour through Europe, but we saw no Paris beauties or glamor here. Our division assembly area was in the apple orchard region of Normandy and we lined up our pup tents in these small orchards, each surrounded by high hedgerows. We soon became accustomed to sleeping on the ground and learned that a drink of Calvados, the French firewater, would keep you warm all night. It worked pretty well in your cigarette lighter, too.

During the two weeks that we were there we took many walks about the countryside, looking at old German emplacements, pillboxes down at the beach, and the bombed-out town of Valognes. We were always careful where we walked for only the roads had been cleared of mines. The usual method of testing a field was to send a few cows through it.

Normandy Beachhead, D plus 91

There were no big towns and little night life, although the arrival of several movies did wonders in relieving the monotony. A USO show came around one day, and then a Red Cross donut wagon; it certainly was good to see those American girls again.

The more venturesome among us dug out our French Language Guides, and, after an hour of maltreating the language, managed to convince some housewife that we would give her soap, chocolate bars, coffee, etc., if she would wash our clothes. Then we wondered if we had been wise when we watched her take it down to a stream and beat the clothes against the rocks with a stick.

Pfc. W. H. MacCrellish, Jr., 3d Battalion, 415th Infantry, gives the inside on fraternization: "As to the women the problem was not then as we later found it in Germany, one of not being allowed to fraternize, but mainly finding a girl who seemed desirable for fraternization. We weren't too ecstatic over the plump Norman maidens in their wooden shoes and dirty aprons."

It took the Signal Company no time at all to discover that humorous incidents observe no international boundaries. The simple Normandy countryside provided the background for many hearty laughs. They are constantly remembering the farmer's wife, who arrived in their bivouac area, bearing a floral wreath to place on the cross over the mound of earth in the corner bearing the recently interred remains of "Monsieur Closed Latrine, 11 September 1944." Their gallant cook, Sergeant Jean Alzugarat, a native-born Frenchman, arose to meet this international crisis. With continental savoir faire he explained the true significance of the cross-covered mound and the confused woman made a hasty retreat. However, the traditional Gallic humor was revealed a few days later, with the appearance of a second cross, marked, "What a pity, another American soldier laid to rest."

When orders were received on 16 September 1944 from Communications Zone Headquarters that the Division would organize twelve truck companies to assist in the supply of front-line troops, the forecast rumors were: "Communications Zone troops" and "Army of Occupa-

41

tion." Under the able leadership of Colonel William P. Evans, Executive Officer, 104th Division Artillery, with the assistance of the Division and Division Artillery staff, the Timberwolves quickly and efficiently organized the twelve truck companies. Drivers from all units were enrolled and immediately began the great task of running supplies from the shores of Normandy to the front lines in Belgium, France, and Germany. During the next four weeks the Division contributed much to the success of the Red Ball Express. Staff Sergeant George B. McEwen of Headquarters Battery, 387th Field Artillery Battalion, tells his experiences as follows:

Driving a truck for the Red Ball Express may have sounded dull and uninteresting at one time to some of us who had the opportunity to drive for that organization, but by the time we had finished, all of us had some never-to-be-forgotten memories. Besides the initial mission of hauling badly needed supplies to the front line troops, it afforded most Timberwolves their first and only opportunity to see a little French life at close range.

We operated on an around the clock schedule, making runs to the Normandy beaches to pick up supplies, then driving the return trip to deliver them to the various railheads and supply depots in northeastern France. Long hours of driving and working in all kinds of weather, however, were not without their compensations—for instance there was Paris. Luckily someone thought of making Paris one of the supply railheads for the Red Ball, and if you were fortunate, you made a run to that fair city occasionally. Viewing Paris from the cab of a two and a half ton GMC might not sound like the ideal sightseeing tour, but then a GI can't be too particular. My first impression of the French capital was a favorable one—not so much for the broad, tree-lined boulevards or the historic landmarks, but from the abundance of young and very beautiful women living there. Probably one of the strangest sights for all of us was to see some sweet young thing dressed like an advertisement in *Vogue* magazine pedaling a beat-up bicycle down one of the famous boulevards. Even stranger yet was the fact that they were all very friendly. Had it not been for the business-like attitude of the Red Ball, or the fact that our stays in Paris were limited to such a very short time—I am confident that we could have lived up to our slogan, "Nothing In Hell Can Stop The Timberwolves."

The Red Ball proved its versatility time and again by hauling anything that was needed. A few of the things usually associated with war that were hauled included: ammunition, tires, gasoline, blankets, food, clothing, shoes, signal equipment and medical supplies. Not content with transporting all this, the Red Ball carried enough miscellaneous items to stock a chain of cut-rate drug stores. Occasionally, they handled human cargoes as well. On my first trip to Rheims, our convoy brought back a load of German prisoners of war just taken in the drive toward the Siegfried Line. On a moment's notice the Germans were packed into GI trucks and bounced over 200 miles of rough French roads to Chartres, all this happening so suddenly that most of them had hardly recovered from the shock of being captured before arriving at their destination. At any rate it gave the Germans a sample of the spirit and ingenuity behind an organization like the Red Ball and they knew what to expect in the future.

Two of the most interesting details were drawn by Technician Fifth Grade Francis H. Williams and Pfc. Norwood Pipkin, of the 804th Ordnance. Williams drove for a USO show in the Paris area and "Pip" was an interpreter in a German prisoner of war camp.

Other missions were assigned to units within the Division. The 1st Battalion, 414th Infantry, under command of Lieutenant Colonel Robert Clark II, guarded the rear installations of Communications Zone Headquarters in the vicinity of Valognes. Upon successful completion of its mission, it rejoined its regiment on 27 September. On 21 September the 415th Infantry, under the command of Colonel John Cochran, with orders to shoot to kill, assumed the important role of guarding vital army installations, including railroads, pipelines, pumping stations, and warehouse docks. All units of the regiment were employed on this important mission in the vicinity of Cherbourg, Surdon, Valognes, Quequerville, Lessay, Granville, St. Lo and Le Mans. Black market looters had been tapping thousands of gallons of gasoline out of the pipelines, hijackers had been raiding trains and trucks for army food and cigaretes. It was not long until the "Old Faithful" Regiment had reduced these losses to a mere trickle. The Regiment was recalled by Division on 10 October.

The Division, less 415th Infantry and 1st Battalion, 414th Infantry, moved by foot and motor from the vicinity of Valognes to its new bivouac area in the vicinity of Barneville sur Mer on 26 September. The Seagull and Mountaineer infantrymen made one of the longest marches in their history, a distance of thirty miles. From our new bivouac areas we overlooked the English Channel and the Jersey Islands ten miles out to sea. Upon the Jersey Islands was located a strong German garrison, which in the past had conducted raids on the shores of France.

The 104th Reconnaissance Troop, under the command of Captain Arthur S. Laundon, immediately established outposts and patrols along the shoreline to prevent further raids by the Nazis. Mobile reserves were established in each unit with the mission of being prepared to assist in driving off any landing force. The war was definitely coming closer to the Timberwolves.

Throughout our stay in Normandy we were busy being fully equipped and trained for combat. Road marches, detection and removal of mines, firing of weapons and night fighting were stressed.

MOVED UP

The seventh day in October 1944 was the day that the Timberwolf Division became earmarked for combat. At 1030 Division Headquarters received the following warning order from III Corps: "Be prepared to move the Division by rail and motor forward on or about 15 October. Communications Zone will submit detailed order on movement later selecting routes, bivouac areas, class I and III Distributing Points and time for movement. Prepare to move Division by rail—6,000 infantry with duffel bags, by motor—Division (—). Other details:

1. Basic load of ammunition, gas, oil, repairs and tools.
2. Seven rations per man.
3. All vehicles must be fully loaded.
4. Foot troops will move by rail from either Barneville, Valognes or La Haye du Puits."

Immediately the warning order was dispatched to all units and the troops knew that combat was near. On this same date the 692d Tank Destroyer Battalion (Towed), under the command of Lieutenant Colonel S. S. Morse, and the 555th Antiaircraft Artillery (Automatic Weapons) Battalion (Mobile), under the command of Lieutenant Colonel Robert J. Rowse, were attached to the Division. The Division troops engaged in other missions were immediately recalled. There was still speculation as to the destination of the Division because the order had only described that the Division be prepared to move forward.

On 11 October the Commanding General III Corps communicated with Major General Terry Allen, informing him that the Division would move on 15 and 16 October by rail and on 16 and 17 October by motor; La Haye du Puits had been designated as the entraining point, and the Division would move without its attachments. General Allen at 1100 on 12 October conducted a conference with all of his commanders during which he stressed warning orders must be issued at all times by all branches and services to give both lower and higher headquarters notice of impending events, that messages contain only what, when and where, and that security be established at all times.

At 0600, 14 October the advance party, composed of officers and enlisted men from all Division units, moved out. On this same date the Division was informed that it would move to the vicinity of Vilvorde, Belgium, north of Brussels.

On 15 and 16 October, 6,523 doughboys from the 413th, 414th, and 415th Infantry Regiments and from Division Special Troops boarded dilapidated 40 and 8 freight cars at La Haye du Puits. Many of us recalled the experiences told by friends and relatives, veterans of the last World War. Pfc. Edward J. Apple, Jr., of Company L, 414th Infantry Regiment, describes the trip very realistically with his poem:

104th Division Command Post near Barneville, France, 28 September 1944

We read of travel problems now, and know how those things are;
When civilians rave, because they crave a streamlined Pullman car.
We sympathize in every way, when the train's an hour late;
But no doubt the new French system, would bring things up to date.

It was something like a Pullman car, that left La Haye du Puits;
And took us up to Mechelin, from "Sunny" Normandy.
A few hundred miles to Belgium, wasn't going to be so far;
And then they only put just thirty men in every car.

These "sleepers" that they gave us tho', had all other sleepers beat;
We found as we crawled in the door and saw—not one damn seat.
And it wasn't quite a normal size, as we could plainly tell,
But one thing was for certain—air-conditioning was swell.

The racks were missing from the top, no fountains at the end;
And the Colonel spoiled the whole damp trip—"Each car gets ten more men."
We realized—with forty hommes—what the sign had said was so,
And wondered where the hell they'd put the missing eight chevaux.

When rations, packs, and duffel bags, and weapons came in too,
We wondered if they'd bitten off—too much for us to chew.
When some "kill-joy" mentioned sleep just then, we realized our plight;
And decided that three-fourths of us would spend a sleepless night.

As we hung our packs and helmets (we felt sure that it would work),
Something told us we were moving—must have been the awful jerk.
We were started on our journey, now it wouldn't be so bad;
But that little tho't of pleasure, was the last one we had.

It's funny how soon darkness came—and without the slightest peep,
Forty men looked all around them, for a little place to sleep.
As the "looie" crawled into his roll, spread out upon the floors,
He said, I quote, "Now you must keep a guard on both those doors."

One night!—who were we kidding, it would take a week, we bet;
After all our night of riding, we weren't off the coastline yet.
Though it seemed we stopped for hours, one just didn't have to go,
But just get in the position, and the whistle had to blow.

The dirt collected on our faces—the beards were doing fine.
Then came the dreaded order, "Wash and shave by half past nine!"
Oh! wasn't this all lovely—so we took the chorus up,
Forty-eight, forty-nine and fifty—shaving in a canteen cup.

When we came to a big city, we would always draw a crowd.
We were their liberators—and were we ever proud.
Cigarettes for fifty francs a pack—was ended just like that.
"Get back in those damn box cars, AND TAKE OFF THAT WOOL KNIT
        CAP."

Our puptents seemed like heaven, you could set them any place;
Where one could sleep in peace, without a foot smack in the face.
Where one didn't get a shower, from the holes up overhead,
Or have a helmet hit the "dome," just as we got in bed.

We were rugged individuals—we were on our way to war.
Now we've beaten up the Germans, and won't ride that way no more.
That's what we tho't till we started back to the States,
We rode back into France again—hell yes! in forty-eights.

On 16 and 17 October the balance of the Division moved by motor
following the route—La Haye du Puits, Carentan, Bayeux, Caen,
Lisieux, Evereaux (first night bivouac), Rouen, Beauvais, Amiens,
Cambrai (final bivouac area) all in Belgium. In the words of Staff
Sergeant Jack O. Ellis of 104th Reconnaissance Troop:

The troops moved out from Barneville, France, the morning of 17 October
1944, headed for Vilvorde, Belgium, and an eventual baptism of fire. It was a
cool sunny day as the convoy of four line platoons and headquarters platoon
formed for the march. An advance party consisting of three jeeps preceded the
main body for the purpose of marking the route and clearing the native traffic
hazards. As the column moved out and on to good roads and speeded up, it
became apparent that we were in for a fine sightseeing tour of France that would
cost a mere civilian a pretty penny.
    As we progressed down the highways past apple orchards and hedgerows and
farmlands, the fair citizens of the country extended their good will by pelting us
about the head and shoulders with apples.
    We made good progress on the trip, stopping every two hours for a ten

minute break and an hour at noon and evening for meals. We halted at night to bed down and rest. The first night we spent in a muddy beet field beneath a torrential downpour much reminiscent of beloved Oregon maneuvers. Patience was short as men pitched pup tents and crawled between wet blankets to relax. Other unfortunates tripped in the dark and fell into flooded foxholes, much to the amusement of their companions One of our advance jeeps had missed a right turn that evening and gone fifty miles to Amiens where wine and beer were plentiful. Upon their return the occupants of the jeep claimed they had lost their road map. The "fortunes" of war no doubt.

Enroute the next day we were amazed and awed by the havoc which had been wrought to the country The gigantic masses of rubble which had once been houses, wrecked equipment of all sorts, blown bridges, crater filled fields, small rows of crosses here and there marking the graves of the dead—all mute testimony to the power of war.

The morning of the third day of our march we crossed into Belgium where we received friendly greetings and salutes from the inhabitants. It was here in Belgium where we got our first good look at British men and equipment. Most of the English material was condemned by the men as having no comparison whatsoever to our own. We were proud of what we had been given to fight the enemy.

By now farmlands and small houses had become a familiar sight to us all, and so it was with eager expectancy that we entered Brussels late that afternoon. It reminded us of home more than any place we had been since arriving in Europe. The city itself seemed untouched by war. Hundreds of persons milling in the streets, street cars clanging along, coffee shops, and crowded restaurants.

Reluctantly we pushed on through Brussels, through the quiet town of Mechelin and thence to Vilvorde, our destination.

At 0930 on 16 October Brigadier General Bryant E. Moore, Assistant Division Commander, and the Division G-3 reported to Headquarters, First Canadian Army at Antwerp. There orders were received that the Division was attached to the First Canadian Army and was a part of the I British Corps. At 1730 on 18 October the Division was informed by SHAEF that the 692d Tank Destroyer Battalion (Towed), 555th Antiaircraft Artillery Automatic Weapons Battalion (Mobile) and 750th Tank Battalion were attached to the Division effective upon their arrival in Belgium.

The Division closed in its new bivouac area in the vicinity of Vilvorde and Mechelin (Malignes) on 20 October. During our short stay we had an opportunity to visit Mechelin, Vilvorde, and other smaller communities. We found the people hospitable and friendly.

It was here that final preparations for combat were made, vehicles and weapons given their last tune-up. Wonderment and anticipation could be clearly perceived among all of us. Morale was good and spirits high. We soon became familiar with the buzz bomb—thousands of which were to pass over us during our operations in Holland. They were all bound for Antwerp . . . and according to the testimony of Quartermaster Staff Sergeant Nicholas Maggio, "We learned to tell time by the damned things and used a little body english on them to steer them some other way."

PHASE III

BATTLE OF THE DIKES

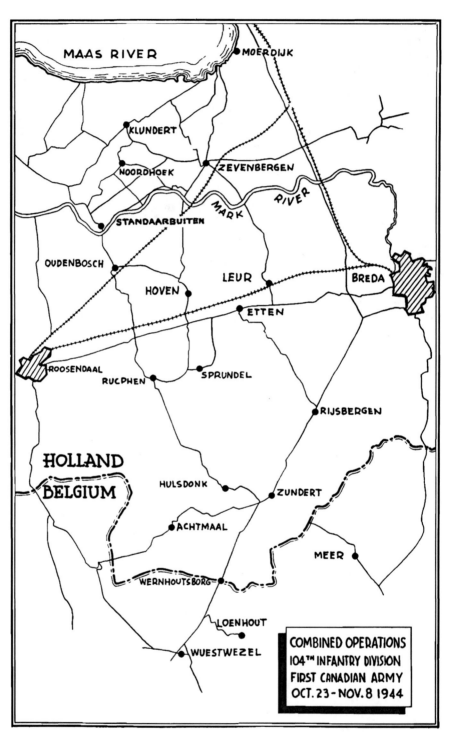

MAAS RIVER

MOERDIJK

KLUNDERT

NOORDHOEK

ZEVENBERGEN

MARK RIVER

STANDAARBUITEN

OUDENBOSCH

LEUR

BREDA

HOVEN

ETTEN

ROOSENDAAL

SPRUNDEL

RUCPHEN

RIJSBERGEN

HOLLAND
BELGIUM

HULSDONK

ZUNDERT

ACHTMAAL

MEER

WERNHOUTSBORG

LOENHOUT

WUESTWEZEL

COMBINED OPERATIONS
104TH INFANTRY DIVISION
FIRST CANADIAN ARMY
OCT. 23 - NOV. 8 1944

IN THE LINE

AT 1730 on 20 October in the historic castle of Belgium's Prince Bernhardt in the vicinity of Elewyt, the Division commander and all unit commanders and staff officers were assembled. "Our mission is to be prepared to relieve elements of the 49th Infantry Division (British) within the next few days," slowly and firmly spoke Major General Terry Allen. After an orientation by staff officers, Lieutenant General Guy G. Simonds, commander of the First Canadian Army, spoke to the assembled officers. He pointed out that while Allied troops held the city of Antwerp, the great port was not available for use because the Germans blocked the northern approaches. The mission of the First Canadian Army was to clear these northern approaches and to throw the Germans back north of the Maas Estuary.

The great American breakthrough from Normandy through France had halted on the western edge of the Siegfried Line for lack of supplies. It was imperative that the First Canadian Army accomplish its mission in order that the largest port on the European continent be cleared for use as a supply base for all Allied armies on the Western Front. At the time of the airborne thrust north, at Arnhem and Nijmegen, the 49th Infantry Division (British) was covering the left flank south of Tilburg and northeast of Antwerp. When the Arnhem salient ceased to extend, the 49th Infantry Division on 19 October was moved to positions across the main Breda-Antwerp road north of Wuestwezel, thirty-five miles northwest of Antwerp. Canadian troops were heavily engaged east of Antwerp. In the briefing, he continued that the 104th Infantry Division would probably be used in relieving the 49th Infantry Division west of Wuestwezel. From General Simonds' remarks it was evident that the Timberwolf Division was soon to be launched into combat in one of the most vital operations of the war.

On 22 October the I British Corps, under the command of Major General John A. Crocker, directed that the 104th Infantry Division relieve the 49th Infantry Division during the period 23-25 October, and establish strong defensive positions in the vicinity of Wuestwezel. Orders were issued by all units, and troops packed their duffel bags, checked their weapons and ammunition and wrote last-minute letters— we were moving into the line.

The front to be occupied by the Division faced north to the Maas-Waal Estuary twenty-two miles away, and in width extended approximately 8,000 yards on each side of the main highway running northeast from Wuestwezel to Zundert and Breda. The land was flat with an imperceptible slope to the northwest. Under the sandy surface, impervious

Lieutenant General G. G. Simonds and Major General Terry Allen in conference at Antwerp, Belgium, 20 October 1944

clay prevented standing water from draining and necessitated ditching not only of the roads but of the fields. Grain, sugar beets, turnips and potatoes were grown where the ground was not too marshy. Elsewhere was rough pasture and small but numerous planting of pine woods in various stages of growth. Vehicular traffic was road-bound. The principal highways were of stone construction and were good; all others were narrow and incapable of two-way military traffic. The buildings and steeples of numerous villages provided the only observation.

In the early hours of 23 October, Regimental Combat Team 413 moved from its bivouac area to the vicinity of Wuestwezel. Commanded by Colonel Welcome P. Waltz, the combat team was composed of the Seagull Regiment, 385th Field Artillery Battalion, Company A, 329th Medical Battalion, 1st Platoon, Company A, 329th Engineer Battalion, and a Signal Detachment of the 104th Signal Company. From right to left, the 1st, 2d and 3d Battalions occupied the 8,000-yard sector, completing the relief of the 56th Brigade (British) at 1700. At 1745 the 385th Field Artillery Battalion registered in. The first night in the line was quiet; however, the jitters normal to new troops caused some firing at menacing shadows. Vigorous patrolling by the 413th Infantry Regiment during the night 23-24 October disclosed no enemy in the imme-

diate sector. The Division command post, consisting of Division Headquarters and 104th Headquarters Company, 104th Signal Company,
Headquarters and Headquarters Battery, 104th Division Artillery, and
the 104th Reconnaissance Troop, 104th Quartermaster Company, 804th
Ordnance Company and 329th Engineer (Combat) Battalion moved
from their bivouac area to the vicinity of Wuestwezel. Sergeant Leo
Powers and Pfc. Craydon Nickols of Company A, 413th Infantry, while
on outpost duty 500 yards in front of the lines captured the first Nazi
soldier. Private Hubert L. Merritt of Company A, 413th Infantry
Regiment, was the first casualty.

The next day, 24 October, Regimental Combat Team 414 relieved
the 147th Infantry Brigade in a zone extending 3,000 yards across the
Breda road on the left of the 413th Infantry Regiment. Under command
of Colonel Anthony J. Touart, the combat team was composed of the
Mountaineer Regiment, 386th Field Artillery Battalion, Company B,
329th Medical Battalion, 1st Platoon Company B, 329th Engineer Battalion, and a Signal Detachment of the 104th Signal Company. From
right to left the 1st and 2d Battalions moved into the line, completing
the relief at 1600. The 3d Battalion was held in regimental reserve.
During the night of 24-25 October patrols of the 414th Infantry Regiment and 413th Infantry Regiment pushed out vigorously. Patrols of
the Mountaineer Regiment entered Holland at 2350.

Occupation of the Division sector was completed at 0930, 25 October
when Regimental Combat Team 415 relieved the 154th Infantry Brigade
on the left part of the Division sector. Under the command of Colonel
John H. Cochran, the combat team was composed of the Old Faithful
Regiment, 929th Field Artillery Battalion, Company C, 329th Medical
Battalion, 1st Platoon Company C, 329th Engineer (Combat) Battalion,
and a Signal Detachment of the 104th Signal Company. Two battalions
entered the line, the 1st on the right and the 3d on the left, with the
2d Battalion in regimental reserve.

The 147th Tank Regiment (British) was attached to the Division,
one squadron being placed in support of each combat team. In addition
the 103d Antitank Battery was attached to the 414th Infantry Regiment.

What was your impression of first combat? Private First Class James
K. Lenihan, Company F, 413th Infantry Regiment, says of his baptism
of fire:

On Sunday night, 22 October 1944, the executive officer of F Company, 413th
Infantry Regiment, Lieutenant Strebel, called the platoon sergeants to the company command post and told them "tomorrow night at this time you'll be in the
front lines."

The news spread quickly through the company and men gathered in groups to talk it over. The general feeling was one of excitement rather than fear. Never having heard a German shell fall or never having had someone trying hard to kill you, we didn't know we should be sober and apprehensive instead of chattering.

We were as confident as we were ignorant. Sure, war is hell; men lose their arms, their legs, their sight, their mind, but certainly none of us. Men would be killed but not the guy next to you, whom you had known for two years and was as close as a brother. Men would die but it would be "other" men, not us, not our best friends.

We moved by truck from the vicinity of Mechelin to within five miles of Haegstsaeten, Belgium, where we were to relieve an English brigade.

Twenty minutes after we de-trucked we started down a road that would terminate only on the Mulde River, Germany.

My first small taste of war came when my eye was attracted to a mound of dirt some ten yards off the road. The cross standing there and the helmet hanging from it made no impression on me for a minute. I suddenly realized that there was an Englishman that would never again drink " 'is Majesty's 'ealth."

We relieved the English and settled down to figure a few things out. One thing that was annoying me was the sight of four Belgian civilians digging a grave for a partly decomposed cow, 200 yards in front of our positions. Now what in thunder is this? Isn't this the front? Isn't there a war going on? Then what are civilians doing out 200 yards in no-man's land burying a cow? That question was one of the few that was to puzzle us before we finally got to know the score.

As night came on, word was received that no man was to leave his hole unless sent for. Men are nervous at night and this night was a particularly scary one. It was very cold and a thin mist hung above the ground. The absence of the moon limited vision to a few feet so you couldn't see the men in the hole next to you. These factors plus the idea that it was our first night in combat contributed greatly to the reason for so many shots being fired that night.

For a few hours after dark the silence was so heavy, it was stifling. Suddenly a shot rang out from over on our right, then another. Now, one from our left. Was there a patrol coming near or was it trigger happy GI's shooting at shadows? We didn't know but we strained our eyes trying to pierce that black, looking for what we hoped we wouldn't find—Germans.

Now a machine gun started chattering angrily and we unsnapped the safeties on our rifles. A lone rifleman might shoot at shadows but certainly a machine-gun grew must have seen something—we thought. After a short time the machine gun stopped firing but we didn't relax our vigilance. If Germans were sneaking up on us, scared as we were we intended to do some shooting.

As the night wore on the shots increased and we became used to them. After straining all our senses for five hours our bodies were making more persistent demands on us and we'd go off into short naps that would end suddenly.

Around four o'clock in the morning two shells exploded some 500 yards over to our left. We asked one another a question recruits would ask us many times before the shooting stopped—"Theirs or ours?"

The two hours before dawn were spent dozing off and waking every other minute.

We were glad when the day came as we thought we put in a bad night. We lived to learn that with the shooting, all by GI's, with all our nervousness and with all our sweating, our first night in combat was one of the quickest and easiest nights we had.

What was your impression of first combat? Private First Class George V. Boyle, Jr., Company F, 415th Infantry Regiment, says:

Upon entering the Army all of us had some idea of this somewhere in the back of our minds. We were here to do a job that would eventually end in fighting for our country. It was something that didn't bother us much as long as we were still in the States—we had too many other diversions. Nevertheless the day was coming.

When the Division was first committed to combat the thought that was uppermost in our minds was that this was the test, the final test of our training and ourselves. Questions raced through our minds, "Will I be able to stand it?" "Will I be wounded?" "Will I be killed?" The answer to all of these was soon to come.

On a rather ordinary October day we were alerted to move out at noon. Just where we were going we didn't know, but rumor had it that we were going into the line. There was the usual amount of confusion as we prepared to move. After a half hour delay we finally began the march that we would never forget. We had been marching steadily for about six hours and the question of where we were going began to circulate. Bets were being laid as to whether or not we would see combat.

Being a private in a rifle company, my own impressions of the first night of combat are probably much the same as those of the rest of the men.

During the approach march I didn't have much to think about because it was still daylight and we were allowed to smoke and talk. Then as night fell and smoking and talking were prohibited my imagination began to run riot. "Where are we going?" "Why?" "Are we going to fight?" Then a halt was called and we were ordered to leave all equipment we didn't need behind. I knew then that this was it. At first I was a little frightened and the slightest noise grated on my nerves. Then I got a grip on myself and decided that it was something that had to come sooner or later. About that time the order came to move out.

We had been moving for quite some time. I was near the end of the column with the executive officer, trying to keep from being sleepy. Several times we left the column to check dugouts and buildings but found nothing. Finding nothing made me feel much better although I don't know why. I knew it would have been for the best to have flushed out a couple of the enemy to see what they looked like.

I then got a chance to ride a jeep trailer for awhile and get a rest. I was about half asleep when the first shell hit the column. Without any knowledge of having moved I found myself in a ditch listening to shells come whistling in. My first thought was that this was the end and that every shell coming over had my name and address on it. Then I began to pray. That didn't last long because in ten seconds all prayers I ever learned became three words, "God protect me."

The shelling lessened for a few minutes and I got my first idea of what a shell could do to a man. There had been several direct hits on the column and the Medics had taken most of them. I went back to help render first aid. The Medics had not even been around and yet they had been shelled and wounded

regardless of their noncombatant status. This had instilled in me a deep hatred for the enemy.

I was amazed that any resemblance of order could be maintained through our first shelling. However the companies started to move out once more. What made me feel better than anything right then was seeing the regimental commander walking down the road as if nothing out of the ordinary was happening.

The interesting part of my first night of combat was the way in which all my training came back to me instinctively. I remembered lessons that I once thought were very unnecessary. I learned to my surprise that they were very essential indeed.

However my most lasting impressions of the first night of combat was what it is like to have fear. One cannot put into words just exactly what fear is and what it does to you, for words are merely meaningless sounds and fear is very real to the newly initiated.

In a post V-E Day letter to his parents Sergeant David Malachowsky,

Company D, 329th Medical Battalion, reminisces on the actual events as they took place that day:

Dear Folks,

For the last two years we had all been saying "this is it" and that certain afternoon it happened. Our Division went into action for the first time and only two days later, all the novelty and excitement of a new thing had worn off and we all felt as though we had been handling casualties for a lifetime.

We moved up to a little green field outside of Ostmalle, Belgium, just before dusk and set up our tent station. The usual admissions and walking wounded tent, the evacuation tent, the two surgical tents, and one medical set-up, just in case. It took just twenty minutes from the time we pulled in our two-and-a-halfs that we were ready for our first battle casualties. But all was still and none came . . . at first.

There we waited and every few minutes we'd jump a mile as a British artillery unit would cut loose with a round or so, from the woods behind us. Us "greenies" were sure each shell was meant for us, and it took hours before we got accustomed to the blast of the guns and the eerie whining of the shells on their way towards the German 15th Army opposing us.

But outside of that all was quiet. An occasional "meat wagon" from collecting would roll in over our rutty, winding road following our clearing station signs and we'd gather around it like vultures, expectant and yet a bit leery of our first sight of blood and guts. But "no luck," only a GI with diarrhea and another with nasopharyngitis, mod., sv., c.u., the same stuff we'd been handling since Oregon maneuvers.

It wasn't until almost midnight that our first casualty came in. He was an old dirty looking Dutchman with an M-1 slug in the place where you and I usually sit. One of our infantrymen cautiously advancing through Hans' backyard had stumbled over the poor fellow while he was using his version of our slit trench, and not taking any chances, GI Joe had pulled the trigger first and asked questions later.

But the old man's popularity soon passed, because from then on our own boys started to roll in. Ambulance after ambulance painfully crawled along the bumpy cowpath in the blackness of the moonless night, to come to rest before the blacked out admission tent, already loaded with our wounded. EMT tags were checked, completed and their wounds examined. Those needing further treatment were carried into our surgery where after plasma had been given or a splint adjusted, they would eventually arrive at the evacuation tent to await the long trip back to the evacuation hospital in the rear.

It was new to us. Completely new to all of us. It was something that one did not meet in civilian life and we didn't even know how we would react to the sight of blood and mangled limbs. But after the first load of casualties had come in . . . we knew. There wasn't even a choice of how to react. The tired eyes, the dull, pale, dirt-smeared faces, the broken bodies, and the ever present red of their blood seeping through their clothes and onto their litters gave us the incentive. What these men were facing up ahead was as new to them as our job was to us, despite the thousands of dry runs we'd had. The least we could do was the job expected of us. And that we did for the next ten hours, handling a steady stream of our boys through station and out again to the rear as fast and as safely as possible. We were too rushed and too tired to think of resting. All I could see after awhile was B. C. WIA, Sv PEN W LT. CHEST. . . . BC WIA . . . SV . . . BULLET . . . BC . . . SHRAPNEL . . . WIA . . . SV. AMMUNITION LEG RT MINE . . . BC WIA . . . but we kept them rolling, we just had to.

By afternoon, our Division had advanced past Wustwezel and were almost at the Dutch border. At this point our other clearing platoon moved out of our set-up and opened station in a small apple orchard near Wustwezel, thus finally relieving us.

We tore down in blackout, loaded our trucks and moved into the orchard to await the next move.

Well, folks, I'd better stop now and grab a few winks. I'm okay so don't worry.

Your loving son,

Dave.

What was your impression of first combat? Sergeant Felix A. McRan, Company B, 329th Engineer Battalion, says:

There was a lot of miles in behind us. Miles that seemed torturously long because we always wondered when the truck would slowly stop, and somebody would yell "unload."

Strangely I abhorred the idea. All the magnificent movies and adventurous tales of glory and honor, I failed to remember. And the war, that until now seemed so far away, suddenly had become very close and personal. Maybe I was a little scared. But somebody had already told me it was a natural feeling. Like the first uncomfortable day at a new school,—only more so. How much more so, they never said. "You'll get used to it." It's possible to grin now as I remember the words.

The booming of the guns had become louder. Now and then the truck would pass small groups of British Tommies walking in the same direction. Some would grin feebly, occasionally one would wave. I often pondered whether they meant "hello" or "goodbye."

There was very little said that trip. We silently stared at crumbled buildings, knocked-out tanks, and long lines of civilians, slowly and painfully making their way toward us. Then the truck stopped. The truck, that we had hoped might run forever, had stopped, and we were off, digging foxholes. Nobody told us how deep—no one had to.

We didn't do much that afternoon. Cleaned our rifles, tried to sleep. Frequently we'd jump when our guns directly behind us fired. Realizing our mistake we'd grin sheepishly. At intervals a stray German shell fell close. None of us got hurt. Oh, war wasn't too bad.

We had already begun preparing our shelter halves for bed, when we heard the familiar sound of our platoon jeep pulling in and stopping in our area. From that day, I held a secret hatred for the sound of that jeep. A road to be cleared. Mines? Maybe. Road block? Definitely.

Climbing into the truck we took off. We'd be back soon. The cobblestone road in Belgium, just this side of the Holland border, was probably a pretty road in more pleasant days. But now it was cluttered with broken branches, scattered parts of German tanks, and the dirty black of shell bursts. Where we stood British tanks huddled near battered homes—ahead, who knows? Our troops

were up ahead about three or four miles. Then what the hell were we worried about? "Let's go." Mine detectors are unloaded and tuned, men assigned, and we're off. Straight and upright (I never learned any other way) we go, swinging and swaying with our little detectors.

We were doing all right I thought. At least a mile of road cleared. No mines yet, up ahead the road block. Frequently a shell landed close. Strays we thought . . . or liked to think anyway.

Somebody coming in behind. Long lines of infantrymen were slowly making their way forward, hugging the ditches, occasionally crawling—always low.

When finally they reached us, one of our men asked, "Where you guys going? Relieving somebody?"

"Relieving somebody, hell. We come to take this road."

"You mean ahead there's nobody? We're first—holy cats!"

I remembered standing upright in the middle of the road, my nonchalance, and thought, "If ever ignorance was bliss." The situation had taken a new slant. Our self-confidence became badly shaken. The recent shells and rifle fire were becoming explainable. A realization of uncertainty, that now maybe tomorrow, and we were all so small in comparison. It was getting dark and there was still a road block to remove.

The trees were huge, I remember. The Jerries had done a good job too. We checked the fallen trees, removed a few charges in the limbs, and began to work. We winched with a truck, tugged, pulled, chopped, and the job went slow, impatiently slow. Then darkness.

Somebody raised an axe, a limb fell, then a deafening explosion, a moan and a stumble in the dark. Everybody swallowed hard and knew. A booby trap. We all became mad at somebody, or something. Yet few knew who or what.

It was all very vague, but we knew it was out in the night somewhere. One man hurt. In the face. Nobody knew how bad yet. The next few minutes seemed like forever. The uncertain next step. Were there any more? If there were, who can see them now?

The road block was finally cleared and internally everybody sighed deeply. The tension broke a little as we went back, yet nobody talked much,—it began to rain. It wasn't a very tasty supper that night. The hash and coffee were cold, and we jabbed aimlessly in the dark at it, while the rain ran down our necks and into our messkits. But we were hungry. And a bit cold now. One of the cooks remarked that a whole company of ours was wiped out, and we wondered, bewildered and confused, groping for answers we couldn't find.

The guns barked into the night flashing brilliantly. The guard was posted, and we went to sleep, not knowing whether forever or just for another day.

What was your impression of first combat? Sergeant Roger Ries, Company D, 329th Medical Battalion, has this to say:

The clearing company moved out of its bivouac area near Brussels. We were going into combat. We had set up our station and run through simulated patients hundreds of times during our training and maneuvers, but this was the real thing.

Nerves were on edge. Your brain was working overtime to think of a good joke or some funny happening. What you needed was a good laugh to relieve the anxiety and tenseness, but try as you might, all you could think of were the coming events. What would be your reaction to the first battle casualty? How would the people you worked with react? What were our chances in the case of an air raid, shelling, or if one of those buzz bombs, which we had been watching on their way to Antwerp, should decide to cut out above us?

It wasn't long before all of these questions had been answered. Everyone's reaction to the first battle casualty was to help. There was a guy that needed the kind of help that only we could give, and as far as our chances were concerned it was "To hell with that. We're helping guys who take more chances in a minute than we take in a month."

We learned more in one day on the Belgium-Holland border than we had in all those months of maneuvering in Oregon and California. There were no doubts as to how the individual or the group as a whole would work. As far as our type of work went, we were veterans. I'll never forget those first few hours, and the satisfaction I got because we were able to help when we were really needed.

What was your impression of first combat? Sergeant Harry V. Frampton, Battery A, 385th Field Artillery Battalion, says:

Belgium in October. . . . In the language of Mauldin's Willie, "That's where we were kissed." The first days of combat. Everyone felt the pressure to some extent. Things were double checked and reexplained. The night after crossing the Dutch boundary the 385th commander came belting up to an infantry position in a jeep. The headquarters wire team was coming in with 110. Someone remarked "It is almost like maneuvers." However, few men spent any time talking about the comparison once things got really warm. It certainly was not like maneuvers when the 3d Battalion of the 143d Infantry Regiment had their first real German counterattack. The artillery liaison officer was using the battalion command post as a check point from which to fire his mission. Computers in fire direction center were saying "Charge one," and they could hear for the first time the rattle of Nazi burp guns. If they weren't uneasy, they at least knew that the outfit was definitely in action.

When the first rounds came over A Battery, the Battery Commander yelled "Here they come." Every man automatically on the ground or in a hole. When reports started coming in to the command post about the casualties among our own forward observer crews, reality set in quickly. Nothing makes the actual participation in combat as significant as a casualty report. Especially when men are killed with whom you have had a personal acquaintance through the many months of preparation and training. A feeling of satisfaction and relief results from watching men "swing to" and do their jobs the right way. Maybe you didn't particularly like this fellow—perhaps you felt that some other individual would not be worth his weight in combat. Yet there they are, getting it done. A few times it wasn't easy, but the team clicked. Some funny things happened at times. Lots of perspectives changed. Things like having an extra twenty bucks in your pocket didn't mean a thing, but a letter from home or a couple of chocolate bars could be a red letter day for any man.

For the artillerymen it wasn't so much the baptism of fire as it was the realization that there is no transition period between being a soldier who reads about it—and one who does what somebody else reads about.

THE FIRST ATTACK

At 1010 on 25 October a patrol of Company E, 414th Infantry Regiment—Lieutenant Cramer, Sergeant Joseph and Pfc. Fortner—gained contact with the enemy in the vicinity of the Custom House on the Wuestwezel-Breda highway just north of the Holland frontier. There they were fired on by the enemy employing a platoon armed with light machine guns. Banked ditches beside the road, groups of trees from which all the leaves had not yet fallen, and numerous scattered buildings furnished cover in which the enemy personnel and gun emplacements could be concealed with excellent fields of fire across the surrounding flat open meadows. This situation was characteristic of the positions in which the enemy was encountered throughout the operations in Belgium and Holland. With this patrol action began the development which led to the successful attack on Zundert two days later. It appeared that the enemy was withdrawing his main forces, but it was uncertain to what extent the withdrawal had proceeded.

Field Marshal Sir B. L. Montgomery, commander of the 21st Allied Army Group, with Lieutenant General John A. Crocker, commander of the I British Corps, visited the assembled commanders and staff officers at the Division command post in the vicinity of Hoogenheide at 1130. Field Marshal Montgomery expressed his desire that the Division thrust forward without delay, engaging the enemy firmly

Allied negotiations near Hoogenheide, 25 October 1944. (1) Field Marshal Sir B. L. Montgomery, Commander, 21st Army Group; (2) Lieut. General John A. Crocker, Commander, British I Corps; (3) Major General Terry Allen; (4) Brigadier General Bryant E. Moore; (5) Brigadier General William Woodward; (6) Colonel Welcome P. Waltz, Commander, 413th Infantry; (7) Colonel John H. Cochran, Commander, 415th Infantry; (8) Colonel B. R. DeGraff, Chief of Staff, 104th Infantry Division; (9) Major T. E. D. Kidd; (10) Major Wilson; (11) Lieutenant Colonel Scott T. Rex, G-1; (12) Lieutenant Colonel Mark Plaisted, G-2; (13) Lieutenant Colonel Leo A. Hoegh, G-3; (14) Lieutenant Colonel Clyde Pennington, G-4.

and driving him northward with all possible speed. General Crocker expressed it: "The Boche is softening all around, and we don't want to miss an opportunity." General Crocker further directed the Division to push in the enemy outposts and clear the main road through Zundert, gaining control of the road junction and the city on 27 October.

Toward this end the Division, by warning orders on the afternoon of the 24th, followed by Field Order 5 at 2300, had already directed the regiments to gain and maintain contact with the enemy and to initially secure a line just north of the Belgium-Holland frontier designated as phase line A. On the morning of the 25th the advance began as planned. Scattered resistance appeared along the front. The 413th Infantry Regiment, which had the greatest distance to reach phase line

A, moved the 2d and 3d Battalions out at 0600. Soon they met the fire of machine guns and came under mortar fire. Throughout the day the resistance was not enough to halt their advance. A gap was created between the Division's right flank and the BOB force (a British composite force). At 1400 the 104th Reconnaissance Troop was dispatched to strengthen that area. At 1700 strong opposition including artillery fire on the 3d Battalion halted the regiment just short of phase line A.

In the center, along the Breda road, progress was also made without initial difficulty. The 414th Infantry Regiment, ably supported by the 386th Field Artillery Battalion and 329th Engineer Battalion, advanced at 0900 and reached phase line A at 1430. Shortly prior to noon some confusion was caused to the advancing troops by great numbers of civilians being driven through the lines by the Germans. At 1600, with the 1st and 2d Battalions up, the 414th Infantry Regiment jumped off to continue the advance. Now the opposition was considerably heavier and progress slow. Company B was stopped by fire from the vicinity of Wernhoutsvourg. Company A bypassed the source of fire and continued to phase line B, where it remained during the night. When the 2d Battalion had advanced 1,000 yards it met heavy machine gun fire from concrete works in the path of its advance, and was forced to withdraw to phase line A and reorganize.

In the Division left zone the 415th Infantry reached phase line A at 1600. The 1st and 3d Battalions encountered small arms fire during the latter part of their advance.

As night fell, about 1800, the Division was substantially where it had planned to be. The enemy, however, remained elusive; his main forces had not yet been encountered. The Division plan as directed by higher headquarters was to maintain constant pressure—specifically this time by night operations.

After the conference with Field Marshal Montgomery and General Crocker, General Allen directed the regiments to advance north a distance of approximately 3,000 yards beyond phase line A to phase line B.

The 413th Infantry Regiment, with the 2d and 3d Battalions in line, advanced at 2230, with Division artillery support firing on known enemy installations. The night was overcast and dark; the regimental commander described the movement as an infiltration. After an advance of 800 to 900 yards against the enemy, strongly organized and dug in, the Seagulls buttoned up. In the center zone the 1st Battalion of the 414th Infantry held its ground, phase line B, as directed. On its left the 2d Battalion advanced toward phase line B, but was held without gain. The 415th Infantry progressed slowly through difficult terrain. The ground was marshy, with diked ditches four feet in width and in depth. The men were wet to their armpits; rations and ammunition were being carried up by hand. During the night advance, Lieutenant Colonel John H. Elliott, commander of the 1st Battalion, was injured by enemy artillery. Captain Martin Preuics immediately assumed command. Two days later Lieutenant Colonel Fred Needham (then Major) assumed command of the battalion. Both battalions had encountered stiff resistance during the night, but by morning had advanced 1,600 yards. Late in the afternoon of the 25th, when a section of British Churchills came to the support of the 3d Battalion, 413th and I Company launched an attack on Heilbloom. The first battle was nearly over and the 3d Battalion buttoned up around crackling flames set by the six-pounders of the Churchill tanks. The enemy had dug in in a perimeter defense around Heilbloom, right on the border between Belgium and Holland. Their main line of defense was a series of heavily defended strongpoints made up of trenches, bunkers, field fortifications, 20mm flak guns and machine guns. The sector of fire from one strongpoint would lap the sector of fire from another strongpoint. This was the German principle of defense and this series of mutually supporting strongpoints was a line of defense which the enemy had no intention of abandoning. The mission of the German 15th Army was to prevent the Allies from reaching the estuary of the Maas River at all costs.

Early the night of the 25th, after the fall of Heilbloom, the 3d Battalion reorganized. I and K Companies buttoned up around Heilbloom only 600 to 800 yards away from the enemy's main defense positions, which were well hidden in thick forest around a group of buildings designated on the map as Goorkins, Holland. The 2d Battalion was in flat, open fields to the right of the 3d Battalion. Elements of the 414th Infantry were on the left of the 2d Battalion. Just as the units were buttoning up, the order was received to reach phase line B by dawn. Phase line B was an entirely arbitrary line 2,500 yards away through a forest area. It was impossible to bypass the forest, and there was only one road in the 413th sector, and that was unimproved. Time for the night movement was 2230.

At 2230, L Company, which had been in reserve, was selected to lead the 3d Battalion, a shift which delayed the jumpoff to a more favorable hour. To further safeguard the battalion from ambush, L Company was to send out a platoon strength patrol as advance guard, which the company was to follow at 1,000 yards.

The advance guard in patrol formation was stopped by intense automatic fire fifty yards from the enemy lines. The company closed up to within 100 yards of the patrol and deployed to attack the now definitely located strongpoint at dawn.

At dawn, L Company assaulted the strongpoint but was thrown back with heavy losses. Several daylight assaults also met with failure. Casualties were mounting. About 200 yards of open field without cover or concealment had to be crossed to reach the strongpoint. In addition the enemy was so well concealed and camouflaged that our men could not locate targets, while the enemy sharpshooters were having a field day.

Meanwhile the 3d Platoon of G Company jumped off at 0700 on 26 October, and crossed 600 yards of open field against fire from 20mm and 40mm flak guns, dug-in 88mm's, and machine guns. For the first time Seagulls saw Germans machine gun their own men—eight Jerries who tried to surrender were picked off by their Wehrmacht buddies. The 2d Battalion was making no outstanding progress. At 1800 the battalion was counterattacked when E Company started to lead the battalion across the fields. The counterattack was repulsed and the 2d Battalion captured a 40mm flak gun intact and the battalion buttoned up in the woods but still short of phase line B. Ahead of them lay a huge castle defended by a large force of Jerries, but it was decided to leave this until the next day.

About 1500 the enemy launched a strong counterattack against the 414th Infantry and a reinforced platoon passed to the left of and behind I and K Companies and attacked the 3d Battalion CP, around which were most of the 3d Battalion vehicles, ammunition dump, the 81mm mortars, and other miscellaneous elements. A defense was hastily organized by 1st Sergeant Gazzaway of M Company, Staff Sergeant Nardi of the Intelligence Section, and Lieutenant Gimbel, Communications Officer. Captain Schaps, 385th Liaison Officer, called down a huge volume of artillery fire to support the defense. A series of attacks by the enemy were repulsed and a vital communications and supply route was saved.

With British tanks in support, L and K Companies, which had passed through I Company, overran the Goorkins strongpoint. Two flak guns were captured along with their crews. Lieutenant Gene Clark of K Company bagged a half-dozen PW's when he "just for the hell of it" tossed some hand grenades in a dugout, and about thirty startled Jerries tumbled out of the buildings at Goorkins after the tanks had set fire to the shelters. The rest of the defending force of some 200 Germans took off through the woods with K and L Companies in hot pursuit. It was here that the 413th first employed marching fire. K Company went into the darkening woods shooting at any and everything until they halted on phase line B to button up for the night. It was a dark night and darker still in the woods, and the defense was the tightest ever used by the 413th, a battalion dug-in in less than a 200-yard circle. It was so dark that you had to feel your way around. An M Company sentry reached into a foxhole to wake up his relief, but touched two Germans instead. The Germans promptly surrendered. Resistance in this area had not been the "I wanta quit" Volkssturm variety. Two Germans continued sniping in one area for over twenty-four hours until searching doughboys found them. They gave their ages as fourteen and sixteen years.

The 329th Engineer Battalion was busily engaged throughout the period in clearing mine-infested areas and in the construction of bridges and culverts.

The Division in strength had driven the enemy out of Belgium and was now well established in Holland. On 26 October the infantry, ably supported by its artillery, completed the envelopment of the enemy positions.

The Attack on Zundert, Holland

Lieutenant Colonel Mark S. Plaisted, the Division G-2, estimated the total enemy strength along the Division front the morning of 26 October at seven infantry battalions with an average strength of 200 to 300 men each and with two battalions in reserve. Supporting the foot troops it was estimated there were two brigades of self-propelled guns believed to consist of forty guns each. Weapons in use by these units included 20mm antiaircraft guns used as ground pieces, 88mm and 76mm self-propelled guns. All units further developed the enemy positions on 26 October, forcing the enemy to abandon his position late that day.

The surprising efficiency of the Dutch "underground" which flourished in the Netherlands despite Nazi attempts to root it out, is illustrated by the following narrative of Lieutenant Colonel Kelleher, of the 415th Infantry, concerning the discovery of secret documents of incalculable importance to the First Canadian Army:

On October 27, 1944 I entered the town of Achtenwaal with the advance guard of the 3d Battalion of the 415th Infantry. At first the town seemed deserted. At the main intersection a uniformed man came out to meet us. He identified himself as a Dutch police officer and asked for the senior Allied commander. When I made myself known he asked me for identification and then showed me his identification which was operator (No. —) of the Dutch underground. He then brought me into a house. In the living room on the ground floor he shoved back a stove which hung on a hinge. Where the stove had been was a concrete slab. This he removed and brought out a large neatly wrapped bundle of papers which had been given to him by Dutch underground operator

(No. —), with orders to turn them over to the first Allied officer he met. I immediately sent these back to the Division.

The "papers" upon inspection proved to be two bulky volumes of maps, overlays, and logistical data, which detailed, town by town, the entire defense system of the Nazis in Holland. This priceless find was rushed by G-2 to First Canadian Army Headquarters on the outskirts of Antwerp, where the data saved many lives and insured the success of the final British drive through the Netherlands seven months later.

The 414th and 415th Infantry Regiments maintained pressure on the enemy in the center and in the left zone, while the 413th Infantry warily attacked toward Zundert. After a strong artillery preparation, which was devastating judging from the amount of dead found and from statements made by shell-shocked prisoners, the Seagulls jumped off promptly at 0640. The right-hook action of Colonel Waltz's men was strongly supported by the 385th, 387th and 68th (British) Field Artillery Battalions, a squadron of the 147th Tank Battalion, the 2d Battalion of the 415th Infantry Regiment, and the 104th Reconnaissance Troop. The attack was spearheaded by the 3d while the 2d Battalion was held up by mortar and small arms fire from a castle to the left front. Patrols from Company F supported by 81mm mortars silenced the fire and brought in three prisoners. The fire of enemy artillery and self-propelled guns was light, replaced by heavy mortar fire, while snipers operated continuously.

At 1230 the Seagulls seized the intermediate objective, and after a brief reorganization the regiment again drove further to the north at 1515. The 329th Engineer Battalion hurriedly constructed a sixty-foot Bailey bridge to permit the advance of tanks into Zundert. At 1730 the 3d Battalion, 413th Infantry Regiment, entered the city of Zundert and prior to 1800 had its objective buttoned up. The 2d Battalion was in the position north of Zundert cutting the Zundert-Breda highway while the 1st Battalion took up position between the two battalions. The first critical objective assigned to the Division had been seized and it was prepared to continue its advance on further orders.

Associated Press dispatches in the United States carried the following banner and story about the initial action of the Division:

TIMBERWOLVES NOW IN BATTLE

First Prisoners Reported Taken by 104th Timberwolf Division in Netherlands Fighting

The rough and ready 104th Infantry Division which has taken its first enemy prisoner in Holland, was whipped into tough fighting trim at Camp Carson,

Lt. Chronister
Abilene,
Ks.

4th Platoon
K - 413 Inf.

Colorado by Major General Terry Allen who inspired his men with the slogan, "Nothing in Hell Can Stop the Timberwolves." The 104th Division moved into the line on the Dutch-Belgian border the night of 23 October, under Canadian Army command. The Division was the first American Division to be shipped from the United States directly to Cherbourg. The Division is now across the Dutch border and fast settling into the routine of combat.

The General said, "So far everything has gone according to schedule. I can't ask for anything more at this point. I cannot say too much in praise of the Canadian units and the British who are supporting us with tanks and artillery."

Last June Under-Secretary of War Robert P. Patterson and members of the Military Affairs Committee reviewed the Division while stationed at Camp Carson. Secretary Patterson stated at that time, "I am certain that the 104th Infantry Division will do its share in upholding the traditions of the Army of the United States." He said he was greatly impressed by the Division when it staged a sham battle.

The Division had inflicted great casualties on the enemy, had suffered first casualties in combat, had learned to distinguish the incoming shells from outgoing shells; we knew the sharp crack a bullet makes when it goes close by; we could distinguish the rattling rapid fire of the German machine guns from the slower American guns, and we knew when to duck. It had now been proven to us that the training under the able leadership of Major General Gilbert R. Cook and Major General Terry Allen was profitable and paying big dividends. The mock battles that we had fought on the rugged Oregon and California deserts had been a real prelude to the grim reality of war. Among those of us who had looked forward to entering combat, none could say that he had any further unsatisfied desire. The grimness and terror of war were at hand.

The gratitude of the Dutch people for their liberation in Zundert was shown by both the flying of flags and by the rousing cheers given our men. The haggard looks, the joyous cries and the hospitality shown us made our suffering seem somewhat worthwhile.

DRIVE TO THE MAAS

RIJSBERGEN. At 0300 on 28 October the Division issued Field Order No. 6, which directed the following:

1. The Division will mop-up, retain its hold on Zundert and maintain contact with the enemy by vigorously patrolling the axis, Zundert-Breda.

2. Rucphen will be secured by the 414th Infantry, reinforced.

3. The Division will be prepared to advance on Breda, northwest through Rucphen.

4. The 413th Infantry will be in Division reserve, prepared to spearhead attack on Breda.

5. The 415th Infantry will protect the right flank of the 414th Infantry on the latter's advance to Rucphen. The Division was reinforced during the day by the attachment of the 555th Antiaircraft Automatic Weapons Battalion (Mobile) and 692d Tank Destroyer Battalion (Towed).

At approximately 0845 the Division received a Corps directive informing it not to go to Rucphen, but to drive for Breda. The 414th Infantry was given this mission at 0900. The 414th Infantry with the 3d Battalion as advance guard moved out from its position southwest of Zundert at 1100. In the early afternoon the regiment passed through the 413th Infantry at Zundert. Enemy in small groups surrendered to the advancing infantrymen. A few rounds of light artillery fell on the troops just south of Rijsbergen.

At 1700 the operation was again changed by a Corps directive which stated: "Stop your advance toward Breda at Rijsbergen and be prepared to swing north and march on the Mark River." Colonel Anthony Touart of the 414th Infantry was immediately told to stop his troops at Rijsbergen and be prepared to move north towards the Breda-Roosendaal highway, four miles north of his present position. The 414th had contacted the enemy just short of Rijsbergen, and after a quick envelopment by K Company the 3d Battalion moved in and seized the objectives before nightfall. The regiment closed in the vicinity of Rijsbergen that night and prepared plans to swing to the north the following morning.

While the 413th Infantry Regiment remained in Division reserve at Zundert the 415th Infantry advanced to position of readiness just southwest of Zundert at Biggelaar prior to 1700.

BREDA-ROOSENDAAL ROAD . . . At 1700 Cochran's Old Faithful Combat Team, with the 107th Tank Squadron (British); Battery C, 555th AAA Automatic Weapons Battalion; 1st Platoon, 104th Reconnaissance Troop; and the 929th Field Artillery Battalion attached had been directed to cut the Breda-Roosendaal highway. When the Corps directive sent the 414th Infantry Regiment northeast instead of into Breda the 415th Regiment was given its new mission. The 1st Battalion, under command of Major Fred Needham, preceded by the regimental Intelligence and Reconnaissance Platoon under Lieutenant Pruit, advanced over the route on the right. Good progress was made until shortly prior to midnight, when artillery and machine gun fire held up the column south of Sprundel. Four hours later the battalion mortars and the supporting artillery fire from the 929th Field Artillery Battalion forced the enemy to abandon his position. The remainder

Award of Distinguished Service Cross. By direction of the President, under the provisions of AR 600-45, 22 September 1943, as amended, and under the authority contained in Circular No. 32, Headquarters European Theater of Operations, United States Army, 20 March 1944, as amended, the Distinguished Service Cross is awarded to:

Private First Class BEVERLY TIPTON (Army Serial No. 35670069), Infantry, Company I, 413th Infantry, United States Army, for extraordinary heroism in connection with military operations against the enemy in Holland on 25 October 1945. On 25 October 1944 the platoon to which Private TIPTON was assigned was advancing across flat, open terrain in the face of intense, accurate enemy fire from well prepared dug-in defensive positions in the sparse hedgerows and from points of vantage in the few surrounding buildings. Two squads were pinned down by grazing heavy machine gun, mortar, and small arms fire, and the first scout of Private TIPTON's squad was killed. Private TIPTON immediately assumed the duties of the first scout, and while leading the squad along a hedgerow to the enemy's flank under the heavy harassing fire, he saw an enemy machine gun. Halting the squad, he worked his way back to the automatic rifleman, obtained the automatic rifle, and moved toward the enemy machine gun nest. Courageously advancing to within six feet of the enemy position, he opened fire, shooting from the hip, killing the members of the machine gun crew and capturing the enemy weapon. Throughout the entire action visibility was good, and Private TIPTON was subjected to direct, aimed fire from three enemy snipers. His spontaneous aggressiveness, bold tenacity, and bravery set an inspiring example for the men of his unit and facilitated the subsequent advance of his unit. Private TIPTON's courageous actions, above and beyond the ordinary call of duty, were in keeping with the finest traditions of the armed forces of the United States. Entered military service from Upper Lexington, Kentucky.

of the regiment, preceded by the 1st Platoon, 104th Reconnaissance Troop, advanced over the route on the left. At 2230 the advance was halted while Company C, 329th Engineer Battalion, removed a large road block of fallen trees in the vicinity of Hulsdonk. After an hour's delay progress was resumed. In the vicinity of St. Willabrord the column was subjected to heavy artillery fire. Vehicles were immediately dispersed and later continued on by infiltration, still subject to mortar and artillery fire. The foot columns were not halted but continued their relentless pressure throughout the night. At daylight both columns had reached positions just south of the Breda-Roosendaal highway and by fire had denied the enemy use of this important axis.

VAART CANAL . . . On 29 October, while the 415th Infantry was improving its position in the control of the Breda-Roosendaal highway, the 414th Infantry made its assault to the north. Company L took the lead and advanced beyond the northern outskirts of Rijsbergen, where the enemy was contacted in force along the wide Vaart Canal. The enemy had established a strong defensive position at the canal with an estimated force of four infantry battalions supported by an engineer battalion, an antitank battalion, an artillery regiment, and a brigade of self-propelled guns. The west end of this position had given way, surprised by the night operations of the 415th Infantry, but the east portion held firmly. The 386th Field Artillery Battalion, reinforced by the 385th and 387th Field Artillery Battalions, laid down a heavy artillery barrage, which with the skillful maneuver of infantry forced the enemy to give up his positions at 1730. The 3d Battalion, gaining the north bank of the Vaart Canal, reorganized, and the 1st Battalion passed through advancing on Leur. Company C moved out first commencing at 2100 and marched north for a distance of three miles through heavy woods, bypassing all resistance, reaching its position just south of Leur. The balance of the battalion closed on the position without incident. Shortly after daylight on 30 October the 1st and 2d Battalions of the 414th Infantry had seized Leur and Etten, with the 3d Battalion in reserve south of Leur.

The main body of the 413th Infantry remained in Division reserve, moving under cover of darkness to its newly assigned position in the vicinity of Sprundel on 29 October. The 1st Battalion, under Major John White, while the 414th Infantry was engaged on the Vaart Canal, was directed to protect the Division right flank, and by midnight it had accomplished its mission. At 1600 small arms fire slowed but did not halt the advance. At 0745 on 30 October the battalion made contact with the 1st Polish Armored Division two miles west of Breda. Very shortly thereafter it rejoined its regiment at Oudenbosch. Here, Captain Dyer, F Company, 415th Infantry, describes the warm, enthusiastic welcome accorded the men of "Old Faithful":

The thin lines of soldiers on either side of the cobblestoned road were tired, mud-splattered, but sharp-eyed and alert as they followed the turning, twisting road toward Oudenbosch.

It was large and red and made of brick, that building on the left. The door opened and a timid head poked questioningly out. Another head appeared, and moments later a group of black-frocked priests were gathered at the side of the road, staring wide-eyed at the approaching troops. Then from somewhere appeared grapes, apples, and pitchers of cider, eagerly offered to the *Ameri-kaner* by the now smiling, chattering Fathers. It was the first introduction of the 2d Battalion, 415th Infantry, to the friendly Hollanders of Oudenbosch, but only the beginning.

Around the bend, across the railroad tracks, and then the troops were in the town, where a people, after four years under the German iron heel, awaited them.

It was a wildly cheering throng that choked the sidewalks and spilled over into the street; a crying, laughing throng that broke out long-hidden flags of orange and waved them as if making up for the last four years. A large banner of black cloth with crude letters in orange, "Welcome, our Liberators," was brought out and quickly stretched across the street.

He must have been seventy or eighty, but now he walked with the spring of youth, the stimulant of reborn freedom, as he approached the soldiers. "We have been waiting four years," he said in his heavy English. "This I have saved for you when you should come." He pressed the slim bar of a famous Dutch chocolate into the soldier's hand and waited anxiously as the American un-wrapped it and bit into it. Both smiled at the same time, and the soldier fumbled at his belt. "Here, Pop," he handed the pack to the old man.

"Heavens, it is Camels," the old man gasped. "Momma, Momma, Camels it is," he called as he turned to the buxom old lady on the porch.

Cookies, cakes, apples, grapes, and pitcher after pitcher of cider made their appearance and rapid disappearance as the soldiers eagerly accepted them.

"Have you seen our Princess in America?" a little sixteen-year-old asked, tugging at her light pigtails nervously.

"Sorry, m'am," the big sergeant from Texas told her, "but we were pretty busy over there before we left, and I guess I missed her."

"Will she be back soon now?" the youngster asked earnestly.

"Lady," the sergeant grinned, "now that we're here, she can come home— anytime."

Pitchers of hot milk, with butter floating on top, were brought out, and quickly finished before the lines of soldiers began to move again.

On the other side of town the bridges were blown, the roads and approaches mined or blocked by the fleeing enemy. The battalion dug in for the night and started to work to clear the way forward. The city of Oudenbosch was free again and liberated without bloodshed.

In a dark, candle-lit, shuttered room, Lieutenant Colonel Denisevich met with the nameless leaders of those living dead who had never given up. All through the night shadowy figures moved silently here and there. Locations, installations, routes, all began to appear on the battalion operations map. The muffled tread of horses' hoofs, the shuffle of wooden-clad feet, the soft slither of saws began to sound throughout the town.

The next morning there was a bridge up, the road blocks were gone, and the mines either removed or plainly marked. A quiet mute tribute to the work of those unknowns who never gave up, in their desire to be free.

Prior to daylight on 30 October, after a nine-mile night march, the 413th Infantry, less the 1st Battalion, had closed in the vicinity of Sprundel. The 415th Infantry and the 414th Infantry now had complete control of the Breda-Roosendaal road within the Division zone. The operations had completely destroyed and overrun the Vaart Canal defensive positions of the enemy. Only one more position south of the Maas River was available to the Germans—the Mark River. With the 415th Infantry on the left and the 414th Infantry on the right, the Division commenced its drive to the Mark River at 1245. The I British Corps had directed the clearance of mines from the Breda-Roosendaal highway which was performed by the 329th Engineer Battalion and the ammunition platoons of both regiments.

CROSSING THE MARK

The Division right boundary was exclusive of the woods north of the main highway. In the woods there were four active enemy batteries. The 386th Field Artillery Battalion learned the location of the hostile batteries and requested permission to fire on them. Because the positions were in the 1st Polish Armored Division's zone, permission was not granted by Corps Headquarters. Corps had asked the Division whether it would assume responsibility for the additional zone, to which G-3 replied: "Leave the boundary as it is, and have the Poles clear out the woods immediately." Shortly thereafter Sherman tanks raced out of the woods toward the right flank of the 414th Infantry. The antitank guns and the attached tank destroyers of the regiment were loaded and aimed. Fortunately before the fire order had been directed it was discovered that the Poles occupied the tanks. At 0900 infantrymen of the 414th were being embraced by Polish tankers.

The 30th of October was a cold, bleak, windy day with intermittent showers—visibility was very poor. The 415th Infantry advanced over two routes in its drive to the Mark, 3d Battalion on the left and the 1st Battalion on the right. Its mission was to seize the Standaarbuiten-Oudenbosch crossing over the Mark River. The movement forward was made with only minor resistance being encountered. The main routes to Oudenbosch were blocked by railroad cars heavily mined and booby-trapped. These constituted the principal harassing activities of

Award of Distinguished Service Cross. By direction of the President, under the provisions of AR 600-45, 22 September 1943, as amended, and under the authority contained in Circular No. 32, Headquarters European Theater of Operations, United States Army, 20 March 1944, as amended, the Distinguished Service Cross is awarded to:

Sergeant CLIFFORD P. HINKEL, 36709357, (then Private) Infantry, 415th Infantry Regiment, 104th Infantry Division, United States Army, for extraordinary heroism in connection with military operations against the enemy. On 26 October 1944, the battalion in which Sergeant HINKEL was a machine gunner was subjected to an enemy counterattack which had encompassed the left flank of their position. The enemy had brought forward machine guns and, with intense fire, pinned Sergeant HINKEL and his fellow soldiers to the ground. Entirely on his own initiative Sergeant HINKEL seized his own heavy machine gun and, without fear or hesitation dragged it forward more than one hundred yards through intense enemy machine gun and sniper fire. Completely disregarding his own personal safety, he set up his weapon within plain view of the enemy and opened fire. For more than thirty minutes he poured fire into the enemy position, causing many casualties and neutralizing the enemy fire in that sector. Through the valiant, voluntary act of Sergeant HINKEL, a grave threat to his battalion was averted. The extraordinary heroism and courageous actions of Sergeant HINKEL reflect great credit upon himself and are in keeping with the highest traditions of the military service. Entered military service from Illinois.

the enemy in addition to occasional rounds of mortar and artillery. The 3d Battalion at 1900 arrived at the bridge site of Standaarbuiten. Here they found a road block constructed of steel cross-jacks about 200 yards short of the bridge. K Company drew fire from a machine gun and several machine pistols that were protecting the road block. As patrols rushed the bridge great confusion was observed among the enemy groups. They were shouting and running about in the vicinity of the bridge. Seconds later the bridge was blown. The sneak attack by Lieutenant Colonel Kelleher's 3d Battalion barely failed in seizing the bridge intact. All resistance on the south bank of the river was eliminated prior to 2030. Fierce fire of all types from the north bank continued throughout the night.

During the day the 413th Infantry moved to positions southwest of Oudenbosch in the vicinity of Seppe.

The Division had closed on the Mark River. The 49th Infantry Division (British) on the left was three miles short of the river and on the right the 1st Polish Armored Division was just short of the river line. In view of the successful pursuit action of the Division and the surprise effected, Corps directed the Division to continue in pursuit of the enemy and force a crossing of the Mark River. The chance of success of such a hasty piecemeal effort was of course problematical, but the advantages in sight prompted I British Corps to press the attempt. The Division directed the 415th Infantry to force a crossing prior to daylight on 31 October. Throughout the night heavy mortar and artillery fire fell on our positions. The 1st Battalion, 415th Infantry, was designated by Colonel Cochran to cross the river and establish a bridgehead 2,500 yards east of Standaarbuiten. Reconnaissance for the crossing was made under difficult conditions—the flat meadows enclosed within their surrounding dykes gave no cover from enemy fire and the dykes themselves were heavily mined.

On the right the 414th Infantry likewise made reconnaissance. Both bridges in its zone were found damaged beyond use. At no point did the approach to the water offer solid footing for the equipment necessary to cross it. Crossing by the 414th Infantry was therefore cancelled.

At 0630 on 31 October the 1st Battalion, 415th Infantry, under the command of Major Fred Needham, commenced the crossing of the Mark River. Company B, the first wave, crossed the water under grazing machine gun fire. Most of the troops clung to the sides of the assault boats to avoid being hit. On the north bank a strip of meadow at water-level had to be crossed before the men reached the cover of the first dyke. From this position they were able to return fire and to cover crossings of additional waves. Company B was closely followed by

By authority of Appendix B, Ninth United States Army, Sheet No. 1, enclosure to letter 200.62/67-116 GNMAG, Ninth United States Army, subject: "Announcement of Immediate British Combat Awards", Dated 6 April 1945.

The Distinguished Service Order is awarded to Colonel GERALD C. KELLEHER, (then Lieutenant Colonel) 0310994, Infantry, 415th Infantry Regiment, 104th Infantry Division, United States Army, for extraordinary heroism in connection with military operations against the enemy. On 29 October 1944 Colonel KELLEHER was in command of a battalion making an advance against the enemy in Holland, when the forward elements were halted by enemy artillery and mortar fire. Realizing the danger of remaining there, Colonel KELLEHER, with total disregard for his own personal safety, ran quickly to the head of the column and rallied his men, then personally led the advance by acting as the point. When he observed an enemy patrol of approximately ten men approaching, he ran forward, armed only with a pistol, charged the patrol, capturing two and forcing the remainder to withdraw. As the advance continued, his executive officer became wounded. Courageously and heedless of the enemy artillery and sniper fire, Colonel KELLEHER, without hesitation, ran to the fallen officer and carried him to the cover of a nearby building. The valor and superior leadership of Colonel KELLEHER contributed in a large measure to the success of the drive. His extraordinary heroism and courageous actions reflect great credit upon himself and are in keeping with the highest traditions of the military service. Entered military service from New York.

Company C. Initially Company A was pinned down before it reached the river bank. At 0900 the three rifle companies reinforced by D Company were on the north side of the river and had pushed forward a distance of 1,400 yards on a 1,000-yard front. With Company A on the left, B on the right and C in reserve, it soon developed that all companies became heavily engaged.

The weather remained cold with a heavy mist that limited visibility to an extremely close range. Occasionally through the day the mist changed into rain. Little support for the bridgehead troops was possible. There was no way to get the supporting arms across the river and the 81mm mortars could not go into position for lack of observation and because of constant counterbattery fire. Wire communications could not be maintained, the use of radio brought down immediate and accurate fire, and weather conditions would not permit the use of artillery observation planes—therefore artillery support was materially limited. Enemy observers, occupying concealed positions in the dykes, accounted for the accuracy of hostile fire until they could be spotted and eliminated. It was planned to follow the initial crossing immediately with the 2d Battalion. This plan was abandoned for the reasons just noted and for the further reason that many of the assault boats had been destroyed and constant heavy shelling continued, including accurate fire from self-propelled guns. The boggy ground also made any further crossing virtually impossible.

Early in the afternoon the 1st Battalion received enemy fire from the rear. Company F was quickly committed to clean out the resistance and protect the bridgehead from the south side of the crossing. About 1600 the battalion was surrounded by hostile tanks which overran the position and fired into individual foxholes. With most of the assault boats destroyed and the river behind them, the men put up a determined fight which saved many lives that appeared doomed. Further assault boats were requested from Corps but were not immediately available. In these circumstances, it was evident that the rifle elements in the bridgehead could not maintain it. They alone in the entire Corps zone were north of the river, subject to the concentrated power of all the German resources. The effect of violent surprise had been lost.

That evening the I British Corps directed that the 1st Battalion be withdrawn to the south side of the river and the Division was to prepare plans for a coordinated Corps attack. Lieutenant Colonel Peter Denisevich, commanding the 2d Battalion, and Captain Felkins, commander of Battery C, 387th Field Artillery Battalion, with a reinforced platoon of F Company, under command of Sergeant Scott, advanced with additional bazookas and ammunition in an attempt to provide antitank protection for the withdrawal of the infantry. About 500 yards north of the river bank the relief party encountered an enemy patrol and machine gun fire. The party was unable to reach Companies A and B but assisted in evacuating the wounded. Lieutenant William C. Tufts of Company C requested and was granted permission to lead a patrol forward with aid-men and antitank weapons. Under most hazardous conditions he was successful in opening a wedge in the enemy lines, permitting the withdrawal of the bulk of the 1st Battalion. The heroism of the officers and men of the 1st Battalion was outstanding. The action was not in vain, as the boldness of the attack had prompted the Germans to withdraw their main forces north of the Maas River. The heroic deeds of the officers and men, particularly Lieutenant William C. Tufts, Captain Felkins, Lieutenant Robert G. Neill, Pfc. Dahlmon, Pfc. B. E. Fiedler, Jr., Sergeant Boswell, Pfc. Gross, Sergeant Mohrman, and many others will never be forgotten. Two days later it was discovered that sixty-five officers and men who had remained on the north side of the river had sustained themselves and held their ground against a much larger force. Company C of the 329th Engineer Battalion had rendered outstanding support in assisting the crossing of the 1st Battalion.

On 1 and 2 November the Division prepared plans in line with the Corps directive for a coordinated attack on the Mark River. In the early afternoon of 1 November a conference was conducted by Lieutenant General John A. Crocker at his I Corps headquarters at Roosendaal.

In addition to General Allen, the division commander of the British 49th Infantry Division, Major General Barker, and the 1st Polish Armored Division commander were in attendance. The following directive was issued by General Crocker:

1. At 2100 on the evening of 2 November the I British Corps, with the 104th Infantry Division making the main effort, will force crossings over the River Mark. The 104th Infantry Division is to cross in the vicinity of Standaarbuiten, secure the Corps Bridgehead, develop its operation and secure Zevenbergen, and exploit within its boundaries as far north as the Maas River (Holland's Diep).
2. The 49th Division is directed to attack at the same time on the left of the 104th Infantry Division and the 1st Polish Armored Division is to force a crossing in the eastern part of the Corps Zone.

At 1800 on 1 November all commanders were assembled at Division headquarters in Hoeven, where General Allen issued the following directive:

1. The 413th will make the main effort, crossing the Mark River west of

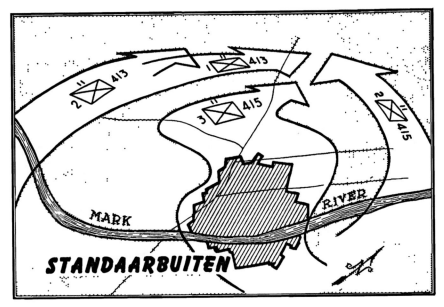

Operational Plan For Mark River Crossing

Standaarbuiten with the mission of seizing Phase Line F prior to darkness on
3 November.

2. The 415th Infantry will cross the river at Standaarbuiten and to the east
thereof with the mission of seizing Standaarbuiten blocking routes to the east
as far as point 22.

3. The 414th Infantry will make a feint and be prepared to later follow the
assaulting regiments.

4. The 329th Engineer Battalion will assist the crossing of infantry elements
with assault boats and foot bridges and will construct bridges across the river
and maintain roads and clear obstacles.

The terrain north of the Mark River consisted of boggy fields, for
the most part below sea-level, bounded by numerous ditches containing
water between steep dykes. The few roads in the region ran on bare
dykes high above the surrounding meadows.

The 413th Infantry sent four three-man patrols to reconnoiter the
north bank of the Mark River in its zone the night of 1-2 November.
At 0300 the patrols returned with prisoners and information concerning the disposition of the enemy. The enemy's determination to hold
the river line was disclosed by the statement of the prisoners that 200
replacements had arrived in the area on 30 October and that troops in
the line were threatened with force to remain and fight to the last man.
Throughout 1 and 2 November the Division artillery, reinforced by the
65th Medium Regiment, 75th Medium Regiment, 60th and 115th HAA

(all British), fired heavy concentrations on Standaarbuiten, Zevenbergen and the main routes of communications. Artillery planes reported road blocks, barbed wire, enemy observation positions and freshly dug foxholes in the vicinity of Standaarbuiten. At 1900 air observation determined that many enemy emplacements were unoccupied.

To amplify the feint by the 414th Infantry during the afternoon of 2 November, over 100 members of the Division headquarters rear echelon, a squadron of tanks, and sixty vehicles from 104th Quartermaster and Division Headquarters moved into assembly positions in the 414th regimental zone, simulating assembly of a large body of troops. After nightfall they were withdrawn by infiltration.

By 2000 the assault battalions of the 413th and 415th were in position, and a preparatory one-hour barrage by the Division and Corps artillery began. At 2100 the attack jumped off.

In discussing the artillery preparation for the Mark River crossing, Technical Sergeant Herbert Goins of Headquarters Battery, 929th Field Artillery Battalion, stated:

Our Command Post was a barn, complete with straw, a couple of hogs and one lone goat; typical of all Dutch barns in that it had a series of windows in the roof that consistently defied our attempts at blackout.

Our guns had the mission of neutralizing the area immediately across the river and sealing off the road into the town of Standaarbuiten, while our medium battalion was to neutralize the town itself. Shortly before the preparation, one of the observers reported an enemy column on the road leading out of the town. We adjusted one gun until we had zeroed in. Naturally the Heinies had left their wagons in the road and taken cover. After all our guns were laid on the area, we loaded and waited. Shortly, the observer reported that the Heinies had loaded up and were preparing to move. We gave the order to fire. They never knew what hit them. This was by no means new tactics in artillery but it was my first experience with it.

About an hour before the initial barrage, the fire plan had been completed and was enroute to the firing batteries. The men in my section were dog tired and yet no one made an effort to get any sleep. We wanted to see the results of our barrage and whether or not the infantry would have trouble in crossing. I went out into the orchard about fifty yards to the right of our forward battery. There was a light haze in the sky and now and then a searchlight swept from north to south somewhere far to the west. It was quiet, in the hush that comes before all hell breaks loose, when I heard the order "Fire" at the battery.

Our battalion fired almost as one gun and shortly after, the 5.5's of the Royal Artillery opened up. I heard the rifle-crack of the 3-inch tank destroyers and then the air was filled with the whirr and whine of shells. To the northwest, the sky was a dull, red glow that suddenly became long sheets of flame. The town was afire and a German ammunition train on the north road had been hit. I could see round after round of time fire bursting at a perfect height across the river.

The effect of our barrage was apparent the next day by the devastation in the town and the fact that so many Heinies were caught unprepared and lay dead in the roads and fields surrounding it.

The high explosives of the artillery, tank destroyers, and cannon companies were ripping up Standaarbuiten, and the town seemed to rise and fall with each successive barrage as though it were undergoing a series of earthquakes. The fierce time fire inundated the fields with a flood of lethal steel. Promptly at 2100 the first infantry assault boats were placed into the slow-moving Mark River. On the left, the 2d Battalion, 413th Infantry, commanded by Lieutenant Colonel Collins Perry, had completely crossed by 2124 and was pushing through the darkness toward Kreek. The men had to move over a high dyke on the south side of the river to reach the water's edge and were exposed to a rain of small arms fire as they scrambled over the broad earthen dykes into waiting assault boats. A few yards beyond the river itself was another stream almost as wide as the fifty-foot Mark River and about four feet deep. The open area between the two streams was flat and exposed to grazing small arms fire. Mortar and small arms fire was intense, but by advancing in short rushes the battalion reached phase line E at 2140. The 1st Battalion, under Major John White, followed the 2d Battalion, completing its crossing at 2145. By midnight the 413th Infantry was entirely across. At 0007 phase line F was secured and by 0620 the Division objective, phase line L, had been seized.

Although the defense was sporadic it was necessary to use grenades and bayonets in mopping up cleverly concealed snipers. Standaarbuiten, like many Dutch towns, was strung out for nearly a mile along a highway with a row of houses on each side of the road. Most of these houses were in the 413th Infantry zone. Machine guns at each end of the road swept it with intermittent fire but the infantry successfully crossed by squad rushes. On the other side of the highway the troops reached the first of the many drainage ditches (canals) which were to keep the men soaking wet for the rest of the Holland campaign. This first one, all the others being similar, was about eight feet wide and waist-deep, with a double-strand barbed wire fence running down the middle. The men, loaded with ammunition, plunged pellmell over the road into the ditch and many of them became tangled up in the wire, with all of them cursing the travel folders of scenic Holland. The whole area between the Mark River and the Maas Estuary is flat. Each farmer's field is bounded by ditches, and the larger areas fenced in by dykes with roads built along the top. Everyone was wet to the skin all the time. Whenever a foxhole was dug it immediately filled with water. The constant sniper fire as well as the shelling by mortars and artillery

The President of the United States takes pleasure in awarding the Medal of Honor to First Lieutenant CECIL H. BOLTON, Infantry, United States Army, for service as set forth in the following citation:

Lieutenant BOLTON, leader of the weapons platoon of Company E, 413th Infantry, on the night of 2 November 1944 fought gallantly in a pitched battle which followed the crossing of the Mark River in Holland. When two machine guns pinned down his company, he tried to eliminate, with mortar fire, their grazing fire which was inflicting serious casualties and preventing the company's advance from an area rocked by artillery shelling. In the moonlight it was impossible for him to locate accurately the enemy's camouflaged positions; but he continued to direct fire until wounded severely in the legs and rendered unconscious by a German shell. When he recovered consciousness, he instructed his unit and then crawled to the forward rifle platoon positions. Taking a two-man bazooka team on his voluntary mission, he advanced chest-deep in chilling water along a canal toward one enemy machine gun. While the bazooka team covered him, he approached alone to within fifteen yards of the hostile emplacement in a house. He charged the remaining distance and killed the two gunners with hand grenades. Returning to his men, he led them through intense fire over open ground to assault the second German machine gun. An enemy sniper who tried to block the way was dispatched, and the trio moved on. When discovered by the machine gun crew and subjected to direct fire, Lieutenant BOLTON killed one of the three gunners with

First Lieutenant Cecil H. Bolton, awarded the Medal of Honor for outstanding heroism during the forcing of the Mark River

carbine fire, and his two comrades shot the others. Continuing to disregard his wounds he led the bazooka team toward an 88 millimeter artillery piece which was having telling effect on the American ranks, approaching once more through icy canal water until he could dimly make out the gun's silhouette. Under his fire direction, the two soldiers knocked out the enemy weapon with rockets. On the way back to his own lines he was again wounded. To prevent his men's being longer subjected to deadly fire, he refused aid and ordered them back to safety, painfully crawling after them until he reached his lines, where he collapsed. Lieutenant BOLTON's heroic assaults in the face of vicious fire, his inspiring leadership and continued aggressiveness even though suffering from serious wounds, contributed in large measure to overcoming strong enemy resistance and made it possible for his battalion to reach its objective.

HARRY S. TRUMAN

pinned all to their foxholes when not actually attacking. Straw piles and burning buildings were attractive, but many of them were booby-trapped—tug on a bundle and you activated hidden grenades. At midnight, when Companies G and F had passed through Kreek they encountered a force of six enemy tanks with infantry. Promptly the 385th Field Artillery Battalion laid heavy fire on the enemy tanks, forcing them back.

The crossing of the 415th Infantry had proceeded with equal dispatch. Company K crossed the river at Standaarbuiten heavily armed with grenades and mines. It quickly seized the town, obtained the bridgehead and cleaned out all resistance. A terrific toll had been taken of the German troops who had occupied the town. The men from K Company had used the word "Kayo" to identify each other in the darkness. Next morning, as citizens crawled from their cellars or from the debris of what was their homes, they queried "Are you a Kayo?" Further east, the 2d Battalion, under the command of Lieutenant Colonel Peter Denisevich, crossed with E and G Companies while F Company made a feint. It was necessary for these infantrymen to carry their boats over 900 yards of swampy ground to the river bank. The boats, skillfully operated by the men of the 329th Engineer Battalion, were subjected to heavy machine gun and sniper fire. The regimental Intelligence and Reconnaissance Platoon did excellent work in this operation in cleaning out many machine gun nests on the north bank of the river. By 2235 the initial objectives assigned to the 415th were seized. Standaarbuiten had yielded many prisoners and enemy dead. At 0100 four enemy tanks and infantry counterattacked Company G, but the devastating fire of the 929th Field Artillery Battalion and supporting artillery units stopped them in their tracks. Prior to daylight phase line L had been secured and the Division had taken its assigned objectives.

Construction of bridges across the Mark River was essential to insure that the troops would be adequately supplied and supported by tanks and tank destroyers. The 329th Engineer Battalion reinforced by a Royal Engineer Company (British) had been assigned this mission and promptly began its work after the leading assault elements had crossed the river. Construction of the Class 9 bridge (nine-ton capacity) near Standaarbuiten proceeded with difficulty. Hostile mortar and artillery fire on the bridge site was extremely accurate. At 0115 the bridge was completed and the engineers started construction of the Bailey bridge (forty-ton capacity) along the main Oudenbosch-Standaarbuiten road. At 0315 one bay of the Class 9 bridge was destroyed by enemy artillery, but was quickly repaired by the engineers. Each time the engineers returned to work on the bridge they were heavily and accurately shelled. When there were no engineers near the bridge the fire ceased. Brigadier General Moore, while visiting the site, was convinced that the enemy had an observer concealed in the immediate vicinity. The 3d Battalion, 415th Infantry, was directed to make a thorough search, and a German officer and sergeant were found concealed under the abutment of the old bridge directing fire by radio. After they were disposed of, the accuracy of the fire ceased. At daylight on 3 November the nine-ton bridge was in use and by 1300 the Bailey bridge was completed. Thus the supplies and heavy supporting weapons were able to get to the advancing troops.

While the 413th Infantry and 415th Infantry were assaulting the Mark River the 414th Infantry on the south bank of the river supported by fire the attack of the 2d Battalion, 415th Infantry.

About 0900 on 3 November Lieutenants Fox and Squires and approximately sixty-five men of Companies A and B of the 415th Infantry were encountered in their advanced position north of the river. They had held these positions since 0900 31 October, the morning of the first crossing, despite heavy odds in favor of the enemy. These gallant men had subsisted on turnips and sugar beets. In addition to being under enemy fire, they had also been under severe friendly artillery fire. By maintaining superior discipline and morale and by the excellent use of cover they had not suffered a single casualty during their isolation from the rest of the battalion.

Before noon of 3 November it was apparent that the German line on the Mark River had been broken. No further delaying positions remained for the enemy south of the Maas River. Throughout the day hostile artillery fire became lighter as the enemy withdrew his heavy equipment to the escape route over the bridge at Moerdijk in the zone of the 1st Polish Armored Division. However, the 88s and self-propelled guns supported by infantry that were left behind employed hit-and-run tactics, necessitating skillful maneuver by our troops. The Germans customarily dug in on the reverse slopes of the dykes and set up positions in the houses along the roads. They massed their mortars behind houses, making it extremely difficult to knock them out. Machine guns were set up in culverts at road junctions and in holes beside houses as well as at each end of the drainage ditches. Tanks fired from dug-in positions.

Private First Class Tommy Boles of Company F, 413th Infantry Regiment, vividly describes the feelings and the actions of all infantrymen who participated in this great assault:

Award, Posthumous, of Distinguished Service Cross. Under the provisions of AR 600-45, 22 September 1943, as amended, and pursuant to authority contained in paragraph 3c, Section I, Circular No. 32, Headquarters European Theater of Operations, United States Army, 20 March 1944, as amended, the Distinguished Service Cross is posthumously awarded to the following officer:

Captain WILLIAM C. FELKINS, JR., 387th Field Artillery Battalion, United States Army, for extraordinary heroism in action against the enemy on 31 October 1944 and 1 November 1944, in Holland. Captain FELKINS, displaying great personal courage, voluntarily led a patrol across a river and into dangerous enemy territory to drive off hostile troops and tanks which had taken a heavy toll of an isolated infantry battalion. He personally adjusted a devastating artillery concentration upon the enemy positions which killed many Germans and forced the withdrawal of several tanks. As the artillery fire lifted, Captain FELKINS, with complete disregard for his own personal safety, advanced far ahead of the patrol while subjected to intense machine gun fire. As he prepared to lead a charge upon the enemy, he was fatally wounded. Captain FELKINS' heroic actions resulted in the safe withdrawal of 120 men, many of whom were severely wounded, and enabled two companies to maintain their critical position until the main bridgehead was later established. Entered military service from Alabama.

It started as a rumor, but later I was to find that it was not a rumor, but actually a river crossing, and ours was the company that had been selected to make it.

We had not been in this business of war very long, and what few casualties we had suffered—well, the number seemed large. That is what the doughboy thinks of most—the number of casualties, and it is quite natural that he does, because of endless hours and days he gambles with death.

It was a beautiful November day in Holland when I heard this vicious rumor that sent my morale zooming to a new low. The pit of my stomach must have done a somersault because I had no appetite until after the whole affair was over. A battalion runner told me that there was a river up ahead of us, and that the night before, some other outfit had tried crossing it and had great difficulty. This, I thought, was really the end, and right then and there I started preparing myself for it—mentally, physically, and spiritually, because by this time I realized that my fate wasn't up to me.

Most unpleasant things that start as rumors have a habit of turning out to be true, and this was no exception. We did receive an order to cross the river, and at once preparations got under way. There were countless orientations and each one left us feeling just a little more confident that it couldn't be so hard as most of us were inclined to believe. During the short time that we had to prepare for the ordeal, most of us had practically made ourselves regain the confidence that we had lost, so that when the time came we were ready and anxious to get it over with. Finally the order came to move out—we grabbed our equipment and got started. Never before have I walked in such an indirect route to go such a short distance. This I learned later was to confuse the enemy, so he wouldn't know just what we were up to. We walked for hours, and finally wound up at the assembly area. Incidentally, we had no idea that we were so close to the river. It was cold—muddy, cold and wet as only Holland can be. But each step forward was a step towards home, so with that thought in the back of our heads, we tried to soothe our feelings.

Suddenly there was a terrific roar, such as I had never heard before, and frankly, I was scared. A crash, boom, pow, that was entirely new to my ears. Then I looked up over the bank ahead of me. The sky was a glorious red—balls of fire exploding in mid-air with a guttural, splitting sound—explosions on the ground throwing earth, rocks and hot steel in every direction. Ah, that is beautiful, I said to myself, just like Fourth of July at home, except we never had this mud, and these dikes to put up with.

Then, after a few minutes, we were ordered to move up further and get ready to jump in a boat and cross. All this under that murderous artillery barrage that only Montgomery knows how to lay down. We were told ahead of time that a wire fence along the river had been cut, so all we had to do was to get in a boat, and glide across. So we moved forward to the point of departure. So far I had made it all in fine style, and I remarked on this to a friend, when splash! I found myself wading a "small canal" that happened to be neck high. Well, I was all wet, all the way through. Now what else could happen to make me feel worse?

After that artillery had put the fear of God into the Germans for awhile longer, we received the order to grab a boat, help take it the few remaining yards to the river, and go across. "Well, here we go," I said to myself, "I sure hope

I live to tell this one." So we started to the river lugging one of those heavy boats. And we stopped.

"Now what the hell is wrong?" someone asked. I looked ahead, and there it was. The fence was still there and no one seemed to have wire cutters. "Now we really do get it," I said to myself, but at that moment someone came up with the wire cutters and made a gap in the fence, and we managed to get to the river with the boat. Just as we started across, splat! something hit the water, and my heart sank, for I thought the Jerries had spotted us this time sure. But as luck would have it, this was nothing more than a piece of shrapnel from our own artillery, and I was very relieved to find it out, because in those days, I hadn't learned that our artillery could get us as well as Jerry's. Silently we glided across the river, and as the boat stopped almost everyone made a dash for the bank. I think that everyone had the same thought then—we were not amphibious and were better able to take care of ourselves if we had our feet on solid ground. Anyway, the thought seemed to boost our sagging confidence. Me, I took it easy, and stepped gingerly from the boat onto the bank, expecting every step that my foot would make connections with a mine. After a few minutes, I found the company commander, and we started forward with the outfit. Going forward was always the thing we wanted to do, but this time, even though we didn't meet anything that could be called opposition, it was not as easy as some people would have you believe. Just as we were going at a fairly rapid pace, what should loom ahead but a ditch—full of water and too wide to jump. "Well, here we go again" I said bitterly and plunged right into the middle of it, getting myself and all my equipment soaked to the skin. After that, with everything water-logged, I was carrying about twice the ordinary load, so I let go a few remarks against the people who had caused this, and threw everything except my rifle as far as I could send it, and hoped that I would never see it again.

Again we got started, and a few minutes later we came to a larger ditch, and of course, jumped in again. I felt just like a duck. I don't think that I would have done it, but at times the fear of getting lost is worse than the fear of getting hit, and this was one of those times. So I got through that one, and later two or three others just like it.

Slowly we moved on toward our objective. When we thought we were there, we called the Battalion Commander, and told him the situation. He promptly replied that we couldn't be there yet, because we hadn't had enough time. So with the usual grumbling we started plodding on. The comments on this were many and varied. Amid the mumbling, I overheard one person say, "That's a helluva note, they expect us to win the war all by ourselves, and in not more than twenty-four hours."

"Well," I thought, "we are moving, and this is going to be a cinch compared to what I expected, if only they would let a fellow get a little sleep, and quit trying to win the war in one day." Jerry had different ideas, I suppose, for at dawn, he cut loose with everything he had—tanks, artillery, mortars, and small arms—completely covering almost every inch of the area that we occupied. This time I really got down in my hole, and prayed as never before. This was the blackest moment of my life, and I am not ashamed to say that I was scared— plenty scared. There was no escape, for the terrain was as flat as a tabletop, and it appeared that the Germans were looking down our throats, judging from the way they were placing that artillery. .So all I could do was dig, and I really went down fast.

God must have been on our side during those days, for we finally succeeded in pushing the Jerries out of their excellent positions, in the face of extremely difficult opposition. It appeared that Jerry had sat back and allowed us to walk right into a trap, but we somehow managed to come out of it alive—most of us. Then came the welcome news. We were being relieved. What we didn't know was that we had established ourselves as a high-ranking combat outfit, and were on our way to take our place alongside of a crack outfit for more of what we had just gone through.

As far as personal reactions are concerned, I don't think that the average doughboy is capable of putting all those reactions into words. They are inside of you, and you get a sort of personal satisfaction in knowing that you were in on a job—a hard, dirty job, a job that cost lives, but yet you know that you did your part toward victory, and you get a sense of happiness that the job was well done.

Private First Class Charles J. Golden of Company K, 415th Infantry Regiment, gives this on the same action:

The 415th Infantry Regiment reached the Mark River 30 October. Company K dug in on the reverse slope of the dike and awaited orders to move on. Word was passed down early on the 1st of November that tonight was the night—at 2100 hours. Father Quinn went from foxhole to foxhole along the dike hearing confessions and giving the men a spiritual pat on the back. The muddy doughs checked their weapons and equipment and listened carefully to the well-planned assault information brought back from the command post by the noncoms. Then at 1900 word reached the line that the attack had been postponed twenty-four hours. Company K lay back down in the mud and sweated this one out.

The next day passed as the others had. Very little small arms fire, but the steady crash of German 88s along the dike and in the fields beyond. The noncoms ran back through the low, wet land to the farmhouse command post and were briefed again on the coming assault. The 1st Platoon objective was the center of the village; the 2d to check six houses on the right of town, then establish a road block to prevent German armor from counterattacking; the 3d Platoon aided the 1st, as did one machine gun squad. The other machine gun squad was attached to the 2d. Company headquarters sent an advance command post across the river under the command of Lieutenant Ray Collins. The mortar section remained in battery on the west bank and the rear command post group waited on the dike and maintained radio contact with all the assault elements.

It was a moonless night, but by 2015 hours the town of Standaarbuiten burned red and the scene across the dike was a holocaust of artillery-made daylight. The nerve-center was the command post farmhouse. Company K officers, the M Company Commanding Officer, the Battalion Commander, and thirty enlisted men waited there, talking quietly and listening to the steady blast of artillery falling across the Mark. At 2030 the platoon leaders left and the headquarters group prepared to move up to position on the dike. Up over the dike, down the gentle slope to the bank where the assault boats rested easily in the

water. A column of twos, well dispersed, then bunching quickly to load. Excited commands whispered—four boats moved toward the far bank—then four
more—and four more. . . .

Now the 1st Platoon was moving rapidly toward the burning sugar foundry
on the edge of town—the 2d out across the wet field toward their six houses.
The artillery was quiet now—an occasional round over the town—and no small
arms fire as yet. Then the angry spitting of a BAR from the sugar foundry.
Tracers burned the wet air. Still nothing from the 2d Platoon and now the
BAR was silent. Seconds passed and the headquarters group watched anxiously
from the dike. No radio contact yet. A blurt and the white tracers of a German
machine gun sent the 1st to the ground. But it was too late. They were at the
edge of the building. Rifles, automatic rifles, and grenades spoke. On the right
the 2d Platoon broke into flame and slashed their way into the houses. The 3d,
following the 1st, moved on through the sugar foundry, across the intersection,
and started slowly up the street toward the high-steepled church, blasting each
house with grenades and rifle fire. The 1st hung in on the left and kept pace.
Behind in the sugar foundry the enemy machine gun was silent.

The 2d Platoon houses were cleared now and prisoners—brand-new prisoners
—were being marched back toward the river. Radio contact was established and
the platoon dug in to protect the town flank. John Day, 2d Platoon BAR man,
was the company's only casualty that night. He was killed by short-range rifle
fire. While the 2d dug in, the 1st and 3d finished their advance through the
town and reached the church. Outposts were established and strategic positions
in the town buildings manned. At 2250 hours, less than two hours after the
jumpoff, Standaarbuiten was secured. The only indications of a counterattack
were a few high-angle 88 shells that dropped harmlessly past the town in the
fields. By midnight all enemy activity had ceased. The objective was taken
and the Mark River crossed.

Throughout 3 November the infantry elements shoved forward. By
nightfall the 413th Infantry had Noordhoek and Checkpoints 16 and
21, while the 415th Infantry had gained Checkpoint 22—the bridgehead was definitely established. Late in the afternoon the 49th Infantry
Division (British) had not yet been able to construct a bridge in its
zone and therefore many British trucks carrying troops and supporting
weapons were rushed across the 104th bridges at Standaarbuiten in
order to assist in the drive on our left flank.

The action was stiffly opposed, with many short skirmishes occurring
between our troops on one side of a dyke and the Germans on the
other. In one instance a German rifle company, attempting to outflank
Company A, 413th Infantry, walked straight into the guns of Company B and was cut down without warning as B's riflemen and attached
Company D machine gunners opened up on them at thirty-yard range.
The enemy was defending each house, barn, and shed. It was necessary
to blast the intervening buildings and the walls with direct fire and
then rush the occupants within the building. After vicious close-in
bayonet and grenade duels the defenders would be put out of action.

Mark River Bridge, Standaarbuiten

All kinds of ruses were employed by the Germans. One machine gun would place overhead fire down a highway, and when a doughboy attempted to cross the road he would be cut down by another machine gun firing grazing fire. They attempted to make us lose confidence in our own artillery by shelling us as soon as our artillery would open up on them, timing their barrages so that we might blame our own guns for short rounds. There were several instances of Germans yelling "Kamerad," and then opening fire as the infantryman stuck his head up. Shouting wildly and firing into the air, Germans would attempt to frighten our troops or make them give away their positions. Roads were frequently mined, shattered jeeps being a common sight. As the Germans retreated they liberally sowed the restricted avenues of movement with various types of mines and booby-traps. Many of the booby-traps were improvised with beet roots. The sugar beet harvest had just been gathered and the ground was literally covered, and to mine them an antipersonnel charge was inserted in the center of the root.

PURSUIT TO THE MAAS

Across this bleak and forbidding marsh-ridden plain, intersected everywhere by obstacles of canals and dykes and swept by high winds penetratingly cold, the pursuit continued for three days and nights.

Oral orders were issued early in the afternoon of 3 November by Division headquarters directing the 413th Infantry and 415th Infantry to continue the attack to the north at 1000 on 4 November with the mission of seizing a line running through Klundert and just south of Zevenbergen. When that line was seized the 414th Infantry would pass through the 413th Infantry and 415th Infantry and continue the attack to the Maas River. As the weather was clearing, air attacks on Klundert and Zevenbergen were frequent.

During the early hours of 4 November, a fifty-man counterattack was launched by the enemy against the 1st Battalion, 413th Infantry, the attack being supported by small arms, mortar and machine gun fire. The counterattack was quickly repulsed with the aid of Division artillery. The enemy, true to form, was counterattacking frequently, but good communications and quick response to firing requests sent back by the infantry enabled our artillery to keep the enemy dispersed.

As planned, the Division attacked at 1000. On the right the 415th assaulted, with Companies E and F leading. The 3d Battalion, which had been relieved in Standaarbuiten by the 1st Battalion, took over the positions formerly occupied by the 2d Battalion. By 1820 Lieutenant Colonel Denisevich's men were in complete occupation of the regimental objective and the Old Faithful Regiment had the city of Zevenbergen to themselves.

On the left the advancing 413th Infantry, with two battalions abreast, the 1st and 3d, had Klundert contained by 2000. Heavy resistance was encountered and repulsed by the 3d Battalion, which was being harassed throughout most of the day by self-propelled guns and tanks.

Shortly after noon the 414th Infantry moved across the bridge at Standaarbuiten in column of battalions, the 3d leading, followed closely by the 1st and 2d. At 1600 the Mountaineers passed through the 415th Infantry on the Zevenbergen-Klundert road. Immediately to its front 1,000 yards a strong enemy position was destroyed by thirty-six Spitfires of the Royal Air Force. This effective strike enabled the regiment to proceed to the north against moderate resistance. Throughout the day Spitfires of the Royal Air Force made numerous attacks on Zevenbergen, Klundert, Zandberg and other German strongpoints, assisting greatly in the neutralizing and destruction of these fortresses.

On the night of 4-5 November the 414th Infantry with the 1st Battalion on the left and the 3d Battalion on the right continued its advance. Again the Division was striking at night—a tactic which throughout its campaign had proven successful. On 5 November it continued its drive north of Zevenbergen through Zandberg and at 1615 patrols from the 1st Battalion had reached the Maas River. Lieutenant Arthur Levin led the patrol consisting of the 3d Platoon, Company C, 414th Infantry, to the river. Technical Sergeant Dinges writes of this experience:

We had been moving all night, and were tired and cold when Lieutenant Levin informed us we were to go to the Maas. As we moved forward over soft muddy ground we checked each house and barn in our path. No enemy was encountered and we finally reached the river to be greeted by civilians coming from their shelters between the last dike and the river. Water was dipped from the Maas with a canteen cup—it was a great relief to know we had reached our objective.

At 1800 on 5 November the 2d Battalion, 415th Infantry, moved on Zevenbergen against scattered resistance while the 3d Battalion came up on the right. At 1500 one company of each battalion converged on the town from the west and southwest. No hostile infantry were encountered and the mines sown along the approaches were bypassed. At 1800 Zevenbergen had been secured.

The 413th Infantry with its 1st Battalion reached its objective, Zwanenhoes, by 0900. As planned, the Seagulls held their positions for the remainder of the day, terminating their combat mission in the Holland campaign. The relentless pressure by the 414th Infantry had driven the enemy out of the Division zone towards Moerdijk. In the late afternoon the Moerdijk bridge was so closely threatened that the Germans could no longer risk leaving it intact. In a thorough job of demolition they completely destroyed the three center spans of this large bridge, one of the longest spans in the world.

On 5 November the 104th Division Headquarters received a TWX from Headquarters First United States Army, directing it to move to the vicinity of Aachen, Germany, with the least practicable delay, as soon as released by the First Canadian Army. On 5 November the Division was ordered to move into assembly positions in the vicinity of Aachen commencing 6 November.

At 1440, the afternoon of 5 November, the I British Corps assigned the Timberwolf Division an additional mission: "to assist the 1st Polish Armored Division in securing Moerdijk." Because the 414th Infantry was the only unit in contact with the enemy, the Division Commander directed Colonel Touart to remain in position and to prepare for the accomplishment of the newly assigned mission. The 386th Field Artillery Battalion, commanded by Lieutenant Colonel Urey W. Alexander; the 1st Platoon, Company B, 329th Engineer Battalion; and Company B of the 692d Tank Destroyer Battalion were attached to the 414th Infantry for this operation. On 6 and 7 November the remainder of the Division moved to Aachen.

When the 1st Battalion of the 414th Infantry reached the Maas River the only escape route over the Maas from the west was severed. The 1st Polish Armored Division on our right had been unable to proceed as rapidly as the Timberwolves, therefore the escape route from the east over the Maas River had not been denied to the Germans and they were stubbornly defending this site to the last man. On the night of 5-6 November the 2d Battalion, 414th Infantry, moved into position

By direction of the President, under the provisions of AR 600-45, 22 September 1943, as amended, and under authority contained in Circular No. 32, Headquarters European Theater of Operations, United States Army, 20 March 1944, as amended, the Distinguished Service Cross is awarded to:

Technical Sergeant HENRY A. MALONE, 34355017, (then Private First Class), Infantry, 413th Infantry Regiment, 104th Infantry Division, United States Army, for extraordinary heroism in connection with military operations in Germany on 3 November 1944. When the assault elements of his battalion met five enemy tanks and one tank pinned his company down at close range, Sergeant MALONE immediately took aggressive action with his rocket launcher. Exposing himself to enemy sniper fire, he made his way to a coverless position within sixty yards of the enemy tank. Despite intense small arms fire which his action drew, Sergeant MALONE fired four well aimed rounds, setting the tank afire and forcing it to withdraw. The extraordinary heroism and courageous action of Sergeant MALONE reflect great credit upon himself and are in keeping with the highest traditions of the military service. Entered military service from Georgia.

Mountaineer machine gunner covers the advance on Moerdijk.

about 1,000 yards southwest of Moerdijk. This citadel was protected by a canal, 600 yards of flat flooded marshland, and by an eight-foot concrete wall. In the early morning the battalion forced a crossing of the canal and moved against Moerdijk with one company. The attack was met with heavy grazing machine gun fire from the wall and by artillery and mortar fire from the north banks of the Maas River. The battalion was unable to enter the city, but with effective artillery support from the 386th and by use of regimental mortars it maintained pressure on Moerdijk throughout the day while the 1st Polish Armored Division was moving on the town from the south and southwest.

On 7 November the 2d Battalion again launched an attack, advancing 400 yards in its mission to maintain pressure on Moerdijk. Again it met heavy enemy fire. Later in the afternoon preparations were completed for a third assault in conjunction with elements of the 1st Polish Armored Division. Just prior to the attack the regiment received orders to move immediately to the vicinity of Aachen and rejoin the Division. The 2d Battalion was relieved by the 2d Essex Scottish Regiment of the

97

First Canadian Army and moved to assembly position prepared to rejoin the Division. Other elements of the regiment started their movement for Germany from Oudenbosch at 1700.

The Holland campaign had concluded with the release of the great port of Antwerp for Allied use and by the destruction of the German forces south of the Maas River. During this campaign the Division suffered casualties totaling 1,300 officers and men—of these 179 were killed, 856 wounded and 356 missing, but of the missing personnel one officer and thirty-four men were recaptured by the British in December. The Division captured 658 prisoners, who testified that their casualties had been exceptionally high because our artillery fire and tactics were more devastating than anything they had encountered on other fronts.

The Dutch underground "Delta" proved most useful and reliable in giving the location of enemy troops, mines, artillery and radios.

The association with the First Canadian Army and the I British Corps and their supporting troops was most pleasant. At all times the commanders, staffs, officers and men were cooperative and helpful. We had learned by experience that the fighting men of the Canadian and British Armies were skillful and that they were determined to destroy Naziism.

In tribute to the Division's successful operations in Holland, Field Marshal Bernard L. Montgomery, Commander of the Twenty-first Army Group, and Lieutenant General G. G. Simonds, Commander of the First Canadian Army, forwarded the following commendations:

TAC HEADQUARTERS
21 ARMY GROUP
B.L.A.
3 November 1944

Lieut-Gen Guy Simonds,
Comd, First Canadian Army.

1. Now that the operations designed to give us the free use of the port of Antwerp are nearly completed, I want to express to you personally and to all commanders and troops in the Canadian Army, my admiration for the way in which you have all carried out the very difficult task given to you.

2. The operations were conducted under the most appalling conditions of ground—and water—and the advantage in these respects favoured the enemy. But in spite of great difficulties you slowly and relentlessly wore down the enemy resistance, drove him back, and captured great numbers of prisoners.

It has been a fine performance, and one that could have been carried out only by first class troops.

3. The Canadian Army is composed of troops from many different nations and countries. But the way in which you have all pulled together, and operated as one fighting machine, has been an inspiration to us all.

4. I congratulate you personally.

And I also congratulate all commanders and troops serving under your command. Please tell all your formations and units how very pleased I am with the splendid work they have done.

> (Sgd.) B. L. Montgomery,
> Field-Marshal,
> C-in-C,
> 21 Army Group.

> Main HQ First Cdn Army
> 4 November 1944

I am in receipt of a letter from Field-Marshal Montgomery, a copy of which I attach. I would like to thank you, personally, for the loyal and able support I have received from yourself and your troops during these difficult operations.

> /s/ G. G. Simonds
> /t/(G. G. Simonds) Lt-Gen.
> A/GOC-in-C, First Cdn Army

> 2d Ind.

(3 November 1944)
Headquarters, 104th Infantry Division, APO #104, U. S. Army, 11 November 1944.

To: Commanding Officers, all units and attached units, 104th
Infantry Division, APO #104, U. S. Army.

The Division Commander takes pleasure in forwarding the commendation of Field-Marshal Montgomery and Lieutenant General Simonds for work well done by the Timberwolf Division.

By command of Major General ALLEN:

> /s/ MELVIN M. KERNAN
> /t/ MELVIN M. KERNAN.
> Major, A. G. D.
> Adjutant General.

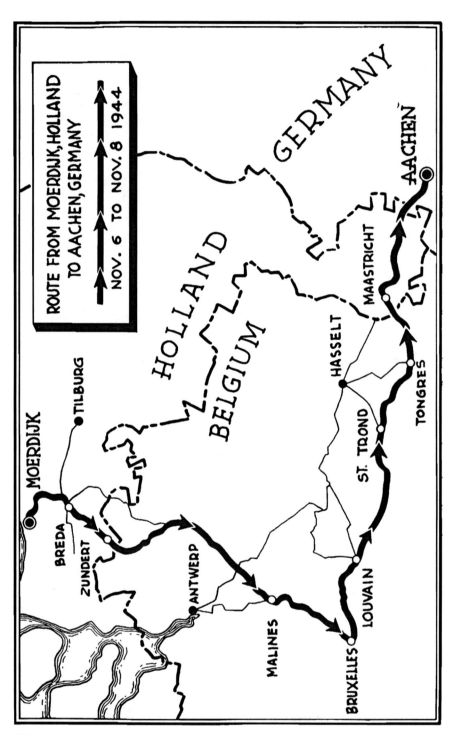

ROUTE FROM MOERDIJK, HOLLAND
TO AACHEN, GERMANY
NOV. 6 TO NOV. 8 1944

GERMANY

HOLLAND

BELGIUM

AACHEN

MAASTRICHT

TONGRES

HASSELT

ST. TROND

LOUVAIN

BRUXELLES

MALINES

ANTWERP

MOERDIJK

TILBURG

BREDA

ZUNDERT

R-E-S-T-R-I-C-T-E-D
HEADQUARTERS, FIRST CANADIAN ARMY
Commander-in-Chief, 21st Army Group.   — 7 November 1944
104 US INFANTRY DIVISION.

1. On behalf of First Canadian Army will you kindly express to the C-in-C 12 Army Group my appreciation of the services of 104 US Infantry Division while under command.

2. I realize that it is not easy for a division to have its introduction to battle in an Army other than its own. Nevertheless, once the "Timberwolves" got their teeth into the Boche, they showed great dash, and British and Canadian troops on their flanks expressed the greatest admiration for their courage and enthusiasm.

3. During the time 104 US Infantry Division has served in First Canadian Army relations have been most cordial and we have received the utmost cooperation from General Allen, his Staff and all commanders. I am sorry that they are leaving us and feel sure that when they again meet the Boche "all hell cannot stop the Timberwolves."

Sincerely,

(Sgd.) G. G. Simonds, Lt-General
A/GOC-in-C, First Canadian Army

*   *   *   *

200.6 (A) HEADQUARTERS, FIRST UNITED STATES ARMY,
APO 230—15 November 1944

SUBJECT: Commendation — 104th Infantry Division.
TO   :   Commanding General, 104th Infantry Division.

1. Field Marshal Montgomery recently forwarded to the Commanding General, Twelfth Army Group, the attached copy of a letter from Lieutenant General Simonds, First Canadian Army, expressing the latter's appreciation of the splendid services of the 104th Infantry Division while under his command.

2. I am very pleased to learn of the high esteem in which both British and Canadian troops hold your division, and am confident that it will continue to maintain the high standard of battle conduct which it has established.

(Sgd.) COURTNEY H. HODGES,

Lt. Gen., U. S. Army, Commanding

*   *   *   *

201.22 (19 Nov 44)   2nd Ind.
HEADQUARTERS VII CORPS, APO 307, U. S. ARMY
TO: Commanding General, 104th Infantry Division,
APO 104 U. S. Army.

1. Your attention is invited to preceding indorsement.

2. The Timberwolf Division has indeed made an enviable record in Holland and is daily adding distinction to its reputation in the current operation.

(Sgd.) J. LAWTON COLLINS,
Maj. Gen., U. S. Army, Commanding.

*   *   *   *

HEADQUARTERS 104TH (TIMBERWOLF) INFANTRY
DIVISION

28 November 1944

To All Timberwolves:

The above commendations have been received by this Division.

The tenacity and courage of our infantry, the skillful support of our artillery, the cooperation of our engineers, the proficiency of our signal personnel, the vigilance of our reconnaissance elements, and the team-work of all units, have been basically responsible for our successful performance in battle. The devotion to duty of our medical, quarter-master, ordnance, headquarters and military police personnel, has been outstanding. I wish to express my sincere personal thanks to you all.

We must maintain our high standards of discipline, training, physical fitness, AND PRIDE IN OUR UNITS. NOTHING IN HELL MUST STOP THE TIMBERWOLVES.

(Sgd.) TERRY ALLEN
/t/   TERRY ALLEN

R-E-S-T-R-I-C-T-E-D

PHASE IV

BEYOND THE SIEGFRIED LINE

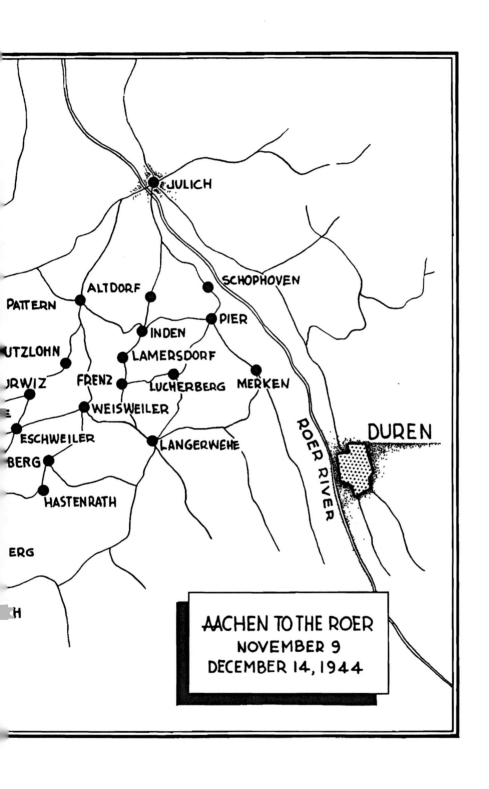

JULICH

SCHOPHOVEN

ALTDORF

PATTERN

PIER

INDEN

UTZLOHN

LAMERSDORF

FRENZ

JRWIZ

LUCHERBERG

MERKEN

WEISWEILER

ROER RIVER

DUREN

ESCHWEILER

LANGERWEHE

BERG

HASTENRATH

ERG

H

AACHEN TO THE ROER
NOVEMBER 9
DECEMBER 14, 1944

THE INFANTRY

A salute to the Infantry—the God-damned Infantry, as they like to call themselves.

I loved the infantry because they were the underdogs. They were the mud-rain-frost-and-wind boys. They had no comforts and they even learned to live without the necessities. And in the end they were the guys without whom the Battle could not have been won.

I wish you could have seen one of the unforgetable sights I saw . . . A narrow path wound like a ribbon over a hill miles away, down a long slope, across a creek, up a slope and over another hill. All along the length of that ribbon was a thin line of men. For four days and nights, they had fought hard, eaten little, washed none and slept hardly at all. Their nights had been violent with attack, fright, butchery; their days sleepless and miserable with the crash of artillery.

The men were walking. They were fifty feet apart for dispersal. Their walk was slow, for they were dead weary, as a person could tell even when looking at them from behind. Every line and sag of their bodies spoke of their inhuman exhaustion. On their shoulders and backs they carried heavy steel tripods, machine gun barrels, leaden boxes of ammunition. Their feet seemed to sink into the ground from the overload they were bearing.

They didn't slouch. It was the terrible deliberation of each step that spelled out their appalling tiredness. Their faces were black and unshaved. They were young men, but the grime, whiskers and exhaustion made them look middle aged. In their eyes as they passed was no hatred, no excitement, no despair, no tonic of their victory. There was just the simple expression of being there as if they had been there doing that forever, nothing else.

The line moved on seemingly endless . . . It was one long tired line of ant-like men. There was agony in your heart and you felt almost ashamed to look at them.

They were just guys from Broadway and Main Street, but you wouldn't remember them. They were too far away now. They were too tired. Their world can never be known to you, but if you had seen them just once, just for an instant, you would know no matter how hard people were working back home, they never kept pace with those infantrymen.

—Ernie Pyle

AACHEN

URING the latter days of October, discussions had been held in the vicinity of Wuestwezel with a representative from the G-3 Section, First United States Army, concerning the probable use of the 104th Infantry Division in Germany in the vicinity of Aachen. On 4 November, the TWX from First Army stated that the 104th Division would move to the vicinity of Aachen as soon as it was released by the First Canadian Army. On 5 November, First Army directed the Division to move to Aachen, commencing on 6 November.

As we have seen, the 414th Combat Team under Colonel Touart remained in action in Holland while the rest of the Division was withdrawn to assembly positions in preparation for the move to its new destination. The 555th Antiaircraft Battalion (Mobile) and the 692d Tank Destroyer Battalion (Towed) (less one company) and the Division rear echelon units began their movement early on 6 November. The 750th Tank Battalion, commanded by Lieutenant Colonel White, had been attached to the Division on 3 November, but had not been committed in the operation in Holland. It also moved to the Division assembly area near Aachen on 6 November. An advance party led by Major Harold Fosnot, Assistant Division G-2, informed Division Headquarters that First Army was anxious to have the Division close on 7 November so that it could go into the line that night. Many of us had erroneously thought that we would receive several days of rest prior to being committed in this new sector. We recalled the maneuver days when a two or three days' rest period was in effect after "the problem ended." During the day the 413th and 415th Infantrys closed in their assembly areas in the vicinity of Oudenbosch. Most of the men got their first hot shower since entering combat at the shower units and schoolhouses in Oudenbosch.

At 0100 7 November, tactical reconnaissance parties from all units left for Germany. At daylight the Division began to move, clearing the area by 1430. By 2200 the Division (less the 414th Infantry) closed in its new assembly area south of Aachen in the vicinity of Grenzhof. All the troops had moved the 165-mile distance in trucks. It was a long, tedious ride. Pfc. Donald Von Raden of A Battery, 387th Field Artillery Battalion, describes the trip as follows:

The mud, rain, and blackness were our enemy all that night, but the alertness and skill of our drivers and maintenance crews took it in stride. We had a bit of luck, for we later learned that we had driven right through the middle of a minefield during a change of route. Our only guide was a faint red dot in the black ahead of us. We hugged the Belgian border as the night passed and awoke many a Dutch village with the roar of our trucks on quaint cobblestones. We were routed through Maastricht and entered Belgium as daylight cut the mist.

At 0935 hours, the battalion crossed the German border and everyone gazed at the tank-trap dragons' teeth and pillboxes of the Siegfried Line. Having just missed a German barrage reception in Aachen the "Cats" rolled through and on to a rendezvous position in a wooded area near Brand where we met our reconnaissance party who had arrived the night before. After another battle with the mud we moved a short way up the road and into position just vacated by the 5th Field Artillery Battalion of the 1st Infantry Division. By 1630 the battalion made its first registration on the pay dirt of Germany. Despite the rough trip of 140 vibrating miles and the switch to an entirely different battlefront, the 387th had not missed firing at the enemy for a single day.

For the Military Police Platoon it was a rugged trip from start to finish. Richard V. Marks tells us:

The traffic section, acting as road-guides for the movement, never took a beating like that one. There were a lot of sad-looking, mud-covered, rain-soaked, frozen, unhappy MP's that day. We moved into Brand and the first real hot tub-bath on the continent. We never did go back to our helmet wash-bowl-bathtubs again, and weren't sorry in the least.

At 1000 on 7 November the reconnaissance parties reached the Division command post at Grenzhof just a short distance beyond the dragons' teeth protecting the borders of Germany. At once Colonel Waltz, Colonel Cochran, Lieutenant Colonel Shinkle, commander of the 385th Field Artillery Battalion, Lieutenant Colonel Gilbert, commander of the 929th Field Artillery Battalion, and Lieutenant Colonel Leo A. Hoegh, G-3, were ushered to the command post of the 1st Division, where they were briefed on the situation by the Division Commander. "The 104th Division is to relieve the 1st Division in its eight-mile sector southwest of Aachen the nights of 8-9 November and be prepared to attack on the 11th," was the directive of the VII Corps, First Army. The 1st was the division that General Allen had successfully led through North Africa and Sicily. We were attached to the VII Corps and were now a part of the First Army, under General Courtney Hodges. This was an entirely new sector and there was much work to be done.

In the hurried briefing Major General Huebner, then commander of the 1st Division, related the dramatic story of the drive from Normandy through France into Germany and the seizure of the first great German city, Aachen. We were now on the front where the great Red Ball Express had delivered the badly needed supplies. We recalled the many newspaper reports about this great action and how it bogged down because of the lack of supplies. The Allied powers had just missed finishing off the German armies in the west during the summer months. Since early September the Germans had had time to reorganize their battered formations, raise reinforcements from the civilian population and strengthen the Siegfried Line. Outside of the seizure of Aachen the month of October all along the western front had been relatively quiet. The Allied forces were concentrating for an all-out effort to drive into the heart of Germany, and the 104th Division had been selected to join in this great offensive. When the objectives of Stolberg, Eschweiler, Durwiz, Inden and Weisweiler were mentioned we were not particularly impressed, thinking that they were just German cities that had to be taken, little realizing that they were strongly organized fortresses.

After the briefing the reconnaissance parties went forward to make their plans with the units of the 1st Division.

The 415th Infantry officers went to the 16th Infantry command post at Steinbruck, where all commanders were oriented thoroughly by the commanding officer. The officers of the 413th Infantry went to the 18th Infantry command post, where they also were briefed. By the end of the day all plans for the relief of the 1st Division had been completed.

When the troops arrived late that night they went into bivouac in assembly areas south of Aachen. Again the troops lived in their puptents, this time on the damp soil of Germany.

According to Corporal Robert Lieberman, 385th Field Artillery Battalion, it happened just outside of Aachen, in the first position occupied by the 385th Field Artillery since the switch to the German border:

> The night was pitch black, overhanging clouds raced low, blotting out the feeble efforts of the moon to illuminate the landscape. Lieutenant Lee B. Sanders, executive of C Battery, plodded along through the mud, down a fence-lined trail. His senses were alert, for walking at night in an enemy country was something new to Lieutenant Sanders.
>
> Suddenly he stopped. Someone was moving in the bushes to his flank. His heavy .45 fairly leaped out of its holster and with the reassuring feeling of the weapon in his hand he called out, "Halt! Halt! Halt!" The stillness was split with a roar. Some, hearing the noise, swore that a German machine gun was creating havoc behind our lines, others just held their guns more tightly and waited. The dawn unfolded a scene of death. Out of the seven rounds Lieutenant Sanders had fired, the cow had been hit in the head five times. Some steak, eh?

The Division was disposed as follows on 7 November: The Division (less the 414th Infantry) was assembled late in the evening near

Aachen, the 414th Infantry (less the 2d Battalion) was enroute to Germany, and the 2d Battalion, 414th Infantry, with Colonel Alexander's 386th Field Artillery Battalion was engaged in battle with a stubborn German garrison at Moerdijk, 150 miles northwest of Aachen.

At 1600 on 8 November relief of the 16th Infantry began by the 415th, being completed by 0025 9 November. Company C of the 750th Tank Battalion; Company B, 692d Tank Destroyer Battalion; and Company C, 329th Engineer Battalion, were attached to Colonel Cochran's forces.

During the past two months warfare on this front had been stabilized and during the interim both forces strengthened their positions and laid in huge stores of ammunition and supplies. The terrain was hilly with spots of timber here and there over the entire area, pillboxes being situated on critical terrain features. Factories with high smokestacks afforded the enemy excellent observation. The 3d Battalion, 415th Infantry, was in the west edge of Stolberg, with the enemy holding the remainder of the city. The German units facing the 415th Infantry included the 3d Battalion, 27th Regiment; 2d Battalion, 89th Regiment, and the 246th Fusilier Battalion. During the day the remainder of the Division closed into assembly position.

On 9 November the 413th Infantry began its relief of the 18th Infantry. Attached to Colonel Waltz's forces were Company A, 750th Tank Battalion; Company A, 692d Tank Destroyer Battalion and Company A of the 329th Engineer Battalion. As the men moved into the pillboxes which were to be their homes for the next few days they were well aware that the positions were not the place for a rest cure. German direct-fire weapons continuously bounced armor-piercing rounds off the reinforced concrete emplacements. High-explosive mortar shells dug new holes in the mud and the rapid-firing machine guns clipped twigs from the already torn trees which blanketed the rolling hills. As was true with the 415th Infantry, the scheduled relief was accomplished without casualty.

During the day, plans for the Division attack under the VII Corps were completed. At 1400 all commanders and staffs assembled at the Division command post and were thoroughly briefed on the coming operation. From left to right the VII Corps troops on the line consisted of the 413th Infantry and the 415th Infantry of the 104th Infantry Division, one combat command of the 3d Armored Division, the 1st Infantry Division, the 4th Infantry Division, and the 4th Cavalry Group. The remainder of the 3d Armored Division was in Corps reserve. The 30th Infantry Division, a part of the XIX Corps (Ninth United States Army), was on the immediate left of our Division. The

Major General Allen and General Bradley, 12th Army Group Commander, with General of the Army Eisenhower at Grenzhof

VII Corps, in conjunction with the forces of the Ninth Army to the north, the other forces of the First Army and the Third Army on its right, would attack in the direction of Duren and Cologne to penetrate the enemy's main defenses. This all-out assault would be preceded by a large-scale bombing by 2,400 United States and British bombers.

"The 104th Infantry Division, with the following units attached: 750th Tank Battalion, 692d Tank Destroyer Battalion, 555th AAA AW Battalion (Mobile), 188th Field Artillery Battalion (155 How.), will attack, making its main effort on the right to seize assigned objectives and destroy all enemy west of the line Weisweiler-Inden. D-Day and H-Hour to be announced," was the VII Corps order.

The Division Field Order No. 10, issued on 9 November, further directed the 414th Infantry, with Company B, assault gun platoon and mortar platoon of the 750th Tank Battalion attached, and with Company C, 692d Tank Destroyer, and Company B, 329th Engineer Battalion, in direct support, to move to assembly positions southwest of Stolberg the night prior to the jump-off, and attack and seize objective "A"—unforgettable Hill 287—and continue its advance to eventually seize Weisweiler and Frenz. Colonel Touart's men were assigned the additional mission of protecting the Division right flank and maintaining contact with elements of the 3d Armored Division and the 1st Infantry Division. For the initial operation the 1st Battalion of the 415th Infantry would be attached to the 414th Infantry to seize the high ground just south of Stolberg and northeast of Hill 287.

The 415th Infantry was assigned the mission of seizing the fortress

111

city of Stolberg and the industrial city of Eschweiler. To assist Colonel Cochran's forces Company C of the 750th Tank Battalion was attached and Company B of 692d Tank Destroyer Battalion and Company C, 329th Engineer Battalion, were in direct support.

The 413th Infantry, Company A, 750th Tank Battalion attached, and Companies A of 692d Tank Destroyer Battalion and 329th Engineer Battalion in direct support, was to attack on the Division left and seize the successive objectives to the northeast, including the many pillboxes, plus Rohe, Durwiz, Helrath, Putzlohn, Inden and Lamersdorf. It was assigned the additional mission of protecting the Division left flank and maintaining contact with the 30th Infantry Division. General Woodward's artillery was to support the attack and the 104th Reconnaissance Troop was to be prepared to secure the Division right flank and assist the 414th Infantry in maintaining contact with the 3d Armored and the 1st Infantry Divisions.

Colonel Taggart's medical battalion, as in all operations, was to have its collecting companies in direct support of each regiment.

The dominating terrain in the Division area was a high hill in the zone of the 414th Infantry known as Hill 287. The units on the line prior to the Division arrival had on three occasions attempted to seize this important terrain feature, but in each instance were repulsed. It was apparent that the strongly defended observation point would have to be seized before any substantial gains by the Division could be made Therefore it was determined that at H-Hour on D-Day, the mass of the Division strength would be committed in the 414th Infantry zone in order that this important hill and the high ground just west of Hestenrath could be seized quickly.

. Shortly before noon on 10 November General Dwight D. Eisen hower, Commander of all Allied Forces in the European Theater; Gen eral Bradley, Commander of the Twelfth Army Group, and Lieutenant General J. Lawton Collins, Commander of the VII Corps, called on the Division Commander at Grenzhof. During the conference General Eisenhower stressed the importance of the coming assault. It was pointed out that the bulk of the German armies was deployed west of the Rhine in front of the industrial and coal-producing regions of the Ruhr and Saar, both together forming the industrial heart of Germany. The German armies must save the Ruhr and Saar Basin or starve for lack of supplies. It was a bitter time for fighting, with the freezing cold and rain seldom letting up, and the battlefields were oceans of mud. Such conditions would hurt our forces and favor the Germans because they greatly interfered with our greatest battle asset—mobility on the ground and use of air forces. The choice for attack had been

Each house was treacherous—the mud thick and slimy.

made, accepting these depressing conditions and trying for a knockout blow rather than leaving the Germans free to scheme and improvise until the coming spring.

Hitler had managed to get roughly 1,000,000 troops for his West Wall, which was to the immediate front of the poised armies. The V-1 buzz-bomb and V-2 were evil and dangerous weapons. It was essential that Germany be beaten before it perfected all of its future possibilities for these weapons of revenge. The stakes of the winter battle were large and the losses were bound to be heavy. Most of the divisions that were in the line had been in combat since D-Day; all were battle-weary and footsore. The 104th Infantry Division was one of several new divisions to be committed in this drive. The operation of the Division and other similar units was soon to determine the effectiveness as a fighting force of the selective service men—could they withstand murderous combat against professional enemy troops? The answer to this vital question was soon answered in the affirmative by the hard-hitting Timberwolf doughs.

The attack which was to have commenced on 11 November was postponed late the night of the 10th owing to poor flying conditions. During the next five days the weather was miserable; the cold, rain, and snow, in addition to the tenseness of the coming attack, added materially to the discomfort of the men. Life in a pillbox, a dilapidated building, in sour basements, and in wet foxholes was nervecracking. Although the men now were seasoned veterans after their successful entry into combat in Belgium and Holland, they still grew apprehensive when darkness fell. The extensive minefields and booby-traps around the defensive positions of our own troops and those of the Germans made it difficult for patrol action at night. Artillery constantly pounded observed enemy positions and the men stood constantly on the alert in muddy foxhole outposts. Local skirmishes between the patrols continued throughout the period.

To the front of the 413th Infantry were rows of strong steel reinforced pillboxes, well dug-in and camouflaged, all being mutually supported by emplaced machine guns. Many of them appeared like innocent dwellings or haphazard piles of debris. To the immediate front of the 415th Infantry lay Stolberg, industrial center, with all its factories, cellars, and buildings turned into strongpoints. Most of the buildings had been heavily shelled by Allied artillery. Around the industrial section the Germans made fortresses of the great slagpiles, which also provided them with good observation. Roads leading into the city were narrow and winding, and mines covered by small arms fire made formidable road blocks.

While the patrols did not capture any prisoners, they were able to obtain valuable information about location of minefields, booby-trapped defenses, movements of enemy troops, and the location of pillboxes. The enemy set up loud-speakers and broadcast bits of propaganda which provided much amusement for the front-line rifle troops. Popular American recorded dance music was interspersed with juicy tidbits like "Gentlemen prefer blondes, but blondes prefer men who are not crippled."

Staff Sergeant Charles Henderson of Company A, 413th Infantry, relates his feelings during this period of anxious waiting:

There are many things that make war hell; the sheer physical exhaustion that comes after days of walking; the torment, after being cold for hours; going into a warm building only to go back into the biting cold. There is the hunger that comes after days of eating the same cold food, the disgust one gets when he smells his own stinking body and tastes his own filthy mouth. There is the beard, the dirty clothes, and the dead weight of pack and equipment. I could go on indefinitely but the worst is the "sweating out" that precedes every attack.

The sweating out of the first attack is not too bad. The troops are green, true, but they are physically and mentally in good shape. Their buddies are all there. They have not seen men ripped apart by shrapnel, or their guts torn out by a bullet. They have not heard men scream after a mine has blown off their legs. They have the happy, care-free, attitude of the naive.

After the first attack they know. They know—but they lie to themselves. "Poor Joe," they say. "It can never happen to me," they tell each other. It's not too bad—yet. Only a few aren't with them any more. They know what a battle is and how to take care of themselves. The enemy has been met, killed, captured, or forced to retreat.

The attacks continue. The original men become fewer. Private First Class Smith, the boy who said, "They'll never get me," has been killed. The ones who are left say to themselves, "Why don't you stop kidding yourself? I'll be very, very lucky to come out of this in one piece."

DRIVE TO THE RUHR

At 0325 the G-3 at Division Headquarters received the following message from VII Corps: "This is D-Day, H-Hour is at 1245." The biggest Allied attack since the St. Lo breakthrough was to commence in nine hours and twenty minutes. All units were notified immediately, and with all plans completed the Timberwolf Division awaited the zero hour.

At 1105 you heard distant continuous thunder like Niagara Falls, very far away. It was the heavy bombers of the 8th Air Force and the Royal Air Force arriving on schedule from England; simultaneously more than 1,000 cannon began to punctuate the monotonous drone of the bombers. This was the beginning of the biggest air assault of World War II. For the next ninety minutes, 2,400 medium and heavy bombers passed over the front line to bomb the strategic targets of Eschweiler, Duren, and Julich. The artillery concentrations had been carefully prepared by General Woodward and his battalion commanders and had been coordinated with the many guns of Corps and Army. Every gun had its specific target and observation from the ground or air on that target. Far back you could hear the deep blast of bigger artillery pieces and throughout the area the Division 105's and 155's were blasting sharply. From orchards, from behind buildings, from backyards, gun muzzles spat flame and smoke into the frosty air. All along the front, the tanks, tank destroyers, mortars and infantry cannon took up the incessant roar. Promptly at 1245 the 414th, 413th and 415th Infantry Regiments launched their attacks.

HILL 287 . . . The 3d Battalion, 414th Infantry, under Lieutenant Colonel Leon Rouge, led in the main effort with Companies K and L. As had been experienced by other units in previous weeks, the enemy resisted stubbornly with murderous mortar, machine gun and artillery fire. Each building lying southwest of this key observation was heavily fortified with concrete pillboxes and dugouts. The enemy's reinforced fortifications withstood the air and artillery bombardment and as soon as our fire lifted the Germans would hurriedly man their defensive positions, and the rushes of the 3d Battalion were repulsed. At 1500 Colonel Clark's 1st Battalion moved on the right of the 3d Battalion and after ferocious fighting had pushed forward 400 yards prior to "buttoning up" at 2300. The 1st Battalion, 415th Infantry, which was attached to the 414th Infantry for the initial attack, lunged forward at 1245 over the open ground along the south edge of Stolberg. They likewise met heavy resistance but were successful in reaching the southern edge of their objective by 2300, a distance of 900 yards.

Again on 17 November the attack was resumed by the 414th Infantry. Constant pressure was maintained against Hill 287 throughout the day and with effective use of smoke and heavy artillery concentrations I Company was able to surround a massive pillbox which was the key to the entire defense of the sector. However, the enemy again withstood the assaults by our infantrymen, but his position was becoming more precarious hourly. Shortly after daylight on the 17th the 2d Battalion of the 414th Infantry under Lieutenant Colonel Cummins moved forward to an assembly position 400 yards to the right rear of the 1st Battalion. At 1230 the 2d Battalion attacked abreast of the 1st Battalion and at dark had made an advance of 900 yards against stiff resistance.

The 1st Battalion, 415th Infantry, under Lieutenant Colonel Fred Needham, repulsed several vicious counterattacks against its positions and after heavy fighting had reached its objective, which overlooked Stolberg and was located north and west of Hill 287.

On 18 November the Germans were driven from Hill 287 and the 414th Infantry now held the dominating terrain with observation over Stolberg and Eschweiler. Only effective coordination and teamwork by the tanks, artillery, air, engineers, and the determined fighting infantrymen enabled the regiment to seize the fiercely defended Hill 287 by 1230. In the words of Staff Sergeant John W. Craver and Corporal Kale F. King, 414th Infantry, two members of I Company, one of the assault units, the attack on Hill 287 will always remain an outstanding example of the best infantry tactics:

The night of 15-16 November was one of those pitch-black ones—where you can hardly see your hand six inches in front of your face. I can remember moving onto the road near Lieutenant Leroy E. Willis, my platoon leader, for whom I was a messenger, and being barely able to see the two white strips of tape on his harness. The speed of the column in moving out—led by Company I and Lieutenant Lawrence W. Smith, our company commander—was adjusted to the slickness of the pavement over which we had to move. There were stretches of rough cobblestone, and some of slick paving brick, each equally hard to move over after a rain. Winding around, up and down hills, through villages and quiet hamlets where only occasional lights flickered, the column was quiet, watchful, wondering if the enemy knew we were moving closer. This was a new adventure, for this was the first time we had moved toward the enemy over his own ground. Heretofore we were on friendly soil, fighting the Kraut on territory that was not too receptive to his trespassing. We were moving along a road somewhere near the famed dragon's teeth of the Siegfried Line. Then we neared a town. From behind us our artillery was sending over shell after shell into enemy lines. From in front the enemy was sending us one of his shells for every one of ours; punctuating his short barrages with spasms of machine gun fire. Company I moved along the streets of the town, around a curve in the road to a two-storied, white, stucco house on the edge of a slight gulch. As we moved into position to dig in we were met with several shells that fortunately landed off to our right a few hundred yards. This was our welcome to Buschbach.

Dawn came, and the hour for attack had been set at 1230. This was 16 November 1944, a day never to be forgotten by the men of Company I and of the 3d Battalion of the 414th, for this was our initial move into Germany proper. As the hour for attack approached a force of Flying Fortresses and P-38 fighters moved over us toward Eschweiler, where the Germans were expected to show stiff resistance. What a pleasant sight those 1,000 bombers were.

The 1st and 2d Battalions led the attack on Stolberg and were held up momentarily by mortar fire. This caused our battalion, of which Company I was the support company, to move quite slowly through the town of Buschbach and into the streets of Stolberg, only part of which was held by the 3d Armored Division. Company I remained in support until the other two rifle companies were pinned down south of Hill 287 by small arms fire. Our objective then was to flank the hill. We approached the hill from the front about dark and dug in about three hundred yards from the top.

Hill 287 was a well defined dominating point in the town. From the pillbox at the top of the hill a person could see nearly all the western approaches to the town as well as those to the north and east. The superhighway leading to Eschweiler and part of the town itself could be seen from the observation platform of the pillbox. Northwest of this particular box, along a ridge that extended into the town, were two more boxes, which covered a large portion of the town of Stolberg. However, at this time those two were in our hands. Communication trenches led from the top-most box to several lesser boxes, and to a church a few hundred yards north of the crest of the hill. The church was used as storage space for munitions until it was hit by our shells, and then the rubble became cover for machine gunners.

Near where the company dug in were several houses along a small road. One of these houses was used for a command post by an outpost of the 3d Armored Division, which had been forced to abandon its vehicles and revert to infantry tactics. This same house was used by us as our command post and it was here that orders were received to move the company across the open ground to the church, and if no opposition were met, to dig in there until morning. Before moving, the company commander had a patrol organized from the 2d Platoon, which had been reserve platoon during this movement. The patrol consisted of Staff Sergeant Charles Kuczka, and nine men. The men were to move toward the church, learn whether or not any enemy was in that direction, and return to advise the company commander as to whether or not the troops should be moved to that locale.

Less than two hundred yards from the command post the patrol was ambushed by two machine guns covering a minefield. One man was killed and several were wounded; nevertheless all but two men returned safely to the CP. One of those men was killed, the other was seriously wounded and was taken in by the enemy troops and treated for his wounds as best they could. Later he was recaptured by men from the company. The company remained on the hill the remainder of the night and at dawn found themselves at the mercy of the enemy artillery observer on the pillbox. For the next ten hours we were pounded nearly every minute of the day by heavy concentrations of artillery and mortar fire but with only one direct hit in all that time. Several times shells exploded just in front of or to the rear of a foxhole, causing no casualties. Throughout the entire night and the following day the four platoon messengers, Pfcs. Francis E. Swiggum, Russell Leeds, Jerome S. Tobin, and Kale F. King, were required to carry on their duties under fire, crossing the fire-swept ground between their platoons and the company command post time after time.

As darkness came on the night of the 17th the company received orders to withdraw to a large building several hundred yards to the rear in order to reorganize and rest up for an early dawn attack. The platoons moved off at five-minute intervals to reach the building where 1st Sergeant George A. Ricker had arranged for the men to bed down for the night, get good hot chow, and be all ready to move off the following morning.

Dawn of 18 November found the company moving back to the right of the hill behind L Company. As L Company took its objective—a row of houses to the right of the box—Company I would move toward the front of the pillbox, with the 1st Platoon going to the rear of the baby fortress, within hand grenade range. Orders were that the pillbox would be taken with the weapons at hand: bazookas, flame throwers, automatic rifles, hand grenades, and satchel charges. This proved impossible, so a 105mm gun was drawn up in front of the box after a platoon of tanks had assaulted the box and a tank-dozer had been brought up to cover the rear entrance. A series of satchel charges were exploded against the rear doors. Entrance was made to the box only to find that the enemy had escaped down the communication trench, quietly slipping past members of the 3d Platoon who had remained on guard all that night.

Proof of the desperate position in which the enemy found himself is the fact that as they escaped from the pillbox they set a booby-trap on one of our own dead, the explosion of which caused several casualties in the company following the capture of the pillbox. However, information found in the box in the form of sketches aided materially in the removal of the minefield in front of the pillbox. Several copies of field orders, together with a list of the passwords for over a week proved that these troops were members of units met by other outfits in the same area and positively identified several enemy commanders.

During this operation against the pillbox two of Company I's officers were injured. Lieutenant Smith, the company commander, and Lieutenant Raymond C. Doan, the weapons platoon leader, were both evacuated.

Casualties were heavy but the incident was but a living proof that before the battle is won, the war-weary dogface must grasp every inch of ground.

The Germans had now lost their observation for the first time since the great assault had commenced. The stubbornness of the defenders and their determination not to give up this key terrain was evidenced by the rubble and ruins of all buildings and pillboxes and the great numbers of enemy dead in the path of our advance. As soon as Hill 287 fell, the 414th Infantry was quick to exploit success by pushing forward Colonel Clark's battalion towards Objective No. 1, the high ground northwest of Hastenrath, 1,500 yards east of Hill 287. Two squadrons of fighter-bombers preceded the assault at 1700 by striking the defensive positions which lay in the battalion zone of advance. Striking at night, the 1st Battalion advanced 1,500 yards, passing

House-to-house fighting through Stolberg's rubble-lined streets.

through a number of enemy strongpoints without drawing fire. Shortly after midnight it was firmly established on Objective No. 1 after its sneak attack through the formidable Siegfried Line. The 2d Battalion was advancing on the right of the 1st Battalion and in the morning of 19 November it was abreast of the 1st Battalion. The 414th Infantry immediately prepared plans to continue its attack on Volkenrath.

STOLBERG . . . The 2d and 3d Battalions of the 415th Infantry attacked at 1245 on 16 November. The 2d Battalion had the mission of seizing the high ground north and east of Stolberg, with the 3d Battalion given the important assignment of taking Stolberg. As was true in the zones of the 413th and 414th Infantry Regiments, dense minefields and all types of antipersonnel mines and devices hampered the advance of the 415th Infantry. Using tank-infantry-engineer teams, the 2d Battalion, in conjunction with the 413th Infantry, made an advance of 800 yards on the left. Several pillboxes, all being mutually supported by fire, blocked further advance of Colonel Denisevich's battalion. That night Staff Sergeant Bradshaw of Company E led an eight-man patrol to Pillbox 113, a few hundred feet in front of the battalion's position. One hundred yards south of the pillbox they surprised the two Germans who were outposting it. Two more Germans, the relief for the outposts, were also captured. One man was sent to the rear with the prisoners while the remaining seven inched forward and saw Germans sitting outside the pillbox. The sergeant called to them to surrender, but they answered with grenades. One of the patrol members launched a rifle grenade and the Germans scurried inside. A "beehive" was placed against the door and blew it off the hinges. The blast blew open a second door but the Germans threw more grenades and immediately called for artillery fire on the area. It was necessary for the patrol to take cover in nearby trenches. When the enemy fire lifted a German medic approached crying "Kaput." Not being familiar with the German language, they sent him back. From prisoner of war statements it was determined that there were forty men occupying the pillbox. On 17 November the 2d Battalion continued the attack against the pillboxes in its zone. Pillbox 113 was taken and an assault was made on 114, also protected by many smaller pillboxes. In front of these fortifications barbed wire had been strung to a depth of twenty-five yards and hundreds of Schü mines were strewn throughout the area. Enemy weapons were accurately zeroed on the approaches to the pillboxes, making it a difficult task to close in on these strong positions. By 19 November the pillboxes which had retarded the 2d Battalion's advance were captured, heavy casualties having been suffered by both sides.

The 3d Battalion, under Lieutenant Colonel Kelleher, had been constantly engaged in hand-to-hand combat in the fortress city of Stolberg since 16 November. All companies were committed, and with the use of pole charges, satchel charges and all types of demolitions and with the effective support of self-propelled 155mm guns of Battery A, 987th Field Artillery Battalion, the high-velocity weapons of Company B, 692d Tank Destroyer Battalion, they forced their advance from building to building. The tall chimneys, factories and buildings were shelled extensively and gradually Stolberg was pulverized. Entrances had to be blasted into each building by self-propelled guns or demolitions. As soon as one block had been cleared by Colonel Kelleher's infantrymen, vicious counterattacks were thrown against the newly gained positions by the fanatic Germans. For three days and nights the battalion edged forward from house to house. Staff Sergeant Charles M. Todd, 929th Field Artillery Battalion, recounts the close infantry-artillery coordination that enabled the doughs to advance against the heavily fortressed city:

Several days before the attack were spent in poring over maps and air photos, searching out any possible strongpoints where artillery fire would have to be delivered rapidly and accurately. This study revealed that throughout the area were numerous hills and ravines which all added to the problem of delivering

Award of Distinguished Service Cross. By direction of the President, under the provisions of AR 600-45, 22 September 1943, as amended, and under the authority contained in Circular No. 32, Headquarters European Theater of Operations, United States Army, 20 March 1944, as amended, the Distinguished Service Cross is awarded to:

First Lieutenant GEORGE T. VAN GIESEN, 01306023, Infantry, 414th Infantry Regiment, 104th Infantry Division, United States Army, for extraordinary heroism in connection with military operations against the enemy. On 8 November 1944, Lieutenant VAN GIESEN, a platoon leader, volunteered to lead a combat patrol against enemy positions which he had located the previous night while on a reconnaissance patrol. While skillfully leading his men over the same route he had passed the night before, he and his men were suddenly subjected to intense machine gun fire which caused many casualties. Realizing that maneuver was impossible, he ordered his men to withdraw while he, completely disregarding his own personal safety, moved among his wounded men, rendering first aid and moving them to safer positions. This courageous act was done without thought for himself and amid intense machine gun fire which took his life. Lieutenant VAN GIESEN demonstrated a spirit of unselfishness and fearless devotion for his comrades that is an inspiring example for all. The extraordinary heroism and courageous actions of Lieutenant VAN GIESEN reflect great credit upon himself and are in keeping with the highest traditions of the military service. Entered military service from California.

accurate fire. Careful inspection of the air photos in conjunction with information supplied by 415th Infantry patrols determined the location of many pillboxes which were then added to the firing charts. Throughout these days of preparation the artillery liaison officers were continuously coordinating the efforts of the artillery and infantry battalion operations sections. As the plans of movement changed it was necessary that artillery fire plans be revised so as to give the maximum support. These trips from one command post to another were made over roads which the enemy was covering with very accurate harassing fire.

When the fire plans were finally completed all important points from the high ridge, which ran perpendicular to the route of advance, to the east side of Stolberg had been carefully plotted on all firing points. Targets were assigned to each battalion to be fired "on call" should any unit need additional support.

For the best part of an hour before the time our doughboys were to move forward, the surrounding buildings shook as the Division artillery and supporting units stomped the targets which had been so carefully located and plotted. Among the most important of these was the famous Hill 287, called "the Pimple." All high buildings and factory smokestacks were also denied to the enemy as points of observation.

As the troops moved forward all fires were "on call" and were employed very successfully by using a system of geographic points referred to as "George points." These points, important terrain features, were numbered so that any observer could get rapid, accurate fire where he wanted it. This system proved to be very useful and was in continuous use throughout our following campaigns.

When the infantry buttoned up for the first night, detailed defensive fires were planned to protect them against counterattack by the enemy. All main roads entering the city were pinpointed so that efforts by Jerry to bring up reinforcements would prove very costly.

Many pillboxes and fortifications, well camouflaged in buildings, made it necessary during the battle for the city to employ eight-inch howitzers to neutralize them. The skill and courage of our forward observers and their sections made the use of these weapons very effective in softening up and destroying many of these obstacles.

Throughout the entire operation shell reports were made by the infantry to the artillery, making possible the location of various enemy weapons. Liaison officers coordinated the firing of mortars and artillery.

On 18 November, after the 414th Infantry had seized Hill 287, the 1st Battalion of the 415th Infantry reverted to the control of Colonel Cochran. Early on 19 November the 415th Infantry launched an attack, with three battalions abreast. The 1st Battalion, under the cover of air protection, moved forward rapidly and was on its objective, the high ground southeast of Stolberg, at 1100. The close air support of the 8th Air Force fighter-bombers, effectively bombing and strafing enemy positions during the period, enabled the battalion to advance with little or no enemy mortar fire. Colonel Needham's battalion was now in a position to block the enemy's escape from Stolberg. The 3d Battalion increased the fighting tempo in Stolberg and by 2300 it firmly

held the once great German industrial city. The 2d Battalion had destroyed the remaining pillboxes in its zone and at dark was abreast of the 3d Battalion.

The regiment dug in and made preparations for exploiting its success the next day.

ROHE-HELRATH . . . On D-Day, 16 November, simultaneously with the 414th and 415th Infantry Regiments, Colonel Waltz's Seagulls had launched their attack. The 2d Battalion, under Lieutenant Colonel Neilson, was on the left and Colonel Bill Summers' 3d Battalion was on the right. The 1st Battalion, which had been on the line, was withdrawn into regimental reserve, prepared to support the attack. Many of the fortress pillboxes in the Siegfried Line lay in the path of the 413th Infantry. The infantry-artillery-engineer teams were effective in the assault, and after three hours of heavy fighting the 3d Battalion had destroyed several of the pillboxes and had entered the town of Verlantenheide, completing an advance of 800 yards prior to nightfall. The next day all of the remaining pillboxes were seized and Verlantenheide had been thoroughly mopped up. The lead companies, E and G of the 2d Battalion, and I and L of the 3d, were frequently held up by fire from the left flank. During the next day the positions were consolidated and the main activities were conducted by patrols reconnoitering Rohe and Helrath, the regiment's next objectives. To approach these towns, however, the villages of Wamvach and Verweden had to be secured. After extensive patrolling the 2d and 3d Battalions renewed their attack at 0800 on 18 November. The advance was steady and was subjected only to sporadic mortar and machine gun fire, and by 1000 the two villages had been taken. During the night a cold rain soaked the countryside, turning all roads into mires of mud. It was still raining the morning of the 19th when Colonel Neilson's battalion sloshed through the slippery mud and driving rain to assault Rohe. In its advance of 4,000 yards the battalion had met stiff pockets of resistance but by dusk it held the intermediate objective overlooking Rohe. The 1st Battalion was moved up on the left of the 2d Battalion, getting into position for its assault on Helrath. The day ended with the regiment having gained 5,000 yards. The 3d Battalion went into regimental reserve.

The fighting continued on 20 November, with the 2d Battalion advancing against its objective, Rohe. At 1335 in the driving rain and ankle-deep mud, Colonel Neilson's men, advancing under the covering fire from Company C, 750th Tank Battalion, stormed the town. After heavy fighting from house to house and room to room the battalion

Medic ! !

seized its objective and promptly consolidated its gains. The enemy was determined not to give up and constantly counterattacked the battalion throughout the remainder of the day and morning of the 21st. Shortly after noon on the 21st the enemy had been thoroughly repulsed.

During the afternoon the 1st Battalion, under Lieutenant Colonel John White, with Company A leading, passed through the lines of the Division on our left and executed a daring flanking maneuver against the town of Helrath. Supported by one platoon of tanks, Company A alone entered the town at dusk and before total darkness had gained the central part of the town. That night the enemy infiltrated behind the lines and cut off Company A from the rest of the battalion. However, at daylight on 20 November the rest of the battalion joined Company A in the beleaguered town and systematically cleared it in a series of bitterly contested house-to-house battles.

In four days the Division had smashed five miles beyond its line of departure, had inflicted heavy casualties on the fanatic Nazis who were determined to protect their "Sacred Soil," and had broken through the Siegfried Line, capturing the ground dominating the great industrial city of Eschweiler. The Division had kept abreast of the many veteran divisions on the line and at this time was spearheading the drive for the Roer River. Selective service personnel making up the fighting men of the 104th Infantry Division had proven to higher headquarters that they not only could take it but could dish it out.

The Chicago *Daily Tribune*, on 27 November, carried the following article by its war correspondent, William Strand:

104TH DOING OKAY, SAYS FIGHTING FIRST

With the United States First Army in Germany: It is now possible to disclose the divisions in the First Army which have participated in the present offensive. They include the famed 1st, the 4th, the 3d Armored and 104th. The 104th is commanded by Major General Terry Allen, who led the 1st through North Africa and Sicily. The 104th fought its first battle here beside the 1st Division veterans who say the 104th is doing okay.

The 104th was the first to enter Eschweiler after taking the towns of Helrath and Rohe and cleaning up Stolberg.

The 104th had preliminary battle experience fighting with the Canadian First Army to clear the Port of Antwerp. Later they became the first Allied troops to reach the Maas River.

The great offensive had not been without sacrifice. Sergeant Mack Morriss, *Yank* correspondent, in an article published in the Army weekly on 29 December 1944, paid tribute to the splendid work of the battalion aid station of the 3d Battalion, 415th Infantry. The high praise for the efficient work of the medical men was applicable to all medical personnel of the Division.

BATTALION AID STATION

Stolberg, Germany—The attack was a day old. The door opened at Battalion Aid, and two or three walking wounded lurched through and then the man with the arm came in. He paused at the door, a short little guy with very pale gray eyes. His eyes looked almost colorless now because his face, like the faces of the other wounded, was black with the dirt of Germany.

The guy stood at the door looking around the room and then he walked over to a davenport and sat down. A man next to him lit a cigarette and gave it to him, and he said "Thanks" and smiled. His right arm had been severed below the elbow and the stump of his arm leaked blood through a tight battle compress. He sat on the davenport and smoked with his left hand while the medics looked at the other patients. Then they made out a casualty tag for him and a medic said: "What hit you?" He looked up and grinned: "Shrapnel, I guess." Then he looked down at the stump and added: "Whatever it was, it was big."

As he waited to be evacuated to the clearing station, he yawned and said to nobody in particular: "I sure am sleepy. I ain't had no sleep for two nights now. I could stretch out right here and sleep a week." But instead, he sat very straight on the davenport so that the bloody bandage on his forearm did not touch the cushioned seat, and he blinked his eyes when the lids drooped from sheer exhaustion. When the time came, he got up and walked out to the ambulance that was to take him and others to the rear.

Lt. Ralph Weiber, MAC, of Chicago, Ill., assistant to the battalion surgeon, had treated the man just after he was hit. The lieutenant told about it.

"He came over and said: 'Say Doc, would you mind cutting this off? It's not doing me much good anymore.' So I cut two ligaments that were holding his lower arm and hand and put on the bandage. One of our medics hid the hand under the rug so the others wouldn't see it. The man walked by himself, still under fire, back to where we had the ambulance. It was about 500 yards. You saw him come in here. He had absolutely no shock. I have never seen a man with more guts."

So another casualty had passed through Battalion Aid. There was a break and the medics poured gin into glasses of grapefruit juice and drank. Business at Battalion Aid is always heaviest during an attack, and this was a big attack. Everybody had been sweating. Gin and juice helped the medics because they rarely drink it themselves. They usually ration it out to the casualties coming in. The casualties take gin and hot water or gin and juice or straight shots of Scotch, depending on their condition. Now Battalion Aid poured itself a drink and almost apologized for it.

A litter-bearer came in and Lt. Weiber asked: "Where's Lamar?" The litter-bearer answered: "Dead, I think." Weiber looked at him for a moment and said: "Not Lamar. Lord, not Lamar."

The litter-bearer said: "We got in front of our own lines and got pinned down. We finally made it back and some infantry guy said: 'A medic just got it right behind you.' Lamar was behind me. I don't know what happened to him." Lt. Weiber swore and went into the next room.

The medics were quiet. Their outfit had lost a third of its 30 men. Lamar was the tenth casualty—the second in three days.

A few hours later they brought Lamar into Battalion Aid. He wasn't dead. They carried him in and laid him down on the floor and went to work on him. He seemed almost gone but was still conscious. Blood, dried and ugly, spread across his eye from the bridge of his nose and down the left side of his face. The right sleeve of his overcoat was ripped and bloody.

Lamar knew where he was. "Hello, Doc," he grinned. "Hello, Lamar," said Capt. John Mitschke of Helena, Mont., the battalion surgeon. "Did you take your wound tablets?"

"No, I didn't, Doc," said Lamar.

"I ought to bust you for that," Capt. Mitschke said as he cut away the heavy clothes.

"I didn't even put on a compress," Lamar said.

"I *will* bust you," said Mitschke with a grin. "Did you bleed much, Lamar?"

"Well, I thought I did, Doc," he answered. "I could hear it sloshing around inside my coat and it sort of scared me for a while."

Scissors snipped away at the clothes on his right shoulder. They cut through his overcoat, then his field jacket, then his shirt, then his winter underwear. Mitschke laughed. "You've got more clothes than an infantryman," he said.

Lamar pursed his lips. "I just keep putting 'em on, Doc."

Finally and delicately the clothing was parted from the wound. A rifle bullet had ripped into the long muscle of the upper arm above the bicep and destroyed it. Lamar had three wounds—the one in his shoulder, a hole in his right fore-arm and the bridge of his nose shot away. They wiped his face with cotton and daubed tenderly at his nose.

Lamar, his eyes closed, caught some conversation about his left eye. He said calmly: "It's okay, Doc. I know it's gone." Actually his eye, blinded by blood, was all right.

They gave him plasma. He felt better. He said: "You know what happened? I got hit and I rolled down into a ditch. I stayed there for a while and then I heard somebody call to me. It was a German. He spoke good English and he said: 'Come over to me.' Well, I wasn't so sure who he was but I thought he was a German. Anyway, it was hot around there, and I decided I might as well go over to him. I started toward him. He shot me."

Lamar lay on the floor for a while longer while plasma ran down a tube into his left arm. Then he said: "Wait till my mother hears about this. It will scare her to death." He paused and then his face twisted in recollection. "She could never figure out why I wanted to be a doctor. She said people had enough trouble without being a doctor and seeing all the terrible things that can happen to other people. She couldn't even go into a hospital without having a fainting spell. By the way, Doc, how are the nurses back up the line?"

Mitschke laughed: "They're wonderful. You'll like 'em."

"Yeah," said Lamar, "but the question is, will they like me? I've been telling the patients how good they are, and now you tell me."

"They're swell," said Mitschke.

Lamar was quiet. Then he said: "Say, Doc, I want you to do me a favor." Mitschke said: "Sure, what?"

"I'm going to get a fruit cake for Christmas," Lamar said. "When it gets here, I want you all to eat it. Will you do that for me?"

"You know we will," said Mitschke, "and we'll think of you when we do."

Then Lamar was evacuated.

Battalion Aid began to fill again. Pfc. Milton Schillion of Paducah, Ky., brought in four men. After he had deposited them he went over to the Jerry can and drank. He was sweating.

When Schillion had gone back to where K Company was having it rough, Lt. Weiber said: "There is a man with guts. Our first day in combat, they pulled him off the line and made a litter-bearer out of him. He was one guy who wasn't afraid to go out and bring men in. He's always been a rugged character. Back in the States he used to go up to the regimental CO and tell him he was going over the hill."

Capt. Mitschke talked about Schillion, too, when there was time. "We made a litter-bearer out of him at first, but he's done such good work that we use him now to coordinate litter squads. He roams from company to company. If he thinks it's too hot for the squad to go out, he holds them until things quiet down a little. He's very valuable to us."

Then the doc said: "It takes a lot of courage to be a litter-bearer and more courage to be an aid man. An infantryman has a hole and he stays in it, but when there's a casualty, the aid man has to leave what little protection he has and get out in the open. A mortar shell or 88 doesn't recognize the Red Cross on a helmet.

"We've had varied treatment from the Jerries. You heard what Lamar said about being shot when he started toward this German. On the other hand, we had this happen yesterday. There was a Jerry machine gun about 100 yards to the right and there were three wounded men out front. A lieutenant showed the litter squad where they were and went running over to them. The machine

"Then Father Quinn went out to pick up some of the kid's buddies on the field . . ."

gun opened up on him. The litter squad followed and there was no fire. The litter-bearers made two trips and didn't get shot at. But the third casualty could walk so they left an aid man and the lieutenant to help bring him in. When the lieutenant started back with the aid man, both of them helping the casualty, they were all shot at."

And if you stayed long enough at Battalion Aid you'd see that the strain told on the medics, too.

A kid stumbled into the room, crying, and they sat him down in a chair. He wore a Red Cross brassard. S/Sgt. John W. Green of Greensboro, N. C., tried to calm him down, but it was no use for the moment. He burst out with a stream of words: "Noise, too much noise, all noise, too much noise." They took him into the next room and gave him something that made him sleep. Next day he was all right. Green said: "He's just a kid."

Another one came in. They put him on cushions on the floor, and he lay on his belly and held his ears. A shell had exploded and killed the men standing beside him, and the noise of it had hurt his eardrums. But the death of the men beside him had done more than that. Father Quinn—Capt. Gerald Quinn of Hoboken, N. J.,—came in and saw him on the floor and said: "There is a man who was tough. But he's been through a lot in two days."

Then Father Quinn went out to pick up some of the kid's buddies on the field. Mitschke said to him: "Father, it's not safe to go out there now." Father Quinn said: "Oh, it's all right."

When he had gone, Weiber told a few stories about the chaplain, who in his first month of combat had already won the Silver Star.

131

A third medic came in. "Doc," he said, "I've got a hunk of something back here." He dropped his pants and pulled up his shirt and there was a small hole in his backside. "I was sitting behind a wall," he said, "and a shell hit the other side. I didn't have time to stop and besides I didn't think it amounted to anything."

"Hum," Doc said. "Well, it has pus in it. I'm going to evacuate you." So the medic bent over and Mitschke probed the wound for the shell fragment, or piece of rock, or whatever it was inside. The probing was painful in the raw wound, but the medic stood bent over and let it go on without a word. His mouth froze into a queer grimace and remained that way.

As the probing went deeper, the medic raised his head and gazed intently at the pin-ups—some German and some American—that smiled down at him from the wall with their magnificent civilian indifference.

ESCHWEILER . . . Stolberg having been taken on 19 November, the 415th resumed its relentless drive towards Eschweiler. The 2d Battalion, on the left, advanced 3,000 yards through the dense Propster Wald, meticulously mopping up all resistance in its zone. By nightfall it had reached the northwestern outskirts of Eschweiler. On the right the 1st Battalion moved hard and fast through the woods down the axial ridge into Eschweiler. Isolated groups of snipers impeded the movement at times and had to be flushed out, but many prisoners were taken and much abandoned material was captured. Company C of the 329th Engineer Battalion played an important role during the day's operations clearing the important Stolberg-Eschweiler road of mines, repairing damaged sections and replacing demolished bridges to insure a continuous flow of antitank weapons, ammunition and supplies to the forward troops. Patrols from this battalion entered Eschweiler at 1120, and at 1640, with three companies abreast, the battalion was in the outskirts of Eschweiler. In the 20 November 1944 issue of *Stars and Stripes*, G. K. Hodenfield wrote:

HODGES' MEN IN ESCHWEILER

With the First U. S. Army: Under the brightest skies since the present offensive began, the First U. S. Army pushed forward today on all fronts and advanced in some places as much as four miles. There were patrols in the outskirts of Eschweiler. They could look down into the city of 50,000 persons which had been on the receiving end of continuous air and artillery bombardment for almost a month. Four large buildings in Eschweiler had roofs which were draped with huge red crosses.

Three-day passes out of the front lines were encouraged all through even the hardest fighting. Psychological effects of battle claimed almost as many combat fatigue cases as did physical injuries incurred in action. In order to hold down the amount of such incidents, short duration leaves were arranged to give the doughboy a chance to ease his mind and body, get clean clothes, and generally change his atmosphere to a more pleasing locale for a few days. Paris was the leave that most of the weary Joes hoped for. . . . Paris might not be as glamorous as in pre-war days but it still held not a little fascination for each and every fighting man. First Sergeant Albert R. Parker of Headquarters Company, 3d Battalion, 413th Regiment, affirms that his excursion to "Gay Paree" was an unforgettable experience:

On 21 November 1944 the platoon is shacked up in a nice safe reinforced paper factory. The guard is fixed and all is set for a decent night's sleep. That is, until 0200 when the CO calls for three men and a truck-load of antitank mines to be delivered to K Company. So off we go into a pitch-black night to the rifle front. At battalion headquarters the old man tells me to send the boys on up with a guide. As for me, I'm to go to Paris on the first forty-eight hour pass. There must be a catch, but no, it's true. Thanksgiving Day finds me in the safety of Service Company eating a turkey dinner and getting a much needed haircut from 1st Sergeant Langstrom. Then a quick drive to Belgium for a shower and clean clothes; well, almost clean. Finance makes a mistake and cuts loose with three months pay and I'm off—on a cold and miserable 550-mile trip to Gay Paree.

Two days and a night. One night stay in Rheims—the home of champagne. It was here Sergeant Herbert Hawkins had such fun sleeping on the hard floor after his hardships in German beds. Then on to Paris. After getting the convoy lost in the immensity of Paris, we park in a business district, and from every window beautiful illusions begin to appear. Before a chance is had to get acquainted the convoy rolls on to our hotel. We register and take an automatic elevator to our rooms. Such luxury, such beds, and the bathroom was something to shout about. An enormous tub and beaucoup hot water. There is no question about the first thing to do. Fill the tub and loll in its wonderful warmth.

Then downstairs for supper. Food furnished by the Army, cooked by French chefs, and supervised by the Red Cross. What a chef can do to spam and powdered eggs is out of this world. And for a tip of a cigarette the waiter couldn't bring you enough. Now we were ready to tackle the town. We're in luck; by an odd coincidence it is the local Sadie Hawkins Day, or to be exact St. Catherine's Day. Females of all shapes and sizes in mass formations down the streets. Anything resembling a man was fair game for a round of kisses by the mademoiselles. Naturally this loosened the strings to our candy bar pockets which in turn caused us to be hoisted on the shoulders of shouting kids and paraded through a huge Metro station. This went on a couple of hours before Sergeant Grover Preston and myself decided to break away and see some nite-club life. We had heard this was located in a sectoin of Paris known as Pigalle. Don't ever try to walk straight to any place in Paris. It is much quicker to just wander around aimlessly. Paris consists of miles and miles of six-story stone buildings and cobble-stone streets that meander around town in no particular direction. Eventually we got to Pigalle and decided on a likely-looking bistro. It was a nice place. Quiet music, almost American style, waiters in evening dress, and champagne at only 500 francs a bottle. Then very quietly out of the side of the waiter's mouth came the words "If you wish real Scotch, it can be had—for three dollars a shot." Army men were selling their liquor ration for a tidy sum it seemed.

And so we whiled away our forty-eight hours in all parts of that historic city doing whatever struck our fancy. I know no one was sorry he had come. The French were swell to us and the Red Cross gals did a wonderful job of arranging accommodations for the battle-weary troops.

The trip back was not as pleasant as the one going. We knew what awaited our return. And we weren't mistaken. Paris became nothing but a dream my first night back but it was an experience I'll never forget, even the few parts I neglected to mention.

The 413th and 414th Infantry Regiments on 21 November held the important terrain which dominated the city from the northwest and southwest. Throughout 21 November the 1st and 2d Battalions of the 415th Infantry continued their attack against Eschweiler. The 2d Battalion, working on the left, gained more than 400 yards over its thickly mined and heavily shelled zone. The greatest number of casualties of the day were caused by S-mines scattered throughout the area. Among the dead was Chaplain Clarence Stump, killed by an S-mine while evacuating casualties. The feelings of the men were expressed by one who said, "Someone will pay dearly for this." The fighting encountered by the 1st Battalion within Eschweiler was heavy. Its advance was greatly hampered by continuous fields of mines and booby-traps covered by long-range mortars and artillery. At dusk it had gained a strong toehold in the south end of Eschweiler.

Because enemy mortar and artillery fire was accurately placed on the advance of the infantry during the day, the 415th Infantry prepared for a continuance of its attack at night. At 0300 on 22 November, Company C, led by Lieutenant Jerry Hooker, moved into the inky, black streets and headed for the railroad that divided Eschweiler. At the same time Company A, commanded by Lieutenant Ernest Fox, moved up on the right, with its objective the key road junction. Three Germans were caught asleep and at 0500 the companies were abreast along the railroad. The surprise was further evidenced by the fact that enemy mortar and artillery fire continued raining on the positions formerly occupied by the companies before their jump-off. The underpass in C Company's zone of advance had been demolished and caved in. At dawn the men swarmed over the embankment and in conjunction with Company A they continued their unceasing attack against Eschweiler. Company B was following closely behind, mopping up scattered pockets of resistance. At 1100 the 1st Battalion had reached the north outskirts of Eschweiler, to be joined by the 2d Battalion at 1130. Only scattered resistance had been encountered by both battalions. The great industrial city of Eschweiler, the largest city between Aachen and the Roer River, had fallen.

Company C of the 329th Engineer Battalion was busily engaged in clearing the roads of mines and rubble. A sturdy "cat" immediately began to clear the demolished overpass along the main route of supply. The operator had taken three scoops off the mound of debris when he observed two empty T-mine crates. Detectors and probing parties went to work and suspicious registrations appeared. A few fifty-pound charges of dynamite sunk in the pile were detonated. The explosions revealed that the debris had been heavily mined. When the "cat" resumed work and reached the street surface, layer after layer of plastic mines were discovered. Other Division engineers bridged the Inde River in Eschweiler. It was a typical engineer-infantry day.

Don Whitehead of the Associated Press released the following story on the 104th Division:

FIRST INTO CITY
ESCHWEILER IS ENTERED BY THE U. S. 104TH INFANTRY DIVISION
OUTSTANDING IS THE DESCRIPTION OF THE TIMBERWOLVES IN EARLY ACTION

With U. S. First Army in Germany (AP): The U. S. 104th Infantry Division, commanded by Major General Terry Allen, who led the 1st Division through North Africa and Sicily, was the first American outfit to enter Eschweiler.

Even in the short time they have been in action with the First Army, the Timberwolves proved themselves to be an outstanding Division as they drove to Eschweiler. Allen often was at the front personally directing the operations and giving instructions to battalion and regimental commanders—and company commanders. The Timberwolf Division is composed of personnel drawn from all sections of the United States.

The 415th Infantry continued to occupy Eschweiler in division reserve until it was again committed on 29 November, while the 413th and 414th Infantry Regiments on its left and right continued their advance.

DURWIZ . . . While the 415th Infantry was assaulting Eschweiler, Durwiz was pounded flat by fighter-bombers under Division control. Where many of the houses of Durwiz had stood there were now only bomb craters. In spite of the paralyzing bombardment it was soon learned that the Germans in the town would fight viciously behind every room and wall. After a quick reorganization by the 1st Battalion, 413th Infantry, on its newly seized objective, Helrath, it lunged forward in the morning of 21 November toward Durwiz, 1,200 yards to the east. Four hundred yards west of Durwiz the terrific volume of

"WESTERN FRONT"
(*Time*, November 27, 1944)

As in Normandy . . .

Generalfeldmarschall Gerd von Rundstedt well knew which was the most vulnerable sector: the Aachen area where Lieut. General Courtney Hicks Hodges' U. S. First Army had already sunk a spearhead aimed at the Cologne plain. The Germans had watched for nearly two months as the Americans moved in 1,000 guns, massed a whole new army—the U. S. Ninth.

Lieut. General Omar Nelson Bradley well knew that the Germans had bolstered their fortifications and had had time to mass their own guns. As in Normandy, it would take a coordinated attack by all forces to make a break. Bradley knew that great results are produced only by great battles. This was to be the greatest battle the Americans had fought in Europe. They had superiority: two men to the Germans' one, four guns to one, five tanks to one, several hundred planes to one.

As in Normandy, the aim was to smash the German Army, to finish off the war in the west by quick exploitation of a break. For the Germans it was a case of stand and die—to make so many American and British soldiers die that another such battle could not be fought this winter.

As in Normandy, General Bradley tightened the pressure—on two relatively small areas, probing for a weak spot. On a 15-mile sector—from behind Geilenkirchen to the Aachen-Duren hills—the German sky throbbed to the thunder of more than 4,000 aircraft, the German earth shook under the bolts of 10,000 tons of bombs, the blows of 20 tons of shells a minute. How any German could stand up to battle after the opening blow was beyond the belief of those who watched.

But Germans did stand up to fight and die, to cling tenaciously to the German soil, to patch the breaches with more men against a grinding weight that expanded and extended northward to the British Venlo sector as the battle went through three smoke-clouded days and fiery nights.

By this week cracks had begun to show in the hard German crust. By the fifth day the Americans could count their advances in miles instead of hundreds of yards.

On the ten-mile sector east of Aachen, battle-wise First Army troops lunged upon Eschweiler, nearly midway between Aachen and Duren and astride the six-lane Adolf Hitler Highway to Cologne, only 28 miles away.

Eschweiler Crumbled

mortar, machine gun and artillery fire held up the battalion's advance. All guns of the II Corps artillery were concentrated against the stubborn defenders, and with coordinated attack of infantry, tanks and artillery, the battalion forced its way into the city at 1335. By 1800 it had gained the center of Durwiz and by 1600 the following day the battalion had completed its mission and mopped up all enemy resistance. Outside Durwiz was the four-lane autobahn which led to Cologne and one end of a ten-mile tank trap thirty feet deep which had to be bridged and fought for like a river.

PUTZLOHN . . . On 21 November, the 3d Battalion of the 413th Infantry had closed in Helrath. The orders were that when Durwiz had been taken the 413th Infantry would continue its eastern drive by taking the town of Putzlohn and the high ground south of it. Because of the large coal pit just west of Durwiz which had necessitated the flanking action by the 1st Battalion, it was necessary to maneuver the 3d Battalion through the lines of the 30th Division on our immediate left. In column of companies, with Company L forward, the battalion moved out late in the afternoon and closed in its assembly position 1,000 yards northeast of Durwiz at 1955. At 0800 the next day the battalion attacked. It moved against heavy resistance, being forced by savage artillery and tank fire to halt the attack along the outskirts of the town.

The next morning, 23 November, K Company attacked in the pre-

Award of Distinguished Service Cross. By direction of the President, under the provisions of AR 600-45, 22 September 1943, as amended, and under authority contained in Circular No. 32, Headquarters European Theater of Operations, United States Army, 20 March 1944, as amended, the Distinguished Service Cross is awarded to:

Private HOWARD E. BROHMAN, JR., 35892705, Infantry, 415th Infantry Regiment, 104th Infantry Division, United States Army, for extraordinary heroism in connection with military operations against the enemy. On 19 November 1944, Private BROHMAN volunteered to clear an enemy mine field in Germany after two of his comrades had been killed by exploding mines in attempting to reach an enemy pillbox. Heedless of the known dangers of his mission and disregarding his own personal safety, Private BROHMAN crawled forward in the face of enemy mortar, machine gun, and sniper fire to clear a path for an assault team. By his courageous act, Private BROHMAN personally located and deactivated twenty-five enemy mines and cut his way through dense wire entanglements. When he had successfully completed this tedious and dangerous task, the path was then cleared for an assault team to reduce an enemy pillbox, thereby permitting the advance of the attacking troops. The extraordinary heroism and courageous action of Private BROHMAN reflect great credit upon himself and are in keeping with the highest traditions of the military service. Entered military service from Indiana.

Cautious advance through Eschweiler's sniper-filled streets.

dawn darkness and forced its way into the southwest corner of Putzlohn. Simultaneously L Company also advanced on Hill 272. Vicious infantry counterattacks were received from the northeast by K Company, but each was repulsed. Company L stopped numerous ferocious attacks of infantry and tanks coming from the vicinity of Weisweiler— one of the counterattacks penetrated a platoon area but was driven back in some of the most severe fighting in the area. Although disorganized by the strong resistance and murderous counterattacks, the 3d Battalion continued its valiant struggle for the town. Shortly after noon Company C moved out from Durwiz and made contact with Company L at 1330. At 1500 it advanced on and seized Hill 272. The balance of the 1st Battalion under cover of darkness moved up to take over from the 3d Battalion in Putzlohn. Shortly before noon on the 24th the 1st Battalion had thoroughly mopped up Putzlohn, held Hill 272, and had strong outposts 500 yards to the east.

The Division now held the ground which overlooked the fast-flowing Inde River two miles to the east. During the Putzlohn operation the enemy had committed numerous concentrated tank attacks closely followed by infantry. Again the stout-hearted infantryman, with the close support of his own tanks, tank destroyers, and artillery, had held his ground and had inflicted great casualties on enemy tanks and personnel. For the next three days the 413th Infantry remained in the vicinity of Putzlohn and Durwiz, making preparations for its assault against Lamersdorf and Inden, on the west banks of the Inde River.

139

VOLKENRATH, NORTHBERG and WEISWEILER . . . While the 415th
Infantry was attacking Eschweiler from the west and the 413th Infantry was driving towards Rohe-Durwiz and Putzlohn, north of Eschweiler, the 414th Infantry was attacking to the northeast with the mission of securing Weisweiler. This great industrial center was protected
by the towns of Volkenrath and Northberg, a canal and a large factory
area between Northberg and Weisweiler. From its position on the
high ground northwest of Hastenrath the 2d Battalion, with the 1st
Battalion on its left, commenced the attack at 1100 on 20 November.
The attack was held up for three hours by murderous artillery and
mortar fire from Volkenrath. At 1500 two Corps artillery TOT concentrations were placed to the immediate front of our troops, assisting
the regiment in continuing its advance. At dusk the 2d Battalion made
its final rush across 1,000 yards of open ground into the town of Volkenrath. The attack was spearheaded by a platoon of tanks of the 750th
Tank Battalion followed by Companies E and G. By midnight the
2d Battalion had completed mopping up the town, taking over one
hundred prisoners and forcing the remainder of the enemy garrison to
withdraw.

At midnight, following the fall of Volkenrath, the 1st Battalion
passed through the 2d Battalion and continued toward Northberg.
Intense artillery fire held the battalion at the southern portion of its
objective. Throughout 21 November, the battalion was heavily engaged. Its progress was severely hampered by fire coming from Hill
187, outside of the Division zone to the east. At dusk, another 300
yards had been gained, and Colonel Touart's men halted and consolidated their hard-won gains.

Early on 22 November, the 1st Battalion again attacked, fighting its
way from house to house, and by 1700 it securely held not only the
town of Northberg, but the high slagpile which overlooked Weisweiler.
The 2d Battalion on this same day jumped off for the high ground east
of Eschweiler, and by 1800, after an advance of 2,500 yards, firmly
held this ground. The 3d Battalion of the 414th Infantry was moved
from its assembly area at 1430, passing through the forward elements
of the 2d Battalion at 1800. It continued its advance towards objective
Weisweiler. During the night it reached a position 1,500 yards west
of its assigned objective, where it was held up by heavy fire from a
large slagheap to its left flank and from Weisweiler itself.

With the 1st Battalion in the east edge of Eschweiler, the 2d Battalion in Northberg and the 3d Battalion 1,500 yards short of Weisweiler, the 414th Infantry had gained all of its objectives with the
exception of Weisweiler. It had now developed that the slagpile to

the east of Eschweiler must be taken before the 3d Battalion could make a further advance. Therefore plans were immediately made on 23 November for the seizure of the slagheap which dominated all of the surrounding. terrain, particularly Weisweiler. The slagpile was eighty feet high, 1,000 yards square, with wooded edges. Prior reconnaissance and study of aerial photos enabled the unit to secure the exact location of enemy weapons and defensive positions. At dusk, preceded by an intensive half-hour artillery barrage, two companies attacked—C on the left and E on the right. With infantry rapidly following the supporting fires at seventy-five yards, they were on top of the enemy before they could come out of their holes. Within forty-five minutes the objective was seized, with only three casualties, after liquidating many of the enemy and capturing ninety-three prisoners. It was not possible for the 3d Battalion to continue its advance on Weisweiler without flanking enemy fire from this strongpoint.

At 1830, the 3d Battalion began its attack again, and by 2200 held the southwest outskirts of the town. Throughout 24 November Colonel Rouge's men were heavily engaged in hand-to-hand combat, fighting for each house, building, and wall, and at times for each room, with machine guns, bazookas and grenades. Enemy artillery and mortar fire fell like hail on the positions and inflicted heavy casualties on the battalion. During the attack the communications platoon worked day and night in a vain effort to maintain wire communication. At one time nine separate lines had been laid across the fire-swept ground, but even then, radios were the only effective means of communication. Lieutenant Perry's platoon of Company K sneaked behind the enemy's lines and remained there for forty-eight hours, sniping and demoralizing the enemy, killing fifty-five Nazis and contributing greatly to the success of the attacks on Weisweiler.

The 3d Battalion was concentrating its power on the southwest portion of Weisweiler. On the northwest edge of Weisweiler stood a large power plant and other huge factories. On the night of 24-25 November the 1st Battalion advanced due east of the slagpile against these large factories. Company B, under command of Captain Charles Glotzbach, in its daring night attack, wrote an unforgettable piece of Timberwolf history:

"THEY FIGHT BY NIGHT"
AL NEWMAN, *Newsweek* War Correspondent
(December 11, 1944)
(From the front before Cologne, Al Newman, *Newsweek* war correspondent, sends this story of a fresh division and a fight by night.)

Maj. Gen. Terry de la Mesa Allen, once the famous commander of the

Award of Distinguished Service Cross. By direction of the President, under the provisions of AR 600-45, 22 September 1943, as amended, and under authority contained in Circular No. 32, Headquarters European Theater of Operations, United States Army, 20 March 1944, as amended, the Distinguished Service Cross is awarded to:

Technician Fourth Grade JESS T. RENTERIA, 37354648, Medical Detachment, 414th Infantry, United States Army, for extraordinary heroism in action against the enemy on 18 and 23 November 1944, in Germany. Technician Fourth Grade RENTERIA voluntarily left a position of comparative safety, crossed fifty yards of fire-swept terrain, and in the face of intense small arms fire, carried an injured soldier out of danger. Several days later Technician Fourth Grade RENTERIA again braved fierce enemy mortar and machine gun fire as he made five trips over open terrain and evacuated seven severely wounded soldiers. Technician Fourth Grade RENTERIA's actions resulted in the saving of many lives and reflect great credit upon himself and the military service. Entered military service from Colorado.

*   *   *   *   *

Award of Distinguished Service Cross. By direction of the President, under the provisions of AR 600-45, 22 September 1943, as amended, and under authority contained in Circular No. 32, Headquarters European Theater of Operations, United States Army, 20 March 1944, as amended, the Distinguished Service Cross is awarded to:

Captain ROGER S. REES, 0349468, 413th Infantry, United States Army, for extraordinary heroism in action against the enemy on 19 and 20 November 1944, in Germany. When a rifle company became disorganized by enemy artillery fire and suffered heavy casualties, Captain REES moved through vicious fire to the company, reorganized and rallied the men, and led a successful attack against a strongly defended village. The following day, Captain REES assumed command of a platoon of tanks, and moving on foot through devastating fire, directed a coordinated tank-infantry attack against a second heavily fortified town. By his personal courage, inspirational leadership, and sound tactical decisions, Captain REES enabled his battalion to successfully capture its objective with a minimum of casualties. Entered military service from California.

1st Division of North African fame, recently popped up in the thickest of the fighting on the western front with his new division—the 104th, which wears a shoulder patch depicting a gray timber wolf howling at a nonexistent moon in a green sky. They were in fast company, for to their south sat some of the greatest divisions of the United States Army—the 1st, 3d Armored, 9th, and 4th.

Until they saw action in October with the Canadians north of Antwerp, the 104th had never even undergone an air raid. The first division to land directly at Cherbourg, they missed Britain completely.

But by this third week of the big push, it became apparent that Terry Allen had trained a very good division indeed. Jumping off on Nov. 16 into the long-disputed town of Stolberg, they had fought their way by the bloody yard over the ridge into Eschweiler, turned east to Weisweiler, then northeast to Inden.

Nightmares at Arms: Allen taught his Timberwolves some new tricks along with the old, for as the Germans on their sector have discovered, the 104th is a body of night-fighting specialists. Strangely enough, this is a little-developed technique in modern warfare, for most commanders fear mixups which result in friend slaughtering friend in a deadly game of blind man's buff. Means of identification are highly important, but, most vital of all, each man must keep his head and act decisively and quickly under the nightmare conditions.

Concrete proof that Allen's smart insomniacs could do just that was furnished in the taking of Weisweiler, a German stronghold just east of Eschweiler.

Under cover of the early winter darkness, at 1900 in the evening, Capt Charles Glotzbach of Paxico, Kan., sneaked his company (Company B, 414th Infantry) up to the western outskirts of Weisweiler and into the inky blackness of the huge power plant, whence they could emerge for attack from within the town at dawn.

Once inside the building, the captain's first concern was to find a suitable command post. He found his room all right, but it held six Germans who fortunately were cowed into surrender. Moreover, it quickly became apparent that the building was alive with Krauts—two companies, it later turned out. Still more embarrassing was the fact that they had been aroused by the minor row. Glotzbach could hear them assembling at points in the building and in the courtyard.

Death in the Moonlight: The obvious thing to do was to retreat quickly, taking along prisoners and hoping for as few casualties as possible. But successful officers are not always those who do the obvious thing. Instead, the captain turned to his forward artillery observer, Lt. Warren Conrad, of Ashland, Ore., "Order a concentration on this building," he snapped. "Hurry!"

"Fire on control point so and so," said Conrad into his telephone, for guns already had been registered on the power plant. There was a pause, then a startled reply. "That's your present position," said a voice from the 105mm battery in the back of pounded Eschweiler. "Right. But fire anyway and hurry," said Conrad.

As the black minutes ticked away, Glotzbach got his company down into the cellar. Finally, "On the way" came over Conrad's phone. Seconds passed, then hell broke loose overhead. There were screams and startled shouts in German and the sound of running feet as troops sought shelter.

Then came the nerve-cracking wait, but finally a German commander, obviously believing the concentration an accident and never dreaming his American opponent would call for fire on his own position, once more began to assemble his men—in the courtyard. It was a bad mistake, because Glotzbach glimpsed them there as the full moon flashed briefly through the clouds.

This time he called for timed fire—for the shrapnel air bursts so fatal to troops caught in the open. The terrible, cracking bursts proved too much for the enemy. For once and for all they got away from that accursed building, and Glotzbach's company had a fairly quiet night.

The cold sun of the following morning looked down palely on eighty German corpses in the courtyard.

On 25 November, with the 1st Battalion now on the left and the 3d Battalion on the right, the 414th Infantry continued hammering at Weisweiler, gradually forcing the enemy to withdraw from the city fortress. At 0825 Companies L and K were reported by the battalion as surrounded. The skillful fighting of the companies, reinforced with tanks and a platoon of the reconnaissance troop, by 1215 had repulsed the enemy's attempt at encirclement. The action was culminated for the 3d Battalion when the 2d passed through it at 1520 to continue the advance abreast of the 1st Battalion. More than half of the city had been seized after a bitter and exhausting battle had routed the enemy from each house and strongpoint. At 0730 on 26 November, the 414th Infantry jumped off again, and by 0930 had taken the prized possession, Weisweiler, now a mass of debris and ruins.

FRENZ . . . On 25 November, the 3d Battalion, 415th Infantry, had been alerted by Division Headquarters to be prepared to pass through the 414th Infantry after it seized Weisweiler. Its mission was the seizure of Frenz, another German fortress lying on the west banks of the Inde River, 3,000 yards east of Weisweiler. At 1000 on 26 November Colonel Touart of the 414th Infantry requested permission to continue the attack to the east. The request was granted and Companies C and E of the 414th continued east towards Frenz. At 1125 both companies had gained another 500 yards when they were pinned down by heavy mortar and small arms fire. Following a heavy artillery barrage, the infantry at 1500 pushed forward and by 1900 were in Frenz. That night and early the 27th were spent by the companies in mopping up their newly gained objective.

LAMERSDORF . . . On 26 November, when the 414th Infantry was attacking Frenz, the 2d Battalion, 413th Infantry, moved from Durwiz, closing into Weisweiler at 1230. Throughout the day it maintained liaison with lead elements of the 414th, preparatory to its attack on Lamersdorf. The 413th Infantry, after seizing Putzlohn with its commanding ground in that vicinity on 22 November, had been directed to be prepared for the attack on Lamersdorf and Inden on Division order. Now that the key city of Eschweiler had been taken, the Seagulls were getting into position.

Prior to daylight on the 27th the 2d Battalion moved through Weisweiler towards Frenz. Enroute it was subjected to intense mortar and artillery fire, and after long rushes it reached Frenz, where it passed through elements of the 414th. At 1000 the battalion launched its first coordinated attack against Lamersdorf, 1,200 yards to the north of Frenz. Prior to the jumpoff, Lieutenant Colonel Tom Neilson, commander of the 2d Battalion, was killed by hostile artillery. Captain Reese immediately assumed command, with Captain Sanford Bush taking over later in the day. The battalion had hardly emerged from the outskirts of Frenz before the German guns let loose. Machine guns swept the flat open fields, and incoming artillery reached a concentration of sixty rounds per minute. The battalion was held with a gain of 300 yards and all day long it was subjected to terrifying artillery barrages. The Division and Corps artillery heavily countered the forty-one enemy gun positions which had been located by infantry and artillery observers.

Fierce fighting ensued during the next thirty-six hours with the battalion finally securing a toehold in Lamersdorf by nightfall on 28 November. The advance was subjected immediately to a series of vicious counterattacks by tanks and infantry. The intense fire from the high ground around Lucherberg was greatly restricting the movement of the battalion. At 1500 on the 29th half of Lamersdorf had been secured. In the tank attack of the 750th Tank Battalion which was then advancing against Inden, five tanks peeled off and joined the 2d Battalion in Lamersdorf. A coordinated infantry-tank attack was launched at 1730. Again the men crouched in doorways and searched out each room and cellar for Jerries. Little by little the battalion inched its way toward the northern outskirts of Lamersdorf, and by 2130 it had fully penetrated the city. During the night, bypassed snipers were mopped up and the Timberwolves had taken another German fortress.

INDEN . . . While the 2d Battalion, 413th Infantry attacked Lamersdorf the Seagull 1st and 3d Battalions struck for Inden. At 0430 on 28 November, under cover of darkness the 1st Battalion moved out of positions near Lohn and Putzlohn over the muddy fields toward Inden. Prior to their departure, K Company had secured a line of departure for them, 1,000 yards out of the town proper. Company C, under Captain Ralph Gleason, swept to the northern portion of the town unobserved prior to daylight. Before B Company could reach the town it was discovered and was subjected to heavy machine gun and mortar

DAILY NEWS
NEW YORK'S PICTURE NEWSPAPER

104TH, GREEN BUT TOUGH, GETS A GULP OF BATTLE

By GRAHAM MILLER
(Staff Correspondent of *The New York Daily News*)

Weisweiler, Germany, Nov. 26.—Under a mottled blue sky and with the comforting drumming of their own aircraft overhead, troops of the U. S. First Army fought their way forward again today as their offensive entered its second week.

There was even sunshine at times and all over this front GIs lifted grimy faces skyward and blinked bloodshot eyes almost unbelievingly at the sight of sun, blue sky and air support.

We took the town of Weisweiler today, occupied it thoroughly, cleaned out cellars with bomb and bayonet and moved through in the direction of Frenz, the next shabby German town along the road.

There isn't much to the town of Weisweiler. It looks pretty much like any other beaten German town. The same smashed houses, splintered furniture and dead horses along the roadside. But there is this about Weisweiler—it was taken by a "green" division, Major Gen. (Terrible Terry) Allen's 104th, which was a little unsure of itself until now.

A week ago, when I first met these boys they were frankly suffering from stage fright. They found themselves in the line alongside Major Gen. Clarence Huebner's famous 1st Division—the finest division this correspondent has seen in this war—and they wondered how they'd make out. They had had a short tour up in Holland with the British and Canadians on either side of them to get used to the sound of gunfire, but this was their first solo show. They needn't have worried. They did all right and other leathery-faced troops in tough divisions are talking respectfully of the 104th.

A DULL, DRAB DUMP

You come into Weisweiler along a bumpy, shell-pocked road from Eschweiler. You leave your jeep under the lee of what you hope is a strong wall, turn right and find yourself in the town's main street, which runs slightly downhill. It's a dull, drab dump and God knows why anybody ever lived there in peacetime but the present occupants are Americans, quite a lot of them from New York.

German Paratrooper, captured near Eschweiler, sullen in defeat.

fire over the flat naked ground. During the advance of Company A, enemy small arms fire forced it to change direction, and at daylight it was in the town of Altdorf, one mile north of Inden, where it joined elements of the 30th Division's 120th Regiment which was then attacking that town. It was not until nightfall that A Company was able to reach Inden to join elements of Company C.

Previous aerial bombardment and heavy artillery concentrations had reduced Inden to rubble. However, the enemy had elected to hold the fortress and deny us the crossings over the Inde River. It was soon discovered that the Germans were to fight to the last man in a desperate effort to hold this key road center. Throughout the day C Company alone fought off the fanatic Nazis, by this time strongly reinforced with tanks.

The horror and despair that can come to an infantry soldier upon the knowledge that he is cut off from his other units is well described in the words of Pfc. Broadbent, Company C, 413th Infantry, a new reinforcement at the time:

We approached Inden in the early morning hours across what seemed like endless miles of muddy beet fields. As we drew nearer the city the artillery started plastering every square inch of the town—under this terrific barrage we got right up to the outskirts of town before being detected. When the artillery lifted we were well situated in close to Inden. At this time we met our first

147

Award of Distinguished Service Cross. By direction of the President, under the provisions of AR 600-45, 22 September 1943, as amended, and under authority contained under Circular 32, Headquarters European Theater of Operations, United States Army, 20 March 1944, as amended, the Distinguished Service Cross is awarded to:

Sergeant DAVID L. COLOMBE (then Private), 37486968, 414th Infantry, United States Army, for extraordinary heroism in action against the enemy on 26 November 1944, in Germany. Armed only with a trench knife after his rifle had been shattered by shell fragments, Sergeant COLOMBE leaped into an enemy foxhole and singlehandedly captured two Germans. Securing a hostile automatic rifle from the emplacement, he voluntarily worked his way behind enemy lines. As pressure was exerted upon the enemy stronghold by his company, Sergeant COLOMBE killed seven Germans and wounded many more as they attempted to withdraw. His deadly fire demoralized the enemy force, resulting in the collapse of their defenses. Sergeant COLOMBE's valorous actions, performed at great personal risk, reflected the highest traditions of the armed forces. Entered military service from S. D.

resistance—we ran into several German outposts but quickly took care of them. We then commenced digging in, being interrupted several times as first one German tank and then another started up right ahead of us, cruised around and then took off into the town. They gave us quite a few anxious minutes before they departed, but we were prepared to greet them with our only antitank weapons—two bazookas and several Molotov cocktails. I was BAR man at the time and those tanks rumbling around right up ahead of me really gave me my first real good scare and sent chills up and down my spine—this was my first real action since joining the Division in Aachen and—well, I was plenty bewildered by all the noise and confusion.

Just before daylight we took off into Inden. My platoon (3d Platoon, C Company) led the attack. I was the sixth man into town and I was all prepared to use my BAR for the first time. However we passed through the first phase line with little opposition—only occasional sniper fire from quite a ways off to our right. We advanced up one of the main streets and at the first intersection we finally met some opposition. We took over several large buildings and formed all-around security. I was given the rear courtyard to guard with the assistant BAR man.

It was at this point that we discovered we had been cut off from the rest of C Company. After we passed the first phase line (a main street) a Tiger tank pulled up at the street end and started firing pointblank down the street, thus preventing the other platoons from continuing on with us. Well, anyway, there we were almost in the center of Inden and practically surrounded. Before dark we set up a defense centered around our two buildings—one on either side of the street and right at the intersection. We had a good position and had good observation in all directions and several routes of withdrawal. My BAR was set up on the second story and I had a clear field of fire for several hundred yards up two different streets. As darkness came we got ready—for what, we didn't know. The platoon leader and platoon sergeant told us to hold our fire unless we had to fight our way out. It was the only sensible thing to do because we were surrounded and greatly outnumbered.

The next two days and three nights was a nightmare. At nights the German tanks would rumble up and down the streets, surrounded by German infantrymen. Several times the tanks passed right under my window and I was plenty worried. The first night the Germans counterattacked the balance of C Company and the other companies held up along the first phase line. Their tanks and infantry went right past our positions but there was nothing we could do about it. Why they missed us, I'll never know. Each night we sent out patrols trying to contact the balance of the battalion and finally we made a connection. In the early morning of the fourth day we were rescued by several other companies.

During that night I Company moved up to relieve Company B, which had been severely trampled on the open ground short of Inden. Shortly after midnight, C Company was subjected to strong counterattacks supported by German air, artillery and tanks. Throughout that night, C Company was constantly pounded by artillery and suicide rushes of fanatic German infantry. The company was separated by the attacks, and a part of it under Captain Gleason was forced into surrender shortly before daylight. German tanks had rolled up and pushed their

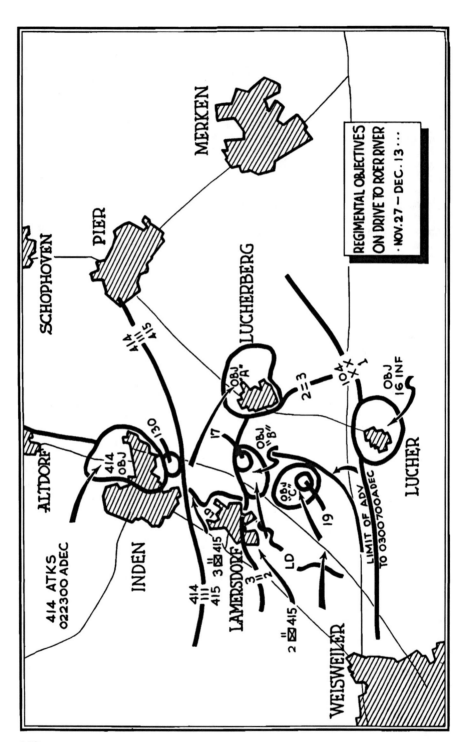

REGIMENTAL OBJECTIVES
ON DRIVE TO ROER RIVER
· NOV. 27 – DEC. 13 · · ·

MERKEN

SCHOPHOVEN

PIER

LUCHERBERG

ALTDORF

414
OBJ

OBJ "A"

414 ATKS
022300 ADEC

INDEN

114
415
111

130

415
414
111

OBJ
"B"

OBJ 16 INF

LUCHER

2=3

17

LAMERSDORF

415 3
111

19

OBJ
"C"

2=3

LD

LIMIT OF ADV
TO 030 0700 ADEC

2 415

WEISWEILER

150

long 88's directly into the buildings occupied by this group of men and fired pointblank for several minutes before our troops gave up the position as untenable. Captain Gleason and the men who were captured that night were later liberated by the Russians. Company A also had been fiercely attacked but the gallant stand by this unit repulsed every thrust of the enemy.

The 1st Battalion wire crew was kept extremely busy trying to keep in the lines. Despite the driving rain these men were constantly working on communications trying to keep the lines in repair. Private First Class Daniel McDougall said: "No line has ever given the wire crew more trouble than that laid from the town of Inden to the battalion CP in rear thereof. The line was subjected to constant artillery fire for a forty-eight hour period and was never in for more than twenty minutes at a stretch. To keep lines from going out, linemen ran them overhead, tried to run them through fields rather than along roads, but shrapnel doesn't know the difference between overhead lines and one on the ground; no field is sacred to a GI truck or tank."

This same story could be told by all wire teams within the Division. These brave men played an important role in each action of the Division. Without superb communications the attack or the defense could not succeed.

The battle continued throughout the 29th. Tanks of the 750th Tank Battalion had tried to enter the town to support the heavily engaged companies but were driven off each time by the murderous direct fire guns which were entrenched in fortified positions in the southwest part of Inden. The barren ground between Putzlohn and Inden was covered by accurate artillery fires directed from the observation held by the enemy in the vicinity of Lucherberg. Reinforcements could not be made in the daytime, but the 3d Battalion, on the night of the 29th, was able to advance into the town to assist the 1st Battalion in its fight against Inden. Supplies were brought into the town at night, with first priority given to ammunition. At 1500 on 20 November a coordinated attack was planned for the employment of both battalions, with support of two companies of the 750th Tank Battalion. The tanks were to sweep into Inden from the southwest and northwest, with an additional light tank company carrying men from Company B in from the west. Promptly at the time fixed, the attack was launched. Some of the tanks were destroyed enroute by direct-fire weapons, some bogged down in the mud; however, the remaining two tanks did enter Inden to join the infantry, who had simultaneously pressed their attack. That night all friendly units completed their reorganization after gaining two additional blocks of the gutted buildings.

Award of Distinguished Service Cross. By direction of the President, under the provisions of AR 600-45, 22 September 1943, as amended, and under authority contained in Circular No. 32, Headquarters European Theater of Operations, United States Army, 20 March 1944, as amended, the Distinguished Service Cross is awarded to:

First Lieutenant JERRY M. PAGE (then Second Lieutenant) (Army Serial No. 0539364), Infantry, United States Army, for extraordinary heroism in connection with military operations against an armed enemy, as a platoon leader and Company Commander, Company C, 413th Infantry Regiment, 104th Infantry Division, on 28 November 1944. When heavy enemy fire from a nearby house threatened his platoon's position on the west side of the Inde River, Lieutenant PAGE, with two other soldiers, charged the enemy stronghold and captured ten of the enemy. Although forced back across the river, he effected a brilliant recrossing and, when enemy fire was encountered from the same house, he and two companions once more assaulted the position, forcing the surrender of twenty-eight of the enemy. Lieutenant PAGE's courageous and inspiring actions were, in a large measure, responsible for the successful fulfilment of his platoon's mission and exemplify the finest traditions of the military service. Entered military service from Michigan.

"Hit the dirt — incoming mail ! !"

On 1 December the 413th Infantry task force, composed of the 3d and 1st Battalions and Company G, two platoons of tanks of the 750th Tank Battalion and two platoons of Company A, 692d Tank Destroyer Battalion, under the command of Lieutenant Colonel William Summers, was subjected to the heaviest concentration of enemy artillery yet encountered by the Division. The rate of this devastating fire, consisting of shells ranging from 105mm to 210mm, at times reached sixty rounds per minute. Enemy tanks dug in on the east bank of the Inde River were a constant harassment; nevertheless the bitter house-to-house fighting continued, with the task force holding the north half of Inden prior to darkness. Thirty-five new hostile gun positions were located during the period by our observers. Our own artillery was heavily engaged not only in laying supporting barrages for the infantry but also in counterbattery duels with the enemy.

Orders were received by regimental headquarters that Inden had to be taken prior to 1700 on 2 December. The Division had formulated plans to cross the Inde River under cover of darkness the 2d of December, with the 414th passing through the 413th to seize that part of Inden located on the east banks of the Inde River and with the 415th on the right seizing the factory area opposite Lamersdorf and Lucherberg, sitting on the commanding heights overlooking the Inde River. The assault on Lucherberg required the part of Inden west of the Inde River be completely cleared in order that the crossing could be made without flanking fire and in order that bridge sites could be secured.

On the early morning of 2 December, the 413th Infantry launched its final attack. Again it was met by heavy fire, but our infantry, closely

153

Progress was slow and torturous as we neared Inden

supported by tanks and tank destroyers, pushed strongly forward, and at 1700 Inden was taken. A reinforced platoon of Company L, 415th Infantry, had advanced from its position at Lamersdorf against the factory just south of Inden and quickly drove the enemy back to make contact with the 413th shortly after 1700. With this contact established, the west banks of the Inde River were securely in our hands. The night attack as planned for the 414th Infantry and 415th Infantry would be in effect. The 413th Infantry was to be placed in Division reserve. However, late in the afternoon on 2 December it was determined from interrogation of German prisoners that a large-scale German offensive was imminent in the vicinity of Inden. A Panzer division, located east of the Roer River, had made plans to slice through our defenses within the next twenty-four hours in an attempt to drive to Aachen. After this critical information was obtained the Division directed the 413th Infantry to take up defensive positions at the vicinity of Putzlohn and Durwiz after the 414th had passed through its lines.

On 3 December, after our own offensive action had proven successful, eliminating the threat of the German attack, the 413th Infantry went into Division reserve at Helrath, Lohn and Durwiz.

By motor on 2 December the 3d Battalion, 414th Infantry, moved to the small town of Lohn, its assembly area. Throughout the day active reconnaissance went on of the approaches to the river and of crossing sites over the Inde River at Inden. At dusk the companies were moved into Inden, relieving elements of the 413th Infantry, and at 2300, in conjunction with the attack of the 415th, the battalion began crossing the river, K Company leading off, followed by L and later by I. All supporting weapons of the 414th and those of the 413th located in Inden massed their fires against the enemy's positions east of the river. By 0015 Companies K and L were across and were fighting house-to-house, slowly pushing back the enemy. Many hand-to-hand battles were fought in the houses, cellars, and on the streets.

154

Prior to daylight the battalion had established a 500-yard bridgehead. At 0300 the 329th Engineer Battalion commenced to build the important Bailey bridge which was so essential for a successful bridgehead. Under continuous mortar and artillery fire the gallant engineers finally completed the job at 0300 on 4 December. Immediately tanks, tank destroyers, and other supporting arms and supplies were rushed forward to assist the infantry in holding its hard-gained bridgehead. Throughout 3-4 December the 3d Battalion deepened and strengthened its bridgehead against the stubborn enemy. Counterattack after counterattack was repulsed with great casualties to the German forces. With the exception of a large factory and a dairy on the eastern edge of Inden, the town had been cleared of all enemy resistance by 5 December.

LUCHERBERG . . . Lucherberg, a town of seventy-five buildings, was situated on a high hill, 2,000 yards east of the Inde River. From the hill on which the village stands, the Germans had observation and therefore could dominate the countryside to the west, including the towns of Inden, Lamersdorf and Frenz, and to the east, including Merken, Pier and Schophoven and the west banks of the Roer River. The VII Corps' drive to the Roer could not be accomplished without taking this key position. To insure the advance to the Roer, Lucherberg must fall.

The all-around German defenses consisted of an elaborate and well-planned system of trenches. To advance on Lucherberg it was necessary to cross the fast-flowing Inde River. There were three routes of approach that could be used in the attack. From the south, the attacking force could come east along the Autobahn highway or across the open fields from Frenz, but the huge coal pit lying on the southwest part of the town formed an excellent natural barrier which would prevent envelopment from the south. In addition to this barrier, the fortress was further protected from the south by a large mound of dirt (apparently taken from the strip mine) which gave the defenders good observation and excellent fields of fire.

The approaches from the west had both natural and man-made obstacles; first, the Inde River, which was then overflowing and was too deep to permit crossing of vehicles or armor. A few hundred yards beyond the river stood a large factory area, to the west of which were open fields which provided excellent fields of fire to any enemy barricaded in the large factory. The coal factory itself was sturdy and the thick walls and heavy machinery could provide good cover. Even after the river had been crossed and the factory seized, the attacking force would run into another slagpile with its many dug-in guns and defen-

THE ALLIES GRIND AHEAD IN THE WEST
(From *Life*, December 18, 1944)

At the end of the third week the strain of the great gray battle of Germany's Western Front was beginning to tell on both sides. Hospital trains of ashen-faced wounded were pouring steadily into Paris and presumably into German cities. But the monstrous struggle for a decision in the west continued despite the casualties, despite the cold and rain and mud.

In most places along the 450-mile front the fighting was the same as it had been since the first day, but in some it had changed. In the south the headlong dash of the U. S. Seventh and French First Armies was over. The troops fought slowly to clear the Germans from the Vosges pocket. The U. S. Third, also a ground-gainer from the start of the Big Push, had swung a strong arm northeast of Metz to the Saar Basin and was now battering against dense German defenses. In the seething 25 miles facing Cologne and the Ruhr the U. S. First and Ninth Armies and the British Second still worked ahead yard by yard.

The battle on this front had become a corrosive test of strength, reminiscent of the dogged fighting in Flanders and the Meuse-Argonne during the last war. On the thickly populated plain which leads to the Rhine the Germans fought ferociously for every house and trench. The three Allied armies ground forward by the weight of men and arms in what the as-yet-unreleased casualty lists will probably prove the most costly fighting since Verdun in 1916. At the end of last week their deepest gain, which was made on the First Army front, was seven of the 35 miles to the Rhine.

The great sweeps of this war have moved over enormous expanses of land, but now and then the armies have stopped and fought where each yard meant a separate battle. Struggles like these made blackened battlefields of Stalingrad, Cassino and Normandy. Now for the first time the war is making such a battlefield in Germany.

The battlefield of Germany is at present a 30-mile strip of the Rhineland near Cologne where four Allied and German armies have been fighting to decide how long Germany can avoid defeat. It is a battlefield of gouged farmland and of scattered woods. But mostly it is a battlefield of devastated towns because the Germans have elected to fight, regardless of cost, for every house and factory west of the Rhine. There Allied and German troops have fought most of the savage individual battles of the Allied winter offensive.

In the battle for the Rhineland towns neither side has yet accomplished its original objective. The aim of the Allied drive was to break down the German military power before it could grow stronger by desperate last-minute mobilizations. The aim of the German defense was to hold off the Allies and to bleed Allied armies so they would not be able to begin another offensive before spring. At the end of three weeks of bone-crushing attack and defense, the German power still appeared intact and the Allies still seemed capable of prolonging the winter offensive.

156

sive positions. Along the road from the factory to Lucherberg the advance could be hampered by the stone houses on the southern edge of the road and by the woods, heavily mined, on the north.

The approaches from the north were along flat open ground and there were no natural obstacles. Realizing this weakness, the enemy had dug many trenches from which machine guns could deliver murderous grazing fire along the flat ground. The Germans knew the significance of holding Lucherberg and had fully prepared it for all-around defense.

Lucherberg was a village of only 400 inhabitants. The church spire dominated the entire town and surrounding area and later was to become the focal area of the fight. All of the buildings were of brick and stone and all had thick, reinforced cellars.

Detailed plans and preparations for the attack on Lucherberg had been going on for several days between 28 November and 2 December, while units of the 413th Infantry completed the seizure of Inden and Lamersdorf. During this time all leaders down to and including the platoons made aerial reconnaissance in artillery observation planes of the terrain in addition to making intensive map and aerial photo studies. All men were thoroughly briefed in the part they were to play in this important operation. Everything was in readiness.

On 29 November the 3d Battalion, 415th Infantry, moved from Weisweiler to Frenz, relieving elements of the 414th Infantry. The next day the 3d Battalion moved into Lamersdorf, relieving the 2d Battalion, 413th Infantry. The battalion mopped up isolated enemy strongpoints in the vicinity of both towns. In the afternoon of 1 December, a reinforced platoon of Company L advanced to the north of Lamersdorf, seizing the large factory in the south end of Inden in order to facilitate its crossing that night. At 1700 it made contact with elements of the 413th Infantry in Inden.

The Division plan of attack directed the 414th Infantry to force a crossing at Inden with one battalion, and the 415th with two battalions abreast to force crossings opposite Frenz and Lamersdorf commencing at 2300 on 2 December. The 415th was to attack with the 3d Battalion on the north and the 2d Battalion on the south.

In conjunction with the 3d Battalion, 414th Infantry, the 2d Battalion was to attack at 2300, two companies abreast, with the mission of securing the large factory at checkpoint 17 and the enemy strongpoint at checkpoint 19, objectives B and C, respectively. The 3d Battalion was to move at 2400 with companies in column directly on Lucherberg. The 104th Division artillery, augmented by fire from the VII Corps, 30th, and 1st Infantry Division artillery, was to support the

Sniper Vigil

attack in addition to all weapons of the infantry, attached tanks, tank destroyers, and the 555th AAA AW Battalion. By interrogation of prisoners late in the afternoon of 2 December it had been determined that there were 500 to 600 infantry with tanks garrisoned in and around Lucherberg. It also was determined that a German Panzer division east of the Roer River had made plans to attack our positions in a drive towards Aachen. The Timberwolves were determined to proceed with the attack despite these alarming reports and, as planned, the assault was launched.

At H minus sixty (2200) the artillery guns began their heavy preparatory fires against the enemy positions. The fire plans had been meticulously prepared by the 929th Field Artillery Battalion and the Division artillery. These plans called for not only heavy concentrations on known enemy defenses but also on road blocks along the approaches leading to Lucherberg from the east. All Division artillery battalions and attached and supporting battalions of adjoining divisions and the VII Corps participated in the stomp, each battalion being assigned definite and fixed targets. The last artillery round to be fired on Lucherberg was to be a white phosphorous round on call, indicating that the assault company was in position to move into the objective.

As the guns rained shells upon the enemy the 2d Battalion, 415th Infantry, was moving to its line of departure on the Inde River. Company G, commanded by Lieutenant James Milliner, and Company E, under Captain Ruch, jumped off for their assigned objectives as soon as the artillery fires lifted at 2300. Both companies, closely following behind the artillery barrages, crossed the icy, waist-deep Inde and drove hard against the enemy. No weapons were loaded, each man having been ordered not to fire, but to use instead hand grenades and bayonets. Company E rushed its objective C, including checkpoint 19, a large chateau, reaching it without encountering any enemy resistance, and by 2345 it was secured. The enemy was surprised and dazed and fell easy prey to our men. As the company CP was moving into the chateau two Germans walked into the command post, apparently unaware as to what had gone on. They were much too surprised to counter the fast-thinking doughs, who quickly disposed of them. Company G raced across the flat, open ground in the pitch-black night and assaulted the factory buildings, objective B. The enemy, surprised by the suddenness of the attack and the terrific fire, was overrun on the floors and in the cellars of the large factory and quickly subdued by bayonets and hand grenades. Our infantrymen knew that anyone who fired was an enemy and he was quickly dealt with. Company G's Sergeant O'Connor recounts this surprise attack in vivid detail:

Award of Distinguished Service Cross. By direction of the President, under the provisions of AR 600-45, 22 September 1943, as amended, and under authority contained in Circular No. 32, Headquarters European Theater of Operations, United States Army, 20 March 1944, as amended, the Distinguished Service Cross is awarded to:

Private First Class JAMES V. POLIO (Army Serial No. 33299528), Infantry, 413th Infantry Regiment, United States Army, for extraordinary heroism in action against the enemy in Germany on 28 November 1944. On the afternoon of 28 November 1944 elements of the company to which Private POLIO was assigned were advancing toward their objective when they were suddenly pinned to the ground by heavy machine gun and sniper fire from well concealed enemy positions 300 yards to their immediate front. Private POLIO, voluntarily and on his own initiative, crawled from his covered position and, at great risk to his life, advanced toward the enemy, exposing himself to the merciless fire in order to locate the enemy positions. After ascertaining the enemy's disposition and relaying this information to his company commander, he nevertheless continued to advance on the hostile positions in the face of intense fire, attacking and eliminating a machine gun nest with a rifle grenade. He then continued on into the enemy positions, using his rifle and hand grenades to wipe out a second machine gun nest before being killed by sniper fire. His heroic sacrifice undoubtedly saved the lives of many of his comrades in the subsequent advance of the company. His action, far above and beyond the ordinary call of duty, is in keeping with the finest traditions of the armed forces of the United States and reflects the highest credit on Private POLIO and the military service. Entered military service from Hazlehurst, Penna.

"Another block taken!"

About two minutes before 2300 when the artillery was to cease firing, Lieutenant James A. Milliner of Madison, Florida, saw that we had to cross an open field approximately two hundred yards wide, so without waiting, gave the order to move out, as he realized the Jerries wouldn't be expecting visitors at least until the artillery ceased. When our first platoons stepped off into the river, they found that it was much deeper than the twelve inches we'd been told, and it later turned out that the Germans had blown up a dam further upstream. As more and more men plunged into the freezing, swiftly flowing water of the Inde River, they found the water over their waists but, holding their rifles high over their heads, they all surged on. Now we were crossing the open field and were still undetected. Just a company of grim, determined men, and with each step forward we were that much nearer another goal. Out of the darkness on the other side of the field Pfc. Claudie L. Soape spotted two emplacements and figured they were occupied, so without hesitating, he made a one-man assault on the first one, threw two grenades, instantly killing its two occupants, and another grenade into the second, wounding two more and taking their desire to fight right out of them. By his actions it was later shown that Pfc. Soape had knocked out two machine gun nests that were laid in on the river and had perfect grazing fire directly across the rest of the company's entire front, but because of our early jump-off they had not had time to man their weapons after the artillery ceased.

The fight was now on, and as we moved into the factory, we wanted to be as quiet as possible so refrained from opening up and engaging in any fire fights. The artillery in our immediate vicinity had now stopped so the only noise was that of someone's stumbling through the darkness or the report of a grenade being thrown in some doubtful spot. In the next fifteen minutes we moved on

161

into the rest of the factory, clearing it out as we went along and setting up a
hasty defense. From all appearances we had caught Jerry off guard as we merely
walked in on them and gave them the familiar "hände-hoch" before they could
tell us from their own men. So far we'd captured some thirty-five prisoners,
killed many more, and the factory was ours. About this time they launched their
one real attempt at a counterattack which was quickly repulsed after our defense
had done an effective job of eliminating them as they showed themselves, but
another twenty prisoners were taken without a single casualty inflicted on our
forces. The rest of the night was spent with every man on the alert and ready
for business and with the advent of dawn came a realization that we'd done a
good job, relieved the pressure on our adjacent units, and were now just that
much nearer to complete victory.

German survivors then rallied, and until dawn bloody hand-to-hand
battles ensued. Just as it became daylight, a German patrol of seven
men led by a major came down toward the factory. It was fired on
and several of the enemy were killed and wounded. Upon searching
the major, he was found to carry an order which gave his mission:
1. Find out what was beyond the bridge over the Inde.
2. Contact units on left and right.
3. Evacuate all dead and wounded.
His mission would not be accomplished.
Shortly prior to noon on 3 December the 2d Battalion held firmly in
its possession both of its assigned objectives, and as the enemy was seen
shifting positions near the slagpile they were quickly brought under fire.
To the north of the 2d Battalion, Lieutenant Colonel Kelleher's 3d
Battalion was making final preparations for its assault on Lucherberg.
At 2300 a reinforced platoon of L Company planked the railroad bridge
across the Inde River just south of Inden to make a crossing available
for I Company. It then advanced on the factory area, in a position to
protect the left rear flank of Company I, which was to make the initial
assault on Lucherberg.
At midnight, I Company under Lieutenant John Olsen crossed the
railroad bridge without incident and started for Lucherberg, selecting
the steepest and most difficult approach. Just after crossing the railroad
tracks the leading elements encountered a three-strand barbed wire
fence, and as the men stooped to go through the fence they were subjected to rifle and automatic weapons plunging fire. A now alert enemy
opened fire with several other machine guns. Realizing that surprise
was lost, Lieutenant Olsen shouted out to the men, "I am making a
rush to the town. Come if you like, or stay and be wiped out by artillery fire in the morning." The two platoons rushed over the uneven
ground through the enemy's fire up the steep cliff into Lucherberg.
There was a tank in the western part of the town which fired almost

pointblank at the advancing men, but after several rounds of bazooka fire the tank withdrew. The leading elements got into several houses in the northwest part of the town and another group with Sergeant Miller took up positions in a double house surrounded by an orchard, about one hundred yards west of the church. Lieutenant Olsen took a group of men forward to a house near the church and after a twenty-minute battle cleaned out the house and placed his men inside to hold it. Olsen then returned to his initial building and realizing the company's critical situation sent a radio message for help and dispatched a patrol to get the rest of Company I forward. Then Olsen with his squad of men returned to the church area and attacked another house, where they captured fifteen prisoners in the basement. After he had led the men in clearing this house, he started through a hole in the wall of an adjacent house and was mortally wounded.

Lieutenant Verelle assumed command of the company, which now had a foothold on Lucherberg consisting of four buildings that were held by his fifty men, not including casualties. Sergeant Cheatam observed a column of men coming up the street from the southeast. At first his platoon was ordered to hold its fire since it was thought these might be friendly troops. However, they were soon discovered to be enemy and all guns fired upon them, killing many of them. About 0400 an enemy medical officer asked for a truce so that his men could evacuate the German dead and wounded, of which there were many. The truce was soon worked out between Lieutenant Verelle and the German officer, although neither knew the other's language well. While the terms were being discussed Lieutenant Verelle called to Cheatam to cease firing. Sergeant Cheatam and his men came out of the house and assisted in administering aid to the wounded.

As mortar observer, Lieutenant John Shipley brought up the 3d Platoon and machine gun section to the base of the cliff, where he met the three messengers who had been dispatched by Lieutenant Olsen for help. On the western outskirts of the town he organized a strongpoint in a lone brick house and sent a patrol of five men forward toward the church. In the strongpoint the machine guns were set in walls to provide all-around defense. All three floors were so organized. Later Lieutenant Shipley with two other men went to the church area, and when they arrived the truce was still on.

During the truce period there were about forty enemy and approximately twenty men of the 1st Platoon and twenty-five of the 2d Platoon in the vicinity. All of them were busily evacuating the wounded. A German captain and about forty Nazi soldiers suddenly appeared and began firing on the Americans. The firing ceased while the German officers and Lieutenant Sheridan and Sergeant Marokus were discussing the matter, but the new group of enemy continued to surround the American troops. They acted as if they thought the American soldiers wanted to surrender and started to take up the arms and ammunition of our men. There were now approximately one hundred enemy in the immediate vicinity and others were heard in the town.

An argument started between Sergeant Marokus and the German captain, the sergeant pointing out that "In an army which prides itself upon its discipline, the captain should obey the major, who was still maintaining that the truce was at his request." The captain claimed the major was a medic and therefore had no right to command. In fanatic rage the captain overruled the major and shouted to our men that they had fifteen minutes to get out of town. While this was going on, the enemy apparently grabbed off one or two American soldiers at a time, and it is thought that Lieutenant Verelle disappeared in this fashion. The captain kept Lieutenant Sheridan as a hostage while Sergeant Marokus had the major. Just before the end of the truce, Lieutenant Sheridan and the major were freed to return to their respective lines.

Lieutenant Shipley now took command and he quickly organized his command post in the basement of the lone double house on the northwest outskirts of town. A quick check on the strength of Company I showed that there were forty-five men available for action, twenty-two were missing, and several others had been injured. At daylight the defense of the double house was more carefully organized. Men were stationed so they could observe in all directions. By use of the SCR 300 brought by Lieutenant Shipley and the "300" of Sergeant Miller, the men were able to call in both mortar and artillery fire.

It was here that Corporal George R. Smith, 929th Field Artillery Battalion, recalls the heroic action of Lieutenant Ulmer, working as FO with the assault units. During the early morning hours of 3 December, the enemy launched seven savage counterattacks, which were effectively repulsed not only by the efforts of the infantry but by the murderous artillery fire rained down on the Germans by Lieutenant Ulmer. It was in great part through his efforts that our troops were able to move ahead and take the objective.

Shortly after daylight, the enemy in great force moved against Company I's position. As the enemy came in, Lieutenant Shipley and Lieutenant Ulmer called for 81mm mortar and artillery fire on their own positions. Boyd Lewis, United Press war correspondent, stated:

The story of how Company I of the 415th Infantry Regiment of Maj. Gen. Terry Allen's 104th Division called down American artillery fire on its own position and withstood the shelling for seven hours was told today by the men who gave the order to fire.

They were 1st Lt. Arthur A. Ulmer, Portland, and Lt. John D. Shipley, Appleton, Wis.

The story was told in the buttressed steel-doored factory basement—a building which recently was a backstop of the Siegfried Line but which now is a shelter for American troops.

Ulmer, a smiling, jet-haired man with big hands and a slow manner of speech, explained that he was an artillery spotter working with Company I in the embattled town of Lucherberg.

Ulmer was stationed on the third floor of a house while the doughboys of Company I fought it out in a moonlight battle with a group of German paratroopers.

At his post Ulmer heard a German medical major give a command to cease shooting. He understood German well enough to gather that the German major had ordered a truce to permit the exchange of wounded prisoners, among whom was the Company I commander, who was critically hurt.

Descending to investigate, Ulmer emerged from the door and two Germans jammed a rifle into his ribs, demanding his pistol. When he surrendered it they rushed away and darted back into the house, where he saw that the paratroopers were paying no attention to the German medical major, but were disarming the Americans, who were heavily outnumbered.

The German major was shouting and arguing and trying to make the paratroopers stick to the truce. Ulmer said, "But he was getting nowhere, so I went back to my observation post, grabbed my radio and climbed out the back window."

I withdrew to the edge of town, where a platoon of Company I was defending a house. A bunch of soldiers came running by without any weapons, saying the Krauts had disarmed them and given them fifteen minutes to leave town.

While this was going on the Company I commander died for lack of attention on the floor of a church where the Germans had placed him.

Shipley then rallied the fleeing soldiers and got them into the house. Within fifteen minutes they were armed with two bazookas. The Germans started to blast holes in the house, attacking with machine gun fire and grenades.

Outnumbered three to one, Ulmer and Shipley took a desperate decision. They decided to call down American artillery on their own position.

They believed that the Germans were more exposed and would suffer much greater losses than the Americans would. They got most of their men into a heavy basement which had thick fortress-like walls, posted riflemen at slits picked out of the brick walls.

Then, Ulmer radioed his artillery to crash down on the town with everything available.

Ulmer kept yelling at us all day long, "Keep shooting," said Capt. James Nealon, who was at the receiving end of the calls. "We gave it to him for seven hours."

The ground around the besieged company rocked with the concussion of its own shells. But toward the end of the day German resistance collapsed while Ulmer was still calling for more fire. By 1615 Company I—what was left of it—was able to mop up the town with virtually no difficulty. Some 200 German dead lay in the streets.

The two "300" radios proved invaluable because by their use all the guns in the VII Corps could come to the rescue of beleaguered I Company. Every rifleman was busy throughout the day sniping at the fanatic enemy. Time after time rushes against the double house were stopped cold in their tracks by bazookas, hand grenades, machine gun and artillery fire. On several occasions when Lieutenant Shipley was asked to report on the situation, he replied: "Everything going okay. My only trouble is getting a place to see and shoot with all these dead Jerries piling up in front of the cellar windows." Each man was determined to hold Lucherberg—Company I did not give ground.

In the original plan of attack, L Company was to follow Company I. Because of the withering fire sweeping over the area it was not possible for L Company to advance, so the company was moved back to Lamersdorf. At 1200, L Company crossed the Inde and joined with Company G in the factory area. Company F of the 2d Battalion also moved up to the factory area, and at 1500 Companies L and F made a coordinated attack from the west on Lucherberg. Determined to reach Company I, the men of L Company scaled the large slagpile and fought desperately, finally making contact at 1630. Shortly thereafter, F Company gained the southern edge of Lucherberg, and three companies— I, L, and F—slashed through the town. At 1715 Colonel Cochran reported that his regiment held Lucherberg. Throughout the night 3-4 December there were frequent local skirmishes.

In the twenty-four hour period, our Division and attached artillery battalions, not including the supporting guns of VII Corps and adjoining divisions, fired 370 missions with a total of 18,950 rounds.

Before the attack could be completely assured of success, it was necessary that bridges be constructed immediately in order that much-needed supplies, tanks, tank destroyers and other supporting weapons could be brought to the forward positions. Shortly after the attack began, the 329th Engineers made reconnaissance for construction of bridges in the vicinity of Lamersdorf. The site was constantly under terrific mortar and artillery fire, therefore work could not be commenced in this area. At 0100, Company C began construction of a ford south of the bridge site, completing it by 0400. The river then began to rise, and throughout the morning of 3 December it was necessary to reinforce the ford. At 1400 one of the tanks of the 750th Tank Battalion tried to cross the river over the matting of the ford, but bogged down in the fast-flowing stream, with only the turret above the water. The route was now blocked.

Despite the devastating enemy fire, the engineers continued their work on the Bailey bridge, but construction was greatly hampered.

Main Street — Merken, Germany

After surmounting formidable obstacles of terrain and observed enemy fire, the engineers completed the forty-ton bridge in the early afternoon of 4 December. Immediately antitank weapons of the regiment were rushed across the bridge and tanks and tank destroyers followed, so that by nightfall on 4 December, Lucherberg was strongly reinforced and in a position to withstand attacks. At 0400 on 4 December, prior to the arrival of our antitank weapons, the Germans launched a strong counterattack with tanks and 200 infantry against our positions in Lucherberg. Our mortar and artillery completely disrupted the attack, with great loss to the enemy. Heavy enemy mortar and artillery fire kept falling on Lucherberg during 4, 5, and 6 December, and during this period Lucherberg was subjected to five strong counterattacks. Following an extremely heavy enemy artillery barrage of one hour's duration, another sharp counterattack of 150 infantry and ten tanks struck from the southeast against Lucherberg before dawn on 5 December. Four tanks were destroyed by antitank and tank fire and the remainder withdrew towards Pier and Merken. The counterattack was completely repulsed by 0910.

The surprise and the strength of the night attack made by the 415th Infantry was clearly demonstrated by the statement of one German prisoner of the 10th Company, 8th Paratroop Regiment: "We didn't know we were being attacked, until grenades dropped in our foxholes." The loss of Lucherberg was keenly felt by the enemy, as was evidenced

167

BATTLE OF THE ROER
(*Time*, December 11, 1944)

The Germans fought for the Roer River, between Aachen and Cologne, as if it were the Meuse, the Marne and the Somme of the last war all rolled into one. German radio broadcasts called it "the most terrible and ferocious battle in the history of all wars."

Hardly more than a creek in summer, the Roer was now swollen by rain. The Germans increased the flood by blowing dams and opening sluice gates, until the shallow brown water in one place spread almost a mile across the plain. Lieut. General William ("Texas Bill") Simpson's Ninth Army inched painfully forward until it held a 20-mile stretch on the west bank. On his right, Courtney Hodges' First Army had to cross a smaller stream, the Inde, before it could come up to the Roer. The Germans fought like wild men for the Inde also. Driven out of the town of Inden, they lanced back in with armor and crack infantry, blew up a bridge. Ousted again, they put down an artillery barrage in which the Yanks counted 60 shells a minute.

STEADY SLUGGING YANKS PUSH INTO INDUSTRIAL RUHR VALLEY
(*Army Times*, December 9, 1944)

WASHINGTON.—Steady slugging by American and British infantry and armor have carried the Allied forces across two of the Reich's main barriers, the Saar and the Inde Rivers, and forced the Germans back to the Maas and the Roer in mounting battles opposite the Ruhr Valley, a center of Nazi coal and steel production.

Correspondents predict that the coming battle of the Roer will see the bloodiest fighting yet experienced on the Western Front since the Germans have tossed in all their strength to protect the Ruhr factories.

by the many counterattacks directed against the fortress in futile attempts to regain it and by confirmed reports that General Model (commander in chief of the German forces on the Western Front) had personally ordered the recapture of Lucherberg while he was in Duren. The known enemy losses included 204 killed, 209 prisoners, two Tiger tanks, two Panther tanks, one self-propelled gun, five 75mm antitank guns, and vast stores of ammunition and supplies. In addition, approximately 400 to 500 German troops had been wounded. The skillful use of night operations limited our losses to twenty-five killed, fifty-nine wounded, and twenty-one missing. Although the German Panzer division had not been committed en masse, many of its troops had been destroyed in piecemeal counterattacks. This costly experience proved to Model and his forces that the Timberwolves would not give ground.

Lieutenant Colonel Max Kahn was succeeded by Lieutenant Colonel Robert P. Tabb as commander of the 329th Engineer Battalion on 5 December. On the same date Colonel Charles T. Lanham (later Brigadier General) took over his duties as Assistant Division Commander.

On 4 December, Lieutenant General J. Lawton Collins, commander of the VII Corps, sent the following telegram to the Division:

FROM: CG,   VII CORPS
TO   :   CG,   104TH INFANTRY DIVISION
CONGRATULATIONS TO THE 104TH DIVISION ON ITS SUPERB PERFORMANCE IN CAPTURING LUCHERBERG
(SGD) COLLINS

On 7 December General Allen issued the following commendation:

To All Timberwolves:
The above commendation has been received by this Division.
The successful attack on Lucherberg was made possible by the stubborn fighting of the 413th Infantry in first taking Lamersdorf and Inden, and the quick crossing of the Inde River by the 3d Battalion, 414th Infantry. In the actual night attack on Lucherberg, involving a river crossing and the assault of a strongly fortified town, the troop leading and dash of the 2d and 3d Battalions, 415th Infantry, were outstanding. The functioning of the forward artillery observers and the close artillery support was highly effective. The troop leading, dash, and tenacious fighting of Company I, 415th Infantry, in its night attack to seize the north edge of Lucherberg and in retaining its position thereat until its timely support by the 2d and 3d Battalions, was particularly outstanding.
My personal congratulations to you all for again earning a well-deserved commendation for your combat accomplishments. NOTHING IN HELL MUST STOP THE TIMBERWOLVES.
/s/   TERRY ALLEN
/t/   TERRY ALLEN

Medic gives first aid to wounded bazooka man.

For the heroic action of the men in the 2d and 3d Battalions, 415th Infantry, the following unit citations under the provisions of Section 4, Circular No. 333, War Department, 1943, were awarded:

The 3D BATTALION, 415TH INFANTRY REGIMENT, is cited for extraordinary heroism and outstanding performance of duty in armed conflict with the enemy between 2 and 6 December 1944. The 3D BATTALION, 415TH INFANTRY, assaulted and captured the dominating fortified area of Lucherberg, Germany, and, by their gallant action, facilitated the continued advance of all units in the sector. On 2 December 1944, a reinforced company of the 3D BATTALION forced a crossing of the River Inde and without delay advanced boldly through active, emplaced enemy positions up the hill towards Lucherberg under a withering hail of automatic weapons, heavy mortar, and artillery fire. Three hours later rifle elements daringly entered the perimeter fortifications of the town and blasted their way through the walls of three houses, giving the 3D BATTALION a toehold in Lucherberg proper. Without hesitation, and totally disregarding their isolated and seemingly untenable position, these slender forces spurned an enemy ultimatum to withdraw within fifteen minutes or be destroyed. With complete disregard for safety, these troops directed the fire of the Division artillery on and around their own positions, thereby assisting in repelling the enemy's successive furious counterattacks. A company of the 3D BATTALION, which had found its way blocked after crossing the River Inde, returned under heavy mortar and artillery fire and for the third time crossed that swollen stream, wading waist-deep in the fast flowing, icy water. Without halting, it assaulted the heavy fortifications of a factory area to the west of Lucherberg, advancing courageously throughout the morning in the buildings and passages while under observed enemy fire. In a successful frontal attack against the perimeter defenses of the hill-top town, these elements established contact with the initial troops still holding out in the houses, enabling the combined force to defend the vital ground through the night. At dawn on 4 December 1944 enemy reinforcements totalling two hundred men moved to the east side of Lucherberg, where battalion mortars and infantry pinned them down. The reserve company of the 3D BATTALION was committed at this time, displaying the highest courage, and by prompt and decisive action denied this reinforcement to the garrison of Lucherberg and enlarged the area held by the battalion. On the morning of 5 December 1944, following an enemy artillery barrage on the battalion positions lasting over an hour, the enemy counterattacked with one hundred additional fresh infantry troops mounted on ten tanks. Upon dismounting, the German infantry in furious action suffered heavy losses and a crushing defeat. The Tiger tanks were put out of action, one by a rifleman armed with a rocket launcher. Throughout the action the officers and men of the 3D BATTALION consistently distinguished themselves by exceptional initiative and individual bravery, and by the highest form of combat discipline. These heroic and gallant actions of all elements of the 3D BATTALION, 415TH INFANTRY REGIMENT, were carried out, despite its severe losses of officers and men, without wavering in the continued bloody battle to a decisive conclusion, inflicting terrific losses on the enemy and gaining complete command of the key terrain of the region. The cool courage, combat skill, and esprit de corps displayed by the members of 3D BATTALION, 415TH INFANTRY REGIMENT, contributed materially to the success of their Division and reflect the highest traditions of the armed forces of the United States.

The 2D BATTALION, 415TH INFANTRY REGIMENT, is cited for extraordinary heroism and outstanding performance of duty in armed conflict with the enemy during the period from 2 to 4 December 1944 in the vicinity of Lucherberg, Germany. During this period the 2D BATTALION, 415TH INFANTRY REGIMENT, distinguished itself by its skillful and fearless performance of an extremely difficult mission, assaulting and securing the Goldsteingrube factory area and the Lutzeber chateau area. Their gallant action facilitated the continued advance of all units in the sector. Two companies of the battalion attacked on the night of 2 December 1944, silently waded the freezing, waist-deep Inde River, and, by stealth, approached the long prepared, determined and powerfully emplaced enemy. To effect surprise, and for close-in combat, rifles were left unloaded, bayonets were fixed, and each man carried six hand grenades. In the face of extremely heavy automatic weapons fire, these units closed with the powerful enemy force, subdued it, and organized the objectives without firing a shot. During the early morning hours of 3 December 1944, the enemy launched savage counterattacks, which were courageously and effectively repelled by the units of the 2D BATTALION, 415TH INFANTRY REGIMENT. The attack was so skillfully executed that the objective was secured with the loss of only four men. One enemy 75mm antitank gun, fifteen machine guns, a large number of machine pistols, and fifty-four prisoners were captured, and thirty-five enemy soldiers were killed. During the daylight hours of 3 December 1944 the remainder of the 2D BATTALION, under continuous heavy enemy artillery and mortar fire, infiltrated across the Inde River, reached the outskirts of Lucherberg, and despite intense small arms, bazooka, and mortar fire, tenaciously held their position throughout the night. The following morning (4 December 1944) the 2D BATTALION completed mopping up their sectors and pushed forward to establish more favorable positions, thus denying the enemy any possible entrance into Lucherberg from the south. Throughout the action, the officers and men of the 2D BATTALION, 415TH INFANTRY, distinguished themselves by great determination, outstanding aggressiveness, and superior combat discipline, gaining exceedingly difficult objectives with a minimum of casualties. The initiative, courage, and esprit de corps displayed by the battalion reflected the finest traditions of the armed forces of the United States.

PIER-SCHOPHOVEN . . . On 4 December, Lieutenant Colonel Clark's 1st Battalion, 414th Infantry, closed in Inden and Putzlohn, joining Colonel Rouge's Battalion, which now held most of the town of Inden east of the river. Company A moved to the left flank of the 3d Battalion to secure the Division left flank, making contact with the adjacent unit at 0100, 5 December. Because of the ferocious fighting going on to the south at Lucherberg, Company B and one platoon of tanks from the 750th Tank Battalion were alerted as a task force to be prepared to move on Lucherberg. When the tide of battle turned, the task force was taken off its alert status.

Enemy air was more active and on four occasions on 6 December, Inden, Lamersdorf, and Lucherberg were subjected to bombing and strafing. Artillery fire was still falling heavily in Inden and Lucherberg, often reaching the rate of forty rounds per minute. On 5 December, Division Headquarters directed the 414th Infantry to launch an attack on Pier and Schophoven on 10 December and that the 415th would prepare itself to assault Merken, the remaining barriers on the west banks of the Roer River. To secure a suitable area of departure for the 414th's attack against Pier, at 1500 on 6 December, the 3d Battalion, 414th Infantry, advanced on the factory just east of the railroad tracks beyond Inden. The plan of attack included heavy artillery preparation by the 386th Field Artillery Battalion, reinforced by the Division and Corps artillery, heavy concentrations of eight-inch gun fire as well as long-range machine gun and mortar fires by Company M. Tanks and tank destroyers were rolled forward to open up concrete and brick walls of the factory. Companies K and L maintained frontal pressure while Company I moved to the right and struck from the right flank. The enemy was caught by surprise and within two hours the battalion had its objective, capturing 176 prisoners.

Just how effective the surprise attack was, is illustrated by the fabulous incident of Captain "Jock" Whitney, I Company's Commanding Officer, who singlehandedly, with no more lethal a weapon than a map case, captured fifteen German warriors.

The only obstacle between the 414th Infantry and Pier that remained was the dairy lying 400 yards to the east. Again on 7 December the 3d Battalion continued its attack at 1130, after it had repulsed a fierce counterattack launched against the factory shortly after daylight. The new objective was fiercely defended but fell to Lieutenant Colonel Rouge's men at 1210.

The area of departure was now cleared and the 414th perfected its plans for the assault on Pier. During 7, 8, and 9 December, active reconnaissance was conducted by the 414th Infantry on the left and the 415th Infantry on the right. The Division's positions were strengthened and long-range artillery duels were in progress during most of the period. Counterattacks against our front line positions continued but in each instance they were repulsed with heavy losses to the enemy. Forty active gun, battery and mortar positions were reported and the Division artillery was massed on these positions, resulting in a great lessening of artillery fires on Inden and Lucherberg. On 9 December, Company K, 415th Infantry, moved 400 yards to the east of Lucherberg, taking up its positions by 2100. The 1st Battalion, 414th Infantry, completed its plans to move through the 3d Battalion for its attack on Pier.

December 10th was a cloudy and misty day. At 0745, with Companies A and B abreast, the 1st Battalion, 414th, commenced its advance on Pier. Sergeant Walter M. Phillips, forward observer from the 386th Field Artillery with Company B, controlled the advance of the infantry by a rolling barrage. The effectiveness of the fire enabled B Company to advance 1,200 yards over the open ground to the edge of its objective (Pier) in forty-five minutes and forced the enemy to withdraw to prepared positions within the town. The infantrymen had crossed the flat open ground with few casualties, but owing to the heavy enemy fire from prepared positions within Pier only one platoon was able to get a foothold in the edge of the town. Simultaneously with the attack of the 1st Battalion, the 3d Battalion on the left advanced from Inden towards Schophoven. Initially the advance was against small arms resistance, but as it neared the objective heavy artillery fire forced the battalion to halt and reorganize on the high ground 800 yards west of Schophoven. The battle raged furiously for the next forty-eight hours. Repeated counterattacks were made by the enemy in a futile effort to push our advancing troops back into Inden. Heavy fighting went on

Award of Distinguished Service Cross. By direction of the President, under the provisions of AR 600-45, 22 September 1943, as amended, and under authority contained in Circular No. 32, Headquarters European Theater of Operations, United States Army, 20 March 1944, as amended, the Distinguished Service Cross is awarded to:

Private First Class FRANK MORALEZ, 37326029, Infantry, 413th Infantry Regiment, 104th Infantry Division, United States Army, for extraordinary heroism in connection with military operations against the enemy. On 31 November 1944 in Germany, an enemy tank, supported by infantry, moved into positions held by the platoon in which Private MORALEZ was an assistant squad leader. Realizing the futility of his position and the danger of his comrades, Private MORALEZ faced the enemy fire to secure a more advantageous position. From this position, he exchanged fire with the enemy tank. His fourth rifle grenade found its mark and the tank was forced to withdraw, but not before it had fired a direct hit on his position taking his life. The heroic efforts of Private MORALEZ undoubtedly saved the lives of many fellow soldiers. The extraordinary heroism and courageous actions of Private MORALEZ reflect great credit upon himself and are in keeping with the highest traditions of the military service. Entered military service from Minnesota.

Not a stone upon a stone — Pier, Germany

not only by the infantry but also by tanks. On 11 December Companies
C and E relieved the beleaguered Companies A and B.

Private First Class George Field, Company B, 414th Infantry, tells a
tale that only a war could bring . . . a story that taxes the imagination.
It happened during the 1st Battalion's attack on Pier, and in the words
of Pfc. Field:

I was a new replacement in the 1st Platoon of B Company, my first time
under fire. The Germans had very good observation points, and as we advanced
over a thousand yards of open field they threw everything at us. I eventually
got into the town and the only people I found there were a couple of men from
my company whose names I didn't know, a squad leader who was later to become my platoon sergeant and an officer from A Company. The squad leader,
Sergeant Serposs, told me to go over to a barn and fire my BAR. He assigned a
target but by the time I got to the barn I'd forgotten what it was. I climbed a
haystack and started to shoot. I didn't care or know what I was shooting at but
fired just the same. After shooting twenty rounds the weapon jammed, so I
pulled back into the first building I saw, and tried to fix the stoppage. I worked
on it a long time but it was no use. I was conscious of firing going on around
me, but by now my ears were so numbed that I didn't pay any attention to it,
and didn't jump a mile every time a round went off.

By this time it was growing dark, and since there was no change of orders
that we knew of, we decided to button up for the night. Six of us, two from
B and four from A Company, were sent down to a cellar of a ruined house to
guard a road that ran through the village. The cellar we found consisted of two
rooms. One was obviously occupied by the two men whose bodies we found in
the other room. They were killed by our artillery fire that preceded the attack
on the town. We covered their faces with a towel. The bodies were laying
right in the middle of the door that connected the two rooms, their feet in
one and their bodies in the other. There was also a little opening through
which we had a view of the street we were supposed to guard. We had to crawl
over the two bodies and a pile of bricks to get to that window. By the time my
turn came for guard it was already dark. I climbed over the bodies up to the

window and settled down for a two-hour stretch. I piled some loose bricks in front of me and to the sides but left an opening large enough to look through and to fire if necessary. It wasn't more than a half hour when I heard a rumbling noise down the street. At first I didn't know what it was, but soon realized it was a tank, and a large one, coming right at us.

"Hey guys! There is a tank coming this way," I heard someone holler and then realized it was me.

"Let's keep quiet—maybe it'll go away" seemed the universal opinion. But it stopped right in front of our window, and we heard a couple of men get out.

"*Kommen Sie raus!*" penetrated the still night.

We were scared. . . . Plenty scared. No answer. . . . I doubt that we even breathed.

"*Kommen Sie raus oder du bist todt.*"

There were a couple of moments of silence and then came the flash and concussion of a grenade. There weren't any fragments, so it must have been a concussion grenade. There was another explosion and another. . . . Then quiet.

"They think we're dead," I whispered.

"I am not sure whether we are or not" came out of the blackness. Then came fifteen minutes of hell. The gun on the tank started firing through our house. Just the muzzle blast of that gun had us bouncing off the walls. When it finally ceased we heard a couple of men crawl down the window. We listened to them talking, and decided if one of them should come into the room we would give up, because in a case like this it would be no use fighting. So we sat back and waited, hardly daring to breathe, listening to those two so-called "Supermen." One of the Germans noticed the two dead men in the doorway and stopped. He called his buddy over, and there they stood talking, none of them taking another step. Finally they quit lighting matches and settled down, probably to spend the night. We spent a very quiet and slightly jumpy night with the two Heinies in the next room. Around five o'clock in the morning they left.

The place was quiet. The sort of quiet you can hear—close and suffocating. There was no noise of artillery shells coming in, there was no chatter of machine guns, not even footsteps. We knew for sure that our companies were forced back, but we didn't know when they would try again. The only thing left for us to do was to sit tight and wait.

I don't know how long we were there but one morning we heard a lot of commotion. We weren't sure who was coming but all of us hoped and prayed that our men had come back to take the town and this time for good. Someone came in through that same window. He also saw the two dead bodies. Again we were tense until he yelled out to his buddy, "Hey, Joe, throw down a flashlight."

That was the most welcome sound I ever heard or will hear.

Further attacks by our forces were repulsed by the enemy, still holding behind his battered positions. At 0645 on 12 December, Company G, supported by a platoon of tanks from the 750th Tank Battalion, swept into Pier from the southwest while Companies C and E pressed hard and attacked from the northwest. G Company quickly gained a foothold and the tanks stormed into the town. In close hand-to-hand fighting from building to building and from room to room the stout-hearted infantrymen pressed on, gaining the objective by 1200.

At 0630, 13 December, Companies L and K of the 414th attacked Schophoven frontally in conjunction with a right hook by Company F from Pier.

That right hook turned out to be one of the most expensive endeavors of the entire campaign. An unusually high price in American blood and human misery was paid for ancient, moated Mullenark Castle, which was Company F's objective. Staff Sergeant Frank Perozzi recounts a vivid story of that costly venture:

On the cold dark morning of 13 December 1944 at 0500 Fox Company crossed the line of departure out of Inden, heading cross-country toward Phase Line 1. This would bring us on line with K and L Companies, who were en-trenched on the crest of the gentle hill between Inden and our objective. Onward from Phase Line 1 meant crossing practically a mile of billiard-table country.

The mile to this crest had been a miserable trek. We were loaded wtih ban-doleers, grenades and various types of ammunition which did not ease our way through the darkness, ankle-deep mud, and water-filled craters. Anyone who fell in the deep mud required the assistance of two men to set him back on his feet. Since the chateau was surrounded by a moat, we had crossed the line of departure carrying an eighteen-foot plank by which we would span the water barrier. Well, it was impossible to keep the plank moving with the company, which forced the carrying party to either rid themselves of the plank or get lost. The heavy beam sank into the thick mud.

It was 0630 when the artillery barrage opened up, together with H Com-pany's mortars and overhead heavy machine gun fire. We would wait ten min-utes before starting across the open plain. The barrage was a spectacle, beautiful but devastating—the flashes of our "automatic artillery" would race in two seconds time from one flank of our objective to the other. The tracers of our harassing machine gun fire from Inden would burn out just overhead—as though they were afraid to advance beyond the infantry units.

Finally, F, K and L Companies moved out with the 1st Platoon of F Company on the extreme right flank.

Jerry had been awakened by the terrific barrage and was now throwing in "searching" mortar shells. He did not know from what direction infantry was advancing, if at all. We moved as fast and as quietly as possible, stumbling over the turnips and sugar beets of the rain-flooded fields. We kept visual contact with our squads only by dropping low and silhouetting the men against the sky.

We were approximately 300 yards from our objective when our artillery lifted—a little too soon for the majority of us. Our only concern now was not to be caught in the open by enemy low trajectory fire—we had to reach our objective but quick! We would never be able to defend ourselves if trapped in these fields. To fall under enemy fire at this moment would have made retreat hopeless, for dawn and its light was nearing.

As we approached the moat and were clearing a stack of baled straw, we

Award of Distinguished Service Cross. By direction of the President, under the provisions of AR 600-45, 22 September 1943, as amended, and under authority contained in Circular No. 32, Headquarters European Theater of Operations, United States Army, 20 March 1944, as amended, the Distinguished Service Cross is awarded to:

Captain WILLIAM B. WHITNEY, 01289180, AUS (Infantry), 414th Infantry Regiment, 104th Infantry Division, United States Army, for extraordinary heroism in connection with military operations in Germany on 4 December 1944. Discovering that two of his men were missing, Captain WHITNEY immediately advanced into the fire-swept area, searched the foxholes and shell-craters, found the two wounded men and personally carried them to safety. Realizing that a frontal assault on an enemy held railroad embankment would result in heavy casualties, Captain WHITNEY decided to try a bluff. Unarmed and carrying a small, celluloid map-board, Captain WHITNEY briskly walked down the track. Nearing an enemy trench, Captain WHITNEY motioned with his map-board and one enemy rose from his position and surrendered. He continued this action until a total of fifteen of the enemy had surrendered to him. The extraordinary heroism and courageous actions of Captain WHITNEY reflect great credit upon himself and are in keeping with the highest traditions of the military service. Entered military service from Mississippi.

The Master Race?

heard the first enemy machine gun fire over in the K and L Company area. Would we be next?

The 1st Platoon was to clear four "sheds" as shown on the aerial photo, then set up a defensive position around the right edge of a small pond situated seventy-five yards right of the chateau.

Dawn broke as the men of the first and second squads alternately slid into the cold, chest-high water. Luckily, the moat was at "low" tide; we had expected a depth of eight feet. As we emerged over the opposite bank and advanced for our "sheds," we found that sugar beet mounds resemble sheds in an aerial photo. The third squad had advanced past the first and second before we could warn them of the situation. By then, it had started!

Enemy snipers were picking away at us from windows of Mullenark and were zeroing in their mortars. The second squad was pinned where it stood, forcing the men to dig in on the spot. The first squad managed to maneuver around the pond and set up on the dike. Men paid the price of one enemy slug toward them with each shovelful of dirt dug from life-saving foxholes. Men were drenched and cold and lay in water, unable to sit up and afraid to smoke a sneaked cigarette. Men tore off overshoes and untied shoes to lessen the pain on water-soaked feet. Men were wounded; there were no medics. Those attempting to locate medical help never came back. Our own artillery was firing again; air bursts too close for comfort! From upper windows Jerry rifle grenades were easily dropped against our parapets. The second squad BAR man lessened enemy resistance by knocking out a machine gun in a tower to the rear of Mullenark.

The third squad had gone too far to turn back and miraculously made its way to a one-room, ground level shelter behind the chateau. The six-man squad had twelve prisoners before Heinie mortars began to fall outside the entrance. With each mortar round or machine gun burst at the doorway, Jerries and Americans would simultaneously hit the straw floor in one grand mixup. Eventually, two of the men were able to contact a tank from Schophoven and, with covering fire

179

from the tank, the rest of the third squad maneuvered into town. Schophoven had fallen by 1030.

The 2d Platoon was dug in on the chateau bank of the moat and bore the brunt of the enemy mortar fire. Many casualties were the result of tree bursts that sent whistling shrapnel into their water-filled holes.

The 3d Platoon was moving in on Mullenark from the left. We were to wait and hold until they cleared the fort, but heavy enemy resistance was encountered in the buildings before the chateau, and the platoon was unable to carry on after suffering heavy losses.

Existing throughout the day under murderous mortar and grenade fire, word finally came in the quiet early morning of the next day that we would move out. At 0400, 14 December, F Company moved around Mullenark and into Schophoven. Because of unknown resistance in our left flank movement into town we were forced to leave the many casualties behind. As we recrossed the moat, we told the wounded that litter bearers would be sent to them.

Company F remained in town until 1500 the same day. Chateau Mullenark was still to be taken. A combat patrol was formed of the remainder of both platoons—a total of sixteen men. After a small tank barrage, the patrol moved across 150 yards of open terrain out of town and into the buildings which stood before the chateau. Taking all precautions, the patrol dashed across the main bridge into the main entrance of the fort. We spent approximately an hour completely clearing the place and, to our surprise, captured but four prisoners. The rest had taken off. Chateau Mullenark was ours.

The 3d Battalion troops stormed Schophoven and soon gained a foothold in the citadel. The enemy tenaciously defended each building, room, and wall, but by 1730 K and L, in close-in fighting, had destroyed the German garrison and gained their objective, Schophoven. The advance of the company on the right to Schophoven was halted by devastating fire from the Mullenark Castle southwest of Schophoven.

By 1500, 14 December, the castle fell, and the Division now held the west banks of the Roer River throughout its zone, the 415th having cleared its area on the right.

MERKEN . . . Thirty-two hundred yards east of Lucherberg lay Merken, a strongly held town of over one hundred stone and brick houses. The terrain was an open, slightly rolling ground which provided the enemy with superior fields of fire. It was not possible to approach Merken without being exposed to deadly flanking fire. To avoid excessive losses it was directed that the assault on Merken be made at night. Prior to the attack, careful terrain study by key personnel was made from excellent observation posts in Lucherberg. Detailed preparations of plans included study of photo interpretation maps and each unit was assigned zones of advance.

On 9 December, Company K, 415th Infantry, had advanced east of Lucherberg to secure the line of departure to be used by the 1st Bat-

Artillery support from deep in the Hurtgen Forest

talion in its night attack. At 0400 on 11 December, Lieutenant Colonel Needham's 1st Battalion jumped off on the objective in a column of companies echeloned to the left: B, C and a reinforced platoon of Company A. Following closely the rolling barrages of the 929th Field Artillery, the advancing infantry quickly overran the surprised outposts, and prior to daylight B and C Companies had a firm hold on the outskirts of Merken. Since Pier had not as yet been taken, a reinforced platoon of Company A under Lieutenant Arbogaste was directed to secure the battalion's left flank and seize Vilbenich, located northwest of Merken. Striking swiftly against a disorganized enemy, Lieutenant Arbogaste's men captured seventy-eight prisoners before they could reach their weapons. The Pier-Merken road was effectively cut and blocked by the quick seizure of this strongpoint. With our left flank secure, Company C under Lieutenant Hooker and Company B under Captain Raymond Garino commenced their bitter house-to-house fighting within Merken at 0700.

The enemy was still dazed, and before nightfall more than two-thirds of Merken had been seized with three casualties to our troops and with the capture of 160 prisoners and over one hundred casualties to the enemy. Infantry and tank teams continued their operation the next day, completing the seizure of Merken prior to nightfall. The enemy still had not given up the west bank of the Roer River, since he held the

181

Award of Distinguished Service Cross. By direction of the President, under the provisions of AR 600-45, 22 September 1943, as amended, and under authority contained in Circular No. 32, Headquarters European Theater of Operations, United States Army, 20 March 1944, as amended, the Distinguished Service Cross is awarded to:

Sergeant GEORGE E. BURNS (Army Serial No. 32780093), Infantry, 415th Infantry Regiment, United States Army, for extraordinary heroism in action against the enemy in Germany on 5 December 1944. On the morning of 5 December 1944 the enemy launched a vicious counter attack with tanks and infantry on the company to which Sergeant BURNS was assigned. An enemy tank penetrated the company's position, knocking out the antitank defense, delivering direct fire on the company command post, destroying all communications and wounding the company commander. Realizing that his platoon's bazookas had been destroyed, Sergeant BURNS, at great risk to his life and in the face of direct fire from the enemy tank and supporting infantry, ran from house to house until he found a bazooka and ammunition. Unable to find a covered position providing a field of fire, Sergeant BURNS fired the bazooka from a point in the open street, seeking cover only to load his weapon. He fired a total of 10 rounds at the enemy tank, killing eight of the supporting infantrymen and setting the tank on fire with a well-aimed round through the tank's ventilator. The tank was forced to withdraw, and, at great risk to his life, Sergeant BURNS courageously pursued it down the open street, stopped the tank with his last round, and killed the crew with his rifle as they abandoned the burning tank. His courageous actions, far above and beyond the ordinary call of duty, are in keeping with the finest traditions of the military service and reflect the highest credit on Sergeant BURNS and the armed forces of the United States. Entered military service from New York City, New York.

paper factory southeast of Merken. At daylight on the 23d, Colonel Needham's men assaulted this last stronghold, clearing it prior to 1100. In addition to the enemy having suffered heavy casualties, he lost large stores of supplies, ammunition, and weapons, including four antitank guns, two self-propelled weapons and fifteen machine guns.

From the shelled and shattered remnants of Pier, Merken and Schophoven, dirty, weary dogfaces slogged back to the rear for a few days' rest off the line. They hardly looked the part of triumphant soldiers. Here was no glamour . . . no adventure. In its place was much anguish, fatigue and pain. Technical Sergeant Ramo Parola, L Company, 414th Infantry, seems to catch the spirit of each dough on his return through the hell of a yesterday:

It was late afternoon. You were sitting in a cellar in Schophoven. You had reached the Roer. It was ten days since the night you jumped across the Inde River at Inden. You were tired, beaten down, shaky. You were everything that ten days of fighting could make you.

Then the word came down. The company was being relieved that night. Goin' back! Yeah, you were goin' back for a rest. Where? Inden, for sure—maybe to Weisweiler.

Weisweiler! Your mind traveled back. It was only a few miles, but in your mind it was dozens of mortar and artillery barrages; it was three jump-offs; it was one river crossing; it was innumerable carrying parties; it was night marches through mud; it was lots of private hells; it was nights of fighting and shivering in foxholes; it was planned attacks that never formed; it was counterattacks beaten off; it was lots of casualties; and it was three company commanders back down that long hard road that led deeper into the heart of Germany.

Weisweiler, sure you remembered it. That's where you lost your first CO. Yeah, Cap'n Nelson. Confident and courageous in a manner that inspired his men, a past-master of coordinated attacks, that was the Cap'n. You wondered how the company would get along after it lost him, didn't you? But the company got along. The Cap'n would be back in England in a hospital by this time, you figured. Then you remembered others who weren't so lucky. You remembered that Lieutenant Kenyon died at Weisweiler. Kenyon with a wife and kid and you wondered why it should have to be Kenyon; and there was Krause, and Reitz and Buchanan and Lacy and Folse. Yeah, you'd remember Weisweiler.

The company was lining up in the dark out on the road now, getting ready to leave Schophoven. Goin' back for a rest. You looked over that thin, double line of dark shapes. Hardly more than a platoon, the remnant of a line company that had accomplished its mission. You moved out, staggering and stumbling in the mire of the rutted road. You didn't mind. You were goin' back for a rest. You were gettin' off the line.

Remember how you came into this town? In the darkness just before dawn, following your own artillery barrage so close it got a couple of the boys, that's how you came in. Holland, only an arm's length from you, carrying a machine gun, died coming into this town. His last words had been words of encouragement to bolster the confidence of a faltering buddy. Remember? Pierce was hit too. He was carrying the radio. It was right there that morning in the dark

Award of Distinguished Service Cross. By direction of the President, under the provisions of AR 600-45, 22 September 1943, as amended, and under authority contained in Circular No. 32, Headquarters European Theater of Operations, United States Army, 20 March 1944, as amended, the Distinguished Service Cross is awarded to:

Private First Class FRANCIS T. CHASE, JR., 32942130, 414th Infantry, United States Army, for extraordinary heroism in action against the enemy on 3 December 1944, in Germany. When his company was pinned down by intense enemy automatic rifle and cannon fire, Private First Class CHASE raced across fifty yards of open, fire-swept terrain and gained the entrance to a large factory. Moving from window to window, he placed devastating rocket fire upon the hostile positions, permitting his company to occupy the building without casualties. As an enemy self-propelled gun advanced and placed point-blank direct fire upon the structure, Private First Class CHASE occupied an exposed position outside the building and fired two rockets into the enemy vehicle. The weapon fired directly at Private First Class CHASE, painfully wounding him. Despite his wounds, he continued to fire and forced the vehicle to withdraw. A second self-propelled gun approached, followed by foot troops. Firing his rocket launcher, Private First Class CHASE forced the vehicle back, then fired upon the attacking infantry, inflicting severe casualties and halting the assault. Entered military service from New York.

with your own artillery burstin' around you, and the wounded guys groanin' and Lieutenant Teig strugglin' to get the radio off the wounded Pierce. Yeah, it was there that you knew that Teig was good enough for your money, come Heinies, hell, or high water. Yeah, Teig, your newest CO. (God, but new CO's were becoming a common occurrence of late.) You knew then that he was one of those referred to when the CO said, "Nothing in hell ―――――." You never saw a man stay so cool in a spot, work so fast, and cuss a colonel so volubly all at the same time.

A flash of bursting Heinie ack-ack broke your reverie. Scared you, didn't it? You thought at first it was time fire comin' in. You wondered if the other guys had noticed that ack-ack; you wondered if they too thought it was time fire; and you wondered why somebody didn't say something about it, and you figured they, like you, were afraid to mention it for fear of alarming the others.

You were passing beet piles now. You remembered it wasn't so far off to your left there that the whole battalion was forced to hole up three days and nights before it was possible to force an entry into Schophoven. It was there that Bennett and Dove, inadequately armed, courageously went out and got themselves five bunkers and fifteen Heinie prisoners. You remember it was there that you sweated out three days and nights in holes. Trench foot got some of the guys, mortar and small arms got some of 'em. Couldn't get out of your hole most of the time except at night. And you recalled bitterly the futile attempts to form and launch daylight attacks from those positions.

You caught sight of a dim tree line ahead, marking the main road from Inden to Pier and Schophoven. You couldn't see 'em, but you knew that up that road to your left were the burnt out hulks of our tanks. Knocked out while forcing an entry into Pier. It was good to get the solid surface of the road underfoot and swing on toward Inden. You felt better. You weren't alone in this feeling because even the stragglers caught up to the column now.

Then, there it was―that damned German SP that had given the boys in the factory so much hell, sittin' there on the road where it was knocked out. Its crew likewise was knocked out. Kirbie had seen to that―Kirbie and his BAR.

There was our factory too. Yes, *our* factory. God knows it was bought dearly enough. You still marveled at the tenacity with which the 1st and 3d Platoons and their attached machine guns held onto that chunk of hell despite self-propelled weapons, artillery, mortar, and pitched small arms assaults. Even with the damn thing falling in around their ears they stuck. It was their factory. They kept it. And when that SP pulled up and practically stuck the muzzle into a window, Chase and Jasnosz manning a bazooka fought it off, forced it to withdraw. You remembered the litter cases and the walking wounded that came back from that factory and some men who refused to be evacuated until they had been hit two or three times. Yeah, and Van Orman died there. It was a helluva price to pay for a factory, but with the factory you got a town.

There was the railroad. Right down there to the right was the plate factory. You remember the night you spent there. Over in the next building Kirbie had mowed down the crew of that SP early the next morning. Cap'n Whitney had run down that same railroad armed only with a map board and came back with a dozen Heinies. The big white house was down that way too. Remember, the one Short went over to take that night. Yeah, he finally had to pull back, but not without raising plenty of hell and leaving dead Jerries lying around.

There was the house used as a CP, clearing station, and DP for chow and

Shell fire always managed to find our communication lines.

water. You remembered how Laird used to come up every night with his carrying parties loaded with chow and water, panting from the exertion. You paid tribute to those men performing an obscure service. It was a job well done. You remembered the night they brought up fried chicken, mail, and *Stars and Stripes* and you saw the dirty, bearded, tired, strained faces around you light up again. Just a brief interlude in all the sordid business but it meant a helluva lot. You remembered the night Bricker came up to that house—just back from a rest camp, and you thought what a thing it was for a guy to come back to, but you were glad to see him. It gave you new confidence, and you shared a feeling with the rest of the guys in the platoon. A feeling that Ol' Brick was back, everything would be okay.

Yeah, and there was the house where the CO died; and you wondered why it had to be Lieutenant Weed; and you wondered about Mrs. Weed and the anticipated heir; and you realized again that it had been your privilege to soldier with real men, some of the best that had ever fought and died.

There was the big house—the first one you took that night of the attack. The house where Mielke died. Struck down as you spoke to him in a low whisper. Your face only inches from his. Soft-spoken, dependable Mielke—liked by everybody. Why him? You kept asking yourself that question time after time as other men died, and you decided that the forces of death were no respecters of persons, rank, creeds, or colors; and besides that, you decided that a doughfoot wasn't supposed to be able to figure out why. But you didn't like it.

Now you turned right along the river until you reached the bridge. It was a Bailey bridge now, constructed by our engineers. You remembered crossing the damaged original the night of the jump-off. It had been a real night attack in true Timberwolf style and it had paid dividends.

The colonel and CO had told you what to do before the jump-off. It sounded easy down at the battalion CP. "Within thirty minutes after you crossed the

186

bridge you'd have that factory buttoned up." It had taken considerably longer but what remained of that factory was finally buttoned up.

You were back across the river now. You were in Inden. You were back with the rear echelons, the CP's, the kitchens. Where in the hell were the guides to lead you to your billets? You and the rest of that weary column cussed the first sergeant for his inefficiency. The guides were found and they led you to the shell-damaged building you were to occupy. There was hot chow. The supply sergeant had cigarettes and blankets! There were plenty blankets. Yeah, lotta guys hadn't come back to use theirs.

You didn't realize it then but you had played a major role in crushing the German military might. Your activities had been duplicated along the length of the Roer by other Timberwolf units and by other outfits.

Not until you had crossed the Roer and were well on your way to Cologne were you to know what work you had wrought. Then Jaffe was to read to you from an old copy of a German newspaper the anguished cry of the Nazi hierarchy for a new resistance which would avenge the tremendous slaughter inflicted upon the ranks of the "Nazi Supermen" in the engagements from the Inde to the Roer.

But for the present you were content with the knowledge that you were getting a rest, hot chow three times a day every day for a few days and maybe even a shower and clean clothes. For the next few nights at least you could look forward to the luxury of a nice dry floor to sleep on.

Had you been capable of high resolve at that time you might have remembered those who did not come back to this rest; and for those whose lives had been terminated yet unfulfilled, you might have resolved to make, in the fulfillment of your own, a project worthy of their approval, in order that they should not have died in vain.

The 104th Infantry Division, now known throughout the Western Front as the fighting Timberwolves, had successfully completed its drive to the Roer River. The gallant fighting infantrymen of the 413th, 414th and 415th Infantry Regiments, with the indomitable support of the Division artillery, the hard-hitting 750th Tank Battalion and 692d Tank Destroyer Battalion, put the Division in its commanding position on the Roer. The close support by our engineers, who worked unceasingly to clear obstacles and to construct vital bridges across the Inde, coupled with the untiring efforts of the 329th Medical Battalion, contributed much. The 555th AAA AW Battalion (Mobile) had not only protected our troops from enemy air attacks, but had also supported many of the operations by placing its deadly .50-caliber machine guns and 40mm guns against enemy strongpoints. The 104th Reconnaissance Troop skillfully maintained contact with units outside the Division zone and blocked in position in order to free infantrymen for the continued advance. Communications were constantly maintained between Division Headquarters and lower units by Captain Schwartz's Quartermaster Company, and Captain Smith's 804th Ordnance Company kept the supplies of food, ammunition and clothing rolling to the

Award of Distinguished Service Cross. By direction of the President, under the provisions of AR 600-45, 22 September 1943, as amended, and under authority contained in Circular No. 32, Headquarters European Theater of Operations, United States Army, 20 March 1944, as amended, the Distinguished Service Cross is awarded to:

First Lieutenant JOHN OLSEN (Army Serial No. 01289308), Infantry, 415th Infantry Regiment, United States Army, for extraordinary heroism in action against the enemy in Germany on 2 and 3 December 1944. On the night of 2-3 December 1944 the company which Lieutenant OLSEN commanded was given the mission of assaulting and capturing a strongly defended town. Shortly after launching the attack, Lieutenant OLSEN's company was pinned to the ground by extremely heavy machine gun fire. Realizing the need for prompt action in maintaining the impetus of the attack, Lieutenant OLSEN, with complete disregard for his personal safety, ran to the head of his company, completely exposing himself to the heavy enemy fire, to shout encouragement to his men and lead the advance. Inspired by the bravery of their leader, the men of the company rose to their feet and followed him up the hill and into the outskirts of the town, advancing against heavy enemy fire. Lieutenant OLSEN then reorganized the company and, at great risk to his life, constantly exposed himself to enemy fire in leading his men in clearing the town. In this operation Lieutenant OLSEN was seriously wounded, but he continued to lead the advance until his company had gained a firm foothold in the town. Lieutenant OLSEN's courage, tenacity of purpose, and inspiring leadership, above and beyond the ordinary call of duty, is in keeping with the finest traditions of the military service and reflect the highest credit on himself and the armed forces of the United States. Entered military service from N. Y.

The welcome trek back off the line

front. The teamwork and the determination to win of all Division and attached units was outstanding.

Lieutenant General J. Lawton Collins, commander of the VII Corps, commended the Division for its heroic action by a letter dated 26 December 1944:

Major General Terry Allen
Commanding, 104th Infantry Division
APO #104, United States Army

Dear Terry:

I am taking advantage of the first lull in our current fighting to acknowledge receipt of your fine letter, and to express to you and the officers and men of the 104th Infantry Division my admiration and keen appreciation of the magnificent work you did for the VII Corps during our recent campaign.

The mission of seizing the great industrial area Eschweiler-Weisweiler-Stolberg, which was assigned to the 104th Division in the first phase of our operations, was a difficult nasty task. The Division cleared this important area in much shorter time than I had expected and with the minimum of loss. The speed with which this was accomplished is a tribute to the leadership, dash and sound training of the Division.

The second phase involving the crossing of the Inde River and the advance to the Roer was even more difficult, but with characteristic skill and dash, in a series of brilliant night attacks, the 104th Division forced a crossing of the Inde and in a few days had cleared its entire sector to the Roer River. I regard the operation which involved the seizure of Lamersdorf-Inden-Lucherberg as one of

189

the finest single pieces of work accomplished by any unit of the VII Corps since D-day.

During the entire time that the 104th Division was under my command, I and my staff were tremendously impressed with the cooperative spirit and exceptional fighting ability of the officers and men of all ranks. We regard the Timberwolf Division as one of the finest assault divisions we have ever had in this Corps. I only hope that you will rejoin us before long for the advance to the Rhine. Meanwhile, please convey to your officers and men my warmest greetings and best wishes for 1945.

> (Sgd.) Joe Collins
> J. LAWTON COLLINS
> Major General, U. S. Army

TO: All Timberwolves and All Attached Units.

The above letter was received by this Division. Your devotion to duty and true combat discipline have earned this latest commendation for your battle accomplishments. My personal congratulations to you all.

There will be other rivers to cross and more objectives to take before final victory is attained. Our standards of discipline, training and physical toughness must be maintained. We must *all* be imbued with the fighting spirit of our Division and an intensive belief in our units. NOTHING IN HELL MUST STOP THE TIMBERWOLVES.

My warmest greetings and best wishes to you all for the New Year:

> s/   TERRY ALLEN

STOLBERG

V

OBJECTIVE: COLOGNE

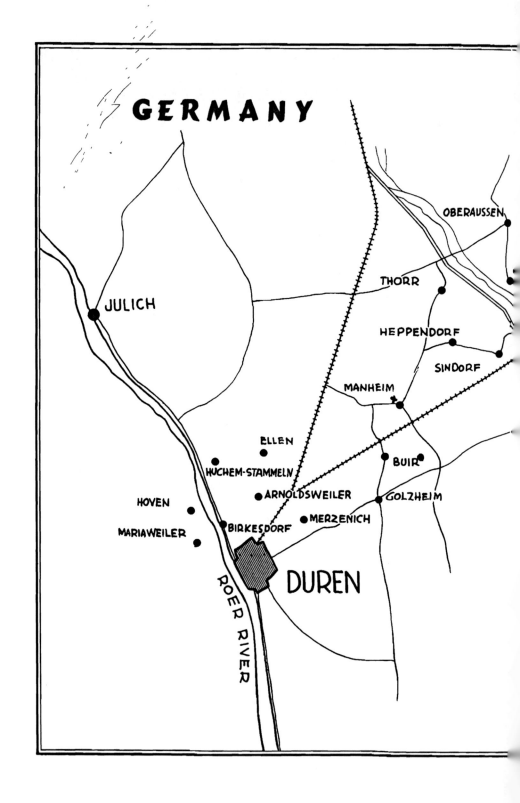

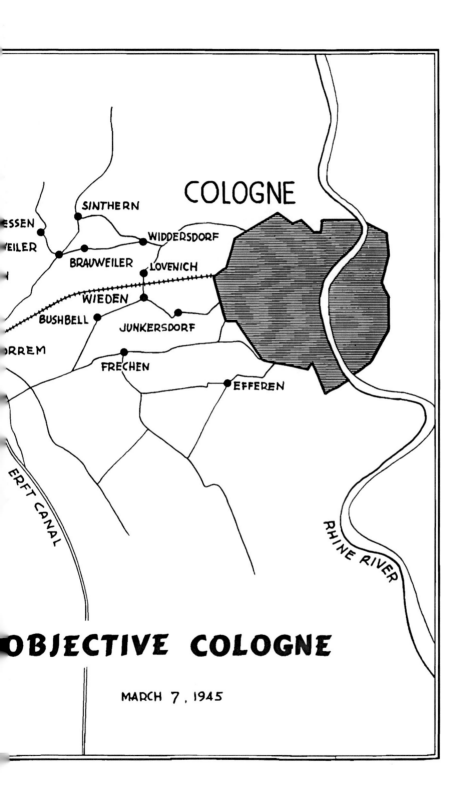

COLOGNE

SINTHERN

WIDDERSDORF

ESSEN

WEILER

BRAUWEILER

LOVENICH

WIEDEN

BUSHBELL

JUNKERSDORF

ORREM

FRECHEN

EFFEREN

ERFT CANAL

RHINE RIVER

OBJECTIVE COLOGNE

MARCH 7, 1945

A famous war correspondent once remarked that in all his exhausting travels through war torn Europe, he had probably seen enough unusual signs representing units' command posts, fire direction centers, main supply routes and airstrips to compile a history of the war using a collection of just such signposts. He also made note of the fact that while many of these direction finders were cryptically unimaginative, no matter where he went in the First Army zone of Advance, one sign always stood out from all the rest—"Timberwolf Up!"

The birth of the Division signpost took place shortly after the move from the battlefields of Holland into Deutschland. The creation, attributed to the 104th Signal Company, came at a very opportune time. The result was a trail of "Timberwolf Up's" hundreds of miles long that are as definite a part of our achievements as the doughboy trudging many miles of scorched earth. Years from now, should anyone be interested enough to make an investigation, some lone tree or backyard fence will undoubtedly still bear mute testimony of the tide that swept across Germany like a whirlwind. As one GI put it, "when the smoke of battle cleared away and we look around to find out who was on top, the 104th always found the situation to be—TIMBERWOLF UP!!"

ON THE ROER

ON 12 December, during the final hours of the drive to the Roer River, Lieutenant General J. Lawton Collins, Commanding General of the VII Corps, in conference with the Division commander and Division G-3, outlined the Corps plan for the crossing of the Roer. Therefore, as soon as the Division had seized the west banks of the Roer on 14 December, active reconnaissance by infantry patrols and the 329th Engineer Battalion reconnaissance sections went on along the banks of the river to determine the most suitable crossing sites. On the night of 15 December the first patrol, led by Staff Sergeant John D. Rindfleish and Staff Sergeant Felix J. Weingart, both of Company B, 415th Infantry, crossed the Roer River at the site of the Autobahn bridge and returned with information pertaining to the enemy's activities without having been fired on.

Continuous enemy artillery and sporadic mortar fire was falling on all the towns immediately west of the river on 15, 16, and 17 December. During the night of 16-17 December, active aerial operations were conducted by the enemy throughout the Division zone. Two enemy JU 52's were shot down by the accurate guns of the 555th AAA (AW) Battalion. This aerial operation was in conjunction with the strong German offensive which had been launched the morning of 16 December in the sector to the south of the 104th Division—the Battle of the Ardennes or "The Bulge." On 17 December, it became increasingly apparent that this action to the south was an offensive of great magnitude. The situation began to have a distinct effect on the actions of the VII Corps, and greatly influenced the activities of the Division from 17 December to the middle of February.

The crossings of the Roer became an operation for the distant rather than the immediate future. The Division was directed to prepare an all-out defense of its sector and was given responsibilities of an enlarged area. Between the 17th and 24th of December, the Division relieved the 9th Infantry Division on its immediate right and elements of the 83d Infantry Division opposite Duren, while on the north elements of the 29th Infantry Division relieved our troops at Schophoven, Pier and Inden. The defensive area of the Division throughout December, January and most of February included the 16,000-yard front along the Roer from Merken to south of Duren.

Enemy air continued active the 17th, 18th, 19th, and 20th of December. Vigorous patrolling was conducted by all units in the Division to locate enemy parachutists who had landed in its sector during this period. It was difficult to locate the troopers in the cold black night, but each morning the units thoroughly searched every building, haystack and crevice in its sector, and twenty-one parachutists were captured.

Reports came from the south that German troops were using American uniforms and equipment. Checkpoints were set up along all important arteries to stop and interrogate the occupants of each vehicle. There was much tenseness all along the line and each unit held alerted mobile reserves for quick deployment against parachutists and any attempted breakthrough in our lines. It had now been determined that the German offensive in the Ardennes was directed at the great Allied supply center of Liege, and that Hitler wanted to present the people of Germany the recapture of Aachen as a Christmas gift. Aachen was sixteen miles to our rear.

From left to right the Division had on the line the 415th Infantry with one battalion up and two battalions back, one of which constituted a mobile Division reserve; the 413th and the 414th Infantry Regiments, each with two battalions up and one battalion back. All units organized their sectors with all-around defense including wire, mines, booby-traps, prepared demolitions and road blocks. The 329th Engineers, with each combat company in direct support of its respective combat team, put in a solid belt of antitank mines across the Division sector, and prepared each bridge and overpass for demolition. All positions were well dug-in, wired and camouflaged. Constant improvement of the defensive positions continued throughout the period until the 7th of February. Over 28,000 mines, most of which were booby-trapped, had been emplaced, over seventy-five miles of wire entanglements had been strung, and each gun emplacement was dug-in and camouflaged. The defense was in great depth and had the enemy struck in force the Division was confident it could repel it. Strong German patrols of twenty and fifty man strength probed our front lines each night between 16 and 27 December and in each instance were quickly repulsed by the devastating fire of our artillery, mortars, and machine guns. Movement on the north-south route through Duren, east of the Roer, was constant and heavy each night. This revealed either a build-up, a possible attack in our sector, or a continuous movement of supplies to the "Bulge."

It was determined that the latter deduction was correct. On 21 December, the 750th Tank Battalion, which had fought so valiantly with the Division during its drive to the Roer River, was assembled and detached from the Division at midnight. It was later moved to the south and engaged in the Battle of the Ardennes. At midnight that same night, the Division was released from the VII Corps and was attached to the XIX Corps. The VII Corps was soon to direct the actions of several divisions in the Battle of the Bulge.

If Hitler was to fulfill his promise to the German people, he would have to drive through the 104th Division to get Aachen. On Christmas day he had not kept his promise and the Timberwolves remained on the alert, prepared to thwart any effort. The attack never materialized, as the Division constantly dominated the Roer River, repulsing any attempts of the Nazis to penetrate our lines while the Timberwolves were actively patrolling east of the river.

On 24 December, Task Force Lion, under the command of Colonel B. R. DeGraff, the Division Chief of Staff, was organized to defend the city of Eschweiler, and the Division left and right rear flanks. The troops comprised the 1115th Engineer Group, and all Corps and Division troops located within Eschweiler. Service companies, maintenance companies, quartermaster elements and all types of rear echelon troops were rallied into fighting units within the Task Force. Major William T. Gordon, as Task Force S-3, coordinated all the work and operations of the eighteen units comprising the force.

Further to the rear, the 104th Division rear echelon, with all personnel sections of the units attached under Lieutenant Colonel Marvin E. Kernan, established all-around defenses in the vicinity of Brand, and it was prepared to assume the offensive to destroy all paratroopers or saboteurs within the area. Bandsmen, clerks, cooks, service troops—as a matter of fact, everyone who was a member of the Division or units attached to it was prepared to stand to the last man against any assault of our positions.

At the time, the 104th Division projected the farthest east into Germany. If the German offensive in the Battle of the Ardennes proved to be successful, it might have meant that the Division would be cut off from its vital supplies. Realizing this possibility, higher headquarters directed the Division to prepare plans to organize and construct defensive positions west of the Roer. The first position was the line running through Putzlohn, Eschweiler and Volkenrath, the second position ran along the line Verlandeheide, Brand and Buschbach. On 29 December, Field Order 16 was issued by the Division directing the units to stake out the positions and prepare to withdraw on Corps order to these new defensive positions. The field order further directed Brigadier General Bryant E. Moore to organize a covering force consisting of approximately one-third of the Division to be prepared to hold the enemy east of the Roer and protect the withdrawal of the Division. Reconnaissance was immediately initiated, and troops from each battalion went back daily to the tentative rear defense positions to prepare

The banks of the Roer remained snow covered for two long months.

them for occupation. Throughout the period from 30 December to 7 February, constant improvement and strengthening of the positions went on by all units. It was difficult for many to understand why this action was necessary, but with the initial pessimistic reports from the Ardennes fight, it soon became evident to all men that no chances should be taken. It was comforting to know that we had not only perfected impregnable defenses along the Roer but that our defenses were in the great depth of sixteen miles to the rear. The Timberwolves were prepared for any eventuality, knowing full well that it was in a position to hold its hard-earned sixty square miles of German soil gained in its drive to the Roer River.

Thanksgiving . . . Christmas . . . New Year's . . . fesitve occasions close to the heart and dear to the memory of every fighting man. For the average Timberwolf on line, each was just another day of fighting, waiting, and hoping. Still, despite war and all its travail, GI ingenuity and sentiment would not allow these days to pass unnoticed.

Quartermaster Sergeant Raymond C. Gremli tells us that "Thanksgiving was celebrated with 'Herr' Talbot's best linen and china, and of course the culinary department helped out by cooking a super dinner. We dined by candlelight, and it started out to be amusing, but that

198

night the thoughts of every man were thousands of miles away. We silently prayed that the next Thanksgiving would find us with our loved ones, but no one would admit to being homesick and we gruffly concealed our emotions."

December 24th found the Roer River front a suitable environment for Bing Crosby's "White Christmas." . . . And come to think of it, we all didn't go musicless during this usually joyous feast day. Corporal Ralph E. Dippel of 414th's Cannon Company recalls how "a very cold Christmas Eve rolled around, finding the boys of the 2d Platoon sitting up all night in their dugouts. In the hut of Sergeant Bocchino, Corporal Nelson, Pfcs. Witanek and Smasal, the night was spent talking of home, girl friends and of the future. Pfc. Delheimer suggested light- ing a candle in celebration of Christmas, and McGinley's very good cooking of the C-ration, greens, etc., helped out. The only touch of Christmas for the boys on duty at the guns perhaps was the music that came over their phones. Pfc. Bickerstaff remembers listening to 'Silent Night,' a German version, which was being piped to the gun positions from Cannon Company's switchboard. Corporal Baily and Pfc. Herch- berg had access to a radio there and regularly relayed radio programs through our switchboard to the boys at the guns. The music helped, but afterward we all wondered if it didn't actually make us feel worse. Thoughts were thousands of miles away as Jerry burp guns sacri- legiously broke the stillness of the holy night."

Regimental Chaplains Murray and Jackson, 414th Infantry, recall hazardous jeep trips to and from units on line bringing the cheer and sanctity that only a Christmas service can instill into the heart of a battle-weary GI. It was definitely a busy season for chaplains. When they hit I and L Companies in Birgel, they found a scene hardly indica- tive of front-line combat, only 300 yards from enemy terrain. Search- ing deserted German homes, the ingenious doughboys had brought forth large numbers of brightly colored ornaments, and each squad outpost boasted a Christmas tree done up in the finest Yuletide fashion.

Most front-line rifle units poke good-natured fun at other outfits behind them, calling them rear echelon groups. Actually, however, each rifle company has a forward echelon, which consists of its fighting doughs, and a rear echelon made up of its service, maintenance, and mess personnel. To show how a member of each of these combat echelons spent Christmas, 1944, we have the commentaries of Corporal Hotchkiss, a cook with B Company, 413th Infantry, and Pfc. Dan L. McLoone, a doughboy with the 415th's 1st Battalion antitank platoon.

Corporal Hotchkiss recounts:

I was a cook in Baker Kitchen of Dagger Red (Company B, 413th Infantry).
Our battalion train was in Langerwehe, between Weisweiler and Duren. Like
most other nights during the long months in combat, on Christmas Eve I spent
most of the night working on food for the following day. The windows of our
small work-room were blacked out with rugs and linoleum, and the heat from
the three field ranges was terrific. Smoke from the diesel oil we were burning
in glass-chimneyed lamps kept the air murky.

Carl and I had been thankful when we had drawn the rations for Christmas
dinner. There were turkeys, cranberries, mincemeat for pies, and all, or almost
all of the traditional foods with which the festive tables of the United States
are loaded on Christmas. Carl (Sergeant Carl J. Ellingson) and Tony (Sergeant
Anton Gruber) and I would give the men of B Company a Christmas such as
their wives and mothers would have liked to prepare for them if it took us
every minute of the time until it must be served, almost twenty-four hours later.
We were proud of our little part of the war that night, and we put every bit of
our effort and skill into the preparation of that meal. Nothing was too good
for those men of that rifle company on line, and we would give them our best.

As the night wore on, fatigue and the terrific heat dulled us. Although the
guard in the doorway said the town was shelled a little during the night and
there was a continual patrol by German reconnaissance planes, I do not remember much except working all night on that dinner, which must be perfect.

As I became sleepy I began to think dreamily about home, and about the
touching beauty of Christmas among my family. I remembered that they must
be having a rare thrill preparing surprises for my red-headed four-year-old
brother. Every man on the line must have had somewhat the same sort of lone-
some thoughts that night.

Sentiment in me swelled the next afternoon to see men luxuriate in the glow
of the party B Company held in a windowless little Gaststube in Mariaweiler.
We had china and glassware and white table linen. There was a piano, and
someone brought a guitar. The men even sang, and someone began to pick out
carols on a chime-like zither he had discovered in the village. Although shells
whistled into the neighborhood all through the afternoon, and two B Company
men became casualties during the serving of Christmas dinner, somehow our
minds broke through the tragedy and destruction around us, and we felt some
of the warmth and fellowship of the Christmas Spirit.

From his defensive position on the Roer, Pfc. McLoone remembers:

"Silent night, holy night, all is calm, all is bright"—you follow in English
the familiar hymn that the Germans are singing on the opposite bank of the
Roer River. You are on guard in a foxhole a few hundred muddy yards from
the river and a thousand dark, barren yards from your "home." This is Christmas Eve, 1944 style. And though you know Christmas and war do not mix
and that your every thought should be of your duty, you cannot help but think
of all those happy Christmas Eves of the past. It seems ironic that your musical
background for these memories should be German.

You are relieved from guard and start to stumble toward "your town." It
makes a striking contrast to your home town. It is hard to believe that there
can be such a town tonight—with holly wreaths in frosted unbroken windows—

Heating bombed out buildings was always something of a problem.

with a church bell that rings from an undamaged steeple—with lights that shine bright from a house with no holes in it.

Your feet turn and twist on pieces of "homes" as you grope for the hole that leads to your cellar, when the route should be lighted by Christmas trees. You are stopped by a guard who should be a Santa Claus on a street corner. You hit the ground as you hear shells coming your way when you should be hitting a carpeted floor playing with the toys you bought for the kids.

You enter the cellar which is decorated with ornaments "liberated" from other houses—and your backyard is decorated too—with well shot rabbits and well chased chickens. They will be tomorrow's dinner. The candlelight throws peaceful shadows on the small and properly erected crib that you found upstairs. There is nothing special about going to bed this Christmas Eve—your rifle is still by your side and your helmet is still by your head.

And there is nothing special about awakening the next morning—your first question is still about war until you realize that this is Christmas and you lie your head back on the floor and dream.

Later, religious services are held in a shell-torn church that was a battleground not long ago. You marvel, as you enter through what you think must have been the doorway, at the large, beautiful crucifix that still remains in place, defying man to ignore God. Organ music for the service is furnished by the German mortar shells.

On returning "home," you find that the boys have cooked the dinner—they have a large table completely set with dishes and silverware borrowed from the neighbors, and a clean white linen tablecloth. There is a solemn moment as everyone bows his head and listens as grace is being said in a sincere tone by one of the more eloquent lads. You are thanking God for the food and for being alive to enjoy it. The Amen is the chow whistle and hands begin to fly. The baked rabbit and roast chicken would tempt the most particular taste. Yes, a GI can celebrate Christmas anywhere.

Sergeants Capone and Gifford remember Christmas Eve, 1944, pretty well too, but for a different reason. That night, Recon made its very successful patrol across the Roer, bringing back a few Jerries to decorate the Lendersdorf Christmas trees. Sergeant Gifford said:

Several times we made trips to the OP. We were going into Lieutenant O'Gara's plan, which was a good one, and each man knew how he fitted in—when the time came—but when would that be?

The morning of the 24th was no different from any other day, though on the ground there was more snow, which had fallen during the night. It looked ripe. That night we would go across.

Snowcapes, ammunition, more plans, aerial photos, sketches in the snow, last-minute instructions and nervous kidding of each other. "Don't forget to have plenty of good hot coffee for us when we get back." "Good luck." "Thanks, we'll need it."

Sergeant Capone recalled:

H-hour was set at 2000. Three minutes of artillery fire boxed in the area of our objective—then we took off. First, the covering force, with Corporal James Capone in charge, ran down to the railroad embankment bordering the river and got into position. Then the patrols, with Lieutenant O'Gara in charge of the first and Sergeant Loyd Hahn with the second, followed.

Passing through the covering force, over the railroad tracks, an agonizing stretch of seventy-five yards to the river's bank, in we went. It was cold and slippery going over the slimy rocks. Then the barbed wire on the Heinie side slowed us up. Once across we hit the trenches. During our crossing, heavy stuff was being thrown at the dug-in position. Now the trenches.

Bob Bryant and Dean Gilchrist were first in, and rounding a turn they saw two German soldiers who had been taking cover from the artillery but were now attempting to man their machine gun that covered the ground the patrol was working. Pfc. Bryant and Corporal Gilchrist "persuaded" the Krauts to surrender.

At this moment Pfcs. Holsinger and Andeway dropped into another trench. As Holsinger was on the firing step, a Heinie rose from the hole, but Holsinger fired first and sent him on his way to Kraut heaven, should there be such a place.

Lieutenant O'Gara and Sergeant Simmons captured another in a trench in their area. He had been wounded by our artillery and had to be carried back to our lines by Spence and Cantrel at great risk to themselves.

The prisoners were hustled back by other members of the patrol as Corporal Gifford, Corporal Rodriguez, and Pfc. Osborn covered their withdrawal.

Timberwolves will always remember the eve of 31 December 1944 as the only New Year's Eve that resembled a Fourth of July. Robert Lieberman, Headquarters Battery, 385th Field Artillery Battalion, has this to say:

About 1800, orders came down through battalion that several extra OPs would be manned throughout the night. We were waiting for the Jerries to pull something and we wanted to be ready.

Three men out of Liaison Section, attached to the 1st Battalion, 414th Infantry, Sanf, Rhubarb, and myself (Corporal LeGore, Sergeant Powell, Corporal Lieberman) were to remain all night in the attic of a paper factory near Baker Company, which overlooked the Roer River, 300 yards away.

The night was cold and clear; it wasn't windy, but it was the sort of a night, mixed with uneasiness, that chilled a person to the bone. About 2030, we heard the dull clack of our taped-up phone bell and we were told that the artillery was preparing an 0600 "Happy New Year" shoot, and at midnight every infantryman on the line was to fire his weapon for five minutes.

We thought that would be something to hear. The hours crept slowly by, and as each passed, we huddled together to preserve our body heat. That didn't help much, and as midnight approached, we were cautiously peering out of our OP windows, watching the ghostly figures of the relieved outpost coming in for a sorely needed rest.

Exactly at midnight, a .50-cal. machine gun began its rhythmic pounding. Taking that as a signal, the whole section opened up at once. We listened and watched the spectacle . . . the healthy banging of numerous M-1's, the lighter pinging of the carbines, the fast blast of our 30's and the intermittent burp of a captured machine pistol. For five minutes the air above the Roer was alive with hot steel.

The Heinies must have expected an attack, because it wasn't long before their calling cards came at us—60's, 80's and 120's.

At 0600 our artillery shoot came in, and were they hopping over there. After that, we had the satisfaction that it may not have been the best New Year, but it sure as blazes was the noisiest.

TRTC

In combat it was soon learned that the reinforcements received by the Division needed additional training from veteran combat officers and sergeants. During the defensive operation, the Division was in a position to give this training. The Division commander directed G-3 to organize the Timberwolf Reinforcement Training Center in order that each reinforcement could receive two weeks' training under combat conditions before entering the front lines. Lieutenant Colonel Edward G. Rager, Major William T. Gordon and Captain Peter H. Nicholas renovated a German barracks in Eschweiler, and on 22 January the first reinforcements began their battle school. The training courses included instruction in weapons, night attacks, and scouting and patrolling. After the two-week "blitz" course given by combat-wise veterans, the first class of over 200 men graduated. The Division continued to maintain the TRTC, graduating its last class in Halle, Germany, in June, 1945, the last of more than 3,000 men to have received this invaluable training.

On 1 February 1945, the *Stars and Stripes* released the following story:

BATTLE-WISE IN 104TH TRAIN GREENHORNS

Reinforcements of this Division will have a much better chance of surviving the coming battles with the Germans because battle-wise veterans are now giving these green men two weeks of intensive training which admittedly is badly needed.

The course is not an innovation because the Timberwolves' CG, Maj. Gen. Terry Allen, used it in North Africa, and some other divisions are also giving reinforcements such training.

Other divisions, however, are throwing new boys right into the line. This latter practice is inevitable when a division is engaged but it would seem inexcusable not to give reinforcements special training when they arrive at a division temporarily inactive. If green men are not given extra training it simply means some little mistake made in battle which could be avoided by a course like the 104th's.

Reinforcements know this and they are all eager to learn every possible battle trick.

Capt. Peter H. Nicholas of Syosset, Long Island, is one of the experienced officers running the training camp. He says, "The men are keen as hell to learn and cuss themselves out for not having learned more in the States. Of course, now it's a matter of their lives."

Lt. Col. Edward Rager of Seward, Pa., school commander, stated that the training emphasized the use of weapons from rifles to machine guns, mortars, night attack, street fighting, patrolling, map reading, and compass work.

T/5 Wayne Morris of Duluth, Minn., has been in the army since 1942 and overseas since last May but "It's a long time since I had any infantry training and I've just about forgotten what I did have. This course is a damned good idea."

Pvt. Jacob Matura of Meriden, Conn., and Leslie Christensen left the States in January after 17 weeks' basic training but they want everything they can get in the way of training. Christensen says, "There's plenty a battle-wise guy can teach you which you don't get from books."

T/4 Francis Rego of Somerville, Mass., says, "I just finished the first weeks of basic and I sure need this training. Until a short time ago I cooked, and I never expected to be a combat infantryman, which means the training I had a long time ago is pretty hazy."

Each group entering the course is welcomed by Allen, who has made an immediate hit with every man. Allen takes the utmost interest in the welfare of his men. One of the reasons the 104th has an excellent record is that slogan from early training, "Get smart and get tough." These are not idle words but are carried out, as this reinforcement training testifies.

The seventy days and nights following the capture of ancient Mullenark Castle, until the Division resumed the offensive on 23 February 1945, were filled with historic events on the Western Front. A hard winter had set in with bitter cold and driving rains, sleet, fog and snow. The time marked the beginning and end of the last all-out effort by the Germans in the Ardennes and included our first Christmas away from the United States and ushered in a New Year. Moreover, the period meant a real test of the Division's ability to secure intelligence through ground patrols under the most adverse conditions.

In the seventy days, sixty-three patrols crossed the eighty-foot wide, swollen Roer River, which at times reached a depth of twelve feet and 325 feet in width. The heroic action of the patrols resulted in several enemy being taken prisoner and returned to our lines for interrogation, at a cost to the Germans of twenty to thirty killed in hand-to-hand combat. Our patrols suffered thirteen wounded, all of whom were evacuated. Two men were reported missing after their rubber boat had capsized in the flooded river. This was the effort and cost that made our knowledge of the enemy across the Roer River so remarkably accurate. It was the bold and daring yet cautious manner in which our front-line officers and men planned and executed their patrolling that dominated the Roer River region. Through their findings we learned the exact location of the enemy's wire barriers, minefields, and entrenchments. Prior to the forcing of the Roer on 23 February, the identification and disposition of enemy troops had been accurately determined.

It was just three days before our jump-off across the Roer when one of our patrols came back with information that led us to believe that a/ complete reorganization, which possibly involved a complete new division, was about to take place in the German line to our front. The following night a deserter from central Germany crossed the swollen river to surrender. Captain William Stelling, chief interrogator, worked hard the next few hours to bring out some bits of information from the prisoner that would shed light on the latest disposition of German troops. Time was running out and the prisoner insisted that he came through the Roer River lines so fast that he didn't have time to talk to

Award of Distinguished Service Cross. By direction of the President, under the provisions of AR 600-45, 22 September 1943, as amended, and under authority contained in Circular No. 32, Headquarters European Theater of Operations, United States Army, 20 March 1944, as amended, the Distinguished Service Cross is awarded to:

First Lieutenant PERRY O. TESTER, JR., 01317703, 413th Infantry, United States Army, for extraordinary heroism in action against the enemy from 28 to 30 November 1944, in Germany. When four enemy machine guns opened fire upon his platoon, First Lieutenant TESTER, throwing hand grenades and firing his carbine, advanced far forward of his men in an assault which resulted in the complete destruction of the weapons and crews in vicious close-in fighting. While his company withdrew to reorganize for a continuation of the attack, he remained behind, and in the face of intense fire carried a wounded soldier 1000 yards to an aid station. Leading another assault two days later, First Lieutenant TESTER was severely wounded by a shell fragment. Administering medical aid to himself, First Lieutenant TESTER, despite his pains, continued to lead his platoon in the attack until he was again hit by artillery fire and mortally wounded. Entered military service from Indiana.

his fellow comrades. The phone rang in the G-2 Section—it was 2200—Captain Stelling had a plan. He continued with his story of how the prisoner wanted to help us. The prisoner would recross the turbulent river that night, sneak into the German lines, and simply ask the outpost guards what unit was in that area. That seemed simple, actually too simple. Was it a ruse? We didn't think so. The man seemed pretty earnest in his desire to help us.

By midnight preparations were completed and Lieutenant Burleigh Sheppard, Engineer Battalion, with the help of six of his fellow engineers, took the prisoner back to the German side of the river. At 0300 the prisoner, according to plan, swam back to our side with complete information. He had checked in with three German outposts and had confirmed the fact that a new division had recently gone into position to our front. In addition to this information, he gave us the identification of the new division and its boundaries. Later, all of the information was found to be incredibly accurate.

This incident of course is an oddity among the many methods used to gather enemy information. Most information was gathered through the efforts of our own foot patrols. Their careful planning, excellent leadership, and courageous aggressiveness is borne out by the eye-witness accounts of some of the patrols related in these pages.

ROER PATROL
By PFC. ED BAYLESS, Company F, 414th Infantry

A group of American doughboys stealthily move through highly defended enemy positions. Their mission: to capture a German outpost guard who can supply the key to the German network of defenses; defenses which have impeded American progress for more than a month. Success in this venture means an American crossing of the now partly frozen Roer with a minimum loss of life and time. Theirs is truly a difficult and important mission.

What of these men upon whose success so much depends? What are their chances against the ostensibly great odds? Are they prepared for the hazards that lie ahead? What are their reactions—what is going on in their minds as they move forward?

The time is four hours earlier, about 1700 the same day. These same seven are huddled around a table covered with maps and aerial photos of the region their patrol will cover that night. The landmarks and possible routes are carefully pointed out so that they will know beforehand where to expect the most opposition, where the easiest and safest places to cross the river are, where the most vulnerable parts of the enemy's fortress-like position are, and all the other vital components of the most essential part of any military move—the orientation. For without this vital pre-analysis, it would be sheer suicide to attempt any patrol; but since such briefing is a most integral part of our Army's strategy, these men are doubly protected.

The platoon leader, Lieutenant Francis Melary, is carefully explaining to his men of F Company, 414th Infantry, every phase the patrol will cover in its endeavor later that evening. He answers the questions which the men eagerly pour forth: the probable size of any opposition that may be encountered,. the quickest and safest routes of withdrawal, the length of time they will be furnished protective artillery, and the choice of weapons, clothing, route, time, and tactics which would govern their actions. And the seven crowd still closer together, as they realize they must cooperate entirely, for the safety of each member and the success of the venture depend upon the experience, alertness, and teamwork of the seven individuals.

As the men look at one another, they are reassured. For every man has been especially chosen for a particular task. In a mission of this sort, each must be trusting of the other's ability, for psychology plays a major part in such endeavors. The deliberate choice of each man is a silent commendation by the leader.

The patrol consists of Technical Sergeant Tom Kendrew, who will lead the men across the river. He is particularly suited for the job because of his proven leadership during previous engagements. Also a highly capable leader is Staff Sergeant Wayne Kirby, the second in command, who has also seen much service as a combat leader and will prove invaluable should anything befall Kendrew. Then there is Pfc. Slim Thompson, who because of a previous patrol through the same sector will prove highly valuable as a guide. The three covering men who can double as getaway men are Pfcs. Jack Jones, Mike Kozak, and Daryl Lutes. They are highly dependable battle veterans. The seventh man is Pfc. Herb Stein, whose knowledge of the German language should prove an invaluable asset in dealing with the enemy. So the patrol is now well prepared in orientation, and is very ably manned with men capable of shouldering the responsibility which each one's mission will entail.

The time for the patrol has been well chosen—a moonless night which will eliminate the danger of possible detection by moving shadows. However it is light enough to insure complete visual contact and there will be no talking; all signals by motion, another safeguard against detection. The choice of weapons is also commendable; since only close contact is anticipated, each member of the patrol is armed with a "grease" gun and four or five hand grenades for flushing foxholes. Lutes carries a carbine. Now the size of the patrol is such that contact can be insured and swiftness is the theme. The formation is also purposeful, with the leader, interpreter, and guide to the front, the assistant leader and one of the cover men in the center for control and cover, and the other two cover men to the rear. The platoon leader and the runner (Ed Bayless) are at the point of departure, equipped with telephone to control the artillery and fire of the rest of the platoon, and dispatch the patrol quickly. It is the duty of the remaining members of the platoon to use their weapons—rifles, BARs, and machine guns—to the best advantage by countering any fire the Germans bring to bear. Now everything is ready for commencing the task. Every detail has been well taken care of so that the men may have the knowledge that they are not entirely alone.

The objective is a long line of foxholes which lie approximately twenty-five yards past the river, and an equal distance in front of a street of buildings, which conceal the enemy's main line of defense. Therefore it is these structures that the bulk of the platoon will try to control with their weapons. That leaves the patrol the main worry of capturing a prisoner from the holes. As the preparatory artillery attempts to discourage observation by the Germans, the GIs cross the line of departure in their snow suits which are suitable for the terrain they must negotiate. The ground vibrates from the weight of the huge shells, and now the use of creeping fire is affording cover for the would-be captors.

But what of the men who are flirting with death in a heroic attempt to save the lives of others? What are their thoughts as they start their journey? Each man is thinking the same thoughts, only the references differ in respect to persons and pleasures. Will there be any short rounds which would bring immediate destruction to the mission and its members? Will any of us see our loved ones again? Are the Germans aware that the shelling is preparatory to a small-scale invasion? Will the enemy detect us first and plan an ambush? Will we be able to capture a prisoner and return safely with him? Will this be only one of numerous patrols and engagements or the beginning of the end of the war and all the terror and discomfort it has brought on me and so many other innocents? And so read the thoughts of the seven-man patrol and of the lieutenant whose responsibility is their safety and success.

Zero hour, and the artillery moves forward to permit the men to start over the river and to the objective. The men climb unhesitatingly into the icy water. They are on their own. The thought that they must go and return before the enemy is fully recovered from the pounding coupled with the startling effects of the icy water on their legs seems to give them more speed and drive, although they should already be fatigued from the initial arduous run over their own bank. Then the thought that the artillery will afford protective creeping fire for only five minutes spurs them swiftly onward.

Once over the river they hurry to the first of the holes. There they stop breathlessly as a surrender ultimatum by the interpreter is directed at the hole. But there are no occupants of that hole. The process is repeated many times, and each halt seems to age them years. Finally, at the eighth or ninth hole success is theirs. A prisoner steps forth, a worthy reward for their perseverance. But the task is only half completed. And as they hurry to recross the icy barrier, more thoughts race through their worried minds. Now that we have been successful, will victory be snatched from our grasp? Didn't the prisoner seem more frightened than we? Though we are very much farther downstream than we intended to go, aren't we within the studied radius of our sector? Will there be an ambush? Can we keep up our fast pace to the safe side? Will the Germans spot us now that we have outlasted our fire support? But the last question is answered with the ping of Jerry machine guns in their vicinity. And all seems lost until they hear the counterbattery from their comrades in the houses across the river. As they wade into the water again, they notice that the accurate predirected fire of the rest of the platoon has silenced the German weapons.

When the patrol returns to the platoon command post a quick checkup reveals that theirs has been the first patrol to cross the river and capture a prisoner without any casualties. After the lieutenant congratulates the men and tells them to change their wet clothes, get something warm in their stomachs, and try to get some sleep, a very wet, tired, and cold bunch of American soldiers happily find their way back to their respective squad houses. And after they relive those trying minutes in enemy territory, they are very thankful that the ten-minute patrol had four hours insurance, as well as the cooperation of so many others.

TIMBERWOLF REWARDED FOR RIVER MISSION
(*The Stars and Stripes*, Feb. 11, 1945)

WITH 104TH INF. DIV.—His regiment found out about enemy troop dispositions. He got a pass to Paris and was invited to dinner with Maj. Gen. Terry Allen, the Division commander.

This came when Lt. Karl H. Stelljes, tech sergeant three weeks ago, took his 413th Inf. patrol successfully across the Roer and back. His orders were to get prisoners. His patrol from Co. G started out in the dark, wrapped in snow capes and carrying weapons camouflaged with white tape.

Sgt. Cecil E. Ross set up a BAR in the dense brush as the others moved up in a skirmish line. Twenty yards ahead there was a trench; fresh tracks in the snow showed that Jerry was using it. So Sgt. Donald R. Weishaupt kept three men in the edge of the thicket as a covering party while Lt. Stelljes moved on with Pfc. Fred W. Slife and T/4 John R. Fowler to investigate.

FIRES MORTAR FLARE

They jumped into the trench, walked down it 20 yards, and a burp gun opened up. Stelljes went back to get Weishaupt as Pfc. Emil Zegerheim fired a green parachute flare to signal for mortars.

The patrol moved 30 more yards through the trench and a sentry challenged. This gave Jerry's location away and the lieutenant tossed a "DeGregoria cocktail" at him. This, a half-pound block of TNT with a five-second grenade fuse "invented" by S/Sgt. Phillip A. DeGregoria, was followed by a white phosphorous grenade.

Stelljes opened fire on the dugout with his Sten gun. He moved on with Weishaupt at his heels pouring tommy gun shells at the Kraut position.

"Kamerad! Don't shoot." Two Germans emerged from their dugout in the end of the trench. One poked his rifle at Weishaupt, but Stelljes was too quick for him. He threw the empty Sten gun at the German, grabbed his rifle, and brought it down on the enemy soldier's head.

That was enough for the Krauts. The Americans took their captives back on the double. One Jerry had an awful headache, but there were no other casualties.

HOW VETS ARE MADE
By TECHNICAL SERGEANT DALE ENGLER, Company L, 413th Infantry

New Year's Day, 1945, found six veterans of the 3d Platoon, Company L, sitting on the bank of the Roer River, across from the town of Duren, Germany, in a defensive position, getting acquainted with the new reinforcements sent down from regiment to bring the platoon up to combat strength. The veterans had many stories to tell about Holland, Hill 287, Inden, and all the rest of the bloody fighting they had been engaged in. The rookies had stories to tell about the States, which some of them had left only a month ago.

That same day an order was received by the new platoon leader, Lieutenant Fred R. White, to make plans for a platoon raid across the river to capture prisoners for the Division. Importance of the mission was stressed, as it was essential to find out if the enemy were moving troops from our sector to aid in their drive in the Bulge, or if they were concentrating for an attack toward Aachen.

The atmosphere immediately changed from one of watchful waiting to one of frenzied activity. The old men knew that much had to be done while the new men seemed to realize for the first time that they were soon going to be trading punches with the Jerries. The opinion of the old men was expressed by Staff Sergeant Vincent Rohay and Staff Sergeant Rolland Ford when they said, "We are worried about what these new men will do. When we had so many new men at Inden the results weren't so good. However, we've had a chance to tell these fellows a few things, and then we didn't even have time to find out their names." Pfc. J. R. Devine said, "I wondered what was coming; I had been in the Army about six months, and there I was in combat. I'll admit I was scared stiff and wishing I had learned a little more back in basic training. Those stories the old boys were telling didn't make me feel much better at the time, but I realize now I picked up some good points from them."

"They told me that we were going to cross the Roer River, and I couldn't sleep," was the view of Pfc. Lawrence Totsky. "When they said I was going to be a member of a team to go across with bangalore torpedoes to breach a mass of barbed wire I really got scared. I had seen a bangalore torpedo in basic, but never thought I'd be using one."

The next few days were spent in checking equipment, ammunition, cleaning rifles, and worrying by most of the new men. Aerial reconnaissance was made and plenty of maps were sent down after the crossing site was selected. A visual reconnaissance was made first by the platoon leader and squad leaders, and later every man in the platoon had a chance to get a good look at where he was going. A detailed plan of action was worked out with particular attention being paid to support of artillery, mortars, and machine guns.

At last everything was ready to go. Then followed a period of anxious waiting as the actual time of the raid was postponed twice due to unfavorable weather conditions. On the 6th of January, word came that this was the day, and at 2030 that night the raid was on. Staff Sergeant Rohay had the first squad and said, "Going down to the river wasn't bad; we went through our own minefields, and the first men had waded nearly half-way across, waist deep in icy water, before we were discovered. Then all hell broke loose. The Jerries cut loose with everything they had, and our own mortars and artillery immediately cut loose, boxing in an area so our Jerries couldn't get away."

Everything went smoothly as planned; although enemy fire was intense, it was ineffective. The wire was breached and everyone moved on. Each squad cleared its designated area. Enemy machine gun nests were cleaned out. Pfc. John Mahan and Pfc. Jesse Elmore saw a Jerry running, trying to get away, so they chased him and ran him down. With the mission accomplished by capturing Germans, the platoon leader called for covering fires, and the platoon started withdrawing across the river with their prisoners.

After crossing the river every man was back, although one casualty had been suffered. Veterans were made that night, and the new men felt they had played no small part in enabling the 3d Platoon to accomplish another outstanding, well-prepared, well-executed mission. Four men won decorations for their outstanding work, and all the men received citations for a job well done.

SLEEPER PATROL
By SERGEANT WILLIAM M. McILVAIN, Company A, 413th Infantry

We had been in a defensive position on the river for six weeks. The Roer

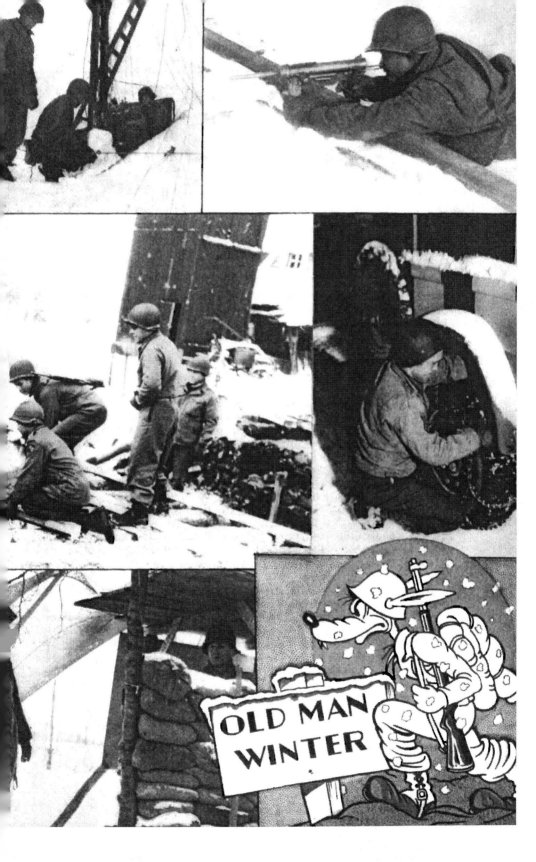

OLD MAN WINTER

TEXAN LEADS PATROL THROUGH HELL, COVERING RETREAT IN HAIL OF FIRE

LIEUTENANT BATTLES FOE WHILE MEN GAIN SAFETY

(The Stars and Stripes, Jan. 5, 1945)

ROER RIVER FOREST, Germany, Jan. 4.—Leaves are tough to obtain on the Western Front but 27-year-old Lt. Everett E. Pruitt, of Munday, Texas, had a 24-hour pass today.

All he had to do to earn it last night was:

Lead a seven-man patrol across the Roer River in moonlight, then through minefields and 400 yards into German positions.

Bring three wounded men back under mortar, rifle, machine gun and artillery fire.

And then bring himself back.

It happened this way. The lieutenant led six men across the river on a scouting expedition. Once across, Pruitt took his men through a minefield and started to outflank a pillbox. Just then he heard an explosion at the rear and he rushed back to find one of his men had stepped on a small mine.

Pruitt went into the minefield after his man. Just as he pulled him out another man stepped on a mine, and in a few seconds a third. With half of his patrol wounded, Pruitt decided to start back.

He sent one man back across the river to get medical men and arrange for artillery fire to cover his retreat. He sent the other two to help the wounded.

Then taking carbine and hand grenades, Pruitt covered the slow, painful withdrawal of his men. The Germans, meanwhile, sent out eight men to attack his patrol. Pruitt held them off—sometimes exposing himself to draw fire away from his men.

The Americans made their way back to the twisted wreckage of a blown bridge, their only escape route, the Germans closing in.

Pruitt took the grenades from the wounded and jumped on top of a bulkhead at the end of the bridge.

"When the enemy raised to firing positions to pick him off, Pruitt heaved grenades into their midst," his commanding officer said.

Pruitt held his position until his men were safely away. Then he dropped down and crawled back across the bridge under fire. Once on the American side he discovered one unwounded man was missing and started back for him, but halfway across he heard calls and found the missing soldier had swum back across.

had been flooded, and at the time of our patrol was a raging flood of unknown fury and seemed an impassable barrier: ~

We were in the little town of Mariaweiler, and were expecting to attack across the river at any time. To say the least, everyone was in a state of nervous expectancy. Therefore, when on the afternoon of 12 February, Captain Peltonen asked for volunteers to go on a sleeper patrol into enemy territory, I volunteered. Later though, when we were on the other side, I wished that I hadn't been quite so hasty.

After several of us had agreed to go, we were sent to the battalion command post. There, four of us were selected: Technical Sergeant Flores was in charge, with Pfc. Bonselaar, Pfc. McCain, and myself. We were then given some last-minute instructions to plan our route of approach. We studied aerial photos, and planned to use a dark night, taking advantage of the dikes and small wooded areas on the enemy side. We even used the map to plan a compass course and picked a house on the other side for our observation post. Heavy artillery was assigned to four point targets around the house to help veil our position.

The last and most important thing was to decide the equipment we should carry. We wanted to travel as light as possible, but at the same time have all the things that we would need for a successful completion of our mission. Deciding to carry only our field jackets, we knew that we would spend an uncomfortable night, but also knew the risk of too much clothing. For weapons, we had three automatic carbines and a Thompson sub. Ammunition was one thing we had in abundance. A flashlight to signal the boat on our return, two carrier pigeons for communication, a pair of wire cutters and a couple of K rations apiece completed our gear.

Up to this time there had been very little time for thought, but now we began to weigh our chances. It seemed they were pretty good, if we got over the river. This was left to the engineers.

We reached the river about ten that night. The boat was waiting to take us across. Then, the river seemed such a monster that no one could possibly survive, but the engineers were more than equal to their task. And in less time than it takes to tell, we were on the enemy side of the river, and the boat had started back. With its disappearance we all felt a personal loss. We turned and started up the bank, but were stopped by a barbed wire fence. The wire cutters fixed that.

We crossed a small ditch, all of us soaked to the skin, but not noticing the cold in our excitement. After creeping and crawling, slipping and sliding through the muck, we became so tired and exhausted, we had no sense of time or feeling. All we knew was to follow—at times the thought of capture seemed a relief. Suddenly Sergeant Flores called us quietly to him. There, only a few feet from us, lay a German sleeping in his foxhole. Leaving McCain with a knife at the throat of the unsuspecting foe, we crept softly away. McCain followed. The sleeping enemy was left unmolested—under different conditions, he would never have seen another sunrise.

The next half hour was just a matter of going forward inch by inch, wondering what might happen the next second. Then, one of our worst fears was realized. Sergeant Flores, being extremely careful, saw antipersonnel mines. We retreated a few yards and planned our next move. At last, we decided to give the area a wide berth. But from there on, we lived with the dread that our

Coffee, doughnuts and American girls. The Red Cross in Eschweiler

next step might activate a mine. It is a horrible feeling to know that you are in territory belonging to the enemy and that if anything goes wrong, there is nothing your friends can do to help. And worst of all, there is very little you can do to help yourself. It is a mixed feeling of hope and futility, of success one moment and despair the next.

After we had passed the minefields, we breathed a little more easily, and began to feel as if everything would go off without a hitch. We were in single file and started for the house we had picked for our command post. Our thoughts of a house were short-lived, however, as we reached the place and saw a crack of light from one of the windows and heard singing from inside. It sounded as though a party were in progress. We had left our formal attire with our buddies, so we retreated to a not-so-cozy but far more healthy shell hole a hundred yards away.

The holes were wet, our field jackets were soaked, and night was passed in a series of chills. We lay there freezing, thinking of the nice warm room we had left of our own free will for a place like this. We lay shivering, blaming ourselves for our sad plight, and waiting for morning to bring us relief from the cold and dampness.

At last it grew light, but instead of a warm sun, we received a cold, dismal sky. We released one of the pigeons, then waited breathlessly until he flew out of sight.

A little later in the morning, our unknowing hosts began to move again. We felt safe in our holes, and if we had been more comfortable, would have enjoyed spying on the unsuspecting foes. It was easy to tell that they had profound respect for our artillery. They exposed themselves as little as possible and did all of their work on the double. We spent some time watching a German working on a motorcycle. From time to time he would hit the dirt as a shell landed close by. At last he gave the job up as hopeless and retired to a cellar nearby.

Our artillery gave us a few anxious moments also. Since we were not in the designated house, we were exposed to the very fire that had been scheduled to give us added protection. During the barrages we laid low. However, we did discover the approximate strength and location of German troops in the vicinity of Duren.

216

The longest day of my life finally ended and we started to release the second pigeon, but he had grown weary of his gas mask cage and flew the coop. We then wearily, but eagerly, returned to the river. We had a few anxious moments when a burp gun opened up, but after a brief hesitation, we decided it was just harassing fire and went on to the river with no more trouble than would be expected, while playing tag with German mines. We even failed to see our sentry that had been having such peaceful dreams the night before.

We reached the river and signaled the boat with our light and in a few minutes we were on our way back to what we had commonly referred to as paradise. And believe me, the coffee we were given when we reached the 1st Battalion command post never tasted so good.

Hundreds of others had similar patrol experiences. Defense along the Roer was not without its humorous and unusual situations. One day troops of the 1st Battalion, 413th Infantry, spotted a group of Germans and opened fire with their 81mm mortars. The enemy heard the weapons go off and dove for their foxholes, remaining there until the shells had arrived and burst. Thereupon they climbed out of their holes and resumed their work. This went on and on and Staff Sergeant Robert Barton and his D Company mortar squad became rather vexed. They tried firing one shell ten seconds after the other, nailed three Germans, but they soon caught on to this too and poked their heads out between bursts. Finally Barton timed the shell in flight. Noting that it was twenty-two seconds from the time of fire until the shell burst, he fired a round, waited twenty-two seconds, and let go with another. The Germans ducked the first one, but the noise of its burst muffled the report of the next one being fired and the Germans crawled out of their holes. In twenty-two seconds the one they hadn't heard showed up and caught them all above the ground.

Staff Sergeant Arthur E. Williams had the strangest little black book in the entire ETO. His men never kidded him about the names of the blondes or brunettes in it, as they knew the grim entries that filled its pages. On their first night of combat Sergeant Williams and his buddy started the night together. In the morning Sergeant Williams was alone. That was the night he swore eternal hatred for the Nazi killers, and since then he made his business the destruction of the enemy whenever and however he could find them. In the little black book, you find the date, "weapon used," and the name of the victim if he had time to get it, and the circumstances surrounding the kill. By 1 February he had twenty-three entries in the book.

The men of the 3d Battalion, 414th Infantry, while occupying their sector north of Duren found that the fleeing Germans had wrecked the power lines and had taken all the candles and oil lamps with them. When Colonel Rouge and Major Ryan found the remains of a water-driven generator in a ruined foundry, they told Pfcs. George Martin and M. F. Redeker to rewire the town and put the generator into operation. Shortly thereafter this newly organized "public utilities" corporation supplied Lendersdorf with steady current. The 3d Battalion Timberwolves living in the town had electric lights and radios. Once when the lights dimmed, a detail of trouble-shooters found a dead cow in the grate which kept debris out of the turbines, but an internal dose of dynamite kept it from sabotaging the "public utility" venture.

Life on the Roer was further described by *The Stars and Stripes* in its 26 February 1945 issue:

A SOW'S EAR IS NOW SILK PURSE . . .

WITH 104TH INF. DIV.—The first platoon was told to make itself at home and the men took the orders literally.

I Co. of the 413th Regt. had moved into a German paper plant still burning from American shell-fire. With little or no roof on what remained of the building and waist-high piles of debris covering the floors, the outlook was dim. But the first platoon took over and, with a few days labor, developed a model for postwar economical home-making.

Pfc. Delbert Erwin, of Kahoka, Mo., worked out an arrangement which turned concrete storage-bins into tight little sleeping-cabins. Home-made double-deck bunks provide room for two or three men in each compartment—with space left for stove, table and chairs. New low board ceilings simplify the heating and lighting problems. Walls are lined with salvaged newsprint for added insulation. A rig of pipes constitutes a rudimentary air-conditioning system. Hand-made stair-cases lead to the small steel doors of each cubicle.

Piles of lumber that had been untouched by the fire went into a construction project under Pfc. Andrew Posey, of Birmingham, Ala. The main job was the building of a complete new bathroom, with tub, heater, and running water.

Using the same home-grown methods of construction, the 60mm mortar section worked up a clubhouse—"Club 60," they dubbed it—furnished with writing table and telephone and decorated with pinups.

"It's a regular Maginot Line," says Posey. "We don't have to leave the building for anything."

Sergeant Louis Silberschutz, 385th Field Artillery Battalion, gives the artilleryman's point of view while on the Roer:

The Huertgen forest in mid-winter looked from a distance like something out of a Christmas card. Appearances, however, were deceiving. The Huertgen had been one of the bloodiest battlegrounds of the war, and weeks after the fighting was over we came upon frozen bodies that had been overlooked and piles of clothing and equipment that had been abandoned.

We came into the forest during the days of the Bulge. Our mission was defensive. We were to help hold the west bank of the Roer. Across the river

Our liaison planes donned skis for winter operations.

lay Duren, once reputedly the home of German millionaires, now a city gutted by bombing and artillery fire.

We were fortunate, we thought, in finding homes in the forest. Others before us had built dugouts roofed with logs. In the course of five weeks, we were to find out that we weren't so fortunate. The logs blocked the wind, but the melted snow just poured through. When a slight thaw set in, the ground water rushed in. Bailing out the dugout was regular morning exercise.

The command post was located in the largest dugout of the lot. It looked much like something out of a World War I movie. Roofing the dugout was quite a problem. There was always a bucket or two on the ground, catching the drippings from the roof.

The area had been mined by the enemy. All personnel were warned to stay on the paths. A few weeks after we had come into position, the engineers came through with "Danger, Mines" signs, right through the middle of our battery area.

The Huertgen days were marked by reduced ammunition allotments. Most of the ammunition was going to the outfits fighting in the Bulge. Most of the time we were reduced to thirty-two rounds per day. However, we did have available to us the battalions of Corps artillery. During the weeks in the forest, we got to know those outfits by their telephone code names very well. There were "Archduke," "Castle," "Avail," "Ardent" and "Cockpit."

Across the Roer, Duren was a kind of ghost city. Occasionally some German would show himself, usually to be greeted by artillery fire. We had forward observers up near the river bank, and an observation post on a hill back of us. The enemy was being watched very carefully, and he knew it.

219

The strangest report from our observers was the 'Duren Express.' Several men reported to us that they had heard train whistles. A train in deserted Duren sounded fantastic. Reports of the train came in regularly, and several times we fired on supposed train locations.

We were "defensive minded" in the forest. The trees of the forest were prepared with dynamite charges so that the roads could be blocked. The S-3's were busy preparing plans. Defensive fires covered every approach of the enemy. We were in front of Aachen, and the Germans, overconfident in the early days of the Ardennes offensive, had said that they would give Hitler Aachen for a Christmas present.

What the enemy planned to do was the big question. Almost every night infantry patrols crossed the river and we fired, sometimes as much as 500 rounds, to cover them. We soon became expert in laying down box barrages, blocking off a stretch of enemy territory with fire so that our patrols could move in.

The enemy was just as worried as to what we were planning. One enemy patrol, in considerable strength, was spotted coming across the river and received the fire planned for such occasions. Observers reported that the shells riccocheting on the frozen ground had terrible effect.

After weeks of waiting in the forest, we learned that we finally were ready to begin the attack across the Roer. We could take up our usual offensive mission. The Bulge had been liquidated. The German move of desperation had failed. It was our turn now.

The Roer crossing had been planned for months. Maps and aerial photos had been carefully studied. Our observers had been watching the enemy painstakingly, and knew the terrain across the river thoroughly. The battalion S-3, Major Marion A. Foreman, consulted our liaison officers with the infantry battalions, our observers, and the infantry. Every possible artillery position, every enemy strongpoint, every crossroad across the river was to be covered with artillery fire.

We left the Huertgen forest just before the jump-off to go to the battered town of Schlich. We took positions and waited for the fateful day.

Finally, after a few delays, we were told that the offensive was about to begin. Fire missions were sent out to the supporting battalions, data was sent down to the guns. Metro corrections were worked out down to H-hour. Finally the word was given.

Those who saw the artillery preparation that went out that night have described it as an awe-inspiring spectacle. The ground seemed to bubble. Everywhere across the river, shells were falling—our next stop was across the Roer.

Ernie Leiser, *Stars and Stripes* correspondent, found the inspiration for his following article in the "Day Room Closest to Berlin":

"COMFORT" ON ROER GETS GI NOD . . .
(*The Stars and Stripes*, Feb. 8, 1945)

WITH 104TH INF. DIV.—The Easy Co. (414th) OP was in a house at the edge of the Roer, rock-tossing distance from the Germans dug in across the river. The crash of Division artillery, adjusting on a building across the river, was the only sound to break the afternoon silence.

Climbing down into the basement after a quick look to see if the Nazis were stirring in the town across the way, Lt. Stanley Golub, Seattle, said, "You know, they damn near had to use force to get the battalion that was here before us to come out of the lines and go back to the rest area. Division finally had to order them back, they liked this place so well."

He led the way up one flight of rickety stairs.

* * * *

The living room, less than 100 yards from enemy lines, was intact. And furnished in perfect taste. It was filled with deep, soft chairs, big tables, rich maroon drapes and other adornments of a comfortable burgher home. Only the broken windows indicated it was anywhere near a war.

We went downstairs and crawled through a series of king-size rat-holes in the basement walls.

"The Jerries had these cut out so they could go through the building under-ground," he explained.

He stood up and walked through a door.

"This," he said, "is the day room. Since we are the U. S. outfit deepest into Germany and this is our most advanced point, we claim it as the day room closest to Berlin."

* * * *

It looked like a garrison in the States. Half a dozen GIs were sitting around reading in over-stuffed chairs. The walls were covered with Petty and Varga girls. A stove kept the room warm and snug. Pfc. Walter Collins of Persis, Calif., looking up from a paper, said he liked it "pretty good" here.

Golub led the way back through the rat-holes to the other end of the basement.

"This is patrol headquarters," he said. It was a room with a big inner-spring mattress in one corner, occupied at the moment by a lieutenant and a private. On the table in the center of the room was some Dresden pottery and in the wall cupboard were vari-colored glasses.

"Fox company has got so much glassware that it uses different glasses for every drink," Golub said. "Yeah, it's a pretty good set-up here. The only reason some of the guys don't prefer it to a rear area rest center is on account of the patrols to the other side of the Roer."

"Patrols or not," said Pfc. E. F. Scacchitt of Scranton, Pa., "it's sure more comfortable here than in a rest area."

* * * *

Golub left the house and led the way back to the battalion CP, screened from the Germans across the river only by fallen branches. He stopped in at Easy Co. CP, down in the basement.

Company Commander Lt. Stanley Blunck of Oakland, Calif., got up from a divan and called Sgt. Robert Heisele, of St. Louis, Mo., to bring over some jam for the bread on the table. Heisele pointed to the shelves on the wall, loaded with jars of vegetables, pickles, relish and jams.

"You can see why the guys in this area hate to leave the front lines for rest areas," he said.

The new year of 1945 was welcomed by all artillery and cannon pieces firing one round of high explosive at 0001. Again at 0600 every weapon in the Division sector sent deadly greetings across the

First Nighters

Roer River. Throughout the defensive period, coordinated harassing "shoots" were directed against the enemy. Often good targets could not be engaged because of the shortage of ammunition which was now being felt all along the line due to necessary priority going to the troops engaged in the Bulge. However the Division never relinquished control of the Roer, constantly maintaining its aggressive defense by patrolling and executing sharp raids against the enemy on the east side of the river. Throughout the operation, not one Timberwolf was taken prisoner by the enemy and his repeated attempts to probe our positions were frustrated. The 784th Tank Battalion, the first colored troops to be attached to our Division, under command of Lieutenant Colonel George C. Dalia, had ably supported the Division in defense during the period 3 January to 3 February. On 6 February, the 750th Tank Battalion, under Lieutenant Colonel John A. White, rejoined the Timberwolves after its fight in the Ardennes. The 784th Tank Battalion then moved north to join troops of the Ninth United States Army.

In the latter part of January, the German offensive to the south had been repulsed and driven back to the line held on 16 December. The VII Corps, having completed its mission in that sector, moved back to its old position near Aachen and again assumed command of the 104th Division on 6 February.

On the bright crisp day of 10 January at 1330, hundreds of B-17's passed over the Division zone in the assault on Cologne and other strategic targets along the Rhine River. It was reassuring to see planes flying toward the east to lay waste strong German defenses, but suddenly the bomb bay doors opened on twelve of the planes. At the

Division CP everyone scurried for cover, but still there was a toll of twenty-four lives and twenty-eight wounded. More than 365 bombs churned the Division CP in the Weisweiler factory and in the area occupied by the 1st Battalion, 415th Infantry. Quickly, the Signal Company and Headquarters Company personnel cleared the debris, and communication with all units was restored within six minutes. Although the accidental bombing caused undue loss of life, the men took it all in their stride. A typical reaction, after the din and confusion of the explosions had terminated, came from Signal Company's Sergeant Poole, who wryly remarked, "I thought I'd given Colonel Hoegh the wrong number again."

Not often can a Piper Cub boast a stenciled swastika on its fuselage but one of the 104th's Grenade Bombers, as they are affectionately known to all doughboys, achieved just such renown one day while patrolling the air along the Roer River front.

It was a routine air reconnaissance mission for the crew of two, who had flown their artillery cub plane in many previous missions. They were Lieutenants Robert C. Dwelly, pilot, and Everett E. Jones, aerial observer, both of the 385th Field Artillery Battalion.

After a few minutes in the air, a light haze closed in and they turned back to the airstrip.

Still two miles from the airstrip at Wrexen, Germany, Lieutenant Jones saw six strange planes through the haze. Hesitantly, nervously, he identified them as Jerries; ME-109's coming his way. As they came in rapidly, Lieutenant Dwelly put the little ship into a steep dive. Before he leveled off, the first Jerry opened up with a burst of machine gun fire, followed closely by the second and third planes. Lieutenant Dwelly skimmed the ground as he flew up a little valley, and the first Jerry followed him down. Unable to pull his high speed craft away from the ground, the Messerschmitt crashed and burst into flames. The following planes fired quickly from a safe altitude and their speed carried them out of range.

With sighs of relief the cub crew landed safely and patched their plane. The event had been witnessed by the battalion commander of the 555th Antiaircraft Artillery, Lieutenant Colonel Farnum, and a certificate was issued to Lieutenant Dwelly, crediting him with the destruction of an enemy pursuit plane, the first in the European Theater of Operations by an artillery cub.

PREPARATION FOR THE OFFENSIVE

On 6 February, the Division was directed to prepare plans for the crossing of the Roer River. The offensive once again was to be re-

sumed by the Allied armies in the drive for the Rhine River. The
Division zone was narrowed by the 8th Infantry Division relieving the
414th Infantry and elements of the 413th Infantry. The 414th Infantry
was placed in Division reserve. Every move or order made by the units
pointed toward the crossing of the formidable Roer. During the next
several days equipment and troops were moved night and day; reconnaissance was conducted and an air of suspense and excitement dominated the whole area. Sergeant H. V. Frampton, Jr., of A Battery,
385th Field Artillery Battalion, recalls how "Five Men" sweated out
the green light that would start what everyone hoped would be the
last large-scale offensive:

Advances of the British and Canadians across the German border from Holland—Spectacular thrusts of onrushing Russians from the East—Relentless pressure of the Seventh and Third—The British offensive in Burma and MacArthur
in the Philippines. These occupied the headlines in February.

Analysts and commentators speculate on a thrust over the Roer, across the
plain to the Rhine along the route of the Duren-Cologne highway, but all is
quiet along the Roer River front in the Duren vicinity. Why? At 1930 on
February 14th, around a large oblong table in a comfortably warm, dimly lit
room, Five Men partake of a sumptuous, unrationed dinner. The menu:
breaded pork chops, green string beans, potatoes, creamed tomato sauce, followed by coffee, cheese, fruitcake, assorted nuts, and mints. Finally, cognac,
all around, as cigars and cigarettes were passed.

Smoke rises from the table amid quiet, earnest discussion of the Lublin
Government in Poland, the trend toward popular left wing governments in
Jugoslavia, Belgium and Greece, and the recently announced fall of Budapest.
Conversation centers on the Western Front.

Facts well known to these men have never been printed in any newspaper,
never broadcast by any newscaster.

Manned by Lieutenant General Courtney Hodges' First Army, the Duren
sector has been considered as the logical point for a spearhead to the Rhine.
The Five Men have been informed by Army information sources as to the turbu-
lence of the Roer, its treacherous speed caused by the German release of water
from the Schwammenauel Dam. Men have been swept off their feet when only
knee-deep in the river. The Five Men know that on the night of 11 February,
when three men attempted to cross and drive stakes for guide ropes, the engineer
officer and one other man were never heard from again.

And on the night of the 13th, a four-man patrol crossed, spent a day hidden
in German territory. A pigeon was used as messenger. The patrol counted
Jerries, located an enemy "120" and a minefield, then returned on the night of
the 14th under enemy machine gun fire. The Five Men know that on the
American-held side of the river a thunderbolt waits to strike. In and near every
building and ditch there are men and vehicles, artillery of all sizes, chemical
battalions, antitank, engineers, tank destroyers, armored outfits, medics, ordnance
units, quartermaster, signal corps, military police, Allied Military Government,
all of the many interdependent groups necessary for movement of a large force.
On the front lines the rifle company doughboys come and go silently in the

always cautious traffic of darkness. They make their way in shifts to and from the outposts. Occasionally, the stillness is broken by "incoming mail"—artillery, mortar coming in, more often going out. Sometimes the deadly "putting" of a robomb is heard headed west. Soon, out of the seemingly lethargic stillness, the last big push for the Rhine will explode and bolt forth from Duren.

The Five Men are relaxed. Smoke rises from the table. Military maps and aerial photos are laid out after glasses are removed. The plans are covered in minute detail. This operation may ring down the curtain on the last war fought by man. Who are these "Five Men"?

Their meeting has not been heralded by the press.

Their names have not been mentioned.

Their opinions have not been quoted.

General Eisenhower has never been present at their meetings.

Could it be possible that these Five Men are the big three plus the "Gissimo" and DeGaulle? No, that would be impossible because the Five Men are just a couple of hundred yards from the Roer River in the Duren sector of the Western Front. They are in a cellar of a former school, the top floor of which serves as their observation post. They enjoyed a dinner that was made up of an accumulation of Army rations and boxes from home saved up for several weeks.

They are just another forward observer crew from the field artillery. One lieutenant and four enlisted men. They will go in the attack with A Company, which is the point rifle company of the battalion to which they are assigned. They are awaiting H-hour, waiting for the word "Go." They are "sweating it out." If, as the doughboys say, the five men should end up "Kaput," they at least had a helluva fine evening.

Assault boat training and the actual practice of crossing men and equipment were conducted by all units along the Inde River in preparation for the coming operations. During this period, the Timberwolf engineers assisted the infantry units in perfecting assault boat technique. Many experiments were conducted by the engineers in order to determine the most expedient means of forcing the turbulent Roer. At a demonstration conducted on 12 February, the engineers successfully demonstrated the use of assault boats, pontons, rafts, and "weasels" with cable attached for quick crossing. It was also shown that rockets and grenade launchers were effective devices in shooting communication wire across the river. The engineers were indeed a versatile combat unit. Not only had the battalion assisted materially in the organization of the Division defenses, maintained important avenues of supplies, and instructed the infantrymen in assault boat crossings, but during most of the period while on the Roer, it had troops occupying defensive positions in the southern part of the Division sector.

During the period 1-10 February, the Division issued Field Order No. 18 and Operations Memoranda 33-38, in which plans and orders for the initial crossing of the Roer were directed. Immediately to the east of the Roer River stood the once thickly inhabited cities of Birkes-dorf and Duren in the southern part of the Division zone. In the northern zone was the town of Huchem-Stammeln. The line running roughly north and south through these cities and including the high ground in the vicinity of the insane asylum in the east section of Duren was designated phase line A. It was necessary to seize this line in order that bridging operations could be started, unhampered by small arms and observed artillery fire. Approximately three miles east of phase line A was the high ground in the Division zone which domi-nated the Roer. A line running through the town of Ellen on the north and Merzenich on the south was designated phase line B—the VII Corps bridgehead. Following a forty-five minute artillery preparation, the 413th Infantry on the right, and the 415th Infantry on the left, were to force crossings and seize phase line A. If resistance was light, the two units would continue in their advance and seize phase line B. The alternate and most likely plan was for the 414th Infantry to pass through the 413th at the A line, and in conjunction with 415th's attack on Ellen, it would seize Merzenich and the southern portion of the B line. In three commanders' conferences during this period, General Allen formed all plans and orders.

Several times D-Day was set, only to be cancelled late in the after-noon prior to the attack. The enemy held the important Schwam-menauel Dam which controlled the flow and depth of the Roer River. To force a crossing with the enemy still in possession of these dams was perilous because it would be possible for the Germans to cut off initial assault forces by demolishing the dams and releasing tons of water.

From the 11th of February, tension mounted daily. While the infan-trymen were nervously waiting, the engineers and all unit service troops continued working on the tremendous problem of logistics. Road, bridge and crossing site data were compiled by the engineers. Traffic control plans were formulated; the medical battalion and all aid stations prepared for any eventuality, and mines and booby-traps in the path of our advance west of the Roer were removed. Finally word was received from higher headquarters that the great offensive was to commence at 0330 on 23 February. The Timberwolves were poised and ready to strike, with the 413th on the right, the 415th on the left and the 414th in Division reserve at Langerwehe and Esch-weiler. For the assault the following units were attached: 750th Tank Battalion; 692d Tank Destroyer Battalion; 555th AAA (AW) Bat-talion (Mobile); Companies A and B, 87th Chemical Battalion; 957th Field Artillery Battalion (155 How.), 87th Armored Field Artillery

A heavy blanket of snow enveloped Duren late in January

Battalion (105 How.); and 283d Field Artillery Battalion (105 How.). The 1106th Engineer Group was in direct support.

Poised on the west banks of the Roer, the United States Ninth and First Armies were prepared to strike against the main German forces defending the Rhine. General Eisenhower had stated that one of the decisive battles of the war was to be fought on the Cologne plain. The purpose of the offensive was to destroy all German power west of the Rhine, the SHAEF commander declared, and then cross the Rhine River, marching to a meeting with the Russian Armies in the East. "There is going to be no cessation of aggressive action on this front," he said. "We are going to fight as violently and aggressively as we are able from now on." Later, the German radios blared, "Eisenhower's armies have launched the greatest offensive ever staged."

At 0245, 23 February 1945, in the black of the night, the Roer River line burst into a ball of fire—the thunderous battle flamed along a twenty-two mile front. Guns from 75mm to 240mm; 60mm, 81mm and 4.2-inch mortars, rockets, direct fire from tanks of the 750th Tank Battalion and from the tank destroyers of the 692d Tank Destroyer Battalion; .50-caliber machine gun and 40mm guns from the 555th AAA (AW) Battalion's multiple mounts—in fact every weapon of the Division and its attached units were hurled against the enemy to stun, kill, or drive him from his positions. For forty-five minutes the earth-shaking barrages continued while doughboys of the 1st and 3d Battalions of the 413th Infantry and the 1st and 3d Battalions of the

227

The turbulent Roer just prior to the Timberwolf crossing.

415th Infantry, accompanied by engineers of the assault boat crews, moved silently up to the line of departure. At 0330 the barrages shifted to the east and the Timberwolves commenced crossing the flooded Roer. The depth of the river in the Timberwolf zone varied from six to twelve feet and the width varied from 130 to 360 feet. The flooded currents raced at the rate of eight to ten miles per hour and the temperature was forty degrees. The Roer provided the enemy with an excellent obstacle, but the Wolves were determined to conquer and crush its defenders.

DUREN . . . Colonel Waltz's Seagulls had the 3d Battalion poised for Duren and the 1st Battalion set for the southern part of Birkesdorf. Company A, 87th Chemical Battalion, Company B, 750th Tank Battalion, were attached. Company A, 692d Tank Destroyer Battalion; 385th Field Artillery Battalion, with reinforced fires of the 386th Field Artillery Battalion; and Company A, 329th Engineer Battalion, were in direct support of the 413th. In the path of Lieutenant Colonel Summers' 3d Battalion, the banks of the Roer rose in height from three to fifteen feet; three to six feet high on the near side and fifteen feet high on the enemy side. The nearest cover on the west side of the river was 300 yards inland. The ground between that point and the river was flat, open, muddy, partly inundated, and devoid of concealment or cover. On the east side of the river, the enemy was in a position to cover with automatic fire all approaches into Duren. The river banks were heavily mined from the river to the trench system which commanded the river. Antipersonnel mines were encountered in the water, on the concertina wire placed along the river's edge, and in front of the trenches. Extensive minefields, including Schü mines and regular

228

trip wire and pressure devices, were throughout the depth of the enemy's position. The portion of Duren (north) assigned to the 3d Battalion was mainly the factory district, a zone 1,500 yards wide and 3,000 yards deep, filled with huge industrial buildings and installations including paper mills, a sugar factory, slaughter houses, municipal electric works, and numerous large foundries and metal works.

Promptly at 0330, the first assault wave of Companies I and K shoved their boats off the west banks of the river and within twenty minutes thereafter the companies held the outer edges of Duren. Several boats overturned in the assault crossings, but the men swam to the enemy banks and, though wet and cold and some without weapons or ammunition, went into action. The swift current greatly hampered the crossings and the engineers were able to return only three of the original thirty-four boats. A cable ferry was hurriedly constructed by the versatile engineers, but the swift current broke the half-inch steel cable. However, by 0830 a ferry was completed and ammunition, supporting weapons and vital communication wire were rushed forward. At 1030 Colonel Summers' men had seized the initial regimental objective and Company I had repelled two counterattacks on the battalion's right. Shortly thereafter the battalion was directed to proceed with its advance through Duren and seize the insane asylum which was located on the eastern edge of Duren on the high ground which overlooked the whole city. Following closely the rolling artillery barrages of the 385th Field Artillery, Companies I and K lunged forward, and at 1453, K Company was reported holding the asylum buildings, and at 1900 the Battalion had eliminated all resistance in the northern half of Duren.

For the heroic action of the men of the 3d Battalion, a unit citation was awarded under the provisions of Section IV, Circular 333, War Department 1943:

The 3D BATTALION, 413TH INFANTRY REGIMENT, is cited for extraordinary heroism and outstanding performance of duty in armed conflict with the enemy during the period from 23 to 25 February 1945 in the vicinity of Duren, Germany. The 3D BATTALION, 413TH INFANTRY REGIMENT, forced a crossing of the Roer River and, without delay, advanced across partially inundated and well mined terrain in the face of devastating fire from well prepared defensive positions. Two companies made the initial crossing, and when several boats overturned, the men swam to the enemy side and though wet and cold and some of them without ammunition or weapons, they went into action. A ferry was swiftly constructed by supporting assault engineers, and badly needed supplies and supporting weapons and ammunition were ferried across, and the wounded and prisoners of war were evacuated. The two companies advanced immediately against huge factory buildings, secured their initial objective after a fierce hand-to-hand battle, and repelled two enemy counter attacks after quickly organizing a defense. At this point the plan of attack was altered and the battalion was ordered to assault and capture an insane asylum, which was the dominating terrain feature in the city of Duren. Quickly resupplying ammunition and weapons and formulating a plan of attack, which was delivered to subordinate commanders without recourse to radio, the battalion subdued fierce resistance in adjacent factories and launched its assault on schedule, capturing the objective in a furious assault. At 0300, 24 February 1945, an enemy counterattack supported by devastating artillery fire was launched by the enemy. The attack was repulsed by the men of the battalion by quick and effective coordination of machine gun, artillery, and mortar fire, inflicting 40 casualties on the enemy force of over 100 men and capturing the remnants of the force. The aggressive actions of the 3D BATTALION, 413TH INFANTRY REGIMENT, successfully established and secured a bridgehead into Duren, penetrating 3000 yards into enemy-held territory. The penetration of successive fixed positions broke the enemy's defenses which had been prepared for over three months and secured observation enabling the placing of observed fires on enemy positions, contributing greatly to the confusion and disorganization of the enemy and facilitating the assault across the plains of Cologne toward the Rhine River. Large quantities of enemy equipment were taken, 178 prisoners captured, and 20 enemy killed by the battalion in this action. Throughout the action, the officers and men of 3D BATTALION, 413TH INFANTRY, distinguished themselves by great determination, outstanding aggressiveness, and superior combat discipline, gaining exceedingly difficult objectives with a minimum of casualties. The initiative, courage, and esprit de corps displayed by the battalion reflects the finest traditions of the armed forces of the United States.

Only the closest coordination between infantry and artillery, an outstanding feature of all 104th attacks, made this maneuver so successful. Lieutenant Colonel Shinkle, commanding the 385th Field Artillery Battalion, gives a short account of how swiftly this teamwork can be effected and how devastating its results:

The 3d Battalion, 413th Infantry, had done well under many difficulties. Their objective was that part of the city of Duren which lay north of the railroad track. They had crossed the Roer in early morning, beaten through their assigned sector, held on their right pending the arrival of the 8th Division, and were organizing to take the insane asylum. The asylum was the key to that sector. It was situated on a hill that commanded the north portion of Duren and much of the area north of that. Its capture was necessary to allow free movement over the bridge and in the area of the 413th Infantry.

At this point Lieutenant Colonel Summers, commanding the 3d Battalion, and Colonel Shinkle talked on the phone. The conversation ran something like this:

"Hello Bill, this is Eddie. When are you going to jump?"

"We'll be ready in about an hour, Eddie. Jump off at 0230."

"OK. I've got your plan. Here is my suggested artillery support. One light battalion across the road, one light battalion on each side of the road, and deepen it with a medium battalion. We will move east to the end of the line of buildings at a rate of one hundred yards every three minutes. When you reach the

end of the buildings we will put all battalions on the hill for five minutes.
When you leave the buildings for the asylum, turning southeast, we will put
two battalions on your left flank and one with the mediums out beyond the
asylum. How's that?"

"OK, Eddie, I'll put it out to the troops."

Colonel Shinkle then called Major Foreman at 385th Field Artillery fire
direction and explained the plan carefully and decided on exact coordinates,
times, and rates of fire. For such a preparation one hour was short notice.
Everyone had to work fast and accurately. Foreman secured the services and
assigned schedules to the 929th, 386th, and 387th Field Artillery Battalions.
All was ready within the hour and as the time drew near for the jumpoff all
data were carefully checked. Gunners and cannoneers checked settings and
charges. Observers were alerted for surveillance. Fire direction carefully
checked their figures. At 1430, forty-eight rounds landed on the first line of
the preparation and were reported as accurate. The earth shook and great clouds
of red and brown dust rose from those last buildings on that side of town.
Sporadic enemy fire ceased in that sector. The infantry moved forward.

The preparation was beautiful and accurate. It went forward exactly as
planned and completely neutralized enemy resistance in a vital area.

At 1455, General Collins, the Corps commander, entered the 413th CP. He
emphasized the importance of seizing the asylum. He asked, "When are you
going to take it?" His answer was immediate and dramatic. A radio message
from Colonel Summers announced to the CP, "We are on the objective."

BIRKESDORF . . . Adjoining Duren to the north lay Birkesdorf. The
1st Battalion, 413th Infantry, was to seize the southern half while the
1st Battalion, 415th Infantry, had the capture of the northern half as
its assignment. Simultaneously with the attack of the 3d Battalion,
413th, these two battalions plunged forward. Lieutenant Colonel
Charles Fernald's 1st Battalion, 413th, assaulted with Companies C
and A, while Lieutenant Colonel Needham's 1st Battalion, 415th Infantry, assaulted with three companies abreast. The swampy banks of the
Roer were zigzagged with trenches manned by the enemy from which
they had a clear field of fire on the long stretches of low ground along
the west side of the river. The accurate barrage of artillery assisted
materially in neutralizing strong enemy defensive positions, enabling
the units to cross with few casualties. The initial objective of the 1st
Battalion, 413th Infantry, was a large factory near the river's edge.
Despite the fact that only two platoons of Company C were able to
cross initially owing to many of the assault boats overturning in the
turbid waters, Captain Andre Wartha's company quickly reduced the
factory. Company A's crossing was made without casualty and, team-
ing up with C Company, pushed forward quickly so that by 1700, the
1st Battalion held the southern edge of Birkesdorf. In the late afternoon, the balance of the 1st Battalion had crossed the river, and by
2400 Lieutenant Colonel Fernald's men had reached phase line A. The

speed of the advance prevented the Germans from utilizing their fortifications.

New York's *PM* and other syndicated papers throughout the country carried the following story in their 26 February editions:

YANKS FEEL THEY'RE GOING PLACES
By C. R. CUNNINGHAM (UP)
PM, New York, February 26

Duren, Germany, Feb. 26.—Major General Terry Allen's Timberwolves of the 104th Infantry Division swept through the last remnants of German resistance in this flattened city yesterday and today they and other units were firmly established on top of the ridge paralleling the Roer River on the East.

They were ready either for another plunge forward or for a counterattack by some of the sizeable German tank and infantry forces between here and the Rhine.

This time the boys feel they are going places. The new spirit reaches from the very front line back to the ordnance boys who are sending up ammunition and the quartermasters who are sending up the clothing.

The three rifle companies of the 1st Battalion, 415th Infantry, successfully crossed the Roer, being subjected to devastating fire from machine guns emplaced near the cloverleaf on the Autobahn highway. At 0340 the three companies reported "Float Three," meaning that they had landed on the east banks of the Roer without initial opposition. Company A, as soon as it reached the east banks of the river, rushed the cloverleaf position and soon eliminated the Nazi machine gunners. Company C drove hard through the northern half of Birkesdorf, with B Company initially in reserve. Fighting fiercely throughout the day against pillboxes, concrete bunkers and mined obstacles, the battalion reached its objective, phase line A, at 1507. Two counterattacks of enemy infantry and tanks were repulsed with heavy losses to the enemy. From a forward exposed position on the ridge Lieutenant Moreno directed continuous fires, promptly breaking up the counterattacks.

HUCHEM-STAMMELN . . . While Colonel Cochran's 1st Battalion assaulted northern Birkesdorf, his 2d Battalion under Lieutenant Colonel Denisevich stormed the Roer northeast of Merken. Company G crossed in the extreme northern part of the Division zone, skirting the canal lying between the Roer and Huchem-Stammeln, and struck the objective from the northeast. Company E forced its crossing directly west of Huchem-Stammeln. In spite of the swift current, G Company made the crossing without casualty, the boats being flung against the

eastern shore with such force that the men were practically cata-
pulted ashore. Closely following the rolling barrage laid by Lieutenant
Colonel Gilbert's 929th Field Artillery Battalion, the men led by Lieutenant Mauldin raced into Stammeln and ran into the enemy entrenched
in fortressed houses. Dug-in 75's and machine gun nests were charged
by the infantrymen firing light machine guns from the hip. Two 75mm
guns were captured and turned around to fire on the Germans. In stiff
house-to-house fighting, G Company overwhelmed the defenders, and
at 0505 had its objective, Stammeln. During its crossing Company E
encountered a murderous crossfire from four machine guns emplaced
near the water's edge. The first wave made a successful crossing but
the succeeding waves were not able to penetrate the murderous fires.
It had originally been intended for Company F to follow Company E,
but because the crossing was governed by enemy fire, it moved to the
site used by Company G. Lieutenant Dyer led his men across the Roer
and advanced against the factory and the machine guns which had
stopped Company E. By late afternoon all resistance within Huchem
had been eliminated.

By midnight of the 23d the 104th Division held phase line A, thus
eliminating enemy pockets along the Roer River. The mighty Roer
had been conquered, with the 413th and the 415th holding firmly the
Division's initial objective. During this twenty-one hour period the
Division artillery, in close support of the assaulting troops, had fired
18,346 rounds, not including Corps and attached artillery battalions.
TOT's (Time on Target) were fired on Oberzier, Ellen, Arnoldsweiler, Merzenich and other targets in the Division zone. As many as
thirteen battalions were massed in the TOT's. To assist in the close
air support the artillery had fired seventeen counterflak and fifteen red
smoke missions.

BRIGHT MOONLIGHT FLOODS ROER RIVER AS YANKS START BIG PUSH CROSSING

By DON WHITEHEAD

WITH AMERICAN INFANTRY ON THE ROER RIVER, Feb. 23 (AP)—The
moon was very bright—too bright—for a night attack. But orders had been
issued for H-hour at 3:30 A. M.

"Hell, the Krauts can see us coming a mile away," a soldier growled.

The men in the battalion command post in a basement near the flooded Roer
didn't have much to do now except to wait for the hour of attack, which had
been held up for days by the Germans releasing water from the dams to the
south. All plans had been made and troops were in position near hidden assault
boats in which they were to cross the river.

Capt. Robert Neilsen of Bloomington, Calif., looked at his watch. His face
was drawn and his eyes red from lack of sleep. It was midnight.

Night Noises Loud

"It will be a lifetime from now till 3 o'clock," Neilsen commented. Outside guns boomed occasionally. There was an undercurrent of tenseness in the little room. A truck idled by outside and the slight noise made everyone look up.

Maj. Ray Waters of Richfield, Utah, laughed. "When I walked down the road a few minutes ago I tried to tip-toe. Those noises sound awfully loud at night with the Jerries just across the river," he said.

A telephone rang and someone reported figures were moving about on our side of the river. Neilsen began checking units to see who they were.

Smudge Pots Set

"We'd feel silly as hell if the Jerries came over and stole our boats," Waters chuckled.

They appeared relaxed and easy, but these men were sweating out those last hours before the attack. There were Neilsen, Waters, Lt. Allen Dean of Phillips, Tex., Capt. Max Eisner of Pittsfield, Mass., and Capt. Frank Schiele of Staten Island, N. Y.

Lt. Col. Fred Needham of Auburn, Calif., slept in the next room, resting up for the hard grind ahead.

Neilsen's check disclosed the men on the river bank were our troops putting out smudge pots to be used if necessary to throw up a smoke screen.

Commander Young

We decided to go down to the command post of Capt. Jerry Hooker of St. Petersburg, Fla., who was to lead one of the assault companies in the river crossing. The road toward the river was deserted and there were no signs of troops waiting inside the dark ruins of houses along the way.

Hooker looked much too young to be commanding a company. He looked younger even than his 24 years as he talked to tall, handsome Lt. Sam Jenkins of Cartersville, Ga., his weapons platoon leader.

"Don't wait for a signal from me," Hooker told Sam. "Three minutes before H-hour, shove 'em off."

Sam said, "Okay, will do," and he went out into the night.

There wasn't much talk here and what there was usually was brief and to the point. With Hooker were Sgt. Charles Courtney, Ft. Worth, Texas; T/Sgt. Robert Ogilvie, S. Pasadena, Calif.; Lt. Francis Ahrnsbrak, of Marshall, Okla.; and Sgt. George L. Woods, Riverside, Calif.

Drink of Scotch Saved

Hooker pulled out a bottle of Scotch with a couple of drinks left in it. "I have been saving this," he explained.

He took a drink and handed the bottle to Ahrnsbrak, saying, "Have one, Francis."

"Thanks, I wish I had those nine bottles I ordered," the Lieutenant replied.

A shell landed nearby and the little house shuddered.

"That one was coming in, pop," said Hooker. "It belongs to us now."

A lamp on the table cast long shadows on the walls and made the youthful faces look old, at times, as a light played across the lean, serious features of the men.

Hooker slung an automatic weapon across his shoulder, folded a single blanket and tied it on his back by criss-crossing a rope around his chest. He said, "I wish it were darker. It's a lot harder to get shot if they can't see you." Then he hung a grenade on his chest strap.

BARRAGE OPENS UP

Suddenly the big guns, which had been firing only occasional rounds, opened up with a mighty roar. The lamp trembled on the table and shadows danced in jitterbug nervousness.

"There the fireworks go," Tufts said.

"Punctuating the booming of the artillery was the clatter of machine guns raking the enemy-held shore. The soft moonlit night turned into a hellish roar of guns, the whispering of shells and the sound of the explosions.

At 3:15 Hooker said quickly: "Okay boys, let's go."

They stepped into the night. Houses were disgorging troops who moved silently in the moonlight.

We climbed into the attic of a battered house some hundreds of yards from the river to watch the attack go in.

SOME BOATS OVERTURN

Artillery shells burst in ripples of flame along the German-held banks of the Roer. Bright red chains of tracer bullets streaked across the leaden waters. There was a continuous pulsing roar of guns and angry outbursts of machine guns that grated the nerves like someone dragging his fingernails across a blackboard.

The dull glow of fire lit the skies and the smoke of explosions drifted upward, forming a fog in the moonlight.

Below us figures materialized from the shadows, lifted assault boats and walked to the river. They slid the craft into the swollen stream and clambered in and began paddling furiously.

The current caught the boats and they seemed to shoot downstream. Most of the boats got across safely, but a few German guns challenged them on the crossing, but some swamped in the swift stream and the men plunged into the icy waters—to be dragged under by the weight of their gear.

PRIVATE SNORES SERENELY

These assault units in this sector were led by Hooker, Lt. Ernest Fox of Salt Lake City, and Capt. Raymond Garino of Hackensack, N. J.

On the shore they began clawing their way against mounting German opposition. Fog began to settle over the river, shielding the movements, but then the German guns began bombarding the river banks and approaches.

The heavy crump of the shells made the old building tremble, and the crash of artillery and explosions became louder. But on the ground floor a youth snored serenely as though it were a quiet spring night. He was Pfc. Allen Clawson, Philadelphia, Pa.

"That guy can sleep through anything," a soldier remarked, and Clawson snored on.

Across the river the fighting raged as the doughboys fought deeper into enemy-held positions.

One more Nazi stronghold added to the swiftly growing list.

Lieutenant Colonel Farnum's 555th Ack-Ack Battalion poured 43,997 rounds of .50-caliber tracer and incendiary ammunition into the initial objectives and materially assisted the doughboys in their advance to phase line A. In addition, it was constantly on the alert for enemy aircraft, thereby preventing any effective bombing or strafing of the bridgehead. Seventeen missions of eight airplanes each were flown by the 9th Air Force, directed by Major Thomas Kiggins, in close support of the advancing infantrymen. Throughout the period the 329th Engineers were constantly busy ferrying the infantry in assault boats, and operating boats for supply and evacuation. No sooner had the small arms fire been taken from the bridgehead on the Roer than the 1106th Engineers started their bridging work. Throughout the night of 23-24 February, the engineers, often working under intense artillery and mortar fire, threw bridges across the Roer. By midnight, two infantry support bridges and one treadway bridge had been completed. Shortly after midnight the supporting weapons and heavy traffic began to roll forward.

Establishing a bridgehead is one of the roughest tasks given a combat outfit and the men of the engineers can recall some nightmarish episodes in connection with the 104th's Roer crossing. Private First Class Morton R. Lieberman, Company A, 329th Engineer Battalion, remembers how:

236

The old men of the outfit had already crossed the Mark River in Holland, and they knew an assault crossing is one of the toughest jobs the engineers have. We had our breakfast at 2100 on the 22d, and drove by truck to within one-quarter mile of our forward command post. Our assault boats had been dumped the previous night, and now we carried them to the command post. It was an eerie quiet, a stillness only broken by an occasional machine gun burst, or a whining shell. The infantry came up and we all huddled in the command post, which was formerly a creamery. Our barrage started at 0245. Rockets swished, shells whined, tanks and TD's whizzed by, mortars screamed, lowering an almost solid curtain of lead and steel on the far-side of the river.

Zero-hour arrived at 0330, and the infantry, plus a crew of engineers, had carried each sixty-pound assault boat to the river's edge. It was no easy job. We were loaded down with full equipment; the boats seemed to get heavier as we moved forward, foot by foot, through the oozing mud along the river bank.

The first wave of men jumped off at the scheduled moment. One engineer was in the bow of the boat setting the stroke, the other in the rear steering against the rush of water. A heavy haze of smoke and fog covered the water, aiding our concealment. The fourteen men in the boat stroked and struggled against the swift waters; finally we scraped the far shore. Luckily the men in my boat suffered no mishap, but there were other casualties from enemy fire. We constructed a ferry across the river to carry heavy equipment needed for supporting our advance. This ferry was maintained until a permanent bridge was constructed by the Corps engineers.

The medics are another combat unit to whom an assault crossing spells trouble. Setting up a route of evacuation and a forward collecting point is indeed a difficult task under such conditions, as Sergeant Eckhoff, C Company, 329th Medics, recalls:

At 0500, 22 February 1945, the company commander of C Company, 329th Medical Battalion, the battalion surgeon, 2d Battalion, 415th Infantry Regiment, and myself were in the church steeple overlooking the Roer River, where the plans were made for evacuating the casualties from the 2d Battalion after they crossed the river. After receiving instructions I started off for the river with medical supplies, two squads of litter bearers from C Company, and two technicians from the 2d Battalion Aid Station, in a weasel which I was driving. As we approached the river the ground was soft and marshy and the weasel was just able to slog its way through the flooded terrain until we reached a branch of the Roer. It was too deep to cross with the weasel so we hunted up and down stream until we found an infantry assault boat which we used to cross the branch. When we got on the other side, there was about 200 yards of flooded lowland to wade through, ankle and knee deep, before we got to the main stream. Here we decided to use another infantry assault boat which could be moved straight across the river because of its attachment to a heavy cable which was stretched from bank to bank. Once on the other side the technicians set up a temporary aid station in a factory about 300 yards from the river. They notified the aid men and litter bearers up front with the companies that they were ready, and our route of evacuation was established. After the first few casualties came through, we knew we had a complicated but efficient chain of evacuation. First step in this chain was from the front line back to the factory; here the technicians gave plasma, morphine, and administered whatever first aid was needed. Litter bearers then carried the casualties from the factory to the river; there another squad took over and pulled the patients across in the assault boat. Then one of the two squads on the other side lifted the litters out and carried them across the flooded terrain to the small branch of the river. Here the process of loading and unloading in an assault boat took place again. I was able to bring the weasel up to the rear bank and direct loading was possible. From here it was about 700 or 800 yards to a forward ambulance loading post; the patients were able to get warm in heated ambulances during their short trip to the collecting station in the basement of a church in Merken.

The litter bearers became fatigued quickly from carrying the litters through the sloshy mud. A group of German PWs were being brought back from the front and I requested their employment to carry the litters across the most difficult terrain. Under guard of infantry, the PWs were used until 0200, when the rate of casualties lessened and our litter bearers took over the relay post. All through the next day PWs were again employed; the line of evacuation continued working smoothly until the following day at 1800, when the collecting company was able to cross the river and the vehicles were able to transport casualties directly from the aid station.

ARNOLDSWEILER and OBERZIER . . . The relentless drive of the Timberwolves had crushed the outer defenses, gathered up 356 prisoners and resulted in the seizure of Huchem-Stammeln, Birkesdorf, and the northern part of Duren. The enemy had been knocked off balance and the Division, determined not to let the enemy get set, drove for Arnoldsweiler and Oberzier at 0300 on the 24th of February.

The 2d Battalion, 415th Infantry, sent strong patrols in the direction of Oberzier in the early morning of the 24th. The Germans had expected a night attack and had laid all night in the prepared defenses waiting for the Timberwolves. They had retired for a peaceful day when the 2d Battalion with Company G on the left and E on the right struck at 1100. Catching the enemy by surprise, the battalion quickly pierced the outer defenses, and after a stubborn house-to-house fight, Oberzier fell at 1700.

At 0300 Lieutenant Colonel Needham's 1st Battalion, with Companies B and C abreast, moved towards Arnoldsweiler. Immediately German resistance was encountered, but the skillful use of night tactics advanced the attacking troops over the 3,000 yards of open terrain into the outskirts of Arnoldsweiler. Upon reaching the edge of town they became engaged in their hardest fight. Arnoldsweiler was one of the key cities in the defense of the Roer. The Germans were determined not to give ground. It was a hand-to-hand fight all the way, with the advancing infantry being forced to bayonet the enemy from well-nigh

Bismarck surveys the ruins of Duren.

impregnable positions. The fighting became so ferocious that the medics were unable to get forward to assist in the evacuation of the wounded.

Finally at dusk the battalion had forced its way through one-third of the city. During the day six enemy counterattacks of infantry and armor had greatly impeded the advance of the battalions. At 0500 on 25 February, Colonel Needham's battalion rallied, launching an all-out attack, and completed the capture of the objective at 0900. After two and a half days of vicious fighting, Arnoldsweiler had fallen and the enemy had lost eight artillery pieces, one tank, two self-propelled guns, 200 dead and over 300 prisoners. The action had prevented the enemy from forming another strong defensive line and assisted materially in the final seizure of the Corps bridgehead.

For this outstanding action the Division commander has recommended the battalion be awarded a unit citation under provisions of Section IV, Circular 333, War Department, 1943:

The 1st BATTALION, 415TH INFANTRY REGIMENT, is cited for extraordinary heroism and outstanding performance of duty in armed conflict with the enemy during the period from 23 to 26 February 1945, in the vicinity of Birkesdorf and Arnoldsweiler, Germany. At 0330, 23 February 1945, the battalion forced a crossing of the violent, flood-swollen waters of the Roer River and over-ran a well established and heavily mined enemy position. Devastating counter fire failed to impede the advance to assigned objectives in Birkesdorf and the adjacent high ground to the north. In hand to hand combat the enemy was killed or routed. The fearless and aggressive drive of our assault elements enabled the medical aid men, during the height of battle, to rush immediately to the aid of the wounded and made it possible also for the assault engineers to construct one of the first bridges across the Roer River, over which weapons, supplies, and troops poured to support and sustain the attacking impetus not only of this unit but also of units to either side. With the battalion's objective well in hand by night, higher headquarters committed the unit to continue the attack another 3,000 yards to the east across unfamiliar terrain, in the blackness of night, until the capture of Arnoldsweiler, Germany, was assured. Without hesitation, the battalion plunged forward, weary, but indomitable. Again the unit met deadly artillery and self-propelled fire, but undaunted, obtained a sure foothold on the objective by dawn. At this point the enemy launched six furious counterattacks heavily supported by self-propelled guns and direct fire weapons emplaced in surrounding terrain. The battalion frustrated all these thrusts, inflicting heavy casualties on enemy personnel, and at the same time firmly entrenched themselves in position to rout the Germans from the town. After two and one half days of savage and relentless fighting, foregoing sleep and exposing themselves ceaselessly to danger, the battalion captured Arnoldsweiler, Germany, taking a toll of 200 dead Germans and over 250 prisoners. The gallant and intrepid battle waged by the battalion enabled the bridgehead of the Roer River to be so firmly and securely established that the enemy was reduced to impotence and stripped of any power to stem the powerful tide of our forces. The officers and men of the 1st BATTALION, 415TH INFANTRY REGIMENT, displayed inspired heroism and unflagging combat spirit against an enemy who offered formidable odds. Their initiative, courage, and esprit de corps reflected the finest traditions of the armed forces of the United States.

PHASE LINE B . . . In the late afternoon of 24 February, the 414th Infantry closed in assembly positions at Duren and Mariaweiler. The 1st and 3d Battalions, 413th Infantry, held phase line A, the 1st Battalion, 415th Infantry, held one-third of Arnoldsweiler, and the 2d Battalion, 415th Infantry, held Oberzier, which was the northern part of phase line B. Orders were issued in Operations Memorandum No.

38 directing the 413th Infantry to seize the great marshalling yards 1,500 yards to the east of Duren, as an area of departure for the attack to be launched by the 414th Infantry against Merzenich at 0300 on 25 February. In conjunction with Colonel Touart's assault, the 413th Infantry would attack from phase line A between the marshalling yards and the still-contested Arnoldsweiler, and seize the high ground and castle in the center of the Division zone along phase line B. The 415th was directed to launch an attack at midnight from Huchem-Stammeln against Ellen. These series of driving, converging and parallel operations required the utmost cooperation of all Timberwolf staff and troops. To completely crush the defenses along the Roer and to gain the Corps bridgehead, phase line B, the night operations must be successful. Much was at stake.

At 2100 Company G of Lieutenant Colonel Koster's 2d Battalion moved through the 1st Battalion outpost line and jumped off in an attack on the marshalling yards. Although they were opposed by heavy machine gun fire, the G-men were on the objective by 1015, and shortly thereafter Colonel Waltz received the message that the area of departure of the 414th had been secured. Between 2300 and 0200 the next morning, two counterattacks were launched against the newly gained position, and G Company repelled them at heavy cost to the enemy.

IRON BISMARCK EYES HIS TRIUMPH: DUREN'S DUST
By Graham Miller

With U. S. First Army Troops in Duren, Feb. 25.—Standing in the main square of the Rhineland city of Duren is a bronze statue of Germany's Iron Chancellor, Bismarck, architect of the policy of German aggression so eagerly adopted by Kaiser Wilhelm and Adolf Hitler. And this statue is the only thing left standing in the square.

There's not a house, not a tree, not a blade of grass, and it's a pity that Bismarck's bronze eyes, as they look out over this scene of ruin, can't record these fruits of aggression and transmit them to the whole German people.

Duren is the most completely smashed town I have ever seen in this war. It is gashed, splintered and torn, with here and there an acre or so of nothing but powdered rubble that grits between your teeth as the cold wind blows it about. And the statue of the Iron Chancellor looks down glumly.

Bodies Rot Underneath

There's the stench of death in Duren, too, for there are long-neglected bodies under the piles of rubble. There are a few fires still burning in the city's skeleton today and not a single civilian in sight.

A little way to the northeast, troops of Major Gen. Terry Allen's 104th Division have occupied the village of Merzenich, which is important because it stands on the highest ground in the Duren area. An advanced reconnaissance party was reported within 15 miles of Cologne.

It's safe to say, after 48 hours of this offensive, that it has been one of the most successful that any American army has ever launched. On this front of Lieut. Gen. Courtney H. Hodges' First Army everything has moved with a beautiful precision.

PLANES SNARL ENEMY

Nothing was left to chance and nothing went wrong. Every section of the gigantic machine of war worked smoothly. Our planes were there whenever they were needed in close support of infantry and they did a fine job of snarling up German troop movements and supplies.

It's good to report that our losses have been light. I can't give you the figures, but when a staff officer tonight announced the off-the-record totals of killed, wounded and missing, the war correspondents whistled with surprise.

It's also good to report that German casualties have been heavy. They couldn't have been otherwise under that terrific barrage of shells and bombings.

TANKS FAIL TO ARRIVE

The Jerries are surrendering easily. Today troops of the 104th Division captured a battalion of panzer grenadiers intact and complete with commander and staff. After a brief exchange of shots the enemy hung out a white flag and were found huddled in the cellars of a medieval castle at Rath, not far from Merzenich.

They didn't have any of their tanks around and when questioned they said they had been waiting for their armor to reach them and then were going to launch a counterattack. But somehow the tanks never arrived.

Tonight the Rhine is 15 miles ahead of the First Army and there is good tank country in front of us. So unless we are suddenly and heavily counterattacked, we may be on the banks of the Rhine sooner than we would have dared hope a month ago.

Three miles to the north, at midnight, Colonel Clough's 3d Battalion of the 415th struck for the citadel of Ellen. Ellen was the key road center in the northern part of the Division zone and its buildings were set on a high ridge and dominated the eastern banks of the Roer. No sooner had K Company jumped off than a German plane flew over and dropped a flare within one hundred yards of the tail of the advancing column. While the flare was burning out during the next ten minutes, K Company was pinned to the ground, but as soon as the flare was extinguished the men continued their advance over the 1,500 yards of open terrain. When 700 yards from the objective, the men rushed the northwest part of the town, employing marching fire. A burning haystack and two burning buildings lighted up the area, silhouetting the men, and making the advance considerably more difficult. By 0100 K Company was in Ellen and started its house-to-house mop-up. Shortly thereafter it was joined by I Company, and after much close combat the city was cleared by 0800. It was a difficult and nasty task. The

Germans, refusing to give up this key ground, launched a counterattack of tanks, SPs and infantry against the position, but the 3d Battalion stood its ground. At 0300, three hours after G Company, 413th Infantry, had seized the marshalling yards, and the 3d Battalion, 415th Infantry, had attacked Ellen, the 1st Battalion, 414th Infantry, and the 2d Battalion, 413th Infantry, attacked Merzenich and Rath respectively. Lieutenant Colonel Clark's 1st Battalion, 414th Infantry, plunged into the fray at 0300, jumping off from its line of departure at the marshalling yards, and advanced behind the rolling barrages of the 386th Field Artillery into Merzenich. It was a converging attack, one company closing in from the north and another from the south. Bewildered and beaten, the enemy surrendered in droves, and by 1230, at a cost of two casualties, Merzenich was in American hands.

Simultaneously Lieutenant Colonel Koster's 2d Battalion, less G Company, lunged forward for the high ground and Castle Rath 300 yards east of Arnoldsweiler. It was vital to seize this large medieval castle, for once in our hands it would isolate the troops defending Arnoldsweiler. Moving on the left flank of G Company, contact was made with the enemy 600 yards northeast of the marshalling yards. Disregarding burp gun and machine gun fire, Company A quickly eliminated the initial resistance and continued its advance, approaching the moated castle from the south. One platoon of Company A raced across a bridge spanning the moat which surrounded the fortress. Inside the wall they encountered five armored half-tracks and one self-propelled gun. Machine guns on the half-tracks swept the invaders. Quickly Captain Leigon sent a platoon to the rear of the castle. They waded the moat and moved in by the west gate. They were met by heavy small arms fire, which was eventually quelled, and the men overran the half-tracks. After spraying the windows and doors, the men moved to the large, sturdily built castle and systematically cleared room after room by throwing concussion grenades and spraying the interior with automatic fire. Company E moved up to the castle and aided in the assault. Although counterattacked several times from outside the castle walls, the companies wrested the fortress from the Germans prior to daylight, and by mid-morning the 2d Battalion, 413th Infantry, controlled it and the surrounding territory, after bagging more than 300 prisoners and accounting for almost as many dead.

At 0900, one hundred hostile infantrymen supported by tanks withdrew east out of Arnoldsweiler as the 1st Battalion, 415th Infantry, cleared the town. Seeing the enemy coming toward their position unaware that American troops were at their rear, Colonel Koster's troops withheld fire until they were fifty yards from them. Then all

With all modern conveniences, an automatic-rifle man of the 1st Battalion, 414th Regiment, tries to keep warm in his well ventilated foxhole.

weapons opened fire on the bewildered and helpless Germans. All were killed or captured. For this outstanding operation the battalion with attached units was awarded a unit citation by the War Department:

The 2D BATTALION, 413TH INFANTRY REGIMENT, reinforced by the following units: 2D PLATOON, ANTITANK COMPANY, 413TH INFANTRY REGIMENT; FO PARTIES (3), 385TH FIELD ARTILLERY BATTALION; LIAISON PARTY, 385TH FIELD ARTILLERY BATTALION; FO PARTY, CANNON COMPANY, 413TH INFANTRY REGIMENT; 2D PLATOON, COMPANY B, 750TH TANK BATTALION; MEDICAL DETACHMENT, 2D BATTALION SECTION, 413TH INFANTRY REGIMENT; FO PARTY, COMPANY A, 87TH CHEMICAL MORTAR BATTALION, is cited for extraordinary heroism and outstanding performance of duty against the enemy in the vicinity of Duren, Germany, during the period 24 to 26 February 1945. In the first of a series of night thrusts, the battalion advanced across 2,000 yards of flat terrain crisscrossed by enemy entrenchments, to seize a railroad marshalling yard, its initial objective. Two hundred enemy troops were killed and captured in the attack. Quickly reorganizing, the 2D BATTALION, 413TH INFANTRY REGIMENT, repulsed, without yielding ground, three enemy counterattacks by German infantry supported by self-propelled guns and mortars. At 0300, 25 February, the battalion again advanced under cover of darkness to seize the next objective, a moated castle 3,000 yards away. Although all the approaches to the castle were defended and the surrounding woods occupied by enemy troops, the

244

2D BATTALION, 413TH INFANTRY REGIMENT, assaulted the strongpoint and engaged in hand-to-hand combat until all resistance was overcome and the garrison either killed or captured. At daylight, the battalion was counterattacked from the rear and front simultaneously by enemy infantry now supported by artillery, as well as self-propelled guns, flak guns, and mortars. Containing the frontal counterattack by fire, the American battalion destroyed the attacking force in its rear. Then by concentrating all fire power to the front, the second enemy force was annihilated. This success was followed up by an aggressive assault, which completely overran the main enemy defenses in the area consisting of elaborate entrenchments and 88mm. guns in concrete emplacements. The final action led to the break-out of American armor onto the Cologne plain. The initiative, courage, and aggressiveness of the 2D BATTALION, 413TH INFANTRY REGIMENT and its attached units are in keeping with the finest traditions of the armed forces of the United States.

By 0900 on 25 February, the 104th had secured phase line B and eliminated all German resistance in its zone extending five miles east of the Roer River. The night attacks on 24-25 February were completed with amazing success and the prisoner of war total had swelled to over 1,500. Only the best troops, skillful in night operations, could have perfected and executed this daring operation. The enemy was caught completely off balance by the vicious night fighting of the Timberwolf veterans.

Headline after headline carried the stories of the Timberwolf Division successes. In the 26 February edition of the Washington *Evening Star*, there appeared the following account by AP's Don Whitehead:

WITH THE UNITED STATES FIRST ARMY IN GERMANY, Feb. 26.—Maj. Gen. Terry Allen, who once led the Fighting 1st Infantry Division, has another red-hot division which now is winning combat laurels. It's the 104th Infantry Division, known as the Timberwolves.

The dark-haired little general's outfit is the talk of the First Army as Lt. Gen. Courtney H. Hodges' men drive toward Cologne after crossing the Roer River in one of the most spectacular night operations of the campaign.

It's a tough, disciplined outfit which has made a specialty of night fighting. It takes well-trained, disciplined, aggressive troops to fight successfully in darkness—troops with a lot of confidence in themselves and their division, and that is what Gen. Allen has achieved with his new command.

INSTILLS CONFIDENCE IN MEN

It isn't a coincidence that the 104th has absorbed a lot of the fighting qualities of its slender leader. Gen. Allen has the knack of instilling confidence and

For this group of Roer River defenders the war was over.

fight into the men under him and making them proud of their unit—and the Timberwolves are being compared now with the veteran Fighting 1st.

Gen. Allen began specializing in night attacks in Tunisia, when his troops attacked at El Guettar in the darkness and routed the Germans.

During the Sicilian campaign, the 1st Division attacked almost solely at night in driving the Germans back toward Messina, and now Gen. Allen has another pack of night prowlers.

In driving from Aachen to the Roer River, the Timberwolves made every major assault during dark and captured many difficult objectives with amazingly light losses. The 104th has probably the lowest casualty rate of any combat division.

CROSSED ROER AT NIGHT

The Roer River crossing was one of the Division's moonlight masterpieces. They swarmed across the river in assault boats behind a terrific artillery barrage and literally clawed their way through enemy positions and established a solid bridgehead alongside the 8th Infantry Division.

Then guns, ammunition, equipment, and supplies flowed smoothly into the bridgehead with hardly a hitch.

Another striking achievement has been Gen. Allen's training of replacements, at combat school near the front lines. Youths who have had no combat experience get actual practice in their front line jobs under direction of veterans.

When they join their units they know where they are going and what to do about it.

Similar news articles told of the 104th's continued achievements:

FIRST ARMY PATH IS CLEAR

Duren, Germany, Feb. 25 (UP)—Maj. Gen. Terry Allen's Timberwolves of the 104th Infantry Division, having swept through the last remnants of German resistance in this flattened city today, were ready for another plunge forward.

246

They are so enthusiastic over their crossing of the formidable Roer that they are looking forward to crashing through to the Rhine.

The country beyond Duren ridge is more or less flat and is suitable for any armor the Americans get across the Roer.

The soldiers are almost buoyant in spirit. Maybe the weather is one reason. The snow has disappeared and the last few days have been bright with a touch of spring. The wind is drying up the ground so that there is good solid terrain. It will make for fast moving.

Duren really has been beaten up. What the Air Force did not do, the artillery completed.

Prisoners taken today report that great Cologne is about as badly beaten as Duren. Civilians remaining in Cologne are living in ruins, they said.

The relentless fighting for fifty-three hours by the infantrymen was skillfully supported by all attached units. Owing to the determination of the Division and the 1106th Engineer Group, the assault boat crossing had been successful, and prior to midnight on the 24th, five bridges consisting of two treadways, one Bailey and two infantry support, were in operation in the Division zone. With utter disregard for their own safety, the engineers worked night and day to provide the advancing troops with adequate supplies and supporting arms. Throughout the 24th, enemy planes constantly attacked the Timberwolf bridges, but the 555th frustrated twenty-six enemy air attacks. During each assault the 750th Tank Battalion, the 692d Tank Destroyer Battalion and the Division artillery were in on the kill.

The heavy traffic over the Roer bridges flowed freely, thanks to the MP's and the paddock system inaugurated by General Allen. Each vehicle had been classified as to the time when it would be needed at the front and was then placed in a "paddock," like a racehorse awaiting call. When the vehicles got the nod, they immediately moved to the river without interference and crossed without waiting to be exposed to enemy artillery and aircraft. All the operations necessitated superior communications, which were constantly maintained by the 104th Signal Company. The 104th Quartermaster Company and the 804th Ordnance Company kept the ammunition, weapons and gasoline rolling to the front. Timberwolf teamwork was paying off.

CATHEDRAL SPIRES IN THE DISTANCE

The VII Corps plan for the assault of the Roer directed the 104th Division and the 8th Infantry Division to make the initial crossing with the 4th Cavalry Group and the 3d Armored Division in Corps Reserve. Upon capture of the Corps bridgehead, the 3d Armored Division would pass through the 8th and the 104th Divisions in its drive for the Erft Canal, and the 4th Cavalry Group would pass through the 415th Infantry and clear the Hambach Forest directly to the east, linking up with the 3d Armored Division just short of the Erft.

The operations had proceeded ahead of schedule, and by 25 February the enemy was reeling, the terrific night attacks of the Timberwolves having kept him constantly off balance. Three miles to the east of the most advanced position of the bridgehead lay two other fortress cities, Morschenich and Golzheim. Lieutenant General Collins, the VII Corps commander, wanted to make certain that when Major General Maurice Rose's 3d Armored Division was committed, it would not be stopped by these strongpoints. It was determined that the Timberwolves should widen the bridgehead in order to assure the unimpeded advance of the armor. The 104th Division was again to attack at night to seize the enlarged bridgehead, with the specific responsibility of eliminating all resistance prior to 0600 on 26 February, at which time the 3d Armored Division would roll through our lines and exploit the success.

MORSCHENICH and GOLZHEIM . . . The Timberwolves again struck at night with the 1st Battalion, 413th Infantry, assaulting Morschenich and with the 2d Battalion, 414th Infantry, attacking Golzheim. At dusk the 1st Battalion left Birkesdorf for its forward assembly position near the castle then held by the 2d Battalion. After the four-mile march through the battered town of Arnoldsweiler and surrounding areas, in the faint glow of an overcast moon, the battalion reached the castle without incident. With final briefing of company commanders completed, A and B Companies abreast started for Morschenich, which lay three miles away on the far side of a deep forest. They were making a frontal assault on the city from the west. Company C, led by the battalion executive officer, Major Marshall Garth, was to sweep in from the right, assaulting the town from the south. Companies A and B, after advancing 800 yards, ran into a storm of fire from small arms, machine guns and SP guns. Our 57's drove off the self-propelled guns, and by employing marching fire, the enemy small arms and machine guns were silenced. Closely following their supporting artillery and 4.2 mortars, the two companies continued their advance until stopped by enemy fire 1,000 yards short of the objective. Company C, guiding on the Duren-Cologne railroad, advanced 3,000 yards, then cut sharply to the left, driving hard on the objective from the south. In its quick thrust the battalion overran three tanks and swept into the city at 0100.

Blasting a path for the infantry

Immediately the Boche counterattacked and was dispersed by fire from the battalion's heavy weapons. Shortly thereafter A and B Companies swept out of the woods, across the plain, and entered the city from the west. By 0545 the objective had been completely mopped up and all resistance had been cleared. The action had netted 315 prisoners including two regimental commanders, their staffs, and several high-ranking officers. The enemy had been dazed by the ferociousness of the attack and the audacity of the night advance. At the very time of their capture the commanders were in the process of completing plans for the defense of the city against a daylight attack. In recognition of its bold and successful attack the battalion has been recommended for a unit citation under the provisions of Section IV, Circular 333, War Department, 1943:

The 1st BATTALION, 413TH INFANTRY REGIMENT, is cited for extraordinary heroism and outstanding performance of duty in armed conflict with the enemy during the period from 23 February to 26 February 1945 in the vicinity of Morschenich, Germany. During this period the 1st BATTALION, 413TH INFAN-TRY REGIMENT, distinguished itself by its skillful and fearless performance of an extremely hazardous and vitally important dual mission of clearing and securing a safe passageway for armor to push through in force, and also to seize and secure the city of Morschenich, only 1,000 yards northeast of a road cut which afforded the enemy excellent fields of fire and superior observation on the only available passageway for the armored columns. On the night of 25 February 1945, the battalion launched a daring night attack on the town simultaneously from front and rear. Two-thirds of the battalion launched a frontal assault, and despite several enemy strongpoints and heavy artillery, they quickly pushed forward, overpowered all opposition, and seized the road cut. Having secured this strategic objective, the force unrelentingly continued its frontal assault on Morschenich. Despite a minefield and severe fire from strongpoints

249

Award of Distinguished Service Cross. By direction of the President, under the provisions of AR 600-45, 22 September 1943, as amended, and under authority contained in Circular No. 32, Headquarters European Theater of Operations, United States Army, 20 March 1944, as amended, the Distinguished Service Cross is awarded to:

First Lieutenant EVERETT E. PRUITT, 01289319, Infantry, 415th Infantry Regiment, 104th Infantry Division, United States Army, for extraordinary heroism in connection with military operations against the enemy. On 30 December 1944, Lieutenant PRUITT, a platoon leader, led a six-man patrol across the remains of a destroyed bridge over the Roer River in Germany. When three of his men stepped on enemy mines, becoming casualties, he rendered first aid and ordered his squad to withdraw, dispatching one man to return for litter bearers. Though the area was now heavily subjected to enemy machine gun and small arms fire, Lieutenant PRUITT, with no thought for his own personal safety, alternately fired upon an advancing enemy patrol and assisted his wounded men. When his carbine became jammed, he hurled hand grenades at the enemy, holding them back while his men crossed the bridge. Learning that one of his men was not present, he courageously started to return to the scene of the fighting, despite the known dangers of the mine field and the lurking enemy troops. As he advanced across the bridge, he heard the missing man call to him, saying that he had reached safety by swimming the river. The devotion to duty and great leadership of Lieutenant PRUITT were an inspiration to all. His extraordinary heroism and courageous actions reflect great credit upon himself and are in keeping with the highest traditions of the military service. Entered military service from Texas.

of resistance, these frontal assault units, utilizing supporting fires in superb manner, successfully beat back all enemy resistance and entered the city from the west. Simultaneously one reinforced company executed a wide sweeping flanking attack, and, although subjected to heavy enemy small arms, machine gun, and SP fire from a strongly entrenched and well prepared enemy, this small task force fought its way to the town from the east. Because of the piercing fire power and outstanding surprise achieved by this daring and well coordinated movement, a total of 315 enemy prisoners and much booty were taken during the course of the operation, including two regimental commanders and their complete staffs. Fierce house-to-house fighting followed and after a period of mopping up the town was completely secured. A defense was quickly organized and two fierce armor-infantry counterattacks in force were repulsed. A traffic control plan was quickly and effectively put into effect, facilitating the movement of vehicles through the area. The conspicuous gallantry, aggressiveness and devotion to duty displayed by the members of the battalion in the performance of an extremely difficult task insured a successful route to the plains of Cologne for the armored forces. The eminently significant accomplishment of this gallant and cohesive fighting force was instrumental in breaching the entire defense system in this sector, enabling the entire Corps to advance uninterruptedly to the Rhine River. The gallant heroism and intrepidity displayed by the officers and men of the 1ST BATTALION, 413TH INFANTRY, are in keeping with the finest of military traditions, reflecting distinct credit upon the armed forces of the United States.

Lieutenant Colonel Cummins' 2d Battalion, 414th Infantry, launched an attack at 2130 against Golzheim with the mission of clearing the town by 0600. The attack was to be launched from Merzenich, which was held by the 1st Battalion. The distance between the two towns was, by direct line, approximately three miles. The ground was flat and capable of being covered by hostile antitank fire with no defilade available. There was no antitank obstacle between the towns and there was a suitable roadnet which made a tank attack possible, unless the roads were mined. The moon was nearly full but the atmosphere was slightly hazy. An object as large as a tank was discernible at about a hundred yards. Colonel Cummins decided to attack the town with tanks, tank destroyers and infantry under the cover of artillery fire. The armor was divided in three parts, each advancing simultaneously over a different route, there being three roads leading into Golzheim from Merzenich. The infantrymen of two companies were carried on the armor, each armored vehicle carrying approximately ten doughboys. The distance between the line of departure and the objective was accurately scaled on each route and the two phase lines were set up by mileage. The column commanders were not to cross the first phase line until ordered by the tank company commander, this order to be given only when all columns had reached the line. The second phase line was fixed at 300 yards from the town, where the armor would deploy, the infantry dismounting for the assault, from which positions the tanks and the tank destroyers would employ their heavy guns. All fire was to open on the town at the tank commander's order. The 386th Field Artillery Battalion would commence firing on the town at 2130 and continue to do so until ordered to cease. Their howitzers not only kept the enemy in the basements, but also gave direction to the attack by dropping occasional rounds of white phosphorous.

At 2130 the night operation proceeded as planned, with the armor, mounted by infantry, converging on the town from three directions. When the second phase line was reached the armor quickly deployed and, for fifteen minutes, fired directly into the city while the infantry dismounted and rushed the objective. As soon as the infantry had reached the town, tanks were led by the doughs to various strongpoints of resistance, and by 0200 this excellent teamwork resulted in the seizure of Golzheim. At the cost of seven casualties, Colonel Cummins' 2d Battalion had captured 227 German prisoners, including a battalion commander and several other officers.

As further evidence of surprise gained in this action we quote John McDermott, in his Washington *Times-Herald* story:

CARELESS LOVE BLOOMS IN RUINS UNDER SHELLFIRE

Golzheim, Germany, Feb. 27 (UP).—Love is a wonderful thing, the grimy sergeant said. Several "slave" workers left behind by the fleeing Germans were so busy catching up with love-making they didn't hear the Yanks arrive.

Sergt. James T. Sobansky, of Washington, Pa., told the story as we sat on a pile of potatoes in a cellar while shells continued to fall around us.

IT WAS THIS WAY

A short time before, tank-riding doughboys of the 104th Infantry Division had stormed this shell-shattered village, which is within sight of Cologne.

Sobansky and his men entered one shell-damaged building searching for any snipers who had remained behind. They weren't expecting what they discovered in one room.

"We found four good-looking but scantily clad babes and four Polish men. The men were stripped down to their long drawers.

"I sort of hated to break up what looked like the warmest lovers' rendezvous in Europe. They weren't paying a bit of attention to the war going on outside," the sergeant said.

"The women and men all were about 25 years old. They were wearing dresses and nothing more. The men, caught in their long, white drawers, looked at us sheepishly.

"I don't think the surprised look on their faces was any greater than those of the soldiers who swarmed into the building to have a look," he said.

So They Were Prisoners

Sobansky's commander, Lieut. Stanley R. Blunck, Oakland, Calif., confirmed that the men were Polish. He didn't know the nationality of the women. No one knew why the eight had been left behind. They believed the men were "slave" workers brought in by the Germans and left behind when their captors fled.

The 104th lost two men killed and several wounded in taking Golzheim. They captured 227 prisoners, including the eight lovers.

"Both men and girls protested being prisoners with so little clothing, but I didn't trust them out of sight. Off they went to the stockade as they were," Sobansky said.

ERFT CANAL . . . Adding the towns of Golzheim and Morschenich to its long list of seizures, the Division had provided a way for the 3d Armored Division's attack through the lines of the 413th and the 414th Infantry Regiments, with both infantry units closely following the armored spearheads. At 1700 the 3d Battalion, 414th, moved from Merzenich to Buir. At 2300 the regiment was in Buir, with K Company occupying two small localities 3,000 yards to the east. The other units of Colonel Touart's aggregation completed the mop-up in their zone, with the 1st and 2d Battalions located in Golzheim.

The Seagulls mopped up all resistance within their area, closing behind the 3d Armored, with the 2d Battalion closing in on Mannheim three miles northeast of Buir. At 0700 the 4th Cavalry Group passed through Colonel Cochran's "Old Faithful" Regiment, and later in the day the 415th Infantry reverted to Division reserve in positions at Arnoldsweiler, Duren and Merzenich. The 3d Armored Division had made excellent progress and the Timberwolves were ably mopping up all bypassed resistance.

On the 27th the 413th and the 414th Infantry Regiments continued their operations of leapfrogging battalions from town to town closely behind the onrushing armor while the 415th Infantry remained in Division reserve. Over 2,000 German civilians were wandering aimlessly and hopelessly within the Division zone and for the first time the Military Government and counterintelligence corps personnel were confronted with the difficult problem of civilian control. Late in the afternoon the 3d Armored Division, which had advanced due east of Buir, had moved through Sindorf and Heppendorf and then cut north out of the Division zone. Colonel Cummins' 2d Battalion of the 414th Infantry, closely following the 3d Armored, quickly eliminated resistance. On the north the 2d Battalion, 413th Infantry, now under the command of Lieutenant Colonel Irvine (Lieutenant Colonel Koster had been wounded by strafing planes on 26 February), advanced to Heppendorf, and by 1430 had rid the town of all resistance. Immediately the 413th and the 414th Infantry Regiments shot patrols forward to the Erft Canal. All resistance in the Division zone had been crushed and now plans for crossing the obstacle were already in preparation.

At 1828 on 27 February, Corporal Zalowsky of the 2d Platoon, Company C, 692d Tank Destroyer Battalion, fired three rounds of high explosive 90mm into Cologne at a range of 19,000 yards. At 1835, seven minutes later, two platoons of Company A fired three platoon volleys into the cathedral city. Optimism ran high; the Timberwolves were now within range of Germany's third largest city, and everyone was confident that it would soon fall prey to the hard-hitting 104th.

On the left was the 3d Armored, and on the right the 8th Infantry closed along the Erft Canal the following day. The next operation for the VII Corps was to force a crossing of the Erft Canal. This barrier consisted of three canals approximately three feet deep and ranging from twelve to thirty feet in width. It was essential that the crossing be made with the least delay so as to take further advantage of a disorganized enemy. After receiving its directive from the VII Corps, Division issued its operations memoranda and field orders detailing the plans for the final assault on Cologne. The terrain was flat and swampy, and immediately to the east of the canal lay the towns of Quadrath, Ichendorf and Horrem. Just behind the towns was a high ridge running from north to south across the Division front. The approaches to the ridge were obstructed by large pits and slagpiles which would canalize any frontal attack on the Vorgebirge Hills. It looked like an impossible task.

James L. Kilgallen, International News Service, speaks of the drive to the Erft Canal in his 27 February story:

BEATEN NAZIS PICKED UP BY THOUSANDS
Driving U. S. Armies Engulf Rhine Foe; Push on Erft River

Paris, Feb. 27 (Tuesday).—Two powerful American Armies, scooping up prisoners by the thousands, shattered German defenses before the Rhine and thrust strong spearheads to within 10 miles of Cologne yesterday as artillerymen of the First Army hurled heavy shells into that Rhineland bastion for the first time in the war.

Spilling over the breached Cologne plain defenses in a swelling tide, the U. S. First and Ninth Armies lunged to within three miles of the Erft River after seizing the defense center of Blatzheim and racing two miles farther east. Blatzheim is 12 miles from the great fortress of Cologne on the Rhine.

3,000 Prisoners a Day Captured

International News Service Staff Correspondent Lee Carson, with the American troops on the Cologne plain, reported whole battalions of Germans were falling into the American net as the Yanks rode roughshod over weakening enemy resistance.

"Since the First and Ninth Armies crossed the Roer, 69 towns have been captured and the prisoner count has averaged 3,000 daily, but today the number of prisoners was impossible to count," she reported. "Entire battalions (normally numbering around 1,000 men) are being engulfed," she said.

"It is obvious that Field Marshal Karl Gerd von Rundstedt considers the military situation hopeless," the dispatch said, pointing out that the enemy now could not expect to make a major stand along the Erft, last barrier before the Rhine itself.

LIGHTNING THRUST BAGS DOZEN TOWNS

After Major General Terry Allen's Timberwolf Division of the First Army seized Golzheim, 14 miles west of Cologne, American infantry struck out in a lightning-like thrust that swiftly enveloped at least another dozen towns.

One strongpoint after another was toppled by the teams of infantry and armor that encircled and then seized their objectives with almost monotonous regularity.

Driving enemy infantry and panzers before them as they raced for the Rhine, American First Army tanks threw a curling arm around the towns and villages in their path. Then the infantry swept in to complete the job.

At least 30 more towns and villages thus fell to the Yanks along an erupting front east of the Roer now widened to 35 miles.

The Corps plan had directed crossings by the 3d Armored on our left and the 8th Infantry Division on our right in a coordinated attack to commence in the early morning of 1 March. For the 104th Division, the 413th and the 414th Infantry Regiments were directed to force crossings and seize the towns of Quadrath, Ichendorf and Horrem. As soon as the 413th Infantry and the right flank elements of the 3d Armored Division had cleared the high ground in the northern part of our zone, the 415th Infantry would pass through the "Seagulls," and after reaching the Vorgebirge Hills would swing south and clear the high ridge east of the pits and the slagpiles. This operation, as planned, would eliminate the necessity of a frontal attack against the commanding hills which overlooked the distant spires of Cologne. Through the 28th of February, all Division units coiled behind the Erft in preparation for the assault. The 2d Battalion, 413th Infantry, advanced on Ahe, just west of the Erft, and by 1400 held it firmly. The 1st Battalion closed into Heppendorf at 1640. The 329th Engineers completed clearing the debris in Mannheim, Sindorf, Buir and Heppendorf. They also put all roads in condition preparatory for the attack. Throughout the day engineer reconnaissance parties were determining the most suitable sites for crossing. Just prior to nightfall, at the Division command post in Buir, General Allen and the Assistant Division Commander, Colonel George A. Smith, Jr., formed all plans and orders with unit commanders. Colonel Smith had joined the Division on 26 February, relieving Brigadier General Moore, who had assumed command of the 8th Infantry Division. At dark, patrols from the 413th and the 414th Infantry went forward to make last-minute checks on the crossing sites. W. C. Heinz describes this patrol action in the New York *Sun*, 2 March 1945:

PATROL FOUND BRIDGE ACROSS ERFT

Good Night's Work Helped Americans Get Over Last Water Barrier Before Rhine

With the 104th Division on the Cologne Plain, March 2.—As beaten-up Rhineland towns go, Sindorf got off quite easily, and in one of the better cellars the colonel and his staff were sweating out the patrol.

"Let's get them in here," the colonel said, "as soon as they come in."

Every time the Americans move out on an attack, every time they push forward, there have to be a few Americans who go first. Sometimes they go out in strength and they try to draw enemy fire and to see how far they can get—and then they are a combat patrol. Sometimes they go out, three or four or five of them, to find out where the enemy is or perhaps to find out if there is still a bridge across a river—and then they are a reconnaissance patrol, which is what this patrol was that the colonel was waiting for.

Patrolling is business as sticky as it is important, and if the officers in the battalion command post were sweating out the patrol it was not because they were afraid the kids had dropped into a neighborhood movie or were around the corner shooting pool. They had started out toward the Germans, five of them, in the darkness at 9 o'clock, and now it was 11 o'clock, and in the command post of the 1st Battalion of the 414th Infantry Regiment of this Timberwolf Division the officers were waiting.

What the colonel—Lieut. Col. Robert Clark of St. Joseph, Mo.—was going to try to do was to put his men across the last water barrier between the Americans and the Rhine, the Erft canals. Outside they had assault boats and wooden planks waiting, and what the colonel was trying to find out was whether they were going to be able to plank the railroad bridge or whether the Germans had blown up the bridge, making it necessary to put the infantry across in assault boats, which would be a more difficult thing.

Corporal Reports

Now when the corporal who has been with the patrol came in it was about 11:10, and of course nobody said they were glad to see him or that they'd been sweating him out, although both those things were true. The corporal—Fred Wagoner of Gibsonville, N. C.—just came in and took off his helmet and stood there for a minute, a big guy with big hands, and then Lieut. John Hurley of Dorchester, Mass., who is with the 104th Engineers, asked him what they'd found out.

"The railroad bridge is blown," Wagoner said, "but I think we can cross if we lay some heavy timbers on it."

"You mean you actually saw the bridge?" the lieutenant said. "You mean you can show me on the map?"

The corporal said that he could. There was a dusty, old, red plush, gold-brocaded couch against one wall, and the lieutenant motioned the corporal down on the couch next to him and they went over the map, the corporal talking and pointing with his heavy finger.

"We walked up here to the edge of the woods and saw all this flooded area," the corporal said. "We couldn't find any place to put a bridge in that other place."

TELLS ABOUT THE BRIDGE

"Yeah, yeah," the lieutenant said, "but what about the railroad bridge? Are you sure we can put a whole company across? What does it look like? How big a hole has it got in it?"

"Well, sir," the corporal said, and he talked very slowly, "Mikon and I both saw it. A few twelve-foot planks will do the job. One side is blown off and that's dropped down and is lying in the bed."

"Mikon," the lieutenant said. "Get Mikon before he gets away."

Wagoner turned to the man sitting next to him on the couch. The man was Lieut. Mort Kauffman of 66 West 88th street, New York, who is public relations officer for the Timberwolves but who very often goes up to see for himself what it's all about.

"I was really sweatin'," Wagoner said. The lieutenant said he believed him.

When Sgt. Felix Mikon of Beaver Falls, Pa., came in, the three other men who were also on the patrol came in with him. They were Staff Sergt. James Dioquino of Norfolk, Va., Sergt. Ralph Repp of Lancaster, Pa., and Sergt. Fred Hill of Moro, Ark., and they looked tired and their faces were wan in the yellow light from the one bare bulb hanging from the middle of the ceiling.

What Mikon said was just what Wagoner had said, and the lieutenant seemed satisfied, and the colonel, who had been listening, went back to his map. At 3 o'clock in the morning the American infantry pushed off across the last water barrier between them and the Rhine, and when they went they knew where they were going and how they were going because another American patrol had done another night's work in this war.

Prior to midnight General Allen and his aides, Captain James Eastman and Lieutenant Collins, and Colonel Smith went forward to the 414th Infantry CP, then located in Sindorf, to direct the coming operations. At 0240 the Division artillery started its preparatory fires and the infantry and the engineers moved to the west bank of the first canal.

Just prior to 0300, a heavy artillery shell demolished the 2d Battalion, 414th Infantry, command post, killing three of the senior officers. The Assistant Division Commander, Colonel George A. Smith, Jr.; the Commanding Officer of the 414th Infantry, Colonel Anthony J. Touart; and the Commanding Officer of the 2d Battalion, 414th Infantry, Lieutenant Colonel Joseph M. Cummins, Jr., were instantly killed while directing operations. During the brief time that Colonel Smith had been with the Timberwolves he had earned the respect and admiration of the Division for his fearlessness and unswerving devotion to duty. Colonel Touart had commanded the 414th Infantry since

its activation in September 1942, and his death was a severe blow to the Mountaineers and to all those who knew him through the many tedious days of training and hard months of relentless combat. The Timberwolves lost a gallant leader and a true friend in "Tony." Lieutenant Colonel Cummins had commanded the 2d Battalion, 414th Infantry, since the spring of 1944, and was a proven combat leader. With Lieutenant Colonel Aurand E. Linker immediately assuming command of the regiment and Major Melhop taking over the 2d Battalion, the operations proceeded as planned. At 0530 Colonel Gerald C. Kelleher, executive officer of 415th Infantry, took command of the 414th.

Not only did enemy artillery take its toll that night in Sindorf, but the Luftwaffe struck harassing blows that in some cases had telling effects. To bomb installations was bad enough, but when Jerry started eliminating kitchens, that was too much for Corporal Williams Rogers, of the 414th Infantry's Cannon Company:

It was one of those cold, windy nights in March—the Cannon Company CP was located in the heart of the city of Sindorf, Germany, approximately one mile from the gun positions. As usual the Luftwaffe was up, although in small numbers. Unopposed, they continually dropped flares in order to pick their targets. Then in a seemingly leisurely and methodical manner, they would dive on their objectives. This practice continued throughout the night extensively until about 0400, when the majority of the planes seemed to vanish, leaving only one for harassing purposes. . . . Then it happened.

This lone enemy plane dropped his stick of bombs near the company headquarters. One bomb struck the building which housed the kitchen and its personnel. After the whistle of the last bomb, nothing was heard except the terrifying screams of the kitchen crew. Due to the fact that there was no cellar in the house, all of the occupants were trapped. The entire roof of the building was destroyed and all the rooms were sprayed with bomb fragments.

Immediately after seeing what had happened, I ran out to my jeep with the intention of going for an ambulance, only to find all the tires punctured by shrapnel. As there was no other alternative, I drove the jeep in this condition until I reached the regimental aid station, where I secured an ambulance. As I returned to the scene of the tragedy, I could still hear the faint sound of the plane overhead circling around.

Lieutenant Baker, who was in charge of company headquarters, later made a survey of the kitchen equipment, only to find that ninety per cent had been damaged beyond repair. Even though the kitchen was practically demolished, the kitchen personnel were ready to move on to the next position within a few hours fully prepared to serve a hot meal to the men.

At 0300 the Timberwolves charged recklessly into the enemy fire, crossing in assault boats at some points, splashing through the shallows on foot in others, and even swimming the canal to get closer to the enemy. There was no stopping them . . . the 1st and 2d Battalions,

Regimental commanders receive the Silver Star. Left to right: Colonel Waltz (413th Infantry), Colonel Touart (414th Infantry), and Colonel Cochran (415th Infantry)

414th Infantry, with the 1st Battalion on the right, pushed across the canal barrier, and by 1300 seized the industrial city of Horrem. Fighting against enemy small arms, mortar and artillery fire, the battalions moved steadily ahead. On the left, the 2d Battalion, 413th Infantry, with Company B attached, swiftly crossed the Erft barriers. Company E led off, quickly followed by F and G, and by 0320 the canal obstacles were behind them. A Class 40 bridge across the main channel was captured intact. By 0410 all company objectives had been taken, including the large castle on the east banks of the canal and the twin city area of Quadrath-Ichendorf.

It was not until 0710 that a thoroughly confused Boche garrison tried a counterattack. It came in from the north in strength of about a hundred infantrymen, but was quickly smashed by the 385th and 387th Field Artillery Battalions. Although the town had been taken, there were still German troops in the nearby hills, and the slow job of digging them out was completed at 1600. Incoming artillery and mortar fire increased in tempo as the day went on, blasting the town and its surrounding approaches.

Company B, 329th Engineer Battalion, constructed foot-bridges and operated assault boats across the Erft in support of the 414th Infantry while Company A rendered the same support to the 413th Infantry. A fifty-foot Bailey bridge was completed by C Company of the 329th Engineers at 1330 and another Bailey bridge was completed in the 413th Infantry area by the 1106th Engineers. Immediately tanks, tank destroyers, and infantry supporting weapons were moved across the waterways. The 415th Infantry remained in Division reserve, but throughout the day all commanders were busily occupied in reconnaissance and planning for the future employment of the regiment.

To the men of Company F, 413th Infantry, fell Von Oppenheim's castle, the fifth castle in five days. In fact, Sergeant Ed Cunningham, *Yank* feature writer, calls this the "Castle Company":

Schloss Schlenderhan, Germany—The room was dark except for the glowing coals in the fireplace which threw off just enough heat and light to make it an ideal setting for some story-telling. Everybody was comfortable, lounging in overstuffed chairs or stretched out on the two long divans which flanked the fireplace. They listened intently to the story being told by Capt. Walter Leigon of Clifton, Tex., CO of F Company of this regiment of the 104th Infantry Division. All of them knew it by heart because they had made the story. But this was one of those tales that improved with repetition.

"This is the second German castle we've captured in five days," Capt. Leigon said. "Our first was at Arnoldsweiler just east of the Roer River. That one was right out of King Arthur's Knights of the Round Table. It was a big red brick building with turrets on each side and a 15-yard moat around it that was filled with water three or four feet deep. Then, yesterday, we took this one, which is just the opposite. It's as modern as anything you'd find back in the States. It belongs to a Baron Von Oppenheim, a Cologne banker, and has 40 rooms with 10 baths and a stable of racing horses that is supposed to be one of the best in Europe."

"This is strictly a classy joint," Pfc. Robert Myers, the company runner from St. Louis, Mo., chimed in. "It's even got a wine cellar downstairs."

"You mean it had a wine cellar," interrupted Pfc. Rydal Stone of Cortland, N. Y. "When those tank guys left here they cleaned it out."

"Okay," Meyers agreed. "But anyhow, this was a pushover compared to that Arnoldsweiler deal. You gotta admit that."

"You sure seemed to think it was a breeze," Capt. Leigon said to Myers. Turning to the rest of us, he explained: "I went into the music room, right after our platoon buttoned up this main building, and found Myers in there. The other platoon was still fighting down in the stables and artillery shells were falling all over the place. But there was Myers, standing by the window with his gun, looking for stray Jerries and at the same time winding a Heinie victrola that was playing 'Silent Night'."

Lt. Calvin Walker of Denver, Colo., got in the conversation: "I agree with Myers about Arnoldsweiler. That was a rough deal."

At Capt. Leigon's suggestion, Walker gave his version of the capture of Schloss Rath, the medieval castle on the outskirts of Arnoldsweiler that was taken in a night attack. F Company was sent to take the castle, six miles east of Arnoldsweiler, while the rest of the regiment cleaned out the town.

Reaching Schloss Rath, the 1st Platoon established themselves in the nearby woods. The 2d Platoon attempted to assault the main gateway and got in by surprise before the Germans could get set. The plan worked—up to a point. A Jerry sentry, guarding the wire gates in front of the first bridge across the 15-yard-wide moat, was surprised and killed by the 2d Platoon's lead scout. The rest of the platoon rushed the gates. Seconds later, four half-tracks mounting flak guns and two SPs opened up on them from within the castle grounds. They were promptly pinned down against the walls of a stable.

Meanwhile Lt. Walker's 3d Platoon had come up behind the castle. They managed to get across the moat and into the grounds before being discovered and secured all the buildings on the estate except the castle itself. Separating them from their objective was another bridge, which led across the moat into the main archway of the Schloss. In some ancient day, the bridge had evidently been a drawbridge which could be pulled up to the wall in case of enemy attack. But the castle's later owners had abandoned this in favor of the ordinary bridge type, not foreseeing the day when F Company would be storming its gates.

Lt. Walker assembled his forces for the attack on the archway. Under cover of BAR fire which kept enemy gunners away from the castle windows, the 3d Platoon cleared the bridge. The platoon sergeant leading the attack fell midway on the bridge, fatally injured by a blast from a Jerry burp gun. But Pfc. Harris, right behind, killed the Jerry who got the sergeant. The rest of the platoon followed him through the archway.

Storming into the castle, the 3d Platoon chased the Germans from one room to the other. Finally they cornered them in the cellar. A concussion grenade took the last bit of resistance out of the Jerries. Speaking in English, one of them called up that they were ready to surrender. When Lt. Walker went down to collect his prisoners, he found he had bagged the staff of the 1st Battalion of the 10th Panzer Grenadier Regiment: a lieutenant colonel, six lieutenants and 100 men. The haul also included 12 American PWs from another regiment of the 104th Division, captured in Arnoldsweiler earlier in the day.

"The situation looked pretty good right then," Walker said. "But it didn't last long. The Jerries who were getting shoved out of Arnoldsweiler decided to retreat and make a last stand in the castle, not knowing we were there. When they found out, they turned their six SPs on us and started raising almighty hell. Then this Jerry lieutenant who could speak English started getting arrogant as hell. I wanted to drill him right there but I decided against it, figuring the tables might be turned any minute with all those Heinies closing in on us. I could only spare three men to guard the 107 Jerry PWs. The rest of us, reinforced by the 12 GIs we had recaptured, had to get ready to beat off the Jerries. Fortunately, the 1st Platoon took care of the retreating Krauts, but for a couple of hours there it was anybody's ball game."

The 1st Platoon really took care of the back-pedaling Jerry force of 200 men. T/Sgt. Oscar S. Lycksel, who had taken over the platoon when his platoon leader was killed, held fire until the Germans came into an open field that adjoined the woods where his men were located. Then he gave the order to fire.

"They killed Germans until it almost made them sick," Walker said. "We're not sure just how many but our total for the night was 105 and the 1st Platoon got most of them."

Meanwhile a German 88 dug in a hill overlooking the castle, started firing directly at the archway. That tied down the Americans who had been mopping up around the grounds. But it didn't hold them long. F Company men, S/Sgt. Brock and Sgt. Smick, found an 80mm German mortar and started experimenting. It didn't have a sight but Brock and Smick set it up and started firing.

"They were adjusting it by Kentucky windage," T/Sgt. Denis Earhart of Staunton, Va., platoon sergeant of the 2d Platoon, said. "It worked, because they got a direct hit on the 88 after a few rounds. Right after that two Heinies came down the hill waving a pair of white underwear, the Long John type. They said there were 12 more Germans back there who wanted to surrender. So we sent the two back to collect the rest and all 14 of them came back. Our total for the night, our company, that is, was 396 prisoners plus the 175 killed. We also got four armored half-tracks. That's not a bad night's work for one company."

"I still think that castle needs a 'W' in front of that 'R' in Rath," Lt. Walker said. "It would be more aptly named, particularly the way it looks now after that Jerry 88 and those SPs and our bazookas got through with it."

Earhart got up and put some more coal on the fire, dimming the room's light until only the shadowy figures of the occupants were visible. Somebody in the next room started playing a piano. He began with what sounded like a classical composition, then switched over to popular music. Several voices joined in, singing "I Wanna Dance with a Dolly with a Hole in Her Stocking."

"That's Boles," (Pfc. Thomas Boles of Greenville, Tenn.), Myers explained. "He studied to be a concert pianist. He's nuts about the Steinway piano they got here in this castle. But the guys make him play swing stuff because none of them know the words to those other songs."

Schloss Schlenderhan was a damned sight easier to take than Schloss Rath," Capt. Leigon said, resuming the story of how F Company captured its second German castle. "We started moving up the hill on it at 0400 yesterday. We ran into some small arms fire at the gate-keeper's house but we flushed them out pretty quick. Then we started getting some really heavy fire from the right wing of this castle and the trenches out in front. We pulled up and threw time-fire on the building, waiting for the tanks to catch up with us. When they arrived, we rushed the castle."

Although the castle is one of Germany's showplaces and was formerly used for conferences by the German General Staff, the Krauts made only token resistance here. F Company captured one company commander and 57 men, besides wiping out the entire platoon of 25 Germans outposting the castle when the attack started.

The Jerry company commander and two other Krauts were nabbed by Pfc. Robert D. Green of Center, Tex. Green was outposting one end of the stables at the rear of the castle, standing at a window on the first floor. He spotted a German captain, armed with a rifle and a hand grenade, sneaking around the corner of the stable. Waiting until the German was directly in front of him, Green pulled the trigger of his M-1. A loud click was the only result. Green didn't wait around to investigate why. He made a flying leap at the German and pinned him to the ground. The officer dropped his weapons and surrendered. Then he called out two of his men who were hiding behind a tree and ordered them to do likewise. Green and Sgt. Manuel Garcia of Los Angeles, Calif., who had been attracted by the scuffle, carted the trio of Jerries off to the company's PW cage.

"All three of those Jerries promptly produced those surrender pamphlets which Gen. Eisenhower had dropped over enemy lines, claiming it entitled them to the food and treatment he promised them in the pamphlet," Capt. Leigon said. "But when we found several of them on each one, they admitted they had been issued a batch of the pamphlets for use as toilet paper. They figured on using it when their pants were down all right, but not quite in the same circumstances that Green caught them in."

Along with the batch of 58 prisoners, the men of F Company fell heir to some 300-odd German civilians when they captured Schloss Schlenderhan. These included members of the household staff and their families, together with relatives from the nearby village of Quadrath who had sought shelter in the Schloss bomb cellars when the Americans attacked their village. To keep them under surveillance until the authorities arrived to screen them, Capt. Leigon ordered them to remain in the bomb cellars. He permitted the cooks and kitchen help to remain at their jobs to provide food for the internees. He also ordered the grooms and stable boys to exercise and tend the string of fine racing horses which Baron Von Oppenheim had here. Many horses in his stable, which included 40 mares, eight studs and 22 yearlings, were killed by mortar and artillery shells during the battle for the castle. According to information given by the household staff, the Von Oppenheim stable is Germany's most famous stud farm.

The staff of the household also provided F Company with some interesting information on the Baron himself, together with background on the Schloss. Waldemar Von Oppenheim was a member of one of Germany's first families and prominent in the nation's politics until the Nazis came to power in 1933. His mother was an American, the former Florence Hutchins of New York City; his father was half-Jewish, a fact which put the present Baron in disfavor when Hitler launched his anti-Semitic program. That eventually forced Von Oppenheim to change the name of the family bank in Cologne from Sal. Oppenheim Companie to one with a more "Aryan" sound.

Right after the fall of France, the German Army took over Schloss Schlenderhan, the Oppenheims' 220-year-old ancestral home. However, they permitted the Oppenheims to occupy part of the castle. But the Baron and his family went into hiding several months ago to escape arrest by the Nazis.

The SS High Command took a particular fancy not only to Schlenderhan's pine-treed, well-kept acres but to the racing stable as well. They summarily appropriated many of Von Oppenheim's finest horses. Later, they announced the castle would become permanent SS property after the war. That was at a time when the fortunes of war showed no indication that American GIs from Texas and Missouri would be occupying it in the late winter of 1945.

Just before the German breakthrough in the Ardennes last December, Gen. Model held several military conferences at Schloss Schlenderhan which were attended by Gen. Sepp Dietrich and his Chief of Staff, Brig. Fuehrer Draemer. After they left, the staff of the SS Frunsberg Division made the castle its headquarters. Two weeks before its capture by the Americans, the staff of the 86th German Corps was quartered there. They were followed by a panzer division staff which pulled out fast when the Yanks crossed the Roer River, leaving only a handful of troops to defend the estate which the SS chiefs looked upon so fondly.

"This makes the fifth castle we've been in since we crossed the Roer," Myers, the company runner, said, yawning and then sinking a little deeper in the cushions of the divan. "But we only had to fight for two of them. The other three we just mopped up after the armor had knocked them off. It's getting to be a habit with us. Guess we should change our name to Castle Company instead of F Company. Then maybe we could get Capt. Leigon promoted to a Baron."

"Yeah," the captain said. He didn't sound enthused at the prospect.

Out in the other room, Boles, the guy who studied to be a concert pianist and wound up being an infantryman in Germany, was playing "Deep in the

Heart of Texas." He was getting plenty of support from the baritones and tenors, not good but loud.

Everybody around the fireplace seemed to be enjoying the music. They slumped down a little more into the overstuffed chairs, just listening. It sounded good, plenty good; particularly when you remembered that only a few hours ago some Jerries were probably singing "Deutschland über Alles" to the accompaniment of this same Steinway piano.

On 2 March, while the adjoining divisions were securing their bridgeheads across the Erft, the 104th Division remained in position, with the 415th Infantry moving into Thorr, Ahe and Quadrath. In accordance with the Division directive, the 413th and the 414th Infantry Regiments had gained their objectives in the afternoon of 1 March, and before the 415th Infantry could be committed on its envelopment operation it was necessary for the bridgehead on the left to be established. This terrain made it necessary for the Division to seize the Vorgebirge Hills from the north, as the numerous coal pits and slagpiles could not be assaulted frontally without heavy loss. The front line regiments maintained constant pressure. Throughout this period enemy air activities increased materially. The Germans were reluctant to give up the outer defenses of Cologne without shooting the works. John Wilhelm of the Chicago *Sun* tells of the heroic work by Lieutenant Colonel Farnum's 555th AAA (AW) Battalion in his story of 2 March:

JET BOMBERS HARASS DRIVE FOR COLOGNE
U. S. GUN CREWS HANDICAPPED BY TARGETS' SPEED

With 104th Infantry Division in Front of Cologne, March 2.—German jet planes—especially the now notorious Messerschmitt-262, a bomb-carrying version—are becoming increasingly active on the Cologne battlefields.

Last night and early this morning, enemy jet planes were overhead every five minutes, cutting their motors and gliding down in silent dives that enabled them to loose their bombs or shoot up forward American ground units without a second's warning.

Our antiaircraft put up a furious barrage every time a jet was reported in the skies overhead.

BARRAGE "BEATS CASSINO"

Ed Clark of *Stars and Stripes*, Army newspaper, said: "This barrage beats anything we used to throw up at Cassino in Italy."

The·jet raiders hit with bombs and blazing guns at our troops strung out along the Erft canal before Cologne.

Anxious to see our antiaircraft striking back, I left the command post and joined a gun crew of one of the most famous antiaircraft battalions, the "Mr. Five-by-Five" battalion that works with Maj. Gen. Terry Allen's Timberwolf Division.

CHICAGOAN COMMANDS BATTERY

The battery, sitting out on the flat plain in a stubby wheat field, was commanded by Capt. Fred D. Waters, son of Col. Fred Waters of Chicago. The captain's wife, Opal, works at the University of Chicago library, he said.

He took me over to one of the gun crews that at that moment was firing at an enemy jet plane, shooting through the clear blue skies overhead.

Too Fast for Range Finder

"Give him hell, boys. Give him hell," said my jeep driver, a rough and tough Missourian, Corp. Billy Todd of Aldrich, as the big gun, which can toss two-inch shells at the rate of 120 a minute, hurled big puffs of smoke that were clearly breaking around the jet.

"Cripes, those things are fast," complained Corp. Joe Idasek of 3119 S. 53d St., Cicero, whose job is to set the range and keep bursts ahead of the plane, like a duck shooter leading a duck.

The jet job moved out of range and soon its bombs could be seen drifting earthward behind us, followed by a blurb of yellow flames in the distance, and our gun ceased firing.

Idasek, who was a student at Saint Mary's College in Winona, Minn., before the war, explained:

Gunners Spot Them Now

"Jets are something new. The first we saw actually fire was on Feb. 22 and since then we've seen more every day. The first warning is a queer rumbling noise if the jet is on. But no warning at all if the jet is off and the plane is gliding."

Idasek said they now know the jet silhouette and can spot it far off or even by moonlight.

"But it sure is the fastest thing you ever saw," Idasek said.

Jet Planes Can Be Hit

These jet planes are run by jet motors similar to those used in robot bombs. The motors are shut on and off in spurts to lengthen the flying time. They usually shoot up to an extreme height, using jet propulsion, then glide like great swallows, reapplying the jet for more altitude or to escape from Allied interceptors.

The "Mr. Five-by-Five" anti-aircraft battery, whose identifying symbol is a fat little man with can, looking something like Old Dutch Cleanser's Dutch girl trademark, said the jet-propelled planes are the hardest to shoot, but definitely can be hit, provided they can be brought within range.

While I had primarily gone over to watch the guns battling the jet, it was good to find the crack "Five-by-Five" antiaircraft outfit.

.50-Calibers Fire on Troops

It had gained fame during the Roer River crossing by turning its quadruple 50-calibers (four machine guns on one mount) away from the skies and down to a horizontal bearing, where they fired directly on German ground troops with considerable success.

On 3 March, fighting forward through the day and most of the night for gains up to four miles, the Division seized positions three miles from the outskirts of Cologne. Two more towns, Glessen and Damsweiler, had fallen and over 300 prisoners were captured. The

415th Infantry led off with the 2d Battalion at 0500 and closed into Oberaussen in the northeast part of the Division zone at 0900. At 1100 it commenced its sweep over the Vorgebirge Mountains. By 1520 the battalion had mopped up the wooded ridge and was in possession of the great barrier which not only dominated the Erft but overlooked Cologne. The battalion was led in its successful advance by Lieutenant Colonel Dean. Colonel Dean had replaced Lieutenant Colonel Peter Denisevich, who had become the 415th regimental executive officer. On the 2d Battalion's left Colonel Clough led his 3d Battalion against Glessen and Dannsweiler, taking the former at 1204 and the latter at 1800. In its advance it repelled two counterattacks and advanced stubbornly against heavy enemy mortar and artillery fire.

To prepare for its advances across the high ridge in order to link up with the 415th Infantry at 1200, Colonel Kelleher sent his 1st Battalion against the high ground approximately 1,000 yards east of Horrem. Facing heavy fire, Captain Radlinsky's A and Captain Barker's C Companies were able to reach the objective by 1600 and shortly after dark completed mopping up the area. In the afternoon the 2d Battalion secured its line of departure 3,000 yards east of Horrem, in preparation for the coming attack on Koenigsdorf. This was accomplished without incident and the battalion was set for its midnight attack against Koenigsdorf just east of the Vorgebirge Hills. Southeast of Koenigsdorf lay Buschbell, which was to be assaulted by the 3d Battalion at the same time. At 0001 on 4 March the 2d and 3d Battalions jumped off. The 2d Battalion met little resistance and by 0930 it had secured its objective. The 3d Battalion, then commanded by Major Ryan (Colonel Rouge had been injured at Sindorf), passed through the 1st Battalion at midnight and seized Buschbell prior to 0930. To the east, 3,000 yards of Buschbell, was Weiden, which commanded an important approach to Cologne. Throughout the afternoon of 4 March, the enemy fought with every weapon at his disposal, even antiaircraft guns, in a desperate effort to stop the determined Wolves. By 2330, the strategically located objective was taken.

The 413th Infantry was directed to follow the 3d Armored on the Division's left and to mop up the remaining enemy resistance on 3 and 4 March. Colonel Welcome P. Waltz, commander of the 413th Infantry Seagulls since September, 1942, had been directed to report to First Army Headquarters for a new assignment. The 413th Infantry Regiment had lost a great leader. On 4 March Lieutenant Colonel Lonning assumed command of the regiment. The Seagulls continued in their stride, and by the end of 4 March they had advanced a distance of ten miles through the towns of Buzzdorf, Flesteden, Sinthern, Monstedten and Geyen.

Lieutenant Colonel Needham's 1st Battalion and Lieutenant Colonel Clough's 3d Battalion of the 415th Infantry continued their drive on Cologne, capturing the bitterly contested cities of Brauweiler, Freimeisdorf and Lovenich. As the advance was closing on Cologne, resistance became more stubborn. The Division was now only two miles outside the city limits, with the 413th on the left, the 415th in the center, and the 414th on the right. Two important highways leading into the Rhineland city were under control of the Timberwolves. During the last three days the enemy had fought tenaciously and their artillery was frequently heavy. Now it appeared that the enemy was getting set to pull out.

The defense of Cologne had been elaborately planned, as evidenced by four semi-circular lines of trenches and strongpoints in and around the city. Cologne was besieged by a semi-circle of three divisions, the 3d Armored Division on the left, the 104th Infantry Division in the center, and the 8th Infantry Division on the right. Throughout the cold, cloudy day of 4 March, with snow flurries and intermittent rains, the Timberwolves seized six more large towns and one large factory area in their steady advance toward Cologne. The sustained night and day fighting by the Timberwolves had carried the 104th Division in record time to the outer edges of Cologne. The fall of the city was imminent. The prize was the third largest city in Germany, the strongest yet approached by the Allies, and an important industrial center.

The VII Corps had directed the 3d Armored Division and the 104th Division to close on Cologne, with the 8th Division striking for the west bank of the Rhine south of Cologne. On 5 March the Division lunged forward, with the 414th on the right, the 415th on the left, against the southern half of the metropolis, with the 413th initially in reserve.

COLOGNE IS OURS

At 0923 the Timberwolves drove into Cologne, and by 2100 four battalions had a firm grip on the great industrial center, having pierced the city limits by 4,000 yards. Colonel Kelleher's Mountaineers, with L Company in the lead, crossed the city limits at 0923. Lieutenant Mervin Tieg, Staff Sergeant Fred Hoover, Sergeant J. B. Kerbie and Pfc. James Smith were the first to enter.

Let Staff Sergeant George Dove tell of the exhilaration felt by the men of L Company, 414th Infantry, as they became the first American troops to enter the great city of Cologne:

Troops of the now famous Timberwolf Division entered the great Rhine city at 0923 this morning, 4 March 1945.

Staff Sergeant Fred Hoover and his squad of the 2d Platoon, L Company, 414th Infantry, made the eventful entry into the great city of Cologne, climaxing the Timberwolves' eight-day drive which began at the Roer River on 24 February 1945.

Headline news! That's what it was. This is what the people back in the States were reading on the front pages of their local papers. Well—weren't the eyes of the world on this new offensive drive? Wasn't everyone watching Cologne, with dozens of British and American correspondents watching our every move? And L Company right out there leading the whole drive. Oh, it wasn't the only time that L Company had been the first to enter an enemy-held city. This was news to the world, but it wasn't new to us.

Yes, news headlines, but the story behind the story started around March 3d, the night before; after hiking through the densest forest I had ever seen, we stumbled into the outskirts of Buschbell. Then, trying to overtake the fleeing Jerries in the damp mist, we arrived at a huge hot-house. I can remember how fascinating it seemed to us—winter outside, flaming red peonies blooming and dying inside. If I only could have sent some to Mom for Easter; or better yet— let her know that I was still okay. We had just missed the Germans by a few minutes and were ordered to "button up" for future orders. We were dead on our feet—exhausted—and did I sleep—and dream.

We were moving down into another town, along a highway lined with huge trees and flanked with foxholes that had poles and straw sticking up from them. Everything was deathly quiet and we were expecting the worst at any minute. It began with a few sniper shots, then machine guns, and finally 20mm and mortar fire chimed in. We headed into a lone house that was the entrance to the town. A ramshackle affair that looked like the largest fortress to us at the moment. One of our tanks came up the road, caught in the open by surprise. Sergeant Williams tried to stop the tank, but with the noise and the excitement it rolled right by. Suddenly the tank shot in the air, and a cloud of smoke enveloped the infantrymen in the rear. The mines laid across the road had proved effective and the men astride the tank quickly took cover in the foxholes alongside. The firing seemed to be quieting down, and the 1st Platoon had already left for town.

It was our turn next; slipping and sneaking up a ditch, we entered the next house, then another; never knowing for sure what would be behind the next door, what kind of wine would be found in the next cellar. It would soon be night and we wondered how much further we would have to go; probably to the intersection of town. Artillery was once again coming in pretty heavily, but we finally saw the intersection. Huge blocks of cement loomed up on both sides of the road, defying vehicles to get through, and perhaps covered by an SP or mortar fire. We came up to it, and through it, just like that. Evidently the Jerries left it only to retard tanks.

After an uneventful night and an appreciated breakfast of hotcakes, L Company again prepared to move out in the lead. At 0900 we continued the advance from this town of Weiden, down the Autobahn leading to Cologne. Amid light

enemy artillery barrages, completely missing their mark, Hoover's squad led the company within the city limits of the once great town, to a suburb called Junkersdorf. Here for the first time in any of our city fighting, there were civilians, all doubtfully watching our approach; staring eyes, an occasional smile, perhaps now for them the war would be over. A civilian steps forward to warn us of a minefield on the right side of the road. The houses were in excellent condition. Here were no signs of devastation and ruin. The main enemy force had withdrawn to the middle of the city; stragglers were quickly rounded up. Newsreel cameras shuttered as prisoners, tramping to the rear, scuffed over a swastika spread out upon the ground. Each cellar had its supply of wine, and as the company held up to reorganize, my squad had a dinner of sauerkraut and wienies, found simmering and abandoned on a welcome cookstove.

The twisted rubble that was once a great city was now in our hands. Its once beautiful streets were now mere wagon paths; with broken sewer pipes and gutted buildings; block after block of devastated and leveled business sections—this was our prize—this was Cologne.

The 3d Battalion mopped up Junkersdorf and the large Sportsplatz, with the 1st Battalion on its right clearing up a large barracks and outer residential section. Colonel Cochran's regiment, with the 1st Battalion on the right and the 2d Battalion on the left, steadily advanced against scattered resistance, neutralizing the large residential area and factories in its path.

Iris Carpenter, *Herald* war reporter, on 6 March released the following story amid Cologne's destruction:

COLOGNE HANGS OUT WHITE FLAGS
LAST 1,000 DEFENDERS FALL BACK TO THE RHINE

We are in Cologne. Once capital of the Rhineland, now third largest rubble pile in Germany, it is being mopped up by General Maurice Rose's 3d Armored Division and General Terry Allen's famous Timberwolves.

They fought their way block by block through the northern and western suburbs as the 8th Infantry were clearing up southern suburbs.

Tonight a fifth of Cologne was ours, and a staff officer estimated that only 1,000 defenders were left.

These last-ditchers were withdrawing to the old town on the Rhine bank for a sacrificial last stand.

The Germans had fought desperately to delay us. They poured a withering shower of artillery, mortar and small arms fire on our troops, but nothing could stop men so exhilarated—and men supported by thunderwaves of fire-power.

ROAD BLOCK—FIVE TRAMS

They blazed forward, tanks scrunching their way through, men scrambling over what used to be parkland in some of the finest residential parts.

At one point the Germans had made a road block of five trams, reinforced by steel rails driven into the street. Our tanks drove straight through.

White flags hung from the windows. Civilians stood in groups to watch the Americans advance—or, clutching their goods, set out for our rear lines.

Outside the city refugees were straggling forlornly along the roads, gazing in dazed despair at shells erupting in tall pillars of white smoke all along the horizon.

Over narrow, muddy roads cows wandered, lowing miserably, with no one to milk them. Horses and sheep got caught up in the river of our armor and supply trucks.

SPECTACLE OF MISERY

I have seen nothing in all Europe to compare with today's spectacle of utter misery—hundreds of refugees, mostly old people and cripples, being evacuated from a basement and directed to a collecting point.

Off they went, carrying their few remaining possessions, into the new life that Hitler built for them.

Some had bicycles, or prams or handcarts on which were hurriedly stacked blankets, a big jug of water, a few cooking pots.

For these are the essentials for living when you have brought living to this pass.

I saw women with a baby in one arm and a bundle of food in the other, children carrying loaves of bread, plates and cups, and crying as they stumbled along in icy wind and driving rain.

We have waited a long time, and gone through much, to bring home to the German people this horror of refugee columns and all the rest of what war means. But we are certainly doing it now.

This is utter defeat, the relentless shattering of Germany in a Nemesis that was never more deserved.

Seeing it would satisfy even the civilians the Germans drove on the roads before Dunkirk. But I don't think even the most bitter of them would enjoy it.

Another war reporter cabled:

Ruined Cologne is another Aachen. The only familiar sight today was the Cathedral.

Great billows of smoke were rising on both sides of the Cathedral towers. It appeared that a petrol dump was blazing.

Most buildings on the outskirts were still standing but as we rolled farther in more and more devastation greeted our eyes.

Buildings were lying all over the streets as a result of the air and artillery bombardment of the last few days.

Tonight we are more than a mile inside Cologne and street fighting is raging.

COLOGNE FALLS
By GRAHAM MILLER

With U. S. First Army in Germany, March 5—Units of Lieut. Gen. Courtney H. Hodges' First Army crashed into Cologne from five directions today, entering from the directions of Ossendorf, Longerich, Bickendorf, Mungersdorf and Junkersdorf. And among the first senior officers to enter was Col. Gerald Kelleher of Albany.

Opposition from German ground troops has been patchy so far, but in some places the enemy is using antiaircraft artillery, so fusing the shells that they burst 100 feet or so over our heads, sending white hot splinters of flak downward with terrific force. It was these lethal splinters that kept me from writing under a Cologne dateline tonight.

Antitank gun position in the shadow of the Dom Cathedral

PIPER CUBS OVERHEAD

Early this afternoon I came to the last of a cluster of houses on a road leading into the city. Eight hundred yards ahead, across the completely flat plain, were the first houses of Cologne, then a darker mass of buildings and, rising above and beyond them, the twin spires of the cathedral.

Perfectly ranged and bursting above the road, the enemy shells were putting down a tenuous but deadly curtain of white hot steel. There wasn't a scrap of cover along the road, but up ahead were the forward elements of our battalions.

I huddled in the doorway of the last house with a few GIs who were also waiting for the shelling to slacken before going up forward. We watched two Piper Cubs fluttering about the sky like wind-blown leaves as they avoided the bursts and tried to spot the locations of the enemy batteries at the same time.

DODGE OWN SHELLS

It was a gray day with smoke drifting across our front from a burning building somewhere on our left. There were dead cattle dotting the fields ahead and two dead Germans were lying nearby, both of them with their faces in the mud. They had been killed an hour or so before by one grenade.

Our own artillery was firing over our heads now and we thought that maybe those Piper Cubs had a line on the German gun positions. Our shells passed so close over our heads that, even though we knew they were ours, we crouched instinctively. Gray dust as light as pollen fell on us as the house trembled.

I went back down the line and found a group of infantrymen eating K rations in the yard of a house. An 8-year-old German boy named Oscar was watching the GIs with wide-eyed wonder.

273

MISERY AND HUMILIATION

Two old men, smoking those long, curved pipes that you see in illustrations of Grimm's fairy tales and almost nowhere else except in the Rhineland and Bavaria, were also standing in the yard. Their faces expressed misery, humiliation and dislike.

A frozen-faced woman in shabby black clothes came up the cellar steps and whisked the howling Oscar away.

Less than a dozen hours earlier German soldiers had been standing in that same yard.

Across the narrow street an old German was reading a notice just posted by the military government authorities. Tears ran down his face.

GIs PLEASED AT NEWS

The GIs, completely unperturbed by the sullen faces of the surrendering civilians, munched their K rations and asked me how things were going up forward. I told them about the shell bursts and also that we had entered Cologne at five points.

The faces of those boys lit up like Chinese lanterns when they heard that news and three of them, who are New Yorkers, asked me to tell their folks back home that they and Terry Allen (Major Gen. Terry Allen, commander of the 104th Division) were helping to take Cologne. They were Benedict Tusa, 208 Wyona St., Brooklyn; Karl Herman, 123 Neptune Ave., Brooklyn, and Knight Velmot, 14812, 115th Ave., Jamaica, Queens.

Through incessant rainy weather the Division continued its steady advance through the streets of Cologne. At 1400 a Timberwolf patrol from the 415th Infantry Regiment composed of Pfcs. Charles E. Cheatham and Francis H. Wilbur, stood on the west bank of the stately Rhine River. These men had reached this strategic point which overlooked the great Hohenzollern Bridge not only by their own ability, but because of the fighting strength of the entire Timberwolf team. The combat fighting and cooperation of infantry, artillery, tanks, engineers, tank destroyers, antiaircraft, medics, ordnance, signal, headquarters, military police and quartermaster, had enabled this patrol to stand at the historic Rhine as a living symbol that "NOTHING IN HELL CAN STOP THE TIMBERWOLVES."

Private First Class William C. Buck, F Company, 415th Infantry, tells a tale of the tense action leading up to that memorable event:

On the morning of 4 March our battalion moved into Dannsweiler following a miserable night spent in foxholes at the edge of a heavy woods outside the town. We had rested the next day until that evening, when we were alerted at the report of Jerry massing sixty tanks, supposedly trapped between us and the Rhine. Rumor had it that the armor could not retreat because the bridges were blown and that they were preparing an assault to repel our drive on Cologne. After a not too easy night, we set out the next day for what was to be the attack on Cologne, the queen city of the Rhine and the once proud center of a great industrial area. As we marched through the small villages

The Cathedral City witnessed bitter street fighting.

towards Cologne, we were unopposed. The supposedly arrogant Nazi German stood in amazement at the entrances of his air-raid shelters and gawked at the American *Soldaten*. Many German children were obviously happy at seeing us. They seemed to think it was a parade, and they waved. The older ones were different. They were curious; but more than that, they were afraid. What did the coming of the Americans mean? Where were the secret weapons their Führer had promised them? When would their glorious Wehrmacht drive these *Amerikanische Schweinhunde* from the sacred soil of Germany? There must have been revolution in their minds when they first began to realize that we were there to stay.

We marched on through, soon reaching the town from which we were to launch our attack. Here we held up till the appointed hour for the attack— 1600. We all knew that ahead of us was 4,000 yards of open field before we could reach the first building. Two miles without cover; two miles of wide, open space. A lot could happen in two miles. Constant aerial attack by our air forces and the day and night shelling of Cologne was said to have many Germans trapped on this side of the Rhine, ready to make a suicidal stand. The hour set was 1600, and 1600 hours saw the lead scout start out across the two miles of open fields. The twin towers of the famous Cathedral of Cologne were now plainly visible, but that two miles of open farmland attracted far more attention.

We moved on out in a staggered line across the open field. The tanks were holding up behind us; this was a job for the infantry. If the Germans were going to do anything, this was the time to do it. When would the 88's start flying? Where were those damned screaming meemies, the sound of which was so terrifying? The past few days we have been unopposed, the Jerries had fallen back to Cologne. They were ready for this. Those 88's had plenty of

275

time to zero in on these fields. Yes, setting out across open fields was a sweat job, and glory was the farthest thing from a dogface's mind. We moved on across at a rapid pace. Nothing happened. We kept moving. Still nothing happened. What were they waiting for? Why in hell didn't they fire! We kept moving boldly forward in our staggered line, not knowing if the next step would set off a "Schü mine" and blow off a leg, or when and where the first shell would land.

When we had reached a point just 200 yards from the nearest house we had a set of railroad tracks to cross. Was this it? Would the Jerries open up now? What a mess Jerry machine guns could make. Their artillery was fairly quiet, no shells landing in our immediate vicinity, and there were only a few American volleys going over. But there were those artillery observation planes buzzing overhead, ready to direct fire in our support. It was a comfort just to have them there.

We crossed the tracks and hurried on as fast as we could go. No use hesitating then. It was now or never. We dashed on in among the first row of houses. Finding many houses locked, we broke in the doors or rifled the locks, and found most of them empty. There was a great deal of relief to find no organized resistance. It was almost time to start our "souvenir hunting." It was logical to expect scattered resistance, so our first job was to put the civilians where we could control them. We rounded them up and kept moving them into a large *Luftschutzbunker* (air raid shelter). There were mostly women and children, but there were some old men around. Continuing our search of houses, we reached the phase line at which we were to hold up. We organized our defense, and by late evening everyone had gotten around to eating a cold K-ration and between shifts at the outposts we were catching cat-naps. The house searching had been so successful for some men that they were able to celebrate in style.

In rounding up the civilians we had time to take notice of this suburb, which was our objective. The houses were part of a federal housing project, and formed a model, well laid out community. The town square was surrounded by a modern school, church, bakery, grocery, meat market, air raid shelter, and of course a hofbrau, in which some schnapps and cognac were found.

We had taken our objective. We had done our share. Now we had time for rest—a good night's rest. But the word rest just wasn't in the book. About eleven that evening, when everyone but the guards had gotten settled, the order came. "Get ready to move out!" We were to move up to the next phase line and hold up. It was plenty dark and everyone was tired, but as soon as the company had assembled we set out down a rubble-strewn street under a dark, foreboding underpass which had been half blocked off with brickwork, evidently for the purpose of serving as an air raid shelter. Moving up a curving road, we passed the storage yards of the remains of an industrial plant. The movement was as quiet as possible. We soon reached the next phase line. On our right was what we later identified as a street car barn. On our left was a six or eight story apartment house which had been shelled and was windowless. We moved into the building. There were some frightened civilians in the cellar, but the rest of the apartment house, which was hardly inhabitable, was vacant. We searched the place. There were no Jerries there, so our next job was to find a place to sleep. Bedding was scarce, but we managed somhow, though we had no sleeping bags or blankets with us. Still it wasn't time for everyone to sleep.

The doc relaxes

A patrol was sent out through the dark, bomb-cratered streets to contact friendly elements on our right. Another group went back to lead the battalion wire men up. We had a lot of trouble with communications. The telephone went out as soon as the wires were strung. A stray artillery shell had hit the line. Then the radio wouldn't work. The wire men worked on the telephone line. Then later the contact patrol came in. Somehow, between guard shifts, we managed a few winks of sleep.

At daybreak everyone was awakened for another day of advance through gutted Cologne. This day was somewhat more eventful, for as we advanced, some elements received sniper fire. War correspondents were around, because Cologne was big news. There was some plenty big Jerry artillery coming in. The advance was held up several times. We moved the civilians to the rear as we encountered them. It was on this afternoon of 7 March that a small patrol from F Company ventured beyond our phase line, going all the way to the Rhine, being the first infantry troops to reach the Rhine River at Cologne.

The destruction which our air forces had brought to Cologne was beyond imagination. There remained only shells of most buildings or vast heaps of rubble.

Company F reached the Cologne Opera House late that afternoon. And it was here that the body of the company held up. The Opera House had been bombed, but we found or made suitable quarters for ourselves in the basement. To our surprise, it still had electric lights. Electric lights among all this ruin where there were no utilities working was unbelievable. It happened that the house had its own power plant underground which somehow escaped the intense bombings. During the next few days we patrolled adjacent sections of the city searching out assigned sectors. We had taken Cologne. It was a job well done.

In a few days, passersby noticed a sign erected in the square in front of the Opera House. Printed both in German and English, its prophecy read:

GIVE ME FIVE YEARS AND YOU WILL NOT RECOGNIZE GERMANY AGAIN. Signed: Adolf Hitler.

Commencing at 0645, on the 6th, the 414th Infantry and the 415th Infantry started their grim, slow advance through the rubbled streets. In addition to the mortar, small arms, and self-propelled fire against which our troops had to advance, swarms of civilians blocked all approaches, and determining civilians from enemy soldiers proved difficult. By nightfall the 1st and 3d Battalions of the 414th Infantry were 1,000 yards east of the Rhine, while the 1st and 2d Battalions of the 415th Infantry had 500 yards to go. Advancing abreast, the four battalions pushed forward through the bursting flak and the whine of sniper bullets. Since the Division zone had been extended further south, Major Melhop's 2d Battalion was directed to launch an attack against Effern on the southwest border of Cologne. Striking at 0200 in a bold night attack, the battalion caught the enemy bewildered and disorganized, resulting in the seizure of the town and numerous self-propelled guns and tanks. The 413th Infantry was directed to take over the extended zone and press the attack to the Rhine River in the southern edges of Cologne. The Seagulls' 2d Battalion relieved the 2d Battalion, 414th Infantry, in Effern, and the 3d Battalion, now under the command of Lieutenant Colonel George O'Connor, took up positions to the north late in the afternoon of the 6th.

Again at 0645 on 7 March, the Timberwolves, with three regiments abreast, mopped up the remaining yardage. At 0900 the 1st and 2d Battalions, 415th Infantry, were on the Rhine. By 1229 the 3d Battalion, 413th Infantry, had pushed through the southern outskirts and had reached the Rhine. The 3d Battalion, 414th Infantry, reported K Company on the Rhine at 0745, and by 0945 the 414th Infantry was closed on the river's edge. In forty-eight hours the Timberwolves had driven from the outskirts of Cologne through the heart of the city to the west banks of the Rhine. The great industrial city of Western Germany was ours.

Iris Carpenter, *Herald* war reporter, sent this story from Cologne on 7 March:

COLOGNE OURS
WHITE FLAGS FLYING

Cologne, the Rhine's greatest city, is ours. American First Army tanks and infantry have just fought their way through its ruins to reach the river.

Streets are chequered with white surrender flags. All resistance had been crushed, apart from sporadic fighting in the southeast corner of the city, by 8 o'clock tonight.

The few German soldiers who have not been trapped are trying to escape down the west bank of the Rhine to Bonn.

No Place for Tourists

Now that we are finally here nothing is working out as we expected to find it, except possibly the fact that the cathedral is, as the Air Forces have always claimed, relatively undamaged.

I got a look at it this afternoon as I jeeped near. A quick look because this inner city area was then most definitely no place for leisured sightseeing.

There was artillery, mortar, small arms fire, sniping.

We stayed only long enough to note that the twin Gothic spires were still looking just the same as they do in guide books, and that the structure was not hurt beyond pock-marking from bomb splinters.

What does the rest of it look like?

From a quick glimpse I should say that the center of the city looks just the way you would expect it to look after 42,000 tons of bombs had been dropped on it.

The suburbs look very much like any badly bombed bit of London.

There is a surprising number of whole buildings left in spite of all that obviously hit them.

In Ehrenfeld, for instance, which we badly bombed, there is hardly a window out of several acres of workmen's modern luxury flats.

Along the Venloer-strasse the familiar red facade of Woolworth's store is all right except for glass and the fact an "O" is askew.

Once past the strip of park by the Cologne West Railway station, however, it is a different story.

The station clock has stopped at a quarter past eight.

It is about the only easily recognizable station feature.

You see tangled and rusted cars, dozens of cream-colored tramcars toppled sideways or jammed under bridges for shelter, and yellow and white and gray stone houses either rubble piles or gaunt shells, on which here and there, only a blue enamel street nameplate is left.

Much more striking than the bomb damage, however, was the attitude of the civilians.

So long we have dreamed of it—of being on the Rhine, in Cologne, having the enemy on the run, and all it would mean to the defeated German citizens.

Well, here we were, only to find that the civilians, instead of being huddled, terrified in their cellars, as we had expected, are wandering about the streets in spite of the fighting and our orders to them to stay inside.

They insist on treating us as liberators rather than as victors.

"Give me five years and you will not recognize Germany again."—Adolf Hitler

"Fire a few shots down the street and see if that helps," said one harassed sergeant as he tried to get a dozen people down in their cellars while our tanks rumbled through.

The shots made them dive into doorways, but half a minute later out on the street they were again, watching the battle as though it were a stage show.

Outside Willi Beucham's wine shop on Venloer-strasse there were 18 people, far more interested in looting wine than the fact that they might be mortared any minute by their own countrymen just across the Rhine.

Wilhelm Scheribh, a miserable-looking ginger-moustached man, wearing baggy trousers and a dirty celluloid collar with a dingy black tie, came to greet me in English with a "We've been waiting for you to come a long time."

During the campaign which began at the Roer 23 February, and was concluded with the seizure of Cologne 7 March, the Timberwolves had cleared 115 square miles of the German Reich, capturing ninety-seven towns and communities and bagging 4,899 prisoners, at a loss of 377 killed and 1,121 wounded. This historic victory, culminating in the joint seizure of Cologne by the 3d Armored Division and the 104th

This "88" guarded Cologne's front door.

Division, is a fitting tribute to every fighting man who played a part.

During the next twelve days, 8-19 March, the Division actively defended the west banks of the Rhine River in its sector, which initially included the southern half of Cologne and five miles to the south. In the latter part of the period, it included the entire city. Observation posts were set up adjacent to the river and aggressive patrolling was conducted throughout the area by all units.

Company H, 414th Infantry, covered one assigned part of the river with heavy machine guns and mortars. At the same time, they ingeniously set up quite a domestic haven for themselves while keeping the east side of the Rhine hot for any ambitious Jerries.

"Cologne—Köln as the Germans spell—was to us a long looked-for goal," relates Sergeant Randolph Coleman:

I was communications sergeant of H Company, a heavy weapons company. This job kept me in contact with most of the men, so I knew just about what they were looking forward to. The power play from the Roer was fast and tiring, with the many night movements and attacks which so successfully did the job, but it left us all pretty well fagged out, so it was with high hopes we looked forward to our mission of holding a line along the Rhine. After the fighting was over we settled down to enjoy ourselves as well as accomplish our mission of defending our sector along the river.

We had fun—at least compared to the life that we had been living, this was definitely it! The part of the town where we were quartered was a very rich residential section with large houses, some of which reached castle proportions. Our 2d Platoon CP and one of our heavy machine gun sections were set up in a mansion. You see this whole area had not been too badly beat up, as there was no military value in the section. The machine gun was set up on the fourth floor of the mansion so that it could cover the river and about 2,000 yards on the other side. The men had placed it on what was once a beautiful piece of mahogany furniture, set back from the window so that they could fire out without being seen. Twenty-four hours a day there was someone on that gun and the chief sport was trying to knock some ambitious Jerries off their bicycles at extreme range. One man would wait with the glasses and when he saw one coming he would give the word to fire. I went up there one day when Sergeant Mike Martin was there along with Pfc. Bufford Wiggins; I heard Mike say "Oh boy, there comes one. Wait—wait—now, let him have it." Wiggins let go a burst. Mike hollered "Hot dog—I don't know if we got him but if we didn't, that bike sure does well without a rider!" I then went downstairs to what had once been a study, in which Lieutenant Richard Paul had his CP set up. What luxury; two large double beds had been installed, a kitchen stove was set up, and a pot of coffee gave forth a pleasant aroma. On a magnificent desk which must have belonged to a high party official were a couple of phones that contacted the other squads and the company CP.

The walls were of beautifully finished oak, with the upper part covered with an expensive-looking tapestry. Assorted and choice souvenirs were piled up along with carbines and the usual doughboy's equipment. Best of all, the liquor cabinet overflowed with the best that Cologne possessed. Chianti, Cognac; not at all like that which the Frenchies sold us back in Normandy; Champagne, and real Rhine wines. This was it. It was about noontime and Lieutenant Paul and Corporal Zealy were dexterously peeling some fried potatoes and thin slices of fried K-rations. I sat down to a white linen-covered table, with crystal glasses and fine solid silver cutlery. With one ear cocked for shells and the other for the sound of the phone, we enjoyed a pleasant meal.

My next job was to go down to the Club Cologne, where Sergeant Eugene MacParland was proprietor and genial host. However, I did not make the mistake of taking the road that led along the river bank in plain sight of the Germans. I had been warned about it by Captain Francis L. Novack, our CO. He made a trip on this road by mistake one day and found his jeep attempting to outrun an 88 shell. Thus duly warned, I arrived without mishap at the Club Cologne. The doorman, Pfc. Turman "Termite" Smith, welcomed me, and having given the correct password, I went down the cellar stairs to the club's main room. There, seated under the club sign, was Sergeant MacParland dispensing good cheer. Most of the men from his machine gun section were seated around shooting the breeze in the SOP manner. The cellar was nicely furnished with tables, chairs, soft beds and a well-stocked bar. Just in case there is some misunderstanding about the situation I had better explain. The doorman was in reality not a doorman, but on duty with the gun which was sandbagged in on the porch, with one of the best fields of fire I had ever seen. The "Club" was situated about one hundred yards from the river with almost 180 degrees of unobstructed field of fire.

After a few quick ones and a short visit, I fixed the phone, which actually was my reason for coming down. I very carefully made my way back to the 1st Platoon CP, where Lieutenant Spencer Stewart, Corporal James Bennett and

Unit Commanders Conference, March 1945

Pfc. John MacMartin, the platoon runner, were holed up. Again I found a very nice arrangement. They were set up by one of the medieval watch towers and lighthouses that are found along the river. Lieutenant Stewart was looking at a picture showing the might and equipment of the German Army and carrying on a conversation with MacMartin about the ingenious Kraut devils. Between exchanges of views Mac was indulging in an unnecessary shave; Mac's beard, even after six days, was hardly worth mentioning. Corporal Bennett was working on a generator in order that they could have electric light. He had liberated a German car and was hooking up a generator to the back wheels. When I later visited them, they had lights and a radio; the only question being, would it not draw fire? It was getting late, so I started back to the 3d Platoon to see if they needed anything. Since the roads were wooded and we were on the high bank of the river, once we were away from the bank we had very good concealment and were able to move around without fear of observation. In the evening when the lights were dim one could almost think that he was walking down some street in Winnetka or Highland Park. The streets with their even border of trees, the houses with their gardens and driveways, gave an illusion of home.

The 81mm mortars were dug in around some classy homes in such a way that their flash was masked from the Germans and they could fire at any time of night without being picked up. When I arrived at the CP I found Instrument Corporal James McKinly and Lieutenant William Hackler plotting the fire data for the night's firing. The night before, some activity was observed near one of the knocked out bridges, so they were planning a warm reception for any Jerries that ventured forth that night. In the next room Pfc. Albert Bouckus, the SCR-300 operator, was just putting a knife-edge crease in the dirtiest pair of pants with a couple of Jerry flatirons and some fraulein's ironing board. Hanging nearby was a shirt with the neatest set of military creases that I had seen since Camp Adair. Staff Sergeant Tom D. Allen came in at that time to arrange a trade with me for two flashlight batteries. In exchange I would get a bottle of recently acquired champagne—with an unbroken seal. Going over to the house occupied by his squad to complete the transaction, I found Pfc. Marion

Flags of the VII Corps' divisions fly in the Cologne Sports Platz, marking the fall of the Rhine city to the Timberwolves

Hunt busily manipulating a foot-powered sewing machine, repairing his shirt.

After stopping by the kitchen for chow I went on to the company CP. The generator, furnished by the German Signal Corps, was chugging merrily along and when I got inside the lights were on and the radio playing. After reporting in to 1st Sergeant Robert W. Kates, who was putting clean sheets on our bed, and finding out if there was any late dope or assignments, I went upstairs and had a hot bath. Yes, a real hot running water bath in a real modern bathroom. The Military Government had gotten the water running in some parts of the town and we had steam heat and hot water.

That was Cologne as I remember it. It was pretty much what we had looked forward to: a chance to get some needed rest, clean up, eat good food, and at the same time accomplish our mission of protecting our side of the river and getting ready for the time when we should again be called to the attack.

Not only the three infantry regiments and the 104th Reconnaissance Troop which were on the line, but each artillery battalion, engineers, service troops and headquarters personnel were required to patrol their

Award of the Distinguished Service Cross. By direction of the President, under the provisions of AR 600-45, 22 September 1943, as amended, and under authority contained in Circular No. 32, Headquarters European Theater of Operations, United States Army, 20 March 1944, as amended, the Distinguished Service Cross is awarded to:

Second Lieutenant ARCHER L. BRADSHAW, 02000965, Infantry, 415th Infantry Regiment, 104th Infantry Division, United States Army, for extraordinary heroism in connection with military operations in Germany on 25 February 1945. Lieutenant BRADSHAW crossed a mine field, charged an enemy position and forced the surrender of an enemy machine gun crew. With two other men, Lieutenant BRADSHAW advanced and forced the enemy from trenches, bunkers and haystacks. After setting fire to a haystack, Lieutenant BRADSHAW and his companions outflanked the enemy concealed therein and forced them to surrender. Lieutenant BRADSHAW killed two, captured nineteen of the enemy and wiped out numerous enemy installations which had temporarily halted his platoon. The extraordinary heroism and courageous actions of Lieutenant BRADSHAW reflect great credit upon himself and are in keeping with the highest traditions of the military service. Entered military service from Oregon.

Watch on the Rhine

respective areas to prevent infiltration and sabotage. To facilitate the patrol action at night, "artificial moonlight" was employed for the first time by the Division. The large searchlights of the "Five-by-Five" anti-aircraft battalion threw their beams upon the clouded skies which reflected on the ground throughout the area. Guards were placed on the vital communication and strategic installations in Cologne and each regiment designated one motorized rifle company for anti-saboteur, anti-raid and fire-fighting action.

When Headquarters Company, Special Troops, moved out of Duren it hardly seemed likely that they would hit another CP which would suit their mood as well as the Duren insane asylum. But that five-day trek to Brauweiler was long enough to make everyone feel fully qualified for the old folks' home. And that is just where they set up their Cologne CP. The home, as did the asylum in Duren, had to be cleaned up, but there, instead of shovels and brooms, DDT powder was in demand.

Enemy artillery fell in and about Cologne daily, but was generally of a light and strictly harassing nature. Observation posts along the Rhine, artillery cubs and photo interpretation teams reported continuous defense preparations, although no large groups were either seen or believed to be present on the east bank. Occasional enemy deserters came over the river by night and were quickly taken captive.

How the occupation of the largest German metropolis yet captured by the Allies impressed its invaders is best expressed in the words of Ralph E. Dippel, of 414th Cannon Company:

Award of Distinguished Service Cross. By direction of the President, under the provisions of AR 600-45, 22 September 1943, as amended, and under authority contained in Circular No. 32, Headquarters European Theater of Operations, United States Army, 20 March 1944, as amended, the Distinguished Service Cross is awarded to:

First Lieutenant KENNETH U. EAKENS, 0526512, Infantry, 413th Infantry Regiment, 104th Infantry Division, United States Army, for extraordinary heroism in connection with military operations in Germany on 26 February 1945. Although twice wounded, Lieutenant EAKENS led his platoon in assaulting a huge, strongly defended enemy castle. Defying intense enemy fire, his small group routed the enemy and captured the objective by the sheer force and audacity of his platoon's onslaught. After securing the objective Lieutenant EAKENS encountered two enemy sentries who, from hidden positions, commanded him to halt. Although unarmed, wounded, and suffering from exhaustion, he flung himself upon the two enemy soldiers, disarmed and captured both. The extraordinary heroism and courageous action of Lieutenant EAKENS reflect great credit upon himself and are in keeping with the highest traditions of the military service. Entered military service from New Mexico.

Cologne was the largest German city to be occupied by the Allied troops up to that time. It was a different experience for us. In the outer city were modern apartment buildings, large parks, and all present-day conveniences that you would find in an American city. The older, inner city was something out of medieval days. And of course in the center was the cathedral.

But the city was badly wounded from the war. Only a very small fraction of the original population remained. Very few streets were open to traffic because of debris. As you looked around the surrounding landscape from the blown-out roof-top of any large apartment house, the spectacle of the bombed-out factories with their numerous smokestacks standing out against the skyline looked just like many dead insects lying on their backs, stiff legs pointing to the sky.

Although the cathedral was north of our area, many of the fellows "goofed off" when they had a chance to go to see the famous landmark. As you approached it through the ancient, narrow, rubble-filled streets you saw a sign put up by one of our outfits defending that sector of the river-front to the effect: "Sightseers keep out. Fighting men ahead." Yet they came—you can't keep curious GI's away. The condition of the cathedral was wonderful when you compared it with the immediate surrounding buildings which were in almost complete ruin. The railroad station and the huge, demolished Hohenzollern Bridge across the Rhine, both but a stone's throw from where you were, had been the targets of many bombings—yet the cathedral stood generally intact.

After the Timberwolves took Cologne, things were rather quiet for us. Cannon Company's battery was set up in a large vacant lot beside a railroad yard. During our stay we gave training in the direction of fire to many officers and non-coms of the regiment from our OP's on the Rhine. For targets we used suspected enemy installations and personnel on the east side of the river. About the only things the Jerries sent back our way were buzz-bombs, and they kept going west, coming evidently from a location across the river.

Here in Cologne we had our first real contact with German city dwellers. Here for the first time we really learned the extent of our strategic bombing. Going into the cellar of an apartment, our 2d Platoon found a German woman who had been married to an American master sergeant. Since his death several years ago, she had lived in Germany. She told our boys of the fear and panic that our bombers caused day and night in Cologne; told of how the people huddled for hours in the cellars praying that the next bomb wouldn't hit them; and showed them in her basement a 500-pound bomb which hadn't detonated.

In Cologne we found a meek, frightened, whimpering, self-pitying super-race. They gave little trouble outside of continually asking permission to go somewhere or do something. This became annoying at times, so we put a sign in German on the door of the apartment house, wherein our fire direction center was located, stating: "If you think we are tough on you, wait till 'Uncle Joe' comes," followed by the Russian hammer and sickle. That did a good job of keeping the whining civilians away.

At 1500 on 11 March, personnel of the Timberwolf Division participated in the formal flag-raising ceremony at the Sports Palace in Cologne. In the great sports arena where Hitler had many times glorified the Nazi war machine, Lieutenant General Collins, VII Corps commander, heralded the conquest of Cologne as a forerunner of inevitable and complete German collapse within the immediate future.

It was during the drive on Cologne that the 3d Battalion, 414th Infantry, gave birth to a unique organization. Patterned after the old Wolf Scout aggregation, this unit was a compact, highly mobile, hard-hitting group of fifteen infantrymen, brought together for the expressed purpose of handling all of the combat and reconnaissance patrols for their battalion. Formed at the insistence of Lieutenant Colonel Leon D. Rouge, and named Rouge's Raiders after the 3d Battalion commander, the group was a hand-picked combination of close combat fighters, specially trained in the use of automatic weapons, demolition, scouting and patrolling. Led by Lieutenant Howard Doyle, the Raiders drew their men from all rifle companies in the battalion and numbered among its members outstanding Timberwolves like Sergeants Verdell Short, Jerry Martinez and Norman Hooker. The little group proved highly effective, causing other commands to organize units of like caliber.

The Timberwolf Reinforcement Training Center (TRTC) continued training new groups of reinforcements in a new locale. Included among the trainees were three platoons of colored infantrymen that were assigned to the Division to constitute a fifth platoon of one rifle company in each regiment.

The 692d Tank Destroyer Battalion, commanded by Lieutenant Colonel S. S. Morse, left the Division on 13 March 1945. Since it had joined the Timberwolves in Holland on 28 October 1944, the battalion had rendered close infantry support in addition to its role of antitank protection. On many occasions by indirect and direct fire it had capably supported and reinforced the 104th Division artillery.

COLOGNE

PHASE VI

SPEARHEAD

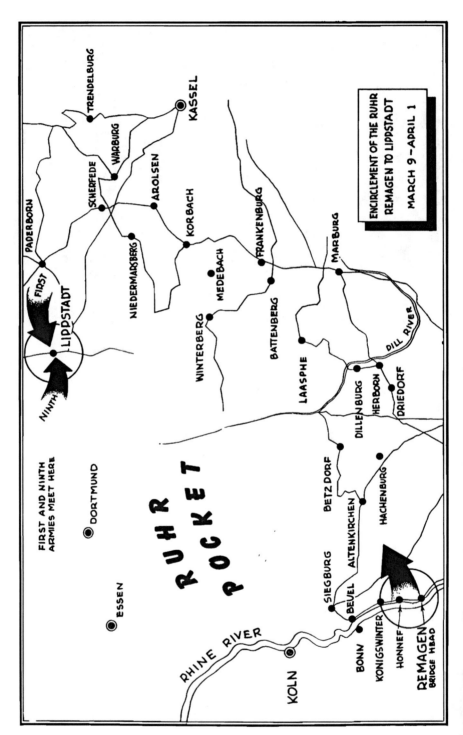

ENCIRCLEMENT OF THE RUHR
REMAGEN TO LIPPSTADT
MARCH 9 – APRIL 1

TRENDELBURG

KASSEL

WARBURG

SCHERFEDE

AROLSEN

PADERBORN

KORBACH

FRANKENBURG

MARBURG

FIRST

LIPPSTADT

NIEDERMARSBERG

MEDEBACH

DILL RIVER

NINTH

WINTERBERG

BATTENBERG

LAASPHE

DILLENBURG

HERBORN

DRIEDORF

FIRST AND NINTH
ARMIES MEET HERE

DORTMUND

R U H R

P O C K E T

BETZDORF

ALTENKIRCHEN

HACHENBURG

ESSEN

SIEGBURG

BEUEL

RHINE RIVER

BONN

KONIGSWINTER

HONNEF

REMAGEN
BRIDGE HEAD

KOLN

ENCIRCLEMENT OF THE RUHR

REMAGEN BRIDGEHEAD . . . What were our future plans? Would we force crossings of the great Rhine River at Cologne? Would the Germans give up, thus eliminating any further combat? What about the Remagen bridgehead? These were some of the many questions in the minds of the Timberwolves.

The banks of the Rhine were filled. It was by far the most formidable water obstacle yet confronted by the Allies, its width varying from 650 to 1,500 feet and the lowest depth generally exceeding six or eight feet. The velocity of the current varied from four to seven feet per second and could reach as high as fifteen feet per second if it were flooded. It was not possible to effectively raise or lower the water level by artificial means, but the spring rains would soon come, putting the river in a flood stage. The most favorable period for crossing the Rhine was the immediate future. Because of the great width and the consequent difficulty of making assault crossings, we knew that airborne troops would be used. However, it would not eliminate the demand for infantry divisions to make joint assaults. Realizing that the 104th Division might be called upon to assist in the forcing of the river, all infantry troops, under the supervision of the 329th Engineers, were trained in loading, unloading, and use of storm boats. The training was conducted in the large lake located in the northwest part of Cologne with the engineer storm boats, double half boats, and full field infantry equipment. Throughout the period, each day one infantry battalion was trained first at daylight and then in darkness.

The second question: were the Germans "Kaput"? That had really been answered during our advance to the Rhine River. The stubborn resistance and the tenacious fighting for each strongpoint indicated clearly that the Nazi party did not want to fall victim to the Allied armies. While it was true that many civilians wanted peace, their blind following of Hitler and his puppets would rally them to make another stand in defense of "Greater Germany." It was apparent that the German cause was hopeless; we hoped they had had enough, but our determination to crush them was adamant. Nazism must be obliterated, and the Timberwolves prepared themselves for this end.

On 7 March 1945, elements of the 9th Armored Division had surprised the Germans by seizing the Ludendorff Bridge near Remagen. The First Army quickly exploited the seizure of the bridge by establishing a firm bridgehead east of the Rhine, fifty miles south of Cologne. It was evident in our observation along the river that the enemy had realized the grave importance of the Remagen bridgehead and had dispatched much of his available strength to that area. Badly battered German divisions had been hastily patched together and thrown into the melee in a vain attempt to stem the tide. No doubt the First Army would further its crossing at Remagen, and it appeared very likely that the 104th Division would be committed in the operation. On 18 March our questions were answered. Commencing 21 March the 104th Division was directed by VII Corps to move to the Remagen bridgehead in the vicinity of Honnef.

On the night of 19-20 March, elements of the 8th Infantry Division relieved the 413th Infantry in the southern part of the Division zone. On the 20th the 413th Combat Team, consisting of the 413th Infantry, 385th Field Artillery Battalion; Battery A, 555th Antiaircraft Battalion; Company A, 329th Engineer Battalion; Company A, 329th Medical Battalion; Company B, 750th Tank Battalion; and Company C, 644th Tank Destroyer Battalion, concentrated in the vicinity of Jungersdorf and made final preparations for its movement to the Remagen bridgehead. The remainder of the Division maintained its position along the Rhine. Early on the 21st, the Seagulls rolled south. The truck convoy halted deep in the Rhine Valley just south of Honnef while smoke generators on each side of the river laid down a thick blanket to screen the ponton bridge from hostile aircraft. The men of the 413th Combat Team got their first glimpse of real castles on the Rhine perched on the high, wooded cliffs. Then the vehicles rolled over the lengthy ponton bridge and the long-awaited Rhine crossing was just a memory. Koenigswinter, deeply steeped in old German mythology, was the site of the initial crossing. Drachenfels, the castle of Siegfried, looked down solemnly upon another invading horde. The 413th moved into positions in the bridgehead that night, relieving the 26th Regiment of the 1st Infantry Division. Lieutenant Colonel Koster's 2d Battalion and Lieutenant Colonel O'Connor's 3d Battalion dug in east of the Cologne-Frankfurt superhighway, while Lieutenant Colonel Fernald's 1st Battalion went into reserve near a captured German airport. Over 500 artillery shells fell in the regimental zone and air bursts flashed throughout the night of 21-22 March.

The Big Red One's capture of the German airbase was a real loss to the enemy. In fact, as Staff Sergeant Frank Marius, C Company, 413th Regiment, recalls:

This was the first airfield captured east of the Rhine and we were soon to discover that the Jerries wanted it back badly. Under cover of darkness, we moved up to relieve the 1st Division. The job was slowed down somewhat by a Luftwaffe strafing attack while we were coming up. Shortly after we were in position we were fired upon by two ack-ack guns. Our outposts attempted to zero in artillery on them but couldn't accurately locate their positions, so the grazing ack-ack fire continued most of the night. About midnight the Germans pulled up a large-scale attack supported by tanks, artillery, and ack-ack fire. Our very effective artillery, directed by the men manning the outposts, broke up this attack when it was within 200 yards of our lines. The Krauts made several more attempts to pierce our lines that night, but none of their attacks could gain momentum. The following day was relatively quiet, with occasional exchanges of artillery barrages.

That night the Jerries tried again, but with little more success than the previous eve. They managed to get one tank on line with the 3d Platoon outpost. The outpost called for and got artillery, and after three zeroing-in rounds, the tank was knocked out.

While the Seagulls occupied front line positions in the bridgehead to the south, the Division was being relieved by the 8th Infantry Division in Cologne. Shortly after midnight on 21-22 March, the relief was completed. At 0600 on 22 March the 414th Regiment (less its Cannon Company) and Company B, 329th Medical Battalion, were attached to the 3d Armored Division. Lieutenant Colonel Clark's 1st Battalion joined Combat Command A; Lieutenant Colonel Ragar's 2d Battalion, Combat Command B; and Lieutenant Colonel Rouge's 3d Battalion, Combat Command R. Beginning at 0300 on the 22d the Division, less the 414th Infantry and Combat Team 413, moved by motor from Cologne to assembly positions east of the Rhine River, approximately ten miles out of Honnef. By midnight the 415th Infantry took its place on the line to the left of the 413th Infantry, after relieving elements of the 1st Division. The 413th Infantry, which had initially been attached to the 1st Division, reverted to the control of the 104th. On our right was the 9th Division, on our left the 1st Division, and concentrated to our rear was the 3d Armored Division, reinforced by the 414th Infantry.

The VII Corps directed the Division to extend the bridgehead to the east and immediately plans were formulated for the 413th and 415th to resume the offensive with night attacks on 23-24 March. At 2300 Company B of the 413th Infantry attacked with the mission of seizing the high ground 400 yards to the front of its present position. By 2355 the objective was taken against light resistance. At 2100 the 1st and 3d Battalions of the 415th attacked against strong small arms and artillery resistance, and prior to daylight on March 24th, after an advance in excess of 1,000 yards the assigned objectives had been secured. At 0830 Lieutenant Colonel Dean's 2d Battalion attacked to further extend the bridgehead. After fierce fighting Company F took the assigned objective, capturing fifty-eight prisoners. The colored platoon of this company in its bayonet rush on an intermediate objective sang "Right in der Führer's Face," and nobly accounted for itself in its first action by quickly seizing the objective and capturing twenty-eight prisoners. Again on the night of 24 March at 2300 the 1st Battalion, 413th Infantry, attacked, gaining its objective 1,000 yards to the east by 0600. All attacks had been successfully concluded, once again ahead of schedule.

Shortly after the Division had moved into the line a German document was captured, revealing the enemy's intentions—"The mission for all committed units is the defense and the holding of the MLR. Penetrations are to be cleaned out at the very beginning with counterattacks by reserves in connection with armor . . . not one meter of ground is to be given up." The terrain east of the Rhine was rugged and well suited for defense and during the first two days of breaking through the crust, our forces had met stiff resistance. Heavy concentrations of artillery, rockets and mortars were placed constantly in the Division zone.

To the Dill River

The VII Corps plan of attack had directed the 1st Division and the 104th Division to break the surface of German defense immediately to the east, and this had now been accomplished. The 3d Armored Division, with the 414th attached, was directed to pass through the 1st Division and the 104th at 0400 on 25 March to seize Altenkirchen, twenty-five miles to the east, and to be prepared to continue its advance to the Dill River, fifty miles beyond Altenkirchen. The 1st Division was to protect the Corps left flank while the Timberwolves would closely follow the armor, destroying all enemy within its zone. The 104th had the further mission of securing the Corps right flank. The Division directed the 413th on the right and 415th on the left to continue their attack, closely following the 3d Armored Division. In addition to fixed objectives a series of phase lines were designated.

It is worthwhile noting at this point the terrain that lay before us beyond the east banks of the Rhine. The countryside reminded one of Oregon with its high, wooded, rolling hills. They gave the enemy excellent defensive positions which would make it difficult for the advancing troops. Ninety miles east of the Rhine River, the Dill River flowed across our projected zone. Hundreds of villages and communities would have to be entered and cleared before the Dill could be reached. Twenty-five miles to the east was Altenkirchen, situated in the Westerwald Forest on the River Wied. It was an industrial town of 2,900 inhabitants, its main resources coming from the surrounding iron and lead mines. The important railroad between Hachenberg and Limburg ran through the city. The Westerwald appeared mountainous

Victor and vanquished.

because of the many streams which had cut gorges through the terrain. Twenty miles further east was Hachenberg, a village of 2,500 inhabitants. Situated on the Dill River were Herborn and Dillenberg. Herborn, a busy town of 4,800 population, was surrounded by four ancient wall towers which were visible from a great distance. It was an old city with many houses dating from the sixteenth century; the city hall had been built in 1590. A castle with many towers, built in the thirteenth century, was situated above the town; it had formerly been owned and occupied by the Duke of Nassau, but was now used as a seminary. Eight miles to the north, Dillenberg, the seat of the House of Nassau from the sixteenth to the eighteenth centuries, was the present capital of the district, possessing 6,100 inhabitants. Its industries consisted of foundries, tobacco, leather tanning, and a mining school. The forty-meter high Wilhelms tower on the ruins of the Dillenberg castle was a prominent landmark in the city.

Thirty-five miles northeast of the Dill River, the large town of Marburg, with 22,000 population, and seat of the Landkreis Marburg, was situated in the Lahn River Valley. This city was famous for its university, founded in 1527, and an important institute for experimental therapy. Historically Marburg recalls the religious discussions by Luther and Zwingli in 1529. Its industries consisted principally of the manufacture of surgical instruments and serums. Over one hundred miles to the north of the Dill River was the 32.000-population city of Paderborn. The River Pader had its source underneath the cathedral and gave the town its name, Paderborn (source of the Pader). The landmarks consisted of the eight old city gates and the twelfth century cathedral. It was here that Karl the Great and Pope Leo III had held their historic meeting in 799.

At the Corps command post in Konigswinter on 24 March Lieutenant General Collins emphasized to his Division Commanders that the coming operation was destined to crush Germany. Tension ran high and all troops anxiously waited for the jump-off. During the night of 24-25 March the 413th continued its attack to the east, and after furious fighting overran three strongpoints immediately to its front. Promptly at 0400 on 25 March, Major General Rose's 3d Armored Division, with Colonel Kelleher's infantrymen mounted on the tanks, plunged through the front lines of the 413th and 415th. Progress initially was slow, but with the Mountaineers dismounting and blasting paths for the advance of the armor, the Spearhead tanks fought their way to within six miles of Altenkirchen. Brilliantly exploiting the breakthrough, the 413th and 415th quickly mopped up the bewildered Germans caught in the smoking wake of the tanks. By nightfall our front lines had advanced five miles deeper into Germany, with the 415th Infantry beyond Limbach, the 413th immediately in rear of Combat Team A, and the 104th Reconnaissance Troop, with Company D of the 750th Tank Battalion attached, abreast of the 413th, guarding the Division's right flank. Since the advancing armor restricted its progress to fixed routes and bypassed resistance whenever possible, sporadic and at times bitter resistance was encountered by our foot troops.

On 26 March the Timberwolves continued their aggressive advances, closely supporting the 3d Armored and mopping up the area as they pushed forward for total gains of twelve miles. Marching on the shoulders of roads and cross-country, the infantrymen pressed forward rapidly. Taking routes between the armored columns, the 415th doughboys, supported by tanks of the 750th Tank Battalion, at one time moved with such speed that they found themselves spearheading the armor, which had encountered strong enemy resistance in the vicinity of Heiberg, and ended the day by seizing Hemmelzen. The 104th Reconnaissance Task Force brushed aside resistance within its zone and continued to secure the Division right flank.

Acceleration of the advance and expected further rapid exploitation made it desirable to increase to the maximum the mobility of the infantry units. Forty-two 2½-ton trucks with trailers were secured from the

VII Corps and twenty of these were attached to each regiment to augment its organic transportation for motorizing and shuttling troops.

Division Operations Memorandum No. 57, issued at 0300 on 27 March, directed that Task Force Laundon be constituted to include the 104th Reconnaissance Troop, Company D (Light Tanks), and one platoon of the 329th Engineer Battalion. The Task Force was assigned the mission to continue protecting the right flank until it reached objective No. 35, then to turn north with the mission of securing the Division left flank. It was now evident that the left flank was becoming more vulnerable since the 1st Division was meeting heavy resistance in its zone. This necessitated the 415th be echeloned to the left rear, with the 413th on the right front. It had also become necessary to safeguard the supply line to the rear, and Task Force Knight was organized to fulfill this mission. The Task Force included Company B and Company C, less the 1st Platoon, of the 329th Engineer Battalion, and one platoon of medium tanks from Company A, 750th Tank Battalion. The regiments were directed to continue their advance. The 413th maintained steady advance behind Task Forces Kane and Doan of the 3d Armored Division, being unimpeded by any stiff resistance. Lieutenant Colonel O'Connor's 3d Battalion made the spectacular advance of fifty miles, commencing from a position west of Altenkirchen and ending the day at Guntersdorf, three miles short of the Dill River. The remaining Seagulls had closed in the vicinity of Driedorf and Marionberg. The 415th encountered stiffened resistance on the left but was able to force its way to Elkenroth and Kotzenroth by the end of the day. Task Force Laundon had swung to the north prior to noon and had joined the 415th Infantry in the protection of the Division left flank. With the 414th mounted on the tanks, the 3d Armored Division had elements along the Dill River and as far northeast as Marburg. In Marburg alone 3,000 prisoners were captured.

Encountering no resistance, the 413th Infantry on the 28th closed on the Dill River, with one battalion seven miles to the east of the river. The 415th and Task Force Laundon continued the difficult task of mopping up behind the armor and guarding the fluctuating north flank of the Division. It was necessary to deploy the infantry on several occasions in order to clean out pockets of resistance and repulse attempted penetrations into the Division zone. "Old Faithful" ended its drive for the day in position at Dillenburg, Langenbauch, Holzhausen and Niederdresselndorf. The Division command post closed in Herborn late that afternoon and all commanders assembled there that night. During the day the Spearhead Division resupplied and completed its plans to push to the north towards Paderborn. The VII Corps had

"Dismount your doughs — there's a Kraut tank up the road."

ordered the 104th Infantry Division to continue its advance behind the 3d Armored commencing early the 29th of March. The Division Commander directed the 413th to continue on the right, with the 415th remaining on the left. To assist the 415th Infantry in its vital role of securing the constantly threatened left flank, Task Force Laundon was attached to Colonel Cochran's regiment.

The Division had completed its eastward push, having pierced ninety miles deeper into Germany, and was now to swing to the north behind the 3d Armored in a sustained drive for Paderborn. It was now disclosed that First Army, with the 3d Armored and 104th in the spearhead role, would link up with the Ninth Army in the vicinity of Paderborn, thus encircling the great Ruhr industrial section. Preliminary estimates by higher headquarters disclosed that this action, if successful, would encircle 100,000 German troops. (Later it was discovered that over 335,000 German troops were cut off in this bold and aggressive maneuver.) Since 24 March the Division had taken 1,830 prisoners, not including the 3,000 which were captured by the 414th and the 3d Armored at Marburg. It was becoming more evident each day that the German Army was collapsing. However, there was still much fighting to be encountered.

SWING TO THE NORTH

Early on 29 March the 2d Battalion, 415th Infantry, battled its way

300

through the town of Haiger, destroying six self-propelled guns and capturing one hundred infantry. The regiment, keeping a watchful eye on the Division's left flank, pushed on, with its forward element closing at Laasphe and Strasseberbach prior to midnight. Stiff resistance was encountered at Eibelshausen, where between 200 and 300 enemy infantry and seven tanks were engaged and destroyed after a fire fight by the 3d Battalion. Because of necessity for the regiment to cover a large area in protecting the Division left flank, another task force was organized: Task Force Salsbury (TFS), comprising Company C, 329th Engineer Battalion, and one platoon of light tanks from the 750th Tank Battalion. At Laasphe, Task Force Salsbury became engaged in a stubborn fire fight, but soon overwhelmed the enemy, capturing two 88mm guns and 130 prisoners. The 413th continued its rapid advance closely behind the armor. Mopping up all resistance within its zone and bagging over 2,000 prisoners, the Seagulls buttoned up north of Frankenburg after the spectacular advance of fifty miles. The Division command post closed behind the 413th at Friendendorf and that night directed all units to continue on their mission early on 30 March. The 413th was assigned the additional mission of protecting the Division right flank, which now lay exposed.

The Division was then confronted with not only pushing forward rapidly in order to secure the supply routes of the 3d Armored, but with the additional responsibility of protecting both flanks. The 413th, alternately moving by foot and by motor, continued on its drive toward the key city of Paderborn. Prior to midnight on 30 March the Seagulls' lead elements closed at Arslsonaw, an advance of another forty miles. It was now watching not only to the front but also to its right to make certain that no hostile force penetrated its zone.

The 415th fought viciously on the left flank and was successful in clearing its zone fifty-five miles to the north, with the 1st Battalion closing into Medebach at 2000, and the 2d Battalion at Hallenburg. Task Force Laundon held Usseln late in the day and blocked the main east-west road running through the town. The Division command post opened up in Medebach late in the afternoon of 30 March. Lieutenant Weber and Lieutenant Mudge, with the 104th Headquarters Company Defense Platoon, had cleared the town shortly before. It was an extremely fluid situation, and all the units of the Division not normally combat units, such as Division headquarters, unit headquarters, medics, service companies, quartermaster, ordnance and signal units, were required to assume a combat role. The Division was extended on a wide front and in great depth. The constant threat on the left flank, which was exposed to attack by enemy troops bottled up in the encirclement, made it necessary for the Division to be echeloned to the left rear; the 413th up well in advance on the right with the 415th echeloned behind. The advance was proceeding as planned, but it called for constant vigilance by all personnel in order to prevent infiltration, sabotage and ambush. Some ambushes did cause damage to personnel and property but were soon eliminated, thus enabling the supplies to continue rolling forward to not only our own troops but those of the 3d Armored as well. On the night of 30 March, VII Corps directed that the Division occupy Brilon, twenty miles to the north, and establish a strong defensive position in that city and immediate vicinity to prevent any breakthrough along the important axial road, Brilon-Nieder Marsburg-Warburg. All of the Division troops were then employed, but the 415th was in a position to release Task Force Laundon by having its own Task Force, TFS, relieve the Reconnaissance Troop at Usseln. This being accomplished by 2300, Task Force Laundon was directed to proceed immediately for Brilon. Division Headquarters also received information of certain enemy dispositions and movements from prisoners and civilians which indicated that the enemy would make attempts to break out of the Ruhr pocket through our lines. Directives were issued to the units to establish strong road blocks to eliminate this threat.

All syndicated papers carried an Associated Press release which aptly told of the desperate efforts of the Germans to break out of the iron band that was slowly but surely strangling their last escape route.

SUICIDE BY TORTURED INCHES

(AP)—The German armies in the west are committing suicide—suicide by tortured inches.

There is no way out through the American lines. In the last three days this correspondent has traveled along the entire First Army battlefront from the Rhine to Paderborn and can testify that there is no loophole on the southern pincer to smash through.

Behind the greatest tank force ever massed under the leadership of a British or American Army commander in this war, Lt. Gen. Courtney H. Hodges has grouped some of the finest veteran infantry divisions in the European theater.

The most the enemy can now hope to accomplish is to break into elastic defenses for a few miles with small armored raiding parties which will be promptly pinched off.

"TIMBERWOLVES" MARCH

Last night, when the pocketed and alarmed Germans began trying to smash at least one avenue through which they could pour troops, Maj. Gen. Terry Allen's 104th Infantry "Timberwolf" Division sent a force of tanks and doughboys to clamp a strong roadblock on Brilon, highway center 25 miles southwest of Paderborn.

"There's a force of enemy tanks and mobile guns in the woods nearby that wants to fight," a staff officer told Capt. Arthur Laundon, a former partner in a Cleveland, Ohio, brokerage firm. "We better send you there by a round-about route."

"How many of them are there?" Capt. Laundon asked.

"At least 100 troops," was the answer.

"Send me by the direct route—I will give them a fight if they are looking for one," said Capt. Laundon.

Capt. Laundon set out with his tanks and men at 10 p.m. in a night march of the kind for which the Timberwolf Division is famous.

SENDS BACK 1,500 PRISONERS

"By 5:30 a.m. this morning he had his roadblock firmly secured," Lt. Col. Leo A. Hoegh of Chariton, Iowa, said, "and that was after a heavy fight that wiped out enemy resistance in the woods on the way. Instead of the 100 or less prisoners that we expected, Capt. Laundon sent back 1,500. He gave them more of a fight than they wanted."

This morning another German column tried to break out from another wood in a small village only a mile from the "Timberwolf" Division's command post. They shot up a jeep carrying Lt. William R. Vanderbilt of Short Hills, N. J., but he escaped uninjured by running across fields.

There was one light tank and five scout cars containing 15 reconnoitering Germans in the column.

"They cut loose on me at about 150 yards with machine guns and got my jeep, but I got away," said Lt. Vanderbilt, who was reluctant to discuss his experience because he didn't want his family to worry about him.

"Then they rolled into a small village and shot up some maintenance vehicles repairing several of our trucks," Lt. Vanderbilt said. "The firing woke up some doughboys sleeping in the houses in the village. They came out with bazookas and rifles and killed or captured every German."

MANY SMALL-SCALE SCRAPS

Numerous such small-scale scraps are taking place all along the perimeter of the pocket—which has shaped up exactly like the battles of Mons and the Falaise Gap last summer—but the chief breakout blows by the Nazis against First Army troops are being concentrated in the Paderborn vicinity.

"They are trying with everything they can put together to push through to Paderborn to the North German plains to try to salvage what they have left of their armies," said Capt. Dan Magnussen, of Green Bay, Wis. "They particularly want to get their heavy armored stuff out and if they try to by-pass Paderborn on the north their tanks bog down in the marshes."

To reach the critical Paderborn road net—American tanks can interdict the escape highways by fire from the outskirts of the city—the 3d Armored "Spearhead" Division set a new record for an armored division in combat by traveling 115 miles in a 24-hour march.

German soldiers by the hundreds are deserting and changing into civilian clothing hoping to escape becoming prisoners. Other units are destroying and abandoning their equipment and then are trying to march across American lines on foot. But they still are organized as fighting units and carry enough automatic weapons to put up a scrap.

APPEAL TO GERMANS' THRIFT

To clean out the villages where these outfits enter and hole up after American armor passes through, the "Timberwolf" Division has formed 15 to 20 infantry and tank forces which comb them out minutely.

In some they have had bitter fights, but they have found it easier to appeal to the German civilian's municipal and personal thrift and his love of property.

"We just roll through a town and bottle up all roads leading out," said Lt. Col. Hoegh. "Then the task force commander calls on the burgomeister or another leading civilian and tells him: 'Either you will immediately deliver up all German soldiers hiding in your village or we will fight our way through it with tanks street by street and house by house—and in that case your village will be destroyed.'

"And in no time at all," said Col. Hoegh, "the civilians have their soldiers coming out with their hands up and piling their rifles and machine guns in the center of the streets. That saves lives all around."

MEDEBACH . . . The 413th continued to maintain contact with the 3d Armored and advanced an additional thirty-five miles during the day. A strong road block at Rimbach was established by 0800 and the important Brilon-Warburg road was blocked not only from the west but from the east. During the day it developed that the 415th would not be in a position to advance further to the north but would have to go into defensive positions to secure the threatened left flank. The regiment was deployed over a forty-mile front, and therefore the Division directed the 3d Battalion of the 413th, reinforced by tanks and artillery, to be motorized and placed in Division reserve at Adorf. Later the regiment was contracted to a twenty-mile front. The 3d Battalion, 413th, was to be prepared for a counterattack role against any penetrations made by the Germans from the west and to be prepared to assist the 413th in case pressure increased from the east. Early on 31 March the Division command post moved from Medebach to Nieder Marsburg, thirty-five miles further to the north, where it could more closely direct the actions of TFL and the 413th, leaving Brigadier General Woodward and a small detachment from Division Headquarters and Headquarters Battery with the 415th. The Germans showed their hand, confirming earlier reports that they would attempt a break through our lines, when messengers and liaison officers were ambushed between Medebach and Medelon. The 2d Battalion attacked Liessen and the 1st Battalion cleared the road between Medebach and Medelon. The opposition consisted chiefly of infantry supported by self-propelled guns. By mid-afternoon all infiltrated Germans had been eliminated. This sporadic, isolated type of warfare created by so many enemy break-out attempts made combat infantry out of just about every unit in the Division. For the artillery, moving too fast to fire any missions, this was something altogether different. That fact is evidenced in the words of Technical Sergeant Tim Casey of the 386th Field Artillery Battalion Headquarters:

We fired very few missions. The armored and infantry advance was too rapid. Then about the 1st of April a sizeable counterattack was discovered forming not too far from our advanced position. The enemy was trying to make an escape route for his encircled troops. The battalion jockeyed positions around the threatened area, occupying various tongue-twisters like Niederingelbach, Goddelsheim, Dudinghausen, and Dalwigksthal. It was necessary to change positions many times in this area because of the wide defensive sector we were assigned. At one time the enemy attack completely bypassed the defending infantry and succeeded in reaching our artillery positions. On the night of 2 April an enemy platoon attacked Charlie Battery's position but were either killed, captured or wounded by the direct fire of the cannoneers who employed grenades, carbines and .50-caliber machine guns. Laying wire to our supported infantry in this area was accomplished with extreme difficulty due to the fact that enemy troops were between our positions and the infantry. At one time fifty enemy soldiers were held at bay by "multiple fifties" while the wire was repaired less than one hundred yards from their position.

The desperate plight of the German Army is reflected in the words of Staff Sergeant Louis Kurtz, C Battery, 386th Field Artillery Battalion, as he tells of that sneak attack the night of April 2d:

On an early April evening, the skies sullen with rain, the black, forbidding forest loomed ahead with the terror of the unknown. From the bosom of the forest crept angry men—men indoctrinated by the hate of Naziism—the hate of Hitler. Men who were rationed on the brown, molding bread of a country that dispatched them into combat without ample preparation for the grim reality of modern warfare. Men who crept into the fold of the enemy for food, for protection—but with the hopeless idea of securing those basic necessities of life by overpowering and outwitting a wary foe.

The shimmering curtain of rain was suddenly pierced by the noise of a machine gun as Pfc. Bertram Levitan began a metallic duet with Corporal Anthony "Moose" Ferraro. Levitan and Ferraro figuratively nudged their slumbering comrades with their cold duet of steel. En masse a hundred men vaulted from their dreams of home.

First Sergeant Ray Hornbuckle and Staff Sergeant Earnest C. Liles mustered their men into immediate action. A battery skirmish line was formed as the foe advanced on hands and knees. The courage of Battery C proved the stumbling block to these men of Hitler. Staff Sergeant Perry L. Thomas grouped his men with the natural instinct of a soldier, deploying them in advantageous positions. And the men recalled companions lying on hospital beds wounded by the counterparts of the men who now faced them. The men of Charlie Battery recalled such comrades as Gabb, Walters, Kulikowski—and others; men who had been taken by the enemy, their fates unknown—men captured—Lieutenant Allison, Argulewicz, Buckingham. These thoughts instilled desire to vanquish the enemy.

Alone, Lieutenant Marvin Nobis approached the enemy to ascertain their strength. He found a handful of desperate, starving men that had been recruited from civil life but two weeks prior. The battle was brief. The overwhelming odds of seven to one soon triumphed over the soldiers of Hitlerism. A straggling group of morose, beaten men, under armed guard, marched down the drenched lane to their predestined hole—a PW cage. Hungry men—to be fed. Men to be cared for. But one man required no food, no attention. For his still form lay on an unfertile field.

Captured Germans confirmed the previous reports that the enemy had a large concentration of infantry and tanks at Winterberg and that they were prepared to make a break-out attempt that night, making their efforts against Hollendberg and Medebach.

The terrain in the vicinity of Medebach was a series of wooded hills threaded by a vital system of roads offering better than average means of maneuver. Off roads the only access to high ground was on foot. The rate of advance denied our troops full opportunity for reconnaissance, while the enemy was able to base his plan on concealment and the maximum use of surprise in his operation on familiar grounds.

On arrival in hours of darkness in the Medebach area, active reconnaissance and resulting intelligence indicated that a strong enemy force was deployed for a break-out in the vicinity of Winterberg. Identified was the 130th Panzer Lehr Division, with evidences of the 3d Panzer Grenadier Division and other general purpose German units also in the vicinity. By an estimate the enemy force was easily superior in number with greater armor strength than the 415th Infantry in that area. The regiment deployed for defense over a twenty-mile front and organized key towns in order to safeguard the routes of communication for the 3d Armored and 104th Divisions. Loss of control of these routes would have placed the right spearhead in a precarious position since the 3d Armored Division was heavily engaged at Paderborn and in constant need of fuel and ammunition.

The enemy's first attack materialized at Liessen on the morning of 31 March when approximately fifty infantry, four personnel carriers, and three SP's attempted to take the locality. In repeated actions throughout that day he was repulsed by the 2d Battalion based at Hallendberg. Enemy losses numbered one SP and one personnel carrier together with half the initial personnel strength killed or captured.

Simultaneously in the Medebach area the 1st Battalion clashed with SS troops harassing supply and maintenance installations between Medebach and Medelon. The harassing attacks grew in strength until at dawn the enemy, in company strength, reinforced by SP's, advanced boldly toward Medelon, where it was met by a stranded platoon of infantry from A Company, 414th Infantry. At 1328 the battalion based at Medebach reported the break-out attempt completely frustrated.

There's an interesting tale about this gallant band of doughs who fought off a numerically superior enemy in the little town of Medelon. Task Force Q they were later dubbed. Staff Sergeant Chris Cullen, a member of TFQ, tells the following story:

The first thing I heard that morning was one of the Polish slave laborers running around yelling, "Panzer! Panzer!" Then as I started to go back to sleep mumbling to myself about that "damn crazy Polack," I heard the unmistakable sound of a German machine gun. That fixed the sleep.

While I was cramming on my boots, one of our men came in for ammo and I asked him what was going on. "Plenty," he said. "There's a Kraut tank coming down the street." People exaggerate when they are excited. I would go look for myself before I got excited.

I got excited. About forty yards away and coming slowly forward was a German SP with a gun on it that looked as large as a telephone pole.

About a week before we had been in on the breakthrough at the Remagen bridgehead. "We" means the 2d Platoon, A Company, 414th Infantry. Our regiment was riding the 3d Armored tanks. Thirty-six hours before we had been right on the spearhead. Then our tanks had broken down and we had been left behind for maintenance in the small town of Medelon, six miles from Medebach. Our spearhead elements were moving so rapidly that a gap of about fifty miles existed between them and our mop-up regiments. The country was just crawling with Krauts and their vehicles trying to break out of the pocket. We were mighty anxious to get the tanks repaired and get going again.

Our group consisted of just sixteen infantrymen, two tanks and their crews. Lieutenant Howard Doyle, our platoon leader, was in command. The doughs were from the first and second squads of the 2d. Platoon. Sergeants Jose Luna and Bill Doramus were the two squad leaders. Vadie Brown, our platoon radio man, and myself, Chris Cullen, acting platoon sergeant, rounded out our meager crew.

We got into the town about sunset. At dusk a third tank came limping in and nearly scared us to death. It was one of our own SP's with a broken clutch. We positioned the tanks to cover the approaches and sweated out the first night. When daylight came things looked much better. The boys remembered they were hungry and started hunting eggs. As soon as the Krauts saw what was happening they began locking the hen-house doors. They lost more doors and locks that way. Lieutenant Doyle sent two men out looking for a good OP and they found a big house on top of a hill which belonged to the burgomeister. We went up to the attic and looked over the countryside and on our way down noticed some hams hanging from a rafter. As "Shorty" Smith said, "Eggs are no damn good without ham."

We had just gotten back to our house when the burgomeister came stomping in with an interpreter. It seemed that some soldier had purloined a ham of his and he authoritatively demanded to see an officer. Lieutenant Doyle is an Irishman and a mean man with the blarney. Before the burgomeister left he was thoroughly convinced that the meat Shorty was cutting up was beef.

Some of the civilians told us of a large build-up of German soldiers in a nearby town called Winterberg, so we anxiously awaited the 3d Armored maintenance crew so we could get patched up and on our way to rejoin the column.

The night passed uneventfully and the next thing I knew that damned Kraut tank was out in the street. Our guards had somewhat relaxed at daylight in an attempt at arranging something to eat. The Krauts didn't shoot until they got into town and they caught us with our guard down. Our small numbers made the situation a little rough. We were greatly outnumbered and bottled up in one house. Our tanks were covered by the German tank and never did get into action. Sergeant "Hub" Turley was out in his tank, but he was alone and couldn't maneuver his Pershing into firing position and shoot at the same time.

Sergeant Luna made a dash out to the nearest of our tanks and got an extra bag of bazooka rounds, as we were low on ammo. That little guy sure could move fast when the spit was flying.

By this time, the German tank had moved up to our front door and proceeded to knock out our unmanned SP. Then the Krauts rushed us. Things at this point took on a Hollywood aspect. Everyone started shooting as fast as he could and the lead really began to fly. Pfc. Schultz went into action with his bazooka from an upstairs window. He wasn't at all excited, but I never before heard of anyone putting a bazooka shell in backwards. However, he finally got straightened out and began blasting from above.

Those Krauts were pretty hopped up. They were yelling and hollering just as loud as they could. When they knocked out our SP the German tank commander stuck his head out and yelled "Héil Hitler!" Following a shot at another of our tanks, he raised his head from the turret again. That was just once too often, and Shorty nailed him.

When Schultz opened up, a Nazi armed with a panzerfaust took aim at our bazooka. Vadie Brown dropped him. That was the biggest Kraut I ever saw. He landed spreadeagled in the street and looked seven feet tall.

Upstairs Bill Doramus was beefing at the top of his lungs. He had just stopped a Jerry, but was sore because his automatic carbine would fire only one round at a time. Seremino and Furrow were burning up their BAR's. I heard Beaver yell "I think I got that machine gunner. The bastard isn't moving any more."

All this and a lot more I didn't see happened in a very short while. Then we were over the hump. Schultz's deliberate and accurate plunging fire was slowly wrecking the German tank and we had stopped all their infantry leaders and tank commander. The Krauts had had enough and started to pull back.

Once they started giving ground we ran them right out of town. To get out of town they had to move along an open road up a hill towards Winterberg. Using a German machine gun captured in the fray, we really made that road hot for its ex-owners.

When we took the score we found Krauts lying all over the road. Ten were dead and twenty-six lying wounded right in town. We could see many lying on the road out of town and there were more both dead and wounded in the ditches. We learned from the enemy officer we captured that the Nazi force had consisted of eighty-four men and four tanks. With our sixteen doughboys we had killed about fifteen, wounded and captured twenty-six, and seriously damaged one of their tanks. The only casualty we sustained was Pfc. McBride, who got a slight wound in the leg.

That afternoon our maintenance truck came along and in the evening we moved on to Medebach, Medelon becoming just another fight along the line. Its outstanding feature was that we had stopped cold one of the first attempts at a break-out of the Ruhr pocket aimed at the larger town of Medebach.

On 1 April at 0610 the 1st Battalion, 415th, was again beset by the enemy, this time in the vicinity of Medebach. Four tanks and 150 infantry in advance guard action approached the defense area via the Dustelberg-Medebach road. Two of the tanks succeeded in entering the western outskirts of the town, where they were destroyed, one by the antitank company and the other by rifle and bazooka fire. By 0730 the attack was repulsed.

Through prisoners taken in these early actions and other feeler attacks along the flank in this area, the enemy's intention was ascertained. Realizing his plight if the VII Corps spearhead linked with the Ninth Army advance to encircle the Ruhr, the enemy had massed two divisions, reinforced with all the armor strength he could muster, to break out in the area of Hallendberg, Frankenberg, Marburg, or along the axial route Medebach-Korbach-Kassel. Either thrust would isolate the troops embattled at Paderborn and provide a path of escape for the 335,000 Germans cut off in the Ruhr.

With the 3d Battalion enroute from Ebeishausen 1 April, the regiment was able to contract to a seventeen-mile front. The 1st Battalion, 415th Infantry (less Company A), was still based in the Medebach area. The 3d Battalion was assembled as a mobile reserve centrally located in the area Godelsheim-Nordenbeck. The night of 1 April the 817th Tank Destroyer Battalion arrived and was deployed in darkness to augment antitank defenses.

Communications and supply were under great strain. In one action along the supply route connecting the battalions, a Service Company convoy was engaged by an enemy ambush on 1 April. Using their individual weapons, the regimental maintenance officer and his drivers fought off an equal force equipped with automatic weapons and saved the fuel convoy.

At 0600, 2 April, Medebach was subjected to a second heavy assault. One component of the enemy force infiltrated the east end of town under cover of darkness, and at daybreak this group attempted to join the main body which was driving on the defenders from the west. Companies C and I, which occupied the town, held fast against the crossfire, killing thirty enemy and capturing sixty-one.

Meanwhile interrogation of PW's had established that the several assaults sustained by 1st and 2d Battalions were made by units of three divisions, 3d Volks-Grenadier Division, 130th Panzer Lehr, and the

176th Infantry Division, all of whose main forces were grouped in the vicinity of Kustelberg. The enemy, if he retained the initiative, might develop a very serious threat with this number of troops at his disposal. Accordingly, on the morning of 2 April, the 415th Infantry prepared for the offensive. Kustelberg, Beifeld, and Titmaringhausen were designated objectives one, two and three respectively. The 1st Battalion was to stand fast in the vicinity of Medebach; 2d Battalion moved into position to attack west; 3d Battalion assembled north of Medebach. Elements of the 9th Infantry Division had relieved the 2d Battalion at Hallendberg and were also moving in the offensive.

The 2d Battalion jumped off for objectives two and three at 1400, with F and G Companies in the assault. Company F met scattered opposition in the approach to Beifeld. At the town itself it was necessary to put mortar and artillery fire on defenders before the troops could force an entry. Mop-up of the objectives was completed by 1900. Company E also met resistance in entering Diefeld, which was nonetheless secured by 1725.

The 3d Battalion was assigned the difficult task of Kustelberg. At 1500 I and K Companies crossed the line of departure and advanced through a wooded sector to within two kilometers of the objectives, where it encountered very stiff resistance consisting of automatic and direct fire. The tanks which were supporting the advance drew fire from the enemy batteries. Barrages fell upon the infantry's position in the woods, where the danger of tree bursts forced the battalion to halt its attack temporarily and dig in. The troops remained in the woods for the night, where their hardships were increased by a driving rain.

The next morning, 3 April, during the final hours of darkness, the 3d Battalion was hit by a succession of determined counterattacks. These were all beaten off and by 0730 the attackers were able to resume their drive for the key center of Kustelberg. Throughout the morning the battalion fought the capable enemy, who poured automatic and direct fire from his favorable defensive position. Company K found the roughest sledding as the battalion assaulted Kustelberg. Private First Class Charles Golden remembers the hot and heavy encounter as one of the company's most bitter skirmishes:

April 3d began as a dry day, with the sun lost behind dark clouds. At 0900 Captain Kimball and his executive officer, Lieutenant Lee Kashmitter, called the platoon leaders to the CP. There were on hand Lieutenant Homer Bryan, 1st Platoon; Lieutenant "Wild Bill" Gallagher, 2d Platoon; Lieutenant Albert Jacobelli, 3d Platoon; and Lieutenant Joe Kelly, Weapons Platoon. The company was up and alert, awaiting the result of the meeting. In a half hour the platoon leaders returned. Company K was going to attack due west—directly toward the Rhine.

Right after the noon meal the company entrucked and rode seven kilometers west to Hillerhausen, assembly point for the battalion. The wait here lasted from 1300 to nearly 1500. Packs were dropped in a large barn and the troops went into houses, ready for the jump-off.

At 1500, K Company left Hillerhausen, moving out in the approach march. At the edge of town, I Company waited, on either side of the road, while K passed through. Ahead an open field, and then the woods, stretching ominously across slight rises. Tanks weaved through the doughs and clanked on into the trees. The objective, Kustelben, lay six miles ahead. In those six miles waited a regiment of the enemy, poised for a break-out.

On the right, Sergeant John Bednarowicz led his squad into the fringe of the woods. A German phone operator there had already called back his valuable information. He surrendered at once and K Company took its first prisoner from the woods. The men were apprehensive now, fearing artillery fire. None came.

The advance continued slowly as the 2d and 3d Platoons moved into a wide skirmish line. Behind the 3d in line came the 1st, Weapons, and Company Headquarters. They pressed on more rapidly, hoping to secure Kustelberg before the night closed in. Then on the right a German machine gun barked! Searing flank fire pinned the 3d Platoon to the ground. The 2d, coming up next to the 3d, paused for a moment, then moved off quickly to the right flank. Working through the thick growth, they found the Jerry machine gun and silenced it. No casualties yet.

Now the advance continued more slowly and cautiously. Suddenly all along the line a fire-fight broke out. The Jerries had dug in deep and were cleverly concealed.

Both forces were pinned by the tremendous volume of fire. Company I left the road and swung in on the left in an attempted flanking movement. They met the same stiff resistance and the entire advance was stopped dead. Tanks rumbled up the road and leveled their cannons. Answering their first tree-shattering bursts, a new enemy menace made itself known. Four German SP guns poked their noses over the ridge to the rear of the enemy position and opened fire. Two of the American tanks, firing from completely exposed positions on the road, were knocked out of action before they could return a single round—the other was withdrawn at once because of the overwhelming odds.

The enemy armor now turned its attention to the doughboys. This proved poor strategy, however, for under the murderous fire K Company was forced to move. When they moved, they moved forward. The German line swayed and broke. The 1st and 2d Platoons, supported by the light machine gun section, came ahead, employing marching fire. Germans died and were wounded, and as their infantry withdrew the SP guns turned and disappeared into the woods behind the ridge. Then it was quiet again, and after a swift reorganization the battalion moved ahead once more.

Two miles were behind—then two and a half. It was nearly dark now and an icy rain was falling. The speed of the advance quickened. Kustelberg was still three miles away. Suddenly the men stopped. The shriek of a mortar shell ripped the air and a second later it crashed to the rear of the company. Others were falling in now. The evening was thick and black and the rain had increased.

Dig in—dig in for the night, word was passed back! A night in the woods— with no protection from the deadly mortars except a mud-lined foxhole, The crashing of the enemy shells continued, but by 2000 K Company was dug in.

The 1st Platoon and a machine gun section were forward and to the left, bounded by a fence that separated the woods from a road. On their right was the 3d Platoon, the 2d directly behind them. To the left and rear of the 2d the mortar section and company headquarters crouched on the edge of a clearing.

By 2100 the enemy mortar fire had come to a standstill. Following Joe Kelly, the mortar section filed past the ammo truck and picked up bandoliers and boxes of ammunition. They were to carry these forward to the entrenched riflemen and machine gunners, who had expended the greater part of their original supply in the concentrated fire-fight.

It was black dark in the woods as the mortar section moved slowly on through the trees. They reached the fence and started along the inside—less than 200 yards to go. Then there was the flash and bang of an SP gun a few hundred yards to the left front. The shell crashed into the I Company sector across the road. Kelly halted the mortar men and they fell flat against the rain-soaked, freezing ground. The shell casing clanged as it left the breech and then the flash came again. This round struck one hundred yards closer. The doughs held their breath as the breech clanged again. Kelly passed back word not to dig—it would give away their position. The third round was a blinding burst of fire, and shrapnel whizzed from a spot seventy-five yards to the left of the road. Kelly was on his feet now, running along the fence checking the men. Near the end of the column crouched Colonel Clough, the battalion commander, and next to him his executive officer, Captain Hallahan. They were in the fight too, wet and chilled to the bone, and cursing the SP.

The fourth round crashed farther back to the left, and the SP continued its traverse in that direction. Three more rounds and the breech clanged shut for the last time. It was quiet again.

The 1st Platoon sent patrols forward, skirting the edge of the woods, seeking enemy positions. Shortly afterwards, shadowy figures made their way back down the road, along the fence. They passed the 1st and continued on opposite the mortar men. Suddenly Kelly leaped to his feet and fired his pistol. He shouted a command and the pistols and carbines all broke into flame. The colonel was on his knees, firing a forty-five over the fence. One of the figures on the road screamed and fell. Another fired a short burst from his machine pistol, then turned and joined his comrades in frantic flight across the field.

Then, except for the rain, it was quiet again. Company K remained alert at first, but fought drowsiness as the night wore on. They were wet and miserable—and the rain continued.

The morning of the 4th came, gray and cold. At 0630 the colonel called I Company and then contacted Kimball. Orders were to move ahead again at 0700. The men were eager to reach Kustelberg. They stood up and stomped their feet and blew on their hands. The morning mist lifted slowly and it was still and quiet in the woods.

Company I moved ahead to the left of the road, K Company to the right. In K Company it was the 1st and 3d Platoons forward, as skirmishers, with a machine gun section attached. Following the initial battle line came the 2d Platoon, mortar section, and company headquarters.

The first mile was uneventful and the day was breaking clear and bright now. Then the Jerry mortar sang again. Nearly all the rounds hit left of the road in the I Company sector and too far to the rear to inflict casualties. The battalion increased its speed.

Just a mile to go now the word came back—but Jerry was waiting in that last mile. It started in the I Company sector—the staccato barking of small arms. Then the 1st and 3d hit another line of entrenched, fighting Germans. This line was thin now, however. The enemy had suffered heavy losses on the previous day.

The volume of fire from K and I Companies was tremendous. Every man fired and fired all he had. The 2d Platoon flanked to the right again, and then all three moved in on the enemy positions. The tempo of fire and movement made surrendering an impossibility, for the Germans broke and ran, and the majority left their weapons behind. The 1st and 2d pressed ahead, up onto a high ridge. Past that ridge lay the outskirts of Kustelberg.

But Jerry was not through yet. On a small hill beyond the first houses an SP gun waited, and behind that hill a heavy mortar section. As K Company stood looking down on the buildings, the enemy opened fire. The 1st moved to the forward slope of the ridge and returned the fire, while the 2d and 3d ran to the right, still in the woods, then swung forward in an attempt to locate and silence the SP and mortars. Round after round crashed in among the doughs and serious casualties were inflicted. The 1st Platoon was hit hardest, losing Lieutenant Bryand and one entire squad in a single salvo of mortar shells. They fought up the street, house to house, until all were off the ridge and the outskirts of Kustelberg were secure.

The 2d Platoon and machine gun section remained on the high ridge to the right of town, defending against possible counterattacks. The sky was gray again and thick wet snow began falling. TD's rumbled down the street, past K Company's houses and on into the main part of town. I and L Companies followed. K Company had secured the outskirts by 1200, and by 1400 Kustelberg was taken, the one remaining SP knocked out, and the mortar crew captured intact.

The Battle of the Woods and capture of Kustelberg was successfully completed. An entire regiment of the enemy had been accounted for, and this threat of a break-out from the Ruhr pocket was gone. K Company had paid for their victory with one killed and sixteen wounded, but it made the Germans pay dearly for these fine men.

The night of 4 April was spent in Kustelberg—hot chow again, and dry clothes for most of us. Early next morning we boarded trucks and headed north.

The enemy's will to carry on had been broken—the best that the Wehrmacht had was not enough. A captured German commander shook his head in amazement, "How is it possible that such an attack could be made on us by troops we have smashed again and again during the past two days?"

For this outstanding action the Division Commander has recommended that the regiment be awarded a unit citation. The proposed citation states:

The 415TH INFANTRY REGIMENT (Reinforced) is cited for extraordinary heroism and outstanding performance of duty in armed conflict with the enemy during the period from 31 March to 4 April 1945, in the vicinity of Kustelberg, Medebach, Winterberg, and Neiderfeld, Germany. On 31 March 1945, the regiment fulfilled its mission of securing the left flank of the armored thrust to Paderborn, Germany, by moving fifty-four miles and repulsing successive attacks in the vicinity of Neidebach, Liessen, and Medelon, Germany. While advancing in this fluid situation, the lead elements of the regiment came into direct contact with three enemy divisions—the 3d Volksgrenadier, the 130th Panzer Lehr, and the 176th Infantry Division—which were massed near Kustelberg, Medebach, Winterberg, and Neiderfeld. Extended over forty-two miles at the time, the regiment quickly redisposed along a twelve-mile front to cover possible areas of penetration into the VII Corps' vital left flank. During the next two days, the enemy put three heavy concentrations of armor, artillery, and infantry against the 415TH INFANTRY REGIMENT line in a fruitless attempt to break out of en-circlement by the United States First and Ninth Armies. In crushing this attack, the 415TH INFANTRY REGIMENT not only exacted heavy losses in men and materiel, but also deprived the enemy once and forever of his opportunity to retreat into central Germany for a new stand. Successful in defense, the regi-ment, on the afternoon of 2 April 1945, wrested the initiative from the foe in a thrust for Kustelberg, Beifeld, and Titmaringhausen, and attained the fiercely defended objectives by the following night. In a five-day period, the 415TH INFANTRY REGIMENT first repelled a major break-out attempt by large forces trapped in the Ruhr pocket, and then commenced an attack which was the first action to reduce the pocket, which eventually yielded over 300,000 troops. Throughout the action, the officers and men of the 415TH INFANTRY REGIMENT distinguished themselves by their exceptional initiative, individual bravery, and gallant action. Their great determination, superior combat discipline, courage, and esprit de corps reflect the finest traditions of the armed forces of the United States.

The Division had been fighting since 25 March. At that time Com-pany C, 644th Tank Destroyer Battalion, reverted to the VII Corps. It was evident that this important direct fire weapon was needed to assist in repelling the concentrated tank attack then forming at Winterberg. Late on 31 March the 817th Tank Destroyer Battalion, under Lieutenant Colonel William H. Bardes, arrived in the Division zone, having been attached to the Division by VII Corps. The complete battalion was attached to the 415th Infantry.

During the next five days, 31 March to 4 April, the 415th crushed numerous attacks and completely frustrated the enemy's attempt to break through our lines.

Easter Sunday and April Fool's Day passed in the same twenty-four hours, both practically unnoticed. To some units, however, it meant a slight breathing spell, a chance to catch up on much-needed sleep and much-hoped-for mail from home. A continuance of Pfc. Golden's nar-rative tells of an Easter spent amid a dreary desolation:

Easter Sunday dawned wet and cold on Captain Frank Kimball's K Company. They were dug in at the German farm town of Braunshausen, anticipating pos-sible counterattacks from the trapped enemy in the Ruhr pocket. The drive was

Recon joins infantry on the advance into Paderborn

north and east from the Rhine into the heart of Germany, and K Company was tired—but they were anxious too. Ahead lay Berlin, the Russians—and home.

Looking down on the town from the north stood a steep, wooded slope. Along the ridge the riflemen and machine gunners had dug positions. All this in the slow, cold drizzle of rain.

Mail and packages caught the company in Braunshausen. Corporal Joe Kuta sat in a small German living room separating the staggering pile of letters into platoon stacks. Everyone in the company, except the newest replacements, read letters that Easter Sunday.

Later in the afternoon the sky cleared and the sun broke through. A dozen cameras came into use. The doughs began to talk more and laugh—maybe Jerry would quit soon.

Easter night the ridge positions were only partially manned. The balance of the company slept well—slept well in Braunshausen's beds. . . . An American ambulance slid to the edge of the muddy road just outside the town that night, struck an antitank mine, and was knocked out.

Colonel Cochran's forces were reinforced during this period with the following units being attached: Companies A and C, 750th Tank Battalion; Cannon Company, 414th Infantry; Company C, 329th Engineer Battalion; 817th Tank Destroyer Battalion; Batteries B and C, 555th AAA Battalion; 929th Field Artillery Battalion; 386th Field Artillery Battalion; Battery B, 387th Field Artillery Battalion; and the 104th Reconnaissance Troop.

PADERBORN . . . At 1400 on 1 April the 3d Armored's TFY, with the 1st Battalion, 414th Infantry, mounted on its tanks, linked up with the

2d Armored Division of the Ninth Army at Lippstadt. The iron ring of infantry and tanks was locked around the Ruhr. Over 335,000 German troops had been encircled and the great industrial area no longer could support the Hitler war machine. Paderborn fell to the 2d Battalion, 414th Infantry, and the 3d Armored troops that morning.

For the vital role the 414th Infantry Regiment played in protecting the 3d Armored Division and in neutralizing enemy resistance in the path of the First Army's spearhead of 200 miles in eight days, the Division Commander recommended that the regiment be awarded a unit citation as provided in Section IV, Circular No. 333, War Department, 1943.

The proposed citation states:

The 414TH INFANTRY REGIMENT (minus Cannon Company) is cited for outstanding performance of duties in action against the enemy during the period 25 March 1945 to 1 April 1945, in which the extraordinary heroism, determination, and brilliant team action of its individual members contributed greatly in the closing of the Ruhr pocket during the historic drive of the First United States Army from the Rhine to the Elbe River in Germany. During this eight-day period the 414TH REGIMENT, attached to the 3d Armored Division, slashed through enemy defenses for more than 200 miles, moving from one center of resistance to another atop tanks. The regiment started the drive in a daring night attack resulting in the taking of the remaining high ground east of the Remagen bridgehead, and the securing of a bridgehead over the Weide River. In a series of hazardous and difficult attacks involving river crossings, house-to-house fighting, and night attacks, one enemy stronghold after another fell to the courageous men of the regiment. Despite their great fatigue from nearly continuous fighting and from riding the armor, when given a mission the 414TH INFANTRY REGIMENT performed in a highly aggressive and admirable manner. After hard, bitter fighting the objectives Altenkirchen and Marburg fell, and on 31 March 1945, the regiment was in front of the key city of Paderborn. This was an SS school, heavily defended by SS troops. Although greatly outnumbered the weary but aggressive troops of the 414TH INFANTRY REGIMENT once again attacked and on 1 April 1945 Paderborn fell, contact was made with units of the Ninth United States Army, and thus the pocket was closed. The daring and determined spirit exhibited by the battle-weary and exhausted men of the regiment in maintaining the momentum of the lightning advance resulted in 1,323 of the enemy being killed, 11,781 prisoners of war taken, and the capture or destruction of great quantities of enemy equipment, with a minimum loss of personnel and equipment. The gallantry, devotion and esprit de corps of the officers and men of the 414TH INFANTRY REGIMENT reflect the highest credit upon themselves and the military service of the United States.

The 414th made limited attacks moving through the dense woods northeast of Rimbeck. It encountered fanatical resistance from the Nazi-indoctrinated SS trainees from the SS replacement and school units of Paderborn. These were thoroughly familiar with the terrain, having maneuvered over the same ground many times in school problems.

One of the heaviest brushes with these Nazi die-hards fell to the men of K Company, 414th, in the little town of Wewer, about two and a half miles southwest of Paderborn. According to Staff Sergeant Thomas Schwind:

> Everything went smoothly until about eleven o'clock, when the forward elements contacted about seventy-five enemy soldiers defending a small town. The position was cleaned out in short order with light casualties. The column reorganized and started off towards Wewer, a small unimportant town no one ever heard about and which will be remembered only by those few that went in there that afternoon. It wasn't until later that it was learned that a small group of SS students had been left for a delaying action while a trap could be formed further ahead. As we came upon Wewer it looked small and peaceful, as if the people never knew of war. The quietness should have been a warning, but the column headed in without reconnaissance. They never got very much farther than three or four houses when the trap sprung. Before anyone knew the enemy was there our four leading tanks had been hit and the leading platoon of infantry practically wiped out. Then began some of the worst house-to-house fighting of the campaign. Before nightfall streets were littered with both enemy and our dead, and we had advanced only a few hundred yards. It was give and take, and each house was bloodily paid for before it was occupied.

Sergeant Walter Snethern remembers how he, O'Leary, Davis and Burner were blasted right off the tank they rode into Wewer:

> The tanks we were riding moved fast to get into town. The boys and myself were on the second tank. We were speeding along through town when several bazooka rounds hit our tank, throwing all of us from the speeding vehicle. Two of us were wounded in the legs but it didn't bother us much at the time because the action was such that we didn't have time to think about it. Wewer was just another small town along the road to Berlin, but it will be long remembered by King Company.

The 104th had completed its 193-mile advance from the Rhine River to Paderborn in nine days. By now the familiar cry "Mount your doughs and move out" was standard operating procedure. The Timberwolves had cleared 4,100 square miles, had captured hundreds upon hundreds of enemy weapons and vehicles, and 6,456 prisoners had passed through the Division cages. The area over which the Division had fought its way consisted of rugged, hilly and densely forested upland over which vehicular movement had been considerably restricted. Altitude of the hill-tops had ranged from 300 to 675 meters. Since the defensive positions along the outer edge of the Remagen bridgehead were crushed on 24-25 March, the Germans had not been able to form a defensive position of sufficient strength to stop the crushing attacks by armor and infantry. The Nazis were vainly attempting to rally, as evidenced by their futile efforts to commit sabotage. A document setting forth the basic rules for sabotage had been found at Brenzhausen. Translated, it reads as follows:

BASIC RULES FOR SABOTAGE

1. Sugar in the gas tank. Piston will burn, engine cannot be used.
2. Sand in gasoline. Connections and air vents will clog up, engine will be out of order for some time.
3. Tar in the greasepoints of engine and wheels (on RR cars). Bearings will burn out, cars will be unusable.
4. Erection of steel street obstacles during darkness (at curves). Tires will burst, cars will be out of control.
5. Stretching of wire across road during darkness (see to it that the color blends in the darkness). Cars and especially motorcyclists will have accidents.
6. Putting nails on boards in street curves. Same results as under paragraph 4.
7. Jamming RR switches with stones. Trains are derailed or collide. The enemy will have heavy casualties.
8. Put obstacles on RR tracks. Trains are derailed.
9. Disconnection of wires on RR signals. Trains will pass signals and derail or collide.
10. Connection of high tension wire and telephone wire by throwing third wire over both. All connected telephones will be out of order.
11. Perforation of diaphragm of telephone with a pointed pencil or a needle or other sharp objects. You hear but the other end won't hear anything.
12. Breaking of telephone wires. Interruption of enemy signal operators.
13. Take anything from the enemy that you can—weapons, ammunition, equipment, parts of uniforms, food, gasoline; in short, everything that belongs to him and that serves him. Destroy it in a quiet corner so that he cannot punish you when he finds it. The enemy will have difficulties.

To conclude:

The enemy must use his front-line troops to safeguard his rear area.

The enemy loses important war materiel and cannot use it against our soldiers.

The enemy has to replace the lost materiel in his factories instead of forging new weapons to fight our soldiers.

The enemy has to draw front-line troops from the battle zone in order to repair the damage done to the road system.

The enemy cannot use the roads destroyed by you to send more troops against our soldiers.

EVERYTHING THAT HURTS THE ENEMY WILL BENEFIT OUR SOLDIERS

A lieutenant of the 741st Jäger Regiment, twenty years of age, who had been exposed to the full blast of Naziism from the age of nine, when he joined the Hitler Youth, talked freely when captured. He reveals the attitude of the Hitler Youth and the SS troopers, if not of all Germany:

Germany is going to win the war, if not immediately and glamorously at least in the long run, you may rest assured. The Allies may succeed in occupying all of Germany north of Wuerttemberg, Bavaria and Moravia. The Russians and the Anglo-Americans may join at the Elbe River. We shall then entrench ourselves in impenetrable mountains and forests of Southern Germany and Austria, and hold whatever can be held of Italy. As a matter of fact, the war in Italy can go on for several years. But, whatever stretches of land you may occupy in Germany, you will never conquer or defeat the German nation. As long as there is a German alive he will fight you. In the occupied parts of Germany we shall fight a partisan war of nerves against you. No Allied soldier will ever feel safe on German soil. There will be no traitor, no collaborationist. Although outwardly we may smile and bend under the Allied yoke, we shall resort relentlessly to ambushes and tricks of guerrilla warfare until in the end every inch of sacred German soil is freed from the hated invader. A master race born to govern cannot be held down eternally.

Do not underestimate us Germans. We have learned to hate a world of nations that is denying us living space. Great deeds inspired by this immortal and sacred hatred have been performed in the past out of this hatred. New war ruses will be born and new methods of fighting. Soldierdom and domination are the two avocations of Germany, and we Germans shall not rest until we fulfill Germany's mission. This mission is closely linked with the fate of National Socialism, and if you want to destroy the National Socialism you must exterminate the German people first (and by this I mean every living German). We shall never capitulate!! A Herrenvolk may fail in the completion of its mission and thereafter have a wrecked existence (*verkrachte existenz*), but it does not capitulate.

And then, there are our secret weapons. In his last speech the Fuehrer said: "God Almighty may pardon me the last moments of this war." Even if Germany should be utterly defeated, our submarines will continue to harass Allied shipping, and our secret weapons, striking from concealed sites in the mountains, will spit death and destruction on the hated invader. We may even follow the example of our national hero, Arminius (Hermann), the Germanic prince, who, posing as a friend of the Romans, went through the Roman educational institutions and War Academy to acquire the military knowledge and leadership which, in the end, enabled him to ambush the Roman Legions of Varus in the Teutoburg Forest in 9 A.D. to free his enslaved tribe from the Roman yoke. There are thousands of fanatical German youngsters who are willing to sacrifice everything for the liberation of a defeated Fatherland, and who, posing as

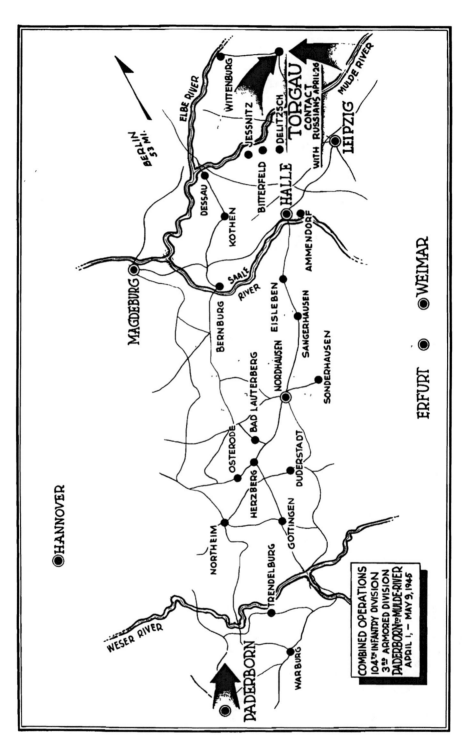

COMBINED OPERATIONS
104TH INFANTRY DIVISION
3RD ARMORED DIVISION
PADERBORN to MULDE-RIVER
APRIL 1, — MAY 9, 1945

TORGAU
CONTACT
WITH RUSSIANS APRIL-26

BERLIN
53 MI.

ELBE RIVER
MULDE RIVER
SAALE RIVER
WESER RIVER

WITTENBURG
JESSNITZ
DELITZSCH
LEIPZIG
BITTERFELD
HALLE
DESSAU
KOTHEN
MAGDEBURG
BERNBURG
AMMENDORF
SANGERHAUSEN
EISLEBEN
SONDERHAUSEN
NORDHAUSEN
BAD LAUTERBERG
OSTERODE
HERZBERG
DUDERSTADT
GOTTINGEN
NORTHEIM
TRENDELBURG
WARBURG
PADERBORN

ERFURT
WEIMAR
HANNOVER

friends of the Allies, will infiltrate into the Allied military government administration. These men will acquire data on possible traitors which will lead to the
punishment of these traitors. They will risk their anonymous lives in sabotaging
every Allied effort. They will act as informants and contact men for the underground.

One man and the spirit he created will always be the guide of our youth:
our Fuehrer. Hitler united us as a nation. Hitler made Germany conscious of
her mission and strength. Hitler may die, but the ideals he created will always
live in the hearts and works of German people. The British say: "Right or
wrong my country." We Germans say: "Right or wrong, our Fuehrer." Stronger
than any clearly defined philosophy, our National Socialism has the power of
myth. It does not appeal to cold reasoning. It appeals to the warm depth of our
feeling and emotions, it overwhelms us by its twilight effects. We do not think.
We feel, we believe, we act. We have faith in our Fatherland. And this faith
will give us the strength not to capitulate, no matter how much of Germany the
enemy may occupy. We shall always fight back, no matter with what weapons,
no matter with what ruses, no matter for how long a period, until the last
invader is killed or driven from Germany.

The VII Corps had successfully completed its mission for the First
Army, but there remained the nasty task of mopping up all resistance
within the zone and checking any hostile attempt to break out of the
encirclement. While the 415th, reinforced, was engaged in the Medebach action, the 413th and the 104th Reconnaissance Troop completed
their assigned missions of clearing all enemy from the Division zone.
The coordinated attack of the Seagulls, now commanded by Colonel
William Summers, had destroyed the SS troops in their path, clearing
and occupying Scherfede, Holtheim and Kleinenberg, all in the northeastern part of the Division zone.

It was during these skirmishes with Hitler's fanatical Elite Corps that
the all-Negro platoon attached to the regiment had their first taste of
combat and handled themselves so commendably. Ann Stringer, United
Press foreign correspondent, recounts the incident in a 3 April release:

WITH 104TH TIMBERWOLF DIVISION SOUTH OF PADERBORN, GERMANY,
April 3—Delayed—UP—The "Dusky Devastators"—an all-Negro platoon—
saw action for the first time today—and licked Adolf Hitler's supermen.

Within a few hours, these eager infantrymen, armed with only rifles and
Sten guns, captured or killed 40 crack Nazi SS troops, cleared two thickly wooded
hills and chalked up a record to make any veteran battle group envious.

The platoon, led by Staff Sgt. Harvey Moseley of Mansfield, O., was sent in
this morning to clear Nazis from two hills inside Hardahausen forest. They
cleared the hills in record time and came back asking for more.

SS MEN IN WOODS

"We'd been told there were SS men in these woods. We'd been told that
many times," said Pfc. Bent T. Brown of Charleston, W. Va., a tall slim Negro

nicknamed "Big Slim." "We didn't know exactly what they were—but we found out mighty quick."

Big Slim, the hero of the day, didn't want to tell about it. But a buddy of his did.

"We were just making an attack across the hill," said Slim's buddy. "Slim and another guy were taking the right flank of our assault. And Big Slim did about one of the bravest things I ever saw. So did the other guy."

"Yessuh," broke in Slim, "that guy was a pretty brave man all right.

BULLETS FLY FAST

"I was walking along beside him when suddenly he shouted at me to drop. I dropped. The Germans had opened up on us and bullets were flying thick and fast.

"Then I saw he was wounded. He fell down flat on his face. I started firing faster than ever then."

Slim's buddy took up the tale.

"I saw Big Slim start toward him. The wounded guy stood up and with his good arm started spraying the Nazis with lead, covering Big Slim.

"It was a good thing he did too, for just about then a German shell hit Slim's rifle and knocked the shell clip completely off. But that didn't stop Slim. He kept right on going."

Here Slim took up the story.

PINNED DOWN BY FOE

"I reached him (the wounded man) and started tugging him to a ditch behind us. I pulled him out as far as I could. That's all I could do. Then both of us were pinned down again by the Nazis."

Others in the platoon finally came to Slim's aid and helped rescue the wounded man, who is in a serious condition with bullet wounds in the arm, shoulder and back.

But that is just one instance of bravery among these Negro troops who, in their first time in action, ran into desperate, trapped, crack Nazi troops.

One of the platoon's prides is big Sgt. Howard Williams of Detroit, Mich., who visited Germany in 1936 as an alternate boxer. He was a Golden Gloves champion in 1938-39.

Williams, who neither drinks nor smokes, always carries four toothbrushes. He explained he brushes his teeth five times a day.

On 31 March the Division front had been extended further to the west and on April 1st the 4th Cavalry Group, under Colonel McDonald, was attached to the Division to assist in mopping up the new area. Colonel McDonald's troops relieved the 104th Reconnaissance Troop at Brilon and during the next four days eliminated all resistance within the Brilon area.

Combat Command A of the 7th Armored Division was attached to the Division late on 2 April. It closed in a reserve position at Medebach prior to midnight. After the 415th had cleared Kustelberg, Combat Command A relieved the 3d Battalion of the 415th in the city and was attached to the 9th Division, which was then advancing north on the left rear of the 415th Infantry.

TO THE MULDE

On 4 April all organized resistance within the Division zone had been reduced and the Division was hurriedly regrouped in preparation for further advance. The 9th Armored and 2d Infantry Divisions were now on the right of the 104th; the 9th Infantry Division on the left rear; the 1st Infantry Division, at the Dill River, was now on the Division's left; and the 3d Armored Division was coiled, with the 414th attached, around Paderborn. With the Lippstadt-Paderborn-Warburg area cleared, the next natural and seemingly logical defense line was the Weser River, forty-five miles to the east. The VII Corps had been directed by First Army to turn east, force a crossing of the Weser River, and drive for the heart of Germany. Again the 104th and the 3d Armored would spearhead the advance of the VII Corps. On 5 April, the 413th relieved elements of the 9th Armored Division and the 2d Infantry Division at Teutonia, Bonneburg and Borlinghausen, ten miles east of its former position. The 415th, after having completed its task on 4-5 April of eliminating the remaining resistance in its zone, moved into position on the right of the 413th, closing in the early afternoon of the 6th in and northeast of Warburg. Throughout the day patrols of the 413th and 415th Infantry Regiments probed enemy positions to the east, preparatory for the attack on 7 April.

The Division Commander had directed the attack to be resumed on 7 April with the 104th Reconnaissance Troop (Task Force Laundon), reinforced with tanks and tank destroyers preceding the advance of the two regiments. During the day the Division made plans to exploit its success by rapid movement to force crossings over the Weser River. To insure rapidity TFL was to be followed by a motorized reinforced battalion in each regimental zone. To the left of the Corps zone were elements of the Ninth Army and on the right was First Army's 2d Infantry Division operating under V Corps. At 0630 on the 7th, Task Force Laundon crossed the line of departure headed for the Weser. The rapidly disintegrating enemy forces yielded to the Division's advances, leaving numerous undefended road blocks in their retreat. The task force encountered abatis road blocks (large felled trees) defended by small arms fire from scattered groups of enemy. While the resistance slowed the advance at times, the task force, closely followed by the advancing 413th and 415th, crushed the defenders and reached the bridge over the Weser at Gleselwerde at 1500. The 3d Battalion

THE STARS AND STRIPES

BRIDGE BLOWN BUT INFANTRY CLEARS WESER

By G. K. HODENFIELD

(*Stars and Stripes* Staff Writer)

WITH 104TH DIV. EAST OF WESER RIVER, Apr. 8 (Delayed)—The Jerries blew up the bridge across the Weser River yesterday almost right in the face of Lt. Col. Bill Summers, of Tulsa, Okla., but today doughs of his 413th Regt. of the 104th "Timberwolf" Div. are across the 80-yard-wide obstacle and headed east.

The 413th entered this town yesterday at 1500 hours and five minutes later the bridge went into the river, leaving one German tank and about 50 infantrymen trapped on the west side.

By 1630 hours the fight inside the town was over, with the Jerries rounded up and the tank abandoned.

L Company's 3d Bn. Commander, Maj. George O'Connor, of Brooklyn, hit the river bank and found that although he couldn't advance he could still kill Germans. The Germans on the other side were dashing around like crazy, apparently headed for a house.

Capt. Joe Peevey, of Texas, called for direct fire on the house and Lt. Hugo Tofnelli, of San Francisco, commanding the antitank platoon of the 3d Bn., let go with several rounds.

When the house was hit the Jerries left in a hurry. L Co. sharpshooters picked them off like ducks on a pond.

Not a man of the 413th was hurt.

All during the night huge trucks rolled into town, carrying assault boats, and at 0425 hours this morning, L Co. started across the river. By 0500 all of L Co. and most of I Co. were across and advancing against practically no resistance.

The 329th Engr. Combat Bn. went to work on a foot bridge and before it was light enough for any Jerries to fire on the project, Lt. Roberts Fields, of Jackson, Miss., and his men had completed the span, and K Co. was ready to move across. Eastbound traffic was halted for a few minutes to allow the first passengers across. Westbound were three prisoners—terrified SS men.

Meanwhile, the 2d Bn., commanded by Lt. Col. Samuel Koster, of West Liberty, Iowa, crossed the Weser downstream. From a little village could be heard sounds of battle as snipers tried to defend the town against steadily advancing Americans.

Those snipers who bothered to look back could see the wrecked bridge, the bridge that was supposed to keep the Americans west of the Weser.

of the 413th dashed madly for the bridge, only to see it demolished in their faces, a few seconds before they reached it.

The 413th and the 415th closed on the west banks of the Weser River by nightfall after having eliminated all resistance within their respective zones. The 414th was again mounted on the 3d Armored Division tanks and were operating to the left of the Division zone, also closing on the Weser that night. Enemy artillery became active and heavy intermittent concentrations fell throughout the remainder of the day.

It was essential that the Weser River be crossed quickly before the enemy could get set in his defensive position. The high ridge line two miles to the east of the Weser dominated the crossing sites, and if it were properly organized and manned, the enemy could inflict great casualties upon our advancing troops. At his command post in Trendelberg, General Allen directed the troops to force crossings prior to daylight on 8 April with the 413th on the left and 415th on the right. At Munden, Germany, the Rivers Falda and Werra joined to form the River Weser, which flows, after a course of 750 kilometers, into the North Sea above Bremen. The average depth of the river was fifteen feet and the width varied from 150 to 280 feet. It was a formidable obstacle running through a narrow valley which was closed to the east and the west by high wooded hills. Near the bridge site the ground to the east sloped gently toward the ridge line two miles away. The enemy could rain devastating fire on all attempted crossings.

At 0400 the next morning the 3d Battalion, 413th Infantry, crossed the Weser in assault boats and was quickly followed by the 2d Battalion. Initially opposition was light. However, the 2d Battalion met heavy resistance in its drive to the northeast to clear the enemy from the bridgehead. Prior to midnight the 413th had accomplished its mission, clearing all Germans six miles east of the river. Simultaneously the 415th had forced crossings, with one battalion moving over the 2d Division bridge to the south and the other battalions crossing in the Division zone. It likewise had cleared its zone prior to midnight. Resistance in some localities had been intense, but the Timberwolves had attained their objective—the Corps bridgehead—capturing over 200 prisoners and thirteen more German towns and communities. East of the Weser the routes of advance of the 3d Armored Division, which had been paralleling the 104th zone to the north, entered our zone, and ran through it to the east. The VII Corps plan had directed the 3d Armored Division to cross over the bridges constructed in the 104th zone and to pass through the Division prior to 1400 on the 9th. The 1st Division, which had now been released from the Paderborn area,

was moved up on our left, and again the three divisions were to head east together. The Timberwolves' mission was to closely follow the armor, advancing rapidly and eliminating all resistance within its zone. The Division plan provided that the 413th with Company A, 87th Chemical Battalion, Company A, 750th Tank Battalion, 1st Platoon, 329th Engineer Battalion, and elements of the 817th Tank Destroyers in support, advance in the north portion of the zone. Together with carrying out the Division mission, the regiment was directed to maintain contact with the 1st Division and protect the 104th's left flank. In the south portion of the Division zone, the 415th, with Company B, 87th Chemical Battalion, Company C, 750th Tank Battalion, Cannon Company, 414th Infantry, 1st Platoon of Company C, 329th Engineers, and elements of the 817th Tank Destroyer Battalion in support, was to advance, maintaining contact with the 2d Division. Task Force Laundon, initially in reserve, was prepared to secure the Division left rear.

Shortly after noon on the 8th, the VII Corps engineers had completed construction of the bridges within the Division zone. The Weser bridgehead was an excellent springboard for another armored drive, and late that night the Spearhead Division's tanks and half-tracks rolled through our lines, passing over the Beverungen bridge bumper to bumper. The German civilians at first stared haughtily, then as the columns filed by in a never-ending stream, their outlook changed to panic-stricken confusion. Miles of American armor mounted by the tough fighting infantrymen of the 414th were too much for the usually arrogant Nazis. Only the slave laborers stayed by the side of the road to gaze at the unending torrent. By midafternoon on the 9th, the tail of the 3d Armored column had cleared the front lines. Again in close teamwork with the tankers, the Timberwolves resumed the advance to the east. Prior to midnight the lead elements of the Division buttoned up twenty miles east of the Weser, with the Division command post established in Adelebsen. Until 6 April the German Eleventh Army Headquarters had been located in the Adelebsen castle, now occupied by the Timberwolf staff.

NORDHAUSEN . . . It was anticipated that the 3d Armored and mounted 414th would reach Nordhausen on 10 April. Nordhausen was located on the River Zorge at the southern foothills of the Harz Mountains, forty-seven miles to the east. In our path stood many towns, including Duderstadt of over 6,500 inhabitants, and the southern edges of the Harz Mountains. (The Harz Mountains are the northern-most mountains in Germany and cover an area of 2,000 square kilometers, extending over ninety kilometers by thirty kilometers. The range was completely isolated from any other mountain chain and rose abruptly from the northern German plain. The highest peak in the group is called Broekn, with an elevation of 1,141 meters. Along the southern edge of the mountains the many streams had formed deep gorges and ravines.)

The regimental missions remained unchanged, but since the 1st Division was encountering stiff resistance on our left, Task Force Laundon was directed to move to the left flank and maintain contact between the 413th and the 1st Division. Our front lines were just short of the north-south line through Goettingen, the large university city situated on the River Leine. Early on 10 April the 413th and 415th continued their relentless drive eastward. The infantry piled onto tanks and into captured Wehrmacht vehicles and took off down the highways mopping up the dispirited Jerries bypassed by the armor. There were not enough vehicles to motorize all infantrymen, so companies and battalions alternately walked and rode in the wake of the armor. Even barnyard carts were requisitioned to assist in the rapid movement. Closely following the 3d Armored Division spearheads, the Timberwolves knifed more than forty miles eastward into the Reich during the day. Patrols of the 2d Battalion, 414th, with the 3d Armored had reached Nordhausen, reporting enemy tanks and troops located there. Lead elements of the 415th were seventeen miles short of Nordhausen, having cleared its zone to that position. The 413th was closing on the southwest approaches into the Harz Mountains. Duderstadt had been cleared early in the afternoon by the 415th and the Division command post moved into the city just prior to dark. This town presented a problem to the Military Government personnel because in addition to its normal population, there were 3,200 displaced people, 8,000 refugees, and approximately 1,000 Allied prisoners. Civilians were quickly screened and a civilian police force was appointed to assist in restoring order. Several small riots broke out in the city, but were soon quelled.

Reports from civilians and prisoners indicated that the disorganized enemy had withdrawn to positions in the Harz Mountains, the only remaining natural defense position in the area. Elements of the Ninth Army were sweeping around the northern flank of the mountains and the 3d Armored and the 415th were sweeping around its left. The 1st Division had reached the western edge of the mountains and was meeting stiff resistance. To make certain that the enemy within the Harz Mountains would not break out into the Division zone, General Allen directed the 413th to establish and maintain strong road blocks at the southern exits. To assist in this strategic mission the 817th Tank Destroyer Battalion, less Company C, was attached to the regiment in addition to its former reinforcements.

As the eastward drive of the 3d Armored paused briefly on Corps order on 11 April, the tempo of the advance of the Timberwolves temporarily slowed. Maintaining close liaison with elements of the 3d Armored and the 1st Division, the Seagulls established their road blocks along the approaches to the Harz Mountains while the 415th completed clearing its zone up to and including Nordhausen. Task Force Laundon remained active in its blocking role, between the 1st Division and the 413th Infantry.

In Nordhausen the Division found a large German concentration camp for political prisoners, discovering 5,000 corpses among the 6,000 inmates in various stages of decay. The corpses were scattered throughout the buildings and grounds of the large camp and all of them appeared to have been starved to such an extent that they were mere skeletons wrapped in skin. Most of the bodies apparently lay untouched since death had overtaken them, but some were stacked like cordwood under stairways. In almost all bunkers and buildings the living were found lying among the dead. In one corner was a pile of arms and legs. All medical personnel that could be spared in the Division were rushed to the scene to give medical aid. The burgomeister of Nordhausen having fled, his assistant was contacted by the Military Government and given explicit instructions regarding laws and ordnances and the responsibility placed on him. Neither he nor any other civilian would admit knowledge of the concentration camp. Hundreds of the male citizens of the town were ordered to the camp, where under guard, they worked several days carrying litter cases and collecting corpses by hand. They dug mass graves on a prominent hill near the camp and carried the corpses through the town to the graves.

Sergeant Ragene Farris of the 329th Medical Battalion relates the impact of the gruesome sights at Nordhausen upon the men of the 104th:

For days and weeks, even months afterwards, the word Nordhausen brought us a mixed response of emotions. We were battle-tired and combat-wise medics, and we thought there was nothing left in the books we didn't know. Blood and bandages and all kinds of hell was daily routine. Plasma bottles—cases of them, surgery, shock and death, all these on a twenty-four hour basis, and I for one, in order to keep working efficiently and smoothly, had grown callous. Yet in a short period of two days I and many others of the Division saw and lived a story we shall never forget.

The strongly Nazified town of Nordhausen fell before air-armor and night attack on 11 April. Our S-2, Captain Johnson, brought the news that we were needed to evacuate patients from a concentration camp in one of the large factory

Emaciated corpses laid out in Nordhausen Concentration Camp

areas of the city. Lying among the multitudes of dead were reported to be a few living "beings," and with quick medical attention some might be saved. Colonel Taggart called into action, early 12 April, the litter bearers and medical technicians as well as any other men available from duties with our own wounded. In a caravan of trucks we rushed into a job which proved fantastic and unbelievable to an American; a job distasteful and sobering; one created by the fanatical inhuman Nazi machine. We found out the full meaning of the words "Concentration Camp."

Coming into the area, I noticed first the similarity of the buildings to a huge college campus. The large two-story structures had been Luftwaffe and SS motor pools and shops until six weeks prior to the fall of Nordhausen, when the buildings were used as pens for various nationalist political prisoners who had been in forced-labor groups working in the V-1 and V-2 underground factories nearby.

We dismounted, litters in hand, and started for the nearest building with a sense of morbid anxiety. It was a sharp sting of reality which met us at the first doorway. Bombs had ground flesh and bones into the cement floor. Rows upon rows of skin-covered skeletons met our eyes. Men lay as they had starved, discolored, and lying in indescribable human filth. Their striped coats and prison numbers hung to their frames as a last token or symbol of those who enslaved and killed them. In this large motor shop there were no living beings; only the distorted dead. We went to the stairs and under the casing were neatly piled about seventy-five bodies, a sight I could never erase from memories. Dying on the second floor were, upon later count, about twenty-five men or half-men.

Some of these, lying in double-decked wooden bedsteads, were grotesquely still, yet hanging tenaciously to life's breath. They were still alive.

We saw, at a quick survey, this was to be as big a medical job as we had been called upon to do. It was a job of action. Speed would save lives, so we fell into a day of evacuation, hospitalization, and feeding, unparalleled to any day of combat. It became evident almost immediately that our few medics could not evacuate hundreds of patients, set up improvised hospital wards, and feed many mouths without help. So, under the leadership of Colonel Jones and Chaplain Steinbeck, who spoke German, we rounded up German civilians on the streets of this Nazi city as we saw them. The order was, "You will work." In this manner, about one hundred German litter bearers were gathered up and rushed to the scene.

My personal job turned out to be gruesomely interesting because I spoke French. I was accosted by a less emaciated prisoner who asked if anyone spoke French. When I answered, he brightened and related that a group of Frenchmen had established a small colony in one of the large cellars of another building, and would I please bring aid to them. This was my signal to get into gear, and off across bomb-cratered grounds we picked our way to this particular building. There were many bodies strewn about. One girl in particular I noticed; I would say she was about seventeen years old. She lay there where she had fallen, gangrened and naked. In my own thoughts I choked up—couldn't quite understand how and why war could do these things. But my job crowded out any serious impressions at the moment. Only later I thought of what I had seen.

Now we approached the cellar stairs leading to the French group. I heard "monsieur" very softly, and at my feet, lying as if dead, was a cadaverous man; he raised up and said, in beautiful Parisian French, that if he were stronger he would honor me by the traditional kiss on either cheek. I learned that he was a captain from France's famous Saint Cyr Military Academy and had received particularly sadistic attention from the SS Troopers. He looked to be seventy-five but was only forty-five. His last step had taken him to the edge of the stairs. He had gone as far as possible to escape the fury of war when the Americans fought into Nordhausen. He lay dust-covered, where he had nearly been crushed by falling walls—yet he displayed remarkable discipline and composure. With care, he was lifted upon a litter and taken to our waiting ambulances. I often wonder if he made it back to life, and if he had ever been able to tell his story.

We went downstairs into a filth indescribable, accompanied by a horrible dead-rot stench. There in beds of crude wood I saw men too weak to move dead comrades from their side. One hunched-down French boy was huddled up against a dead comrade, as if to keep warm, having no concept that the friend had been dead two or three days and was unable to move his own limbs. There were others, in dark cellar rooms, lying in disease and filth, being eaten away by diarrhea and malnutrition. It was like stepping into the Dark Ages to walk into one of these cellar-cells and seek out the living; like walking into a world apart and returning to bring these shadow-men into the environment of a clean American ambulance. I found by questioning some of the stronger men that their ration was one small loaf of black bread per week for seven men. As I later walked over the area, I saw a huge cauldron beside a pile of potatoes. It was evident that a guard had made "soup" for the prisoners by pitch-forking these potatoes into this black pot. To eat this would have been slow poison.

Some of our boys who spoke German, Polish, Czech and Russian were also kept busy. To the German litter bearer squads we all learned quickly to say "Schnell"—and "Tempo you d——— sb's"—in a tone which these Germans did not misunderstand. In one bomb crater lay about twenty bodies. We pulled three or four feebly struggling living ones from the bottom of the pile; they had been struggling for five or six days to get out but the weight of the other bodies piled on them had been too much for their starved, emaciated frames. We saw those on a bank who had been cut down by machine guns in trying to escape the fury of the guards. One incident thrilled me particularly, as we were beginning to get large numbers of patients out into the waiting ambulances. I saw one man feebly stagger to attention and salute us as tears slowly trickled down his cheeks. Too weak to walk, this man was genuinely moved to pay tribute to those who were helping him—showing him the first kind act in years. A few men were able to walk on their swollen, bulging feet; they had no shoes and they were unbelievably dirty. There were lash marks on many of their scantily covered backs—definite proof of beatings and floggings by their inhuman guards. One Parisian business man who had worked in Renault's auto works in Paris prior to the war told me he had been kicked and beaten repeatedly. He was comparatively healthy, as he had been in the camp only three months. He remarked in perfect English that it was "funny" to him to see such healthy, young, clean Americans. He told me that many of the 3,000 dead in the camp had been worked, beaten and forced at top speed until they could work no longer, after which they were starved off or killed outright.

As we worked hour on hour in this fantastic business, we kept a "box score." We ended up that evening, having evacuated about 300 litter patients to our improvised hospitals, and about 400 "walking" patients. Sergeant Leutz, mess sergeant of clearing company, was in charge of feeding these men. I have never before seen the look in the eyes of these men as they came up for coffee, soup, and various foods prescribed by our doctors.

Two miles northwest of Nordhausen a huge underground V-bomb factory was uncovered. Two big tunnels led into the factory, with railroad trains and trucks being able to run directly into the mountain. It was two miles in length, approximately fifty feet in width and height, and was connected laterally by forty-eight smaller tunnels. The work was done in the smaller tunnels, while the two big tunnels served for traffic exclusively. More than 25,000 slave laborers had toiled here for months in production of V-1 and V-2 bombs. The SS were in charge of the factory and the camp, with German criminals as strawbosses. On the slightest suspicion of sabotage the workers were shot. No workers had ever been allowed to leave the camp, and when they became too weak to work, they were abandoned to die and their bodies burned at the crematorium within the grounds. Reports indicated that approximately one hundred bodies were cremated per day, and there were about thirty corpses piled on the ground awaiting such treatment. The bodies showed many signs of beatings, starvation and torture. The huge underground factory had not been damaged, and electric, ventilating and telephone systems were still in operation. Millions of dollars worth of the finest equipment and machinery, thousands of V-bombs and parts of bombs were found within the factory, many loaded on freight cars ready for shipment.

HARZ MOUNTAINS

The enemy had concentrated strong defensive forces in the advantageous terrain of the Harz Mountains to the north of the Division zone, and our progress was slowed. Concurrent rapid advance in the Division zone (fifty-five miles in two days) gave the Division an extended left flank. The 414th, which had been attached to the 3d Armored since 22 March, was to revert to the 104th midnight 11 April. The 2d Battalion of the 414th remained attached to the armored division. The reversion was timely because of the extended front, and General Allen immediately directed Colonel Kelleher's regiment (less the 2d Battalion) to take up positions facing the Harz Mountains north of Nordhausen. It was directed to block all approaches into the mountains north of Nordhausen on 12 April and to maintain the same until relieved by the 9th Infantry Division, which had been placed under command of the VII Corps. With the 413th, the 104th Reconnaissance Troop and the 414th blocking all avenues of escape from the Harz Mountains area over a sixty-mile front, the 415th would continue its progress east behind the 3d Armored.

Colonel Cochran's regiment resumed the advance on 12 April, eliminating all resistance within the Division zone for a distance of twenty-three miles beyond Nordhausen. Colonel Summers' men met continued resistance in their zone throughout the day. Before noon the 3d Battalion had seized Bad Lauterberg, having fought against heavy artillery, mortar, and small arms fire. The 1st Battalion held Bad Sachsa and the 2d Battalion occupied Walkenrich and Ellerich. The 385th, 387th, 802d, 957th and 981st Field Artillery Battalions supported the coordinated attacks of the 413th. The enemy had stubbornly held on to their positions, and only relinquished them after resisting fiercely with artillery, mortar, small arms and tanks. The 414th improved their positions during this period.

April 13th brought a severe shock to the men of the 104th. At about noon that day, news came that told of our Commander-in-Chief's passing. Momentarily, political differences were forgotten, and all felt a rather personal loss.

In the vicinity of Nordhausen the first German general officer to be captured by the Timberwolves was seized—*Generalleutnant Freiherr von Bonneburg*, ex-Military Governor of Paris. Also Dr. Albin Sawatsky was apprehended by Captain Julian's 104th CIC detachment on 13 April at the underground factory. The Doctor was reported to be the inventor of both the V-1 and V-2 rocket bombs and was one of the foremost scientists of Nazi Germany, having been assigned to this area early in 1944 to supervise the completion of the underground factory as well as both V-weapons. In April of 1944 a final test of the weapon was made and a conference was held with Himmler, Goering, Goebbels, Army and Party officials at the plant site. As a result mass production was approved. Plant superviser Sawatsky also coordinated the construction of Junkers airplane engines which were produced in another section of the plant. Among his personal papers were found commendations and recommendations from the Mauser and Junkers concerns. The Doctor portrayed the typical Nazi character—he was slightly stooped, round-shouldered, apologetic, and wore thick-lensed glasses.

It is interesting to note the story told by one of the prisoners captured by the Division on 13 April. He stated that on 7 May 1943 he had been captured by the Americans during the African campaign where he had served as a member of the 92d German Medical Battalion. After his capture he was sent to Fort Custer, Michigan. In the fall of 1944 he together with about 800 Germans was sent to Germany on a prisoner of war exchange. He stated that ninety-nine percent of the 800 would have preferred remaining in the United States. Transfer took place in Goeteborg, Sweden in September 1944. As soon as they arrived in Germany they were interrogated by military authorities. After all of them stated that they were treated by the Americans very well they were cautioned not to talk about it to their comrades to keep them from deserting. They were also requested to give the names of fellow prisoners of war who had proven to be anti-nazi while in American camps.

The 104th Reconnaissance Troop, in the vicinity of Nordhausen, added a few liberated Russian PW's to their rolls. With the aid of clubs and iron pipe, the latter had brought in several SS troopers who had been harassing our men as they advanced. Staff Sergeant Jack O. Ellis recalls how "they wanted to join us and we welcomed them for their value as interpreters and first rate fighters. We soon found they could kill their quota of Krauts with one hand and drink their weight in vodka with the other. With the Russian and Polish feminine DP's— well, Valentino would gape with envy. Michael Motuski spent his spare time hunting on his own and usually chalked up a couple of scores for our side. When it came to finding food and liquid refreshments he was Class 1. Formerly a lieutenant at sixteen in the Russian Army, he had spent four years in German concentration camps."

Object: Confuse the enemy. A German Mark III chassis mounting an American gun and superstructure

The fighting along the southern border of the Harz Mountains continued 13, 14 and 15 April for Colonel Summers' Seagulls. The enemy was constantly dominated and his attempted infiltrations were quickly mopped up. On 13 April, during the fighting on the outskirts of Bad Lauterberg, the chief of police and a medical officer who presented themselves as emissaries of the people in the town and the military garrison, contacted the 3d Battalion, 413th Infantry. They suggested that the town might surrender and offered to act as intermediaries. The usual unconditional terms were offered and the emissaries were sent back to the town where they presented their case to the German commander. They soon returned, however, requesting that an American officer accompany them to the German commander. Lieutenant Carl L. Johnson, S-3 of the 3d Battalion, volunteered for the mission along with Technical Sergeant Walter O. George as interpreter and Pfc. David L. Acker and Pfc. Richard Klein as flag bearers.

These four together with the two Germans went into the town again

335

and were taken to a company CP. Here the Americans were blindfolded and taken to the battalion command post. The enemy battalion commander indicated his own personal desire to surrender and this feeling was reflected by the men; however, he stated he was under strict orders to hold the town and continue fighting. He called his regimental commander by telephone who likewise indicated his willingness to surrender, but because of his present orders he was unable to do so. The regimental commander then placed a call to his division headquarters and the division commander signified his willingness to capitulate, but withheld his decision until he could contact German Army Headquarters. Two hours later after much passing the buck, the Army commander's decision of refusal to surrender was received and the emissaries returned to their battalion. Lieutenant Johnson reported that all the soldiers and civilians had hoped that a surrender could be effected, and when they heard the Army commander's decision, they seemed crushed. The Germans at the time knew that their situation was hopeless since troops of the Ninth and First Armies had them surrounded.

After completing its mission of holding the German forces within the Harz mountains, and when relieved by elements of the 1st Division and the 4th Cavalry Group, the 413th moved to the east on the afternoon of 15 April, and rejoined the Division which was then along the Saale River. Over 65,000 German troops were later gathered from the Harz Mountain area.

SAALE RIVER OFFENSIVE

On 12 April the VII Corps directed the Division to prepare plans for continuing its drive to the east assigning it the mission of forcing crossings of the Saale River and the seizure of Halle on the east banks of the Saale. Fifty-three miles east of Nordhausen the "golden valley" was crossed by the Saale River. The river flowed north from Fichtelgebirge Mountains joining the Elbe River south of Magdeburg. (The entire length of the Saale was 442 kilometers of which 180 kilometers are navigable from Halle to the Elbe River. The average depth was ten feet, its width 200 to 300 feet.) Over fifty towns and communities had to be cleared before the Saale could be reached. In the path of the Division were the large towns of Sangerhausen with 11,000 inhabitants and just to the north was Eisleben, 23,000 population, the birthplace of Martin Luther. It was realized that aside from the Saale River as a stumbling block in the eastward advance, historic Halle would be a formidable obstacle.

Halle, with a population of over 210,000, was the tenth largest city in Germany and the largest Nazi city spared from allied bombing. Near the close of World War I it was the seat of Germany's internal revolution, a rallying point of communism in Germany; and in 1933 when Hitler came to power, it became a center of Nazi organization. The important salt resources and the many soft-coal strip mines contributed to Halle's wealth. The 16th Century City Hall, many Gothic churches, a university, and several hospitals and orphanage foundations showed the importance of the town. It was the birthplace of the famous composer, Handel.

The 415th was east of Nordhausen, the 414th was blocking the exits of the Harz Mountains north of that city, while the 413th was engaged in holding the Nazis in the Harz Mountains northwest of Nordhausen. The enemy in the Harz Mountains maintained desperate resistance and therefore it was impossible for the Division commander to release the 413th for the proposed assault of the Saale River. Consequently for the second time in the past twenty days, the Timberwolf forces would conduct two widely separated operations. To this end, certain regroupings on the north flank were decided upon, giving responsibility for the sector to the 413th and releasing TFL and the 414th for the attack on Halle. To lead a rapid and powerful Timberwolf attack on Halle, General Allen constituted a Division armored spearhead under command of Colonel Kelleher. The Division directed Task Force Kelleher to be organized and prepared for assembly prior to 0800 on 14 April and that the Task Force consist of the 414th Infantry (less the 2d Battalion which was still operating with the 3d Armored Division); the 750th Tank Battalion (less one company); the 817th Tank Destroyer Battalion (less two companies); Company B, 329th Engineer Battalion; the 386th and 802d Field Artillery Battalions; Battery B, 555th AAA Battalion; the 104th Reconnaissance Troop and Company B of the 87th Chemical Battalion. Eighteen trucks were attached to the Task Force leaving nine with each of the other two regiments. The Division would advance with TF Kelleher spearheading, closely followed by the 415th, with the provision that if the 413th were released, then it would advance behind the task force on the left with the 415th on the right.

The situation in the Harz Mountain so developed that it was necessary for the Division to leave the 413th in its blocking role and to proceed with its attack on the 14th of April without that regiment. On the 13th the Task Force perfected its plan for the assault. It would advance over two routes with Task Force Rouge (the 3d Battalion, 414th Infantry, reinforced), on the north route and Task Force Clark (the 1st Battalion, 414th Infantry, reinforced), on the south.

From a line of departure then held by the 415th twenty-five miles to the east of Nordhausen, the Task Force would commence its drive at 1200, 14 April. The 415th would closely follow and eliminate all bypassed resistance along the twenty-five-mile wide Division zone. The 3d Armored had passed through part of the Division zone 13 April having turned north out of our zone just west of Sangerhausen. It was to continue its atack to the east parallel with the 104th.

HALLE . . . During the night of 13 April and the early morning of 14 April the Task Force assembled and made final preparations for the attack. At 1200, spearheaded by the 104th Reconnaissance Troop, tanks of the 750th and tank destroyers of the 817th Tank Destroyer Battalion mounted by infantry, Task Force Rouge on the left and Task Force Clark on the right, crossed the line of departure and drove rapidly to the east. Limited resistance was encountered initially but when the force was in sight of Halle it encountered heavy flak and 88mm fire. At 1800 Task Force Rouge had reached the Saale on the north and patrols of Task Force Clark on the south had the river under observation. The bridges over the mighty Saale had been destroyed by German defenders. The "Old Faithful" regiment shortly thereafter closed behind the Task Force having cleared the Division zone and captured over 215 prisoners. The boldness and aggressiveness of the Task Force had resulted in the seizure of thirty-two additional towns and over 500 prisoners in an advance of twenty-eight miles.

When it was soon discovered the Germans had strong defensive positions within Halle facing the west and all bridges were destroyed over the Saale, it was determined by the Division commander to envelop Halle from the north. The 3d Armored Division had completed crossings of the Saale earlier in the day and a bridge was available for use within its zone. The commanders of the 414th and the 415th met with the Division commander at the Division command post in Teuschenthal. Colonel Kelleher was directed to move his force to the north under cover of darkness, cross the Saale over the 3d Armored bridge and from an assembly area on the east side of the river, attack the city from the northwest at 0800 on 15 April. Colonel Cochran's regiment would relieve the 414th in its present position and would clear the Division zone up to the west banks of the river and with a minimum force secure the west bank. In addition, it would support by fire the attack of Task Force Kelleher.

During the night 14-15 April, Colonel Kelleher's Task Force skillfully disengaged themselves west of Halle and moved by motor north to the 3d Armored's ponton bridge at Fredeburg. After a hazardous and most difficult night march over unreconnoitered terrain, the Task Force, from its assembly position north of Halle, jumped off in two columns at 0800. Against small arms and bazooka resistance by the fanatical defenders, the Task Force advanced rapidly toward the city. Within the city the resistance stiffened; the enemy employed road blocks, flak guns and panzerfausts. One of the greatest obstacles encountered was the frequent accurate sniper action which necessitated thorough searching of each room and building. By darkness of the first night the Mountaineers had seized one-eighth of the city and had captured over 800 prisoners. The citizens of Halle, having observed the destruction wrought other cities which had chosen to resist, and knowing too well the hopeless situation of the Werhmacht, pleaded in vain with military officials for an open city declaration. Knowledge of this situation had enabled Lieutenant Colonel Plaisted, the Division G-2, to initiate an ultimatum leaflet which prophesied the consequences of the attack. Over 100,000 of the leaflets were dropped by air the morning of 15 April. The document stated:

MEN AND WOMEN OF HALLE!

Complete destruction threatens your city. Either Halle will be surrendered unconditionally or it will be destroyed.

At the present stage of the war, surrender is the only choice. We Americans do not wage war against innocent civilians. Already, millions of your fellow countrymen live peacefully in territory occupied by us and help rebuild Germany. If, however, the military commander and the party leaders do not want to prevent bloodshed, we have no other alternative but to completely destroy Halle.

MEN AND WOMEN OF HALLE!

Your houses are still standing. Your homes still offer you refuge. Until now, your city has been spared the fate of so many other German cities. You can still save yourself and your city, by acting immediately. Go to the responsible authorities to prevent senseless bloodshed and complete destruction. This is the hour to act. The time is short. In a few hours it will be too late. There is only one choice—

SURRENDER OR DESTRUCTION

Major General Fritz De Witt, the military commander of the Halle area, had decided to defend at all cost, which was evident when he directed all Saale River bridges to be blown. The more than 4,000 defenders were steadfast in their vain efforts to stop the advance of the Mountaineers.

With the 413th still blocking the southern exits of the Harz Mountains the Division was stretched out over a front of one hundred miles. Through ingenuity and use of field expedients by the 104th

Signal Company, communication by radio and telephone was constantly maintained between the Division headquarters and the 413th, eighty miles to the west, and with Task Force Kelleher, twenty miles to the east. The Timberwolf signal men employed German wire and four intermediate switchboards in order to maintain the vital communications. In the afternoon of 15 April the 413th was released from its mission and late that day rejoined the Division.

The battle for Halle raged from 0800, 15 April to 1055, 19 April, during which time General De Witt's troops resisted, house to house from the northern to the southern extremities. Artillery fire and air attack were withheld during most of the time because hospitals containing American wounded were known to be in the city. Colonel Clark's 1st Battalion on 16 April established road blocks to the east and south of the city thus preventing any of the trapped Nazis from withdrawing.

Task Force Rouge meanwhile had a bitter five-day struggle through the main streets of the city. Staff Sergeant John P. McLaughlin of Company I, the main prong of TF Rouge's assault, tells how it began as

a slow process of house-to-house fighting, blasting the holed-up Jerries out with hand grenades and cold steel, which the German supermen did not particularly relish. The position of the Task Force was K Company on the right, L Company on the left and I Company making the main effort in the center, supported by heavy machine guns and 81mm mortars of M Company. The second day was a very slow process as we battled for every inch of ground. At 1800 the order for cease firing was given for the purpose of declaring Halle an open city. This was never fulfilled. At 0600 the third day we attacked and met the heaviest resistance of all. After hand to hand fighting and rapid maneuver we fought our way through the German barriers. By darkness we had about two fifths of our mission accomplished. At this point the Germans pulled back to the end of town, and set up a last ditch defense. The fourth day we walked through the heart of town with very little resistance. By 1900 we were again in contact with the enemy. After due reconnaissance it was decided to set up our defense for the night. That night Jerry tried numerous counterattacks but to no avail. The fifth morning we pushed off again to sink our teeth into the remaining portion of Halle. We took block after block by digging our way through rubble-filled cellars and blasting the enemy out with grenades and bayonets. We kept up a relentless attack, hitting now with everything we had, and the German defenders slowly but surely gave ground. When darkness came we were just about at the edge of town. The sixth and final day we jumped off at 0600 and by noon the town was ours, having completely pushed Jerry out of his proud city of Halle.

During the early afternoon of 16 April Count Felix von Luckner, known for his sea-raiding exploits of World War I, a longtime resident of Halle and self-styled Nazi-hater, came through our lines after our troops had captured the northern third of the city to discuss surrender plans and to arrange neutral areas over which civilians and allied prisoners would be contained for safety. The unconditional surrender terms outlined by General Allen and Colonel Kelleher were not accepted by General De Witt because as he stated: "I am afraid of what they might do to my family." However it was agreed that all armed personnel would withdraw to the southern third of the city and resume fighting. The house-to-house fighting was thereby reduced one third. At 1055 on 19 April the 414th had crushed the last bit of resistance in the German metropolis of Halle. SS troopers and die-hard youths of the Hitler Jugend made the German resistance bitter but the aggressive maneuver of our seasoned soldiers, superbly led, was too much for the best the Nazis could offer. The city yielded 2,640 prisoners including General Fritz De Witt, who prior to capture retired to one of the city hospitals to rest his nerves and nurse his stomach ulcers. As soon as the Mountaineers had completed clearing the large city, they turned eastward to link up with the 413th and 415th which had crossed the Saale, and were headed in the direction of the Mulde River.

THE MULDE ADVANCE

The average distance from the Saale to the Mulde was approximately thirty miles, a distance seemingly insignificant when compared with the sweep of over three hundred and fifty miles from the Remagen bridgehead in less than one month. It was realized, however, that aside from the Saale River and Halle, there were many communities including Delitzsch and Bitterfeld which loomed as formidable obstacles. Midway between the two rivers stood Delitzsch, a city of 17,000 population, with several small industries, sugar refineries, flour mills and soap factories. Bitterfeld was located in the province of Saxony on the west banks of the Mulde in the northern part of the Division zone. The 22,000 population city was noted primarily for its industries; chemical works of I. G. Farben, soft-coal strip mines and huge power station. The GI's later discovered that rationed camera film was also plentiful in this city. Duben with its 4,000 inhabitants located on the east banks of the Mulde was famous for its mud and salt baths. (The Mulde River flows in a northwest direction and ends as a tributary of the River Elbe south of Dessau, a few miles to the north of the Division zone. The Mulde is slightly larger than the Saale with a much stronger current. The Elbe River is one of the main arteries of transportation in Germany. The waterway from Bohemia to the North Sea is 1,160 kilometers in length, of which 830 are navigable.)

The Elbe and Mulde Rivers were the last remaining major terrain

NATIVE SONS

Count Felix von Luckner, 58, famed "Sea Devil" scourge of Allied shipping in World War I, turned up behind the Western Front, trying to save his hometown, Halle, from Major General Terry Allen's attack. Previously reported as 1) an active Nazi and 2) in the party's bad graces because of his friendship for America, he exclaimed: "By Jove! I haven't been so happy since I ran the British blockade of 1916!" But General Allen's only terms were unconditional surrender, and three days later Halle fell.

SS MEN IN HALLE KEEP WEHRMACHT C.O. IN LINE
By G. I. HODENFIELD, *Staff Correspondent*

With Task Force Rouge, Halle, Germany, April 18 (Delayed)—Right now the enemy is pinned down in the southern end of the city with no hope of escape, because there are roadblocks on every high- and by-way into the town. Sweating it out down there in the southern suburbs is a high officer of the Wehrmacht who would probably surrender, if he could shake those two SS men reported trailing him with drawn pistols.

Most of this city of 200,000 has been spared—for two reasons. First, there are at least 30 hospitals in the town many containing sick and injured allied PWs. Then, too, the civilians here pleaded with the German commander the other day to get out of here so the city wouldn't be flattened.

Partially because of the civilian pleas, but mostly on account of the dough- boys from the 414th Regt. of the 104 Div., the commander has got out of most of the city.

Tank destroyer and infantry move through the streets of Halle, large Nazi industrial center

obstacles or defense lines between the Eastern and Western Fronts. The Elbe was the easternmost line of advance of the Romans in 9 B.C. and only in 1200 A.D. was the entire west bank in German hands. Since 965 the Elbe was the lifeline of the provinces of Messen and Sechen, the capitals and fortresses on its shores being Dresden, Torgau, and Wittenburg. The surprise crossing of Charles V in 1547 decided the battle of Michlberg, and Yorck's crossing in 1813 made possible the junction of the Silesian and Northern armies. The terrain up to the Mulde was flat leading to gently rolling hills.

On the morning of 15 April, the 2d Battalion of the 414th hit the town of Raguhn and there staged one of the finest examples of air-armor-infantry coordination in battle. Staff Sergeant Jack Scott took an active part in this operation and recalls its highlights quite vividly:

Finally, on 15 April, we came to the town of Raguhn, straddling the Mulde Canal. On the city's outskirts, we ran into a sizable force of dug-in Nazis who were determined to keep us out of Raguhn and retain control of the super-

343

highway near the town, in order to maintain an open escape route across the Mulde Canal for their comrades overrun by our task force "Lovelady".

The way the task force took care of those Heinies was a beautiful combined operation. First, we all took a break while four P-47's gave the town a good, effective strafing. Meanwhile, the infantry had dismounted from the tanks and had spread out. The tanks dispersed through the adjacent fields. Then the self-propelled 105mm guns of the armor rolled up and poured in a terrific time-fire barrage over the enemy's holes. After ten minutes of this, H Co's 81mm mortar platoon took over and with Lieutenant Billy H. Sawyers doing the observing, poured it in for ten minutes at sixty rounds a minute. During this mortar barrage an H Company machine-gun platoon under Lieutenant Dietz which had been guarding the operations CP of the task force, moved up and set up its guns on the flanks.

Now that all this preparation was over, the riflemen were ready to move out on the toughest job of all—cleaning out the holes, one at a time. E Company took the left side of the road, G Company the right. They worked carefully and surely—one man flushing out the hole while the rest of his squad covered him and the flanks.

After about an hour of this tedious housecleaning, the road to town was cleared. The results of the operation were thirty-five Nazis killed or wounded and 120 taken prisoner. We didn't suffer a single casualty.

Before midnight on 15 April the Division was again concentrated within a ten-mile square with the 414th, less its 2d Battalion, on the east banks where it had secured a bridgehead by forcing a crossing prior to midnight. The 413th had closed behind the 415th, prepared to relieve the Old Faithful regiment.

The Division commander directed the 415th to cross the Saale, assigning it objectives on the northern part of the Division zone up to and including Bitterfeld along the Mulde; the 413th to leave one battalion on the western banks of the river with the balance of the regiment moving into the center of the Division zone east of Halle, and the 414th to continue the reduction of Halle. During the period 16-19 April, Colonel Cochran's regiment had cleared its zone up to the western edges of the city of Bitterfeld. Lieutenant Colonel Dean's 2d Battalion on 17 April became heavily engaged during its night attack against Sandersdorf. The fight was bitterly contested with the defenders employing machine guns, panzerfausts and flak guns; however, by 1300 it was taken. The 3d Battalion had forced a crossing over the Saale enabling the 329th Engineers to construct bridges within the Division zone, and after clearing several towns was in position at Reitzsch southwest of Bitterfeld on 19 April. The 1st Battalion had destroyed many strong points and cleaned up several communities before it closed abreast of the 3d on 19 April at Petersroda, just west of Bitterfeld. Colonel Summers' Seagulls initially had left the 1st Battalion on the west banks of the Saale to block any escape from

Halle to the west. The 2d and 3d Battalions had moved into position just northeast of Halle and cleared the center of the Division zone just short of Delitzsch on 19 April. The 3d Battalion, from its position east of Halle, was prepared to assist the 414th in its assault against that city and on 18 April it did relieve elements of the 414th on the road blocks east and southeast of the city. The regiment had cleared nine more towns.

BITTERFELD-DELITZSCH . . . The last resistance in Halle having been reduced, the Division was prepared to make its final assault on the Mulde River with the 415th on the left, the 413th in the center and the 414th on the right. On the night of 19-20 April, at 0130, Colonel Cochran launched his attack against Bitterfeld with the 2d Battalion striking it from the west, the 1st Battalion from the southwest and the 3d Battalion from the southeast. It had been determined by patrol action that Bitterfeld would be heavily defended by its 1,500 troops. To insure the complete destruction of the enemy forces within the city Colonel Cochran had directed the bold maneuver. Heavy fighting took place on the western and southern approaches to the city. The resistance was characterized by the unusually large number of panzerfausts employed. Once in the city the troops met continued heavy small-arms, machine gun, panzerfaust and moderate artillery fire from the 1,500 defenders. During the thirty-six hour battle that ended at 1536 on 21 April several counterattacks had been repulsed and more than 900 prisoners were taken.

The 413th had initially planned to assault Delitzsch at night; however, after having advanced on 20 April against little opposition it decided to attack the city that afternoon. After a heavy preparation stomp by the 385th Field Artillery Battalion, the 2d Battalion rushed the city and by nightfall had captured it, including all of its defenders. On 21 April the Seagulls pressed their advance with all battalions on line and by 1700 they held the west banks of the Mulde in their zone. During the night the 3d Battalion observed numerous enemy in Geuna east of the river. Following a mortar barrage, elements of the battalion crossed the swift river, captured eighty prisoners and returned.

The 414th, mounting its forty-eight captured German half-tracks, dashed swiftly to the east, and after clearing sporadic resistance and gobbling up 181 prisoners had cleared its zone by 1600 on the 21st. The Timberwolves now held the Mulde closing the distance between the 104th and the nearest reported Russian column to eighteen miles.

The Division prepared plans to force crossings over the Mulde and drive for the Elbe, commencing the night of 21 April. In the early afternoon of 21 April all commanders reported to the Commanding General at the Division command post in the chocolate factory at Delitzsch, where they were briefed on the coming operations by General Allen and his staff. All regiments were to force crossings with the 414th to seize Torgau along the Elbe in the southern part of the Division zone, while the 413th in the center and the 415th on the north would secure the west banks of the Elbe. Just as the commanders were preparing to leave for their units, a message was received from VII Corps directing the Division to remain along the west banks of the Mulde until further orders. The offensive action of the Timberwolf Division in World War II had ended.

Since 25 March the Division had advanced 375 miles, had captured 19,152 prisoners and had played a vital role in trapping the 335,000 German troops in the Ruhr pocket and the 65,000 Nazis in the Harz Mountains. The Ruhr pocket was formed on 1 April at 1530 when the 2d Armored Division of the Ninth Army and the 3d Armored Division, with the 414th Infantry attached, established contact at Lippstadt. The lightning advance of both armies had entrapped the German Army Group B and many miscellaneous elements, together with Germany's greatest industrial area—Dortmund, Essen, Hamm, Duisburg, and Dusseldorf—the heart of German war industry. The rapidity of the advance had found the enemy unprepared and disorganized.

With the Ninth Army along the Elbe to the north, the First Army along the Elbe and the Mulde and the Third and Seventh Armies rushing deeper into Germany on the south, the Reich had been cut in half. The battle of pursuit for the First Army was finished, and the fight for annihilation of the remaining pockets was commencing by all Allied Armies. In tribute to the fighting men of the 104th, Lieutenant General J. Lawton Collins, Comander of VII Corps, forwarded to the Division headquarters on 30 May 1945, the following letter of commendation:

HEADQUARTERS 104TH (TIMBERWOLF) INFANTRY DIVISION
OFFICE OF THE COMMANDING GENERAL
TO ALL TIMBERWOLVES: 1 June 1945
The letter quoted below has been received from the Commanding General, VII Corps:
HEADQUARTERS VII CORPS
OFFICE OF THE COMMANDING GENERAL
Major General Terry Allen   30 May 1945
Commanding, 104th Infantry Division
APO #104, United States Army
Dear General Allen:
Anticipating the departure of the 104th Infantry Division in the near future,

I wish to express to you and to all of the officers and men of the Timberwolf Division my deep appreciation for the outstanding work performed by your Division since it joined the VII Corps in November, 1944.

The 104th Infantry Division was one of the mainstays in the VII Corps during the severe fighting that carried us from the Aachen-Stolberg area to the Roer River and from the Roer to the Rhine, culminating in the capture of Cologne. Teamed with the 3d Armored Division, the Timberwolves stormed over the Vorgebirge Hills guarding Cologne and seized the southern half of that key city on 7 March 1945. It was during this campaign across the Inde, the Roer and the Erft in February-March, 1945, that the 104th Division perfected its technique of night operations which has made it one of the outstanding night-fighting divisions in the army.

On 22 March, the Division crossed the Rhine at Honnef, and the following night attacked to the east from the Remagen bridgehead. Mopping up scattered points of resistance and consolidating gains in close support of the 3d Armored Division, the 104th Infantry Division played an important role in the great encircling maneuver which trapped over 335,000 enemy troops in the Ruhr pocket and cut off that vital industrial area from the rest of Germany. With great skill and boldness the 104th Division, though stretched at times over a depth of forty miles, held off the enemy's vicious counterattacks aimed at cutting the VII Corps' line of communications from Marburg to Paderborn. The great advance of the 3d Armored Division to Paderborn was thus made possible largely through the splendid blocking and mopping operations of the Timberwolves.

With the Ruhr pocket securely contained, the 104th Division was relieved by elements of the III Corps and assembled in the Borgentreich-Leibenau area. Again in close support of the 3d Armored Division, the Division renewed its advance to the east on 7 April 1945. By 14 April, the 104th Division had crossed the Weser River, blocked the southern exits from the Harz Mountains area, and advanced 140 miles in one week to the outskirts of Halle.

With the relief of elements of the Division along the south side of the Harz Mountains pocket by the 9th Infantry Division, the Timberwolves crossed the Saale River on 15 April 1945 and attacked Halle from the north. Halle, Delitzsch, and Bitterfeld were captured in rapid succession, and by 21 April, the Division had cleared its entire sector to the Mulde River. While waiting for the Soviet forces to close along the Division front, your vigorous patrolling east of the Mulde River resulted in the capture of 20,375 prisoners of war. The Division established contact with the Soviets at Pretzsch on 26 April 1945.

Every officer and man in the Timberwolf Division may well take great pride in your splendid organization. The great achievements of the 104th Infantry Division have demonstrated the highest order of leadership, tactical skill and fine fighting spirit throughout the Division. With its first engagement in the Eschweiler-Weisweiler area last November, the 104th Division quickly took its place as one of the finest assault divisions that has been with the VII Corps. The entire Corps staff joins me in the hope that our association is only temporarily interrupted, and that we will be together when the last shot is fired in World

War II. Meanwhile, we all wish to every Timberwolf the best of luck and continued success.

Sincerely,

/s/ J. LAWTON COLLINS
/t/ J. LAWTON COLLINS,
Lieutenant General, U. S. Army,
Commanding.

This latest commendation, summarizing your combat operations with the VII Corps, is a deserving tribute to the battle accomplishments of our Timberwolf Division.

Again, my sincere thanks to you all for your continuing loyal support.

NOTHING IN HELL MUST STOP THE TIMBERWOLVES.

/s/ TERRY ALLEN
/t/ TERRY ALLEN.

CONTACT WITH THE RUSSIANS

Orders from higher headquarters had halted the Timberwolves on the Mulde while the Russian forces, an average distance of eighteen miles away, closed up to the Elbe, apparently with corresponding orders to move no further west. In the intervening space of partially wooded rolling farmland, over 20,000 German troops, in complete disintegration, gradually abandoned defense of the Fatherland. Timberwolf patrols were active east of the Mulde with only slight opposition. The first day of occupation of the Mulde was comparatively static, with small arms and occasional artillery exchanged. Early on the second day the enemy showed signs of disorganization, and civilians in great numbers attempted to cross the Mulde to escape the Russian advance. Individual prisoners began to surrender in increasing numbers. Our patrols worked towns east of the Mulde and discovered that no organization of military personnel existed and great confusion was in evidence. Thousands of Allied prisoners roamed at large and a burgomeister sought to surrender his entire town. The task was to organize, canalize and move these hordes of Allied prisoners and German troops into the Division zone, where they could be processed and evacuated.

Leaflets of instruction in German were dropped by Division artillery liaison planes directing the enemy soldiers to present themselves at the river in groups of 500, columns of threes, weapons unloaded, spokesmen preceding, at half-hour intervals. Foot-bridges were constructed by the Division engineers. Enemy groups negotiated with patrols or followed the written directive. Day and night for the next ten days an unending stream poured across the bridges. On 24 April 2,400 prisoners entered the regimental lines; on the 25th, 5,700, including sixteen women soldiers; on the 26th, 4,150; on the 27th, 4,550. A total of

21,964 prisoners surrendered to our troops along the river and to patrols on the east. A Timberwolf camp for the thousands of American and British former Allied prisoners of war was established by the 387th Field Artillery Battalion in Halle. The 415th at Bitterfeld, the 413th at Duben and the 414th at Eilenberg worked feverishly on the new problem of evacuation.

Meanwhile junction with our Russian allies was most happily effected, first by personnel of the Division artillery in its cub liaison planes, next by ground patrols, and then in an exchange of visits by staff officers and commanders. At 2000 on 23 April a liaison cub, piloted by Captain Kenneth A. Morris with Captain Donald B. Gordon as observer, was making reconnaissance east of our lines when a large column was observed moving west near Wurzen, ten miles east of the Mulde. At first it was believed to be a Russian column, but when the plane flew low over the road the men in the column began waving white flags. When Captain Morris landed the plane he was immediately surrounded by 300 armed German troops and several British prisoners. Thousands of German troops were in the general area and all types of vehicles were crowding the roads. It was determined that the column had left the Elbe earlier in the day and that it was believed by the Germans that the Russians were closing on the river. After making arrangements for the Germans to continue marching to our lines for surrender, Captain Morris and Captain Gordon returned safely before dark.

Visual contact between the 104th Division and the Russian forces was first made on 24 April at 1305. Major Clyde M. Turner and Major Richard J. Bestor of the Division artillery had volunteered to fly a cub plane behind the enemy lines in an effort to locate the advancing Russian armies. Fifteen miles east of the Elbe beyond Torgau, they sighted Russian columns advancing west and observed an artillery duel between the Russian and German forces. An effort was made by the officers to land behind the lines of the Russians, but an intensive antiaircraft barrage drove them away after damage had been inflicted to their plane. The Russians had been unable to identify the American aircraft and physical contact was denied. After accurately plotting the location of the Russian and German troops, the officers returned to our lines.

On the evening of 23 April Lieutenant Harlan W. Shank, Sergeant Jack Adler, Corporal Bob Gilfillan and Corporal Sam Stanovich of the 104th Reconnaissance Troop, plus a liberated Russian officer, crossed the Mulde, headed for Torgau on the Elbe. Early the next morning, Lieutenant Shank and his men were in Torgau, and from their observation posts determined that the Russians had not yet reached the town. It was then under intensive Russian artillery fire. The bridges at Torgau were still intact and the city contained many German soldiers. Late in the afternoon of the same day the patrol headed back for the Mulde and reached our lines early the following morning.

It was at Torgau that a patrol from the adjoining 69th Infantry Division met the Russian column on 25 April at 1600. On 26 April Lieutenant Shank returned to Torgau and established contact between the 104th Division and the Russian forces at 1830.

This venture of the 104th's Recon Troop was probably the most interesting patrol of the war for any Timberwolf. Regardless of the many hazards involved, all men felt it a singular honor to be chosen for this history-making patrol joining the armies of two such powerful Allied nations fighting a common aggressor. Blending historical fact with a little humor, Sergeant Gilfillan's words relive the memorable exploit:

At 1330 I walked into the headquarters of the 104th Reconnaissance Troop, where our CO, Captain Arthur S. Laundon, briefed the patrol which included Lieutenant Harland Shank, Sergeant Jack Adler, Corporal Sam Stanovich, a freed Russian lieutenant, and myself on the mission. The map was lying on the table in front of us and as I was being briefed I noticed quite a few green patches on the map which designated wooded areas, and that always meant trouble. It was about this that many questions arose.

Our point of departure was Delitzsch, a town in which our headquarters as well as Division headquarters was stationed. We had friendly troops up to the Mulde River, which was about six to eight kilometers forward on our route to meet the Reds. The German troops lay between the Mulde and the Elbe River, and according to G-2 the Russians were in Pretsch, a town on the west bank of the Elbe.

We reached the Mulde, and because of all bridges being blown out in that sector the jeep was driven on an antiquated barge and pulled across by the current. On reaching the other side we met a few German soldiers that were giving themselves up to our doughboys and also a large group of very nice-looking Luftwaffe girls which briefly took my mind off the patrol.

From here on I could see everyone pondering the fact that we no longer saw the familiar faces of our American buddies. However we did meet a German civilian who could speak some English and wanted a ride to the next town. We put him on the hood of the jeep and used him as an information bureau, and through him we found that the next town had 600 German soldiers in it—which made us feel a bit uneasy. It was here that Old Glory, which was a part of our equipment, came into use. A woman's wash pole from a nearby yard acted as a staff for our flag and up it went on the front of the jeep. The civilian was dropped off at the town, unaware of the fact that the Russian lieutenant was about ready to hop out of the jeep and let him have it because the Kraut had kept telling us how bad the Russians were, not knowing that one of us was Russian. One trouble eliminated and one to go—the 600 German soldiers.

On entering the town we saw the familiar green uniform that we were trying to bury forever. After an inquiry, we found that our worries were groundless—

all of the soldiers were hospital patients. Several of the German soldiers surrounded the jeep and we handed them the pamphlets which we had brought along just for this occasion, telling them how to surrender. Since we were a long way from our objective, we decided to move on. Halfway through the town we met a German colonel who started our first attempts at fast thinking.

During the conversation the colonel told us of 1,200 troops which were under his command just outside of town. I soon found myself saluting beaucoup German brass. We did hit luck, however, for the colonel could speak good English, which helped the delicate bargaining along. Our conversation was about how we wanted to aid the German soldier and he seemed to like it. We mounted our jeep and followed the German officer about two kilometers outside of town, and there coming down the road was a breath-taking sight. Here we saw wagons loaded with guns and ammunition; troops on foot and bicycles coming toward us; these then were the colonel's command. Some waved, others looked at us as though they were ready to do the Fuehrer another favor. On entering the next town the colonel said that he would let us know in the morning whether his troops were our captives or still of the Fatherland.

While Lieutenant Shank was trying to impress the colonel and his officers, I was trying to influence the German people, and I recall one policeman comparing my .45 with his Luger and wondering how soon it would be mine. I was an enemy, but evidently a very honored one, because no matter where I walked, the policeman would always clear a path for me and chase the civilians out of my road.

Leaving this town and all its excitement, we started out again. First we oriented ourselves on the map and faced our first wooded area. After going about two miles I noticed a German outpost, containing a very young boy, and beside him in a culvert twelve to fourteen bicycles. It did not take me long to realize that he had friends nearby, and as I glanced across the clover field I saw enough camouflaged helmets to account for all the bicycles. To our left were many German soldiers running about in a confused manner, and to our front about 500 yards I saw them running across the road into the dark pine forest. It was not the time to turn around, so we advanced to the edge of the woods, and about the time we reached there three rifles "took a bead" that was meant for us. Simultaneously, we all raised our hands and helmets and cheered. No shots were fired. We gave the German soldiers some pamphlets and about then we took off in a hurry, as it appeared these troops were set up to resist and it would take a bit more persuasion to talk surrender to them than we were quite ready for. We turned around, having mollified the guards that had attempted to shoot us, and headed back to the forked road, this time bypassing the woods.

The sun was starting to meet the horizon and our daylight hours were numbered, so the jeep traveled a bit faster. We knew that we were soon to reach the Elbe, but we still had a few towns to pass through. Our next village had only a few disorganized German troops in it, and all of them wanted to know where the Americans were, and how they could surrender. We obliged them.

Soon, the road sign Pretsch confronted us, and according to our instructions we would meet the Russians in this vicinity. I think we were a little more afraid of the Russians than of the Germans, because we were not sure they would recognize us. The jeep slowed down, all eyes covering 360 degrees. Halfway through the town and no Russkis; the other side of town and still no Russkis. The jeep was nearing the top of a hill just outside of Pretsch and there over the crest came four heads—very slowly at first, and then a loud cheer and the American flag had come through again.

I have seen men that have not shaved for months, but they had nothing on these boys. Either they lost their razor or forgot how to use it, because I really felt the bristles scrape my face like sandpaper when they gave us that good old kiss on both cheeks. For about fifteen minutes we, as well as the Russians, were never so happy—the world had been waiting for this for a long while.

As we drove toward the Elbe River, more and more Russian soldiers climbed aboard our jeep.

The Elbe was reached and we found it very wide at this point. This didn't stop our reaching the Russian headquarters, because they had a pontoon barge which was pulled across with a cable. The jeep was put aboard the raft and over we went. On the other side I saw the Russian officer put his men in platoon formation while the soldiers brushed their clothes and tried to appear as neat as possible. As the other bank was reached, cheers rose, and it was then that I found the hand-shaking had only begun. We were heroes for a day.

As we drove toward the headquarters of the 118th Russian Infantry Division of Marshal Ivan Konev's First Ukrainian Army, more cheers rose, and the only Russian word I could understand was "Americanski." Greeting the general was quite an honor, for I got the feeling that I myself was tying a bond that signified the end. We then gave them information concerning the American front.

It was not too long before we were escorted to our dining hall. We ate in what was the officers' dining room, and what a meal. Our menu—raw fat, fish, cookies, some kind of dough patties, food which I never saw before, and vodka. If you ever siphoned gas with a hose and accidentally swallowed some, you know what vodka tastes like. It was poured out in water glasses. I tried to down one and had just about accomplished it when my glass was refilled pronto. Lieutenant Shank and Adler were putting it away while Stanovich and I were wishing we had boots so we could fill them with the stuff. Lieutenant Shank would laugh and say "For gosh sakes, Gilfillan, here comes more, hide the bottles under the table." Each time we thought we were through drinking a toast, a new officer would come in. Well, as far as I was concerned I didn't feel like leading the Russian Army into battle, and as it was I could see about six or eight big windows in the room, but as I recall there was only one small one to begin with. Later I heard a Russian officer using the telephone and trying to explain that he had four Americans he wanted decorated.

That evening, we were taken to a hotel to sleep. Jack and Sam were in one room; I was sleeping with a Russian soldier; and Lieutenant Shank was up most of the night giving information for a broadcast to Moscow. I was trying to fall asleep, and as tired as I was I could not because my bed partner couldn't get his boots off. To end it all I got out of bed and helped yank them off. We were well guarded by sentries posted outside our doors, in the hall, and also outside the hotel.

We had breakfast and again no coffee—no milk—but more vodka. After finishing breakfast many pictures were taken. Churchill had nothing on us but his umbrella, because big cigars were handed out and more pictures snapped. As I was sitting down an officer introduced me to his wife and she pinned the Red Star with the hammer and two sickles on my jacket. She was a very beautiful girl as I recall. We were given bouquets of flowers, and to top it all, the jeep had the Russian flag, flowers, pictures of Stalin, Roosevelt, and Churchill pasted on the windshield.

Flying American and Soviet flags, Lieutenant Shank and his Recon patrol made initial contact with the Red forces beyond the Elbe River

On 27 April Major Clyde M. Turner, Division Artillery air officer, flying in a liaison aircraft, brought to the 104th Division command post at Delitzsch a Russian staff officer from the 118th Russian Infantry Division. That afternoon Colonel John H. Cochran, commanding the 415th Infantry, Lieutenant Colonel Leo A. Hoegh, Division G-3, Major Turner and Sergeant Pete Sitnik, 415th Regiment's interpreter, flying by Division artillery liaison planes, crossed the Mulde and Elbe Rivers and landed at Annaburg, fifteen miles east of the Elbe River. Here they spent the night at the command post of the 118th Russian Infantry Division and made arrangements for the Russian commander and his staff to visit the Timberwolf Division.

On 28 April Major General Sohanow and his staff were flown by the artillery planes from Annaburg to Delitzsch, where they were formally received by General Allen, his commanders and staffs. Greatest cordiality marked this colorful and significant meeting during which Russo-American relations were furthered. This was quite evident when General Allen appointed General Sohanow an honorary Timberwolf. The 104th Commander removed his shoulder patch in order to place it on the Red general's sleeve. Finding no pins in the gathering crowd, the American general, with great aplomb, loosened his belt, took a pin

Don't bunch up!—sniper—around the corner!

from his shorts, and with this cemented relations with Russia by pin-
ning a Timberwolf patch on the shoulder of the Soviet leader. Red
Army soldiers applauded and cheered, willing to give the American
commander anything he desired but unable to provide him with his
simplest necessity—a means of holding his shorts up.

Corporal William Yatcilla of Headquarters Battery, Division artillery, also found himself a hero during the Russo-American contact.
Yatcilla, the Russian interpreter for Divarty, made many trips to Russian installations over active German positions, for which he was cited
by the commanding general of the 118th Russian Division. "Wearing
the medal while acting as interpreter for Major Hausell of the 386th
Field Artillery Battalion, during an inspection of displaced persons
camps at Erfurt and Mulhausen," relates Corporal Yatcilla, "I was
treated like a war hero . . . was kissed by many young Russian girls
and handshaked by the Russian men." His observation on Russian
liquor tastes: "They like our gin far better than our scotch."

On one thing, all American doughs seem in agreement. The words of Norman H. Filbert, F Company, 414th Infantry, reflected a universal opinion when he said, "The Russians are the best drinkers in the world. They claim—'if you fight with us, you'll drink with us'—and they certainly strive mightily to live up to both parts of that arrangement."

The regiments had established contact by ground patrols with Russian forces which had now closed on the Elbe.

These patrols found varying episodes in the hazardous territory lying between the Mulde and Elbe Rivers. Sergeants Mannix and Dyer, C Company, 414th Infantry, recall that regiment's attempt at contacting the forces of the Red Army:

Lieutenant Vic Willard, platoon commander of our 3d Platoon, volunteered to lead us across hostile territory to establish contact with the Russians. Our company was in a small town called Pressen, a few miles from the Mulde, expecting the end of the war to be announced any day. About 2000 in the evening of 25 April Lieutenant Willard called the platoon together and told us that he had volunteered our platoon for this mission. He put the patrol on a voluntary basis, knowing our feelings about taking such a risk so near the end of the war.

At 2100 that evening the platoon leader and platoon noncoms went to battalion headquarters and received the necessary information and equipment such as signal flares and maps from Lieutenant Colonel Clark, the battalion CO. Colonel Clark told us that no contact had been established thus far with the Russian forces along the entire front, but they were reported to be across the Elbe at Torgau. On the morning of 26 April at 0700 we moved through the forward elements of our battalion and were quickly shuttled across the river by the 329th Engineers.

Extremely heavy fog made it impossible to follow our originally planned route and forced us to proceed by compass directly east. We moved cautiously though quickly in order to cover as much ground as possible before dawn.

Our route was strewn with enemy vehicles, equipment, and even carefully camouflaged planes which the Germans were unable to get off the ground due to lack of fuel.

Dawn found our patrol on the outskirts of a small village about seven miles from the Elbe River. Our route for several miles had been through woods and we were now near a small farmhouse overlooking an airfield which was not on our map.

From the woods surrounding the farmhouses we observed several enemy outposts of two or three men each. At 0600 we entered the farmhouse to question the civilians concerning the disposition and number of enemy troops in the area. Our interpreter, Pfc. Schueppel, was busy questioning the civilians when three horse-drawn wagons loaded with ammo and equipment came rolling into the farmyard. The morning was very chilly and one of the soldiers started toward the house to get warmed up. We let him enter the house, took him prisoner, and forced him to lay on the floor. After a few minutes his comrades, becoming curious, started for the house. We quickly captured them as they entered and began interrogating them. From these prisoners we learned that there were 250

Red Army commanders received at Division CP, Delitzsch, Germany

Luftwaffe men stationed in that neighborhood in addition to the infantry whose outposts we had infiltrated.

The time was now about 0700 and the road in front of the farmhouse was buzzing with activity. Our new plans were to circle around the airfield's outposts and the town and proceed east on our mission. We were fortunate that the woods came close to the house as we were able to withdraw with comparative safety. Our fear of exposure by the prisoners forced us to take them along. After our platoon was reformed safely in the woods we started on our original mission. The woods provided excellent concealment as we guided on a road around the town. An occasional enemy half-track, truck or foot soldier made our movement slow, as we had to lay low till they passed. Our luck did not hold out for long, however, and finally after approximately a mile we came to the edge of the woods. To proceed on our mission we would have to cross this open ground. From this point we observed a few foot soldiers with panzerfausts and machine guns moving on a road 200 yards to our front. Lieutenant Willard decided to hold the patrol and observe a while longer before crossing the opening. This decision proved to be a wise one, because a few minutes later a heavily armored half-track and several trucks loaded with soldiers came down the road along with more foot troops. This unexpected number of vehicles and troops in this area made a deeper penetration towards the Russians impossible. Lieutenant Willard decided to start the patrol back toward our lines.

We headed dead west this time and kept our scouts way out. Progress back to our own lines proved much more difficult than the movement forward had been as enemy troops were constantly on the move over the roads. Keen obser-

Under Secretary of War Patterson and Brigadier General Woodward leave 104th Command Post at Delitzsch, Germany

vation on the part of our scouts and rear guard kept us out of many a fire-fight which would have meant the end of our small patrol. The woods again provided us excellent cover but there were times when we were forced to cross stretches of open terrain. On one occasion when we were forced to cross a road our Russian interpreter, Pfc. Malafka, was almost run down by a Jerry motor-cyclist.

After much dodging we finally made it to the clearing before the Mulde. Staff Sergeant Limbaugh did excellent work in guiding us back to the spot where we made the river crossing.

On the other hand, Pfc. Raymond E. McGowan, a member of the 415th Infantry's contact patrol, found the situation a lot less hostile and recalls how they reached the Elbe River without too much inter-

Airbase at Polenz, Germany. Wrecked German jet fighter and . . . .

ference and solidified relations with the Russian Bear in their regimental zone:

At 0700 on the morning of 26 April 1945, we left Puchau. Six jeeps from Company D, 415th Infantry, participated in the patrol. Machine guns were mounted on four jeeps to provide security for the trip, which extended about forty miles through towns and villages which had never been entered by our own or Allied forces. The other two jeeps carried interpreters.

It was a cold morning and the jeeps offered scant protection from the biting wind. We crossed the Mulde River and moved out of Wurzen, which was the line of departure, at 0800. When we left the sun was just rising and lighted up the American flag mounted on the lead jeep. The flag had been made by a Polish woman who had been a slave laborer under the Germans for several years. It not only served as a means of identification but was also the first target for the many cameras which had been so graciously "loaned" by the Germans.

We proceeded through farm country which was dotted by numerous small villages. In each town the burgomeister was contacted and questioned as to the presence of German soldiers and arms of any sort. The civilians seemed very surprised to see us and the less timid were very anxious to learn whether our forces or the feared Russians were to occupy their zone.

Streams of liberated prisoners and slave laborers, traveling in both directions, were seen along our route to the Elbe. The hour for which we had so long waited and traveled so far had finally arrived. The bridge was out, but in a few minutes several Russian soldiers and liberated Allied POWs, having observed the American flag, crossed the turbulent river. As they neared our bank there was a clicking of cameras as both Russian and our own force posed in small groups for an exchange of snapshots.

There was a mad scramble to greet the Russians and everyone claimed the distinction of being the first to shake hands. The first thing that we noticed was their impressive array of medals and their youthful appearance. They contributed to the momentous occasion by sharing their canteens which contained vodka. Oblivious of the proceedings, the liberated prisoners seemed only interested in our cigarettes and K rations which we passed out so freely.

In anticipation of crossing the Elbe at Torgau, we traveled ten kilometers north, only to learn that the opposite bank was off limits to our troops. There we sighted our first Russian woman MP, who was directing traffic at a busy

. . . . visiting Russian interceptors.

intersection. Even she was subjected to the typical GI whistle. It was in Torgau that we noted the greatest similarity between the Russian Army and our own. A Russian soldier was observed riding a motorcycle and seated behind him was an attractive fraulein. Any amorous intentions harbored by the Russian soldier were abruptly curtailed when an officer stopped him and subjected him to the usual chewing so familiar to GIs the world over.

During the period 1 to 6 May inclusive, the 272d Regiment of the 69th Division was attached to the 104th Division. The regiment had its troops extended from Eilenberg to Torgau immediately in front of our positions with the mission of protecting this important connecting route between the two Allied forces. Corps, Army, and Group Commanders and many other dignitaries passed over the road enroute to the Russians east of the Elbe. On 3 May a Russian column crossed the Elbe at Torgau and moved west, closing in an assembly position halfway between the Mulde and the Elbe. The 395th Russian Infantry Division, a part of the XXIV Corps of the Thirteenth Army, 1st Ukranian Army Group, was preparing to take up its positions along the east banks of the Mulde.

Firm contact had been made between the Division and the Russian forces all along the Elbe, and now that the vastly disorganized and scattered remnants of the once proud Wehrmacht were fast disintegrating between the two great Armies, the Russians had been directed to move up to the Mulde. The enemy continued his group surrenders to our forces until 6 May, when the Russian troops effected a link-up in force with our troops along the Mulde, eliminating all semblance of enemy resistance. The enemy no longer existed as a striking force and our efforts were then directed mainly to the field of counterintelligence and civil control activities.

All of our own troops were now west of the Mulde and regimental and battalion commanders and staffs from all units exchanged visits with the Russians. Our relationship with them was most pleasant and lasting friendships quickly developed.

361

Under Secretary of War Robert P. Patterson visited the Division in early May. At a later date in a letter to General Allen, he wrote:

Major General Terry de la M. Allen,
Commanding General,
104th Infantry Division.
Dear General:

It was a great pleasure . . . to visit the 104th Division in Germany.

The Timberwolf Division has made a great record. The American people are proud of it and I know that you are proud of it.

With best regards, I am,

Sincerely yours,

(sgd.) Robert P. Patterson

Robert P. Patterson,

Under Secretary of War.

TO ALL TIMBERWOLVES:

This commendation from the Under Secretary of War, who was a combat infantry officer with a distinguished record in World War I, is a deserving tribute to your battle accomplishments.

Again, my sincere thanks to you all for your loyal support and for having lived up to your battle slogan:

"NOTHING IN HELL CAN STOP THE TIMBERWOLVES."

/s/ TERRY ALLEN
/t/ TERRY ALLEN

PADERBORN

PHASE VII

BACK TO THE LAIR

I WILL TURN HOME

I will turn home again some day,
Putting my back on all these things
Of war and mud;
Of pain and blood;
Of aching hunger and maddening stings.
I will go back along the way
I came, until I stand once more
Beneath home skies
And see sunrise
Upon my beloved shore.

I will turn home again when war
Is past and honor's call is quiet.
Till then my face
Is set in place
To one established goal in freedom's fight.
I will turn home at last once more,
Knowing that a true soldier's rest,
Once earned is sweet;
His peace complete
Who gave until the last his best.

—*Sgt. R. A. Larsen*

REDEPLOYMENT

THE long anticipated enemy collapse and surrender seemed likely to become a reality as the Timberwolf Division continued its occupation along the Mulde on 1 May. Berlin had fallen. All Allied armies were rapidly mopping up remaining enemy resistance throughout Germany.

On 4 May the 104th Division all along its front established firm contact with Russian troops, and now for the first time since entering combat on 23 October 1944, in Belgium, front line contact with the enemy had been broken. *The Timberwolves had been in front line combat 195 consecutive days.*

During this grueling period the 104th Division had participated in the Holland campaign—23 October to 8 November, the drive through the Siegfried Line from Aachen to the Roer—8 November to 14 December; the active defense on the Roer River—14 December 1944 to 22 February 1945; the drive to Cologne—23 February to 7 March; defense along the Rhine—8 March to 22 March; the drive to Paderborn and encirclement of the Ruhr Valley—22 March to 1 April; the final drive to the Mulde River—1 April to 21 April; and the active defense along the Mulde culminating in contact with the Russians—22 April to 4 May. Our offensive culminated fifty-three miles short of the German capital of Berlin.

Finally at 0940 7 May the Division headquarters received the following TWX from Supreme Headquarters, Allied Expeditionary Force:

1. A REPRESENTATIVE OF THE GERMAN HIGH COMMAND SIGNED THE UNCONDITIONAL SURRENDER OF ALL GERMAN LAND, SEA, AND AIR FORCES IN EUROPE TO THE ALLIED EXPEDITIONARY FORCE AND SIMULTANEOUSLY TO THE SOVIET HIGH COMMAND AT 0141 HOURS CENTRAL EUROPEAN TIME, 7 MAY UNDER WHICH ALL FORCES WILL CEASE ACTIVE OPERATIONS AT 0001 B HOURS 9 MAY.

2. EFFECTIVE IMMEDIATELY ALL OFFENSIVE OPERATIONS BY ALLIED EXPEDITIONARY FORCE WILL CEASE AND TROOPS WILL REMAIN IN PRESENT POSITIONS. MOVES INVOLVED IN OCCUPA-TIONAL DUTIES WILL CONTINUE. DUE TO DIFFICULTIES OF COM-MUNICATION THERE MAY BE SOME DELAY IN SIMILAR ORDERS REACHING ENEMY TROOPS SO FULL DEFENSIVE PRECAUTIONS WILL BE TAKEN.

3. ALL INFORMED DOWN TO AND INCLUDING DIVISIONS, TACTICAL AIR COMMANDS AND GROUPS, BASE SECTIONS, AND EQUIVALENT. NO RELEASE WILL BE MADE TO THE PRESS PEND-

ING AN ANNOUNCEMENT BY THE HEADS OF THE THREE
GOVERNMENTS.

Signed   EISENHOWER

At last victory in Europe had been gained. News broadcasts, moni-
tored by the Division G-2, gave us more details:

TUESDAY IS V-E DAY!

Prime Minister Churchill, with the approval of the American and Russian
governments, will at 1500 Tuesday announce the unconditional surrender of all
German forces in Europe. The King will speak at 2100 and Wednesday will
be a public holiday in England.

A Reuters dispatch reported the surrender pact was signed in Eisenhower's
headquarters at a Rheims schoolhouse. Signing were the American and German
chiefs of staff and representatives of France and Russia. General Eisenhower
was not present during the ceremonies, but met the Germans a short time later.

During the signing of the surrender, Reuters said the Germans were continually asked, "Do you realize the significance and seriousness of what you are
about to do?"

"Yes," they replied. "We will live up to the terms of the surrender agreement."

Earlier today the DNB radio announced that Germany had surrendered unconditionally as it was useless to continue the struggle. The German radio in
Prague, however, ordered German troops in Czechoslovakia to fight on "as long
as it is necessary to protect ourselves from the menace of the Soviet Union."

GI reactions to V-E Day were slow and unimpressive among the men
who had already seen the handwriting on the wall. Indifference seemed
to characterize their receipt of the news. Private Harold Jaynes of H
Company, 413th Infantry, remembers how he had looked forward to
V-E Day. He thought it would be the happiest day of his life; yet
when it came, the Division had been sitting still, waiting so long, the
men couldn't be too overjoyed—it was expected.

In our sector the actual fighting just gradually slowed down. Two weeks
before V-E Day we were so close to the Russians that both fronts were brought
to a halt to keep out of the other's artillery fire. The war was over as far as
we were concerned, but with no formal declaration. V-E Day was just another
day in May—it still scared us to see a jeep cutting the dark night with its head-
lights—and guard went on without the expected merrymaking.

I think I was more excited the first time we made radio contact with the
Russians. We were moving in to take a little town called Lobnitz. It was about
1100, and rain was falling lightly as we took concealment in a patch of woods
overlooking the town. Mortars were throwing in a few rounds on our left, and
one of our jeeps, equipped with a radio, picked up the Russians. They were
only about thirty miles in front of us. This meant there was little or no heavy

Victory in Europe

stuff between us, and it was only a matter of days before the war in our sector was over. That day meant more to me than V-E Day possibly could.

However victory in Europe did give us lots to look forward to. It meant that, with luck, our combat days were over. It meant that if we were redeployed we could look forward to a furlough at home and several months away from the muck and mud, the shells and blood of foxholes and battlefields. It meant that the first decisive steps toward world peace had been taken, and we were that much closer to that final trip home, to enjoy the freedoms for which we fought.

The immediate problems arising from the victory in Europe proclamation were the necessity of rounding up war criminals and the remainder of the Nazi party members, the destruction of Werewolf organizations, and controlling the great influx of displaced persons attempting to return to their homes.

The Division area of occupation was greatly increased on 9 May, with its front extending from north of Dessau along the Elbe to Wurzen along the Mulde, and with its depth from the Elbe and Mulde Rivers to west of Halle. Each Division and attached unit was assigned a zone of responsibility which it actively patrolled, and in which it maintained law and order. Lieutenant Colonel Bardes' 817th Tank Destroyer Battalion was assigned the city of Halle. Here it maintained constant vigilance over the many strategic targets and displaced persons located within the area. Lieutenant Colonel White's 750th Tank Battalion occupied Bernburg and many other communities in that vicinity. Lieutenant Colonel Farnum's 555th Antiaircraft Battalion occupied the important sector just east of Halle and maintained patrols throughout an enlarged area. In addition to all infantry and artillery battalions, the engineers and the 104th Reconnaissance Troop, Captain Moore's 104th Signal Company, Captain Haphey's 104th Headquarters Company, Captain Schwartz's 104th Quartermaster Company and Captain Smith's 804th Ordnance Company each were assigned occupation zones in which they maintained the security of the sector, patrolled and guarded vital installations, and maintained law and order. Many strategic installations were located within the Division zone, among them a film factory, radar stations, chemical factories, large ammunition dumps, food warehouses; large salt mines near Bernburg containing archives, historical records of Germany and large quantities of silver; railroad marshalling yards with many locomotives, freight and passenger cars; sugar refineries, poison gas factories, several large airfields, SS headquarters; and last but not least, seven breweries, including Germany's second largest, in Dessau.

DISPLACED PERSONS

The flow of displaced persons across the Mulde continued in both directions, with hordes awaiting permission to cross the bridges. People of all nationalities with every type of nondescript cart, wagon, trailer and vehicle and flying flags of half a dozen nationalities appeared at the bridges seeking to cross and continue the trip to their homeland. Russian screening teams operated with our own teams at the bridge sites. Germans were not permitted to cross the river in either direction, and only those who were residents of countries to the east were permitted to cross into the Russian lines, with the same policy adopted for those crossing into our lines. As the displaced persons approached the bridge sites they were screened to determine nationality, residence, and authority to cross the Mulde. The thousands of displaced persons who had been enslaved by the Nazis were now free and on their long trek toward home. The Division processed 41,417 displaced persons.

ALLIED PRISONERS OF WAR

The flow of Allied prisoners of war over the Mulde into the Division zone, which began in the latter part of April, continued throughout May and constituted a major problem. The large camp in Halle was handled by Lieutenant Colonel Stangle's 387th Field Artillery Battalion, later assisted by Lieutenant Colonel Alexander's 386th Field Artillery Battalion; the camp at Polentz by Lieutenant Colonel Gilbert's 929th Field Artillery Battalion; and the camps at Dessau, Raguhn, and Bitterfeld by Colonel Cochran's 415th Infantry Regiment.

Staff Sergeant Melvin Charbaneau of the 415th Infantry's 1st Battalion Intelligence Section says:

The town of Bitterfeld was the most modern we had encountered in Germany. The building selected as a German PW enclosure was a modern bank building. This building was organized by the Battalion S-2 and Intelligence Section to receive PW's who were at one time patrons of this bank.

During the advance and mopping up operation of the city, the companies would periodically bring their day's "catch" to the enclosure. The number of PW's would vary from twenty-five to one hundred at a time. After a quick screening to eliminate policemen, firemen, bus drivers, etc., these prisoners were marched into the building, quickly searched and segregated. After the city had been secured and the necessary screening of all the PW's had been accomplished, we had approximately 250 prisoners in the enclosure. Every branch of the Wehrmacht and "soldaten" of every rank and description were represented. Company A, so that they might receive credit for taking the ranking officer of Bitterfeld, brought in on a stretcher the dead commander of troops—a die-hard Nazi colonel who was determined to fight to the death.

Our most notable and prize live catch of the operation was the colonel who headed the draft board of Bitterfeld and vicinity. Upon interrogation he revealed that the greater percentage of troops defending Bitterfeld had been inducted the past week. The remaining troops were a large number of Volkssturm, partially hospitalized cases, and a small number of regular army soldiers.

It was impossible to interrogate all of the PW's, but a few who might be qualified to divulge information regarding subversive activities, armament work, location of storage depots or influential party leaders were selected for interrogation. The information received along with the help of freed Allied prisoners of war proved to be of great value.

Another incident worth mentioning was when a German girl gave herself up to soldiers of our battalion who were escorting other prisoners to an enclosure. This girl ran from a doorway and joined the prisoners while they were walking —she was dressed in a civilian skirt but the jacket appeared military. When the escorting soldiers tried to force her away from the PW's she protested and said she was a Nazi and a "Marina"—a woman marine. Upon interrogation she boasted she was proud to be a Nazi, proferred a few wisecracks, but refused to give us any information other than she was on leave from her assigned organization. The Bitterfeld operation netted us over 500 PW's.

We liberated hundreds of Allied prisoners of war. The information they gave us proved very helpful in leading us to persons who had been responsible for their maltreatment during confinement.

The capture and confinement of enemy uniformed soldiers in Bitterfeld did not complete our task. Our new task was to launch a campaign to clear the town of Wehrmacht deserters, agents, and party members who had been instrumental in making this industrial city of Bitterfeld a nucleus of Nazi party activities.

The greatest problem in the released Allied PW camps was securing enough DDT powder, showers, laundry and fumigation facilities. The men had been mistreated and improperly cared for by the Germans, thus requiring delousing facilities and immediate medical attention. The sanitation and medical treatment within each camp was maintained by the Division medical personnel, and soon many were cured of diarrhea and severe malnutrition.

Staff Sergeant Joseph C. Shock of the 387th Field Artillery Battalion and Sergeant Howard T. Gundry of the 929th Field Artillery described activities in these camps. Staff Sergeant Shock stated:

On 29 April 1945, the 387th Field Artillery Battalion moved from a position on the front lines to Halle and the site of a former German airbase. It was here that we started a casual regiment to take care of the liberated Allied prisoners of war.

Upon reaching our destination we found the camp in chaos and the liberated prisoners there in a pitiful condition, as were others that came later. This was soon remedied.

The battalion immediately set forth a plan of action that was to run smoothly and efficiently. Headquarters Battery was given the assignment of handling the administrative work and each of the three firing batteries set up sleeping quarters to take care of the men as they were sent there. Service Battery performed notably in supplying food and clothing in large quantities.

The liberated prisoners were mostly recaptured by the Russians, and were brought to us in convoys of 2½-ton trucks. Some of these were Russian vehicles and each Russian truck went back to their own lines full of liberated Russian people. The liberated Russians were brought into the airbase on many C-47 troop carriers from other parts of Europe, having been captured by our troops. These planes were then employed in evacuating the liberated soldiers toward home. The American soldiers and French subjects were flown to Rheims and Brussels.

Headquarters Battery knew approximately when a convoy of liberated prisoners would arrive and would greet them at the gate, dividing them up equally, sending each firing battery a third of the group. Upon reaching the firing battery, the prisoners were immediately given special care. Most of these men were suffering from malnutrition and generally were in very poor health. They were given wholesome food, with the result that many became sick, for it was too rich for their shrunken stomachs. Showers were afforded and clean clothes distributed. They were infested with parasites and had to be deloused. We used all the DDT available in that part of Europe and soon the men were lice-free. Those who required medical care were given prompt attention. Barracks were set up, blankets issued, and the men slept comforatbly in clean beds for the first time in many months. In about three to six days after their arrival they were on the way home in C-47 planes.

There were many nationalities: American, Canadian, French, British, and also some British subjects, Gurkhas and Indians. Some of them had been prisoners for four years, having been taken captive at Dunkirk, Dieppe, and in North Africa. Their inhuman treatment by the Germans was very much in evidence, and it will be a long time before they can forget their harrowing experiences.

On 28 May 1945, we were relieved by a battalion of the 7th Armored Division, 16,367 liberated prisoners having passed through our camp on the way home, much better off in spirits and in excellent health, due to the quick, kind care and attention they received from the men of the 104th.

Sergeant Gundry wrote:

On 3 May 1945, we pulled in at Polenz, Germany, with the assignment of administering the Prisoner of War Exchange camp located there. We went to work setting up our camp in a group of German barracks, formerly used to house members of the Luftwaffe.

The buildings were of good brick construction, with all the latest conveniences, including hot and cold running water, and electric power which was still in good working order.

As we were unpacking our equipment, we had seen numerous Allied POW's in the vicinity. French, American, British, Dutch, Polish and Italians seemed to be wandering all over. Only then did we begin to realize we really had a job on our hands. These people were in a serious state and needed help. We quickly got organized and found out we had about 6,500 French, 2,000 American and British, and about 500 Dutch, Polish and Italian prisoners.

The battalion worked in conjunction with the French headquarters of the camp, and quickly succeeded in obtaining medical attention, baths, clean clothes and food, in such quantities for the prisoners that conditions and morale were greatly improved.

While the processing of these POW's was in effect, movies and band concerts were a daily occurrence. Haircuts for everyone were soon provided by a group of German barbers requisitioned from the town. Our work was progressing very nicely, and by 10 May approximately 1,000 POW's were being moved from the camp to the entraining area daily.

The liberated men reported that the Germans had paid no attention to the Geneva Convention; that they had beaten our men with rifle butts, failed to feed them, taken away their clothing, and occasionally refused them medical aid. Here are some of their stories:

Despite temperatures that dropped to ten and twenty degrees below zero the Germans made no effort to heat the prisoners' barracks. Many had frozen feet and fingers which later had to be amputated.

An infantryman who had been captured on 2 January stated:

I was captured during the German breakthrough in Belgium. Along with 200 other Americans I was loaded on a freight train and sent to eastern Germany. We had no food or water on the trip, which took four days and five nights. Our overcoats, blankets, field jackets and shoes were taken away from us, together with other personal belongings. We licked the ice that formed on the hinges of the boxcar for water. There were seventy of us in each car, with no blankets or warm clothes or even straw to sleep on. Just to make sure we didn't get any sleep the German guards would fire a couple of rounds into the car, not trying to hit us because they fired high, but just wanting to keep us awake so that we didn't have the energy to escape.

Another report:

They often put ammunition cars on the end of prisoners' trains. Then when our bombers came over the guards ran off and left us locked up in the cars like trapped rats. It was an awful feeling to be caught like that, but I was lucky because there were never any direct hits on my train.

A terse but dramatic opinion from a somewhat laconic prisoner: "They're all sons of bitches."

At the Polentz camp 7,500 French prisoners were evacuated by train and 4,800 British and American prisoners by air, while at Halle a total of 25,000 British and American prisoners had been evacuated by air when the Division was relieved of operating the camp on 29 May.

PRISONERS

The Interrogation of Prisoners of War (IPW) Team, the Division CIC unit, and the Photo Interpretation (PI) Team were consolidated under Captain Buschager for the purpose of screening all personnel in the occupied area. To further insure complete counter-intelligence control, instructions were given to German linguists of all units, who in turn conducted routine screenings under direction of the Division intelligence officers. Several reports of possible sabotage were investigated during the period and the results proved that there were no organized attempts at subversive activities within the Division area. An investigation was made of a reported buried 10,000 gold Reichmarks. The "buried gold" turned out to be three boxes of food, clothing, and glassware, the treasure of a local resident. During the month of May, 1,864 German soldiers in civilian clothing were apprehended and 528 other persons were held for further investigation. Several persons of noteworthy interest were encountered. Among them was Ernst Henckel, a German marine on special duty with the Skorzeny organization. Henckel had previously committed acts of sabotage behind the Russian line and had been a member of the Skorzeny organization since

The PW cages swelled to capacity

2 December 1944, specializing in ship sabotage. Several SS women were apprehended, some of whom confessed to mistreatment of imprisoned women.

On 12 May the Division headquarters received instructions from the VII Corps that the 104th would be redeployed in the Pacific. The order directed the VII Corps to be prepared to release the Division for movement from its present area on or about 1 June 1945. Our big question, "What is going to happen to us?" had been answered. At first it was not known whether or not we would go to the Pacific directly or via home. However, shortly thereafter we were happily advised that we would receive thirty-day furloughs before being sent against the Japs.

On 21-22 May the 7th Armored Division relieved all elements of the 104th Division except in its assembly area in and around Halle.

ATTACHED UNITS

While the Division had operated in the European Theater many units had been attached to the 104th. Now they were released. All had played an invaluable part in our final victory, and a short account of each unit's activities is appropriate at this time.

555TH ANTIAIRCRAFT AUTOMATIC WEAPONS BATTALION (MOBILE)

The 555th Antiaircraft Battalion had been attached to the Division since October 1944. The battalion, under command of Lieutenant Colonel Robert J. Rowse until 4 December and thereafter Lieutenant Colonel Sayward H. Farnum, had served in combat with the Division

373

continuously. In its antiaircraft role it destroyed eleven enemy planes and was credited with eleven "probables," a total of twenty-two. Bridges over the Roer River had remained undamaged when the battalion defended them against twenty-seven enemy bombing runs. On thirty-four occasions the battalion had rendered close ground support to the infantry, firing over 3,192 rounds of 40mm and 298,335 rounds of caliber .50 in addition to the thousands of rounds fired in its primary function. During the rapid advance east of the Rhine, its half-tracks established effective road blocks and performed valuable guards for our convoys. The men of the Five-by-Five were the first attached troops to wear the Timberwolf patch. On 24 May it was detached from the Division.

750TH TANK BATTALION

The 750th Tank Battalion, under the command of Lieutenant Colonel John A. White, had served with the Division from 7 November 1944 to 22 May 1945, with exception of the period 21 December to 7 February 1945, when it was involved in the Ardennes. Through the bitterly contested action in the industrial cities of Stolberg, Eschweiler, Weisweiler, and the Inde River region, the tanks were a close and valued member of the Timberwolf team. Again in the forcing of the Roer and Erft Rivers and the final seizure of Cologne they had ably supported our assaults. East of the Rhine, in addition to their normal role in infantry tank teams, the battalion on several occasions, specifically in the thrusts to the Weser and the Saale Rivers, spearheaded the Division's rapid advance.

817TH TANK DESTROYER BATTALION (SELF-PROPELLED)

The 817th Tank Destroyer Battalion (SP), commanded by Lieutenant Colonel William H. Bardes, served with the Division from 31 March to 9 June. During its first three days with the Timberwolves when the Division was blocking the escape route of the large German forces trapped in the Ruhr pocket the battalion by prompt and vigorous action overran twelve strongpoints, destroyed eight machine gun nests and several self-propelled guns. During the drive to the Mulde and particularly in Halle, its action was outstanding.

87TH CHEMICAL BATTALION (4.2-INCH MORTAR)

Elements of the 87th Chemical Battalion (4.2-inch mortars), under the command of Lieutenant Colonel James Batt, had rendered effective support during the period 10 December to 22 December 1944, and

9 February to 10 May 1945. The close-in mortar barrages by these D-Day veterans many times neutralized defensive positions, enabling our advance to continue.

Many other skillfully trained units had rendered close support, namely: 692d Tank Destroyer Battalion, commanded by Lieutenant Colonel S. S. Morse—29 October to 13 March 1945; 147th (British) Tank Regiment, commanded by Lieutenant Colonel William Blaine—23 October to 7 November; 103d (British) Antitank Battery, commanded by Major W. Slater—24 October to 7 November; 784th Tank Battalion, commanded by Lieutenant Colonel George C. Dalia—31 December to 3 February 1945; Company C, 644th Tank Destroyer Battalion—21-25 March 1945; 4th Cavalry Group, commanded by Colonel John C. MacDonald—1-6 April 1945; and the 272d Infantry Regiment, commanded by Colonel Walter D. Buie—1-6 May 1945.

Colonel Robert Erlenkotter's 1106th Engineer Group, 9 November to 15 December 1944 and 5 February to 7 March 1945; Colonel John D. Schemerhorn's 1120th Engineer Group, 21 March to 9 May 1945; and Colonel Hodge's 1115th Engineer Group, 15 December 1944 to 5 February 1945, had provided excellent engineer support.

Many field artillery battalions had supported our infantry advances and reinforced the fires of our Division artillery, including:

68th (British) Medium Artillery Regiment.
188th (British) Field Artillery Battalion.
987th (British) Field Artillery Battalion.
87th (British) Armored Field Artillery Battalion.
65th Armored Field Artillery Battalion.
957th Field Artillery Battalion.
283d Field Artillery Battalion.
802d Field Artillery Battalion.
981st Field Artillery Battalion.
13th Forward Observation Battalion (elements).
991st Field Artillery Battalion (elements).
142d Field Artillery Group.

Close air support by fighter-bombers had been furnished by: Fighter-bomber elements of the Royal Air Force, 23 October to 7 November 1944; 365th Fighter Group, IX Tactical Air Command—16 November to 21 December 1944 and 6 February to 9 May 1945; 36th Fighter Group, XXIX Tactical Air Command—21 December to 6 February 1945.

The Division had served most of its period in combat under the VII Corps, commanded by Lieutenant General J. Lawton Collins. The 104th was directed by the following Armies and Corps in its combat operations:

First United States Army—8 November 1944 to 21 December 1944 and 6 February to 6 May 1945.

First Canadian Army—21 October to 8 November 1944.

Ninth United States Army—7 September to 7 November 1944, 21 December 1944 to 6 February 1945, and 6 May to June 1945.

VII Corps—8 November 1944 to 21 December 1944 and 6 February to June 1945.

I British Corps—21 October to 8 November 1944.

XIX Corps—21 December 1944 to 6 February 1945.

III Corps—7 September to 21 October 1944.

That we were going to the Pacific became more certain each day as we read the headlines of U. S. newspapers, "MEN FROM ETO EN ROUTE TO PACIFIC." In our training, emphasis was placed on indoctrination on the Jap soldier, physical conditioning, discipline, scouting and patrolling, mines and night fighting. Our night attacks had worked against the Germans, enabling us to seize objectives quickly with a minimum loss to ourselves. We were now preparing to fight the Jap at night.

All new reinforcements received training at the Timberwolf Reinforcement Training Center, located in the large airport at Halle. On 28 May the last class of 275 men graduated, with a colorful ceremony that included a parade and short talks by General Allen and General Lanham. The front line combat training program for all reinforcements had done much to prepare the men for their entry into combat. Lieutenant Ray Williams, one of the combat veteran instructors, puts it this way: "If we can tell a man how to protect himself, we have done a great deal, and if we save the life of one man then all our work has been worthwhile."

Prior to the release of the three Negro platoons which had joined the Division in March, a presentation ceremony was held for them on 27 May. Brigadier General Benjamin O. Davis congratulated the colored troops who had fought with the Timberwolves: "You have proven white and Negro troops can serve—and fight side by side. You have won the respect and friendship of your comrades." General Allen also expressed his appreciation for the heroic services and excellent combat record of the Negro Timberwolves. The Division commander decorated two men with the Silver Star award and ten with the Bronze Star.

The latter part of May the Division was directed to send to the United States twenty officers to receive amphibious training. Combat in the Pacific drew closer.

Brigadier General Charles K. Gailey succeeded General Lanham as assistant Division commander on 10 June 1945.

ON THE WAY

On 11 June the Division began its movement from Germany to Camp Lucky Strike near Dieppe, twenty-five miles northeast of Le Havre, France. Mounting "40 and 8's" in Leipzig, all troops of the Division moved by rail, 11-14 June, closing at the new destination on 19 June. Private Chalk of A Company, 329th Engineers, tells of the fine job the engineers, quartermasters and the band performed to facilitate the departure from Leipzig:

While attempts at glamorizing the infantry have proved rather fruitless, since no dirty job is ever glamorous, the large amount of publicity has brought the Queen of Battles into the limelight. But this is not the case with the combat engineers. In the more dangerous jobs, the only thanks given them comes from some footslogger who is glad to set a dry foot on what was an enemy-held river bank or walk unafraid through a deactivated minefield. In most cases that thanks is more than sufficient.

This then, was another thankless task. While there was no danger, except for bruised thumbs, it was a job that required ingenuity, foresight, and as usual, sweat. Another job for the engineers, and another opportunity to learn a trade.

The Division was to enter and leave Leipzig in three days. To accomplish this the engineers, the quartermasters and the band set up headquarters near the terminal one day prior to the arrival of the other units. The job of dispatching and loading the Division artillery was given to C Company. Company A was to secure the stoves, build tables and hangers for the kitchen cars, and attempt to make the "40 and 8's" as comfortable as possible. The QM boys were to provision the kitchen cars for the trip across Germany and France and the Division band was to send the boys off with martial music. When the brass wasn't looking they slipped in a few hot licks.

Company A's method for accomplishing this task was to work each of the three line platoons on a twenty-four hour shift. At night the work was done with the aid of flashlights and candles. The materials were gathered from several unhappy German lumbermen, who we shall assume eventually were paid.

Some previous work had been done, but due to playful German urchins between the ages of nineteen and thirty, and the laxity of the Belgian guards, everything was torn up and had to be reconstructed. The rain also dampened the spirits of the men.

In their off-time the various platoons conducted interesting and educational experiments in German folklore. The Division band, grateful for the appreciative engineer audience, presented a private concert outside of the schoolhouse used by the Hairy-Ears for a barracks. The music was so inspiring, a lovely German lass of eighty summers accomplished amazing terpischorean feats. Dozens of German children applauded the band's performance.

That was the lighter side. The work continued for three days. The hammering, the wiring, the chaining progressed rapidly, and all trains departed on time. The engineers boarded the last train and started on the first lap of their journey home. Once again they had been the first to arrive and the last to leave.

Sergeant John Cantwell, Headquarters, 2d Battalion, 415th Infantry, testifies that on the rail trip to France:

They must have been building the track in front of us! That train moved the way the Burlington Zephyr does not—about 700 miles in five days. We rode in the French boxcars—the old "40 and 8" variety. But it wasn't bad because there was room for most of us to stretch out in our sacks at night and sleep; all except the last two guys to turn in. They had to sleep sitting up. Only two meals a day, but there was plenty to eat both times, and at every meal the train pulled off on a siding for a two-hour break. That gave us a chance to get a helmet full of hot water from the locomotive and wash up.

Our route toward Le Havre swung south of the part of Germany we'd advanced across. We went through Weimar and Frankfurt and crossed the Rhine at Mainz. And every freight train we passed was loaded with hundreds of German soldiers bumming home. German women and kids peddled bottles of wine to us for rations and cigarettes when our train stopped. And sometimes a trainload of Russians passed us heading east, their boxcars gayly decorated with tree branches and the hammer and sickle of the USSR.

When we crossed the French border we all yelled like hell at the first French girl we saw. The end of non-fraternization. We saw the big pillboxes in the Maginot Line, about twice the size of those we had experienced in the Siegfried Line. Then we went through Metz and Rheims. The deeper we went into France the easier it was to sell pistols and cameras to the GI's stationed along the rail.

Lucky Strike was windy and dusty and plenty cool at night, but home wasn't far off. Final POM checks, including packing and listing of all arms and personal property, movies and marching occupied our time while at Lucky Strike. Sergeant Weaver, of the engineers, recalls:

None of us really knew what to expect at Lucky Strike, but when the camp came in sight we all had a sort of let-down feeling. Lucky Strike was very definitely a temporary camp. There were seemingly millions of five-man tents, all in neat, orderly rows, with absolutely no trees near enough to offer any relief from the sun. We marched by the kitchens and got our first view of the life of a PW in the rear areas. They used PW's for cooks, KP's, and for every other menial job around the kitchen. That made a lot of us think not so long ago some of these guys were tossing mortar shells at us, and now they were tossing chow at us.

Finally we were assigned to our tent and told to be prepared for a full-field and rifle inspection before turning in our rifles and web equipment, and not to go out of the company area.

Everyone you ask says that an Army moves on its stomach, but the only people who never learn this are the cooks. Since we had PW's for cooks we were all firmly convinced that the German soldier must have griped just as much as we did about his food. The stuff we were told was coffee must have been some concoction of sulphuric acid and vinegar. As for the main course, the Army again lived up to its usual procedure and offered us at least twice a day, beans; and when they ran out of menus printed in English, beans came three times a day.

Our days were spent in either trying to get a sun tan, fighting the doughnut line at the Red Cross Club, or up at the supply tent trying to beat the supply sergeant out of an extra blanket. Whenever one felt lucky, a poker or crap game was started, and the winner wound up with a pocket-full of francs, guilders, marks, and pounds. After two or three days of waiting we were finally called to the supply tent to draw our ETO jackets. This proved to be a mad scramble, each one trying to get a strangle-hold on as many jackets of different sizes as possible, to insure getting one that didn't resemble a zoot affair with a drape shape.

There was one outstanding feature of entertainment at Lucky Strike. It was a show composed of French girls and actors. None of the girls had legs that could compare with Grable nor were the actors very talented, but nevertheless the laughs were plentiful. The biggest laugh of the whole show came when the chorus came on stage greeted by a bombardment of GI balloons.

When we felt that we had accumulated enough dirt to warrant a shower, we would go to the local Turkish bath. This noted establishment was owned and operated by the quartermaster. Here was a place where consistency was unknown, for after you had used every trick learned from the "Kill or Be Killed" movies to get in, the water was either freezing or boiling. These tents were so crowded that if you forgot your soap you had only to fight your way from one end to the other, find a trickle of water, and emerge glistening with cleanliness.

The usual business executive had invaded the Red Cross tent and had tacked notices on the bulletin boards advising all to invest in good souvenirs—everything from fur coats from Aachen to address books of portable frauleins in Halle.

Finally the big day arrived. Everyone had his ETO jacket on, his combat boots shined, and we were lined up according to rank. The first sergeant called the roll and we were told that if we moved out of the area it was just our tough luck. He reminded us of the night before, when the Articles of War had been read to us, and told us that anyone who went over the hill now would be considered a deserter and would be accused of shirking hazardous duty. And we were going home for a thirty-day furlough!

At the end of the required time allocated by the Army for waiting, our trucks arrived and we piled aboard. They were big eight-ton trailer trucks and the driver must have learned to drive on the Red Ball. The lead truck seemed to be running interference for the convoy and ran a jeep, three carts, and two bicycles off the road.

When we entered Le Havre it seemed just like any other French town, but while riding around trying to find the right road to the dock we passed the section of the city that had been leveled by Allied bombing. When our trucks stopped we found ourselves at the docks, and there to our right was the S.S. *Monterey*, the ship that was to begin our last stage of the journey home. Everyone was happy, but back in our minds was the everlasting memory of all that had happened since that day exactly ten months ago when we had been in the same position on the other side of the Atlantic. One job was done, and we were thankful. But though we were happily anxious to be on our way, we all had a feeling of anxiety about what was to come.

The Division embarked for the United States on two ships, the S.S. *Monterey* sailing 26 June and the S.S. *Ericsson* on 2 July. We left behind us an official combat record second to none. During the 195 consecutive days of combat the Timberwolves had inflicted over 18,000 casualties, in killed and wounded, upon the enemy; captured over 2,000 towns and communities, including the great cities of Cologne, Eschweiler and Halle; had taken 51,724 German prisoners, including four generals, 1,301 officers, 5,397 non-commissioned officers, and 45,022 other soldiers. In clearing over 8,000 square miles of Belgium, Holland, and Germany, the 104th Division had left behind 1,447 comrades, whose supreme sacrifices on the battlefield had contributed so materially to our success. In addition, 4,776 had been wounded and seventy-six were reported missing in action. We had finished a hard, grim fight and had played a vital role in crushing Naziism in Europe. The tenacity, skill, teamwork and devotion to duty of the hard-hitting infantrymen and all combat, service and administrative personnel characterized our combat operations.

Large quantities of supplies had been consumed during the operations. Our vehicles had used 2,100,000 gallons of gasoline, our signalmen had laid 6,901 miles of telephone wire, and 31,200,000 pounds of ammunition had been expended (15,600 tons).

Type of Ammunition	No. Rounds	No. Tons
Carbine	1,138,745	20
Cal. .30, Rifle and MG	6,992,270	249
Cal. .45	852,283	21
Cal. .50	697,878	107
37mm Gun	2,717	7
40mm Gun	11,031	40
57mm Gun	7,629	77
60mm Mortar	101,221	289
75mm Gun	14,269	192
76mm Gun	6,067	102
3-inch Gun	25,892	535
81mm Mortar	148,101	1,008

90mm Gun	1,387	40
105mm M2, Howitzer	281,716	8,448
105mm M3, Howitzer	52,272	1,557
155mm M1, Howitzer	51,548	2,578
Mines	28,470	200
Grenades and Rockets	90,047	136
Total No. of Tons		15,600

HOME AGAIN

On 3 July the S.S. *Monterey* and on 11 July the S.S. *Ericsson* docked near the pier we had left in August 1944. The good old USA looked pretty good. With flags waving and sirens blowing, with Wac and Army bands blaring "There'll Be a Hot Time in the Old Town To-night," we were welcomed back to native soil. After a glass of ARC milk and a few doughnuts we were on our way to Camp Kilmer, New Jersey. Here we were processed and sent on our way to our various locales throughout the United States. None of the countries in Europe could compare with America. As our trains sped across the country the sky seemed bluer, the grass and trees greener, and the cities cleaner. Everywhere we went the people waved and smiled; they were glad to have us with them again. That "some day" we had hoped and prayed for had at last become a reality. William B. James of Company C, 329th Medical Battalion, puts it this way:

After processing at Camp Kilmer, I started my journey home. Being on the last train to leave the camp at any other time would have been cause to gripe. Not now though.

Arriving home, I found things much the same as when I left. Mom—Dad, a little older. Not much though—they looked fine to me. Little brother wasn't "Little Brother" any more. We talked that night—no one could possibly sleep. We spoke of so many foolish things. I experienced a rather awkward feeling—hardly knowing what to say. The sensation seemed mutual. Just being near those I held dear seemed to satisfy all the months-old hunger in my heart. I had thirty days to iron out the rough spots. There was a lot to do. . . . Look up my old friends, see the town, do all the things that I had planned to do for months.

It's easy to fall back in the old swing of things. The family couldn't do enough to please me. Parents are funny that way! Mom tried to overfeed me, and I didn't object. She did a very thorough job of it, believe me! Going to the stadium, window shopping for civilian clothes, taking in the local Saturday Nite Hop; all little unimportant things to anyone else—but it was everything to me. It was home.

The end of the war with Japan brought more serious thoughts to my mind. I hadn't given "going to Japan" much thought before then. My thoughts had been focused to a thirty-day period and not beyond. When V-J Day came it

Home

brought new light on the subject. We were scheduled to go—will we still go? If so, maybe I won't have to stay long. I had plans to fulfill when I was released from the Army. Getting married and having a home was the most important. But if I were to go, then I was ready . . . let's get it over with. Thoughts of me in civilian clothes might materialize sooner than I had expected a month before.

Like all good things, my furlough came to an end. Thirty of the most wonderful days in my life. It seemed as if it had hardly started. Unforgettable—everything I had fought for was in evidence. Leaving had one consolation—I'll be coming back again—this time to stay.

Finale

The Division advance parties reassembled at Camp San Luis Obispo, California, midway between Los Angeles and San Francisco, the first week in August 1945. Shortly thereafter the officers and men began to arrive from their separation centers, to which they had reported after their thirty-day leaves and furloughs.

Scheduled for early combat in the Pacific, the Division went into an intensive training program. On 20 August 1945, when one-half of the

Division had closed in its new camp, the training was renewed. Besides refresher training with weapons, night attacks, Japanese tactics, and scouting and patrolling, the Timberwolves began to singe the California hillsides with flamethrowers. Cooks and drivers went to specialist schools, the medics prepared conferences on tropical diseases; equipment was drawn and the units were preparing themselves for combat against the Nip.

Suddenly, and without warning, the first atomic bomb was dropped on Hiroshima on 5 August 1945. Then a second one fell on Nagasaki, 9 August 1945.

At the Potsdam Conference on 26 July 1945, the President of the United States and the Prime Minister of England had issued an ultimatum to the Japanese forces to surrender or face destruction. Coupled with the second demonstration of Allied atomic power, the Russian Armies were released against the Nips, and in three days had smashed 190 miles into Manchuria.

On 15 August 1945 in General MacArthur's communique came the most welcome news in four years: "Japan Surrenders." The President of the United States on 2 September 1945 announced V-J Day; World War II had ended. Throughout the country millions of Americans wildly acclaimed Japan's capitulation. The Timberwolves were happy that the war had finally ended; however, our order for movement to the Pacific area had not been rescinded. Sergeant Melvin A. Ulrich of Company D, 329th Medical Battalion, expressed our collective feelings:

I was glad the war had finally ended; we are heading for Japan, and it sure helps a lot to know there would not be any more torn-up bodies that would have to be taken care of. I saw too much blood in Europe. I didn't want to see any more in the Pacific. V-J Day meant a lot to all of us.

The entire Division had closed at Camp San Luis Obispo by 29 August. While the war had officially ended, the Timberwolves were still scheduled to proceed to the Pacific for occupational duties. Then came the official announcement by General MacArthur that he would not need any more infantry divisions, and on 30 August official word was received by the Division from higher headquarters that the Timberwolves would not be needed in the Pacific.

During the next six weeks the "Battle of Points" was on. Discharge scores were constantly lowered, the regular military training schedules were amended, and the high-point men were being discharged daily. Specialist teams visited all units for conferences on employment, insurance, investments and education. A battle slogan of the Timberwolves overseas was "Find 'em, Fix 'em, Fight 'em,"—the peacetime slogan

HOLLYWOOD COMES TO CAMP SAN LUIS OBISPO

became, "Know what you want, Know how to get it, Get it." All that was needed was "points" . . . things were rapidly assuming the proportions of a housewife attempting to juggle her rationing coupons.

The daily one-hour classes in various commercial and mechanical subjects, and on the provisions of the GI Bill of Rights, prepared us for civilian life. Timberwolves also attended night schools in San Luis Obispo.

Shot 'n' Shell, official Timberwolf organ at Camp San Luis Obispo, headlined some of the fine USO camp shows that came on from Hollywood to entertain the Division.

JOE E. BROWN BRINGS HOLLYWOOD SHOW HERE SUNDAY AFTERNOON

FRANK MCHUGH HEADS AMPHITHEATRE SHOW THIS AFTERNOON

STRICTLY TERRIFIC WAS THE BOB HOPE SHOW

Also among the notables appearing in the picturesque Ol' Mission Amphitheatre on the camp grounds were Bette Davis, Eddie Bracken, Bob Alda, Arthur Treacher, Frances Langford, Jerry Colonna and Jack Carson. They all brought us back in memory to La Dietrich appearing in her home town of Stolberg and Lily Pons amid Cologne's devastation.

Organized athletics was prominent on our schedules, culminating with the 414th Mountaineers capturing the baseball championship in a hot race with the 413th Seagulls; the Antitank Company of the 415th winning the Division softball title; 413th taking the volleyball crown and also becoming basketball champs.

By direction of the President, a Bronze Oak Leaf Cluster for the Distinguished Service Medal, for exceptionally meritorious and distinguished services in the performance of duties of great responsibility, was awarded to General Allen by the War Department under provisions of the Act of Congress, approved 9 July 1918:

Major General Terry de la M. Allen served with distinction in the highly responsible position of Commanding General, 104th Infantry Division, from 7 November 1944 to 21 April 1945, in Germany. The superb accomplishments of the 104th Infantry Division during the drive to the Roer River, the crossing of the Rhine, and the deep penetration of Germany reflect the consummate tactical skill, inspiring leadership, and great capacity of General Allen. Starting the campaign as a relatively untried division, his command became a superb assault organization, fully demonstrating its ability to accomplish the most difficult missions. The aggressive leadership and sound military judgment displayed by General Allen contributed materially to the defeat of the enemy and reflected great credit upon himself and the Armed Forces.

The Timberwolves were much in demand for parades and community holidays. Convoys carried the 104th men several times to San Francisco, San Luis Obispo, Paso Robles and other cities along the coast.

In October the 413th made a clean sweep in the Division championship firing matches, garnering first place in the carbine, rifle and pistol team matches. The winning carbine team:

> Staff Sergeant Norman H. Filbert
> Staff Sergeant Cole W. Thompson
> Sergeant Samuel E. Holloway
> Sergeant Vernon S. Cheever
> Pfc. Henry C. Grodt
> Pfc. Sanchez Sandalio

The winning M-1 rifle team:

> Staff Sergeant Ernest G. Shafferman
> Staff Sergeant Cole W. Thompson
> Sergeant Edwin H. Lyons
> Sergeant Gene Hawley
> Pfc. David Harris
> Pfc. D. R. Parker

The winning pistol team:

> Pfc. Thomas Scott
> Sergeant Robert Landis
> Pfc. Henry Hall
> Pfc. Edward Rishel
> Private James Johnston
> Pfc. Paul Barger

In individual competition, Pfc. John D. Snyder of the 415th won the high score 187 with the carbine; Staff Sergeant Ernest C. Shafferman of the 413th won the high score 193 for the M-1; and Staff Sergeant Richard J. Jahries of the 386th Field Artillery won the pistol title with 87%.

On 15 September 1945, the 104th Infantry Division on its third birthday passed in final review before its commander, Major General Terry Allen. Over 5,000 friends of the Timberwolves gathered to see the fighting men in their final formation.

THOUSANDS THRILLED BY REVIEW OF 104TH INFANTRYMEN
By Elliot Curry

San Luis Obispo, California, *Telegram-Tribune*
Sept. 15, 1945.

A proud general took the salute of a fighting division this morning at Camp San Luis Obispo when 14,000 men of the 104th passed in review before General Terry Allen.

The gates of the camp were thrown open to the public for the occasion, which may well be the last great military spectacle here of World War II days. Thousands of spectators filled the temporary bleachers and lined the parade ground as the sun came through a late morning fog to glisten on the flags of the Timberwolves.

Third Anniversary

It was the third anniversary of the Division and was made the occasion for presentation of high honors to eight men of the 104th. They were:

Lt. Cecil H. Bolton, Huntsville, Ala., Congressional Medal of Honor. In this case the citation is read but the medal is not presented.

Col. Gerald C. Kelleher, Albany, N. Y., commanding officer, 414th Infantry Regiment, Distinguished Service Order, a British decoration.

T-Sgt. Henry A. Malone, Experiment, Ga., Distinguished Service Cross.

Maj. Francis J. Hallahan, 1st Bn. Executive Officer, 415th Infantry, Richmond Hill, N. Y., British Military Cross.

Maj. Marshall B. Garth, commanding officer, 2d Bn., 413th Infantry, Modesto, Calif., British Military Cross.

Sgt. Jessie M. Barnett, Montpelier, La., British Military Medal.

Col. B. R. DeGraff, Durham, N. H., Legion of Merit.

S-Sgt. Anthony Schukes, Rhodes General Hospital, Utica, N. Y., British Distinguished Conduct Medal.

Troops Assemble

The review opened with the formation of the troops on the parade ground after which General Allen riding in a jeep, passed slowly down the lines. Returning to the reviewing stand, he presented the decorations and made a short address.

As the band played and scores of cameras went into action, the troops passed the reviewing stand.

It was an impressive, rugged military display. No planes roared overhead. No tanks thundered along the line. No mighty machines of war took part. This review was for the men who dug foxholes and fought through mud and water up to their necks. The Timberwolves are not a fancy outfit—just a bunch of guys who went through hell in 195 days of combat with the Nazis and helped to win a war.

Gen. Allen told the history of the Division from its activation on Sept. 15, 1942, at Camp Adair, Ore., through its training and fighting days.

Gen. Allen reflected the pride and spirit of the 104th as he stood at attention, his helmet slightly over one ear in true American fashion, and it was evident that the infantry was proud of their commander.

"Gee," said one, as the commander finished speaking, "did you hear that? The old man had a lump in his throat."

Veteran Timberwolves parade in San Francisco

The last parade brought memories to those men who marched past the reviewing stand that day—to those men who filed by a like reviewing stand mired in Oregon soil three years before. There weren't too many of the old Wolves left, but those who were must have held thoughts that matched the memories of Sergeant Fred Tares, Pfc. Ray Bernd and Pfc. Roy Wittemore, all of I Company, 414th Infantry:

We were cut from the original Timberwolf die. Since our first review in Adair, we have tramped many a weary mile. In the course of all our wanderings we participated in three Division reviews.

We first gathered together as raw recruits, during the fall of forty-two. That initial one wasn't the best—by far the worst. We worked for hours preparing our gear; shined shoes, scrubbed web equipment, polished brass, had haircuts and shaves. We were all ready to go—and so was the rain. The smooth parade ground was transformed into a sea of mud. We were formed at the strike of the band—we stepped off—some never stepped any further, but bogged down in the churning mass. When the battalion passed in review, we slid past at eyes right. Those of you who have ever done a left flank while skidding, and at the same time keeping your piece straight, chin in, eyes off the ground—you alone can appreciate our experience.

Our next review was several months later in Carson. We had endured several months of maneuvers, and if you think combat was rough, try to remember Palen Pass. We weren't garrison troops any more—we were field soldiers. It was hot that day. And those heavy OD blouses. . . . Some of us went so far as to pray for that Oregon mist. Men fell this time too, but from the relentless beat of ol' Sol. We looked great passing in review. No other parade ever equalled that one. It was definitely our day.

San Luis was our final parade. It wasn't the same, somehow. The ranks, though full, to us seemed ghostly—too many oldtimers were missing. We had lost a lot of good men on the way. The new replacements marched well, they covered down, they snapped eyes right, but they weren't the original Timber-

414th Mountaineers, 1945 Division Baseball Champions. Rear row, left to right: Sergeant Edward Guttiers, Pfc James French, Pfc William Cahill, Lieutenant R. Patterson, Sergeant Sloat, Sergeant H. Pierce, Pfc Joe Widak, Staff Sergeant Charles Griffith. Front row, left to right: Pfc Westley Wyrkowski, Technical Sergeant B. Good, Colonel Kelleher, Major General Allen, Staff Sergeant Joe Dobson, Corporal Lewis

wolves—they were intruders in our ranks. That is a vain and selfish attitude—but somehow our deep pride told us that that one at Carson was the *"one."*

In final tribute to the men of his Division, General Allen spoke:

The battle accomplishments of the Timberwolf Division are a matter of official record of which you and your friends and relatives may well be proud. Your combat operations have been characterized by the tenacity, skill, teamwork and devotion to duty of all combat and service elements and by the efficient functioning of all staff sections. The devotion to duty of the service and administrative sections of the Division have contributed materially to the success of the combat units.

In building up the combat efficiency of the Division through many months of arduous training, you have adhered to the four primary objectives of our training: discipline, which involves alertness, cheerful response to orders and directives and unselfish teamwork by all concerned; training, which involves the close application of the most painstaking effort to be experts in the technique of modern battle; physical fitness; and, above all, an intensive belief in your units. In this last item, particularly, our Division has been most outstanding as we all feel completely assured that we are second to none as an American combat unit. The same application of these principles will be equally effective to all of you when the Division is demobilized and you return to civilian pursuits.

We pay tribute to our gallant dead, whose sacrifices made on the battlefield have contributed so materially to our eventual success.

In closing, I wish to express my personal thanks and gratitude to all of you for your unfailing loyal support at all times and particularly during six and a half months of arduous combat. You have lived up to our battle slogan, "NOTHING IN HELL CAN STOP THE TIMBERWOLVES," and . . . NOTHING IN HELL *DID* STOP THE TIMBERWOLVES.

The War Department ordered the inactivation of the 104th Infantry Division effective 20 December 1945. Its mission in World War II had been accomplished.

HEADQUARTERS ARMY GROUND FORCES
OFFICE OF THE COMMANDING GENERAL
WASHINGTON 25, D. C.

20 October 1945

SUBJECT: Letter of Appreciation
    TO: Commanding General, 104th Infantry Division

Our country can ask no more of her people than that they risk their lives in battle in her name. In return, she can never hope to compensate them for their sacrifices and hardships, but she will give to them always her gratitude and esteem. Such is the heartfelt reward which the officers and men of the Timberwolf Division have received from a grateful nation, which feels all too well the inadequacy of its giving.

From its activation in September 1942 in Oregon, during its training in Oregon, California and Colorado, and throughout its brilliant career in combat to its inactivation at the present time, the 104th Infantry Division has always conducted itself in keeping with the finest traditions of our history. After your arrival in Europe early in the fall of 1944, you fought initially in Holland, spearheading the drive to the Maas River. With almost no rest, you turned from this bitter campaign to the struggle for the Roer River line. In February 1945 you crossed the river and swept irresistibly to Cologne. Once over the Rhine, the 104th raced first to Paderborn, then to the Mulde, where contact was made with the Russian Army as the war ended. Your Division had completed its arduous battle assignments with honor and distinction.

Those of you who must now, on your inactivation, receive new tasks will, I am sure, execute them with the same self-reliance, initiative, and loyalty which have become a part of your tradition, until the need for a large Army has passed.

All Americans join me in commending you, with all our hearts, for your heroic contribution to the cause of our country.

/s/ JACOB L. DEVERS
General, USA,
Commanding

APPENDIX 1

THE VALIANT DEAD

The names listed below are a sacred trust in the annals of the 104th Infantry Division. They are our honored dead.

KILLED IN ACTION

Abbott, Sylvester NMI (329th Engr.)
Abrahamsen, Guy O. (415th Inf.)
Achison, Harry NMI (413th Inf.)
Ackerman, Albert L. Jr. (414th Inf.)
Acosta, Roque G. (414th Inf.)
Adams, Graydon L. (413th Inf.)
Adams, William H. (414th Inf.)
Addante, Joe NMI (415th Inf.)
Adkins, John P. (414th Inf.)
Agabo, Joe NMI (414th Inf.)
Agna, Reginald A. (413th Inf.)
Alcantar, Max L. (415th Inf.)
Alemian, Sooren M. (413th Inf.)
Alexander, Russell W. (415th Inf.)
Alford, Jack H. (929th FA)
Alio, Salvatore J. (413th Inf.)
Alioto, John NMI (415th Inf.)
Allen, A. J. (414th Inf.)
Allen, Clark B. Jr. (414th Inf.)
Allen, Jack G. (415th Inf.)
Allen, Roy H. (414th Inf.)
Allgeyer, Thomas R. (414th Inf.)
Allison, John T. Jr. (413th Inf.)
Alloway, Earl L. (413th Inf.)
Alumbaugh, Emmett L. (413th Inf.)
Amolini, Leo J. (413th Inf.)
Anderson, Clayborn E. (414th Inf.)
Anderson, John W. (415th Inf.)
Anderson, Kenneth P. (413th Inf.)
Anderson, Lester E. (929th FA)
Anderson, Wallace K. (413th Inf.)
Andrews, Clifton N. (413th Inf.)
Andrews, Donald R. (415th Inf.)
Angelica, Mike T. (415th Inf.)
Angell, L. C. (414th Inf.)
Anglin, Wayburn F. (415th Inf.)
Antone, Alonzo NMI (413th Inf.)
Aquino, Dominic E. (414th Inf.)
Armen, Albert NMI (413th Inf.)
Arnaiz, Abraham NMI (415th Inf.)
Aronson, Julius NMI (414th Inf.)

Ashby, LeRoy NMI (415th Inf.)
Atkins, Donald L. (414th Inf.)
Atkinson, Loren E. (415th Inf.)
Atkisson, John C. (414th Inf.)
Auerbach, Alfred M. (415th Inf.)
Ault, William R. (413th Inf.)
Ayze, Earl C. (414th Inf.)
Bachinski, Joseph L. (414th Inf.)
Back, Aubrey G. (415th Inf.)
Bagby, Paul D. (414th Inf.)
Baird, Ralph W. (413th Inf.)
Baker, Chester C. (414th Inf.)
Baker, Jack W. (413th Inf.)
Baker, Robert L. (414th Inf.)
Bakken, Kenneth L. (414th Inf.)
Baldridge, Jack B. (413th Inf.)
Baldwin, Allan G. (415th Inf.)
Bales, Elwood E. Jr. (414th Inf.)
Bales, Thomas S. (929th FA)
Baratz, Sol NMI (413th Inf.)
Barker, Robert F. (104th Sig. Co.)
Barlovic, Albert Jr. (413th Inf.)
Barnard, Norris C. Jr. (414th Inf.)
Barnes, Samuel D. (414th Inf.)
Barnett, Jesse W. (415th Inf.)
Barr, Lunie F. (415th Inf.)
Barrett, Clarence D. (415th Inf.)
Barrett, Tom R. (415th Inf.)
Barron, Richard J. Jr. (414th Inf.)
Barry, Victor J. (414th Inf.)
Barshop, Milton NMI (413th Inf.)
Baskin, Sam L. (414th Inf.)
Bast, Henry B. (415th Inf.)
Bates, Robert A. (MP Plat.)
Bauer, Robert S. (413th Inf.)
Baumann, James S. (414th Inf.)
Baxter, George E. (414th Inf.)
Bayer, Arthur NMI (414th Inf.)
Becker, Isidore NMI (415th Inf.)
Becknell, Everett NMI (415th Inf.)
Becraft, Walter G. (413th Inf.)

Belcher, Adrian L. (414th Inf.)
Belfiore, Ross T. (414th Inf.)
Bell, Jack J. (414th Inf.)
Bell, James H. (413th Inf.)
Bellanger, Louis H. (415th Inf.)
Benjamin, Robert E. (414th Inf.)
Bennett, Harvey R. (414th Inf.)
Bennett, Wayne E. (413th Inf.)
Benson, George W. (413th Inf.)
Benson, Joe L. (413th Inf.)
Bentley, James R. (415th Inf.)
Berce, Aloysius J. (415th Inf.)
Berkey, George P. (415th Inf.)
Berman, Stuart NMI (415th Inf.)
Berry, Roy M. (414th Inf.)
Bertoglio, James S. (329th Med.)
Betinger, Frank C. (413th Inf.)
Betke, Henry A. (415th Inf.)
Bevan, Edmond L. (415th Inf.)
Bicker, LaVerle E. (413th Inf.)
Bijeaux, Falton NMI (415th Inf.)
Bisbey, James E. (415th Inf.)
Bisotti, Louis NMI (414th Inf.)
Bisson, Leo D. (414th Inf.)
Bjorgo, Leonard K. (415th Inf.)
Black, James L. (414th Inf.)
Black, Marshall F. (414th Inf.)
Blair, Harry M. (414th Inf.)
Blanschan, Frederick S. (414th Inf.)
Blanton, Fletcher NMI (413th Inf.)
Blanton, James B. (413th Inf.)
Blewer, William F. (413th Inf.)
Blumenthal, Robert L. (415th Inf.)
Boatright, Jasper G. (414th Inf.)
Bob, John K. (414th Inf.)
Bohman, George M. Jr. (413th Inf.)
Bohn, Donald C. (414th Inf.)
Bolechowski, Walter J. (415th Inf.)
Bolin, William T. (413th Inf.)
Boniferro, Benjamin A. (414th Inf.)
Bonkosky, Lester V. (415th Inf.)
Bonner, Leslie M. (413th Inf.)
Boone, Carroll M. (415th Inf.)
Borgner, William J. (414th Inf.)
Boss, John NMI (415th Inf.)
Bouchard, Charles W. (414th Inf.)
Bowden, Charlie D. (414th Inf.)
Bowlds, Auther R. (415th Inf.)
Bowles, Luther C. (413th Inf.)
Boyd, Alvin W. (414th Inf.)

Boyd, Edgar T. (413th Inf.)
Boyte, J. L. (414th Inf.)
Bozeman, Karon L. (413th Inf.)
Braden, William C. (415th Inf.)
Bradley, Milton W. (413th Inf.)
Bradley, Paul H. (413th Inf.)
Bradshaw, John W. (415th Inf.)
Bramel, Bruce M. (415th Inf.)
Bramlett, John T. (414th Inf.)
Brandano, James L. (413th Inf.)
Brandoline, Arthur T. (414th Inf.)
Brann, Clifford C. (415th Inf.)
Brantner, Allison O. Jr. (414th Inf.)
Brasseaux, Albert NMI (414th Inf.)
Braun, George H. (414th Inf.)
Braunstein, Irving D. (414th Inf.)
Bredeson, John R. (414th Inf.)
Breedwell, Wallace F. (413th Inf.)
Brendlinger, Davis A. (415th Inf.)
Brennan, Kenneth G. (413th Inf.)
Brenneisen, Paul NMI (329th Engr.)
Brewster, Ersel J. (413th Inf.)
Bridges, William L. (413th Inf.)
Britton, Eugene W. (414th Inf.)
Brohman, Howard E. Jr. (415th Inf.)
Brothers, Max L. (414th Inf.)
Brotzler, Lawrence E. (413th Inf.)
Brown, Bruce C. (413th Inf.)
Brown, John W. (413th Inf.)
Brown, Kie E. (413th Inf.)
Brown, Ralph M. (415th Inf.)
Brown, Robert F. (413th Inf.)
Bruce, Woodrow L. (415th Inf.)
Bruyere, Marcel NMI (415th Inf.)
Bryant, Jarrell M. (415th Inf.)
Bryant, Robert K. (415th Inf.)
Buchanan, Walter E. (414th Inf.)
Buckowski, Joseph NMI (414th Inf.)
Budraitis, George T. Jr. (415th Inf.)
Buendia, Peter C. (415th Inf.)
Bundy, Peter C. (415th Inf.)
Burge, Oscar E. (415th Inf.)
Burmis, Verlin F. (414th Inf.)
Burns, Leon NMI (414th Inf.)
Bush, Lester A. (413th Inf.)
Bush, Rowland G. (413th Inf.)
Butler, Edward D. (415th Inf.)
Cahill, William P. (414th Inf.)
Calderon, Ralph NMI (414th Inf.)
Calhoun, Forrest L. (415th Inf.)

Calvert, William J. (414th Inf.)
Calvert, William J. (414th Inf.)
Camargo, Elias R. (413th Inf.)
Cameron, Orndorff H. (415th Inf.)
Campaign, Robert D. (415th Inf.)
Campbell, Charles J. (413th Inf.)
Campbell, Frank R. (415th Inf.)
Campbell, Hugh M. (414th Inf.)
Campbell, Vincent T. (415th Inf.)
Campbell, Warner R. (414th Inf.)
Cannon, James D. (413th Inf.)
Cannone, Charles L. (414th Inf.)
Cantrell, Carl E. (329th Engr.)
Cardin, Benjamin R. (413th Inf.)
Cardon, Paul G. (414th Inf.)
Carlson, Clifford G. (414th Inf.)
Carlton, James L. (413th Inf.)
Carothers, Frank K. (414th Inf.)
Carr, Adrian B. (415th Inf.)
Carr, Byron W. (414th Inf.)
Carroll, Ralph B. (415th Inf.)
Carter, Robert A. (413th Inf.)
Carver, Cleve H. (414th Inf.)
Casner, Harold R. (413th Inf.)
Cassady, William E. (414th Inf.)
Castle, Redmond J. (414th Inf.)
Catena, Raymond M. (413th Inf.)
Causey, Rayford H. (413th Inf.)
Ceragioli, Rudolph A. (413th Inf.)
Cernan, Joseph NMI (413th Inf.)
Chambers, Ernest E. (413th Inf.)
Chapman, James J. (413th Inf.)
Chapman, Melvin L. (413th Inf.)
Charron, Gerard P. (414th Inf.)
Chavez, Edward B. (414th Inf.)
Cheney, Chester L. (414th Inf.)
Chevrette, Albert E. (414th Inf.)
Chew, Silas W. (414th Inf.)
Chico, Kee Y. (414th Inf.)
Childress, Herman R. (414th Inf.)
Christoph, Cyril N. (414th Inf.)
Clark, Atwood B. (415th Inf.)
Clark, Eugene J. (413th Inf.)
Clark, Frank W. (413th Inf.)
Clark, Howard NMI (415th Inf.)
Clark, Richard W. (415th Inf.)
Clark, Thomas C. (415th Inf.)
Cline, Robert E. (414th Inf.)
Cobb, Herchul P. (414th Inf.)
Cockerham, Emmitt R. (415th Inf.)

Coffin, Harold E. (413th Inf.)
Cohen, Charles C. (413th Inf.)
Cohen, Morton L. (414th Inf.)
Colbert, George V. (414th Inf.)
Cole, Robert A. (415th Inf.)
Coleman, Robert J. (415th Inf.)
Colley, James A. (415th Inf.)
Commean, William L. (414th Inf.)
Condit, Sherwood W. (414th Inf.)
Condos, Chris NMI (414th Inf.)
Confer, Russell W. (413th Inf.)
Conkin, Earl NMI (413th Inf.)
Conner, James F. (414th Inf.)
Conrad, Warren G. (386th FA)
Conroy, Thomas F. (414th Inf.)
Cook, Edwin E. (415th Inf.)
Cook, Roscoe D. Jr. (414th Inf.)
Cooper, Lee T. (414th Inf.)
Copley, Glen R. (415th Inf.)
Cordero, Frankie U. (414th Inf.)
Corriveau, Donald F. M. (329th Engr.)
Cottone, Jack P. (413th Inf.)
Coviello, Alexander NMI (413th Inf.)
Coviello, Rocco L. (414th Inf.)
Cowen, Robert J. (414th Inf.)
Cox, Harry B. (415th Inf.)
Cox, John P. (414th Inf.)
Coyle, Robert E. (413th Inf.)
Crabb, Raymond L. (413th Inf.)
Craig, Brown A. (415th Inf.)
Crawford, Bruce W. (415th Inf.)
Crawford, Neadie NMI (413th Inf.)
Crenshaw, Robert O (413th Inf.)
Crisp, Albert J. (329th Engr.)
Crosby, Bryce E. (414th Inf.)
Crosby, Floyd R. (804th Ord. Co)
Crosson, Laverne E. (415th Inf.)
Crowder, Richard T. (413th Inf.)
Crowley, Francis L. (414th Inf.)
Crum, Estel H. (414th Inf.)
Cummins, Joseph M. Jr. (414th Inf.)
Currey, James H. (415th Inf.)
Cusack, Leo F. (414th Inf.)
Cvicek, Tom J. (329th Med.)
Czerw, Stanley E. (413th Inf.)
Dalrymple, John P. (415th Inf.)
Danforth, Carter P. (413th Inf.)
D'Antonio, Dario D. (413th Inf.)
Dardar, Sidney F. (415th Inf.)
Davenport, Walter I. (415th Inf.)

Davidson, William L. (415th Inf.)
Davis, Fred R. (413th Inf.)
Davis, William A. (413th Inf.)
Davis, William E. (414th Inf.)
Dawsey, Jewell L. (413th Inf.)
Day, John P. (415th Inf.)
Dean, Robert G. (415th Inf.)
DeAngelo, Armando J. (415th Inf.)
DeBoer, Clifford M. (415th Inf.)
DeCook, Bernard J. (414th Inf.)
Deeter, William H. (415th Inf.)
Deloach, Robert NMI (414th Inf.)
Dench, Francis J. (414th Inf.)
Denniston, Donald W. (413th Inf.)
Denton, William C. (413th Inf.)
Derderian, John N. (415th Inf.)
DeVault, Donald C. (413th Inf.)
DeYoung, Robert G. (414th Inf.)
Dezutti, Vernon J. (415th Inf.)
Dickens, William R. (415th Inf.)
Dickerson, Thomas E. (415th Inf.)
Diedrick, John J. (414th Inf.)
Diercks, Ernest J. (413th Inf.)
Dietz, Royal O. Jr. (414th Inf.)
DiLauro, Louis P. (413th Inf.)
Dinelle, Manuel F. (413th Inf.)
Ditore, Joseph H. (414th Inf.)
Dixon, Robert J. (414th Inf.)
Doane, John NMI (413th Inf.)
Dobbie, John C. (415th Inf.)
Dolson, George H. (414th Inf.)
Donley, Robert G. (415th Inf.)
Donnelly, Glen S. (415th Inf.)
Dosier, James A. (414th Inf.)
Doster, Cecil W. (329th Engr.)
Dougherty, Howard F. (386th FA)
Doyle, James S. Jr. (385th FA)
Dragansky, Edward S. (415th Inf.)
Drake, James H. (414th Inf.)
Draveck, Orest R. (414th Inf.)
Driffill, Charles W. (414th Inf.)
Druyor, Wayne F. (413th Inf.)
Duffey, Edward L. (413th Inf.)
Dugan, Lowell E. (413th Inf.)
Duke, Starling D. (415th Inf.)
Duncan, Henry Jr. (415th Inf.)
Dunkle, Paul E. (413th Inf.)
Dunn, Walter J. (413th Inf.)
Durant, Harry W. (413th Inf.)
Durel, Warren J. (104th Sig. Co.)

Durkin, Charles T. (104th Sig. Co.)
Dwyer, Thomas F. (415th Inf.)
Dye, Willie N. (329th Engr.)
Dyer, Paul B. (415th Inf.)
Dyrdahl, John H. (413th Inf.)
Easley, Joseph M. (413th Inf.)
Eaton, George W. Jr. (415th Inf.)
Ebarb, James J. (414th Inf.)
Eberly, Alan W. (415th Inf.)
Eckert, Clarence E. (415th Inf.)
Edgecombe, Harry E. (413th Inf.)
Edwards, Plen NMI (413th Inf.)
Ehlers, Irvin F. (413th Inf.)
Eichinger, Adam J. (329th Engr.)
Eisenberg, Melvin NMI (385th FA)
Eister, Albert NMI (929th FA)
Elwell, Joseph H. (385th FA)
England, William B. (415th Inf.)
Epperson, Lyndon D. (413th Inf.)
Erickson, Aarne O. (413th Inf.)
Espinosa, Joe NMI (415th Inf.)
Esposito, Dominico T. (415th Inf.)
Eure, Sawney C. (413th Inf.)
Evancho, Peter (413th Inf.)
Evans, Albert J. Jr. (415th Inf.)
Evans, Harry G. (415th Inf.)
Eykholt, John E. (413th Inf.)
Eyler, Llewellyn C. (414th Inf.)
Fahy, Robert J. (415th Inf.)
Fair, Forrest D. (414th Inf.)
Farrell, Thomas J. (413th Inf.)
Faut, David G. (414th Inf.)
Feazell, John W. Jr. (415th Inf.)
Feher, Louis C. (415th Inf.)
Feldblum, Charles V. (414th Inf.)
Felkins, William C. Jr. (387th FA)
Felts, Joseph B. (414th Inf.)
Ferguson, Charles E. Jr. (104th Div. Band)
Fernandes, Henry M. (414th Inf.)
Ferrante, Anthony P. (415th Inf.)
Ferree, Arnold S. (415th Inf.)
Ferrel, Joseph G. (414th Inf.)
Fetzer, Herbert R. (414th Inf.)
Feuer, Philip NMI (413th Inf.)
Fiala, Joseph S. (414th Inf.)
Fiedler, Benjamin E. Jr. (415th Inf.)
Fields, Paul B. (415th Inf.)
Figuli, Samuel J. (414th Inf.)
Fike, Roy L. (414th Inf.)
Filippi, Joseph P. (414th Inf.)

Finch, Perrin L. (415th Inf.)
Finnegan, Henry H. (413th Inf.)
Flanders, Clifford A. (415th Inf.)
Fleischman, Sidney E. (414th Inf.)
Fleming, Robert G. (415th Inf.)
Flores, Telesforo NMI (413th Inf.)
Flores, Tony NMI (413th Inf.)
Flynn, Thomas J. (415th Inf.)
Folse, Wallan O. (414th Inf.)
Fortner, Kenneth J. (414th Inf.)
Fortney, Delbert H. (414th Inf.)
Fosdyck, Morris J. (414th Inf.)
Fossum, Marvin E. (415th Inf.)
Fowler, Oscar B. (413th Inf.)
Fowler, Paul F. (414th Inf.)
Francis, Arthur J. Jr. (413th Inf.)
Frank, Charles J. (413th Inf.)
Frank, Robert H. (415th Inf.)
Frank, William NMI (414th Inf.)
Frederick, Louis B. (415th Inf.)
Frederiksen, Olaf A. (414th Inf.)
Freeborn, Franklin W. (415th Inf.)
Freis, John W. (415th Inf.)
French, Phillip C. (414th Inf.)
Friberg, Alvar NMI (414th Inf.)
Frommelt, James J. (415th Inf.)
Fry, Russell L. (415th Inf.)
Fry, Woodrow NMI (414th Inf.)
Fuhlman, Ralph T. (415th Inf.)
Fulk, Willis R. (414th Inf.)
Furgason, Clifford H. (414th Inf.)
Furrow, Lawrence E. (415th Inf.)
Fyffe, Harold NMI (415th Inf.)
Gabica, Joseph NMI (415th Inf.)
Gajeski, Henry G. (415th Inf.)
Gallegos, Henry E. (415th Inf.)
Galvin, Thomas F. Jr. (414th Inf.)
Gamble, James A. (329th Med.)
Gammill, Charles H. (414th Inf.)
Gapinski, Joseph NMI (414th Inf.)
Garbarini, Charles NMI (414th Inf.)
Gardner, Everett O. (413th Inf.)
Garland, John R. (415th Inf.)
Garner, George C. (414th Inf.)
Garner, Gerald E. (329th Engr.)
Garza, Gilbert G. (414th Inf.)
Gassen, Joseph J. (413th Inf.)
Gentilella, Frank J. (414th Inf.)
George, Lloyd A. (387th FA)
George, Robert E. (413th Inf.)

Gerbasich, Paul A. Jr. (415th Inf.)
Gerrie, Eugene L. (414th Inf.)
Giambarresi, Joseph S. (329th Engr.)
Gibbs, James E. (415th Inf.)
Gil, Triunfo NMI (413th Inf.)
Gilbert, David J. W. (413th Inf.)
Gilbert, Warren L. (329th Engr.)
Gillespie, Warren B. (415th Inf.)
Giovinazzo, Salvatore M. (413th Inf.)
Glawe, Jack W. (414th Inf.)
Gleason, Lloyd E. (415th Inf.)
Goin, Dallas J. (414th Inf.)
Goldman, Melvin I. (415th Inf.)
Goldman, Sam W. (413th Inf.)
Goldstein, Morris W. (414th Inf.)
Golebiewski, Henry F. (414th Inf.)
Golleher, Henry W. (413th Inf.)
Gollender, Warren NMI (414th Inf.)
Gomez, Arnoldo NMI (415th Inf.)
Gongaware, James E. (415th Inf.)
Gonsior, Irvin A. (413th Inf.)
Goodloe, Harry F. (414th Inf.)
Goodrich, Neal J. (413th Inf.)
Goreham, Ray L. (415th Inf.)
Gorman, James R. (414th Inf.)
Gormley, Henry J. (414th Inf.)
Gougeon, Roland H. (414th Inf.)
Gough, Oliver J. (414th Inf.)
Gower, William J. (414th Inf.)
Gould, Aaron R. (414th Inf.)
Grande, Anthony B. (415th Inf.)
Graves, Elexander L. (414th Inf.)
Gray, Alvan P. (413th Inf.)
Gray, Everett C. (414th Inf.)
Gray, Robert H. (386th FA)
Grayson, Edmund K. (414th Inf.)
Grazino, Matthew C. (415th Inf.)
Grebe, Robert L. (414th Inf.)
Green, Ernest C. (414th Inf.)
Greenberg, Martin L. (104th Sig. Co.)
Greene, Rodman T. (414th Inf.)
Gregory, Alfred C. Jr. (414th Inf.)
Gregory, Deword F. (413th Inf.)
Gregory, Forrest S. (415th Inf.)
Griggs, James L. (415th Inf.)
Grogan, Carlin NMI (415th Inf.)
Gromling, Franklin L. (413th Inf.)
Groundwater, Justin J. (414th Inf.)
Guenther, William G. (414th Inf.)
Guerra, Joseph A. (414th Inf.)

Guglietta, John F. (415th Inf.)
Gulino, William J. (413th Inf.)
Gunod, Jerome J. (413th Inf.)
Gunvalson, Ervin W. (414th Inf.)
Guorn, Joseph NMI (415th Inf.)
Gustafson, Donald A. (414th Inf.)
Haas, Merle S. (415th Inf.)
Haffner, Robert P. (415th Inf.)
Hagan, William D. (415th Inf.)
Halbrook, LeRoy F. (414th Inf.)
Haley, Paul E. (413th Inf.)
Hall, Weldon W. (415th Inf.)
Hall, William L. (413th Inf.)
Halley, Edward E. (414th Inf.)
Hamilton, Justin NMI (415th Inf.)
Hammond, James L. (387th FA)
Hampton, James H. (415th Inf.)
Hancock, Donald G. (414th Inf.)
Handman, Jerome J. (414th Inf.)
Hann, Vincent R. (415th Inf.)
Hanna, Leonard L. (414th Inf.)
Hanson, Leon T. (415th Inf.)
Hanson, Robert O. (413th Inf.)
Hanson, Vern L. (413th Inf.)
Harris, Elton G. (415th Inf.)
Harris, Gilbert N. (413th Inf.)
Harris, John M. (414th Inf.)
Harris, Thomas J. (414th Inf.)
Harrison, Robert S. (415th Inf.)
Hart, George E. Jr. (413th Inf.)
Hart, Howard T. (413th Inf.)
Hartwick, Walter J. (415th Inf.)
Hassell, Cecil M. (415th Inf.)
Hastings, William G. (413th Inf.)
Hatmaker, Wilmer W. (415th Inf.)
Hawkins, Estle M. (413th Inf.)
Hawver, Biard F. (415th Inf.)
Hayes, Hugh P. (415th Inf.)
Haynes, Gordon H. Jr. (414th Inf.)
Heckerman, William S. (414th Inf.)
Hedrick, Richard L. (415th Inf.)
Held, James E. (414th Inf.)
Heller, Benjamin NMI (414th Inf.)
Helsabeck, Glenn W. (415th Inf.)
Hemlow, Charles B. (414th Inf.)
Hendricks, Robert L. (329th Engr.)
Hendrix, James E. (413th Inf.)
Henry, Cal N. (414th Inf.)
Henry, Thomas J. (413th Inf.)
Henson, John H. (413th Inf.)

Hermacinski, Ralph W. (414th Inf.)
Hernandez, Lawrence NMI (414th Inf.)
Herring, Roderick J. (415th Inf.)
Hershberger, Hubert NMI (414th Inf.)
Herzer, William A. (414th Inf.)
Hess, Clifford NMI (413th Inf.)
Hessler, Robert M. (329th Engr.)
Hewitt, Alvin M. (415th Inf.)
Heydenreich, William L. (413th Inf.)
Hibbard, Carley NMI (414th Inf.)
Hicks, John P. (413th Inf.)
Higgins, Patrick J. (413th Inf.)
Hilderbran, Donald T. (414th Inf.)
Hill, Edward G. (415th Inf.)
Hill, George F. (414th Inf.)
Hill, Roy C. (415th Inf.)
Hillebrandt, William F. (415th Inf.)
Hinck, Robert X. (413th Inf.)
Hines, Calvin C. (413th Inf.)
Hivner, Hobart B. (413th Inf.)
Hobson, Robert L. (415th Inf.)
Hodge, Everett W. (415th Inf.)
Hodge, Wilfred L. (414th Inf.)
Hodgens, Henry M. J. (415th Inf.)
Hoffman, David M. (413th Inf.)
Hoffpauir, Charles A. (413th Inf.)
Hofmeyer, Willis M. (415th Inf.)
Hogan, Edward E. (415th Inf.)
Hogan, Matthew J. (413th Inf.)
Hogan, Robert E. (413th Inf.)
Hoit, Garner C. (387th FA)
Holland, Charles E. (414th Inf.)
Holland, George E. (414th Inf.)
Holliday, Clarence W. Jr. (413th Inf.)
Hollis, James F. Jr. (413th Inf.)
Holloway, Ernest J. (415th Inf.)
Holt, Alvis J. (414th Inf.)
Hooker, Norman B. (414th Inf.)
Hooks, Ray E. (413th Inf.)
Hooper, Dale C. (415th Inf.)
Hooper, Harold W. (413th Inf.)
Hopkins, Melvin A. (413th Inf.)
Horan, Philip E. Jr. (414th Inf.)
Hord, Thomas C. (414th Inf.)
Horne, John W. (413th Inf.)
Hornyak, Michael C. (415th Inf.)
Horton, Harold J. (415th Inf.)
Horton, Walter R. Jr. (415th Inf.)
Houge, Virgil E. (413th Inf.)
Howard, Albert S. (413th Inf.)

Howard, Clifford H. (414th Inf.)
Howard, Richard G. (413th Inf.)
Hubley, John R. Jr. (413th Inf.)
Huffman, Sylvester J. (415th Inf.)
Hughes, George P. (415th Inf.)
Hughes, Jay J. (415th Inf.)
Hughes, Lealand R. (413th Inf.)
Hulin, Murphy J. (414th Inf.)
Humphrey, Paul S. (413th Inf.)
Hunsucker, Rufus V. (415th Inf.)
Hunter, Alcide J. (104th Sig. Co.)
Hunter, John G. (413th Inf.)
Huntt, Willard M. (413th Inf.)
Hura, William E. (414th Inf.)
Hurtado, Tony Z. (415th Inf.)
Husband, Thomas G. (413th Inf.)
Hutchings, Albert A. (386th FA)
Huwalt, Gerald E. (414th Inf.)
Hyde, Horace L. (414th Inf.)
Hylkema, Richard M. (413th Inf.)
Illingworth, James T. (414th Inf.)
Ingle, Yuven E. (413th Inf.)
Isaac, William B. (413th Inf.)
Ischkum, Joseph P. (414th Inf.)
Isgur, Jack NMI (413th Inf.)
Ivey, James D. (414th Inf.)
Izzo, Frank NMI (415th Inf.)
Jablonski, Joseph A. (415th Inf.)
Jablonski, Walter J. (415th Inf.)
Jackson, Albert NMI (414th Inf.)
Jackson, Bill NMI (413th Inf.)
Jackson, Charles M. (414th Inf.)
Jackson, Claude D. (413th Inf.)
Jackson, Emmitt NMI (414th Inf.)
Jackson, James W. E. (414th Inf.)
Jackson, Robert C. (414th Inf.)
Jackson, William K. (413th Inf.)
Jacobs, Earl J. (415th Inf.)
Jaffee, Irwin B. (414th Inf.)
Jager, Kenneth E. (415th Inf.)
Jakes, George W. (414th Inf.)
James, Willy F. Jr. (413th Inf.)
Jaramillo, Pablo NMI (415th Inf.)
Jaskot, Edward J. (415th Inf.)
Jay, Raymond H. (413th Inf.)
Jeavons, John NMI (415th Inf.)
Jendrzejczak, Sylvester NMI (929th FA)
Jenkins, Joe B. (413th Inf.)
Jennings, LeRoy F. (413th Inf.)
Jensen, Donald R. (415th Inf.)

Jenson, Inghart L. (414th Inf.)
Jenson, John W. (414th Inf.)
Jerzyk, Stanley G. (414th Inf.)
Joens, Harold M. (414th Inf.)
Johansen, Harold A. (414th Inf.)
Johnson, Arvel NMI (415th Inf.)
Johnson, Clayton L. (413th Inf.)
Johnson, Eugene B. (414th Inf.)
Johnson, George F. (415th Inf.)
Johnson, George O. (414th Inf.)
Johnson, Gordon S. (413th Inf.)
Johnson, Harold R. (385th FA)
Johnson, Jesse L. (385th FA)
Johnson, Lawrence C. (415th Inf.)
Johnson, Warren S. (413th Inf.)
Jonas, Ira NMI (415th Inf.)
Jones, David G. (413th Inf.)
Jones, Edmund H. (413th Inf.)
Jones, Joe B. (413th Inf.)
Jones, Leonard G. (414th Inf.)
Jones, Robert NMI (413th Inf.)
Jones, Rolfe D. (414th Inf.)
Jones, William P. (413th Inf.)
Jordan, Harold M. (414th Inf.)
Josephson, Melvin D. (413th Inf.)
Judd, Henry A. (414th Inf.)
Jundt, Lucas NMI (414th Inf.)
Jungling, Walter R. (413th Inf.)
Kachena, Joseph A. (415th Inf.)
Kaiser, Cyril P. (413th Inf.)
Kalvich, Raymond H. (415th Inf.)
Kanczuzewski, Walter A. (415th Inf.)
Kaplan, Joseph NMI (329th Engr.)
Kaplan, Victor F. (414th Inf.)
Keeler, Fred H. (413th Inf.)
Keesling, Fred E. (414th Inf.)
Kelley, John W. (414th Inf.)
Kelly, Harvey W. (413th Inf.)
Kelly, Wallace NMI (415th Inf.)
Kelly, William F. (415th Inf.)
Kempf, Aaron Jr. (414th Inf.)
Kendrew, Thomas V. (414th Inf.)
Kenyon, William J. Jr. (414th Inf.)
Kerr, James W. (414th Inf.)
Kersh, Earnest H. (414th Inf.)
Kershner, Robert L. Jr. (414th Inf.)
Keys, Frank A. (414th Inf.)
Kidder, Bennett C. (415th Inf.)
Killingsworth, Harvel R. (415th Inf.)
Kindle, George H. (413th Inf.)

King, Benjamin F. Jr. (414th Inf.)
King, James L. (415th Inf.)
King, James P. (413th Inf.)
King, Meredith S. Jr. (415th Inf.)
Kingsbury, Donald H. (414th Inf.)
Kinnison, Russel F. (415th Inf.)
Kinsky, Louis NMI Jr. (414th Inf.)
Kirk, Walter F. (386th FA)
Kirschner, Joseph A. (413th Inf.)
Kish, Carl C. (413th Inf.)
Kitchen, Eddie NMI (413th Inf.)
Klar, Sidney NMI (415th Inf.)
Klatt, Henry NMI (414th Inf.)
Klimek, William B. (415th Inf.)
Kling, Oreal P. (414th Inf.)
Kluj, Adam J. (413th Inf.)
Knaus, Frank J. Jr. (413th Inf.)
Knickerbocker, George F. (413th Inf.)
Knight, Homer E. (413th Inf.)
Knorr, Albert W. (413th Inf.)
Knudsen, Frank NMI (414th Inf.)
Kohanke, Donald A. (414th Inf.)
Kohler, James T. (414th Inf.)
Koki, Andrew NMI (415th Inf.)
Kokotoff, Howard H. (414th Inf.)
Kolar, James H. (415th Inf.)
Kolb, William A. Jr. (414th Inf.)
Kolodin, Jerome H. (415th Inf.)
Komnick, Leonard J. (415th Inf.)
Kooky, Samuel NMI (415th Inf.)
Korsnyavi, John NMI (413th Inf.)
Koscianski, Leonard J. (415th Inf.)
Koska, Henry J. (413th Inf.)
Kovala, Leslie J. (413th Inf.)
Kowertz, Ralph L. (414th Inf.)
Kratzer, Eddie NMI (413th Inf.)
Krause, Paul J. (414th Inf.)
Kronstedt, Ernest A. (415th Inf.)
Kruger, Kenneth D. (414th Inf.)
Kuchler, Charles A. (414th Inf.)
Kuebler, Christian NMI (414th Inf.)
Kulisek, Milton J. (415th Inf.)
Kumler, Paul L. (413th Inf.)
Kunes, Ivan C. (414th Inf.)
Kunofsky, Jack NMI (414th Inf.)
Kuzaroff, Stephen C. (415th Inf.)
Kyle, John A. (414th Inf.)
Laceserais, Herman H. (413th Inf.)
Lacy, Thomas S. (414th Inf.)
Lacy, Windsor H. (414th Inf.)

Ladabouch, Robert E. (413th Inf.)
Ladner, Berlin J. (413th Inf.)
Laferriere, Donat L. (414th Inf.)
Lagervall, Lewis M. (414th Inf.)
Lahey, William M. (414th Inf.)
Lamb, James A. (329th Engr.)
Lamson, LaFell R. (804th Ord. Co.)
Landrum, James J. (415th Inf.)
Landry, Leonce J. Jr. (415th Inf.)
Lane, Herbert E. (413th Inf.)
Lane, Robert E. (804th Ord. Co.)
Langlinais, Pierre E. (413th Inf.)
Langston, George E. (415th Inf.)
Lanier, Wilfred J. Jr. (415th Inf.)
Larranaga, Ambrocia M. (413th Inf.)
Lascor, George M. (415th Inf.)
Lasher, Philip K. (413th Inf.)
Laskowski, Donald M. (415th Inf.)
Lassen, Henry NMI (414th Inf.)
Latourette, Lyman T. Jr. (415th Inf.)
Laudeman, Chester J. (414th Inf.)
Laudani, Thomas J. (414th Inf.)
Laughinghouse, Edward S. (414th Inf.)
Lavine, Sanford S. (413th Inf.)
Law, George J. Jr. (414th Inf.)
Lawless, William M. (415th Inf.)
Lawrence, Charles A. (414th Inf.)
Laws, George E. (415th Inf.)
Lawson, Perry D. (414th Inf.)
Leach, Roy E. (414th Inf.)
Lebo, John F. (414th Inf.)
Ledford, William A. (414th Inf.)
Ledoux, Elphie E. (414th Inf.)
Lee, Burton L. (413th Inf.)
Lee, Hewitt D. (414th Inf.)
Lee, Julius E. (414th Inf.)
Lee, Robert C. (413th Inf.)
Lefkowitz, Bernard NMI (415th Inf.)
Legezdh, Frank Jr. (414th Inf.)
Leidy, Morris R. (413th Inf.)
Leon, Walter R. (414th Inf.)
Leonard, Jeremy NMI (415th Inf.)
Leonard, Lawrence P. Jr. (413th Inf.)
Leonhardt, Herbert A. (413th Inf.)
Leppert, Louis A. (414th Inf.)
Lettunich, Edward B. (413th Inf.)
Leum, Paul H. (414th Inf.)
Levan, Harry E. Jr. (413th Inf.)
Levin, Arthur L. (414th Inf.)
Lickel, William M. (414th Inf.)

Lidyard, Herbert NMI (413th Inf.)
Liebman, Seymour A. (415th Inf.)
Liguori, Edward J. (414th Inf.)
Linder, Charles O. Jr. (329th Engr.)
Lindsey, Wendling T. (414th Inf.)
Lindstrom, Stuart B. (415th Inf.)
Link, Winfred N. (415th Inf.)
Listvan, Adam NMI (414th Inf.)
Littrell, Leon G. (413th Inf.)
Livingston, Joseph J. Jr. (413th Inf.)
Livingston, Will J. (413th Inf.)
Lockhart, Troy W. (414th Inf.)
Loftis, William C. (415th Inf.)
Long, William D. (413th Inf.)
Lopez, Esteban C. (415th Inf.)
Lormand, Andrew NMI (414th Inf.)
Love, Matthew J. (414th Inf.)
Lovins, Paul NMI (329th Engr.)
Lowe, James W. (415th Inf.)
Lozich, Nick NMI (413th Inf.)
Luckett, James H. (413th Inf.)
Lucking, Sylvester P. (413th Inf.)
Luking, Donald P. (414th Inf.)
Lundell, Malte NMI (104th Rcn. Tr.)
Lunsford, Joe A. (414th Inf.)
Lunsford, Lonnie S. (415th Inf.)
Luonga, Anthony NMI (415th Inf.)
Luthi, Adolph MI (415th Inf.)
Lux, Louis J. (414th Inf.)
Lynch, Raymond E. (414th Inf.)
Lytle, Harold L. (415th Inf.)
Mabary, Clinton L. (415th Inf.)
Mabe, Millard E. (413th Inf.)
Machlowski, Henry NMI (415th Inf.)
Maddox, Donald W. (387th FA)
Mahlum, Norman K. (413th Inf.)
Main, Thamar J. (413th Inf.)
Malamut, Ira NMI (414th Inf.)
Mallon, Richard F. (415th Inf.)
Mallow, Robert E. (414th Inf.)
Manning, George P. (413th Inf.)
Maraszkiewicz, Paul J. (329th Med.)
March, William M. (414th Inf.)
Marchal, Harould J. (414th Inf.)
Margul, Louis NMI (414th Inf.)
Marino, Paul F. (415th Inf.)
Marshall, John NMI (414th Inf.)
Martin, Elmer L. (415th Inf.)
Martin, Gettys M. (414th Inf.)
Martin, Raymond I. (415th Inf.)

Martinell, Robert B. (413th Inf.)
Martinez, Amador NMI Jr. (414th Inf.)
Martinez, Candelario F. (415th Inf.)
Martinez, John NMI (415th Inf.)
Martinez, Jose L. (413th Inf.)
Martinez, Joseph M. (415th Inf.)
Martinez, Nicholas M. (414th Inf.)
Mask, Merrell C. (414th Inf.)
Massad, Nicholas F. (414th Inf.)
Matteson, Robert L. (414th Inf.)
Matthews, James M. (414th Inf.)
Matthiessen, Hermann R. (104th Sig. Co.)
Mattingly, Herbert T. (414th Inf.)
Maus, Bernard NMI (414th Inf.)
Mayer, Wilbert J. (415th Inf.)
Mays, Richard A. (413th Inf.)
Mazurek, Julian J. (414th Inf.)
Mazzei, Louis NMI (414th Inf.)
McAninch, Clyde E. (414th Inf.)
McCabe, John D. (415th Inf.)
McCain, Kenneth M. (413th Inf.)
McCann, Daniel F. (415th Inf.)
McChesney, Charles R. (415th Inf.)
McCloud, Thomas J. (929th FA)
McCluskey, Harold M. (414th Inf.)
McCreary, James W. (413th Inf.)
McCullough, Charles V. (414th Inf.)
McCurdy, Gerald E. (414th Inf.)
McDonald, James R. (415th Inf.)
McElroy, Charles D. (414th Inf.)
McFall, Howard F. Jr. (414th Inf.)
McGaw, Walter C. (414th Inf.)
McGoldrick, Thomas J. (414th Inf.)
McGrath, Eugene E. (414th Inf.)
McGuigan, William C. (413th Inf.)
McGuire, Denis J. (414th Inf.)
McGuire, Joseph P. (415th Inf.)
McKerney, Bernard F. (415th Inf.)
McKillip, Leslie H. (413th Inf.)
McKinley, David S. (104th Sig. Co.)
McKinley, John R. (413th Inf.)
McKinney, Robert L. (415th Inf.)
McLellan, Reginald W. (415th Inf.)
McLeod, William T. (413th Inf.)
McManus, George A. Jr. (413th Inf.)
McNeal, David D. (413th Inf.)
McNutt, Carl R. (414th Inf.)
McPheron, Clyde V. (413th Inf.)
McQueen, David R. (413th Inf.)
Meader, John R. Jr. (413th Inf.)

Meadows, Dixie NMI (415th Inf.)
Meadows, Johnie J. (415th Inf.)
Meier, John A. (413th Inf.)
Melidones, Spiro C. (415th Inf.)
Melquist, John H. (413th Inf.)
Melson, Vernon L. (415th Inf.)
Mendoza, Simon C. (413th Inf.)
Mendelovitz, Morris NMI (414th Inf.)
Merritt, Hubert L. (413th Inf.)
Messinger, Reid B. (413th Inf.)
Meyring, Herbert A. (329th Engr.)
Miccio, Sylvester A. (413th Inf.)
Michael, Donald G. (415th Inf.)
Michael, Thomas R. (413th Inf.)
Michaels, Arthur NMI (414th Inf.)
Michaels, James F. (413th Inf.)
Middleton, Rex NMI (413th Inf.)
Mielke, Robert J. (414th Inf.)
Mikota, Edwin V. (413th Inf.)
Miles, Herbert A. (929th FA)
Millan, Carlos NMI (413th Inf.)
Miller, Earl E. (415th Inf.)
Miller, Lloyd R. (415th Inf.)
Miller, Luther E. (415th Inf.)
Miller, Raymond H. (413th Inf.)
Miller, Robert U. (414th Inf.)
Miller, Robert V. (414th Inf.)
Miller, Sigmund NMI (415th Inf.)
Millinor, James F. (415th Inf.)
Mingrino, Paul A. (414th Inf.)
Mink, Myron E. (413th Inf.)
Minster, Robert C. (414th Inf.)
Misner, Ralph W. (414th Inf.)
Misquez, Albert NMI (414th Inf.)
Mitchell, Ralph NMI (414th Inf.)
Mitchell, Walter L. (414th Inf.)
Mock, Robert P. (414th Inf.)
Moen, George J. (415th Inf.)
Mohrman, Virgil G. (415th Inf.)
Moland, Myron R. (413th Inf.)
Molandes, Floyd NMI (413th Inf.)
Mooney, John L. Jr. (413th Inf.)
Moore, Donald M. (414th Inf.)
Morales, Roman J. (414th Inf.)
Moralez, Frank NMI (413th Inf.)
Moreno, Eddie R. (414th Inf.)
Morgan, Bill F. (413th Inf.)
Morgan, General L. Sr. (414th Inf.)
Morrill, Robert L. (414th Inf.)
Morriss, Wilbur T. (415th Inf.)

Morrow, Boyd D. (413th Inf.)
Moss, Louis B. (413th Inf.)
Moxley, Kenneth W. (415th Inf.)
Mroz, Edward J. (329th Engr.)
Mugridge, Carl F. (329th Engr.)
Muir, John D. (414th Inf.)
Mullins, Lawrence H. (414th Inf.)
Muncy, William L. Jr. (415th Inf.)
Murphy, Raymond T. (415th Inf.)
Murphy, Richard A. (414th Inf.)
Murray, Johnnie NMI (414th Inf.)
Musacchia, Luke F. Jr. (415th Inf.)
Musser, Lee D. (413th Inf.)
Myers, Oswald K. (413th Inf.)
Myers, Ray E. (413th Inf.)
Myers, Richard L. (415th Inf.)
Maughton, James A. (414th Inf.)
Nazzaro, Benjamin A. (414th Inf.)
Needles, Wayne M. (415th Inf.)
Neilson, Thomas F. (413th Inf.)
Nelan, Terence J. (414th Inf.)
Nelson, Kenneth L. Jr. (413th Inf.)
Nelson, Linneus E. (413th Inf.)
Nelson, Stanley L. (414th Inf.)
Nemeth, Charles H. (413th Inf.)
Newburg, Albert R. (413th Inf.)
Newhook, Ernest R. (413th Inf.)
Nichol, Wallace D. (415th Inf.)
Nicholoff, William P. (414th Inf.)
Nichols, Floyd H. Jr. (413th Inf.)
Nicholson, Clarence D. (414th Inf.)
Nickey, Lee M. Jr. (413th Inf.)
Niday, Merrill E. (413th Inf.)
Nieto, Paul D. (415th Inf.)
Nimmo, Roy E. (413th Inf.)
Nitterhouse, Howard L. Jr. (413th Inf.)
Norton, Manuel L. (413th Inf.)
Norwood, Wayland E. (414th Inf.)
Nunziato, Domenick W. (415th Inf.)
Nurmi, John R. (414th Inf.)
Nycz, Chester NMI (414th Inf.)
Ochs, Robert E. (413th Inf.)
Oelschlager, Vernon W. (415th Inf.)
Olmsted, Robert A. (329th Engr.)
Olsen, John J. (415th Inf.)
Olson, Glenn S. (414th Inf.)
O'Neill, Norbert A. (415th Inf.)
Opava, John N. (385th FA)
Orgeron, Eunice J. (414th Inf.)
Orozco, Crispin E. (414th Inf.)

Orozco, David C. (413th Inf.)
Ort, Milton D. (413th Inf.)
Ortega, Louis O. (414th Inf.)
O'Sias, Mac NMI (104th Recon. Tr.)
Oswalt, Donald NMI (415th Inf.)
Owens, John W. (415th Inf.)
Palermo, Frank L. (414th Inf.)
Pallini, Raymond E. (414th Inf.)
Palmer, Harry NMI Jr. (414th Inf.)
Parise, Frank J. (415th Inf.)
Park, Manuel L. (929th FA)
Parker, Chester A. (413th Inf.)
Parker, Daniel R. (415th Inf.)
Parker, John E. (414th Inf.)
Parnel, Howard L. (415th Inf.)
Partridge, Edwin L. Jr. (413th Inf.)
Partain, Robert E. (415th Inf.)
Pate, Francis A. (413th Inf.)
Patti, Carl A. (414th Inf.)
Paules, Earl M. (414th Inf.)
Peck, Robert F. (413th Inf.)
Pedersen, Lester V. (414th Inf.)
Peebles, James NMI (415th Inf.)
Peeler, Clyde E. (415th Inf.)
Peltonen, Andrew NMI (413th Inf.)
Pendley, Estle M. (414th Inf.)
Peplow, Raymond W. (414th Inf.)
Perasso, George J. (414th Inf.)
Perkins, Charles F. (413th Inf.)
Perry, Elbert R. (415th Inf.)
Perry, William E. (414th Inf.)
Peseka, Peter J. (413th Inf.)
Peter, Melvin J. (414th Inf.)
Petrucco, David (385th FA)
Peters, William B. (415th Inf.)
Petryna, George NMI (414th Inf.)
Pettit, Frank L. Jr. (414th Inf.)
Pettus, Jewell L. (415th Inf.)
Pfaff, Joseph M. (413th Inf.)
Phillips, David A. (329th Engr.)
Phillips, Russell NMI (413th Inf.)
Piepenbrink, Elmer H. (414th Inf.)
Planinc, Edward L. (414th Inf.)
Pierson, Laurance E. (414th Inf.)
Plummer, Lewis G. (414th Inf.)
Polanco, Jesus F. (414th Inf.)
Polio, James V. (413th Inf.)
Pollard, Noah C. (414th Inf.)
Pollitt, Gerrald R. (415th Inf.)
Polos, James NMI (415th Inf.)

Pool, Louis L. (415th Inf.)
Pophal, Norman A. (414th Inf.)
Powell, Ross E. (414th Inf.)
Powers, Andrew NMI (329th Engr.)
Powers, Leo E. (413th Inf.)
Prasil, Edward R. (413th Inf.)
Prater, Clarence G. (413th Inf.)
Pratt, Joseph F. (329th Engr.)
Prefontaine, Albert R. (414th Inf.)
Price, Bernard W. (414th Inf.)
Price, George G. (415th Inf.)
Price, George W. (414th Inf.)
Price, Robert W. (413th Inf.)
Prince, Edgar C. (413th Inf.)
Priore, Walter L. (413th Inf.)
Prosser, John W. (415th Inf.)
Puestow, Raymond F. (415th Inf.)
Pullen, Lloyd W. (414th Inf.)
Pursino, William J. (414th Inf.)
Pusa, Henry W. (414th Inf.)
Qua, Richard M. (414th Inf.)
Qualls, Raymond NMI (414th Inf.)
Queen, Blaine NMI (414th Inf.)
Quenomoen, Julius W. (415th Inf.)
Raffaldt, James L. (413th Inf.)
Ragonese, Ignazio F. (329th Engr.)
Ramirez, Ramon R. (413th Inf.)
Ramsey, Frank A. Jr. (414th Inf.)
Ramstetter, Walter E. (414th Inf.)
Ranney, Richard W. (413th Inf.)
Ransdell, Raymond E. (386th FA)
Ransom, James E. (415th Inf.)
Rapp, Vernon D. (415th Inf.)
Rasmussen, Roland L. (929th FA)
Raught, Gayle E. (414th Inf.)
Rawson, Robert B. (413th Inf.)
Ray, Samuel G. (414th Inf.)
Raynor, Rexford L. (414th Inf.)
Redinger, Frank W. (413th Inf.)
Reese, William R. (385th FA)
Rehfus, John C. (415th Inf.)
Rehker, Donald W. (415th Inf.)
Reid, James NMI (413th Inf.)
Reilly, J. Sheridan (414th Inf.)
Reis, Kenneth R. (413th Inf.)
Reisinger, James M. (415th Inf.)
Reiter, Arlie J. (329th Engr.)
Reitz, Gordon C. (414th Inf.)
Rethorst, Marion T. (414th Inf.)
Rheinheimer, Paul E. (415th Inf.)

Rhoads, Abram M. (415th Inf.)
Richards, John R. J. (415th Inf.)
Riesgo, Alfred G. (414th Inf.)
Riley, Alvin W. (414th Inf.)
Rinaldi, Raymond R. (415th Inf.)
Risen, James K. (414th Inf.)
Risley, Paul S. (415th Inf.)
Rissler, William H. (414th Inf.)
Rist, Harold E. (414th Inf.)
Roberts, Kenneth L. (415th Inf.)
Robertson, Kenneth F. (415th Inf.)
Robinson, Jesse P. (414th Inf.)
Robinson, Willard J. (414th Inf.)
Rodeck, Ewald M. (385th FA)
Roehrich, Fred NMI (414th Inf.)
Roesler, Paul W. (413th Inf.)
Rogers, Carl N. (415th Inf.)
Roose, Benjamin E. (413th Inf.)
Roper, Earl G. (414th Inf.)
Rosalez, Magdaleno C. (413th Inf.)
Rose, Edward A. (415th Inf.)
Rosenbaum, Chester L. (414th Inf.)
Rosencrans, Herbert J. (414th Inf.)
Rosenthal, Irving NMI (415th Inf.)
Roshetko, Mathew L. (414th Inf.)
Rosier, Herbert J. (413th Inf.)
Ross, Harry H. (413th Inf.)
Ross, Kenneth S. (413th Inf.)
Rost, Lowell H. (414th Inf.)
Rost, William E. (413th Inf.)
Roterud, Clarence H. (413th Inf.)
Rothra, Virgil H. (329th Engr.)
Roziger, Walter J. (415th Inf.)
Rule, Leonard F. (413th Inf.)
Russi, Robert W. (415th Inf.)
Russo, Sam J. Jr. (413th Inf.)
Russomano, Ralph C. (413th Inf.)
Rutledge, Carl D. Jr. (415th Inf.)
Sabatini, Dominic NMI (414th Inf.)
Sabinski, Frank J. (414th Inf.)
Sack, Oliver R. (414th Inf.)
Saffert, Leonard J. (414th Inf.)
Salcito, Louis J. (413th Inf.)
Saltzman, Abraham NMI (414th Inf.)
Sammons, Cecil T. (415th Inf.)
Sanders, Michael E. (414th Inf.)
Sanders, Ray H. (413th Inf.)
Sanders, William H. (929th FA)
Sandmoen, Loren R. (415th Inf.)
Sansoucie, Chester C. (415th Inf.)

Sapp, Ernest C. (414th Inf.)
Saul, George A. (414th Inf.)
Saul, Jesse W. (415th Inf.)
Savor, John P. (413th Inf.)
Sawyer, Earl E. (414th Inf.)
Saylor, Orrie A. (415th Inf.)
Sbriglia, Michael A. (415th Inf.)
Scarlata, Remo NMI (415th Inf.)
Schaal, Emmanuel E. (415th Inf.)
Schaefer, Frank W. (415th Inf.)
Schaefer, Herschel M. (413th Inf.)
Schendel, Arthur G. (415th Inf.)
Schiebel, Lawrence J. (414th Inf.)
Schmid, Fredrick C. (415th Inf.)
Schmidt, Thomas NMI (413th Inf.)
Schneider, Arthur A. (415th Inf.)
Schneider, James R. (415th Inf.)
Schnier, Manfred W. (414th Inf.)
Schulman, Isidore NMI (415th Inf.)
Schultz, Harold L. (414th Inf.)
Schwartz, Edward J. (415th Inf.)
Swartz, Leonard H. (414th Inf.)
Sclafani, Dominic J. (415th Inf.)
Scott, Thomas F. (413th Inf.)
Seegmiller, William H. (413th Inf.)
Seeley, Robert S. (413th Inf.)
Seeley, Van L. (414th Inf.)
Seery, Paul M. (414th Inf.)
Seifer, Wayne J. (414th Inf.)
Seiker, David NMI (413th Inf.)
Selleck, Robert A. (415th Inf.)
Seno, Louis J. (415th Inf.)
Sepulvado, Morise Z. (415th Inf.)
Serrabella, Armand J. (413th Inf.)
Shaffer, Elmer NMI (415th Inf.)
Shaffer, Ralph E. (414th Inf.)
Schank, Ralph E. (413th Inf.)
Sharp, Alva D. (413th Inf.)
Shaver, Herbert H. Jr. (415th Inf.)
Sheridan, David L. (415th Inf.)
Sherman, Ewald A. (413th Inf.)
Sherping, Clifford B. (415th Inf.)
Shiplevy, Rudolph NMI (414th Inf.)
Shipman, Odell E. (414th Inf.)
Shively, Nicholas M. Jr. (414th Inf.)
Shoaf, John E. (413th Inf.)
Short, Jack A. (413th Inf.)
Shugert, Howard W. (415th Inf.)
Shy, Newton B. (104th Sig. Co.)
Sieber, William H. (413th Inf.)

Sills, James W. (415th Inf.)
Silva, John Jr. NMI (415th Inf.)
Silver, George NMI (414th Inf.)
Simmons, James H. (413th Inf.)
Simmons, Robert N. (413th Inf.)
Simons, Robert A. (413th Inf.)
Sinclair, Ralph E. (415th Inf.)
Singleton, Charles A. (413th Inf.)
Skaggs, Everett E. (415th Inf.)
Skahill, Bernard L. (413th Inf.)
Skuza, Arnold E. (413th Inf.)
Slater, Henry E. (415th Inf.)
Slay, James E. (414th Inf.)
Slay, William F. (414th Inf.)
Sloan, Darah S. (414th Inf.)
Sloan, Norman J. (415th Inf.)
Small, Edward K. (414th Inf.)
Smith, Charles F. (413th Inf.)
Smith, Clayton E. (413th Inf.)
Smith, David L. (413th Inf.)
Smith, Dumas L. (414th Inf.)
Smith, George A. Jr. (Hq. 104th Div.)
Smith, George E. (413th Inf.)
Smith, Horace S. (413th Inf.)
Smith, James E. (413th Inf.)
Smith, Lester E. (415th Inf.)
Smith, Louis A. (414th Inf.)
Smith, Odell NMI (413th Inf.)
Smith, Quentin D. (415th Inf.)
Smith, Rafe H. (413th Inf.)
Smith, Rexford NMI (415th Inf.)
Smith, Richard M. (413th Inf.)
Smith, Russell W. (413th Inf.)
Smith, William J. (413th Inf.)
Smolan, Morris N. (414th Inf.)
Smoot, Keith H. (414th Inf.)
Snider, John E. (415th Inf.)
Snitzer, James G. (413th Inf.)
Snyder, Eugene P. (413th Inf.)
Snyder, James R. (385th FA)
Snyder, Wilbur D. (414th Inf.)
Sobansky, James T. (414th Inf.)
Sobolta, Richard J. (414th Inf.)
Sokolowski, Anthony T. (413th Inf.)
Solomon, Herbert NMI (415th Inf.)
Sommerville, Robert G. (414th Inf.)
Sorrells, Benjamin F. Jr. (413th Inf.)
Spankus, William R. (414th Inf.)
Speer, Ralph E. (415th Inf.)
Spencer, Gerald R. (414th Inf.)

Stahr, Harold R. (415th Inf.)
Staney, Joseph Jr. NMI (414th Inf.)
Stanley, Allison F. Jr. (413th Inf.)
Stanley, James C. (414th Inf.)
Stanton, Richard J. (415th Inf.)
Stapleton, Francis E. (414th Inf.)
Starliper, Robert C. (414th Inf.)
Staudacher, William A. Jr. (415th Inf.)
Steiger, Robert H. (415th Inf.)
Stein, William F. (415th Inf.)
Stenger, Robert D. (413th Inf.)
Stensrud, William D. (413th Inf.)
Stevens, John NMI (414th Inf.)
Stevens, Norman F. (414th Inf.)
Stewart, James K. (414th Inf.)
Stewart, Robert C. (414th Inf.)
Stewart, Robert C. (414th Inf.)
Stillinger, Phillip E. (414th Inf.)
St. John, Lester A. (414th Inf.)
Stoker, John D. (415th Inf.)
Stoklosa, Michael J. (413th Inf.)
Stoltz, Bernard J. (413th Inf.)
Stone, Francis F. (414th Inf.)
Stone, Ryal G. (413th Inf.)
Storer, George D. Jr. (413th Inf.)
Storm, Joseph D. (413th Inf.)
Stovall, Holton D. (414th Inf.)
Stovall, Jasper NMI (414th Inf.)
Straesser, David R. (385th FA)
Straley, John F. (413th Inf.)
Stratton, Marshall L. (413th Inf.)
Strauss, Kenneth O. (413th Inf.)
Strickland, Alvin NMI (415th Inf.)
Stringer, Paul B. (415th Inf.)
Strittmatter, Harry C. (415th Inf.)
Strong, Scott NMI (413th Inf.)
Stotz, Charles E. (414th Inf.)
Strucienski, Julius J. (415th Inf.)
Stryczek, Edward J. (414th Inf.)
Stump, Clarence G. (415th Inf.)
Sturm, Jack NMI (415th Inf.)
Suhl, Melvin M. (413th Inf.)
Sullivan, Francis T. (413th Inf.)
Surrency, John B. (413th Inf.)
Sutherland, Floyd D. (414th Inf.)
Sutherland, Murton V. (413th Inf.)
Sutton, Benny NMI (414th Inf.)
Swafford, Manis NMI (413th Inf.)
Swanley, Norbert A. (415th Inf.)
Swann, Herschell W. (415th Inf.)

Sweeney, William J. (413th Inf.)
Swenson, Roy B. (415th Inf.)
Swint, James W. (415th Inf.)
Sykes, Joe V. (415th Inf.)
Szewczyk, Ralph P. (413th Inf.)
Szmyd, Aleksander NMI (415th Inf.)
Tabor, Howard NMI (414th Inf.)
Tallman, Fletcher Jr. NMI (415th Inf.)
Tapalansky, John NMI (413th Inf.)
Tarango, Manuel F. (414th Inf.)
Tatlian, Charles M. (413th Inf.)
Tauer, Oldrich NMI (415th Inf.)
Taylor, Bernard B. (415th Inf.)
Taylor, Burtis J. (414th Inf.)
Taylor, Dale O. (414th Inf.)
Taylor, Frank R. (415th Inf.)
Tayman, Eugene T. (414th Inf.)
Teer, Ben J. Jr. (414th Inf.)
Tennery, Oren J. (414th Inf.)
Tester, Perry O. Jr. (413th Inf.)
Thibeault, Bertrand J. (414th Inf.)
Thomas, A. J. (IO) (415th Inf.)
Thomas, David S. (413th Inf.)
Thomas, Elmer W. (104th Sig. Co.)
Thomas, Herbert H. (413th Inf.)
Thomas, Robert NMI (387th FA)
Thompson, Chess M. (414th Inf.)
Thompson, Donnelly O. (414th Inf.)
Thompson, John S. (415th Inf.)
Thompson, John T. (415th Inf.)
Thompson, William F. Jr. (413th Inf.)
Tiburzi, Richard V. (413th Inf.)
Tilson, Jesse D. (415th Inf.)
Tindall, George R. (413th Inf.)
Tito, Vito W. (415th Inf.)
Tjossem, Robert K. (415th Inf.)
Touart, Anthony J. (414th Inf.)
Trahan, Joseph B. (413th Inf.)
Trella, Felix E. (413th Inf.)
Tressler, Chauncey H. (413th Inf.)
Tuck, George E. (415th Inf.)
Tucker, Louis E. (415th Inf.)
Turek, Philip A. (414th Inf.)
Turner, Horace L. (329th Engr.)
Turner, Oscar G. (415th Inf.)
Tynan, Clifford H. (415th Inf.)
Tysinger, John L. (413th Inf.)
Tysl, James A. (415th Inf.)
Tyson, Herschel A. (329th Engr.)
Underwood, Alford L. (414th Inf.)

Urbanowski, Eugene U. (414th Inf.)
Vaccaro, Frank J. (415th Inf.)
Valenta, Raymond J. (415th Inf.)
Van Giesen, George T. (414th Inf.)
Van Orman, Max L. (414th Inf.)
Varela, Manuel NMI (415th Inf.)
Vanadore, Clinton NMI (415th Inf.)
Vasquez, Margarito O. (413th Inf.)
Vaughan, Veldon W. (413th Inf.)
Vawter, Harold B. (414th Inf.)
Veith, James F. (414th Inf.)
Verbanick, Joseph NMI (415th Inf.)
Verble, Oscar M. (413th Inf.)
Vertz, Reuben J. (415th Inf.)
Vevers, Jack B. (413th Inf.)
Viator, Alton NMI (414th Inf.)
Vincent, Mitchell P. (414th Inf.)
Virden, Charles L. (413th Inf.)
Vlahakis, John J. (413th Inf.)
Voelker, John R. (415th Inf.)
Volz, Franklin A. (415th Inf.)
Wachowski, Julius J. (413th Inf.)
Wagner, Charles W. (413th Inf.)
Wald, Morris NMI (413th Inf.)
Waldridge, Robert L. (413th Inf.)
Wales, Wesley E. (414th Inf.)
Walker, Herman R. (415th Inf.)
Walker, James J. (413th Inf.)
Wall, John A. (415th Inf.)
Walsh, John J. (415th Inf.)
Ward, Chester O. (413th Inf.)
Ward, David M. (415th Inf.)
Ward, Emmitt H. (415th Inf.)
Ward, John B. (413th Inf.)
Ward, Lloyd NMI (413th Inf.)
Ward, Sheridan V. F. (329th Engr.)
Wardale, William H. (104th Sig. Co.)
Wardner, Fred G. (414th Inf.)
Warner, Vincent L. (415th Inf.)
Warnock, Wilbur A. Jr. (413th Inf.)
Warszawski, Casimer E. (413th Inf.)
Watson, George T. (414th Inf.)
Waye, Richard A. (413th Inf.)
Weaver, Marion T. (414th Inf.)
Webb, William C. (413th Inf.)
Webber, Ralph L. (329th Engr.)
Weber, Raymond G. (413th Inf.)
Weed, Charles D. (414th Inf.)
Weesner, Ellard M. (414th Inf.)
Wegner, Victor C. (413th Inf.)

Weir, Lloyd K. (413th Inf.)
Wentworth, Aldon N. (413th Inf.)
Werre, John L. (413th Inf.)
Westerman, Harold E. (413th Inf.)
Westmoreland, Thomas R. (413th Inf.)
Wheatley, Bernard B. (414th Inf.)
Wheeler, Bilbo NMI (413th Inf.)
Wheeler, Charles R. (414th Inf.)
White, Glenn R. (413th Inf.)
White, Howard J. (415th Inf.)
White, Walter NMI (413th Inf.)
Whitenack, Theodore W. (414th Inf.)
Whitmer, Dwaine N. (415th Inf.)
Whitten, Archie E. (415th Inf.)
Whorton, Lionel M. (415th Inf.)
Wichniewicz, Joseph NMI (413th Inf.)
Wickard, Edgar J. (413th Inf.)
Widhalm, Carl F. (413th Inf.)
Wielgosh, Edmund R. (414th Inf.)
Wiese, Wilbur F. (414th Inf.)
Wilcox, Henry E. (414th Inf.)
Wilkinson, David C. (413th Inf.)
Will, George NMI (413th Inf.)
Will, Gilmour M. Jr. (415th Inf.)
Williams, Gerald NMI (413th Inf.)
Williams, Keith M. (415th Inf.)
Williams, Raymond W. (414th Inf.)
Williford, Marvin T. (413th Inf.)
Willis, Joe L. (414th Inf.)
Wilson, Denton C. (415th Inf.)
Wilson, James L. Jr. (415th Inf.)
Winn, Raymond L. (414th Inf.)
Winthrop, Paul L. (413th Inf.)

Wire, David M. (415th Inf.)
Wirth, Roy R. (414th Inf.)
Wissinger, Roy V. Jr. (413th Inf.)
Witherite, Guy NMI (414th Inf.)
Wodek, John NMI (413th Inf.)
Wojcik, Leo E. (413th Inf.)
Wolert, Charles J. (413th Inf.)
Wolf, Eugene E. (413th Inf.)
Wolfe, Lester L. (413th Inf.)
Wolfe, Theodore NMI (413th Inf.)
Wolosonovich, Wallace (414th Inf.)
Womack, Kirk Jr. NMI (413th Inf.)
Woods, James C. (415th Inf.)
Woods, Robert L. (415th Inf.)
Woods, Williams F. (104th Sig. Co.)
Worbs, David A. (329th Engr.)
Wozniak, Julius D. (413th Inf.)
Wright, Earl J. (414th Inf.)
Wright, Homer J. (414th Inf.)
Wright, Lyle E. (414th Inf.)
Wright, Wesley J. (413th Inf.)
Wroblewski, Richard E. (415th Inf.)
Yearry, William T. (413th Inf.)
Yeomans, Gerald R. (104th Recon. Tr.)
Yoho, Harry R. (415th Inf.)
Young, Dilworth R. (415th Inf.)
Young, John P. (413th Inf.)
Young, Lester J. (414th Inf.)
Youngland, Kenneth D. (415th Inf.)
Zeigler, James H. (414th Inf.)
Zinn, Sidney NMI (415th Inf.)
Zura, Irwin H. (385th FA)
Zwanetsky, Abe NMI (415th Inf.)

NON-BATTLE DEATHS

Bailey, Richard H. (415th Inf.)
Billhimer, Hiram W. (415th Inf.)
Burger, Theodore G. (413th Inf.)
Casey, Charles W. (413th Inf.)
Castie, Albert C. (413th Inf.)
Chapman, Donald A. (Hq. 104th Div.)
Collum, Benjamin J. (414th Inf.)
Cure, Harold J. (329th Engr.)
Davidson, Omer E. (415th Inf.)
Dwelly, Robert C. Jr. (385th FA)
Effley, Louis F. (415th Inf.)
Garza, Sixto G. (386th FA)
Gessick, John M. (413th Inf.)
Grebene, Stanley S. (329th Engr.)
Halvorson, Robert L. (415th Inf.)

Hart, Eugene E. (414th Inf.)
Henderson, Harold (415th Inf.)
Hobbs, Junior R. (413th Inf.)
Hopkins, David S. (329th Engr.)
Hubert, Frederick J. (415th Inf.)
Huddleston, Lewis D. (414th Inf.)
Huntwork, Ralph C. (413th Inf.)
Johnson, Kieth C. (104th QM Co.)
Kaluza, Virgil R. (415th Inf.)
Kempf, Wayne A. (413th Inf.)
Kirchem, Edward J. (MP Plat.)
Kuemmerle, Christy R. (413th Inf.)
LaCavera, Edward J. (415th Inf.)
Love, John T. Jr. (413th Inf.)
Luscher, Jack J. (413th Inf.)

Maxwell, Virgil W. (929th FA)
Mazie, Stanley NMI (MP Plat.)
Mitchell, Harman A. (MP Plat.)
Morang, George W. (415th Inf.)
Newton, Nelson O. (413th Inf.)
Norton, Joseph D. (413th Inf.)
Pleier, Charles R. (MP Plat.)
Ramirez, Modesto M. (415th Inf.)
Reed, Orval D. (415th Inf.)
Rikansrud, Arthur J. (413th Inf.)
Rubin, Marvin A. (329th Engr.)

Saperstein, Eugene (413th Inf.)
Schorlemer, Felton C. (415th Inf.)
Schreiner, Anthony T. (415th Inf.)
Skolnick, Philip M. (415th Inf.)
Smith, Wayne M. (413th Inf.)
Sullivan, Mortimer L. (415th Inf.)
Thresher, John L. (415th Inf.)
White, Earl NMI (414th Inf.)
Wise, Richard D. (413th Inf.)
Wolford, William R. (413th Inf.)

MISSING IN ACTION

Alaniz, Guadalupe A. (329th Med.)
Aloisio, Joseph M. (415th Inf.)
Amann, Richard J. (413th Inf.)
Anderson, Harry K. (413th Inf.)
Anderson, Howard P. (414th Inf.)
Anschutz, Ralph L. (414th Inf.)
Armond, James M. (413th Inf.)
Arnold, Nelson E. (415th Inf.)
Athey, Ivern NMI (414th Inf.)
Auel, Carl M. (415th Inf.)
Axton, William G. Jr. (413th Inf.)
Balk, Byron M. (414th Inf.)
Bednar, John NMI (413th Inf.)
Broussard, Adam NMI (413th Inf.)
Brown, Earl T. Jr. (414th Inf.)
Burris, William E. (415th Inf.)
Burroughs, William B. (415th Inf.)
Chesnut, William H. (413th Inf.)
Corsini, Victor P. (414th Inf.)
Cossey, Fay D. (415th Inf.)
Cummins, William J. Jr. (414th Inf.)
Dastra, Vincent J. (413th Inf.)
Dietz, Robert S. (413th Inf.)
DiFazio, Joseph J. (415th Inf.)
Dysle, John E. (414th Inf.)
Ellis, Bernard J. (414th Inf.)
Farrington, Parker NMI Jr. (415th Inf.)
Favre, Clarence E. (413th Inf.)
Fenstemaker, John H. (415th Inf.)
Fink, William C. (415th Inf.)
Foresman, Paul W. (413th Inf.)
Fredrickson, Warren E. (414th Inf.)
Gallo, Santo NMI (385th FA)
Gallup, Charles W. (415th Inf.)
Garner, George R. (415th Inf.)
Glanzer, Robert NMI (414th Inf.)
Gleason, Ralph N. (413th Inf.)
Goldring, George V. (413th Inf.)

Gore, Hubert NMI (414th Inf.)
Gumm, Youles S. (413th Inf.)
Hanson, William F. (415th Inf.)
Harlen, Charles Jr. (415th Inf.)
Herrera, Reyes NMI (414th Inf.)
Hickey, Albert C. (415th Inf.)
Hogan, Raymond A. (414th Inf.)
Jackson, Roy E. (413th Inf.)
Jeske, John H. (414th Inf.)
Johnson, Leland H. (415th Inf.)
Jones, Clarence R. (415th Inf.)
Juday, Charles G. (414th Inf.)
Kroll, Stanley A. (414th Inf.)
Lanning, Walter C. (415th Inf.)
Lazore, George F. (414th Inf.)
Mann, Jerry F. (413th Inf.)
Matthews, William C. (413th Inf.)
Michelini, Casimiro NMI (413th Inf.)
Murdock, Claude D. (413th Inf.)
Nichols, Charles B. (414th Inf.)
Podchaski, Walter NMI (413th Inf.)
Price, John J. (415th Inf.)
Reason, Louie NMI (415th Inf.)
Richie, Herbert M. (414th Inf.)
Roberson, Ernest R. (413th Inf.)
Sevigny, John W. (414th Inf.)
Turton, Edgar NMI (415th Inf.)
Urbanowicz, John T. (415th Inf.)
Van Winkle, Arless S. (413th Inf.)
Ventura, Andrew A. (413th Inf.)
Walter, Edward NMI (413th Inf.)
Ward, Bernard J. (414th Inf.)
Wiggins, John L. Jr. (415th Inf.)
Williams, Wesley W. (414th Inf.)
Wilson, Alfred NMI Jr. (415th Inf.)
Yenser, Robert W. (413th Inf.)
Zimmerman, Charlie F. (415th Inf.)
Zulker, Clarence NMI (413th Inf.)

APPENDIX 2

THE NATIONAL TIMBERWOLF ASSOCIATION

Dedicated to preserving the memory of our heroic dead, to prolonging the spirit of fellowship and teamwork with which we have been imbued and to upholding the traditions and ideals for which we fought, the National Timberwolf Association was created on 19 October 1945. On 1 and 2 October on the parade ground at Camp San Luis Obispo,

National Timberwolf Association Founders

California, the Timberwolves from each of the forty-eight states met in their respective groups. State Timberwolf Associations were organized, officers elected, and purposes were outlined. Delegates were directed to meet on 11 October for the formation of the National Association. At this first meeting the State delegates decided to proceed with the organization and drafting of a constitution.

On 19 October the National Timberwolf Association was officially formed, National Officers were elected, and the Constitution and By-Laws were adopted.

A National President, Secretary-Treasurer, and nine Vice-Presidents (representing each of the Army Service Command areas) were elected.

NATIONAL PRESIDENT	NATIONAL SECRETARY
Leo A. Hoegh	Robert R. Clark, II
1st State Bank Bldg.	Quaker Oats
Chariton, Iowa	Cedar Rapids, Iowa

DISTRICT I

Vice-President: Robert D. Haphey, Methuen, Massachusetts

DISTRICT II

Vice-President: Boleslaus B. Kaluzny, 43 Gorski Street, Buffalo, New York

DISTRICT III

Vice-President: Elmer O. Etters, 120 High Street, State College, Pennsylvania

DISTRICT IV

Vice-President: Ben R. Leonard, Donalds, South Carolina

DISTRICT V

Vice-President: James Steedman, 670 Nesslewood Avenue, Toledo, Ohio

DISTRICT VI

Vice-President: John L. Laine, 550 Carrie Street, NE, Grand Rapids, Michigan

DISTRICT VII

Vice-President: D. E. Stevenson, 1511 N. 42d Street, Omaha, Nebraska

DISTRICT VIII

Vice-President: Claude M. Cox, Jr., 314 Cornell Avenue, San Antonio, Texas

DISTRICT IX

Vice-President: Kenneth K. Bell, 403 N. 42d Street, Seattle, Washington

CONSTITUTION OF THE NATIONAL TIMBERWOLF ASSOCIATION

I—PREAMBLE

We, former soldiers of the 104th Timberwolf Infantry Division, bound together by common memories and experiences, resolved to uphold the traditions and ideals for which we fought, associate ourselves in a national organization.

II—NAME

The name of this organization shall be the "National Timberwolf Association."

III—PURPOSES

The Association is a non-profit fraternal organization created to serve these purposes and objectives:

a. To promote the comradeship and re-affirm the friendships established in training and combat.

b. To provide opportunities, through national publications, rosters, and conventions, to maintain and foster personal contact with fellow timberwolves.

c. To keep alive the memories of comrades fallen in battle.

d. To coordinate the activities of the Timberwolf State Associations.

IV—NATURE

The Association shall be civilian in nature. Membership therein does not affect nor increase liability for military service. Rank does not exist.

V—FEES AND DUES

Fees and dues may be assessed when necessary only as set forth in the by-laws.

VI—MEMBERSHIP

All persons who have served honorably as members of the Timberwolf Division are eligible for membership, regardless of the length of their assignment.

VII—OFFICERS

The officers of this Association shall be a president, a first vice-president, a second vice-president, seven third vice-presidents, and a secretary-treasurer. The vice-presidents shall represent the nine service command areas, and all shall be equal in authority, a first and second vice-president being designated by the vice-presidents themselves as successor to the president in the event the president becomes a loss to the association. The president shall have the authority to appoint a secretary-treasurer as a successor to fill any unexpired term of the duly elected secretary-treasurer in the event of his loss, the appointment subject to the approval of the board of governors. The president and the secretary-treasurer shall be elected by the vote of the delegation present at national association meetings. The vice-presidents shall be elected by a vote of the separate states representing a service command. Every member of the National Timberwolf Association shall be eligible to hold office.

VIII—BOARD OF GOVERNORS

There shall be a board of governors of the Association. The board shall consist of the duly elected officers of the associations, with the president of the association acting as chairman.

IX—POWER OF BOARD OF GOVERNORS

The board of governors shall be the administrative body of the association and shall have the power and the authority to do and perform all acts and functions necessary for the conduct of the affairs of the association consistent with the constitution and the by-laws.

X—BY-LAWS

By-laws may be adopted, amended or rescinded by a unanimous vote of the board of governors, or by a majority of the delegation present at any annual meeting.

XI—AMENDMENTS

The constitution may be amended by the affirmative vote of two-thirds of the delegation present at any annual meeting.

XII—ADOPTION

This constitution shall be adopted only after a majority affirmative vote is cast by the duly appointed delegation representing the separate states. This constitution shall take effect immediately upon its adoption.

In order to maintain an active bond among all 104th men, the Association will hold annual conventions in conjunction with one of the larger national veteran organizations, and will issue a publication twice a year containing news of Timberwolves in civilian life. The 34,000 Timberwolves, bound together by common memories and experiences, have associated themselves in a great fraternal organization.

ADDITIONAL COPIES OF

TIMBERWOLF TRACKS

MAY BE OBTAINED THROUGH THE

NATIONAL TIMBERWOLF ASSOCIATION
SECRETARY

ROBERT R. CLARK, II
Cedar Rapids, Iowa

APPENDIX 3
THE INFANTRY DIVISION

I—GENERAL CHARACTERISTICS:

An infantry division is the smallest unit, composed of all the essential ground arms and services, which can conduct by its own means operations of tactical importance. It comprises a Headquarters (104th Headquarters) Company; three Infantry Regiments (413th, 414th, 415th); Division Artillery, Headquarters Battery, three light Field Artillery Battalions (385th, 386th, 929th), one medium Field Artillery Battalion (387th); one Engineer (Combat) Battalion (329th); one Medical Battalion (329th); one Mechanized Reconnaissance Troop (104th); one Quartermaster Company (104th); one Ordnance Company (804th); and one Signal Company (104th). It is an administrative as well as a tactical unit. Personnel consists of 832 officers, forty-four warrant officers, and 13,342 enlisted men.

II—INFANTRY REGIMENT:

Its mission is to close with the enemy and destroy him. When a battle ends, the infantryman pinches himself and tries to realize that he is still alive. It consists of 3,207 men, including 153 officers, five warrant officers, and 3,049 enlisted men. In a regiment there are three battalions and four separate companies. Separate companies are Headquarters, consisting prinpically of communications, intelligence and reconnaissance personnel; Service Company with supply, ordnance and motor maintenance; Antitank Company with nine 57mm antitank guns; and Cannon Company with six 105mm Howitzers for close infantry support. Each company numbers approximately 125 officers and men, with the exception of Antitank Company, which has 165. A Medical Detachment is also a part of the regiment, with its 136 officers and men rendering front line first aid to the foot soldier.

Each Infantry Battalion consists of thirty-five officers and 811 enlisted men, with five companies that include Headquarters company, three Rifle companies and one Heavy Weapons company. The Rifle company, the most forward element of the Division, has six officers and 187 enlisted men in its ranks. It has three rifle platoons and one weapons platoon, the latter being composed of three 60mm mortars and two light machine guns. The Heavy Weapons company, made up of eight officers and 156 enlisted men, has as its principal weapons eight heavy machine guns and six 81mm mortars. The 1st Battalion is made up of A, B and C (rifle) companies, and D (heavy weapons) company; the 2d Battalion has E, F, G and H companies; and the 3d

Battalion has I, K, L and M companies. The first three lettered companies in each battalion are rifle companies, which either lead the attack or are the most forward elements on the defense. D, H and M companies, being the heavy weapons companies, render supporting fire for the rifle elements.

The regiment is armed with:

Weapons	Quantity
M-1 rifles	1,882
Carbines	836
Heavy machine guns	24
Light machine guns	18
57mm guns	18
Browning automatic rifles	81
60mm mortars	27
81mm mortars	18
Rocket antitank launchers (bazooka)	112
Pistols	293
105mm Howitzers	6

III—DIVISION ARTILLERY:

Its primary mission is to support the infantry's advance. Its Headquarters and Headquarters Battery provide the communication, administration and operations for its four battalions. The three light battalions each have thirty-one officers and 501 enlisted men. The 105mm howitzer, of which there are twelve per battalion, renders close fire support to the rifle companies. One battalion usually is in direct support of each regiment, forming a combat team: the 385th Field Artillery Battalion with the 413th Infantry Regiment, the 386th with the 414th, and the 929th with the 415th.

The medium battalion, with thirty officers and 505 enlisted men, has twelve 155mm howitzers. Its primary role is to reinforce the fires of the light battalions. Division Artillery has ten observation liaison planes, two with each battalion and two in Headquarters. Their primary role is air-spotting of the enemy and direction of fires against observed enemy.

With each Infantry Battalion is a forward observer team which accompanies the front line companies and directs, by observation from forward OP's, artillery fire in close support of the advancing units.

The 143 officers, nine warrant officers and 2,029 enlisted men are armed with 1,876 carbines, 166 rocket launchers, 295 pistols and eighty-one caliber .50 machine guns in addition to the thirty-six 105mm howitzers and twelve 155mm howitzers, Divarty's primary weapons.

IV—ENGINEER (COMBAT) BATTALION:

Its primary mission is the repair and maintenance of roads and bridges, removal and passage of enemy obstacles, preparation of obstacles, construction of bridges, and operating assault boats in river crossings. Its twenty-nine officers, three warrant officers and 605 enlisted men are armed with 130 carbines, 549 rifles (M-1), thirty-nine pistols, nine light machine guns and nine caliber .50 machine guns. A, B and C companies are generally in support of each regiment: A with the 413th, B with the 414th, and C with the 415th. Each company comprises five officers and 194 enlisted men. Battalion Headquarters and Headquarters and Service companies provide communications, administration and operation personnel.

V—MEDICAL BATTALION:

It consists of three Collecting companies (A, B and C) and one Clearing company (D). The Collecting companies are always in direct support of an Infantry Regiment: A with the 413th, B with the 414th, and C with the 415th, while the Clearing company evacuates all casualties for the Division. The functions of the battalion are: sanitation and first aid, evacuation and hospitalization. Its thirty-five officers, two warrant officers and 407 enlisted men are not armed.

VI—RECONNAISSANCE TROOP:

Its mission is to gain and report accurate information of the enemy and terrain, to reconnoiter and establish liaison with adjoining units, and to fight delaying actions. It is highly mobile and has more fire power than any other unit for its size. The six officers and 149 enlisted men are armed with thirteen light armored scout cars, twenty-five caliber .50 machine guns, twenty-seven light machine guns, thirteen 37mm guns, three 60mm mortars, eighteen submachine guns, seventy-six M-1 rifles, sixty-two carbines and forty-five pistols.

VII—DIVISION SPECIAL TROOPS:

The Division Special Troops are coordinated by Special Troops Headquarters, consisting of two officers and seven enlisted men. Under its direction and supervision the Division Headquarters company, Signal company, Ordnance and Quartermaster companies operate. Headquarters and Headquarters company consists of thirty-seven officers, eight warrant officers and 195 enlisted men. Within this company is the Commanding General, Assistant Division Commander, and the Division General and Special Staffs. The personnel of the company take care of, feed, transport and defend the Division Headquarters. The personnel is armed with 174 carbines, thirty-three M-1 rifles, ninety-two pistols, four light machine guns, four caliber .50 machine guns and three 57mm antitank guns. In addition to the above personnel the Headquarters company has under its jurisdiction the Military Police Platoon consisting of three officers and sixty-eight enlisted men, whose primary duties are traffic control, evacuation of prisoners of war and police security.

The Signal company provides communication for Division Headquarters, communication from Division Headquarters to its units, to attached units, and to adjacent and higher units. It also supplies signal equipment for the Division. Its nine officers, four warrant officers and 226 enlisted men are armed with 251 carbines and seventy submachine guns.

The Ordnance company with its nine officers, one warrant officer and 141 enlisted men is responsible for the armament, ammunition and motor maintenance within the Division. Its primary weapons are 106 carbines, thirteen submachine guns and sixty-two 1903 rifles.

The Quartermaster company consists of ten officers and 107 enlisted men. Its mission is to feed and clothe the Division and transport supplies. The personnel is armed with 101 carbines, ten pistols and thirty-one M-1 rifles.

VIII—STAFFS:

Each Battalion, Regiment, Division Artillery and the 104th Division have a staff. The duties of staff officers are to provide the commander with basic information and technical advice by which he may arrive at a decision, to develop the basic decision, to prepare adequate plans, translate the plans into orders and insure the compliance of orders by continual inspection.

The Division General Staff comprises the Chief of Staff, who coordinates all actions and plans of the other staff members. The G-1 handles all problems relative to personnel, prisoners of war, casualties, replacements, pay, furloughs and promotions.

The G-2 supervises intelligence training in the Division, keeps the Commanding General apprised of the strength, location, capabilities and probable action of the enemy, and disseminates all information concerning the enemy to the units of the Division.

The G-3 is responsible for training the entire Division, and in combat carries out the policies and commands of the Commanding General by preparing tactical plans, field orders, and coordinating the details of the operations.

The G-4 is responsible for supplying the Division with food, clothing, ammunition and transportation.

In the Battalion, Regimental and Division Artillery Headquarters, the S-1, S-2, S-3 and S-4 have corresponding duties within their respective units.

The Division Special Staff gives technical advice to the Commanding General and the General Staff. The Artillery, Engineer, Signal, Quartermaster and Ordnance representatives have dual responsibilities of command and staff work. The Special Staff is comprised of the Commanding General of the Division Artillery; Engineer, Surgeon and Ordnance Officer; Quartermaster, Adjutant General and Chemical Warfare Officer; Inspector General, Judge Advocate, Finance Officer, Chaplain, Provost Marshal and Headquarters Commandant.

IX—WEAPONS OF AN INFANTRY DIVISION:

Weapon	Quantity	Maximum Effective Range in Yards
Rifle, M-1, caliber .30	6,356	600-800 yards
Rifle, 1903, caliber .30	172	600-800
Carbine, caliber .30	5,279	200-300
Browning Automatic Rifle, caliber .30	243	600
Light Machine Gun, caliber .30	67	1200-2000
Heavy Machine Gun, caliber. 30	90	1600-3000
Machine Gun, caliber .50	236	1600-4000
Submachine Gun, caliber .45	93	200
Pistol, caliber .45	1,157	50
Mortar, 60mm	90	400-600 (max. 1935)
Mortar, 81mm	54	400-1200 (max. 3400)
Antitank Gun, 37mm	13	600-800 (max. 1800)
Antitank Gun, 57mm	57	800-1200 (max. 9000)
Howitzer, 105mm, M-3	18	7000
Howitzer, 105mm, M-2	36	10000
Howitzer, 155mm, M-1	12	16000
Rocket Launchers (Bazooka)	557	100-300

X—DIVISION VEHICLES:

The bulk of the 1,437 vehicles in an Infantry Division are made up of 636 jeeps, 388 two-and-a-half-ton trucks, 251 three-quarter-ton trucks, and 103 one-and-a-half-ton trucks. All personnel of the Division ride except 6,150 infantrymen, who are required to march. To completely motorize the Division, 258 additional 2½-ton trucks are needed. To move the Division by motor one mile, 146 gallons of gasoline are consumed.

XI—MISCELLANEOUS DATA:

A. Road Space—With the Division moving at twenty miles per hour with a hundred-yard interval between vehicles and ten-minute intervals between serials as provided in the Division Standing Operating Procedure, it stretches 220 miles from head to tail, requiring eleven hours for it to pass a fixed point.

B. Rail Movement—To move the personnel and equipment of the Division, forty-eight trains of thirty-five cars each are required.

C. Rations—88,902 pounds of food are consumed by the personnel of an Infantry Division each day.

XII—NORMAL DIVISION ATTACHMENTS:

MEDIUM TANK BATTALIONS

It is composed of a Headquarters company, three Medium Tank companies, one Light Tank company and one Service company. The primary weapons of this unit are the fifty-one medium tanks and seventeen light tanks; in addition, caliber .30 machine guns, caliber .50 machine guns (antiaircraft), 75mm guns, 76mm guns and 105mm guns are available. Its mission is close infantry support. The personnel consists of thirty-six officers, three warrant officers and 653 enlisted men.

ANTIAIRCRAFT ARTILLERY (AUTOMATIC WEAPONS) BATTALION (MOBILE)

Its primary mission is to attack all enemy aircraft within range, to destroy them, cause them to abandon their mission or to decrease the efficiency of their operation. Its secondary role, antimechanized defense and ground support. It consists of four Automatic Weapons Batteries and a Headquarters Battery. Each firing battery has eight 40mm guns and eight caliber .50 machine guns, making a total of thirty-two of each weapon. The 40mm Bofors is mounted on a four-wheeled trailer and towed by a 2½-ton prime mover. The multiple caliber .50 machine guns are mounted on M-16 half-tracks. The personnel consist of thirty-six officers, three warrant officers and 762 enlisted men.

Tank Destroyer Battalion (Self-Propelled)

It has the mission of antitank defense; its secondary role is to give direct support to the infantry by reducing pillboxes and strongpoints, and reinforcing artillery. It consists of thirty-five officers, one warrant officer and 635 enlisted men. Its primary armament is thirty-six three-inch guns mounted on tank chassis. The battalion has five companies, Headquarters and Reconnaissance companies plus three Tank Destroyer companies, with the latter having twelve tank destroyers each.

APPENDIX 4
COMMAND PERSONNEL

COMMANDING GENERAL
Major General Terry de la Mesa Allen

ASSISTANT DIVISION COMMANDERS

Brigadier General Bryant E. Moore	Until 26 February 1945
Colonel George A. Smith, Jr.	26 February to 1 March 1945
Brigadier General Charles T. Lanham	5 March to 13 June 1945
Brigadier General Charles K. Gailey, Jr.	4 August to 20 December 1945

GENERAL STAFF

Chief of Staff	Colonel Bartholomew R. DeGraff
AC of S, G-1	Lieutenant Colonel Scott T. Rex
Assistant G-1	Major Kermit R. Mason
AC of S, G-2	Lieutenant Colonel Mark S. Plaisted
Assistant G-2	Major Harold R. Rosnot
AC of S, G-3	Lieutenant Colonel Leo A. Hoegh
Assistant G-3	Lieutenant Colonel Donald J. Dobbs
AC of S, G-4	Lieutenant Clyde L. Pennington
Assistant G-4	Major Alexander G. Eagle

SPECIAL STAFF

Commanding General, Division Artillery	Brigadier General William R. Woodward
Adjutant General	Lieutenant Colonel Melvin M. Kernan
Finance Officer	Lieutenant Colonel Luther E. Lewis
Chaplain	Lieutenant Colonel Paul C. Mussell
Inspector General	Lieutenant Colonel Russell F. Thompson
Judge Advocate	Lieutenant Colonel James O. Bass
Provost Marshal	Major William C. Nutting
Ordnance Officer	Lieutenant Colonel James D. Williamson
Chemical Warfare Officer	Lieutenant Colonel Richard Hopelain
Engineer Officer	Lieutenant Colonel Max E. Kahn (to 5 Dec. 44)
	Lieutenant Colonel Robert P. Tabb, Jr. (from 5 Dec.)
Postal Officer	Captain Thomas E. Harrington
Quartermaster	Lieutenant Colonel Clyde M. Smith (to 9 Jan. 45)
	Lieutenant Colonel Robert M. Denny (from 9 Jan.)
Signal Officer	Lieutenant Colonel Ralph E. Willey
Special Service Officer	Major Robert C. Duffy
Surgeon	Lieutenant Colonel Hugh W. Jones
CO Special Troops	Lieutenant Colonel Kenneth C. Haycraft

413TH INFANTRY
(23 October 1944)

Commanding Officer	Colonel Welcome P. Waltz
S-1	Major Clinton S. Thompkins
S-2	Captain Samuel W. Koster
S-3	Captain Charles W. Fernald
S-4	Major Richard A. Bush

1st Battalion Commanding Officer	Lieutenant Colonel John W. White
Company A	Captain John A. B. Faggi
Company B	Captain Edward B. Lettunich
Company C	Captain Ralph N. Gleason
Company D	Captain Joseph C. Holloway
Headquarters Company	Captain Ben L. Olcott
2d Battalion Commanding Officer	Lieutenant Colonel Collins R. Perry
Company E	Captain Robert J. Van Egeren
Company F	1st Lieutenant Warren F. Smart
Company G	Captain Marion E. Badgley
Company H	1st Lieutenant John B. Chenoweth
Headquarters Company	Captain Howard H. Hamilton
3d Battalion Commanding Officer	Lieutenant Colonel William M. Summers
Company I	Captain Albert E. Johnston
Company K	Captain James G. Brown
Company L	Captain Marshall B. Garth
Company M	Captain George E. O'Connor
Headquarters Company	Captain Charles W. Casey
Antitank Company	Captain Samuel H. Binder
Cannon Company	Captain Otto E. Feierlein
Service Company	Captain David Frank
Headquarters Company	Captain Marvin E. McCollum

414TH INFANTRY
(23 October 1944)

Commanding Officer	Colonel Anthony J. Touart
S-1	Captain John B. McShane
S-2	Captain Frank R. Gentry
S-3	Major Fred J. Flette
S-4	Captain Elias B. Brand
1st Battalion Commanding Officer	Lieutenant Colonel Robert R. Clark, II
Company A	Captain Paul E. Radlinsky
Company B	Captain Charles J. Glotzbach
Company C	Captain Bernard E. Barker
Company D	Captain Hugh W. Fleischer
Headquarters Company	Captain Wayne E. Powell
2d Battalion Commanding Officer	Lieutenant Colonel Joseph M. Cummins, Jr.
Company E	Captain Cornell E. Bryhn
Company F	Captain Frank R. Bowman
Company G	1st Lieutenant Robert G. Sommerville
Company H	Captain J. Sheridan Reilly
Headquarters Company	Captain Thomas E. Hesselbrock
3d Battalion Commanding Officer	Lieutenant Colonel Leon J. D. Rouge
Company I	Captain Denmon T. Sconyers
Company K	Captain Joseph T. Kusmierz
Company L	Captain Dar Nelson
Company M	Captain Henry A. Cagle

Headquarters Company	Captain Harry D. Malstrom
Antitank Company	Captain Clifford S. Beckett
Cannon Company	Captain Manuel C. Christo
Service Company	Captain Philip E. Horan, Jr.
Headquarters Company	Captain Leonard C. Turner

415TH INFANTRY
(23 October 1944)

Commanding Officer	Colonel John H. Cochran
S-1	Captain John G. Smith, Jr.
S-2	Major John R. Deane, Jr.
S-3	Major Hugh L. Carey
S-4	Major William G. Herbert

1st Battalion Commanding Officer	Lieutenant Colonel John H. Elliott
Company A	Captain Bernard F. McKerney
Company B	Captain Russell Thomas
Company C	Captain Herschel W. Swann
Company D	Captain William D. Gude, Jr.
Headquarters Company	Captain Harold D. Hall

2d Battalion Commanding Officer	Lieutenant Colonel Peter Denisevich
Company E	Captain Kenneth K. Bell
Company F	Captain Charles W. Carroll
Company G	Captain Brown A. Craig
Company H	Captain Arnold J. Strobel
Headquarters Company	Captain Ned U. Bourke

3d Battalion Commanding Officer	Lieutenant Colonel Gerald C. Kelleher
Company I	Captain William W. Barnes
Company K	Captain Raymond D. Collins
Company L	Captain Francis J. Hallahan
Company M	Captain Leland W. Struble
Headquarters Company	Captain William D. Beard

Antitank Company	Captain John G. Vasilake, Jr.
Cannon Company	Captain Forrest L. Gregory
Service Company	Captain George E. Martin
Headquarters Company	Captain Charles H. Allwander

DIVISION ARTILLERY
(23 October 1944)

Commanding General	Brigadier General William R. Woodward
S-1	Major George DeDakis
S-2	Major Richard Bestor
S-3	Lieutenant Colonel Robert C. Ingalls
S-4	Major Nicholas G. DeDakis

Headquarters Battery Commander	Captain Harold Munger

385th Field Artillery Battalion
Commanding Officer   Lieutenant Colonel Edward C. Shinkle
Headquarters Battery   Captain Clement W. Miller
Battery A   Captain Lawrence H. Miles
Battery B   Captain Frank C. Ratcliff
Battery C   Captain Herbert L. Phillips
Service Battery   Captain James A. Hughes

386th Field Artillery Battalion
Commanding Officer   Lieutenant Colonel Urey W. Alexander
Headquarters Battery   Captain Henry A. Dunker
Battery A   Captain Harold L. Ginn
Battery B   Captain Dean H. Stewart
Battery C   Captain Everett D. Nyman
Service Battery   Captain Henry E. Dally

929th Field Artillery Battalion
Commanding Officer   Lieutenant Colonel Vernon G. Gilbert
Headquarters Battery   Captain Merlon R. Richards
Battery A   Captain Albert Eister
Battery B   Captain Norval M. Locke
Battery C   Captain Edmund R. Banks, Jr.
Service Battery   Captain Demar Clayson

387th Field Artillery Battalion
Commanding Officer   Lieutenant Colonel Joseph H. Stangle
Headquarters Battery   Captain John I. Wear
Battery A   Captain Oats A. Pynes, Jr.
Battery B   Captain Joseph E. Cook, Jr.
Battery C   Captain William C. Felkins, Jr.
Service Battery   Captain William H. Forgraves

329TH ENGINEER BATTALION
(23 October 1944)

Commanding Officer   Lieutenant Colonel Max E. Kahn
S-1   Lieutenant Robert Olmstead
S-2   Captain William Roveto
S-3   Captain Robert Lorenz
S-4   Lieutenant William Hackett

Company A   Captain David Price
Company B   Captain Edward Knight
Company C   Captain Max Eisner
Headquarters and Service   Captain Royal Luther

104TH RECONNAISSANCE TROOP
(23 October 1944)
Commanding Officer   Captain Arthur S. Laundon, Cavalry

329TH MEDICAL BATTALION
(23 October 1944)
Commanding Officer   Lieutenant Colonel Samuel R. Taggart (MC)

Company A	Captain Robert R. Pierce (MC)
Company B	Captain Gordon R. Ley (MC)
Company C	Captain George W. Newburn, Jr. (MC)
Company D	Captain Gordon J. Massey (MC)
Headquarters Company	Captain Robert L. Kelley (MAC)

104TH SIGNAL COMANY
(23 October 1944)

| Commanding Officer | Captain Robert G. Moore (SC) |

804TH ORDNANCE COMPANY
(23 October 1944)

| Commanding Officer | Captain Keith E. Smith (QMC) |

104TH QUARTERMASTER COMPANY
(23 October 1944)

| Commanding Officer | Captain Albert J. Schwartz (QMC) |

104TH INFANTRY DIVISION HEADQUARTERS COMPANY
(23 October 1944)

| Commanding Officer | Captain Robert D. Haphey (Inf.) |

104TH MILITARY POLICE PLATOON
(23 October 1944)

| Commanding Officer | Major William C. Nutting (CMP) |

BATTLEFIELD APPOINTMENTS

Throughout the period 28 November 1944 to 18 April 1945, the War Department bestowed battlefield commissions upon 153 men of the 104th Timberwolf Division.

Thirty miles outside of Paris at picturesque Fontainebleau was located a refresher school for future commanders. Here, in German barracks and over Nazi maneuver-tested terrain, the former noncommissioned officers, selected for their superior skill and bravery in contact with the enemy, went through two weeks of intensified training, with emphasis being placed upon the finer points of tactics already experienced by these combat-proven veterans.

The battlefield commissioned officer is the recipient of a signal honor; it is a reflection of the utmost confidence of his superiors in his fighting ability. In many cases, the new second lieutenants had been performing the tasks equivalent to the rank for many months prior to being commissioned in the field, and this proved to be invaluable experience during later campaigns.

These officers of the Timberwolf Division were commissioned from battlefield appointments:

Merlin F. Adams (413th Inf.)
• Jacob C. Akin (413th Inf.)
Jack H. Alford (929th FA)
James R. Allen (414th Inf.)
Alfred G. Anderson (413th Inf.)
Melvin C. Anderson (413th Inf.)
Kenneth A. Andrews (414th Inf.)
Edward P. Arbogast (387th FA)
George W. Avery (386th FA)
Robert B. Bartlett (413th Inf.)
Boone W. Beeman (413th Inf.)
George Belsick (414th Inf.)
Robert O. Berthelsen (387th FA)
Brice R. Bonner, Jr. (386th FA)
Archer L. Bradshaw (415th Inf.)
Charles W. Bricker (414th Inf.)
Edward Bronner (414th Inf.)
Dean H. Brosseau (413th Inf.)
Clark H. Brown (414th Inf.)
Alfred G. Budde (414th Inf.)
George E. Burns (415th Inf.)
William C. Burns (414th Inf.)
Warner R. Campbell (414th Inf.)
Russell D. Cangialosi (414th Inf.)
Armando Capriotti (414th Inf.)
Mark J. Carnall (104th QM Co.)
Edward J. Carroll (415th Inf.)
John P. Casserly (104th CIC)
Lavega Claiborne (414th Inf.)
Frederick A. Clark (414th Inf.)
James E. Conley (415th Inf.)
George T. Cook Jr. (414th Inf.)
Charles W. Crawford (413th Inf.)
John A. Cronin (414th Inf.)
John C. Dahl (413th Inf.)
Jack O. Davis (413th Inf.)
Ben De Leon (415th Inf.)
Clifford H. Dietz (414th Inf.)
Carl L. Dover (414th Inf.)
Leroy Dozier (415th Inf.)
Ralph Duncanson (415th Inf.)
Harry A. Ducat (415th Inf.)
Dennis C. Earhart (413th Inf.)
Hill E. Edwards (413th Inf.)
William Ferency (415th Inf.)
James P. Ferguson (415th Inf.)
Leslie L. Fowler (415th Inf.)
Donald H. Gautereaux (413th Inf.)
Riley C. Gazzaway (413th Inf.)
John Giammarinaro (413th Inf.)

Dale J. Glaze (413th Inf.)
Louis M. Gortz (414th Inf.)
John C. Greenough (413th Inf.)
Paul B. Halstead (329th Engr.)
Stanley M. Hangan (413th Inf.)
David L. Hanna (104th CIC)
• Travis C. Harper (413th Inf.)
George E. Hayden (413th Inf.)
Ray T. Hermanson (415th Inf.)
Muriel R. Hicks (413th Inf.)
Herman H. Hirsch (413th Inf.)
Carter Holcomb (329th Med.)
Walter J. Holder (413th Inf.)
Normall O. Hudson (929th FA)
Francis D. Jackson (413th Inf.)
Russell M. Jehling (387th FA)
Harvey V. Jerles (329th Engr.)
Carrell B. Jones (804th Ord.)
Fred F. Kaiser (415th Inf.)
Leonard F. Kane (413th Inf.)
Richard N. Ketelsen (414th Inf.)
Ord A. Kimmell (414th Inf.)
Robin L. Kirkpatrick (414th Inf.)
Jack H. Knott (Hq. Co. 104th)
Charles R. Knox (414th Inf.)
Herbert C. Knudson (413th Inf.)
Andrew N. Kunkle (Hq. Co. 104th)
Norman K. Larson (415th Inf.)
Houston T. Lipscomb (413th Inf.)
John T. Lowers (414th Inf.)
Oscar C. Lycksell (413th Inf.)
Kenneth A. Mahl (415th Inf.)
John Mancuso (MP Plat.)
Winston L. Markham (413th Inf.)
Randall T. Marshall (929th FA)
Charles R. McChesney (415th Inf.)
Homer A. McDowell (104th Sig. Co.)
James C. McIntosh (415th Inf.)
Emory I. Morgan (415th Inf.)
Leroy E. Morgan (415th Inf.)
Louis B. Moss (413th Inf.)
Rallen B. Nielsen (413th Inf.)
Roy E. Nimmo (413th Inf.)
Wilbert H. Nobles (415th Inf.)
Charles J. O'Gara, Jr. (Recon. Trp.)
Bernard O'Regan (415th Inf.)
Harry L. Palmer (415th Inf.)
John G. Paskus (414th Inf.)
Roy L. Patchin (415th Inf.)
David E. Paul (413th Inf.)

Leon E. Pearce (415th Inf.)
Melvin L. Pechacek (414th Inf.)
Frederick E. Peterson (Hq. Co. 104th)
Walter M. Phillips, Sr. (386th FA)
Nicholas Polivchak (413th Inf.)
Verland C. Proffitt (929th FA)
Robert C. Quinn (415th Inf.)
Maurice J. Quirk (415th Inf.)
ل c Louis Rago (929th FA)
Cecil R. Ramsey (414th Inf.)
Harry L. Rogers (385th FA)
Herbert E. Ruppert (413th Inf.)
James L. Ryburn (Hq. Co. 104th)
Billy H. Sawyers (414th Inf.)
Ralph H. Sawyers (414th Inf.)
John W. Schober (413th Inf.)
Albert Senger (329th Engr.)
W. B. Sheperd (413th Inf.)
Wilfred J. Shields (414th Inf.)
Charles F. Shotts (415th Inf.)
Harlan B. Simmons (Recon. Trp.)
Marion D. Smart (415th Inf.)
Konrad J. Smith (413th Inf.)
Robert L. Sorter, Jr. (415th Inf.)
Harold C. Starr (387th FA)
Karl H. Stellyes (413th Inf.)
John H. Stevens (413th Inf.)

Edward A. Stobaugh (414th Inf.)
Vito D. Tartulli (415th Inf.)
Leroy Thomas (413th Inf.)
Keith V. Thompson (413th Inf.)
Paul W. Thompson (414th Inf.)
John Tirpack (414th Inf.)
James M. Tobin (386th FA)
Louis H. Trog (415th Inf.)
Lawrence D. Tucker (415th Inf.)
Walter C. Tucker (415th Inf.)
Daniel A. VanDetta (414th Inf.)
Frank Vent (415th Inf.)
Joseph Verbanick (415th Inf.)
Oliver R. Vignery (414th Inf.)
Albert Wakefield (413th Inf.)
David M. Ward (415th Inf.)
David Waxman (415th Inf.)
George R. Weaver (415th Inf.)
William Weilby (413th Inf.)
Donald Weishaupt (413th Inf.)
Francis A. Williams (QM Co.)
Howell E. Williamson (415th Inf.)
Peter W. Woyach (929th FA)
Leo Yardley (413th Inf.)
Carl E. Young (Hq. Sp. Trps.)
Ervin W. Young (Sig. Co.)

APPENDIX 5

DECORATIONS AND AWARDS

MEDAL OF HONOR

To earn a Medal of Honor, an individual must perform in action a deed of personal bravery or self-sacrifice involving risk of life or more than *ordinarily* hazardous service so conspicuous as to clearly distinguish him for gallantry and intrepidity above his comrades. This is the highest award bestowed by the United States Government.

Cecil H. Bolton, First Lieutenant, 413th Infantry

DISTINGUISHED SERVICE CROSS

To earn a Distinguished Service Cross, an individual must perform an act or acts of heroism so notable and involving a risk of life so extraordinary as to set him apart from his comrades.

Archer L. Bradshaw, Second Lieutenant, 415th Infantry (Posthumous)
Howard Brohman, Private, 415th Infantry
George E. Burns, Sergeant, 415th Infantry
Francis T. Chase, Jr., Private First Class, 414th Infantry
David L. Colombe, Private, 414th Infantry
William C. Dyer, First Lieutenant, 415th Infantry
Kenneth W. Eakins, First Lieutenant, 415th Infantry
William C. Felkins, Captain, 387th Field Artillery (Posthumous)
Clifford P. Hinkel, Sergeant, 415th Infantry
Henry A. Malone, Technical Sergeant, 413th Infantry
Frank Moralez, Private First Class, 413th Infantry (Posthumous)
John Olsen, First Lieutenant, 413th Infantry (Posthumous)
Jerry M. Page, First Lieutenant, 413th Infantry
James V. Polio, Private First Class, 413th Infantry (Posthumous)
Everett E. Pruitt, First Lieutenant, 415th Infantry
Roger S. Rees, Captain, 413th Infantry
Jess T. Renteria, Technician Fourth Grade, 414th Infantry
Vincent S. Rohays, Staff Sergeant, 413th Infantry*
Joseph M. Schallmoser, Private First Class, 413th Infantry*
Perry O. Tester, First Lieutenant, 413th Infantry (Posthumous)
Beverly Tipton, Private First Class, 413th Infantry
George T. Van Giesen, First Lieutenant, 414th Infantry (Posthumous)
William B. Whitney, Captain, 414th Infantry

DISTINGUISHED SERVICE MEDAL

To earn a Distinguished Service Medal, an individual must distinguish himself by exceptionally meritorious service in a duty of great responsibility, contributing to a high degree to the success of a major

---

*These enlisted men were awarded the D.S.C., but the citations had not been published as this book went to press.

command, installation or project. Superior performance of normal duties does not justify the award.

Terry Allen, Commanding General, 104th Infantry Division
(Oak Leaf Cluster)

SILVER STAR MEDAL

The Silver Star is awarded to individuals who distinguish themselves by gallantry in action to a degree which does not merit the award of the Medal of Honor or the Distinguished Service Cross.

Melvin Adelman, Pfc. (414th Inf.)
*Reginald A. Agna, Pfc. (329th Med.)
Edward T. Aguilar, Sgt. (413th Inf.)
James J. Aiello, Jr., Sgt. (415th Inf.)
Max L. Alcantar, Pfc. (415th Inf.)
Jeddie H. Alderman, T/Sgt. (414th Inf.)
Walter Alexandrow, Pfc. (414th Inf.)
*John Alioto, Sgt. (415th Inf.)
Clark B. Allen, Jr., Pfc. (414th Inf.)
James R. Allen, S/Sgt. (414th Inf.)
John T. Allison, Jr., T/Sgt. (413th Inf.)
Guillermo G. Alvarez, T/4 (329th Med.)
Oliver L. Ammundson, Pfc. (329th Med.)
Alfred G. Anderson, 2d Lt. (413th Inf.)
Melvin C. Anderson, 2d Lt. (413th Inf.)
*Wallace K. Anderson, S/Sgt. (413th Inf.)
Grant J. Andrews, S/Sgt (413th Inf.)
William C. Andrews, Pfc. (414th Inf.)
James S. Atkinson, Pfc. (415th Inf.)
Richard A. Aubrey, 1st Lt. (415th Inf.)
*William R. Ault, 1st Lt. (413th Inf.)
Harvey F. Avery, Sgt. (414th Inf.)
Richard R. Axe, Jr., Pfc. (385th FA)
George H. Axsom, 1st Lt. (413th Inf.)
*Paul D. Bagby, Pfc. (414th Inf.)
Frank D. Bain, Sgt. (329th Engr.)
James G. Baker, S/Sgt. (413th Inf.)
Robert E. Baker, Jr., Pfc. (415th Inf.)
Adolph P. Balinsky, Pfc. (415th Inf.)
Joseph Balistreri, 1st Lt. (413th Inf.)
Bernard E. Barker, Capt. (414th Inf.)
*Adelbert Barlovic, Jr., S/Sgt. (413th Inf.)
Thomas R. Barker, 1st Lt. (386th FA)
†Robert L. Bartlett, 1st Lt. (413th Inf.)
Robert R. Bartlett, 1st Lt. (413th Inf.)

Amos D. Bartz, 1st Lt. (386th FA)
Burton A. Barysh, Pfc. (414th Inf.)
Milton R. Bass, Pvt. (414th Inf.)
Billy Bateman, Sgt. (414th Inf.)
William R. Beaman, Pfc. (414th Inf.)
John L. Beatty, S/Sgt. (413th Inf.)
Walter L. Beery, Pfc. (414th Inf.)
James A. Bennett, Pfc. (414th Inf.)
*James R. Bently, T/Sgt. (415th Inf.)
Donald M. Bertsch, Pfc. (415th Inf.)
Richard J. Beston, Maj. (Hq. 104th)
Marshall E. Bickford, Sgt. (329th Engr.)
J. R. Birmingham, Pfc. (413th Inf.)
Ralph C. Bleier, Sgt. (415th Inf.)
*John K. Bob, T/4 (329th Med.)
*George M. Bohman, 1st Lt. (413th Inf.)
*Donald E. Bohn, 1st Lt. (414th Inf.)
George W. Bollinger, Pfc. (415th Inf.)
Cecil Bolton, 1st Lt. (413th Inf.)
Joseph F. Bonamasso, T/5 (385th FA)
Elvis O. Bone, Pfc. (414th Inf.)
Elwyn L. Bonsall, Pfc. (414th Inf.)
Elmer Bonselaar, Pfc. (413th Inf.)
Samuel E. Booth, Pfc. (329th Engr.)
Lawrence F. Borangno, S/Sgt. (750th Tk.)
Frank M. Borrego, Pfc. (413th Inf.)
*John Boss, Pfc. (415th Inf.)
Louis K. Boswell, Sgt. (415th Inf.)
*Charles W. Bouchard, Pvt. (414th Inf.)
Hayden M. Bower, Capt. (413th Inf.)
Clifford S. Bowersox, T/5 (386th FA)
Paul R. Bowlin, 1st Lt. (415th Inf.)
Frank R. Bowman, Capt. (414th Inf.)
George V. Boyle, Jr., Pfc. (415th Inf.)
Ray G. Bracamonte, Pfc. (413th Inf.)

*—Posthumous.
†—Oak Leaf Cluster.

Archer L. Bradshaw, S/Sgt. (415th Inf.)
L. D. Bragg, Pfc. (414th Inf.)
Robert A. Brandon, Pfc. (929th FA)
*Irving D. Braunstein, Pfc. (329th Med.)
Harry T. Breakison, 1st Lt. (413th Inf.)
Charles W. Bricker, 2d Lt. (414th Inf.)
Leonard E. Bronner, 1/Sgt. (414th Inf.)
†Dean H. Brosseau, 1st Lt. (413th Inf.)
Ben T. Brown, Pfc. (413th Inf.)
†Earl T. Brown, Pfc. (414th Inf.)
Herbert G. Brown, 1st Lt. (413th Inf.)
James G. Brown, Capt. (413th Inf.)
Robert T. Brown, S/Sgt. (414th Inf.)
Roy L. Bryant, T/Sgt. (414th Inf.)
Cornell B. Bryhn, Capt. (414th Inf.)
William H. Buckley, Maj. (413th Inf.)
Troy Buckner, Pvt. (413th Inf.)
Harold D. Burke, Pfc. (413th Inf.)
George E. Burns, 2d Lt. (415th Inf.)
William C. Burns, 1st Lt. (414th Inf.)
*Rowland D. Bush, T/5 (329th Med.)
Edward T. Butcher, 1st Lt. (413th Inf.)
Otto Bytof, Pvt. (387th FA)
Armando Capriotti, 2d Lt. (414th Inf.)
Paul V. Carder, Pfc. (415th Inf.)
Clifford Carlson, Pfc. (415th Inf.)
Leonard I. Carr, 2d Lt. (413th Inf.)
Cecil F. Carter, T/5 (414th Inf.)
James W. Cassidy, Pfc. (387th FA)
Manuel V. Cervantes, T/Sgt. (413th Inf.)
Thomas R. Cheathman, T/Sgt. (415th Inf.)
John B. Chenoweth, Capt. (413th Inf.)
Isadore Chesnick, Sgt. (413th Inf.)
William J. Chilcoat, 1st Lt. (414th Inf.)
*Cyril N. Christopher, T/Sgt. (414th Inf.)
Astere E. Claevssens, Jr., Pfc. (414th Inf.)
Benjamin H. Clark, 1st Lt. (414th Inf.)
Bert T. Clark, Pfc. (413th Inf.)
Richard G. Clark, Pfc. (415th Inf.)
Charles G. Claypool, Pvt. (329th Med.)
†Casper Clough, Jr., Maj. (415th Inf.)
John H. Cochran, Col. (415th Inf.)
Richard E. Coe, T/5 (329th Med.)
*Harold E. Coffin, 1st Lt. (413th Inf.)
Herbert Cohen, 1st Lt. (413th Inf.)
Sydney M. Cohen, Pfc. (415th Inf.)
Raymond D. Collins, Capt. (415th Inf.)
*Benjamin J. Collum, T/Sgt. (414th Inf.)
Harry Coltin, S/Sgt. (415th Inf.)
James E. Conley, 2d Lt. (415th Inf.)

*Warren G. Conrad, 1st Lt. (386th FA)
*Edwin E. Cook, Pfc. (415th Inf.)
William R. Coon, T/5 (386th FA)
Bruce N. Cowan, T/5 (414th Inf.)
John P. Cox, S/Sgt. (414th Inf.)
Herman C. Cramer, 2d Lt. (414th Inf.)
*Meadie Crawford, Pfc. (413th Inf.)
John A. Cronin, T/3 (329th Med.)
*Laverne E. Crosson, Pfc. (415th Inf.)
Paul T. Crowdus, S/Sgt. (414th Inf.)
Christopher B. Cullen, S/Sgt. (414th Inf.)
*Joseph M. Cummins, Jr., Lt. Col. (414th)
Vincent P. Curry, 1st Lt. (413th Inf.)
Normand C. Cyr, T/4 (386th FA)
John C. Dahl, 1st Lt. (413th Inf.)
Herbert W. Dahlman, Pfc. (415th Inf.)
John W. D'Amico, S/Sgt. (415th Inf.)
Thomas E. Danowski, Capt. (415th Inf.)
Arthur N. Dansereau, 1st Lt. (414th Inf.)
Charles R. Daugherty, S/Sgt. (413th Inf.)
Hayden D. Davis, Jr., 2d Lt. (386th FA)
Raymond E. Davis, Pfc. (415th Inf.)
Warren A. Davis, Pfc. (414th Inf.)
John R. Dean, Jr., Maj. (415th Inf.)
Arthur D. Decker, Capt. (413th Inf.)
George B. Decker, 1st Lt. (929th FA)
Theodore F. Decker, Pfc. (329th Engr.)
Houston Deford, S/Sgt. (414th Inf.)
Philip A. DeGregoria, S/Sgt. (413th Inf.)
Grant Denton, Pfc. (414th Inf.)
Garfield A. DeVoss, S/Sgt. (415th Inf.)
Milton H. Dexter, Pfc. (750th Tank)
Harry Diamond, T/Sgt. (413th Inf.)
*Thomas E. Dickerson, Pfc. (415th Inf.)
Sever DiCello, Pfc. (414th Inf.)
Raymond F. Diekroeger, Cpl. (413th Inf.)
William S. Dirker, 1st Lt. (385th FA)
†William S. Dirker, 1st Lt. (385th FA)
Henry Dongvillo, 1st Lt. (413th Inf.)
Michael Donnellan, Jr., Pfc. (414th Inf.)
*Glenn S. Donnelly, Pvt. (415th Inf.)
Ohmer G. Doramus, S/Sgt. (414th Inf.)
Nicholas D. Doseck, S/Sgt. (413th Inf.)
*Howard Dougherty, Cpl. (386th FA)
George B. Dove, Sgt. (414th Inf.)
†Harry J. Doyle, 1st Lt. (414th Inf.)
Howard J. Doyle, 1st Lt. (414th Inf.)
*James S. Doyle, Jr., 2d Lt. (385th FA)
George T. Draper, 1st Lt. (387th FA)
*Charles W. Driffill, 1st Lt. (414th Inf.)

Harry A. Ducat, S/Sgt. (415th Inf.)
*Edward L. Duffy, Pvt. (413th Inf.)
John C. Dwyer, T/Sgt. (414th Inf.)
William C. Dyer, Jr., Capt. (415th Inf.)
Kenneth U. Eakens, 1st Lt. (413th Inf.)
Louie Earls, S/Sgt. (414th Inf.)
Walter L. Eaton, S/Sgt. (413th Inf.)
Royce L. Eaves, 1st Lt. (415th Inf.)
Leonard Effron, S/Sgt. (413th Inf.)
Albert Eister, S/Sgt. (413th Inf.)
Jesse W. Elmore, Pfc. (413th Inf.)
Lloyd M. E. Ensen, 1st Lt. (413th Inf.)
Wolfgang G. Ettinger, Sgt. (386th FA)
James M. Favors, 1st Lt. (413th Inf.)
Stanley A. Felth, S/Sgt. (413th Inf.)
Charles W. Fernwald, Lt. Col. (413th Inf.)
Otto W. Fibranz, Pfc. (415th Inf.)
*Benjamin E. Fiedler, Jf., Pfc. (415th Inf.)
Charles F. Finney, Pfc. (413th Inf.)
Raymond A. Fiscus, T/5 (329th Med.)
Thomas C. Fleury, S/Sgt. (413th Inf.)
Isable M. Flores, S/Sgt. (413th Inf.)
Rolland A. Ford, S/Sgt. (413th Inf.)
*Arthur J. Francis, 1st Lt. (413th Inf.)
*Olof A. Frederiksen, T/3 (413th Inf.)
Charles G. Fulton, Sgt. (415th Inf.)
Wesley A. Gaab, Pfc. (414th Inf.)
Gene T. Gandee, Pvt. (413th Inf.)
David B. Gardiner, Jr., Sgt. (413th Inf.)
Peter L. Gardiner, Pfc. (415th Inf.)
Marshall B. Garth, Capt. (413th Inf.)
Carroll W. Gates, S/Sgt. (329th Med.)
Donald Gautereaux, 2d Lt. (413th Inf.)
Wilford Gaulboard, S/Sgt. (413th Inf.)
Burton S. Gavitt, T/4 (329th Med.)
James W. Gay, 1st Lt. (817th TD)
Riley C. Gazzaway, 2d Lt. (413th Inf.)
*Lloyd A. George, T/5 (387th FA)
Ralph N. Gleason, Capt. (413th Inf.)
James W. Glawson, Pfc. (415th Inf.)
Charles J. Glotzbach, Capt. (414th Inf.)
Stanley D. Golb, 1st Lt. (414th Inf.)
Harry L. Goldberg, Pvt. (414th Inf.)
*Sam W. Goldman, Pfc. (413th Inf.)
*Morris W. Goldstein, Pfc. (414th Inf.)
Wray D. Goode, Sgt. (414th Inf.)
Donald B. Gordon, Capt. (104th Artly.)
*William J. Gower, Pvt. (414th Inf.)
Corado Gozzo, S/Sgt. (414th Inf.)
Gordon L. Graber, 1st Lt. (413th Inf.)

Hunter M. Grady, Sgt. (413th Inf.)
*Elexander L. Graves, Sgt. (414th Inf.)
Arvine W. Gravins, T/5 (385th FA)
Carl L. Gravitt, S/Sgt. (413th Inf.)
Robert T. Gray, T/Sgt. (414th Inf.)
Robert D. Green, Pfc. (413th Inf.)
Lester Greenberg, S/Sgt. (413th Inf.)
James J. Greenday, Sgt. (414th Inf.)
Herbert L. Grewing, 1st Lt. (414th Inf.)
Rollie Griffith, Jr., Pfc. (413th Inf.)
Paul J. Grops, T/Sgt. (413th Inf.)
Fred L. Gross, Pfc. (415th Inf.)
Walter D. Grove, Pfc. (413th Inf.)
Friedrick Gruener, T/Sgt. (413th Inf.)
Edward A. Guttierez, Pfc. (414th Inf.)
Verl G. Haan, S/Sgt. (386th FA)
Wilmer C. Hadley, Pvt. (413th Inf.)
Charles J. Haggarty, 1st Lt. (414th Inf.)
Richard S. Halabrin, S/Sgt. (415th Inf.)
*William L. Hall, Pvt. (413th Inf.)
Willie S. Hall, S/Sgt. (413th Inf.)
Francis J. Hallahan, Capt. (415th Inf.)
Samuel Halloway, S/Sgt. (413th Inf.)
William H. Harbke, Jr., T/4 (329th Med.)
Lucky C. Harkey, Sgt. (413th Inf.)
Barney Harjo, T/Sgt. (413th Inf.)
Jack T. Harmon, Capt. (414th Inf.)
Virgil E. Harrell, Pfc. (413th Inf.)
James D. Harris, Pfc. (413th Inf.)
*Thomas J. Harris, Sgt. (414th Inf.)
*Robert S. Harrison, S/Sgt. (415th Inf.)
†Howard T. Hart, T/Sgt. (413th Inf.)
Bruce H. Harter, Pfc. (415th Inf.)
Lynn W. Hatch, Capt. (414th Inf.)
Sterling S. Hawley, Sgt. (414th Inf.)
George E. Hayden, 1st Lt. (413th Inf.)
*Hugh P. Hayes, Pfc. (329th Med.)
Max O. Hayes, Pfc. (329th Med.)
†Clifford E. Haynes, Sgt. (413th Inf.)
Estle R. Hearn, Sgt. (386th FA)
Frank H. Hedden, 1st Lt. (415th Inf.)
†Robert M. Heisele, S/Sgt. (414th Inf.)
Charley A. Helms, S/Sgt. (414th Inf.)
James W. Henderson, S/Sgt. (413th Inf.)
Ignacio Hermandez, Pfc. (415th Inf.)
*Roy C. Hill, S/Sgt. (329th Med.)
Sylvester L. Hill, T/Sgt. (414th Inf.)
Herman A. Hirsch, T/Sgt. (413th Inf.)
John W. Hoffman, Sgt. (413th Inf.)
Leslie J. Hoffman, S/Sgt. (414th Inf.)

*Matthew J. Hogan, 1st Lt. (413th Inf.)
Joseph G. Holloway, Capt. (413th Inf.)
Thomas G. Holman, 1st Lt. (413th Inf.)
James C. Holt, T/4 (329th Med.)
Jerry S. Hooker, Capt. (415th Inf.)
*Philip E. Horan, Jr., Capt. (414th Inf.)
John Horgdal, Jr., S/Sgt. (413th Inf.)
Donald B. Horton, Pfc. (329th Med.)
Abner E. Howard, T/5 (414th Inf.)
Gordon B. Howell, Capt. (413th Inf.)
John H. Howarth, Pfc. (817th TD)
Vernon Huffman, S/Sgt. (413th Inf.)
Henry W. Hughes, Pfc. (415th Inf.)
*Leland R. Hughes, Pfc. (413th Inf.)
Nils O. Isachsen, Pvt. (329th Med.)
*Joseph A. Jablonski, S/Sgt. (415th Inf.)
Donald G. Jackson, Pfc. (413th Inf.)
Walter A. Jasnosz, Pfc. (414th Inf.)
Carl S. Johnson, Capt. (413th Inf.)
Frederick H. Johnson, Sgt. (413th Inf.)
*Gordon S. Johnson, T/5 (329th Med.)
*George O. Johnson, S/Sgt. (414th Inf.)
Henry O. Johnson, Pfc. (414th Inf.)
Robert W. Johnson, Sgt. (413th Inf.)
Leonard L. Johnston, Pvt. (329th Med.)
William G. Jokkel, T/Sgt. (414th Inf.)
Floyd Jones, Pfc. (414th Inf.)
Hearl Jones, Pfc. (415th Inf.)
Leonard E. Jones, Sgt. (329th Engr.)
*Rolfe D. Jones, 1st Lt. (414th Inf.)
Jack E. Jordan, Pfc. (414th Inf.)
Joseph J. Jordan, Pfc. (387th FA)
William C. Jordan, Sgt. (414th Inf.)
Arthur S. Junger, Pfc. (414th Inf.)
Clifford Kalista, 1st Lt. (413th Inf.)
Edward S. Kalunian, Cpl. (415th Inf.)
Paul C. Kasper, Pfc. (329th Med.)
†Seymour Keith, 1st Lt. (414th Inf.)
John E. Kelly, Pfc. (414th Inf.)
*John W. Kelly, Sgt. (414th Inf.)
Thomas P. Kelly, Capt. (414th Inf.)
Thomas V. Kendrew, T/Sgt. (414th Inf.)
James B. Kendrick, Pfc. (385th FA)
Raymond L. Kerr, Pfc. (413th Inf.)
Irving Kessler, T/5 (329th Med.)
Bennett A. Kilgore, Pfc. (385th FA)
Kenneth S. Kilpatrick, S/Sgt. (415th Inf.)
Frank H. Kimball, 1st Lt. (415th Inf.)
Charles L. Kincheloe, 1st Lt. (414th Inf.)
Ernest W. King, Sgt. (414th Inf.)

Robert J. King, 1st Lt. (413th Inf.)
J. B. Kirbie, Sgt. (414th Inf.)
James E. Kirby, Pvt. (415th Inf.)
Joseph A. Kirschner, 1st Lt. (329th Med.)
Howard R. Kisner, Pfc. (414th Inf.)
Marion A. Klingler, Pfc. (414th Inf.)
Charles A. Knopp, Pfc. (413th Inf.)
*James T. Kohler, S/Sgt. (414th Inf.)
Charles K. Kolarski, Pfc. (414th Inf.)
*William Kolb, Jr., Pfc. (414th Inf.)
Adam Kolodziejski, T/5 (329th Med.)
Samuel W. Koster, Jr., Lt. Col. (413th)
Joseph J. Kristancic, Pfc. (414th Inf.)
George J. Kryc, 1st Lt. (414th Inf.)
Jack R. Kujula, Pfc. (414th Inf.)
*John A. Kyle, Sgt. (414th Inf.)
James S. Lacey, Sgt. (817th TD)
*Thomas S. Lacy, 1st Lt. (414th Inf.)
*Berlin V. Ladner, S/Sgt. (413th Inf.)
*Frank W. Laitinen, Sgt. (750th Tank)
William J. Lamken, S/Sgt. (415th Inf.)
Allen A. Lamond, 1st Lt. (415th Inf.)
Jimmy L. Landress, Pfc. (329th Med.)
Israel Langer, T/5 (387th FA)
Albert A. LaPorte, Pfc. (415th Inf.)
Harry Larsen, T/5 (414th Inf.)
*George J. Law, Jr., Sgt. (329th Med.)
*Roy E. Leach, S/Sgt. (414th Inf.)
Ora J. LeBlanc, T/Sgt. (415th Inf.)
Anthony P. Lenac, Pvt. (413th Inf.)
Robert L. Leonard, Pfc. (414th Inf.)
Pasquale Leonardis, T/5 (413th Inf.)
Paul G. Levie, Sgt. (329th Med.)
Charles J. Levine, 1st Lt. (413th Inf.)
Morris N. Lewis, Sgt. (414th Inf.)
Robert D. Lewis, Pvt. (414th Inf.)
John W. Ligtvoch, Sgt. (415th Inf.)
Walter F. Linette, 1st Lt. (414th Inf.)
Laurence Linn, T/Sgt. (413th Inf.)
*Stuart B. Lindstrom, Sgt. (415th Inf.)
Thurman B. Littreal, Pfc. (329th Engr.)
Cecil M. Logan, 1st Lt. (414th Inf.)
Henry W. Logan, Pfc. (413th Inf.)
James F. Love, Cpl. (329th Engr.)
John T. Lowers, S/Sgt. (414th Inf.)
Joseph W. Luckett, Jr., Sgt. (415th Inf.)
Ned E. Ludlow, T/Sgt. (413th Inf.)
Hugo E. Luedecke, Pfc. (386th FA)
Dale E. Lumsden, Pfc. (414th Inf.)
Edgerton W. Luther, S/Sgt. (929th FA)

John J. Mahoney, T/5 (329th Med.)
Eugene W. Majka, Sgt. (413th Inf.)
†John J. Major, S/Sgt. (415th Inf.)
*Robert E. Mallow, 2d Lt. (414th Inf.)
Frank P. Maliszewski, Pfc. (413th Inf.)
John W. Manan, Pfc. (413th Inf.)
Robert D. Manley, 1st Lt. (414th Inf.)
George P. Manning, S/Sgt. (413th Inf.)
Ernest P. Mannon, Pfc. (414th Inf.)
Joseph F. Mannix, Jr., Sgt. (414th Inf.)
Pete Marınkovich, T/Sgt. (413th Inf.)
Leon Marokus, S/Sgt. (415th Inf.)
Henry L. Marshall, S/Sgt. (415th Inf.)
Randall T. Marshall, 2d Lt. (929th FA)
Nicholas Martinez, Pfc. (414th Inf.)
Patsy C. Mastrocovi, Sgt. (415th Inf.)
Melvin R. Mathias, Pfc. (414th Inf.)
Robert J. Matthews, Pfc. (413th Inf.)
Frank W. Mauerman, Pfc. (415th Inf.)
James A. Mauldin, Capt. (415th Inf.)
William A. Maupin, 2d Lt. (415th Inf.)
Rolland R. Maze, Sgt. (329th Med.)
Lee B. McBride, T/Sgt. (414th Inf.)
Frederick E. McCain, Pfc. (413th Inf.)
John E. McCaslin, Sgt. (413th Inf.)
John W. McColley, Sgt. (413th Inf.)
Marvin E. McCollum, Capt. (413th Inf.)
*Charles E. McCullough, S/Sgt. (414th)
Jack McCullough, T/5 (415th Inf.)
Robert J. McDonald, Pfc. (414th Inf.)
Laurence E. McDowell, S/Sgt. (413th Inf.)
James G. McFarland, 1st Lt. (387th FA)
William McIlvain, Pfc. (413th Inf.)
James S. McKinley, Pfc. (414th Inf.)
Eugene B. McParland, S/Sgt. (414th Inf.)
Mervin T. Medine, S/Sgt. (415th Inf.)
John A. Mehlhop, Maj. (414th Inf.)
*Morris Mendolovitz, Pfc. (414th Inf.)
*Simon C. Mendoza, Pfc. (329th Med.)
William L. Mengebier, 1st Lt. (413th Inf.)
Harold Merims, T/4 (329th Med.)
Marlin E. Meyer, Sgt. (413th Inf.)
†Charles R. Meyers, Pfc. (413th Inf.)
Anthony Mikita, Sgt. (415th Inf.)
Francis Miller, Sgt. (415th Inf.)
Frank L. Miller, Capt. (329th Med.)
Stanley C. Miller, 1st Lt. (329th Med.)
Walter L. Miller, Pfc. (413th Inf.)
Wayne E. Miller, Pfc. (413th Inf.)
James F. Millinor, Capt. (415th Inf.)

Richard K. Miner, Pfc. (414th Inf.)
Victor Miskow, Cpl. (415th Inf.)
Horace T. Mitchell, 1/Sgt. (414th Inf.)
*Virgil C. Mohrman, T/4 (329th Med.)
Francis P. Mojica, Pfc. (414th Inf.)
Stanley W. Moll, T/Sgt. (413th Inf.)
Mario A. Mondelli, Capt. (329th Med.)
*Donald M. Moore, 2d Lt. (414th Inf.)
*Eddie R. Moreno, Pfc. (414th Inf.)
Clayton Morgan, Pfc. (413th Inf.)
†LeRoy E. Morgan, 1st Lt. (413th Inf.)
Michael J. Morgan, 1st Lt. (413th Inf.)
Michael J. Moroz, Pfc. (329th Med.)
Kenneth A. Morris, Capt. (104th Artly.)
Harold E. Morris, Pfc. (413th Inf.)
Melvin E. Morris, T/5 (329th Med.)
Harvey W. Moseley, Pfc. (413th Inf.)
Donald F. Moser, 1/Sgt. (415th Inf.)
*Louis B. Moss, 2d Lt. (413th Inf.)
James D. Mount, 1st Lt. (414th Inf.)
Kenneth L. Mueller, S/Sgt. (414th Inf.)
John Muhar, Sgt. (329th Engr.)
James V. Mullery, 1st Lt. (386th FA)
John B. Murray, Pfc. (413th Inf.)
Dale S. Muskopf, Sgt. (386th FA)
Linford S. Mutter, Sgt. (413th Inf.)
*Oswald K. Myers, Pfc. (413th Inf.)
Robert J. Myers, Pfc. (413th Inf.)
Hugh D. Nally, T/5 (413th Inf.)
Fred E. Needham, Lt. Col. (415th Inf.)
Robert G. Neil, 1st Lt. (415th Inf.)
Frederick C. Nichols, Pfc. (414th Inf.)
Clyde T. Nicholson, S/Sgt. (413th Inf.)
*Thomas F. Neilson, Lt. Col. (413th Inf.)
Harvey A. Niles, 1st Lt. (415th Inf.)
Kenneth P. Nolan, Sgt. (415th Inf.)
†Edward W. Nord, Capt. (414th Inf.)
Thomas G. Notebaert, Pfc. (414th Inf.)
Jonas D. Nunez, T/5 (329th Med.)
Maurice A. O'Connell, T/Sgt. (415th Inf.)
George E. O'Connor, Lt. Col. (413th Inf.)
Charles J. O'Gara, 1st Lt. (104th Recon.)
Jeremiah F. O'Neill, Jr., Cpl. (386th FA)
Leo K. Oren, S/Sgt. (414th Inf.)
Joseph R. Orvino, 1st Lt. (329th Med.)
Frank L. Paddle, Pfc. (413th Inf.)
Fred H. Palmer, Pfc. (413th Inf.)
Irvin Palmer, Pfc. (414th Inf.)
Jerry M. Page, 1st Lt. (413th Inf.)
Delbert R. Parker, 1/Sgt. (413th Inf.)

Herbert O. Parsons, 1st Lt. (385th FA)
Luke U. Patton, Pfc. (415th Inf.)
Paul E. Patton, Pvt. (329th Med.)
Russel Paul, Pfc. (413th Inf.)
Donald A. Peake, 2d Lt. (415th Inf.)
James W. Pearce, Sgt. (692 TD)
Merle J. Peduto, T/5 (329th Med.)
Joe B. Peevey, Capt. (413th Inf.)
*Andrew Peltonen, Capt. (413th Inf.)
James H. Pence, Pfc. (413th Inf.)
Stockwell Pennington, S/Sgt. (413th Inf.)
Ernest L. Petry, Pfc. (414th Inf.)
William T. Phelan, Ptc. (414th Inf.)
Walter M. Phillips, Jr., Sgt. (386th FA)
Pete C. Piazza, Sgt. (386th FA)
Thomas Pierce, Pvt. (413th Inf.)
David W. Piker, Pfc. (415th Inf)
Donald B. Pitts, Pfc. (413th Inf.)
Nicholas Polivchak, S/Sgt. (413th Inf.)
Stanley Poole, Sgt. (414th Inf.)
Ralph S. Potter, Pfc. (415th Inf.)
Jack E. Potter, T/3 (329th Med)
Grover L. Preston, Sgt. (413th Inf.)
Evrett E. Pruitt, 1st Lt. (415th Inf.)
Raymond F. Puestow, S/Sgt. (415th Inf.)
Leonard T. Puryear, T/Sgt. (415th Inf)
Paul E. Radlinsky, Capt. (414th Inf.)
Frederick W. Rancour, Pfc. (414th Inf.)
Kenneth R. Recknagle, S/Sgt. (413th Inf.)
William F. Redman, S/Sgt. (413th Inf.)
William C. Reed, T/5 (329th Med.)
*William R. Reese, Cpl. (385th FA)
Homer S Regan, 1/Sgt. (929th FA)
*Sheridan Reilly, Capt. (414th Inf.)
Joseph J. Reinhofer, Sgt. (415th Inf.)
Harry H. Repman, Capt. (329th Med.)
Frederick D. Reynolds, T/5 (329th Med)
Merlon F. Richards, Capt. (929th FA)
James D. Rifleman, 1st Lt. (415th Inf.)
Richard A. Riis, 1st Lt. (413th Inf)
John J. Rimosukas, 1st Lt. (414th Inf.)
*Harold E. Rist, Pfc. (414th Inf.)
Edward Ritchie, Sgt. (692d TD)
Melville C. Roberson, Pfc. (329th Med)
Myron L. Robison, Pfc. (415th Inf.)
Leo J Rocheleau, Pfc. (329th Med.)
Eugene W. Rodgers, S/Sgt. (415th Inf.)
Vincent S. Rohays, S/Sgt. (413th Inf.)
*Earl G. Roper, Pvt. (414th Inf.)
*Herbert J. Rosencrans, Pfc. (415th Inf.)

*†Kenneth S. Ross, Pfc. (413th Inf.)
Lowell H. Rost, S/Sgt. (414th Inf.)
Charles W. Rotzell, 2d Lt. (329th Med.)
Charles S. Sain, Sgt. (413th Inf.)
Chester C. Sanscoucie, S/Sgt. (415th Inf.)
*Eugene Saperstein, Pfc. (413th Inf.)
Anthony J. Sarrica, Jr., S/Sgt. (415th Inf.)
William R. Satz, T/5 (329th Med.)
Marcell H. Savoie, T/Sgt. (413th Inf.)
Billy H. Sawyer, S/Sgt. (414th Inf.)
Ralph H. Sawyer, S/Sgt. (414th Inf.)
Joseph M. Schallmoser, Pfc. (414th Inf.)
William L. Schemery, 1/Sgt. (414th Inf.)
James H. Schmidt, Pfc. (413th Inf.)
Edward W. Schneider, 1st Lt. (817th TD)
Robert B. Schneider, Cpl. (414th Inf.)
Robert N. Schnell, Capt. (385th FA)
Joseph W. Schober, 2d Lt. (329th Med.)
Anthony J. Schukes, S/Sgt. (414th Inf.)
Thomas C. Schwind, S/Sgt. (414th Inf.)
Willard C. Seffinga, Pvt. (413th Inf.)
John Seifert, S/Sgt. (414th Inf.)
Richard D. Serposs, S/Sgt. (414th Inf.)
*Armand J. Serrabella, 1st Lt. (413th Inf.)
William F. Shaffer, Sgt. (413th Inf.)
Donald B. Shank, Sgt. (413th Inf.)
Eugene A. Shaw, Capt. (929th FA)
Burleigh W. Shepard, 1st Lt. (329th FA)
Wilfred J. Shields, 2d Lt. (414th Inf.)
Paul Shinkewick, T/Sgt. (413th Inf.)
John D. Shipley, 2d Lt. (415th Inf.)
Paul W. Shissler, S/Sgt. (414th Inf.)
Roger F. Shockor, 1st Lt. (415th Inf.)
Charles F. Shotts, T/Sgt. (415th Inf.)
*Howard W. Shugert, Pfc. (415th Inf.)
William H. Shumaker, S/Sgt. (414th Inf.)
*William J. Sieber, Pfc. (413th Inf.)
†James G. Sieben, S/Sgt. (414th Inf.)
Louis Siegel, T/4 (329th Engr.)
Merle T. Simmons, S/Sgt. (415th Inf.)
Lester F. Simon, S/Sgt. (413th Inf.)
Logan W. Skaggs, S/Sgt. (414th Inf.)
*Bernard L. Skabill, Sgt. (413th Inf.)
Paul F. Skinner, 1st Lt. (413th Inf.)
Paul A. Slaughter, T/5 (329th Med.)
Cecil T. Smith, S/Sgt. (414th Inf.)
Joseph J. Smith, Pfc. (413th Inf.)
Konrad J. Smith, 2d Lt. (413th Inf.)
Laurence W. Smith, 1st Lt. (414th Inf.)
*John E. Snider, Sgt. (415th Inf.)

Ralph E. Snider, 2d Lt. (414th Inf.)
David J. Snyder, 1st Lt. (415th Inf.)
Claudie D. Soapes, Pfc. (414th Inf.)
*James T. Sobansky, Sgt. (414th Inf.)
Norman L. Sodman, 1st Lt. (385th FA)
Jacob Solowitz, T/5 (329th Med.)
*Robert G. Sommerville, 1st Lt. (414th)
Martin P. Specht, Pfc. (413th Inf.)
Orville B. Spencer, T/5 (414th Inf.)
Frank P. Sprague, Pfc. (414th Inf.)
John L. Stage, T/Sgt. (415th Inf.)
Coy W. Stainback, Pfc. (413th Inf.)
Lewis E. Stancil, Cpl. (329th Med.)
Joseph J. Stancovich, Pfc. (414th Inf.)
Harold C. Starr, 2d Lt. (387th FA)
Paul G. Stethus, Pfc. (415th Inf.)
Daniel Stapleton, S/Sgt. (413th Inf.)
†Karl H. Stelljes, 1st Lt. (413th Inf.)
Allen A. Stephen, S/Sgt. (414th Inf.)
Robert W. Stevens, T/5 (413th Inf.)
Louis J. Stieritz, Sgt. (386th FA)
Michael J. Stokloss, Pfc. (413th Inf.)
Francis F. Stone, Sgt. (414th Inf.)
*Ryal G. Stone, Pfc. (413th Inf.)
Flem C. Stover, Sgt. (414th Inf.)
*David R. Straesser, 1st Lt. (385th FA)
Floyd W. Stratton, 1st Lt. (414th Inf.)
Hayden L. Strider, S/Sgt. (414th Inf.)
Murray S. Susskind, S/Sgt. (415th Inf)
†William Sugel, 1st Lt. (413th Inf.)
Daniel J. Sullivan, S/Sgt. (414th Inf.)
William A. Summers, Lt. Col. (413th Inf.)
Solomon L. Swain, S/Sgt. (414th Inf.)
*Herschel W. Swann, Capt. (415th Inf.)
George W. Swanson, T/Sgt. (414th Inf)
Fred G. Swartz, Jr., Capt. (329th Med.)
David E. Swindell, Jr., 2d Lt. (386th FA)
Oliver C. Sykes, Pfc. (414th Inf.)
Stephen L. Szabo, S/Sgt. (413th Inf.)
Vito Tarulli, T/Sgt. (415th Inf.)
Emmitt Tate, Pfc. (413th Inf.)
*Burtis J. Taylor, S/Sgt. (414th Inf.)
Howard C. Taylor, Pfc. (413th Inf.)
Robert E. Taylor, Pfc. (415th Inf.)
Mervin Teig, 1st Lt. (414th Inf.)
Charles W. Terrill, S/Sgt. (415th Inf.)
Betrand J. Thibeault, Pvt. (329th Med.)
Joseph Thiebes, Jr., Pfc. (414th Inf.)
Arnold P. Thinstad, 1st Lt. (414th Inf.)
Aubrey W. Thomas, Pfc. (415th Inf.)

*Davis S. Thomas, Sgt. (413th Inf.)
Robert W. Thomas, Jr., 1st Lt. (414th Inf)
Theodore E. Thomas, Capt. (413th Inf.)
Keith V. Thompson, 2d Lt. (329th Med)
Loyce N. Thompson, Pfc. (415th Inf.)
Paul W. Thompson, 2d Lt. (414th Inf.)
James M. Tobin, S/Sgt. (386th FA)
Karl A. Tobusch, Sgt. (414th Inf.)
Gordon Toler, Pfc. (413th Inf.)
Anthony J. Totina, T/5 (329th Med.)
William F. Tufts, 1st Lt. (415th Inf.)
Claude M. Turner, Maj. (104th Artly.)
*Oscar G. Turner, 1st Lt. (415th Inf.)
Arthur Ulmer, 1st Lt. (929th FA)
Daniel Valerio, Sgt. (414th Inf.)
Richard Van Der Hagen, 2d Lt. (750th)
†Daniel A. Van Detta, 2d Lt. (414th Inf.)
Daniel A. Van Detta, 2d Lt. (414th Inf.)
Dudley C. Van Duzer, S/Sgt. (414th Inf.)
*Max L. Van Orman, Pfc. (414th Inf.)
Robert J. Varner, T/Sgt. (414th Inf.)
Frank Vent, 2d Lt. (415th Inf)
Frederick J. Villafranca, Sgt. (415th Inf.)
*Franklin A. Volz, T/3 (329th Med.)
Joseph A. Vosheski, 1st Lt. (414th Inf.)
Dale R. Walrath, Pfc. (414th Inf.)
†Welcome P. Waltz, Col. (413th Inf.)
*Fred G. Wardner, T/4 (329th Med.)
*Vincent L. Warner, Sgt. (415th Inf.)
*Casimer E. Warszawski, S/Sgt. (413th)
Vernon W. Washam, Pfc. (413th Inf.)
James E. Webb, T/Sgt. (413th Inf.)
Walter C. Webb, Jr., S/Sgt. (414th Inf)
Joseph P. Weber, Jr., Pfc. (414th Inf.)
*Charles D. Weed, 1st Lt. (414th Inf.)
Howard F. Weigel, T/5 (329th Med.)
William D. Weilby, 2d Lt. (413th Inf.)
Norman Weinreber, Pvt. (329th Med.)
Donald R. Weishaupt, Sgt. (413th Inf)
Leonard Weiss, Pfc. (329th Med.)
Harold L. Welch, T/5 (386th FA)
Michael Welgan, Pfc. (413th Inf.)
Donald L. West, Capt. (329th Med.)
Fred R. White, 1st Lt. (413th Inf.)
William B. Whitney, Capt. (414th Inf.)
Remo Whitt, S/Sgt. (415th Inf.)
Paul G. Weist, S/Sgt. (413th Inf.)
Thomas D. Wilkinson, Pfc. (414th Inf.)
Victor V. Willard, 1st Lt. (414th Inf.)
Wesley W. Williams, 2d Lt. (414th Inf.)

Donald E. Wilson, Pfc. (Hq. 104th)
James H. Wilson, Pfc. (415th Inf.)
Marvin Winemiller, S/Sgt. (413th Inf.)
Hersal L. Wing, S/Sgt. (414th Inf.)
Laurance G. Wolfe, 1st Lt. (413th Inf.)
Bishop T. Woodson, Pfc. (415th Inf.)
Jerome L. Workman, Pfc. (413th Inf.)
Wallace Worley, Pfc. (413th Inf.)
Karol Wozniak, S/Sgt. (413th Inf.)
Joel W. Wright, 1st Lt. (415th Inf.)
John F. Wright, S/Sgt. (414th Inf.)

William E. Wright, Pfc. (692d TD)
Walter Wyrkowski, Pfc. (414th Inf.)
Clain F. Yohe, Capt. (414th Inf.)
*John P. Young, 1st Lt. (413th Inf.)
William W. Young, S/Sgt. (414th Inf.)
Edward J. Zaliagiris, Pfc. (692d TD)
John A. Zamberlin, Pfc. (415th Inf.)
Anthony P. Zaso, Sgt. (413th Inf.)
Genovevo G. Zapata, Pfc. (929th FA)
Frank Zervas, Pvt. (329th Med.)
William Zupanic, Sgt. (413th Inf.)

LEGION OF MERIT

The Legion of Merit, without reference to degrees, is awarded for exceptionally meritorious conduct in the performance of outstanding services. When awarded to military personnel of friendly foreign nations, the Chief Commander and Commander degrees are comparable to the Distinguished Service Medal awarded to United States military personnel and the Officer and Legionnaire degrees are comparable to the Legion of Merit awarded to United States military personnel.

William R. Woodward, Brigadier General, 104th Division Artillery
Bryant E. Moore, Brigadier General, Headquarters, 104th Infantry Division
Bartholomew R. DeGraff, Colonel, Headquarters, 104th Infantry Division
Anthony J. Touart, Colonel, Headquarters, 414th Infantry
Welcome P. Waltz, Colonel, Headquarters, 413th Infantry
John H. Cochran, Colonel, Headquarters, 415th Infantry

BRONZE STAR MEDAL

The Bronze Star is awarded for minor acts of heroism or achievement or for meritorious service in sustained operational activities or in support of sustained operational activities against the enemy. Though the achievement or service for the award of the Bronze Star is less than that required for the Silver Star or Legion of Merit, it must nevertheless be accomplished with distinction.

Number awarded	3,623
For achievement	2,008
For service	1,615

ORDER OF THE PURPLE HEART

The Purple Heart is awarded to those individuals who receive wounds which necessitate treatment by a medical officer in combat against an enemy of the United States or as a direct result of an act of such enemy.

Number awarded   1,996

AIR MEDAL

The Air Medal is awarded for meritorious achievement while participating in aerial flight, either for a single act of merit or for sustained operational activities against the enemy. The required achievement is less than that for the Distinguished Flying Cross but it must nevertheless be accomplished with distinction.

Number awarded   54

SOLDIER'S MEDAL

The Soldier's Medal is awarded to individuals for an act or acts of heroism involving voluntary risk of life under conditions other than those of conflict with the enemy.

Number awarded   24

FOREIGN AWARDS

French Decorations:

Legion d'Honneur—grade of Chevalier	(2)
Croix de Guerre	(1)

British Decorations:

Distinguished Service Order	(1)
Military Cross	(4)
Military Medal	(5)
Distinguished Conduct Medal	(1)

Soviet Decorations:

Order of Suvorov
Class II (gold) awarded to Major General Terry Allen
Class III (silver) awarded to Colonel William Summers

DISTINGUISHED UNIT (PRESIDENTIAL) CITATIONS

3d Battalion, 413th Infantry—23-26 February 1945

Attached units:

3d Platoon, Antitank Company, 413th Infantry
Forward Observer Party, 87th Chemical Battalion
Forward Observer Parties (2), 385th Field Artillery Battalion

Liaison Party, 385th Field Artillery Battalion
2d and 3d Platoons, Company A, 329th Engineers
Medical Detachment, 3d Battalion Section, 413th Infantry

2d and 3d Battalions, 415th Infantry
    2d Battalion, 2-4 December 1944
    3d Battalion, 2-6 December 1944

414th Infantry Regiment (–Cannon Company)   Pending
    31 March 1945—5 April 1945

Attached units:

4 Forward Observer Teams—
    A Battery, 386th Field Artillery Battalion
    B Battery, 386th Field Artillery Battalion
    C Battery, 386th Field Artillery Battalion
3 Forward Observer Teams—
    Headquarters Battery, 386th Field Artillery Battalion

415th Infantry Regiment   Pending
    31 March 1945—4 April 1945

Attached units:

Companies A and C, 750th Tank Battalion
104th Reconnaissance Troop
Cannon Company, 414th Infantry
Company C, 329th Engineers
817th Tank Destroyer Battalion
Batteries B and C, 555th Antiaircraft Artillery Battalion
386th Field Artillery Battalion

2d Battalion, 413th Infantry Regiment
    24-26 February 1945

Attached units:

2d Platoon, Antitank Company, 413th Infantry
Forward Observer Parties, 385th Field Artillery Battalion
Liaison Party, 385th Field Artillery Battalion
Forward Observer Party, Cannon Company, 413th Infantry
2d Platoon, B Company, 750th Tank Battalion
Medical Detachment, 2d Battalion Section, 413th Infantry
Forward Observer Party, Company A, 87th Chemical Mortar
    Battalion

1st Battalion, 415th Infantry Regiment   Pending
    22-25 February 1945

Attached units:

C Company, 329th Engineers
1st Platoon, Antitank Company, 415th Infantry
C Company, 750th Tank Battalion
A Battery, 555th Antiaircraft Artillery Battalion
2d Platoon, B Company, 692d Tank Destroyer Battalion

2d Battalion, 413th Infantry Regiment   Pending
    24 February 1945

1st Battalion, 413th Infantry Regiment   Pending
    23-26 February 1945

MERITORIOUS SERVICE UNIT PLAQUES

104th Division Band
    28 October 1944—24 March 1945
Star: 25 March—24 September 1945

804th Ordnance Company
    7 September 1944—15 March 1945
Star: 15 March—15 September 1945

329th Medical Battalion
    23 October 1944—31 December 1944
Star: 1 January—30 June 1945

Service Company, 414th Infantry Regiment
    7 September 1944—15 February 1945
Star: 15 February—15 August 1945

Medical Detachment, 413th Infantry Regiment
    23 October 1944—31 December 1944
Star: 1 January—8 May 1945

Medical Detachment, 415th Infantry Regiment
    Belgium—Holland—Germany
Star: 16 February—15 August 1945

104th Signal Company
    7 September 1944—12 February 1945
Star: 12 March—12 August 1945

Service Company, 415th Infantry Regiment
    8 September 1944—25 January 1945
Star: 26 January—25 July 1945

Military Police Platoon, 104th Division
    7 September 1944—15 January 1945
Star: 16 January—15 July 1945

Service Company, 413th Infantry Regiment
    23 October—31 December 1944

Service Battery, 385th Field Artillery Battalion
    23 October 1944—1 March 1945

Medical Detachment, 414th Infantry Regiment
    24 October 1944—1 February 1945

Service Battery, 386th Field Artillery Battalion
    23 October 1944—23 February 1945

Service Battery, 387th Field Artillery Battalion
    16 January 1944—16 March 1945

Service Battery, 929th Field Artillery Battalion
    France, Belgium, Holland and Germany

APPENDIX 6
AMERICAN RED CROSS

Red Cross personnel, consisting of a four-man team, is assigned to a division by the American National Red Cross, upon the request of the Commanding General, and serves within the division as an attached unit functioning under the direction of G-1. The mission of such a unit is to cooperate with the military in any problem relating to the morale, welfare and recreation of servicemen; to serve as a medium of communication between the men in service and their families in case of distress or need at home; to arrange for aid, financial or otherwise, in the solving of personal or family problems. The Army recognizes the fact that if a soldier is worried he cannot properly assimilate and utilize the training skills that he must know nor can he be properly attentive and alert in his work. In fact he may be a source of danger as far as his own life is concerned and the lives of those about him if his mind is concerned about personal problems or affairs at home. By personal counsel and through communication with Red Cross workers in the more than 3,750 chapters which, through their branches, reach every community in the United States, practical assistance, aid and advice can be given. By living with the men of the division, the Red Cross field director makes himself available to the men at any time and at any place the division operates. The fact that the Red Cross field director has no military rank or grade makes it possible for the men to come to him without going through "channels" and also makes it possible for the Field Director to cross-cut channels if need be in attempting to aid the serviceman in the solution of his problem.

During pre-overseas maneuvers and all through the Division's combat in the European Theater, the following ARC men were active in their aid and advice to the GI:

Boyd B. Burnside, field director, had surveillance over the Special and Attached troops, 329th Medical and 329th Engineer Battalions, the 387th Field Artillery Battalion and Division Headquarters. William F. Mackintosh, assistant field director, was associated with the 413th Infantry and 385th Field Artillery. Another assistant field director, William Ritz, worked with the men of the 414th Infantry and 386th Field Artillery. The 415th Infantry and 929th Field Artillery found the services of Daniel H. Strelnick extremely cooperative.

The Divisional team has served 10,802 men of the 104th during the period of 10 December 1942 through 30 September 1945. However, many of these more than 10,000 men have found it necessary to call upon the Red Cross for services in connection with other problems after their initial contact, and 24,198 have been served in all. Many think of the Red Cross in terms of money only. Of these more than 24,000 cases, it has been necessary to make a loan or grant in only 1,946 instances. The total amount of money loaned or granted to men in the Division during the period was $109,840.04.

In January and February 1945, more than 4,500 messages were sent for Valentine's Day, ordering flowers for men who desired to have them delivered in the States. More than $25,000 was transmitted for the men of the Division for Valentine's Day alone. The same service was provided for Mother's Day and Easter.

One of the most enjoyable services was that bringing the Red Cross Clubmobile girls as far forward as safety would permit in order to give many men a chance to talk with a real American girl as well as munch doughnuts along with a cup of hot coffee. Despite rain, mud, and danger, these girls were always willing to come whenever they possibly could, and every Clubmobile unit in the VII and the XIX Corps vied with each other for the chance to serve the Timberwolves, as they always received such a fine reception.

During the long wait at the Roer, when it was impossible, due to the tense situation, for the Division to spare men long enough so that they could take a real pass, a Fatigue Camp was set up at the Division rear. Two very lovely ARC girls did much to brighten up the bare barracks which were converted into a club to provide real home cheer as well as serve coffee and cookies. They helped plan programs for the men and did more than a little dancing. Arita Kelbe and Patricia "Tish" Teage will be remembered by many for their untiring efforts at all hours of the day and night. "Rita" later became the wife of a Timberwolf whom she met at that time.

Among the more pleasant memories is that of the "British-American Red Cross Club" set up at Halle when the Division received the numerous released prisoners of war. The Red Cross was able to provide every man coming through with needed cigarettes, toilet articles and comfort. The presence of an American, a Canadian and a British girl at the club did much for these tired men who had not talked with a girl from home in many long months of internment.

APPENDIX 7
CHAPLAINS

The work of the Chaplains of the Timberwolf Division is a part of the record of the units. Wherever the troops have gone—in training, on maneuvers, or in combat—the Chaplains have gone with them, sharing their life and bringing the ministrations of religious faith.

In August of 1942, a month before the activation of the Division, thirteen Chaplains reported for duty at Camp Adair, Oregon, coming together from a session at the Army Chaplains' School. The following were the original Timberwolf Chaplains:

> Frank J. Worthington (Presbyterian)
> Loren L. Jenks (Disciples of Christ)
> *Paul C. Mussell (Roman Catholic)
> *Paul R. Walker (Congregational)
> Jerome J. Klingsporn (Roman Catholic)
> *Milton E. Berg (Lutheran)
> William A. Norton (Baptist—North)
> *Edmund J. Murray (Roman Catholic)
> *Clair F. Yohe (Methodist)
> Robert A. Boettger (Lutheran)
> *Marvin T. Vick (Methodist)
> Lewis M. Bratcher (Baptist—South)
> Raymond L. Talbot (Roman Catholic)

In the course of time seventeen other Chaplains came into the Division, serving for varying lengths of time:

> *George L. Steinbeck (Lutheran)
> William B. Kenworthy (Episcopal)
> *Gerald A. Quinn (Roman Catholic)
> George A. Downs (Baptist—South)
> Peter Pfeiffer (Baptist—North)
> *Ernest F. Tonsing (Lutheran)
> *Robert B. Frey (Evangelical and Reformed)
> *Robert S. Jackson (Baptist—South)
> *Clarence G. Stump (Baptist—South)
> Arthur E. Bezanson (Baptist—North)

*Elbridge B. Linn (Church of Christ)
*Edward P. Doyle (Roman Catholic)
*Aloys R. Schweitzer (Roman Catholic)
*Wolf G. Plaut (Jewish)
*Harry T. DeHart (Baptist—South)
*William F. Pitman (Disciples of Christ)
*Edmond L. Malone (Episcopal) (attached)

Names marked with an asterisk served with the Division overseas.

Chaplain Clarence G. Stump, serving with the 1st Battalion, 415th Infantry, was killed in action on November 21, 1944, in Stolberg, Germany. Frequently distinguishing himself by his courage and his devotion to the men he served, he has left a heritage of heroism and Christian character which shall be an everlasting memorial.

Three Chaplains were assigned to each Regiment, two to Division Artillery, one to the Medical Battalion, and one to Special Troops. In combat the battalion aid station was the customary location of the individual Chaplain. There he ministered to the wounded and dying, often assisting in simple first aid, in the evacuation of wounded and dead from the battlefield, going out into far forward positions to encourage and cheer the men on the line.

The heroic action and unselfish devotion to duty of all the 104th's Chaplains was speedily recognized by the Division, as is evidenced in the long list of decorations awarded these men of God.

Chaplain (Captain) Gerald A. Quinn—Silver Star, Bronze Star
Chaplain (Captain) Clair F. Yohe—Silver Star, Bronze Star, Purple Heart

Chaplain (Captain) Robert B. Frey—Bronze Star (OLC)
Chaplain (Captain) Milton E. Berg—Bronze Star, Purple Heart
Chaplain (Captain) Edmund J. Murray—Bronze Star
Chaplain (Lieutenant Colonel) Paul C. Mussell—Bronze Star
Chaplain (Captain) Edward P. Doyle—Bronze Star
Chaplain (Major) Paul R. Walker—Bronze Star
Chaplain (Captain) Aloys R. Schweitzer—Bronze Star
Chaplain (Captain) Robert S. Jackson—Bronze Star
Chaplain (Captain) Harry T. DeHart—Bronze Star
Chaplain (Captain) George L. Steinbeck—Bronze Star
Chaplain (Captain) Ernest F. Tonsing—Bronze Star
Chaplain (Captain) Elbridge B. Linn—Bronze Star
Chaplain (Captain) Wolf G. Plaut—Bronze Star

The conducting of religious services was only one of many duties performed, but it was a duty faithfully performed under wide and varied circumstances. During combat operations, whatever place available was used as a chapel. Often the open air, taverns, halls, schools, dugouts and pillboxes. Whenever possible churches were used, and many historic spots were places of worship for men of the Division. Almost any place became a church and every day was Sunday. It is interesting to note that during the six months of combat over three thousand religious services were held, with total attendance of more than one hundred thousand.

Religious work in the Division has always been marked by wholehearted cooperation from all levels of command. It has also showed a splendid spirit of teamwork among the Chaplains themselves. Of varying creeds, they have been one in their faith in God and their desire to serve as soldiers of God and country.

APPENDIX 8
CREDITS

The Staff wishes to convey its thanks to the following organizations for their cooperation and their permission to reproduce articles which appeared in their newspapers, magazines and syndicated columns:

TIME
LIFE
YANK
THE ASSOCIATED PRESS
UNITED PRESS ASSOCIATIONS
INTERNATIONAL NEWS SERVICE
UNITED FEATURE SYNDICATE
THE NEW YORK TIMES
THE NEW YORK DAILY NEWS
THE SUN
PM—DAILY
THE CHICAGO SUN
CHICAGO TRIBUNE
ARMY TIMES
COLORADO SRINGS GAZETTE AND TELEGRAPH
THE PORTLAND OREGONIAN
THE STARS AND STRIPES

Picture credits to:

LIFE
U. S. ARMY SIGNAL CORPS
104TH DIVISION P.R.O.
CAMP CARSON P.R.O.
BALL STUDIOS, CORVALLIS, OREGON
COLORADO SRINGS GAZETTE AND TELEGRAPH
THE PORTLAND OREGONIAN

The Editorial Board expresses its gratitude to Colonel Joseph I. Greene and his *Infantry Journal* Staff (publishers of TIMBERWOLF TRACKS) for their helpful assistance in compiling this history.

CPSIA information can be obtained at www.ICGtesting.com
Printed in the USA
BVOW01s1740290913

332443BV00005B/41/P